GPGPU

Programming
for Games
and Science

GPGPU

Programming
for Games
and Science

David H. Eberly

Geometric Tools LLC, Redmond, Washington, USA

CRC Press
Taylor & Francis Group
Boca Raton London New York

CRC Press is an imprint of the
Taylor & Francis Group, an **informa** business

AN A K PETERS BOOK

CRC Press
Taylor & Francis Group
6000 Broken Sound Parkway NW, Suite 300
Boca Raton, FL 33487-2742

First issued in paperback 2020

© 2015 by Taylor & Francis Group, LLC
CRC Press is an imprint of Taylor & Francis Group, an Informa business

No claim to original U.S. Government works

ISBN-13: 978-1-4665-9535-4 (hbk)
ISBN-13: 978-0-367-65909-7 (pbk)

Library of Congress Cataloging-in-Publication Data

Eberly, David H.
    GPGPU programming for games and science / David H. Eberly.
        pages cm
        Summary: "This in-depth, practical guide describes high-performance computing on general purpose graphics processing units (GPGPUs) using DirectX 11. Suitable for game developers and computing professionals, the book cohesively blends principles, practice, and software engineering and includes many algorithm examples and high-quality source code to illustrate the concepts. A fully featured engine for computing and graphics helps readers avoid having to write a large amount of infrastructure code necessary for even the simplest of applications involving shader programming"-- Provided by publisher.
        Includes bibliographical references and index.
        ISBN 978-1-4665-9535-4 (hardback)
        1. Graphics processing units--Programming. I. Title.

    T385.E37325 2014
    006.6'6--dc23   2014016436

Visit the Taylor & Francis Web site at
http://www.taylorandfrancis.com

and the CRC Press Web site at
http://www.crcpress.com

Contents

List of Figures   xiii

List of Tables   xv

Listings   xvii

Preface   xxv

Trademarks   xxvii

1   Introduction   1

2   CPU Computing   5
   2.1   Numerical Computing   5
     2.1.1   The Curse: An Example from Games   5
     2.1.2   The Curse: An Example from Science   10
     2.1.3   The Need to Understand Floating-Point Systems . . .   11
   2.2   Balancing Robustness, Accuracy, and Speed   14
     2.2.1   Robustness   14
       2.2.1.1   Formal Definitions   14
       2.2.1.2   Algorithms and Implementations   16
       2.2.1.3   Practical Definitions   17
     2.2.2   Accuracy   19
     2.2.3   Speed   20
     2.2.4   Computer Science Is a Study of Trade-offs   20
   2.3   IEEE Floating Point Standard   22
   2.4   Binary Scientific Notation   23
     2.4.1   Conversion from Rational to Binary Scientific Numbers   24
     2.4.2   Arithmetic Properties of Binary Scientific Numbers . .   27
       2.4.2.1   Addition of Binary Scientific Numbers   28
       2.4.2.2   Subtraction of Binary Scientific Numbers . .   28
       2.4.2.3   Multiplication of Binary Scientific Numbers .   28
       2.4.2.4   Division of Binary Scientific Numbers   29
     2.4.3   Algebraic Properties of Binary Scientific Numbers   . .   30
   2.5   Floating-Point Arithmetic   31
     2.5.1   Binary Encodings   32
       2.5.1.1   8-bit Floating-Point Numbers   33

2.5.1.2   16-Bit Floating-Point Numbers   36
2.5.1.3   32-Bit Floating-Point Numbers   39
2.5.1.4   64-Bit Floating-Point Numbers   41
2.5.1.5 n-Bit Floating-Point Numbers   42
2.5.1.6   Classifications of Floating-Point Numbers . . .   45

2.5.2   Rounding and Conversions   50
2.5.2.1   Rounding with Ties-to-Even   51
2.5.2.2   Rounding with Ties-to-Away   52
2.5.2.3   Rounding toward Zero   52
2.5.2.4   Rounding toward Positive   52
2.5.2.5   Rounding toward Negative   53
2.5.2.6   Rounding from Floating-Point to Integral Floating-Point   54
2.5.2.7   Conversion from Integer to Floating-Point .   60
2.5.2.8   Conversion from Floating-Point to Rational .   64
2.5.2.9   Conversion from Rational to Floating-Point .   67
2.5.2.10   Conversion to Wider Format   70
2.5.2.11   Conversion to Narrower Format   73

2.5.3   Arithmetic Operations   81
2.5.4   Mathematical Functions   82
2.5.5   Floating-Point Oddities   83
2.5.5.1   Where Have My Digits Gone?   83
2.5.5.2   Have a Nice Stay!   88
2.5.5.3   The Best I Can Do Is That Bad?   89
2.5.5.4   You Have Been *More* Than Helpful   91
2.5.5.5   Hardware and Optimizing Compiler Issues .   92

3   SIMD Computing   **93**
3.1   Intel Streaming SIMD Extensions   93
3.1.1   Shuffling Components   94
3.1.2   Single-Component versus All-Component Access . . .   95
3.1.3   Load and Store Instructions   95
3.1.4   Logical Instructions   98
3.1.5   Comparison Instructions   99
3.1.6   Arithmetic Instructions   100
3.1.7   Matrix Multiplication and Transpose   100
3.1.8   IEEE Floating-Point Support   103
3.1.9   Keep the Pipeline Running   103
3.1.10   Flattening of Branches   104
3.2   SIMD Wrappers   106
3.3   Function Approximations   107
3.3.1   Minimax Approximations   107
3.3.2   Inverse Square Root Function Using Root Finding . .   110
3.3.3   Square Root Function   111
3.3.4   Inverse Square Root Using a Minimax Algorithm . . .   114

3.3.5   Sine Function 116
3.3.6   Cosine Function   116
3.3.7   Tangent Function 117
3.3.8   Inverse Sine Function   117
3.3.9   Inverse Cosine Function 119
3.3.10 Inverse Tangent Function   119
3.3.11 Exponential Functions 120
3.3.12 Logarithmic Functions 120

4 GPU Computing   123
4.1 Drawing a 3D Object   123
    4.1.1   Model Space   123
    4.1.2   World Space   123
    4.1.3   View Space 124
    4.1.4   Projection Space 125
    4.1.5   Window Space 129
    4.1.6   Summary of the Transformations 130
    4.1.7   Rasterization 131
4.2 High Level Shading Language (HLSL) 134
    4.2.1   Vertex and Pixel Shaders 134
    4.2.2   Geometry Shaders 138
    4.2.3   Compute Shaders 141
    4.2.4   Compiling HLSL Shaders 144
        4.2.4.1   Compiling the Vertex Coloring Shaders . . . 147
        4.2.4.2   Compiling the Texturing Shaders   151
        4.2.4.3   Compiling the Billboard Shaders 152
        4.2.4.4   Compiling the Gaussian Blurring Shaders . . 156
    4.2.5   Reflecting HLSL Shaders   160
4.3 Devices, Contexts, and Swap Chains   168
    4.3.1   Creating a Device and an Immediate Context 168
    4.3.2   Creating Swap Chains   170
    4.3.3   Creating the Back Buffer   171
4.4 Resources 173
    4.4.1   Resource Usage and CPU Access 174
    4.4.2   Resource Views 175
    4.4.3   Subresources 178
    4.4.4   Buffers 179
        4.4.4.1   Constant Buffers 181
        4.4.4.2   Texture Buffers   181
        4.4.4.3   Vertex Buffers   182
        4.4.4.4   Index Buffers 184
        4.4.4.5   Structured Buffers 184
        4.4.4.6   Raw Buffers 187
        4.4.4.7   Indirect-Argument Buffers 189
    4.4.5   Textures 189

4.4.5.1   1D Textures   192
4.4.5.2   2D Textures   193
4.4.5.3   3D Textures   194
4.4.6   Texture Arrays   195
4.4.6.1   1D Texture Arrays   195
4.4.6.2   2D Texture Arrays   196
4.4.6.3   Cubemap Textures   197
4.4.6.4   Cubemap Texture Arrays   198
4.4.7   Draw Targets   198
4.5   States   201
4.6   Shaders   202
4.6.1   Creating Shaders   202
4.6.2   Vertex, Geometry, and Pixel Shader Execution   202
4.6.3   Compute Shader Execution   205
4.7   Copying Data between CPU and GPU   207
4.7.1   Mapped Writes for Dynamic Update   207
4.7.2   Staging Resources   210
4.7.3   Copy from CPU to GPU   211
4.7.4   Copy from GPU to CPU   212
4.7.5   Copy from GPU to GPU   213
4.8   Multiple GPUs   214
4.8.1   Enumerating the Adapters   214
4.8.2   Copying Data between Multiple GPUs   215
4.9   IEEE Floating-Point on the GPU   217

5   **Practical Matters**   **223**
5.1   Engine Design and Architecture   223
5.1.1   A Simple Low-Level D3D11 Application   223
5.1.2   HLSL Compilation in Microsoft Visual Studio   226
5.1.3   Design Goals for the Geometric Tools Engine   227
5.1.3.1   An HLSL Factory   227
5.1.3.2   Resource Bridges   228
5.1.3.3   Visual Effects   230
5.1.3.4   Visual Objects and Scene Graphs   231
5.1.3.5   Cameras   231
5.2   Debugging   232
5.2.1   Debugging on the CPU   232
5.2.2   Debugging on the GPU   233
5.2.3   Be Mindful of Your Surroundings   235
5.2.3.1   An Example of an HLSL Compiler Bug   . . .   236
5.2.3.2   An Example of a Programmer Bug   239
5.3   Performance   241
5.3.1   Performance on the CPU   241
5.3.2   Performance on the GPU   243
5.3.3   Performance Guidelines   247

5.4   Code Testing 249
     5.4.1   Topics in Code Testing 250
     5.4.2   Code Coverage and Unit Testing on the GPU 254

6   Linear and Affine Algebra   257
   6.1   Vectors 257
     6.1.1   Robust Length and Normalization Computations . . . 258
     6.1.2   Orthogonality 260
         6.1.2.1   Orthogonality in 2D 260
         6.1.2.2   Orthogonality in 3D 261
         6.1.2.3   Orthogonality in 4D 262
         6.1.2.4   Gram-Schmidt Orthonormalization 263
     6.1.3   Orthonormal Sets 264
         6.1.3.1   Orthonormal Sets in 2D 265
         6.1.3.2   Orthonormal Sets in 3D 265
         6.1.3.3   Orthonormal Sets in 4D 267
     6.1.4   Barycentric Coordinates 269
     6.1.5   Intrinsic Dimensionality 270
   6.2   Matrices 273
     6.2.1   Matrix Storage and Transfom Conventions 274
     6.2.2   Base Class Matrix Operations 275
     6.2.3   Square Matrix Operations in 2D 278
     6.2.4   Square Matrix Operations in 3D 279
     6.2.5   Square Matrix Operations in 4D 281
     6.2.6   The Laplace Expansion Theorem 282
   6.3   Rotations 288
     6.3.1   Rotation in 2D 288
     6.3.2   Rotation in 3D 289
     6.3.3   Rotation in 4D 292
     6.3.4   Quaternions 294
         6.3.4.1   Algebraic Operations 295
         6.3.4.2   Relationship of Quaternions to Rotations . . 297
         6.3.4.3   Spherical Linear Interpolation of Quaternions 299
     6.3.5   Euler Angles 305
         6.3.5.1   World Coordinates versus Body Coordinates 306
     6.3.6   Conversion between Representations 308
         6.3.6.1   Quaternion to Matrix 309
         6.3.6.2   Matrix to Quaternion 309
         6.3.6.3   Axis-Angle to Matrix 311
         6.3.6.4   Matrix to Axis-Angle 311
         6.3.6.5   Axis-Angle to Quaternion 312
         6.3.6.6   Quaternion to Axis-Angle 312
         6.3.6.7   Euler Angles to Matrix 313
         6.3.6.8   Matrix to Euler Angles 313

| | 6.3.6.9 | Euler Angles to and from Quaternion or Axis-Angle | 317 |

6.4 Coordinate Systems 318
    6.4.1 Geometry and Affine Algebra 319
    6.4.2 Transformations 322
        6.4.2.1 Composition of Affine Transformations . . . 322
        6.4.2.2 Decomposition of Affine Transformations . . 327
        6.4.2.3 A Simple Transformation Factory 330
    6.4.3 Coordinate System Conventions 332
    6.4.4 Converting between Coordinate Systems 336

7 Sample Applications   **341**
7.1 Video Streams 341
    7.1.1 The VideoStream Class 341
    7.1.2 The VideoStreamManager Class 342
7.2 Root Finding 346
    7.2.1 Root Bounding 346
    7.2.2 Bisection 347
    7.2.3 Newton's Method 348
    7.2.4 Exhaustive Evaluation 350
        7.2.4.1 CPU Root Finding Using a Single Thread . . 350
        7.2.4.2 CPU Root Finding Using Multiple Threads . 351
        7.2.4.3 GPU Root Finding 352
7.3 Least Squares Fitting 355
    7.3.1 Fit a Line to 2D Points 355
    7.3.2 Fit a Plane to 3D Points 358
    7.3.3 Orthogonal Regression 359
        7.3.3.1 Fitting with Lines 359
        7.3.3.2 Fitting with Planes 361
    7.3.4 Estimation of Tangent Planes 362
7.4 Partial Sums 364
7.5 All-Pairs Triangle Intersection 368
7.6 Shortest Path in a Weighted Graph 371
7.7 Convolution 377
7.8 Median Filtering 384
    7.8.1 Median by Sorting 385
    7.8.2 Median of 3×3 Using Min-Max Operations 387
    7.8.3 Median of 5×5 Using Min-Max Operations 389
7.9 Level Surface Extraction 392
7.10 Mass-Spring Systems 398
7.11 Fluid Dynamics 400
    7.11.1 Numerical Methods 401
    7.11.2 Solving Fluid Flow in 2D 403
        7.11.2.1 Initialization of State 405
        7.11.2.2 Initialization of External Forces 406

7.11.2.3 Updating the State with Advection 409
7.11.2.4 Applying the State Boundary Conditions . . 410
7.11.2.5 Computing the Divergence of Velocity 413
7.11.2.6 Solving the Poisson Equation 413
7.11.2.7 Updating the Velocity to Be Divergence Free 414
7.11.2.8 Screen Captures from the Simulation 415
7.11.3 Solving Fluid Flow in 3D 416
7.11.3.1 Initialization of State 418
7.11.3.2 Initialization of External Forces 419
7.11.3.3 Updating the State with Advection 422
7.11.3.4 Applying the State Boundary Conditions . . 424
7.11.3.5 Computing the Divergence of Velocity 425
7.11.3.6 Solving the Poisson Equation 425
7.11.3.7 Updating the Velocity to Be Divergence Free 427
7.11.3.8 Screen Captures from the Simulation 427

Bibliography   **429**

Index   **435**

List of Figures

2.1	Colliding circles	7
2.2	Circle interpenetration due to roundoff errors	8
2.3	Circles at last time of contact	10
2.4	Convex hull update (in theory)	11
2.5	Convex hull update (in practice)	12
2.6	Layout of 8-bit floating-point	33
2.7	Distribution of binary8 numbers	36
2.8	Layout of 16-bit floating-point	37
2.9	Layout of 32-bit floating-point	39
2.10	Layout of 64-bit floating-point	41
2.11	Rounding with ties-to-even	51
2.12	Rounding with ties-to-away	52
2.13	Rounding toward zero	52
2.14	Rounding toward positive	53
2.15	Rounding toward negative	53
2.16	Comparison of narrow and wide formats	74
3.1	Initial plot of $g(x) = \sqrt{1+x} - p(x)$	112
3.2	Final plot of $g(x) = \sqrt{1+x} - p(x)$	114
4.1	Eyepoint and view frustum	127
4.2	Symmetric view frustum and faces	128
4.3	1D pixel ownership	132
4.4	2D pixel ownership	132
4.5	Top-left rasterization rule	133
4.6	Vertex coloring and texturing	137
4.7	Billboards using geometry shaders	141
4.8	Dispatch and group thread IDs	143
4.9	Blurring using compute shaders	144
4.10	Mipmaps as subresources	178
4.11	Texture arrays as subresources	179
4.12	Copying data between processors	208
6.1	Visualization of 3×3 determinant	284
6.2	Visual of 4×4 expansion by row 0	285
6.3	Visualization of 4×4 expansion by rows zero and one	287

6.4   Visualization of 3D rotation   289
6.5   Spherical linear interpolation of quaternions   300
6.6   Illustration of affine algebra   320
6.7   Parallelogram law of affine algebra   321
6.8   Counterclockwise rotation in the plane   333
6.9   Left-handed versus right-handed coordinate systems   335
6.10 Conversion from right-handed to left-handed coordinates . .   337
6.11 Commutative diagram for change of basis   339

7.1   Binary expression tree for partial sums   365
7.2   DAG for partial sums of four numbers   366
7.3   DAG for partial sums of eight numbers   367
7.4   Intersection of a meshes for a cylinder and a torus   371
7.5   The directed edges from a point in the grid graph   373
7.6   The directed edges to a point in the grid graph   374
7.7   The breadth-first update of distances in a 5×5 grid   374
7.8   A level surface for a single voxel   392
7.9   Triangle mesh configurations (part 1)   394
7.10 Triangle mesh configurations (part 2)   395
7.11 Surface extraction for two level values   397
7.12 2D fluid screen captures   416
7.13 3D fluid screen captures   428

List of Tables

2.1   The binary encodings for 8-bit floating-point numbers . . .   35
2.2   Quantities of interest for binary8   36
2.3   Quantities of interest for binary16   38
2.4   Quantities of interest for binary32   40
2.5   Quantities of interest for binary64   43

3.1   SIMD comparison operators   99
3.2   SIMD arithmetic operators   100
3.3   Inverse square root accuracy and performance   111
3.4   Minimax polynomial approximations to $\sqrt{1+x}$ 115
3.5   Minimax polynomial approximations to $f(x) = 1/\sqrt{1+x}$ . .   115
3.6   Minimax polynomial approximations to $f(x) = \sin(x)$ 117
3.7   Minimax polynomial approximations to $f(x) = \cos(x)$ . . .   117
3.8   Minimax polynomial approximations to $f(x) = \tan(x)$ . . .   118
3.9   Minimax polynomial approximations to $f(x) = \mathrm{asin}(x)$ . . .   118
3.10 Minimax polynomial approximations to $f(x) = (\pi/2 - \mathrm{asin}(x))/\sqrt{1-x}$ 119
3.11 Minimax polynomial approximations to $f(x) = \mathrm{atan}(x)$ . . .   120
3.12 Minimax polynomial approximations to $f(x) = 2^x$ 121
3.13 Minimax polynomial approximations to $f(x) = \log_2(1+x)$.   121

4.1   The transformation pipeline   130

5.1   Vertex and pixel shader performance measurements   246
5.2   Compute shader performance measurements   247
5.3   Depth, stencil, and culling state performance measurements   248

6.1   Error balancing for several n in the Remez algorithm   304
6.2   Rotation conventions   336

7.1   Numerical ill conditioning for least squares   358
7.2   Performance comparisons for convolution implementations .   382

Listings

2.1 Inexact representation of floating-point inputs 13

2.2 Simple implementation for computing distance between two points 18

2.3 Incorrect distance computation due to input problems 18

2.4 Conversion of rational numbers to binary scientific numbers . 26

2.5 A union is used to allow accessing a floating-point number or manipulating its bits via an unsigned integer 32

2.6 Decoding an 8-bit floating-point number 33

2.7 Decoding a 16-bit floating-point number 37

2.8 Decoding a 32-bit floating-point number 39

2.9 Decoding a 64-bit floating-point number 41

2.10 Integer and unsigned integer quantities that are useful for encoding and decoding floating-point numbers 44

2.11 The general decoding of floating-point numbers 44

2.12 Convenient wrappers for processing encodings of floating-point numbers 45

2.13 Classification of floating-point numbers 45

2.14 Queries about floating-point numbers 46

2.15 An implementation of the nextUp(x) function 48

2.16 An implementation of the nextDown(x) function 49

2.17 An implementation of rounding with ties-to-even 55

2.18 An implementation of rounding with ties-to-away 56

2.19 An implementation of rounding toward zero 57

2.20 An implementation of rounding toward positive 58

2.21 An implementation of rounding toward negative 59

2.22 Conversion of a 32-bit signed integer to a 32-bit floating-point number 62

2.23 Conversion from a 32-bit floating-point number to a rational number 65

2.24 Conversion from a 64-bit floating-point number to a rational number 66

2.25 Conversion from a rational number to a 32-bit floating-point number 68

2.26 Conversion of an 8-bit floating-point number to a 16-bit floating-point number 71

2.27 Conversion of a narrow floating-point format to a wide floating-point format 72

2.28 Conversion from a wide floating-point format to a narrow floating-point format 76

2.29 The conversion of a wide-format number to a narrower format 79

2.30 Correctly rounded result for square root 82

2.31 The standard mathematics library functions 83

2.32 Subtractive cancellation in floating-point arithmetic 84

2.33 Another example of subtractive cancellation and how bad it can be 86

2.34 Numerically incorrect quadratic roots when using the modified quadratic formula 87

2.35 An example of correct root finding, although at first glance they look incorrect 89

2.36 The example of Listing 2.35 but computed using double-precision numbers 90

3.1 Computing a dot product of 4-tuples using SSE2 94

3.2 Computing the matrix-vector product as four row-vector dot products in SSE2 101

3.3 Computing the matrix-vector product as a linear combination of columns in SSE2 101

3.4 Computing the matrix-vector product as four row-vector dot products in SSE4.1 102

3.5 Transpose of a 4×4 matrix using shuffling 103

3.6 Normalizing a vector using SSE2 with a break in the pipeline 103

3.7 Normalizing a vector using SSE2 without a break in the pipeline 104

3.8 The definition of the Select function for flattening branches . 104

3.9 Flattening a single branch 105

3.10 Flattening a two-level branch where the outer-then clause has a nested branch 105

3.11 Flattening a two-level branch where the outer-else clause has a nested branch 105

3.12 Flattening a two-level branch where the outer clauses have nested branches 106

3.13 A fast approximation to 1/sqrt(x) for 32-bit floating-point . . 110

3.14 A fast approximation to 1/sqrt(x) for 64-bit floating-point . . 111

3.15 One Remez iteration for updating the locations of the local extrema 112

4.1 A vertex shader and a pixel shader for simple vertex coloring of geometric primitives 134

4.2 A vertex shader and a pixel shader for simple texturing of geometric primitives 136

4.3 HLSL code to draw square billboards 139

4.4 A compute shader that implements small-scale Gaussian blurring 141

4.5 The output assembly listing for the vertex shader of VertexColoring.hlsl for row-major matrix storage 147

4.6 The output assembly listing for the matrix-vector product of the vertex shader of VertexColoring.hlsl for column-major matrix storage 150

4.7 The output assembly listing for the pixel shader of VertexColoring.hlsl 150

4.8 The output assembly listing for the pixel shader of Texturing.hlsl 151

4.9 The output assembly listing for the vertex shader of Billboards.hlsl 152

4.10 The output assembly listing for the geometry shader of Billboards.hlsl 153

4.11 The output assembly listing for the pixel shader of Billboards.hlsl 155

4.12 The output assembly listing for the compute shader of GaussianBlurring.hlsl 156

4.13 The output assembly listing for the compute shader of GaussianBlurring.hlsl with loop unrolling 158

4.14 The signature for the D3DCompile function 160

4.15 The signature for the D3DReflect function 160

4.16 Compile an HLSL program at runtime and start the shader reflection system 160

4.17 An example of nested structs for which constant buffers have one member layout but structured buffers have another member layout 162

4.18 A modified listing of the FXC output from the compute shader of Listing 4.17 163

4.19 The non-default-value members of D3D11_SHADER_DESC for the compute shader of Listing 4.17 165

4.20 Descriptions about the constant buffers in the compute shader of Listing 4.17 165

4.21 Creating a swap chain for displaying graphics data to a window 170

4.22 Creating a back buffer 171

4.23 Common code for setting the usage and CPU access for a description structure 175

4.24 The description for a shader resource view and the code to create the view 176

4.25 The description for an unordered access view and the code to create the view 176

4.26 The descriptions for render target and depth-stencil views and the code to create the views 177

4.27 Common code for creating an ID3D11Buffer object 180

4.28 Creating a constant buffer 181

4.29 Creating a texture buffer 181

4.30 Creating a vertex buffer 182

4.31 Creating a vertex format via a D3D11_INPUT_ELEMENT_DESC
      structure   182
4.32 Creating an index buffer   184
4.33 Creating a structured buffer   184
4.34 The HLSL file for the AppendConsumeBuffers sample application   185
4.35 The HLSL file for the RawBuffers sample application   187
4.36 Creation of a raw buffer   188
4.37 Creation of an indirect-arguments buffer   189
4.38 Common code for creating an ID3D11Texture<N>D object . .   190
4.39 Creation of a 1D texture   192
4.40 Pseudocode for telling D3D11 to compute mipmap levels after
      the level-0 mipmap is initialized or (later) modified   192
4.41 Creation of a 2D texture for shader input and/or output but
      not for render targets or depth-stencil textures   193
4.42 Code that shows how to share an ID3D11Texture2D object cre-
      ated on one device with another device   194
4.43 Creation of a 3D texture   194
4.44 Creation of a 1D texture array   195
4.45 Creation of a 2D texture array   196
4.46 Creation of a cubemap texture   197
4.47 Creation of a cubemap texture array   198
4.48 Creation of a render target   199
4.49 Creation of a depth-stencil texture   199
4.50 Creation of vertex, geometry, pixel, and compute shaders . .   202
4.51 Typical setup for executing vertex, geometry, and pixel shaders   203
4.52 Using a query to count the number of drawn pixels   205
4.53 Typical setup for executing a compute shader   205
4.54 A query that causes the CPU to wait for the GPU to finish
      executing its current command list   206
4.55 Updating an ID3D11Buffer object using mapped writes   208
4.56 Updating an ID3D11Texture object using mapped writes   208
4.57 Memory copies used by dynamic updates of textures   209
4.58 Creation of a 2D staging texture without multisampling . . .   210
4.59 Copy from CPU to GPU for a buffer resource   211
4.60 Copy from CPU to GPU for a texture resource   211
4.61 Copy from GPU to CPU for a buffer resource   212
4.62 Copy from GPU to CPU for a texture resource   212
4.63 Enumeration of adapters and outputs attached to the adapters   214
4.64 An example of copying a texture from the video memory of one
      GPU to that of another   216
4.65 Verification that float subnormals are flushed to zero when used
      in arithmetic operations   218
4.66 Verification that double subnormals are not flushed to zero when
      used in arithmetic operations   219
5.1   The Application class header file   224

5.2   A compute shader program that fetches a matrix from a struc-
      tured buffer with native type float4x4   236
5.3   The FXC output from the compute shader of Listing 5.2 is the
      same whether you use /Zpr or /Zpc   236
5.4   A compute shader program that fetches a matrix from a struc-
      tured buffer with a struct that has a single member float4x4 .   237
5.5   The FXC output from the compute shader of Listing 5.4 using
      /Zpr   238
5.6   An example of a programmer bug   239
5.7   The output of FXC applied to the code of Listing 5.6   240
5.8   D3D11 code to support timing of execution on the GPU . . .   243
5.9   A simple example to illustrate testing concepts   250
5.10 An example of measuring code coverage on the GPU   254
5.11 An example of code coverage on the GPU where you count how
      many times each block is visited   255
6.1   Computing the length of a vector   258
6.2   Computing the length of a vector robustly   258
6.3   Normalizing a vector   259
6.4   Normalizing a vector robustly   259
6.5   The vector class interface for dot products, length, and normal-
      ization   260
6.6   The 2D vector interface for perpendicular vectors and dot-perp   260
6.7   The vector interface for cross products and dot-cross, where N
      is three or four   262
6.8   The vector interface for hypercross products and dot-hypercross   262
6.9   The vector interface for Gram-Schmidt orthonormalization . .   263
6.10 The 2D vector interface for computing orthogonal complements   265
6.11 The 3D vector interface for computing orthogonal complements   267
6.12 The 4D vector interface for computing orthogonal complements   268
6.13 The 2D vector interface for barycentric coordinates   269
6.14 The 3D vector interface for barycentric coordinates   270
6.15 The 2D vector interface for intrinsic dimensionality   271
6.16 The 3D vector interface for intrinsic dimensionality   272
6.17 Storage for the matrix class   275
6.18 Member accessors for the matrix class   276
6.19 Comparison operators for the matrix class   277
6.20 Matrix-vector products   277
6.21 The class interface for 2×2 matrices   278
6.22 Geometric operations for 2×2 matrices   279
6.23 The class interface for 3×3 matrices   280
6.24 Geometric operations for 3×3 matrices   280
6.25 The class interface for 4×4 matrices   281
6.26 Geometric operations for 4×4 matrices   282
6.27 The Quaternion<Real> interface for the quaternions and algebra
      associated with them   297

6.28 Source code for the rotation of a vector directly by quaternion
      operations   298
6.29 A direct implementation of SLERP   301
6.30 A fast, accurate, and robust implementation of SLERP   304
6.31 An attempt to have compact conversion code   308
6.32 A workaround for the compiler complaints of Listing 6.31 . .   308
6.33 The final conversion code that provides compact code but no
      compiler warnings   308
6.34 Determining the largest-magnitude component of q from the
      products of components   310
6.35 Determining the largest-magnitude component of $\mathbf{U}$ from the
      products of components   311
6.36 Conversion of an axis-angle pair (axis,angle) to a quaternion q   312
6.37 Conversion of a quaternion q to an axis-angle pair (axis,angle)   312
6.38 Conversion of Euler angles e to a rotation matrix r   313
6.39 Conversion of a rotation matrix r to Euler angles e when using
      the vector-on-the-right convention   315
6.40 Conversion of a rotation matrix r to Euler angles e when using
      the vector-on-the-left convention   316
6.41 The Transform class in GTEngine   331
6.42 Incomplete comments describing the form of a 2D rotation ma-
      trix   334
7.1   Acquiring an image and creating a texture from it   342
7.2   Capturing video streams serially   343
7.3   Capturing video streams in parallel   343
7.4   Launching a thread to handle image capturing   344
7.5   Root finding on the CPU using an exhaustive search with a
      single thread   350
7.6   Root finding on the CPU using an exhaustive search with mul-
      tiple threads   351
7.7   Root finding on the GPU using an exhaustive search with $512\times$
      256 thread groups, each group containing 8×8 threads . . .   352
7.8   Program to illustrate ill conditioning in line fitting when the
      mean is not subtracted from the samples   356
7.9   HLSL shader for least-squares plane fitting   362
7.10 A CPU implementation for computing partial sums   365
7.11 The HLSL program for computing partial sums of numbers .   367
7.12 Breadth-first update of distances in an $S \times S$ grid   375
7.13 Convolution with a square filter kernel   378
7.14 Convolution with a square filter kernel and using group-shared
      memory   379
7.15 Convolution with a square filter kernel and using separability   381
7.16 A shader that uses insertion sort to compute the median . . .   385
7.17 Initialization of data for vectorized median filtering   387

7.18 Extracting the minimum and maximum from six numbers with swaps 388

7.19 The compute shader for 3×3 median filtering 388

7.20 Extracting the minimum and maximum from seven numbers with swaps 389

7.21 Extracting the minimum and maximum from eight numbers with swaps 390

7.22 Extracting the minimum and maximum from twelve or sixteen numbers with swaps 390

7.23 The compute shader for 5×5 median filtering 391

7.24 Pseudocode for the high-level fluid simulation 403

7.25 Setup of constant buffers for the 2D fluid simulation 404

7.26 Selection of initial state for 2D fluids 405

7.27 Initial state computations 2D fluids, both for the CPU and the GPU 405

7.28 Setup code for initialization of source forces for 2D fluids . . 407

7.29 HLSL code for generating vortices and other forces in 2D fluids 407

7.30 Shader creation and execution for initializing sources in 2D fluids 408

7.31 HLSL code for updating the 2D fluid state with advection . . 409

7.32 HLSL code for enforcing the boundary conditions for the 2D fluid state 412

7.33 HLSL code for computing the divergence of the velocity for 2D fluids 413

7.34 HLSL code for solving the Poisson equation for 2D fluids . . . 413

7.35 HLSL code for enforcing the boundary conditions after solving the Poisson equation 414

7.36 HLSL code for updating the velocity to be divergence free . . 415

7.37 The pixel shader for visualizing the density of the 2D fluid . . 415

7.38 Setup of constant buffers for the 3D fluid simulation 417

7.39 Selection of initial state for 3D fluids 418

7.40 Initial state computations 3D fluids, both for the CPU and the GPU 418

7.41 Setup code for initialization of source forces for 3D fluids . . 420

7.42 HLSL code for generating vortices and other forces in 3D fluids 420

7.43 Shader creation and execution for initializing sources in 3D fluids 421

7.44 HLSL code for updating the 3D fluid state with advection . . 422

7.45 HLSL code for computing the divergence of the velocity for 3D fluids 425

7.46 HLSL code for solving the Poisson equation for 3D fluids . . . 425

7.47 HLSL code for enforcing the boundary conditions after solving the Poisson equation 426

7.48 HLSL code for updating the velocity to be divergence free . . 427

Preface

The last book I wrote was *Game Physics, 2nd Edition*, which shipped in the Spring of 2010. At that time I decided to take a break from Geometric Tools and book writing and return to industry to work for Microsoft Corporation, in a moderately sized technology group that was part of the research branch of the company. Initially, I worked on a team developing real-time graphics technology using Direct3D 11, but my intended role was to provide a real-time physics engine. A year and one reorganization later, I had not been fully immersed in the engine development and I had not had a chance to improve my graphics education past the Direct3D 9 level. The original team moved to a different part of the company, I stayed with the current technology group, and I found myself involved with a computer vision project that just happened to need a graphics engine with capabilities that only Direct3D 11 could provide. I had a great opportunity to build a new engine—and in a short period of time. After all, anyone working for a large company knows that the deadline for delivery was yesterday. *Didn't you get the memo?*

Fortunately, I had help from a friend and colleague, Alan McIntyre, who also assisted with the physics engine. We were able to produce a reasonable first pass, and I was delighted to see how well thought out Direct3D 11 was compared to Direct3D 9. Several months and yet another reorganization later, the team who owned us was acquired by an even larger team to work on similar computer vision topics but with a hardware component. The graphics engine was soon to get a major facelift—we got the opportunity to learn about GPGPU and compute shaders. The engine evolved over the next year and got a lot of test driving, both from team members and from our own algorithm development.

The current project grew in scope, as did the team size. I discovered that at Microsoft a common mantra is *reorganize early, reorganize often.* As much as I enjoyed working on the advanced technology, the focus of the company was changing enough and the reorganizations, both local and company-wide, were sufficient for me to question whether I had the energy to continue on at Microsoft. In Fall of 2013, the major changes occurring at the leadership level finally trickled down and affected our technology group. Although I had the opportunity to move to other parts of the company and continue working on similar projects, I decided that retirement was a more attractive offer. In my last year, I had once again gotten the urge to write books and do contract work at a small scale, something I prefer because I like to see the fruits of my labor used and I like being held directly accountable for what I do.

So here we go. As my first project, I have written this book on general purpose GPU programming using Direct3D 11. As with all my books, there is a significant source code base that accompanies it. I call this the *Geometric Tools Engine*, which will be the replacement for the Wild Magic source code I have been maintaining for the past 14 years. Much of the book references the source code, which you can download from our site http:\\www.geometrictools.com. The focus of the new engine is robust and accurate source code with implementations on the CPU, using SIMD when that makes sense, and with implementations on the GPU when possible. Although the first pass of the engine uses Direct3D 11 on Microsoft Windows computers, I will soon be writing an OpenGL-based version to support Linux and Macintosh. And like Wild Magic, I will post code updates for the Geometric Tools Engine as I finish them. No one ever said retirement would be easy!

Thanks go to the reviewers of the book proposal: Alan McIntyre, Jason Zink, and Dinesh Manocha; their insights were quite useful. Thanks to Dennis Wenzel, a very long-time friend and colleague who has a knack for poking holes in my ideas and helped me to improve the engine design. Big thanks go to Justin Hunt, a friend in the United Kingdom, who agreed to redraw all my figures for the book. I created them with Windows Paint. He made them look beautiful—and vectorized! And finally, thanks to my editor Rick Adams for his patience while I was behind schedule and to the production team at Taylor & Francis and CRC Press for a great job of finalizing the book.

Trademarks

- Microsoft Windows, DirectX, Direct3D, HLSL, Microsoft Visual Studio, Xbox 360, and Xbox One are trademarks of Microsoft Corporation.

- NVIDIA GeForce, NVIDIA SLI, CUDA, and NVIDIA Nsight are trademarks of NVIDIA Corporation.

- AMD Radeon, AMD Catalyst, and AMD CrossFireX are trademarks of Advanced Micro Devices, Inc.

- Intel Core i7, Intel Streaming SIMD Extensions (SSE), Intel Parallel Studio XE, Intel VTune Amplifier XE, and Intel Inspector XE are trademarks of Intel Corporation.

- PowerPC is a trademark of IBM Corporation.

- Macintosh is a trademark of Apple, Inc.

- OpenGL and GLSL are trademarks of Silicon Graphics, Inc.

- Java is a trademark of Oracle.

- Beyond Compare is a trademark of Scooter Software Inc.

Chapter 1

Introduction

I have been a professional software engineer on many projects, whether as a contractor working for my own company or as a full-time employee for other companies. These projects have involved computer graphics, image analysis and computer vision, and—perhaps most visibly—real-time 3D game engines and games. Although they all have relied heavily on mathematics, geometry, and physics algorithm development, these projects have several requirements that are in the realm of practical computer science and software engineering:

- requirements for robustness,

- requirements for accuracy,

- requirements for speed, and

- requirements for quality source code, ease of maintenance, reusability, and readability.

The main goal of this book is to demonstrate how to achieve some (or all) of these goals for practical problems. With sequential programming, the requirements are not always mutually satisfiable. For example, robustness and accuracy generally come at some cost in additional computing cycles, so it might not be possible to achieve the desired speed. With parallel programming, it might very well be possible to have the desired speed, robustness, and accuracy.

Although the book includes material relevant to programming on a *central processing unit* (CPU), whether single core or multiple cores, the majority of the book is about programming on a *graphics processing unit* (GPU). The evolution of GPUs was driven initially by the video game industry to achieve realistic 3D environments in real time. Recognizing the usefulness of massively parallel processors for other fields, GPUs and the associated shader languages have evolved to meet the need. This is referred to as *general purpose GPU* (GPGPU) programming. I will discuss many of the concepts, including several practical examples relevant to game programming and scientific programming.

The numerical concepts for CPUs apply equally as well to GPUs, so it is only natural to include Chapter 2, a discussion about numerical issues when computing with floating-point arithmetic. Choosing a balance among robustness, accuracy, and speed is invariably the focus when building a software product. Making trade-offs is an important part of computer science. The real number system and floating-point number system are *not the same*. It pays to know the similarities and differences, because you will get into trouble quickly if you were to develop an algorithm or solve a numerical problem as if the computer is using real numbers. This chapter contains a discussion about basic portions of the IEEE 754-2008 Standard for Floating-Point Arithmetic. Even with this amount of coverage, I will not have touched on many of the important features of the standard. The chapter finishes with several examples involving floating-point arithmetic for which the results might be unexpected if you were thinking instead about real arithmetic.

Low-level parallelism for 3D mathematics comes in the way of *single instruction multiple data* (SIMD) extensions to the CPU. This is the topic of Chapter 3. Effectively, you have 128-bit registers to work with, each storing a 4-tuple of 32-bit floating-point numbers. You can perform arithmetic operations and logical comparisons in parallel, four components at a time. With some clever thinking, you can make the SIMD instructions handle more complicated problems. The focus of the book is on the GPU, but GPUs themselves use SIMD, so it helps to understand how SIMD works on CPUs. Moreover, modern GPUs now support 64-bit floating-point numbers, but the instruction sets are limited, not providing for much more than basic arithmetic and comparisons. If you are used to having available on the CPU some of the basic mathematics library functions such as square root, sine, cosine, exponential, and logarithm functions, these are not available natively on the GPU. You must implement accurate approximations yourself, which is not a trivial task. The first part of the chapter is about basic SIMD support. The last part provides a large collection of approximations for standard mathematics functions.

Chapter 4 is the heart of the book, containing a lengthy discussion of the GPU from the perspective of Direct3D 11 (D3D11) and the High Level Shading Language (HLSL). Most game developers have been exposed to a real-time graphics system for drawing. The chapter begins with a summary of drawing 3D objects, including the various matrices that must be computed in order to transform geometric primitives so that they can be projected onto a view plane and rasterized. The various shader types are covered next with several examples of HLSL programs, how they are compiled, and how one obtains information from D3D11 about the shaders in order that they can be set up for execution at runtime. This book covers only vertex, geometry, pixel, and compute shaders. Domain and hull shaders used in conjunction with hardware-based tessellation are not discussed. GPGPU for non-game-related fields are usually heavy on compute shaders.

The chapter continues with details about creating various D3D11 objects to support drawing and computing. Input and output resources for shaders must be created properly. Resource creation for each type of resource with desired runtime characteristics can be daunting at first. Section 4.4 covers nearly every type of resource you can use in D3D11. You will also see how to create global states for blending, depth-stencil buffer manipulation, and rasterization parameters such as culling and solid or wireframe drawing. Shader creation is simple enough but I also provide examples of how to draw using a combination of vertex, geometry, and pixel shaders and how to execute a compute shader.

Copying data between CPU and GPU is almost always a bottleneck in real-time applications. Section 4.7 shows you how to copy data and provides some guidance about parallelizing data transfer when possible.

If you have two or more GPUs in your computer, you can configure them to act as one GPU. You can also configure them to run independently, at least from a programmer's perspective. Section 4.8 shows how to work with multiple GPUs regarding D3D11 adapter enumeration and device creation.

The last section of Chapter 4 discusses the IEEE floating-point support on a GPU. It is important to read this, especially when you are planning on writing compute shaders that require knowledge of how subnormal floating-point numbers are handled.

Chapter 5 is on practical matters when programming a GPU. The amount of low-level D3D11 code needed to accomplish the simplest tasks can be significant. You certainly want to think about wrapping much of the behavior in classes to allow code sharing among applications. Section 5.1 contains a discussion about a simple application built using only the Microsoft Windows and D3D11 APIs to give an idea of how much work is involved. I then discuss how I chose to encapsulate the behavior in the *Geometric Tools Engine* (GTEngine). The design and architecture of this engine have been tested in a commercial environment, albeit in a less evolved form. It has proved useful, especially for rapid prototyping of advanced real-time algorithms.

The remaining sections of Chapter 5 are about performing basic tasks on the GPU that you are used to doing on the CPU. These include debugging applications using shaders, debugging shaders themselves, measuring performance using a CPU profiler and a GPU profiler, and code testing and code coverage. These topics are more in the realm of software engineering than GPGPU algorithm development, but in a commercial environment they are useful and necessary.

The sample applications in this book are heavy on the mathematics. The Geometric Tools Engine has mathematics support—basic and advanced—for the CPU and for SIMD on the CPU. I doubt I could write a book without mathematics, so I included Chapter 6 about vector and matrix algebra, rotations and quaternions, and coordinate systems. There is always a need to understand coordinate systems and how to convert among them.

Finally, Chapter 7 has several sample GPGPU applications on relatively advanced topics. I point out some of the concepts you should pay attention to regarding performance in hopes that when you develop similar algorithms and implementations, you can try the same concepts yourself. In addition to these advanced samples, the source code distribution has a collection of basic samples to show how to use the engine and the resource types in D3D11.

Chapter 2

CPU Computing

2.1 Numerical Computing

The projects I have worked on have a common theme: numerical computing using floating-point arithmetic. It is quite easy to compute numerically using the hardware-supported `float` and `double` data types. The process is simple. Study the mathematics for the problem at hand, develop an abstract algorithm for the solution, code up a few equations, and then compile, link, and execute—the results are at your finger tips. Does the algorithm require computing the roots to a quadratic equation? No problem, just use the quadratic formula. Do you need to compute the distance between two line segments? Again, no problem. Formulate an algorithm to compute the desired distance, code it, and ship it. If it were only that easy!

At times the algorithm development can be complicated, requiring depth of knowledge in many fields. Once you get to the implementation stage, though, numerical computing is quite easy. Right? Of course it is, except for those frequent moments when you find yourself screaming and pulling out your hair because you have once again discovered *The Curse of Floating-Point Arithmetic*. My memorable moments are when I receive yet another bug report about one of my implementations for a geometric algorithm that has failed on some data set. I then painstakingly debug the code to find that once again, floating-point roundoff errors have led to failure in producing an acceptable result.

2.1.1 The Curse: An Example from Games

Although The Curse manifests itself in many ways, one of the most common in geometric applications, especially games, is particularly annoying. Consider the problem of collision detection and response of two circles, one stationary with infinite mass and one moving with constant linear velocity and finite mass. We want to determine the *time of first contact*, when the moving circle collides with the stationary circle. We also want to compute the *contact point*, which is the point of intersection at the time of first contact. At the instant of contact, the two circles intersect *tangentially*—there is no interpenetration of the objects. Finally, we want the moving circle to bounce away from the stationary circle with no loss of energy; that is, the circle's velocity changes direction but not magnitude.

Mathematically, this is a problem whose solution is relatively easy to formulate. To simplify the analysis, let the first circle have radius r_0 and center $\mathbf{C}_0$. Let the second circle have radius r_1 and center $\mathbf{C}_1(t) = \mathbf{P} + t\mathbf{V}$, where $\mathbf{V}$ is a unit-length velocity vector and where $\mathbf{P}$ is the starting location of the circle. Assuming the circles are separated initially, the time of first contact (if any) occurs when the distance between centers is equal to the sum of the radii. Using squared distances, the mathematical equation of interest is

$$F(t) = |\mathbf{\Delta} + t\mathbf{V}|^2 - (r_0 + r_1)^2 = 0 \qquad (2.1)$$

where $\mathbf{\Delta} = \mathbf{P} - \mathbf{C}_0$. The circles intersect tangentially whenever $F(t) = 0$. The function $F(t)$ is quadratic in time, $F(t) = a_2 t^2 + 2a_1 t + a_0$, where $a_2 = |\mathbf{V}|^2 = 1$, $a_1 = \mathbf{V} \cdot \mathbf{\Delta}$, and $a_0 = |\mathbf{\Delta}|^2 - (r_0 + r_1)^2$. We may now use the quadratic formula to compute the smallest positive root T of F; that is, $F(t) > 0$ for $0 \le t < T$ and $F(T) = 0$. At time T, the circles are in tangential contact, so in fact T must be a repeated root of F; thus, $T = -a_1$ and the discriminant of the equation is $a_1^2 - a_0 = 0$.

If it were possible to compute using exact arithmetic (real-valued, infinite precision, no errors), we would expect the behavior shown in Figure 2.1 when the second circle is moving toward the first. Figure 2.1(a) shows the moving circle approaching the stationary circle. As mentioned previously, the first time of contact is $T = -a_1$, a repeated root of $F(t) = 0$. At this time, the moving circle touches the stationary circle at the point $\mathbf{K}$, as shown in Figure 2.1(b). The contact point is on the line segment connecting centers $\mathbf{C}_0$ and $\mathbf{C}_1 = \mathbf{P} + T\mathbf{V}$, so we may write $\mathbf{K} = \mathbf{C}_0 + s(\mathbf{C}_1 - \mathbf{C}_0)$ for some $s \in (0, 1)$. Because $\mathbf{K}$ is on the stationary circle, $r_0 = |\mathbf{K} - \mathbf{C}_0| = sL$, where $L = |\mathbf{C}_1 - \mathbf{C}_0|$. Because $\mathbf{K}$ is on the moving circle, $r_1 = |\mathbf{K} - \mathbf{C}_1| = (1 - s)L$. Thus, $r_0/r_1 = s/(1-s)$, which has solution $s = r_0/(r_0 + r_1)$; the contact point is

$$\mathbf{K} = \frac{r_1}{r_0 + r_1}\mathbf{C}_0 + \frac{r_0}{r_0 + r_1}(\mathbf{P} + T\mathbf{V}) \qquad (2.2)$$

The unit-length, outer-pointing normal vector at the time of contact is the normalized vector difference of the circle centers,

$$\mathbf{N} = \frac{\mathbf{\Delta} + T\mathbf{V}}{|\mathbf{\Delta} + T\mathbf{V}|} \qquad (2.3)$$

The velocity of the moving circle is reflected through the normal to obtain a new velocity

$$\mathbf{V}' = \mathbf{V} - 2(\mathbf{V} \cdot \mathbf{N})\mathbf{N} \qquad (2.4)$$

Figure 2.1(c) shows the moving circle traveling in its new direction, away from the stationary circle. The time T' shown in the figure is the incremental change in time after the contact time T. The center of the circle after $T + T'$ units of time is also shown in the figure.

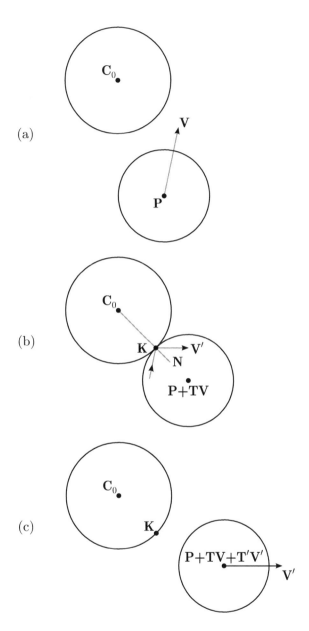

FIGURE 2.1: (a) A circle moving toward the stationary circle. (b) The moving circle's velocity is reflected through the normal vector at the contact point. (c) The circle moves away from the stationary circle in the direction of reflected velocity.

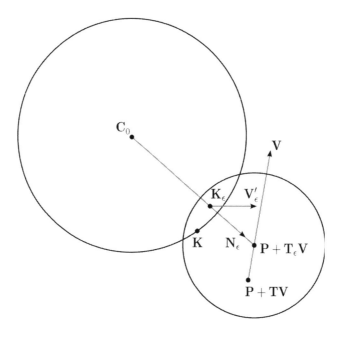

FIGURE 2.2: Numerical roundoff errors cause the circles to interpenetrate by a small amount.

Simple enough? Unfortunately not. When computing using floating-point numbers, you generally cannot compute the exact value of T as a real-valued number with infinite precision. In theory, the discriminant is exactly zero, so there is no reason to compute it numerically—just set $T = -a_1 = -\mathbf{V} \cdot \mathbf{\Delta}$. In practice, roundoff errors may produce the floating-point number $T_\epsilon = T + \epsilon$ for a small error ϵ. If $\epsilon > 0$, you move the circle centers through time T_ϵ after which the circles have a small amount of interpenetration, as illustrated in Figure 2.2.

The point $\mathbf{P} + T\mathbf{V}$ is the theoretical location of the center of the moving circle, but $\mathbf{P} + T_\epsilon \mathbf{V}$ is the numerically computed center. The point $\mathbf{K}$ is the theoretical contact point, but the numerically computed contact point is

$$\mathbf{K}_\epsilon = \frac{r_1}{r_0 + r_1} \mathbf{C}_0 + \frac{r_0}{r_0 + r_1} (\mathbf{P} + T_\epsilon \mathbf{V}) \qquad (2.5)$$

which is a weighted average of the circle centers. Because the circles are not in tangential contact due to roundoff errors, the computed contact point is not necessarily on either circle, as shown in Figure 2.2. The computed normal to be used in the collision response is

$$\mathbf{N}_\epsilon = \frac{\mathbf{\Delta} + T_\epsilon \mathbf{V}}{|\mathbf{\Delta} + T_\epsilon \mathbf{V}|} \qquad (2.6)$$

The new velocity vector for the moving circle is the reflection of $\mathbf{V}$ through this normal,

$$\mathbf{V}'_\epsilon = \mathbf{V} - 2(\mathbf{V} \cdot \mathbf{N}_\epsilon)\mathbf{N}_\epsilon \tag{2.7}$$

As Figure 2.2 demonstrates, the moving circle will travel in a direction that is consistent with our expectations for the theoretical case shown in Figure 2.1. So far, so good—the roundoff errors have not caused us any significant problems. Now that the velocity vector is updated, the collision detection system may start anew.

In the theoretical case, define $\mathbf{Q} = \mathbf{P} + T\mathbf{V} - \mathbf{C}_0$, where $\mathbf{P} + T\mathbf{V}$ is the new starting center for the moving circle. Define $\mathbf{W} = \mathbf{V}'$, which is the new constant linear velocity for the moving circle and is also a unit-length vector, because reflection through the normal does not change the length of the vector. The difference of squared distances is

$$G(t) = |\mathbf{Q} + t\mathbf{W}|^2 - (r_0 + r_1)^2 = t^2 + 2b_1 t + b_0 \tag{2.8}$$

with $G(0) = 0$ because the circles are in tangential contact. However, $G(t) > 0$ for all times $t > 0$ because the moving circle travels away from the stationary circle. They never again intersect.

In the practical case, define $\mathbf{Q} = \mathbf{P} + T_\epsilon \mathbf{V} - \mathbf{C}_0$ and $\mathbf{W} = \mathbf{V}_\epsilon$. The difference of squared distances is still represented by $G(t)$. However, the roundoff errors led to interpenetration, so $G(0) = |\mathbf{Q}|^2 - (r_0 + r_1)^2 < 0$. There is a time $\tau > 0$ for which $G(t) < 0$ for $0 \leq t < \tau$ and $G(\tau) = 0$. Without paying attention to potential problems due to floating-point arithmetic, the collision detection system repeats its algorithm by computing the time of first contact $\tau = -b_1$. The problem is that τ is really the *time of last contact*. The moving circle is moved through that time, as shown in Figure 2.3. The contact point at time τ is $\mathbf{K}'$ and the normal vector at the point is $\mathbf{N}'$. The collision system must now generate a response, which is to compute the new velocity vector $\mathbf{V}''$ by reflecting $\mathbf{V}'_\epsilon$ through the normal. As the figure demonstrates, this will cause the moving circle to re-penetrate the stationary one. It is conceivable—and has happened to the dismay of many physics programmers—that the two circles play tug-of-war trying to un-penetrate and then re-penetrate until the floating-point arithmetic is kind enough to allow them finally to separate.

Building a robust collision detection system is not trivial. In this simple example, the collision detection must be implemented knowing that floating-point roundoff errors can cause problems. The system must recognize that $G(t) < 0$ for $t < \tau$, in which case τ cannot be a time of first contact and collision response is not applied.

The brief lesson of this example is that the most important configuration of a collision detection system is when two objects are in tangential contact. But this is exactly when floating-point arithmetic fails you the most.

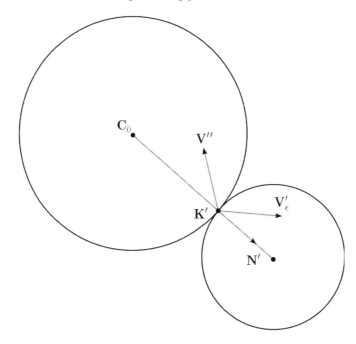

FIGURE 2.3: The moving circle is in contact with the stationary circle, but at the last time of contact.

2.1.2   The Curse: An Example from Science

As I mentioned previously, The Curse strikes regularly in my geometric code. In particular, this can happen in the incremental construction of a convex hull of points whereby the hull triangle faces are updated for each point one at a time. At the core of the construction are visibility tests. Given a point and the current hull, if the point is inside the hull, the point is discarded and the hull remains the same. If the point is outside the hull, it can see some faces of the hull but not other faces. This is akin to an observer on Earth who can see the portion of the Moon facing the Earth but the observer cannot see the dark side of the Moon.

When a point is outside the hull, the faces that are visible to the point are removed from the hull. This collection of faces forms a triangle mesh that is topologically equivalent to a disk, so the mesh boundary is a closed polyline. New faces are added to the hull by inserting triangles, each formed by the point and an edge of the polyline. After each update, the resulting set is a convex hull.

The visibility tests are equivalent to computing the signs of determinants. A point and a triangular face give rise to a determinant Δ. If $\Delta > 0$, the face is visible to the point. If $\Delta < 0$, the face is not visible to the point. If $\Delta = 0$, the face and point are coplanar. The current point is inside the hull when all

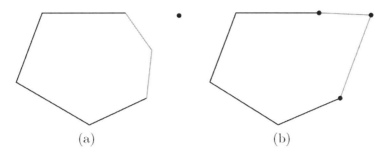

(a)   (b)

FIGURE 2.4: Updating the convex hull (in theory). (a) The visible hull edges are drawn in light gray. The invisible hull edges are drawn in black. The topmost invisible edge is nearly colinear with the current point. (b) The visible hull edges were removed and new edges inserted (drawn in dark gray).

determinants are nonpositive, in which case the point is discarded. If at least one determinant is positive, the hull must be updated. The aforementioned triangle mesh consists of those faces whose corresponding determinants are positive. In theory, one may choose either to include faces whose determinants are zero or to exclude such faces. In practice, determinants that are nearly zero can cause problems due to misclassification of the signs.

The visibility testing is similar for 2D convex hulls. Figure 2.4 illustrates the update of a convex hull when the current point is outside the hull. In theory, exact computation of the determinants ensures that the updated object is a convex hull. In practice, floating-point roundoff errors can cause misclassification of signs, particularly when the theoretical value is very small. If the theoretical value of a determinant is a small positive number, the corresponding edge is visible to the point. The numerically computed value might involve enough roundoff errors that it is a small negative number, causing the program to identify the edge as not visible. Figure 2.5 illustrates the update of a convex hull where an edge nearly colinear with the current point is misclassified as invisible. Once a misclassification occurs, the problems can be compounded because you might now have edges or faces that participate in visibility tests when theoretically those edges or faces should not exist. Conversely, edges or faces might be discarded and do not participate in visibility tests when theoretically those edges or faces do exist and should participate.

The pattern of having to compute signs of numbers without misclassifications is common to geometric computing, so you have plenty of opportunities to see The Curse.

2.1.3 The Need to Understand Floating-Point Systems

The examples discussed here show that you are ill advised to code mathematical equations without concern for the underlying system of numerical

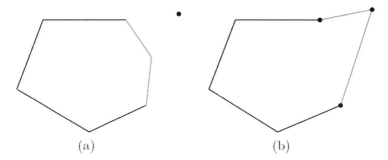

(a)   (b)

FIGURE 2.5: Updating the convex hull (in practice). (a) The visible hull edges are drawn in light gray. The invisible hull edges are drawn in black. The topmost visible edge is nearly colinear with the current point, but misclassified as invisible. (b) The visible hull edges were removed and new edges inserted (drawn in dark gray). Observe that the resulting polygon is not convex.

computation. We all sometimes make the mistake of thinking of numerical computing as real-valued arithmetic with numerical errors that are inconsequential. Floating-point arithmetic is a decent model of numerical computation. It has many similarities to real-valued arithmetic, but it also has some significant differences that can bite you when you least suspect.

One of my favorite examples of unintuitive floating-point behavior is computing roots of quadratic polynomials $f(t) = a_2t^2 + a_1t + a_0$. It is possible to choose 32-bit floating-point coefficients such that a computed root is r with $f(r)$ orders of magnitude larger than zero when the polynomial is evaluated as $f(r) = a_0 + r(a_1 + ra_2)$.

Choose $a_0 = 1.3852034\text{e-}27$, $a_1 = 0.00013351663$, and $a_2 = 3.0170867\text{e-}38$. Using the quadratic formula, the computed root is $r = $ -4.4253494e+33, which is a very large magnitude number, and the polynomial value is $f(r) = $ -2.0068245e+22, which is not close to zero by anyone's imagination. Let r_p be the largest 32-bit floating-point number that is smaller than r (the *previous* number); that is, $r_p < r$ and there are no 32-bit floating-point numbers in the interval (r_p, r). In the example, $r_p = $ -4.4253497e+33. Let r_n be the smallest 32-bit floating-point number that is larger than r (the *next* number); that is, $r_n > r$ and there are no 32-bit floating-point numbers in the interval (r, r_n). In the example, $r_n = $ -4.4253491e+33. Evaluations at these numbers produce $f(r_p) = $ +2.1253151e+22 and $f(r_n) = $ -6.1389634e+22. Observe that $f(r_p)f(r_n) < 0$, $|f(r)| < |f(r_p)|$, and $|f(r)| < |f(r_n)|$, so r_p and r_n bound the infinite-precision root $\hat{r}$ for which r is a 32-bit floating-point approximation. Thus, r is the *best approximation to the root* using 32-bit floating-point numbers.

Without the analysis of the polynomial at the floating-point neighbors of r, you might think your program has a bug. I assure you that your program is not buggy and that this is the best that you can do. In fact, the problem in this example has nothing to do with floating-point roundoff errors; rather, it is the problem of the nonuniform distribution of the floating-point numbers. For large-magnitude numbers such as r, there simply are not enough 32-bit floating-point numbers of that magnitude to produce an accurate result.

In the example mentioned here, you can switch to 64-bit floating-point numbers and obtain a more accurate result because there is a very large quantity of 64-bit floating-point numbers near the 32-bit floating-point number r. If r' is the 64-bit approximation to the root of f, you will find that $f(r') = 1.385203445788650\text{e-}027$. You will also find that $f(r'_p)$ and $f(r'_n)$ are opposite in sign but very large in magnitude. The switch to 64-bit numbers saves the day, but now it is possible to choose 64-bit floating-point coefficients for the quadratic polynomial so that the same problem happens again—the polynomial at the estimated root is orders of magnitude larger than zero.

The bottom line is that you must think about the potential consequences, good or bad, when using floating-point systems, and you must understand the parameters in your mathematical equations and the inputs for those equations to assess whether the numerically computed results will be reasonable. There is no magical solution to all your problems requiring floating-point computations, so it is essential to be detailed in your (error) analysis of your algorithms and their implementations.

I mentioned that you must understand the parameters for your equations. Just when you think that even simple situations are without problems, consider Listing 2.1.

```
// Solve numerically for x in the equation c1*x - c0 = 0.
float  c0 = 0.01f;
float  c1 = 1.0f;
float  x = c0/c1;   // Reported by debugger as 0.0099999998.
```
LISTING 2.1: Inexact representation of floating-point inputs.

Just a moment. The answer should be 0.01, right? Sorry, no. The number 0.01 cannot be exactly represented as a 32-bit floating-point number, even though you can type it exactly as a numeric constant in the source code. In fact, c0/c1 is computed exactly using floating-point arithmetic, but the result x is only an approximation to the infinite-precision result because you cannot exactly represent the *parameter* c0 in the equation. If the parameters and inputs to your equations and algorithms *already have errors in them*, any amount of exact arithmetic cannot change this. Exact arithmetic applied to approximate inputs will lead to approximate outputs.

It is equally important to understand the strengths and limitations of floating-point number systems. For an interesting and entertaining diatribe about floating-point in the Java language, see [19]. In fact, William Kahan was the primary architect of the IEE 754-1985 standard for floating-point computation, so his criticisms are well justified. I found this article while working on a contract that required computing intersections of ellipses and intersections of ellipsoids. As an approximation, I used convex polygons to represent the ellipses and convex polyhedra to represent the ellipsoids. Java was the required programming language, but I first implemented and tested the algorithms in C++ using 32-bit floating-point arithmetic. The tests showed that the code was working correctly, so I ported to Java, still using 32-bit floating-point arithmetic, but did not re-test (oops). After delivering the source code, some time later the client reported a bug for two ellipses that were slightly overlapping, as shown in a graphical display of the objects but the code was reporting no intersection. When I tested this in Java, I was able to reproduce the problem. This is when I learned that, by design (at that time), Java was not using high-precision registers for intermediate floating-point calculations whereas the C++ runtime was. Roundoff errors were significant. Fortunately, the quick-and-dirty solution was to switch to 64-bit floating-point numbers. Lesson learned—test on all relevant platforms and understand the numerical systems of those platforms.

2.2   Balancing Robustness, Accuracy, and Speed

Three important aspects of numerical computing are robustness, accuracy, and speed. These are typically not mutually satisfiable, requiring you to weigh the trade-offs for each option.

2.2.1   Robustness

Researchers have formulated definitions for robustness of geometric algorithms that are typically encountered in the field of computational geometry. The book [20] contains a chapter about robustness and degeneracy that provides a history of the topic, including references to many seminal research papers. The chapter also includes some discussion about floating-point arithmetic, about alternatives, and about how those relate to geometric algorithms. Generally, the book is focused on the theoretical details of geometric problems that one might encounter in applications, and the authors refer the reader to commercial implementations of packages for robust geometric and numerical computing.

2.2.1.1   Formal Definitions

The definitions of [20] are quite formal mathematically. A *geometric problem* is defined to be a function $P : X \to Y$, where $X = \mathbb{R}^{nd}$ is the input space and $Y = C \times \mathbb{R}^m$ is the output space.[1] The set of real numbers is $\mathbb{R}$,

---

[1] The definition includes the concept of *topology*, assigning the standard Euclidean topology to X and discrete topology to C. For the purpose of the brief summary of the definitions, it is not necessary to know what a topology is.

the set of k-tuples of real numbers is $\mathbb{R}^k$, n and d are positive integers, m is a nonnegative integer (if zero, then $Y = C$), and C is a discrete space that is referred to as the combinatorial portion of the output.

A typical example is the problem of computing the convex hull of a finite set of points in two dimensions. In the definition, $d = 2$, which is the dimension of the space containing the points, n is the number of points in the set, and $m = 0$. The input points are indexed with integers 1 through n, and C is the set of all ordered subsets of $\{1, \ldots, n\}$. The output of the convex hull algorithm is an element of C, say, $\{i_1, \ldots, i_q\}$, which represents the ordered vertices of the convex polygon that is the convex hull boundary; mathematically, the hull is the solid polygon that includes points inside as well as on the boundary. If you additionally want the algorithm to compute the area α of the convex hull, you can set $m = 1$ so that the output is a pair $(\{i_1, \ldots, i_q\}, \alpha) \in C \times \mathbb{R}$.

Another example is the problem of computing the points of intersection of pairs of line segments in the plane. We may choose n to be the number of line segments. Each line segment has two endpoints for a total of four real values, so $d = 4$. The combinatorial output is a set of 2-tuples of integers, each of the form (i_1, i_2) indicating that segments i_1 and i_2 intersect. Two segments intersect either in a single point or for an entire interval of points. We may choose always to store a pair of points with the convention that if the two points are equal, there is a single intersection. Thus, we may choose $m = 4$ because a pair of points is represented by four real-valued numbers.

Although the mathematical definition and framework support proving general results about geometric problems, it is not always immediately clear how to formulate a problem according to the definition. Also, the formulation as a geometric problem according to the mathematical definition gives no indication how you would attempt to solve the problem itself. Consider the geometric problem of computing the convex hull for a set of planar disks. At first you might think of this as a problem with an infinite number of inputs—all the points in all the disks. It is not clear how you choose n and d. It is not correct to choose $d = 2$ and $n = \infty$, because the cardinality of the integers is not the same as the cardinality of the reals. The disks have infinitely many points, but that infinity is not the same as the number of positive integers. You may instead think of the inputs as n disks, each disk defined by a center and a radius, so $d = 3$ with each 3-tuple listing the center coordinates and the radius. The output will consist of line segments and arcs of circles whose union is the boundary of the convex hull. The $\mathbb{R}^m$ term in the output space must represent the endpoints of the circular arcs and the combinatorial portion must reflect how the endpoints are ordered as you traverse the boundary.

A geometric problem can be *selective* or *constructive*. The former term says that the output is generated from a selection of elements of the input. For example, the 2D convex hull algorithm for a finite set of points selects points from the input and identifies them as the vertices of the hull. The latter term says that new objects are constructed by the algorithm. For example, the problem of all-pairs intersection of line segments requires construction of points of intersection.

A *geometric algorithm* is a function A that is applied to an input $x \in X$ of a geometric problem and produces an output $A(x) \in Y$. The algorithm *exactly computes P for x* when $A(x) = P(x)$. Of course our goal in practice is to design an algorithm that exactly computes P. However, floating-point arithmetic and other factors such as speed requirements might cause us to design an algorithm for which $A(x) \neq P(x)$ for some inputs x. If this happens, how far off are we from the correct result? The following definitions from [20] attempt to quantify this concept.

A *robust geometric algorithm* A is one such that for each $x \in X$, there is an $x' \in X$ such that $A(x) = P(x')$; that is, the output $A(x)$ of the algorithm is actually the solution to the problem for a different input x'. Additionally, a robust geometric algorithm is said to be *stable* if x' is *near to* x, which says that the output $A(x)$ is the solution to the problem for a different x' and that input x' is a (small) perturbation of x. The measure of nearness is formulated in the following definition. Let $|x|$ denote the maximum norm of x, which is the largest absolute value of the components of x. Let $O(h(N))$ denote the big-oh notation for bounds on a function $h(N)$ as integer N increases without bound. For specified values $N > 0$ and $\varepsilon > 0$, the stable algorithm A has relative error $E(N, \varepsilon)$ if for each $x \in X$ with $|x| \in O(N)$, there is an $x' \in X$ for which $|x - x'|/|x| \leq E(N, \varepsilon)$. The number N is a measure of how large the inputs are and the number ε is a measure of the accuracy of the underlying numerical representation used in the computations. Naturally, we want algorithms for which $E(N, \varepsilon)$ is as small as possible.

To illustrate, consider the incremental algorithm mentioned previously for the construction of the convex hull of a finite set of 2D points. Suppose that the computations are performed with floating-point arithmetic and that x is the input set that led to the incorrect sign classification illustrated in Figure 2.5. Intuitively, we should be able to perturb slightly the input points x to obtain a new set of input points x' for which the sign classifications are correct. In the figure, the offending point would be perturbed so that its vertical component is reduced enough to avoid the misclassification. The incremental algorithm would then correctly compute the convex hull for x', so you would conclude that the algorithm is robust.

2.2.1.2   Algorithms and Implementations

Unfortunately, the formal definition for robustness is not constructive because it tells you nothing about how to avoid problems in the first place. The previous example for incremental convex hull construction illustrated the concept of robustness, but the definition does not help you understand and avoid the misclassification of signs of determinants. Knowing that the algorithm performs correctly on perturbed inputs does not help you generate a correct output for the original data set, and it is not clear how you can prove that an algorithm is robust for all inputs.

The formal definitions also do not explicitly emphasize the distinction between two terms: *algorithms* and *implementations*. A geometric problem is defined as a function whose domain is $\mathbb{R}^{nd}$, the set of nd-tuples whose components are real numbers. A geometric algorithm is a function with the same domain. The standard incremental algorithm for computing the convex hull of a finite set of 2D points with real-valued components is provably correct when using real-valued arithmetic (exact arithmetic). However, if this *algorithm* is implemented on a computer using floating-point arithmetic, the *implementation* does not necessarily produce a theoretically correct output for each input data set. A fundamental principle for numerical computing is that there are algorithms and implementations of algorithms, and the two terms cannot be used interchangeably. The domain for a geometric algorithm is $\mathbb{R}^{nd}$, and the arithmetic operations used in the geometric algorithm are those for tuples of real numbers. However, the domain for an implementation of a geometric algorithm is typically a set of tuples of floating-point numbers, and the arithmetic operations used in the implementation are those for tuples of floating-point numbers. The theoretical correctness of an algorithm does not immediately carry over to a practical implementation, although you would like to create an implementation for which it does.

I do not intend this discussion to belittle the attempts by the theoreticians to quantify the problems inherent in numerical solutions to geometric problems—it is important in the long term to advance the frontier of the theory of computation. However, as practicing software engineers, we are tasked with producing software that solves the problems at hand and that performs according to a set of requirements. Rather than tackling the numerical problems from the perspective of the theory of computation, my goal is to explore the numerical problems on a case-by-case basis, illustrating what goes wrong and then providing analyses, alternate approaches, and perhaps principles and a mind-set that can help avoid these problems or at least reduce the impact on the application when they do arise.

2.2.1.3   Practical Definitions

For the purpose of this book, a nonscientific definition for robustness is used when solving geometric or numerical problems. An algorithm that solves a problem is one that works correctly with exact arithmetic, whether real-valued, rational-valued, or integer-valued. A robust implementation of the algorithm is one that produces *reasonable results* when using inexact arithmetic (floating-point) for an *input domain that makes sense for the practical problem*. You, the application developer, get to decide what reasonable means and what the input domain should be. For example, the geometric problem of computing the distance d between two-dimensional points (x_0, y_0) and (x_1, y_1)

is solved by the algorithm $d = \sqrt{(x_1 - x_0)^2 + (y_1 - y_0)^2}$. An implementation is shown in Listing 2.2.

```
float Distance (float x0, float y0, float x1, float y1)
{
    float dx = x1 − x0, dy = y1 − y0;
    return sqrt(dx*dx + dy*dy);
}
```

LISTING 2.2: Simple implementation for computing distance between two points.

The algorithm works correctly for all real-valued inputs, because we are assuming exact arithmetic (real-valued) and exact computation of the square root function. The implementation uses 32-bit floating-point arithmetic, so the arithmetic operations potentially have some roundoff errors and the square root function will generally produce only an approximation to the theoretical value. However, as long as the value returned from the function is reasonable for the inputs you expect in your application, then for all practical purposes the implementation is robust.

That said, the Listing 2.3 shows that you have to think carefully about your inputs.

```
int i1 = (1 << 30);
float x1 = static_cast <float >(i1 );
float d1 = Distance (0.0f , 0.0f , x1 , 0.0f );
int i2 = i1 + 64;
float x2 = static_cast <float >(i2 );
float d2 = Distance (0.0f , 0.0f , x2 , 0.0f );
float ddiff = d2 − d1;    // 0.0f
int idiff = i2 − i0;     // 64
```

LISTING 2.3: Incorrect distance computation due to input problems.

The input points are all on the x-axis. The distance from $(x_1, 0)$ to $(0, 0)$ is theoretically 2^{30}, the distance from $(x_2, 0)$ to $(0, 0)$ is theoretically $2^{30} + 64$, and so the distance from $(x_1, 0)$ to $(x_2, 0)$ is theoretically 64. The implementation believes the difference of distances is zero, which is incorrect. The problem is that 2^{30} is exactly represented as a 32-bit floating-point number, but $2^{30} + 64$ cannot be exactly represented. The IEEE 754-2008 Standard requires the integer $2^{30} + 64$ to be represented by the closest floating-point number, which is 2^{30}. A consequence is that x1 and x2 are the same floating-point number, as are d1 and d2, thus explaining why ddiff is zero. If you know that your application will produce inputs to Distance with bounded components, say, with absolute values in the interval $[10^{-8}, 10^8]$, then for all practical purposes the implementation Distance is robust. On the other hand, if your application must produce integer-valued inputs that cannot be represented exactly as floating-point numbers, the implementation Distance is not robust and you must come up with a different implementation of the algorithm that satisfies your requirements.

In the example for incremental construction of the convex hull of 2D points, the algorithm uses signs of determinants to determine how to update the current convex hull, identifying faces visible to the current input point, removing those faces, and creating new ones that share the current input point and the terminator polyline from the removed faces. An implementation of the algorithm that misclassifies the signs of determinants is not robust. Equivalently, the implementation is robust when it correctly computes the signs of determinants for the inputs the application expects. There are several approaches to correct classification of the signs, one of those using exact rational arithmetic because a floating-point number represents (exactly) a rational numbers.

2.2.2 Accuracy

The term *accuracy* refers to how close a measurement x_{meas} of a quantity is to its true value x_{true}. The closeness can be computed in terms of *absolute error*, $|x_{\text{meas}} - x_{\text{true}}|$. Closeness also can be measured in terms of *relative error*, $|x_{\text{meas}} - x_{\text{true}}|/|x_{\text{true}}|$, assuming that the true quantity is not zero.

In the context of numerical computing, the term *precision* refers to the number of significant digits or bits that can be represented by a numerical format. As we will see later, 32-bit floating-point numbers (float) have twenty-four bits of precision and 64-bit floating-point numbers (double) have fifty-three bits of precision.

The terms *accuracy* and *precision* are not the same concept, although sometimes people incorrectly use them interchangeably in a scientific context. It is possible to have measurements that are accurate and precise, accurate and not precise, precise and not accurate, and neither accurate nor precise. Typically, statements involving accuracy and precision include reference to number of digits (or bits) and/or comparisons (more accurate than, less precise than). As a simple example, consider measurements to approximate the value of $x = 1/7 = 0.\overline{142857}$, where the overline indicates that the block of digits repeats ad infinitum. The number $x_0 = 0.142857142857$ is an estimate that is accurate and precise to twelve digits. The number $x_1 = 0.142857$ is accurate to six digits but is not as precise an estimate as x_0. The number $x_2 = 0.111111111111$ is precise to twelve digits but not accurate. The number $x_3 = 0.01$ is neither precise (only two digits) nor accurate.

Accuracy and precision are indirectly related, though. Usually, the accuracy of an estimate is related to how precise the number system is. The more accurate you want the measurement, the more precise your number system must be. Of course this is not always a correct relationship. A quantity might be measured using an algorithm that is *ill conditioned*, whereby the output of the algorithm varies greatly with small changes in its inputs. A typical example is in the numerical solution of a linear system whose coefficient matrix is nearly singular. Increasing the precision of the underlying numerical system might help improve the accuracy of the solution for a limited set of inputs, but generally an increase in precision cannot overcome the ill conditioning. The latter is a mathematical issue, and it is quite possible that you might be able to construct an alternate algorithm that is well conditioned.

Naturally, it is desirable to design algorithms and implement them to obtain accurate results in a robust manner. Doing so in a timely and efficient manner may not be easy or even possible.

2.2.3   Speed

Robustness and accuracy do not always come for free. In my computational geometry code, I provide the ability to compute using exact rational arithmetic, treating the input floating-point numbers as rational numbers. The rational arithmetic is based on exact integer arithmetic for integers that have more bits than supported by standard CPUs. This means that the numerical computations are performed in software and are quite slow. This is a problem for a real-time application that must compute convex hulls at runtime. However, it is usually not a problem for a tool that runs offline to produce data to be used in a real-time application. For example, a portalizing tool can compute convex hulls to be used for visibility graphs in a real-time 3D game. All the game needs is to load the hulls for use in visibility tests. Loading costs are a one-time expense—during level loading—but the point-in-hull tests are very fast. The convex hull construction is very slow, but the hulls are computed offline and shipped with the game. The cost of construction is completely divorced from the runtime execution.

2.2.4   Computer Science Is a Study of Trade-offs

Developing algorithms and implementations that are simultaneously robust, accurate, and fast is a serious challenge. In practice, you may select any two of the three and have a chance of meeting those requirements. At the University of North Carolina, I recall hearing many times from Professor Fred Brooks: "Computer science is a study of trade-offs." This has been a dominant theme in all my practical endeavors, sometimes more so than I would like, especially when a potential client wants software that is robust, accurate, and fast. As part of my contract proposals, I try to explain the trade-offs involved in terms of what you gain and lose by each decision.

Generally, my clients want speed. No problem, just let me know how much accuracy you are willing to give up or how limited your input data sets must be to obtain that speed. Assuming the classical model of computing that involves sequential execution on a single processor, the speed-versus-whatever trade-offs play a significant role in the development. The most common trade-off is *space-time*. If you want to compute something quickly, use memory to store precomputed data or to store temporary results to avoid recomputation. If memory is limited, then you are relegated to slower computation time. On a desktop computer, memory is inexpensive and you have lots of it, so exchanging space for faster execution time is a popular choice. But even this choice has consequences to consider, especially when it comes to memory caches. As you increase memory usage for storing precomputed data, you have to be careful in how you access that memory. Data cache misses can be quite costly on modern architectures.

Computer hardware has evolved significantly over the years. These days we have several options to consider. Modern CPUs have SIMD support for vector mathematics; specifically, the CPUs have 128-bit registers that allow us to load four 32-bit floating-point numbers. These registers support fast vector and matrix mathematics. For physics-heavy real-time games, SIMD support is essential because of the extremely large number of vector-matrix operations performed by the physics engine.

Modern CPUs also have multiple cores, each core acting as a separate processor yet sharing main memory. In fact, some dual processor machines allow you to partition the main memory between the processors. This provides us with the ability to develop algorithms with components that may be computed in parallel. Sequential programming is straightforward and is the model of programming that most are used to. Programming on multiple cores requires a different mind-set, because now you have to manage communications between processors, develop parallel algorithms that can be distributed across threads, synchronize threads, and prevent concurrent access. Although nonsequential programming is more difficult to master, it is here to stay. The introduction of formal concurrency support in C++11 makes it easier to program concurrently because it has encapsulated some of the more difficult constructs, making them easier to work with. If you want faster execution of applications, especially to maintain real-time rates, you need multiple processors. The physical limitations of chips have been met—a single CPU can have only so many transistors.

Graphics hardware has also evolved quite rapidly, and GPUs are not just for graphics anymore. With a reasonably priced graphics card, you have at your disposal a massively parallel processing system. General-purpose GPU programming is quite popular. A common use in my contracting involves GPU-based image processing. It is relatively easy to implement GPU-based image filters that significantly outperform their counterparts executed on a single-core CPU. Related to this is the solution of nonlinear partial differential equations. For example, implementing a real-time numerical solver for the Navier–Stokes equations of a 3D fluid is a tractable though nontrivial task.

With all this hardware available, the speed-versus-whatever trade-offs become more interesting. You can use SIMD support for vector-matrix operations. However, you can also queue up a set of operations and perform them in parallel on multiple cores or on a GPU. Part of your algorithm development is now influenced by what hardware platforms you plan to target. Even more importantly these days with smart phones, tablet computers, and other embedded devices, we must now consider trade-offs among computation time, memory usage, and power consumption.

Although robustness-accuracy versus speed is a major player in the business of trade-offs, other trade-offs are perhaps as important. One that I mention to people that causes them to ponder for an instant is development time versus suboptimal algorithm. Sometimes we programmers decide we need an optimal algorithm to solve a problem just because that is what we are trained to do. In an industrial environment, however, that is not always the best choice. For example, suppose you need an algorithm to triangulate simple polygons with large numbers of vertices. The theoretically optimal algorithm in time is linear [5]; that is, for n vertices the computation time is $O(n)$. To my knowledge, no public implementation of this algorithm is available—for that matter, perhaps no implementation is. Linear average-time algorithms are described in [53]. In practice, a randomized linear algorithm might be used [51], which is $O(n \log^* n)$, where $\log^* n$ is the iterated logarithm function. It is a very slowly growing function that for all practical n is a constant, making the algorithm effectively linear. But even this algorithm is difficult to implement. Implementing these algorithms may require a very large amount of development time. A more commonly used algorithm involves ear clipping [26, 11]. With careful implementation, the basic algorithm in [26] runs in $O(n^2)$, and coding a robust implementation requires on the order of a few days. If the performance of an ear-clipping algorithm is acceptable for your applications, then it is worthwhile not spending a large amount of development time on something much more complicated that provides only a moderate improvement to performance.

2.3   IEEE Floating Point Standard

It is natural to expect a programming language to have built-in support for floating-point numbers and arithmetic, especially when the floating-point system has a hardware implementation as is the case on modern CPUs and GPUs. For sake of introducing yet another acronym, the hardware is referred to as a *floating-point unit* (FPU). Less powerful processors such as those on some embedded devices might not have hardware floating-point support, so you have to rely on a software implementation for floating-point arithmetic. Nothing prevents you from rolling your own, especially if you want to support only what your applications need. That said, writing a general-purpose system for floating-point arithmetic is not trivial. If you plan on your applications having the same floating-point behavior on multiple platforms, some with floating-point hardware and some without, you most likely want your software implementation to follow a standard.

The most common floating-point systems follow the IEEE Standard for Floating-Point Arithmetic. As of the time of writing of this book, the most recent version is the IEEE 754-2008 Standard, a seventy-page copyrighted PDF document that is available for purchase online from the IEEE Computer Society. Although a formidable task, it would be useful to see a reference implementation of the standard to which we can compare our own implementations, even if the reference implementation is abstract because it uses a hypothetical programming language. It is possible to infer some of the standard's requirements by writing test programs in a specific runtime environment. Of course, this assumes that the hardware and runtime libraries have an IEEE-compliant implementation of floating-point arithmetic. You also need to be careful, because sometimes you are given control over the behavior of the arithmetic. In Microsoft Visual Studio, you are given control over precision using the compiler option /fp. The default (/fp:precise) allows the 80-bit floating-point registers to be used to store intermediate computations. The final results can be much different from those that use only the number of bits provided by the floating-point type (32-bit or 64-bit). There are also potential issues to be aware of because the ANSI programming language standards are not necessarily disjoint from floating-point standards; for example, register usage in compiled code might involve different size floating-point registers, which makes it difficult to understand the runtime behavior of the code. There is also the potential that, even on the same platform, another compiler will generate floating-point code that behaves differently. Microsoft Visual Studio runtime libraries also provide platform-dependent functions _clearfp and _statusfp that allow you to determine which floating-point exceptions have occurred (if any). This leads to greater understanding of a floating-point number system—you have to understand the underlying model of numerical computation in order to write robust software.

In the sample applications, I will mention whether there are any floating-point concerns and refer to the IEEE 754-2008 Standard document if necessary. Emphasis will be on computing when all expected intermediate computations involve only finite floating-point numbers. A key aspect of the IEEE 754-2008 Standard that is of concern: an implementation of an IEEE-required function must produce a result as if it were computed with infinite precision but then rounded accordingly to a floating-point number. In the vernacular, do the best you can do with the specified precision. The example provided previously about unexpected behavior when computing quadratic roots has this flavor. The computed estimate of a root was the best you could do—the algorithm produced the 32-bit floating-point number nearest to the infinite precision root and with smallest-magnitude function value. If the best you can do is not good enough, you will need to consider other numerical systems or different formulations of your problem that allow more suitable solutions.

2.4   Binary Scientific Notation

Before we investigate the IEEE floating-point numbers, this section will motivate most of the ideas behind them, namely, manipulating binary representations of numbers.

A positive real number r may be written exactly in base-two scientific notation, which I refer to as *binary scientific notation*,

$$r = \left(1 + \sum_{i=0}^{\infty} c_i\, 2^{-(i+1)}\right) 2^p = 1.c * 2^p \tag{2.9}$$

where c_i are the bits, each having a value either zero or one and where $1.c$ is a shorthand notation for one plus the infinite summation.

Allowing an infinite sum, the representation for a rational number is not unique. For example, the number one has a representation $1.0*2^0$, which means the power is $p = 0$ and coefficients are $c_i = 0$ for all i. Another representation is $1.\overline{1}^{\infty} * 2^{-1} = 0.111\ldots$, where the power is $p = -1$ and coefficients are $c_i = 1$ for all i. The notation $\overline{1}^{\infty}$ indicates that the number 1 is repeated an infinite number of times. We obtain uniqueness in one of two ways, either choosing a finite sum (if there is one) or choosing the representation with the smallest power p. Not all numbers have finite representations; for example, $1/3 = 1.\overline{01}^{\infty} * 2^{-2}$, where $\overline{01}^{\infty}$ indicates that the number pair 01 is repeated ad infinitum. Consequently, one-third is an irrational number base 2.

For computing, we will restrict our attention to finite sums,

$$r = \left(1 + \sum_{i=0}^{n} c_i\, 2^{-(i+1)}\right) 2^p = 1.c * 2^p \tag{2.10}$$

where $n \geq 0$. All such finite sums, positive or negative and including zero, are referred to as *binary scientific numbers*. These numbers are necessarily rational. GTEngine provides support for these; see class BSNumber. More detail about binary scientific numbers are provided next.

2.4.1   Conversion from Rational to Binary Scientific Numbers

Consider the rational number $r = n/d$, where n and d are positive integers. The numerator is of the form

$$n = 2^{\ell_n} + \sum_{i=0}^{\ell_n - 1} n_i\, 2^i \tag{2.11}$$

where the high-order 1-bit occurs at index $\ell_n \geq 0$. The coefficients n_i are the remaining bits of the number. If $r = 1$, then $\ell_n = 0$ and the upper limit of the summation in Equation (2.11) is -1. Our convention is that a summation is zero when the upper limit is smaller than the lower limit. Similarly, the denominator is of the form

$$d = 2^{\ell_d} + \sum_{i=0}^{\ell_d - 1} d_i\, 2^i \tag{2.12}$$

where the high-order 1-bit occurs at index $\ell_d \geq 0$. The coefficients d_i are the remaining bits of the number, if any.

We may write r as

$$
\begin{aligned}
r &= \frac{n}{d} = \frac{2^{\ell_n} + \sum_{i=0}^{\ell_n-1} n_i \, 2^i}{2^{\ell_d} + \sum_{i=0}^{\ell_d-1} d_i \, 2^i} \\[2mm]
&= \frac{1 + \sum_{i=0}^{\ell_n-1} n_i \, 2^{i-\ell_n}}{1 + \sum_{i=0}^{\ell_d-1} d_i \, 2^{i-\ell_d}} \, 2^{\ell_n-\ell_d} = \frac{1+\alpha}{1+\beta} \, 2^{\ell_n-\ell_d}
\end{aligned}
\tag{2.13}
$$

where α and β are defined by the last equality and both numbers are necessarily in the interval $[0, 1)$.

When $\alpha \geq \beta$, $(1 + \alpha)/(1 + \beta) \in [1, 2)$ and

$$
\frac{1+\alpha}{1+\beta} = 1 + \sum_{i=0}^{\infty} c_i \, 2^{-(i+1)} = 1.c
\tag{2.14}
$$

When $\alpha < \beta$, $(1 + \alpha)/(1 + \beta) \in (0, 1)$, which implies $2(1 + \alpha)/(1 + \beta) \in (1, 2)$ and

$$
\frac{2(1+\alpha)}{1+\beta} = 1 + \sum_{i=0}^{\infty} c_i \, 2^{-(i+1)} = 1.c
\tag{2.15}
$$

Equations (2.14) and (2.15) may be combined to produce the representation

$$
r = 1.c * 2^{\ell_n-\ell_d-\omega} = 1.c * 2^p
\tag{2.16}
$$

where ω is defined by

$$
\omega = \begin{cases} 0, & 2^{\ell_d-\ell_n} r \geq 1 \\ 1, & 2^{\ell_d-\ell_n} r < 1 \end{cases}
\tag{2.17}
$$

and the power p in Equation (2.9) is

$$
p = \ell_n - \ell_d - \omega
\tag{2.18}
$$

Now consider the rational number

$$
s = 2^{-p} r = 1 + \sum_{i=0}^{\infty} c_i \, 2^{-(i+1)} = 1.c_0 c_1 c_2 \cdots
\tag{2.19}
$$

We construct the bits c_i using an iterative algorithm. Define $s_0 = 2(s - 1) = c_0.c_1 c_2 \cdots$, so c_0 is the integer part of s_0, and define $s_1 = 2(s_0 - c_0) = c_1.c_2 \cdots$, so c_1 is the integer part of s_1. The process is repeated ad infinitum, $s_{i+1} = 2(s_i - c_i) = c_{i+1}.c_{i+2} \cdots$. When using a computer, we will stop the construction after a specified number of bits has been reached. If k bits are requested, then the representation of s is

$$
s = 1.c_0 c_1 \cdots c_{k-1} + \varepsilon_t
\tag{2.20}
$$

where ε_t is the *truncation error*. Observe that the truncation error is bounded by the difference between two consecutive k-bit quantities,

$$\varepsilon_t = \sum_{i=k}^{\infty} \frac{c_i}{2^{i+1}} \in \left[0, 2^{-k}\right] \tag{2.21}$$

We may also choose to round to the nearest k-bit quantity, using a tie-breaking rule when s is equidistant from two such quantities,

$$s = 1.c_0 c_1 \cdots c_{k-1} + \frac{\gamma}{2^k} + \varepsilon_r \tag{2.22}$$

where γ is either 0 or 1 and where ε_r is the *rounding error*. Define $\rho = 0.c_k c_{k+1} \cdots \in [0, 1]$; then

$$\gamma = \begin{cases} 0, & (\rho < 1/2) \text{ or } (\rho = 1/2 \text{ and } c_{k-1} = 0) \\ 1, & (\rho > 1/2) \text{ or } (\rho = 1/2 \text{ and } c_{k-1} = 1) \end{cases} \tag{2.23}$$

The difference of two consecutive k-bit quantities is 2^{-k}, so the rounding error is bounded by

$$\varepsilon_r \in \left[-2^{-(k+1)}, 2^{-(k+1)}\right] \tag{2.24}$$

The tie-breaking rule is referred to as *ties to even*. Consider the binary number $1c_0 \cdots c_{k-1}.c_k c_{k+1} = i.\rho$. If $\rho = 1/2$, the number is equidistant from i and $i+1$. Rounding is to whichever of i or $i + 1$ is even.

Listing 2.4 has pseudocode for handling the conversion of rational numbers to binary scientific numbers. The input rational number is assumed to be positive. The input last index specifies when to terminate the conversion when the rational number base 10 is irrational base 2, in which case the output is only an approximation to the input. The pseudocode uses truncation and, for simplicity of the illustration, assumes that arbitrary-precision integer arithmetic is used; the data type is denoted Integer.

```
void ConvertRationalToBSN (Rational r, int lastIndex, int& p, int& cbits)
{
    // Get the numerator and denominator, both positive numbers.
    Integer n = r.Numerator();
    Integer d = r.Denominator();

    // Get the positions of the leading bits for the numerator and
    // denominator.
    int leadN = GetLeadingBit(n);
    int leadD = GetLeadingBit(d);

    // The first guess at the power.
    p = leadN - leadD;

    // Indirectly compute s = 2^{-p}*r by shifting either the numerator
    // or denominator accordingly.
    if (p > 0)
    {
        d <<= p;
    }
    else
```

```
{
    n <<= -p;
}

// If s < 1, we need to multiply by 2 to obtain 1 < s < 2.
if (n < d)
{
    n <<= 1;
    --p;
}
// s = n/d is in the interval [1,2).

Integer c = 1;
for (Integer mask = (1 << lastIndex); mask > 0; mask >>= 1)
{
    // Indirectly compute s = 2*(s - c); avoid the subtraction
    // when c is zero.
    if (c == 1)
    {
        n -= d;   // s = s - c;
    }
    n <<= 1;       // s = 2*s
    if (n >= d)    // s >= 1
    {
        c = 1;
        cbits |= mask;
    }
    else
    {
        c = 0;
    }
}
}
```

LISTING 2.4: Conversion of rational numbers to binary scientific numbers.

Exercise 2.1 *Modify* ConvertRationalToBSN *to use round-to-nearest rather than truncation.*

2.4.2 Arithmetic Properties of Binary Scientific Numbers

Let B be the set of binary scientific numbers, which consists of numbers of the form in Equation (2.10), both positive and negative and including zero. We may add, subtract, and multiply elements of B, the results also in B. In all cases, the algorithm for performing the arithmetic operation involves modifying the binary scientific notation to obtain a number that is a product of an integers and a power of two.

Specifically, consider $x = 1.u * 2^p$. If $1.u = 1$, define $\hat{u} = 1$. If $1.u > 0$ and u has n bits, then the last bit is a 1-bit. Define $\hat{u} = 1u_0 \ldots u_{n-1}$, where $u_{n-1} = 1$. In either case, $\hat{u}$ is an $(n+1)$-bit odd integer with $n \geq 0$ and we may write $x = \hat{u} * 2^{p-n}$. The GTEngine class BSNumber represents x as the pair $(\hat{u}, p - n)$. In the discussion of binary operations, we will use variables x and y for the inputs, and z for the output. Represent $y = 1.v * 2^q$ using pair $(\hat{v}, q - m)$ and $z = 1.w * 2^r$ using pair $(\hat{w}, r - \ell)$.

2.4.2.1   Addition of Binary Scientific Numbers

Using the previously defined notation, given operands x and y, we need to determine the values of w and r for the sum $z = x + y$. The sum is

$$x + y = 1.u * 2^p + 1.v * 2^q = \hat{u} * 2^{p-n} + \hat{v} * 2^{q-m} \qquad (2.25)$$

If $p - n \geq q - m$,

$$\hat{u} * 2^{p-n} + \hat{v} * 2^{q-m} = \left(\hat{u} * 2^{(p-n)-(q-m)} + \hat{v} \right) * 2^{q-m} = \tilde{w} * 2^{q-m} \qquad (2.26)$$

where the last equality defines $\tilde{w}$, a positive integer. Let the first 1-bit of $\tilde{w}$ occur at index f and the trailing 1-bit occur at index t.

Observe that $\tilde{w}$ is odd when $p - n > q - m$. In this case $t = 0$ and $\hat{w} = \tilde{w}$ with $\ell = f$ and $r = \ell + q - m$. When $p - n = q - m$, $\tilde{w}$ is even. We may shift right the bits of $\tilde{w}$ by t places to obtain $\hat{w}$, an $(\ell + 1)$-bit number with $\ell = f - t$. In fact, the construction applies to the previous case when $t = 0$, in which case there is no shift and $\ell = f$. Thus,

$$x + y = \tilde{w} * 2^{q-m} = \hat{w} * 2^{q-m+t} = 1.w * 2^{q-m+t+\ell} = 1.w * 2^{q-m+f} \qquad (2.27)$$

which implies $r = q - m + f$.

If $p - n < q - m$, a similar construction is applied. We compute $\tilde{w} = \hat{u} + \hat{v} * 2^{(q-m)-(p-n)}$, find the first 1-bit index f of $\tilde{w}$ and the trailing 1-bit index t, shift right $\tilde{w}$ by t bits to obtain $\hat{w}$, set $\ell = f - t$, and finally obtain $z = 1.w * 2^r$ where $r = p - n + f$.

2.4.2.2   Subtraction of Binary Scientific Numbers

The difference $x - y$ is computed similarly to the sum $x + y$ except that the $\tilde{w}$ integer is a difference of positive integers rather than a sum and is potentially negative. The BSNumber class also stores a sign in $\{-1, 0, +1\}$, so when $\tilde{w}$ is negative, the sign member is set to -1.

2.4.2.3   Multiplication of Binary Scientific Numbers

The product of $x = 1.u * 2^p$ and $y = 1.v * 2^q$ is $z = 1.w * 2^r$, where we need to determine the values of w and r. Both $1.u$ and $1.v$ are in the half-open interval $[1, 2)$, so their product is in the half-open interval $[1, 4)$; that is, $1.u * 1.v = b_1 b_0.f$ where $b_1 b_0 \in 1, 2, 3$ and $0.f$ is the fractional part in $[0, 1)$. If $b_1 = 0$, then $b_0 = 1$, $0.w = 0.f$, and $r = p + q$. If $b_1 = 1$, then $0.w = 0.b_0 f$ and $r = p + q + 1$.

If $u = 0$, then $xy = 1.v * 2^{p+q}$. If $v = 0$, then $xy = 1.u * 2^{p+q}$; otherwise, $u > 0$ and $v > 0$, so at least one bit of u is nonzero and at least one bit of v is not zero. Using the notation introduced previously, the product xy is written as

$$xy = 1.u * 2^p * 1.v * 2^q = \hat{u} * \hat{v} * 2^{p-n+q-m} = \hat{w} * 2^{p+q-n-m} \qquad (2.28)$$

where $\hat{w} = \hat{u} * \hat{v}$ is the product of integers. The product of an $(n+1)$-bit odd integer and an $(m+1)$-bit odd integer is an odd integer with either $n+m+1$ or $n+m+2$ bits. For example, consider the case $n = 4$ and $m = 3$. The product of the two smallest odd integers with the specified number of bits is (in binary) $10001 * 1001 = 10011001$, which has $n+m+1 = 8$ bits. The product of the two largest odd integers with the specified number of bits is $11111 * 1111 = 111010001$, which has $n+m+2 = 9$ bits.

We need to convert the right-hand side of Equation (2.28) back to standard form. Define $c = 0$ when the leading bit of $\hat{w}$ is at index $n+m$ or $c = 1$ when the leading bit is at index $n+m+1$, and define $\ell = n+m+c$. Thus, $\hat{w}$ is an $(\ell+1)$-bit odd integer of the form $\hat{w} = 1w_0 \ldots w_{\ell-1} = 1.w_0 \ldots w_{\ell-1} * 2^\ell = 1.w * 2^\ell$, where $w_{\ell-1} = 1$ and the last equality defines w. The product xy is therefore

$$xy = 1.w * 2^{p+q-n-m+\ell} = 1.w * 2^{p+q+c} = 1.w * 2^r \qquad (2.29)$$

The implementation of multiplication in the GTEngine class BSNumber is to multipy $\hat{w} = \hat{u} * \hat{v}$, set c by examining the location of the leading bit of $\hat{w}$, say, ℓ, and computing $r = p + q + c$, finally representing $z = xy$ as the pair $(\hat{w}, r - \ell)$.

2.4.2.4 Division of Binary Scientific Numbers

Although we can define division $x/y = 1.u * 2^p/1.v * q^2$, we would need to apply the algorithm of Section 2.4.1 to obtain the bits of $1.w = 1.u/1.v$. As noted, the sequence of bits can be infinite, so for a computer implementation, we would have to select a maximum number of bits and then round the result. The goal of implementing class BSNumber is to support *exact arithmetic*, so I chose not to implement division. Instead, we can take advantage of abstract algebra and define formal ratios of binary scientific numbers that play the same role as rational numbers do for the integers. For example, the rational number $1/3$ is meaningful and can be manipulated algebraically without ever having to compute a decimal representation $1/3 = 0.3333\ldots$. The same holds true for ratios of binary scientific numbers, which is useful for exact arithmetic in computation geometry. Only at the very end of a geometric algorithm will you potentially need approximations if you decide you need 32-bit or 64-bit floating-point results to report.

Let $x \in B$ and $y \in B$, where B is the set of binary scientific numbers as defined previously. We can define ratios of numbers in B as x/y where $y \neq 0$. Although this suggests division, it is not intended to be that way. The ratios may be defined as the set of 2-tuples $R = \{(x, y) : x \in B, y \in B \setminus \{0\}\}$. The fancy set notation says that y is in the set B but cannot be the element 0. Just as with rational numbers, a single abstract ratio can have multiple representations. For example, $1/3$ and $2/6$ represent the same number. Also, $0/1$ and $0/2$ are both representations for zero.

Given ratios $r_0 = (x_0, y_0) \in R$ and $r_1 = (x_1, y_1) \in R$, *addition* is defined as

$$r_0 + r_1 = (x_0 * y_1 + x_1 * y_0, y_0 * y_1) \qquad (2.30)$$

You are more familiar with the notation using fractions,

$$r_0 + r_1 = \frac{x_0}{y_0} + \frac{x_1}{y_1} = \frac{x_0 y_1 + x_1 y_0}{y_0 y_1} \tag{2.31}$$

where the sum is computed by constructing the common denominator of the two fractions. Observe that the components of the 2-tuple are computed using multiplication and addition of binary scientific numbers, something we already know how to do with a computer implementation (class BSNumber). Subtraction is defined similarly:

$$r_0 - r_1 = (x_0 * y_1 - x_1 * y_0, y_0 * y_1) \tag{2.32}$$

Multiplication of two ratios is defined as

$$r_0 * r_1 = (x_0 * x_1, y_0 * y_1) \tag{2.33}$$

where in fraction notation,

$$r_0 r_1 = \frac{x_0}{y_0} \frac{x_1}{y_1} = \frac{x_0 x_1}{y_0 y_1} \tag{2.34}$$

Division is similarly defined as long as the denominator is not zero,

$$r_0 / r_1 = (x_0 * y_1, x_1 * y_0) \tag{2.35}$$

where in fraction notation,

$$\frac{r_0}{r_1} = \frac{\frac{x_0}{y_0}}{\frac{x_1}{y_1}} = \frac{x_0 y_1}{x_1 y_0} \tag{2.36}$$

As with rational numbers, common factors may be removed from numerator and denominator; that is, for nonzero f, $(f * x, f * y)$ and (x, y) represent the same abstract ratio of R.

The 2-tuple notation is how you represent ratios of binary scientific numbers in a computer program. The GTEngine class BSRational is an implementation of such ratios and the arithmetic that applies to them.

2.4.3   Algebraic Properties of Binary Scientific Numbers

The binary scientific numbers B have abstract algebraic properties of interest. By abstract, I mean in the sense you learn in an undergraduate abstract algebra class about groups, rings, and fields. The set B, together with addition and multiplication, is a *commutative ring with unity*.

1. *Closure under addition:* If $x, y \in B$, then $x + y \in B$.

2. *Associativity of addition:* For $x, y, z\ in B$, $(x + y) + z = x + (y + z)$.

3. *Commutativity of addition:* For $x, y \in B$, $x + y = y + x$.

4. *Additive identity:* The number $0 \in B$ has the property $x + 0 = x$ for all $x \in B$.

5. *Additive inverses:* If $x \in B$, there is an element $y \in B$ for which $x + y = 0$; y is said to be the additive inverse of x. Our notation for the inverse is the unary negation, $y = -x$.

6. *Closure under multiplication:* If $x, y \in B$, then $x * y \in B$.

7. *Associativity of multiplication:* For $x, y, z \in B$, $(x * y) * z = x * (y * z)$.

8. *Commutativity of multiplication:* For $x, y \in B$, $x * y = x * y$.

9. *Multiplicative identity:* The number $1 \in B$ has the property $x * 1 = x$ for all $x \in B$.

10. *Distributivity:* For $x, y, z \in B$, $x * (y + z) = x * y + x * z$.

Elements of B do not necessarily have multiplicative inverses. Recall that we are restricting B to elements $1.u * 2^p$ for which u has a finite number of bits. The number $3 = 1.1 * 2^1$ is in B but does not have a multiplicative inverse in B. If it did, it would have to be the number $1/3$, but this number has representation $1/3 = 1.\bar{01}^\infty * 2^{-2}$, where the bit pairs 01 repeat ad infinitum; there is no representation with a finite number of bits.

The ratios of binary scientific numbers also have abstract algebraic properties of interest. The set R together with addition and multiplication form a *field*. Such an entity is a commutative ring with unity *and* each nonzero $r \in R$ has a *multiplicative inverse*. In our 2-tuple notation, if $r = (x, y)$ with x and y both nonzero elements of B, then the multiplicative inverse is $1/r = (y, x)$. From the definition of Equation (2.33), the product is $r * 1/r = (x * y, x * y)$. Removing the common multiple gives us $(1, 1)$ which is a representation of the multiplicative identity 1.

What do the abstract algebraic properties mean in practice? As long as you have implemented the addition, subtraction, and multiplication operators correctly, you are guaranteed that the implementation will produce exact arithmetic results. As long as two expressions theoretically produce the same number, the implementation will compute the same number.

2.5   Floating-Point Arithmetic

The common floating-point representations for computing are specified in the IEEE 754-2008 Standard for Floating-Point Arithmetic. The native type float has thirty-two bits of storage and is referred to in the standard as binary32. Such numbers are said to provide *single precision*. The native type double has sixty-four bits of storage and is referred to in the standard as binary64. Such numbers are said to provide *double precision*. This chapter provides an overview of IEEE 754-2008 floating-point numbers for the binary encodings but not for the decimal encodings. For significantly more detail, see [14] and [49].

2.5.1   Binary Encodings

The IEEE 754-2008 Standard defines *binary interchange formats* for floating-point numbers. In each format, a floating-point number has a unique encoding. The formats supported by most hardware are 32-bit (C++ type float), referred to as binary32, and 64-bit (C++ type double), referred to as binary64. Also of interest is binary16, because many graphics processors support 16-bit floating-point as a way of reducing memory for vertex buffers and/or reducing the computational load for the arithmetic logic unit.

The first encoding presented here is for 8-bit floating-point numbers, which is not particularly useful on powerful hardware but is helpful to illustrate the general concepts for binary encodings. The other sections contain brief descriptions of the binary encodings for 16-bit, 32-bit, and 64-bit formats. Generally, n-bit encodings are allowed for $n \geq 128$ as long as n is a multiple of thirty-two.

In the discussions, I will use the type name binaryN to represent the N-bit floating-point number. The type will be treated as a C or C++ union; see Listing 2.5.

```
typedef union
{
    UIntegerN encoding;     // the N-bit encoding
    FloatN number;          // the floating-point number
}
binaryN;
```

LISTING 2.5: A union is used to allow accessing a floating-point number or manipulating its bits via an unsigned integer.

This is for convenience of notation by not always having to declare explicitly a union type in the pseudocode that manipulates both the number and its encoding.

The encoding for binaryN has *signed zeros*, $+0$ and -0. At first glance, having two representations for zero might be considered unnecessary, but there are numerical applications where it is important to support this. The encoding also has *signed infinities*, $+\infty$ and $-\infty$. Infinities have special rules applied to them during arithmetic operations. Finally, the encoding has special values, each called *Not-a-Number* (NaN). Some of these are called *quiet NaNs* that are used to provide diagnostic information when unexpected conditions occur during floating-point computations. The others are called *signaling NaNs* and also may provide diagnostic information but might also be used to support the needs of specialized applications. A NaN has an associated *payload* whose

sign exponent   trailing significand

bit   7   6   5   4   3   2   1   0

FIGURE 2.6: The layout of an 8-bit floating-point number.

meaning is at the discretion of the implementer. The IEEE 754-2008 Standard has many requirements regarding the handling of NaNs in numerical computations.

2.5.1.1 8-bit Floating-Point Numbers

The layout of a binary8 number is shown in Figure 2.6. The IEEE 754-2008 Standard does not explicitly mention such an encoding, so I have chosen the encoding that I believe best illustrates the ideas for general encodings. The *sign* of the number is stored in bit seven. A 0-valued bit is used for a nonnegative number and a 1-valued bit is used for a negative number. The exponent is stored in bits four through six but is represented using a bias. If the *biased exponent* stored in the three bits is e, then the actual exponent is $e - 3$. The *trailing significand* is stored in bits zero through three. A *normal* number has an additional 1-valued bit prepended to the trailing significand to form the *significand* of the number; this bit is considered to be hidden in the sense it is not explicitly stored in the 8-bit encoding. A *subnormal* number has an additional 0-valued bit prepended to the trailing significand. To be precise, the 8-bit quantity is interpreted as follows. Let s be the 1-bit sign, let e be the 3-bit biased exponent, and let t be the 4-bit trailing significand. Listing 2.6 shows how to decode the 8-bit pattern.

```
binary8  x = <some 8-bit floating-point number>;
uint8_t  s = (0x80 & x.encoding) >> 7;   // sign
uint8_t  e = (0x70 & x.encoding) >> 4;   // biased exponent
uint8_t  t = (0x0f & x.encoding);        // trailing significand

if (e == 0)
{
    if (t == 0)  // zeros
    {
        // x = (-1)^s * 0   [allows for +0 and -0]
    }
    else  // subnormal numbers
    {
        // x = (-1)^s * 0.t * 2^{-2}
    }
}
else if (e < 7)  // normal numbers
{
    // x = (-1)^s * 1.t * 2^{e-3}
}
else // special numbers
{
    if (t == 0)
```

```
    {
        // x = (-1)^s * infinity
    }
    else
    {
        // Not-a-Number (NaN)
        if (t & 0x08)
        {
            // x = quiet NaN
        }
        else
        {
            // x = signaling NaN
        }
        // payload = t & 0x07
    }
}
```

LISTING 2.6: Decoding an 8-bit floating-point number.

The maximum (unbiased) exponent is $e_{\max} = 3$. The minimum (unbiased) exponent is $e_{\min} = 1 - e_{\max} = -2$. The relationship between the minimum and maximum exponents is required by the IEEE 754-2008 Standard. The number of bits in the significand is $p = 5$, which includes the four bits of the trailing significand and the leading 1-valued bit for normal numbers. The subnormal numbers have a leading 0-valued bit, so the number of significant bits for subnormals is always smaller than p.

The encoding has signed zeros, $+0$ (hex encoding 0x00) and -0 (hex encoding 0x80), and signed infinities, $+\infty$ (hex encoding 0x70) and $-\infty$ (hex encoding 0xf0).

The smallest positive subnormal number is $0.0001 * 2^{-2} = 2^{e_{\min}+1-p} = 2^{-6} = 1/64 = 0.015625$. All finite floating-point numbers are integral multiples of this number. The largest positive subnormal number is $0.1111 * 2^{-2} = 2^{e_{\min}}(1 - 2^{1-p}) = 15/64 = 0.234375$. The smallest positive normal number is $1.0000 * 2^{-2} = 2^{e_{\min}} = 16/64 = 0.25$. The largest positive normal number is $1.1111 * 2^3 = 2^{e_{\max}}(2 - 2^{1-p}) = 992/64 = 15.5$.

The binary encodings and their meanings are listed in Table 2.1 for the 128 numbers with a 0-valued sign bit. The *hex* column lists the encoding of the 8-bit numbers in hexadecimal format. The multiples of $1/64$ (the smallest positive subnormal) for each number is simply the floating-point value times sixty-four. The signaling NaNs are labeled sNaN and the quiet NaNs are labeled qNaN, both with payload values listed.

The finite binary8 numbers live in the real-valued interval $(-16, 16)$. It is important to observe that the distribution of the numbers is *not uniform*. Figure 2.7 shows hash marks at the locations of the binary8 numbers. The subnormals are in the interval $(0.0, 0.25)$. Zero, the subnormals, and the normals in $[0.0, 0.5]$ are uniformly distributed. The normals in $[0.5, 1.0]$ are uniformly distributed but at half the frequency for the numbers in $[0.0, 0.5]$. The normals in $[1.0, 2.0]$ are also uniformly distributed but at half the frequency for the numbers in $[0.5, 1.0]$. The pattern repeats: for each unbiased exponent

TABLE 2.1: The binary encodings for 8-bit floating-point numbers

hex	bsn	value	hex	bsn	value	hex	bsn	value
00	$+0$	0.000000	30	$1.0000 * 2^{+0}$	1.0000	60	$1.0000 * 2^{+3}$	8.0
01	$0.0001 * 2^{-2}$	0.015625	31	$1.0001 * 2^{+0}$	1.0625	61	$1.0001 * 2^{+3}$	8.5
02	$0.0010 * 2^{-2}$	0.031250	32	$1.0010 * 2^{+0}$	1.1250	62	$1.0010 * 2^{+3}$	9.0
03	$0.0011 * 2^{-2}$	0.046875	33	$1.0011 * 2^{+0}$	1.1875	63	$1.0011 * 2^{+3}$	9.5
04	$0.0100 * 2^{-2}$	0.062500	34	$1.0100 * 2^{+0}$	1.2500	64	$1.0100 * 2^{+3}$	10.0
05	$0.0101 * 2^{-2}$	0.078125	35	$1.0101 * 2^{+0}$	1.3125	65	$1.0101 * 2^{+3}$	10.5
06	$0.0110 * 2^{-2}$	0.093750	36	$1.0110 * 2^{+0}$	1.3750	66	$1.0110 * 2^{+3}$	11.0
07	$0.0111 * 2^{-2}$	0.109375	37	$1.0111 * 2^{+0}$	1.4375	67	$1.0111 * 2^{+3}$	11.5
08	$0.1000 * 2^{-2}$	0.125000	38	$1.1000 * 2^{+0}$	1.5000	68	$1.1000 * 2^{+3}$	12.0
09	$0.1001 * 2^{-2}$	0.140625	39	$1.1001 * 2^{+0}$	1.5625	69	$1.1001 * 2^{+3}$	12.5
0A	$0.1010 * 2^{-2}$	0.156250	3A	$1.1010 * 2^{+0}$	1.6250	6A	$1.1010 * 2^{+3}$	13.0
0B	$0.1011 * 2^{-2}$	0.171875	3B	$1.1011 * 2^{+0}$	1.6875	6B	$1.1011 * 2^{+3}$	13.5
0C	$0.1100 * 2^{-2}$	0.187500	3C	$1.1100 * 2^{+0}$	1.7500	6C	$1.1100 * 2^{+3}$	14.0
0D	$0.1101 * 2^{-2}$	0.203125	3D	$1.1101 * 2^{+0}$	1.8125	6D	$1.1101 * 2^{+3}$	14.5
0E	$0.1110 * 2^{-2}$	0.218750	3E	$1.1110 * 2^{+0}$	1.8750	6E	$1.1110 * 2^{+3}$	15.0
0F	$0.1111 * 2^{-2}$	0.234375	3F	$1.1111 * 2^{+0}$	1.9375	6F	$1.1111 * 2^{+3}$	15.5
10	$1.0000 * 2^{-2}$	0.250000	40	$1.0000 * 2^{+1}$	2.000	70	$+\infty$	
11	$1.0001 * 2^{-2}$	0.265625	41	$1.0001 * 2^{+1}$	2.125	71	sNaN, payload 001	
12	$1.0010 * 2^{-2}$	0.281250	42	$1.0010 * 2^{+1}$	2.250	72	sNaN, payload 010	
13	$1.0011 * 2^{-2}$	0.296875	43	$1.0011 * 2^{+1}$	2.375	73	sNaN, payload 011	
14	$1.0100 * 2^{-2}$	0.312500	44	$1.0100 * 2^{+1}$	2.500	74	sNaN, payload 100	
15	$1.0101 * 2^{-2}$	0.328125	45	$1.0101 * 2^{+1}$	2.625	75	sNaN, payload 101	
16	$1.0110 * 2^{-2}$	0.343750	46	$1.0110 * 2^{+1}$	2.750	76	sNaN, payload 110	
17	$1.0111 * 2^{-2}$	0.359375	47	$1.0111 * 2^{+1}$	2.875	77	sNaN, payload 111	
18	$1.1000 * 2^{-2}$	0.375000	48	$1.1000 * 2^{+1}$	3.000	78	qNaN, payload 000	
19	$1.1001 * 2^{-2}$	0.390625	49	$1.1001 * 2^{+1}$	3.125	79	qNaN, payload 001	
1A	$1.1010 * 2^{-2}$	0.406250	4A	$1.1010 * 2^{+1}$	3.250	7A	qNaN, payload 010	
1B	$1.1011 * 2^{-2}$	0.421875	4B	$1.1011 * 2^{+1}$	3.375	7B	qNaN, payload 011	
1C	$1.1100 * 2^{-2}$	0.437500	4C	$1.1100 * 2^{+1}$	3.500	7C	qNaN, payload 100	
1D	$1.1101 * 2^{-2}$	0.453125	4D	$1.1101 * 2^{+1}$	3.625	7D	qNaN, payload 101	
1E	$1.1110 * 2^{-2}$	0.468750	4E	$1.1110 * 2^{+1}$	3.750	7E	qNaN, payload 110	
1F	$1.1111 * 2^{-2}$	0.484375	4F	$1.1111 * 2^{+1}$	3.875	7F	qNaN, payload 111	
20	$1.0000 * 2^{-1}$	0.50000	50	$1.0000 * 2^{+2}$	4.00			
21	$1.0001 * 2^{-1}$	0.53125	51	$1.0001 * 2^{+2}$	4.25			
22	$1.0010 * 2^{-1}$	0.56250	52	$1.0010 * 2^{+2}$	4.50			
23	$1.0011 * 2^{-1}$	0.59375	53	$1.0011 * 2^{+2}$	4.75			
24	$1.0100 * 2^{-1}$	0.62500	54	$1.0100 * 2^{+2}$	5.00			
25	$1.0101 * 2^{-1}$	0.65625	55	$1.0101 * 2^{+2}$	5.25			
26	$1.0110 * 2^{-1}$	0.68750	56	$1.0110 * 2^{+2}$	5.50			
27	$1.0111 * 2^{-1}$	0.71875	57	$1.0111 * 2^{+2}$	5.75			
28	$1.1000 * 2^{-1}$	0.75000	58	$1.1000 * 2^{+2}$	6.00			
29	$1.1001 * 2^{-1}$	0.78125	59	$1.1001 * 2^{+2}$	6.25			
2A	$1.1010 * 2^{-1}$	0.81250	5A	$1.1010 * 2^{+2}$	6.50			
2B	$1.1011 * 2^{-1}$	0.84375	5B	$1.1011 * 2^{+2}$	6.75			
2C	$1.1100 * 2^{-1}$	0.87500	5C	$1.1100 * 2^{+2}$	7.00			
2D	$1.1101 * 2^{-1}$	0.90625	5D	$1.1101 * 2^{+2}$	7.25			
2E	$1.1110 * 2^{-1}$	0.93750	5E	$1.1110 * 2^{+2}$	7.50			
2F	$1.1111 * 2^{-1}$	0.96875	5F	$1.1111 * 2^{+2}$	7.75			

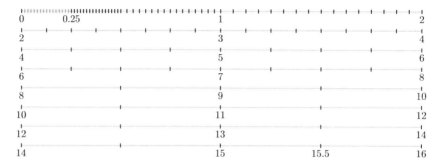

FIGURE 2.7: The distribution of the nonnegative binary8 numbers. The fifteen subnormal numbers are shown with gray hash marks. The normal numbers are shown with black hash marks.

TABLE 2.2: Quantities of interest for binary8

name	value	name	value
F8_NUM_ENCODING_BITS	8	F8_MAX_TRAILING	0x0f
F8_NUM_EXPONENT_BITS	3	F8_SUP_TRAILING	0x10
F8_NUM_SIGNIFICAND_BITS	5	F8_POS_ZERO	0x00
F8_NUM_TRAILING_BITS	4	F8_NEG_ZERO	0x80
F8_EXPONENT_BIAS	3	F8_MIN_SUBNORMAL	0x01
F8_MAX_BIASED_EXPONENT	7	F8_MAX_SUBNORMAL	0x0f
F8_SIGN_MASK	0x80	F8_MIN_NORMAL	0x10
F8_NOT_SIGN_MASK	0x7f	F8_MAX_NORMAL	0x6f
F8_BIASED_EXPONENT_MASK	0x70	F8_INFINITY	0x70
F8_TRAILING_MASK	0x0f		
F8_NAN_QUIET_MASK	0x08		
F8_NAN_PAYLOAD_MASK	0x07		

λ, the numbers with that exponent are uniformly distributed in the interval $[2^\lambda, 2^{\lambda+1}]$ but at half the frequency for the numbers in the interval $[2^{\lambda-1}, 2^\lambda]$.

When implementing floating-point arithmetic in software, it is convenient to define some quantities of interest as listed in Table 2.2. Similar quantities will be defined for other binary encodings. The enumerate F8_INFINITY is assigned to a number that corresponds to the encoding 2^4, but this is not to be considered the value of $+\infty$. Infinities are handled differently from finite floating-point numbers. The enumerate is for bit-pattern testing in the software implementation.

As we explore the properties and arithmetic of floating-point numbers with binary encodings of more bits, it is sometimes instructive to refer back to binary8 as motivation because it is easy to wrap your head around a floating-point number system with so few numbers.

2.5.1.2   16-Bit Floating-Point Numbers

The layout of a binary16 number is shown in Figure 2.8. The *sign* of the number is stored in bit fifteen. A 0-valued bit is used for a nonnegative number and a 1-valued bit is used for a negative number. The exponent is stored

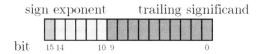

sign exponent   trailing significand

bit   15 14   10 9   0

FIGURE 2.8: The layout of a 16-bit floating-point number.

in bits ten through fourteen, but is represented using a bias. If the *biased exponent* stored in the five bits is e, then the actual exponent is $e - 15$. The *trailing significand* is stored in bits zero through nine. A *normal* number has an additional 1-valued bit prepended to the trailing significand to form the *significand* of the number; this bit is considered to be hidden in the sense it is not explicitly stored in the 16-bit encoding. A *subnormal* number has an additional 0-valued bit prepended to the trailing significand. To be precise, the 16-bit quantity is interpreted as follows. Let s be the 1-bit sign, let e be the 5-bit biased exponent, and let t be the 10-bit trailing significand. Listing 2.7 shows how to decode the 16-bit pattern.

```
binary16 x = <some 16-bit floating-point number>;
uint16_t s = (0x8000 & x.encoding) >> 15;  // sign
uint16_t e = (0x7c00 & x.encoding) >> 10;  // biased exponent
uint16_t t = (0x03ff & x.encoding);        // trailing significand

if (e == 0)
{
    if (t == 0)  // zeros
    {
        // x = (-1)^s * 0  [allows for +0 and -0]
    }
    else  // subnormal numbers
    {
        // x = (-1)^s * 0.t * 2^{-14}
    }
}
else if (e < 31)  // normal numbers
{
    // x = (-1)^s * 1.t * 2^{e-15}
}
else  // special numbers
{
    if (t == 0)
    {
        // x = (-1)^s * infinity
    }
    else
    {
        // Not-a-Number (NaN)
        if (t & 0x0200)
        {
            // x = quiet NaN
        }
        else
        {
            // x = signaling NaN
        }
        // payload = t & 0x01ff
    }
}
```

LISTING 2.7: Decoding a 16-bit floating-point number.

TABLE 2.3: Quantities of interest for binary16

name	value	name	value
F16_NUM_ENCODING_BITS	16	F16_MAX_TRAILING	0x03ff
F16_NUM_EXPONENT_BITS	5	F16_SUP_TRAILING	0x0400
F16_NUM_SIGNIFICAND_BITS	11	F16_POS_ZERO	0x0000
F16_NUM_TRAILING_BITS	10	F16_NEG_ZERO	0x8000
F16_EXPONENT_BIAS	15	F16_MIN_SUBNORMAL	0x0001
F16_MAX_BIASED_EXPONENT	31	F16_MAX_SUBNORMAL	0x03ff
F16_SIGN_MASK	0x8000	F16_MIN_NORMAL	0x0400
F16_NOT_SIGN_MASK	0x7fff	F16_MAX_NORMAL	0x7bff
F16_BIASED_EXPONENT_MASK	0x7c00	F16_INFINITY	0x7c00
F16_TRAILING_MASK	0x03ff		
F16_NAN_QUIET_MASK	0x0200		
F16_NAN_PAYLOAD_MASK	0x01ff		

The maximum (unbiased) exponent is $e_{\max} = 15$. The minimum (unbiased) exponent is $e_{\min} = 1 - e_{\max} = -14$. The relationship between the minimum and maximum exponents is required by the IEEE 754-2008 Standard. The number of bits in the significand is $p = 11$, which includes the ten bits of the trailing significand and the leading 1-valued bit for normal numbers. The subnormal numbers have a leading 0-valued bit, so the number of significant bits for subnormals is always smaller than p.

The encoding has signed zeros, $+0$ (hex encoding 0x0000) and -0 (hex encoding 0x8000), and signed infinities, $+\infty$ (hex encoding 0x7c00) and $-\infty$ (hex encoding 0xfc00).

The smallest positive subnormal number occurs when $e = 0$ and $t = 1$, which is $2^{e_{\min}+1-p} = 2^{-24}$. All finite floating-point numbers are integral multiples of this number. The largest positive subnormal number occurs when $e = 0$ and t has all 1-valued bits, which is $2^{e_{\min}}(1 - 2^{1-p}) = 2^{-14}(1 - 2^{-10})$. The smallest positive normal number occurs when $e = 1$ and $t = 0$, which is $2^{e_{\min}} = 2^{-14}$. The largest positive normal number occurs when $e = 30$ and t has all 1-valued bits, which is $2^{e_{\max}}(2 - 2^{1-p}) = 2^{15}(2 - 2^{-10})$.

The subnormals are in the interval $(0, 2^{-14})$. Zero, the subnormals, and the normals in $[0, 2^{-13}]$ are uniformly distributed. Just as for the 8-bit floating-point numbers, for each unbiased exponent $\lambda > 1$, the numbers with that exponent are uniformly distributed in the interval $[2^{\lambda}, 2^{\lambda+1}]$ but at half the frequency for the numbers in the interval $[2^{\lambda-1}, 2^{\lambda}]$.

When implementing floating-point arithmetic in software, it is convenient to define some quantities of interest as listed in Table 2.3. Similar quantities will be defined for other binary encodings. The enumerate F16_INFINITY is assigned to a number that corresponds to the encoding 2^{16}, but this is not to be considered the value of $+\infty$. Infinities are handled differently from finite floating-point numbers. The enumerate is for bit-pattern testing in the software implementation.

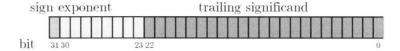

sign exponent   trailing significand

bit   31 30   23 22   0

FIGURE 2.9: The layout of a 32-bit floating-point number.

2.5.1.3   32-Bit Floating-Point Numbers

The layout of a `binary32` number is shown in Figure 2.9. The *sign* of the number is stored in bit thirty-one. A 0-valued bit is used for a nonnegative number and a 1-valued bit is used for a negative number. The exponent is stored in bits twenty-three through thirty, but is represented using a bias. If the *biased exponent* stored in the eight bits is e, then the actual exponent is $e - 127$. The *trailing significand* is stored in bits zero through twenty-two. A *normal* number has an additional 1-valued bit prepended to the trailing significand to form the *significand* of the number; this bit is considered to be hidden in the sense it is not explicitly stored in the 32-bit encoding. A *subnormal* number has an additional 0-valued bit prepended to the trailing significand. To be precise, the 32-bit quantity is interpreted as follows. Let s be the 1-bit sign, let e be the 8-bit biased exponent, and let t be the 23-bit trailing significand. Listing 2.8 shows how to decode the 32-bit pattern.

```
binary32 x = <some 32−bit floating−point number>;
uint32_t s = (0x80000000 & x.encoding) >> 31;   // sign
uint32_t e = (0x7f800000 & x.encoding) >> 23;   // biased exponent
uint32_t t = (0x007fffff & x.encoding);          // trailing significand

if (e == 0)
{
    if (t == 0)  // zeros
    {
        // x = (−1)^s * 0  [allows for +0 and −0]
    }
    else  // subnormal numbers
    {
        // x = (−1)^s * 0.t * 2^{−126}
    }
}
else if (e < 255)  // normal numbers
{
    // x = (−1)^s * 1.t * 2^{e−127}
}
else  // special numbers
{
    if (t == 0)
    {
        // x = (−1)^s * infinity
    }
    else
    {
        // Not−a−Number
        if (t & 0x00400000)
        {
            // x = quiet NaN
```

```
        }
        else
        {
            // x = signaling NaN
        }
        // payload = t & 0x003fffff
    }
}
```

LISTING 2.8: Decoding a 32-bit floating-point number.

The maximum (unbiased) exponent is $e_{\max} = 127$. The minimum (unbiased) exponent is $e_{\min} = 1 - e_{\max} = -126$. The relationship between the minimum and maximum exponents is required by the IEEE 754-2008 Standard. The number of bits in the significand is $p = 24$, which includes the twenty-three bits of the trailing significand and the leading 1-valued bit for normal numbers. The subnormal numbers have a leading 0-valued bit, so the number of significant bits for subnormals is always smaller than p.

The encoding has signed zeros, $+0$ (hex encoding 0x00000000) and -0 (hex encoding 0x80000000), and signed infinities, $+\infty$ (hex encoding 0x7f800000) and $-\infty$ (hex encoding 0xff800000).

The smallest positive subnormal number occurs when $e = 0$ and $t = 1$, which is $2^{e_{\min}+1-p} = 2^{-149}$. All finite floating-point numbers are integral multiples of this number. The largest positive subnormal number occurs when $e = 0$ and t has all 1-valued bits, which is $2^{e_{\min}}(1 - 2^{1-p}) = 2^{-126}(1 - 2^{-23})$. The smallest positive normal number occurs when $e = 1$ and $t = 0$, which is $2^{e_{\min}} = 2^{-126}$. The largest positive normal number occurs when $e = 254$ and t has all 1-valued bits, which is $2^{e_{\max}}(2 - 2^{1-p}) = 2^{127}(2 - 2^{-23})$.

The subnormals are in the interval $(0, 2^{-126})$. Zero, the subnormals, and the normals in $[0, 2^{-125}]$ are uniformly distributed. Just as for the 8-bit floating-point numbers, for each unbiased exponent $\lambda > 1$, the numbers with that exponent are uniformly distributed in the interval $[2^\lambda, 2^{\lambda+1}]$ but at half the frequency for the numbers in the interval $[2^{\lambda-1}, 2^\lambda]$.

When implementing floating-point arithmetic in software, it is convenient to define some quantities of interest as listed in Table 2.4. Similar quantities will be defined for other binary encodings. The enumerate F32_INFINITY is

TABLE 2.4: Quantities of interest for binary32

name	value	name	value
F32_NUM_ENCODING_BITS	32	F32_MAX_TRAILING	0x007fffff
F32_NUM_EXPONENT_BITS	8	F32_SUP_TRAILING	0x00800000
F32_NUM_SIGNIFICAND_BITS	24	F32_POS_ZERO	0x00000000
F32_NUM_TRAILING_BITS	23	F32_NEG_ZERO	0x80000000
F32_EXPONENT_BIAS	127	F32_MIN_SUBNORMAL	0x00000001
F32_MAX_BIASED_EXPONENT	255	F32_MAX_SUBNORMAL	0x007fffff
F32_SIGN_MASK	0x80000000	F32_MIN_NORMAL	0x00800000
F32_NOT_SIGN_MASK	0x7fffffff	F32_MAX_NORMAL	0x7f7fffff
F32_BIASED_EXPONENT_MASK	0x7f800000	F32_INFINITY	0x7f800000
F32_TRAILING_MASK	0x007fffff		
F32_NAN_QUIET_MASK	0x00400000		
F32_NAN_PAYLOAD_MASK	0x003fffff		

sign exponent   trailing significand

bit   63 62   52 51   0

FIGURE 2.10: The layout of a 64-bit floating-point number.

assigned to a number that corresponds to the encoding 2^{128}, but this is not to be considered the value of $+\infty$. Infinities are handled differently from finite floating-point numbers. The enumerate is for bit-pattern testing in the software implementation.

2.5.1.4   64-Bit Floating-Point Numbers

The layout of a binary64 number is shown in Figure 2.10. The *sign* of the number is stored in bit sixty-three. A 0-valued bit is used for a nonnegative number and a 1-valued bit is used for a negative number. The exponent is stored in bits fifty-two through sixty-two, but is represented using a bias. If the *biased exponent* stored in the eleven bits is e, then the actual exponent is $e - 1023$. The *trailing significand* is stored in bits zero through fifty-one. A *normal* number has an additional 1-valued bit prepended to the trailing significand to form the *significand* of the number; this bit is considered to be hidden in the sense it is not explicitly stored in the 32-bit encoding. A *subnormal* number has an additional 0-valued bit prepended to the trailing significand. To be precise, the 64-bit quantity is interpreted as follows. Let s be the 1-bit sign, let e be the 11-bit biased exponent, and let t be the 52-bit trailing significand. Listing 2.9 shows how to decode the 64-bit pattern.

```
binary64 x = <some 64-bit floating-point number>;
uint64_t s = (0x8000000000000000 & x.encoding) >> 63;  // sign
uint64_t e = (0x7ff0000000000000 & x.encoding) >> 52;  // biased exponent
uint64_t t = (0x000fffffffffffff & x.encoding);  // trailing significand

if (e == 0)
{
    if (t == 0)  // zeros
    {
        // x = (-1)^s * 0  [allows for +0 and -0]
    }
    else  // subnormal numbers
    {
        // x = (-1)^s * 0.t * 2^{-1022}
    }
}
else if (e < 2047)  // normal numbers
{
    // x = (-1)^s * 1.t * 2^{e-1023}
}
else  // special numbers
{
    if (t == 0)
    {
        // x = (-1)^s * infinity
```

```
    }
    else
    {
        if (t & 0x0008000000000000)
        {
            // x = quiet NaN
        }
        else
        {
            // x = signaling NaN
        }
        // payload = t & 0x0007ffffffffffff
    }
}
```

LISTING 2.9: Decoding a 64-bit floating-point number.

The maximum (unbiased) exponent is $e_{\max} = 1023$. The minimum (unbiased) exponent is $e_{\min} = 1 - e_{\max} = -1022$. The relationship between the minimum and maximum exponents is required by the IEEE 754-2008 Standard. The number of bits in the significand is $p = 53$, which includes the fifty-two bits of the trailing significand and the leading 1-valued bit for normal numbers. The subnormal numbers have a leading 0-valued bit, so the number of significant bits for subnormals is always smaller than p.

The encoding has signed zeros, $+0$ (hex encoding 0x0000000000000000) and -0 (hex encoding 0x8000000000000000), and signed infinities, $+\infty$ (hex encoding 0x7ff0000000000000) and $-\infty$ (hex encoding 0xfff0000000000000).

The smallest positive subnormal number occurs when $e = 0$ and $t = 1$, which is $2^{e_{\min}+1-p} = 2^{-1074}$. All finite floating-point numbers are integral multiples of this number. The largest positive subnormal number occurs when $e = 0$ and t has all 1-valued bits, which is $2^{e_{\min}}(1 - 2^{1-p}) = 2^{-1022}(1 - 2^{-52})$. The smallest positive normal number occurs when $e = 1$ and $t = 0$, which is $2^{e_{\min}} = 2^{-1022}$. The largest positive normal number occurs when $e = 2046$ and t has all 1-valued bits, which is $2^{e_{\max}}(2 - 2^{1-p}) = 2^{1023}(2 - 2^{-52})$.

The subnormals are in the interval $(0, 2^{-1022})$. Zero, the subnormals, and the normals in $[0, 2^{-1021}]$ are uniformly distributed. Just as for the 8-bit floating-point numbers, for each unbiased exponent $\lambda > 1$, the numbers with that exponent are uniformly distributed in the interval $[2^\lambda, 2^{\lambda+1}]$ but at half the frequency for the numbers in the interval $[2^{\lambda-1}, 2^\lambda]$.

When implementing floating-point arithmetic in software, it is convenient to define some quantities of interest as listed in Table 2.5. Similar quantities will be defined for other binary encodings. The enumerate F64_INFINITY is assigned to a number that corresponds to the encoding 2^{1024}, but this is not to be considered the value of $+\infty$. Infinities are handled differently from finite floating-point numbers. The enumerate is for bit-pattern testing in the software implementation.

2.5.1.5   *n*-Bit Floating-Point Numbers

The IEEE 754-2008 Standard specifies the requirements for binary encodings of *n*-bit numbers for $n \geq 128$ a multiple of thirty-two bits. The sign bit

TABLE 2.5: Quantities of interest for binary64

name	value
F64_NUM_ENCODING_BITS	64
F64_NUM_EXPONENT_BITS	11
F64_NUM_SIGNIFICAND_BITS	53
F64_NUM_TRAILING_BITS	52
F64_EXPONENT_BIAS	1023
F64_MAX_BIASED_EXPONENT	2047
F64_SIGN_MASK	0x8000000000000000
F64_NOT_SIGN_MASK	0x7fffffffffffffff
F64_BIASED_EXPONENT_MASK	0x7ff0000000000000
F64_TRAILING_MASK	0x000fffffffffffff
F64_NAN_QUIET_MASK	0x0008000000000000
F64_NAN_PAYLOAD_MASK	0x0007ffffffffffff
F64_MAX_TRAILING	0x000fffffffffffff
F64_SUP_TRAILING	0x0010000000000000
F64_POS_ZERO	0x0000000000000000
F64_NEG_ZERO	0x8000000000000000
F64_MIN_SUBNORMAL	0x0000000000000001
F64_MAX_SUBNORMAL	0x000fffffffffffff
F64_MIN_NORMAL	0x0010000000000000
F64_MAX_NORMAL	0x7fefffffffffffff
F64_INFINITY	0x7ff0000000000000

is the high-order bit, followed by $w = \mathrm{round}(4\log_2(k)) - 13$ exponent bits, where the rounding function is to the nearest integer. The exponent bits are followed by $t = n - w - 1$ trailing significand bits. The precision (in bits) is $p = t + 1$. The maximum (unbiased) exponent is $e_{\max} = 2^{n-p-1} - 1$, the minimum (unbiased) exponent is $e_{\min} = 1 - e_{\max}$, the exponent bias is $\beta = e_{\max}$, and if e is a biased exponent, the unbiased exponent is $e - \beta$. The number of exponent bits for binary128 is fifteen and the number of trailing significand bits is 112. The number of exponent bits for binary256 is nineteen and the number of trailing significand bits is 236.

The smallest positive subnormal number occurs when $e = 0$ and $t = 1$, which is $2^{e_{\min}+1-p}$. All finite floating-point numbers are integral multiples of this number. The largest positive subnormal number occurs when $e = 0$ and t has all 1-valued bits, which is $2^{e_{\min}}(1 - 2^{1-p})$. The smallest positive normal number occurs when $e = 1$ and $t = 0$, which is $2^{e_{\min}}$. The largest positive normal number occurs when $e = e_{\max}$ and t has all 1-valued bits, which is $2^{e_{\max}}(2 - 2^{1-p})$.

The subnormals are in the interval $(0, 2^{-e_{\min}})$. Zero, the subnormals, and the normals in $[0, 2^{1-e_{\min}}]$ are uniformly distributed. Just as for the 8-bit floating-point numbers, for each unbiased exponent $\lambda > 1$, the numbers with that exponent are uniformly distributed in the interval $[2^\lambda, 2^{\lambda+1}]$ but at half the frequency for the numbers in the interval $[2^{\lambda-1}, 2^\lambda]$.

When implementing floating-point arithmetic in software, it is convenient to define some quantities of interest, as shown in Listing 2.10. The data types Integer (signed integer) and UInteger (unsigned integer) are assumed to use n bits.

```
Integer   NUM_ENCODING_BITS = <number of bits in the encoding>;
Integer   NUM_EXPONENT_BITS = Round(4*log2(NUM_ENCODING_BITS) - 13);
Integer   NUM_SIGNIFICAND_BITS = NUM_ENCODING_BITS - NUM_EXPONENT_BITS;
Integer   NUM_TRAILING_BITS = NUM_SIGNIFICAND_BITS - 1;
Integer   EXPONENT_BIAS = (1 << (NUM_EXPONENT_BITS - 1)) - 1;
Integer   MAX_BIASED_EXPONENT = 2*EXPONENT_BIAS;
UInteger  SIGN_MASK = (1 << (NUM_ENCODING_BITS - 1));
UInteger  NOT_SIGN_MASK = ~SIGN_MASK;
UInteger  SUP_TRAILING = (1 << NUM_TRAILING_BITS);
UInteger  BIASED_EXPONENT_MASK = SIGN_MASK - SUP_TRAILING;
UInteger  TRAILING_MASK = SUP_TRAILING - 1;
UInteger  MAX_TRAILING = TRAILING_MASK;
UInteger  NAN_QUIET_MASK = (1 << (NUM_TRAILING_BITS - 1));
UInteger  NAN_PAYLOAD_MASK = NAN_QUIET_MASK - 1;
UInteger  POS_ZERO = 0;
UInteger  NEG_ZERO = SIGN_MASK;
UInteger  MIN_SUBNORMAL = 1;
UInteger  MAX_SUBNORMAL = TRAILING_MASK;
UInteger  MIN_NORMAL = SUP_TRAILING;
UInteger  MAX_NORMAL = BIASED_EXPONENT_MASK - 1 + MAX_TRAILING;
UInteger  INFINITY = BIASED_EXPONENT_MASK;
```

LISTING 2.10: Integer and unsigned integer quantities that are useful for encoding and decoding floating-point numbers.

The enumerate INFINITY is assigned to a number that corresponds to the encoding 2^{w-1}, but this is not to be considered the value of $+\infty$. Infinities are handled differently from finite floating-point numbers. The enumerate is for bit-pattern testing in the software implementation.

The general decoding of floating-point numbers is shown in Listing 2.11 and is similar to the pseudocode provided for 8-bit, 16-bit, 32-bit, and 64-bit floating-point numbers.

```
binaryN  x = <some n-bit floating-point number>;
UInteger s = (SIGN_MASK & x.encoding) >> (NUM_ENCODING_BITS - 1);
UInteger e = (BIASED_EXPONENT_MASK & x.encoding) >> NUM_TRAILING_BITS;
UInteger t = (TRAILING_MASK & x.encoding);

if (e == 0)
{
    if (t == 0)  // zeros
    {
        // x = (-1)^s * 0 [allows for +0 and -0]
    }
    else  // subnormal numbers
    {
        // x = (-1)^s * 0.t * 2^{1 - EXPONENT_BIAS}
    }
}
else if (e < MAX_BIASED_EXPONENT)  // normal numbers
{
    // x = (-1)^s * 1.t * 2^{e - EXPONENT_BIAS}
}
else  // special numbers
{
    if (t == 0)
    {
        // x = (-1)^s * infinity
    }
    else
    {
        if (t & NAN_QUIET_MASK)
        {
```

```
                //  x  =  quiet  NaN
        }
        else
        {
                //  x  =  signaling  NaN
        }
        //  payload  =  t  &  NAN_PAYLOAD_MASK
    }
}
```

LISTING 2.11: The general decoding of floating-point numbers.

The pseudocode that extracts the sign, biased exponent, and trailing significand may be encapsulated, as shown in Listing 2.12. The combination of parts into a number may also be encapsulated. There is no reason to shift the sign bit into the lowest-order bit.

```
void  GetEncoding  ( binaryN  x,  UInteger&  sign ,  UInteger&  biased ,
    UInteger&  trailing )
{
    sign  =  ( x . encoding  &  SIGN_MASK );
    biased  =  ( x . encoding  &  BIASED_EXPONENT_MASK )  >>  NUM_TRAILING_BITS ;
    trailing  =  ( x . encoding  &  TRAILING_MASK );
}

binaryN  SetEncoding  ( UInteger  sign ,  UInteger  biased ,  UInteger  trailing )
{
    binaryN  x;
    x . encoding  =  sign  |  ( biased  <<  NUM_TRAILING_BITS )  |  trailing ;
    return  x;
}
```

LISTING 2.12: Convenient wrappers for processing encodings of floating-point numbers.

2.5.1.6   Classifications of Floating-Point Numbers

This section contains information about classifying floating-point numbers based on various properties.

Queries for Type of Floating-Point Number. The IEEE 754-2008 Standard requires queries to determine the type of a specified floating-point number. Firstly, an enumeration is required for the various types. Listing 2.13 shows pseudocode that satisfies the requirement.

```
enum  Classification
{
    CLASS_NEG_INFINITY ,
    CLASS_NEG_SUBNORMAL ,
    CLASS_NEG_NORMAL ,
    CLASS_NEG_ZERO ,
    CLASS_POS_ZERO ,
    CLASS_POS_SUBNORMAL ,
    CLASS_POS_NORMAL ,
    CLASS_POS_INFINITY ,
    CLASS_QUIET_NAN ,
    CLASS_SIGNALING_NAN
};

Classification  GetClassification  ( binaryN  x)
{
    UInteger  sign ,  biased ,  trailing ;
```

```
GetEncoding(x, sign, biased, trailing);

if (biased == 0)
{
    if (trailing == 0)
    {
        return (sign != 0 ? CLASS_NEG_ZERO : CLASS_POS_ZERO);
    }
    else
    {
        return (sign != 0 ? CLASS_NEG_SUBNORMAL : CLASS_POS_SUBNORMAL);
    }
}
else if (biased < MAX_BIASED_EXPONENT)
{
    return (sign != 0 ? CLASS_NEG_NORMAL : CLASS_POS_NORMAL);
}
else if (trailing == 0)
{
    return (sign != 0 ? CLASS_NEG_INFINITY : CLASS_POS_INFINITY);
}
else if (trailing & NAN_QUIET_MASK)
{
    return CLASS_QUIET_NAN;
}
else
{
    return CLASS_SIGNALING_NAN;
}
}
```

LISTING 2.13: Classification of floating-point numbers.

Secondly, queries are required for whether the number is finite or infinite, is normal or subnormal, is zero, is a NaN or a signaling NaN, or whether the sign bit is set to one. The queries are trivial to implement using the binary encodings, as shown in Listing 2.14. The enumerates were defined in the sections on binary encodings.

```
// Query whether x is a zero.
bool IsZero (binaryN x)
{
    return x.encoding == POS_ZERO || x.encoding == NEG_ZERO;
}

// Query whether the sign bit of x is set to 1.
bool IsSignMinus (binaryN x)
{
    return (x.encoding & SIGN_MASK) != POS_ZERO;
}

// Query whether x is a subnormal number.
bool IsSubnormal (binaryN x)
{
    UInteger b = (x.encoding & BIASED_EXPONENT_MASK) >> NUM_TRAILING_BITS;
    UInteger t = (x.encoding & TRAILING_MASK);
    return b == POS_ZERO && t > POS_ZERO;
}

// Query whether x is a normal number.
bool IsNormal (binaryN x)
{
    UInteger b = (x.encoding & BIASED_EXPONENT_MASK) >> NUM_TRAILING_BITS;
    return POS_ZERO < b && b < MAX_BIASED_EXPONENT;
}
```

```
// Query whether x is a finite number.
bool IsFinite (binaryN x)
{
    UInteger b = (x.encoding & BIASED_EXPONENT_MASK) >> NUM_TRAILING_BITS;
    return b < MAX_BIASED_EXPONENT;
}

// Query whether x is an infinite number.
bool IsInfinite (binaryN x)
{
    UInteger b = (x.encoding & BIASED_EXPONENT_MASK) >> NUM_TRAILING_BITS;
    UInteger t = (x.encoding & TRAILING_MASK);
    return b == MAX_BIASED_EXPONENT && t == POS_ZERO;
}

// Query whether x is Not-a-Number (quiet or signaling).
bool IsNaN (binaryN x)
{
    UInteger b = (x.encoding & BIASED_EXPONENT_MASK) >> NUM_TRAILING_BITS;
    UInteger t = (x.encoding & TRAILING_MASK);
    return b == MAX_BIASED_EXPONENT && t != POS_ZERO;
}

// Query whether x is a signaling Not-a-Number.
bool IsSignalingNaN (binaryN x)
{
    UInteger b = (x.encoding & BIASED_EXPONENT_MASK) >> NUM_TRAILING_BITS;
    UInteger t = (x.encoding & TRAILING_MASK);
    return b == MAX_BIASED_EXPONENT
        && (t & NAN_QUIET_MASK) == POS_ZERO
        && (t & NAN_PAYLOAD_MASK) != POS_ZERO;
}
```

LISTING 2.14: Queries about floating-point numbers.

Determining Adjacent Floating-Point Numbers. When computing numerically, the classic mind-set is one of coding mathematical equations and implementing algorithms that are formulated at a high level, ignoring or paying little attention to the fact that the underlying numerical system uses floating-point numbers. There is a good chance that you rarely (if ever) write code that requires computing the floating-point numbers that are immediately adjacent to a specified floating-point number.

I had provided an example in the introduction chapter regarding the computation of the roots of a quadratic polynomial. In that example, I mentioned that the computed root appeared to be wrong, but by analyzing the polynomial values at the floating-point numbers adjacent to the computed root, the result was the best we could do. This example shows that validating the results of your calculations might very well require working directly with the floating-point number system rather than relying on yet another high-level mathematical framework that ignores floating-point issues.

The IEEE 754-2008 Standard recognizes that an implementation provide queries to obtain the floating-point values immediately adjacent to a specified floating-point number. The smaller adjacent neighbor is referred to as the *next-down* number and the larger adjacent neighbor is referred to as the *next-up* number.

Let nextUp(x) be the function that computes the next-up value for x. For finite and nonzero x, the next-up value is the obvious choice—the smallest floating-point number that is larger than x. The edge cases are as follows. Let $f_{\min}$ be the smallest positive subnormal number and let $f_{\max}$ be the largest positive normal number; then

$$
\begin{array}{ll}
\text{nextUp}(-\infty) = -f_{\max}, & \text{nextUp}(-f_{\min}) = -0, \\
\text{nextUp}(-0) = f_{\min}, & \text{nextUp}(+0) = f_{\min}, \\
\text{nextUp}(f_{\max}) = +\infty, & \text{nextUp}(+\infty) = +\infty
\end{array}
\tag{2.37}
$$

If x is a quiet NaN, then nextUp(x) returns x and does not signal an exception. If x is a signaling NaN, then nextUp(x) also returns x but signals an invalid operation exception. An implementation is provided by Listing 2.15, where a return of a UInteger implies an implicit conversion to a binaryN.

```
binaryN GetNextUp (binaryN x)
{
    UInteger sign, biased, trailing;
    GetEncoding(x, sign, biased, trailing);

    if (biased == 0)
    {
        if (trailing == 0)
        {
            // The next-up for both -0 and +0 is MIN_SUBNORMAL.
            return MIN_SUBNORMAL;
        }
        else
        {
            if (sign != 0)
            {
                // When trailing is 1, x is -MIN_SUBNORMAL and next-up
                // is -0.
                --trailing;
                return SIGN_MASK | trailing;
            }
            else
            {
                // When trailing is MAX_TRAILING, x is MAX_SUBNORMAL and
                // next-up is MIN_NORMAL.
                ++trailing;
                return trailing;
            }
        }
    }
    else if (biased < MAX_BIASED_EXPONENT)
    {
        UInteger nonnegative = (x.encoding & NOT_SIGN_MASK);
        if (sign != 0)
        {
            --nonnegative;
            return SIGN_MASK | nonnegative;
        }
        else
        {
            ++nonnegative;
            return nonnegative;
        }
    }
    else if (trailing == 0)
    {
```

```
        if (sign != 0)
        {
            // The next−up of −INFINITY is −MAX_NORMAL.
            return SIGN_MASK | MAX_NORMAL;
        }
        else
        {
            // The next−up of +INFINITY is +INFINITY.
            return INFINITY;
        }
    }
    else if (trailing & NAN_QUIET_MASK)
    {
        // x is a quiet NaN; return it (preserving its payload).
        return x;
    }
    else
    {
        // x is a signaling NaN; signal an invalid operation and return
        // it (preserving its payload).
        SignalException(INVALID_OPERATION);
        return x;
    }
}
```

LISTING 2.15: An implementation of the nextUp(x) function.

The nextDown(x) function is similar. For finite and nonzero x, the next-down value is the obvious choice—the largest floating-point number that is smaller than x. The edge cases are

$$
\begin{aligned}
\text{nextDown}(-\infty) &= -\infty, & \text{nextDown}(-f_{\max}) &= -\infty, \\
\text{nextDown}(-0) &= -f_{\min}, & \text{nextDown}(+0) &= -f_{\min}, \\
\text{nextDown}(f_{\min}) &= +0, & \text{nextDown}(+\infty) &= f_{\max}
\end{aligned}
\tag{2.38}
$$

If x is a quiet NaN, then nextDown(x) returns x and does not signal an exception. If x is a signaling NaN, then nextDown(x) also returns x but signals an invalid operation exception. An implementation is provided by Listing 2.16, where a return of a UInteger implies an implicit conversion to a binaryN.

```
binaryN GetNextDown (binaryN x)
{
    UInteger sign, biased, trailing;
    GetEncoding(x, sign, biased, trailing);

    if (biased == 0)
    {
        if (trailing == 0)
        {
            // The next−down for both −0 and +0 is −MIN_SUBNORMAL.
            return SIGN_MASK | MIN_SUBNORMAL;
        }
        else
        {
            if (sign == 0)
            {
                // When trailing is 1, x is MIN_SUBNORMAL and next−down
                // is +0.
                −−trailing;
                return trailing;
            }
            else
```

```
            {
                // When trailing is MAX_TRAILING, x is -MAX_SUBNORMAL and
                // next-down is -MIN_NORMAL.
                ++trailing;
                return SIGN_MASK | trailing;
            }
        }
    }
    else if (biased < MAX_BIASED_EXPONENT)
    {
        UInteger nonnegative = (x.encoding & NOT_SIGN_MASK);
        if (sign == 0)
        {
            --nonnegative;
            return nonnegative;
        }
        else
        {
            ++nonnegative;
            return SIGN_MASK | nonnegative;
        }
    }
    else if (trailing == 0)
    {
        if (sign == 0)
        {
            // The next-down of +INFINITY is +MAX_NORMAL.
            return MAX_NORMAL;
        }
        else
        {
            // The next-down of -INFINITY is -INFINITY.
            return SIGN_MASK | INFINITY;
        }
    }
    else if (trailing & NAN_QUIET_MASK)
    {
        // x is a quiet NaN; return it (preserving its payload).
        return x;
    }
    else
    {
        // x is a signaling NaN; signal an invalid operation and return
        // it (preserving its payload).
        SignalException(INVALID_OPERATION);
        return x;
    }
}
```

LISTING 2.16: An implementation of the nextDown(x) function.

2.5.2   Rounding and Conversions

One of the important aspects of floating-point arithmetic is *rounding*. Most likely you think about rounding when using arithmetic operations such as addition, subtraction, multiplication, and division. Rounding is also of concern when computing mathematical functions. An IEEE 754-2008 Standard requirement that is pervasive throughout floating-point systems is the concept of producing a *correctly rounded result*. For example, addition of two n-bit floating-point numbers should produce an n-bit floating-point number that is closest to the infinitely precise sum. The square root function of an n-bit

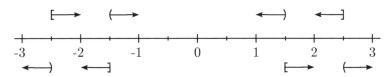

FIGURE 2.11: An illustration of rounding with ties-to-even.

floating-point number should produce an n-bit floating-point number that is closest to the infinitely precise square root.

The concept of *closest* is controllable by programmers in that they may specify a *rounding mode*. The IEEE 754-2008 Standard specifies five different rounding modes: *rounding with ties-to-even* (default), *rounding with ties-to-away*, *rounding toward zero*, *rounding toward positive*, and *rounding toward negative*. These are defined next with application to a number of the form $\sigma d.r$, where σ is $+1$ or -1 (the sign of the number), where d is a nonnegative integer (the integer part of the number), and where r is a nonnegative integer (the fractional part of the number). Although the discussion and figures refer to integers, they are a simplification of the actual situation. The rounding occurs based on the bits that theoretically occur *after* the trailing significand, so in fact you can think of the discussion and figures applying to floating-point numbers with the appropriate shifting of bits (based on some power of two).

After the discussion on rounding, we will consider *conversion* between numbers in various formats, which will involve rounding. In particular, we will look at converting between n-bit and m-bit floating-point formats using rounding with ties-to-even. If $n < m$, then the m-bit format is said to be *wider* than the n-bit format. Equivalently, the n-bit format is said to be *narrower* than the m-bit format.

2.5.2.1   Rounding with Ties-to-Even

This rounding mode is the default and what you are normally taught early in life when rounding numbers. If the fractional part is smaller than half, you round down, and if the fractional part is larger than half, you round up. When the fractional part is exactly half, to avoid bias you round down or up according to whether the integer part is even or odd, respectively. The mathematical summary is

$$\text{round}_e(\sigma d.r) = \begin{cases} \sigma d, & 0.r < 1/2 \text{ or } (0.r = 1/2 \text{ and } d \text{ is even}) \\ \sigma(d+1), & 0.r > 1/2 \text{ or } (0.r = 1/2 \text{ and } d \text{ is odd}) \end{cases} \quad (2.39)$$

Figure 2.11 illustrates this on the number line for several intervals. The use of parentheses and brackets in the figure is consistent with their use in interval notation: a parenthesis excludes the point and a bracket includes the point. Examples are $\text{round}_e(1.1) = 1$, $\text{round}_e(1.9) = 2$, $\text{round}_e(1.5) = 2$, $\text{round}_e(2.5) = 2$, $\text{round}_e(-1.1) = -1$, $\text{round}_e(-1.5) = -2$, and $\text{round}_e(-2.5) = -2$.

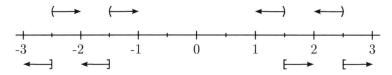

FIGURE 2.12: An illustration of rounding with ties-to-away.

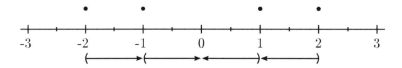

FIGURE 2.13: An illustration of rounding toward zero.

2.5.2.2　Rounding with Ties-to-Away

The rounding mode is similar to ties-to-even in that fractions not equal to half are rounded down or up accordingly. When the fraction is half, the rounding is away from zero, meaning that the rounding is to the largest magnitude integer neighbor. The mathematical summary is

$$\mathrm{round}_a(\sigma d.r) = \begin{cases} \sigma d, & 0.r < 1/2 \\ \sigma(d+1), & 0.r \geq 1/2 \end{cases} \tag{2.40}$$

Figure 2.12 illustrates this on the number line for several intervals. Examples are $\mathrm{round}_a(1.1) = 1$, $\mathrm{round}_a(1.9) = 2$, $\mathrm{round}_a(1.5) = 2$, $\mathrm{round}_a(2.5) = 3$, $\mathrm{round}_a(-1.1) = -1$, $\mathrm{round}_a(-1.5) = -2$, and $\mathrm{round}_a(-2.5) = -3$.

2.5.2.3　Rounding toward Zero

The number is rounded toward zero; that is, it is rounded to the integer neighbor that is smallest in magnitude. You should recognize this as the familiar *truncation* mode. The mathematical summary is

$$\mathrm{round}_z(\sigma d.r) = \sigma d \tag{2.41}$$

Figure 2.13 illustrates this on the number line for several intervals. Some examples are $\mathrm{round}_z(1) = 1$, $\mathrm{round}_z(1.1) = 1$, $\mathrm{round}_z(-1.1) = -1$, $\mathrm{round}_z(-2) = -2$, $\mathrm{round}_z(0.1) = +0$, and $\mathrm{round}_z(-0.1) = -0$. The last two examples emphasize that in floating-point arithmetic, the rounding can produce a signed zero.

2.5.2.4　Rounding toward Positive

When a number is not exactly an integer, the rounding is in the direction of the positive axis. If i is an integer and $x \in (i, i+1)$, the rounded value

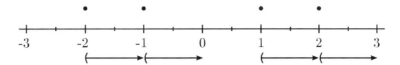

FIGURE 2.14: An illustration of rounding toward positive.

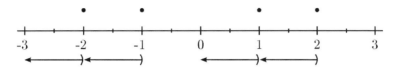

FIGURE 2.15: An illustration of rounding toward negative.

is $\text{round}_p(x) = i + 1$. The equation is more complicated when the number is formulated as $x = \sigma i.f$, but this is necessary to understand the implementation for floating-point numbers. In this mode, the rounded value is d in all cases but one: the number is positive, the fractional part is positive, and the rounded value is $d + 1$. The mathematical summary is

$$\text{round}_p(\sigma i.f) = \begin{cases} \sigma d, & r = 0 \text{ or } (r > 0 \text{ and } \sigma < 0) \\ \sigma d + 1, & r > 0 \text{ and } \sigma > 0 \end{cases} \tag{2.42}$$

Figure 2.14 illustrates this on the number line for several intervals. Some examples are $\text{round}_p(1) = 1$, $\text{round}_p(1.1) = 2$, $\text{round}_p(-1.1) = -1$, $\text{round}_p(-2) = -2$, and $\text{round}_p(-0.7) = -0$. The last example emphasizes that in floating-point arithmetic, the rounding can produce negative zero.

2.5.2.5 Rounding toward Negative

Rounding in the negative direction is similar to that of rounding in the positive direction. If i is an integer and $x \in (i, i + 1)$, the rounded value is $\text{round}_n(x) = i$. In terms of $x = \sigma i.f$ for floating-point rounding, the rounded value is d in all cases but one: the number is negative, the fractional part is positive, and the rounded value is $d - 1$. The mathematical summary is

$$\text{round}_n(\sigma d.r) = \begin{cases} \sigma d, & r = 0 \text{ or } (r > 0 \text{ and } \sigma > 0) \\ \sigma d - 1, & r > 0 \text{ and } \sigma < 0 \end{cases} \tag{2.43}$$

Figure 2.15 illustrates this on the number line for several intervals. Some examples are $\text{round}_n(1) = 1$, $\text{round}_n(1.1) = 1$, $\text{round}_n(-1.1) = -2$, $\text{round}_n(-2) = -2$, and $\text{round}_n(0.7) = +0$. The last example emphasizes that in floating-point arithmetic, the rounding can produce positive zero.

2.5.2.6   Rounding from Floating-Point to Integral Floating-Point

The five rounding modes are illustrated in this section for rounding a floating-point number to a representable integer, itself a floating-point number. In all cases, round($+0$) = $+0$, round(-0) = -0, round($+\infty$) = $+\infty$, and round($-\infty$) = $-\infty$; that is, the sign bits are preserved for the signed zeros and signed infinities. The function names in this section all start with prefix RoundToIntegral and have a suffix that corresponds to the rounding mode.

According to the IEEE 754-2008 Standard, quiet NaNs are mapped to themselves. The invalid operation is signaled when the input is a signaling NaN, and the output is the quieted value for that NaN. No signals are generated for inexact results. The maximum finite floating-point values are already integers, so it is not possible for a rounded result to be infinite (no overflow exception). The IEEE 754-2008 Standard also specifies that an implementation must provide a function RoundToIntegralExact that rounds according to the currently active rounding mode. However, this function does signal the inexact exception. In the pseudocode, I have comments indicating where the signaling occurs, each signal raised via a RaiseFlags function.

Rounding with Ties-To-Even. Consider nonnegative values for x. Similar arguments are made when x is negative. If $0 \leq x < 1/2$, then $\text{round}_e(x) = +0$. The remaining numbers are finite floating-point numbers for which $x \geq 1/2$. These numbers are necessarily normal, so $x = 1.t * 2^e$, where t is the trailing significand and $e \geq -1$ is the unbiased power.

If $e = -1$ and $t = 0$, then $x = 1/2$ and $\text{round}_e(x) = +0$. We round down because x is midway between zero and one, and zero is the closest even integer. If $e = -1$ and $t > 0$, then $x \in (1/2, 1)$ and the closest integer is $\text{round}_e(x) = 1$.

When $e = 0$, the number is $x = 1.t \in [1, 2)$. If $0.t < 1/2$, then x is rounded down to one. If $0.t \geq 1/2$, then x is rounded up to two. When $0.t = 1/2$, the rounding rule says to round to the even integer, which is why 1.5 is rounded to two.

Let $0 < e < n$, where n is the number of bits in the trailing significand. The number x is

$$x = 1t_{n-1} \cdots t_{n-e}.t_{n-e-1} \cdots t_0 = d.r \qquad (2.44)$$

where the last equality defines positive integer d and nonnegative integer r. The number of bits of x is $n + 1$, the number of bits of d is $e + 1$, and the number of bits of r is $n - e$. If $0.r < 1/2$, then x is rounded down to d. If $0.r > 1/2$, then x is rounded up to $d + 1$. If $0.r = 1/2$, then x is rounded down to d when d is even or x is rounded up to $d + 1$ when $d + 1$ is even. In the source code, it turns out that we may combine the last two cases and process all e for which $0 \leq e < n$.

If $e \geq n$, then

$$x = 1.t * 2^n * 2^{e-n} = d * 2^{e-n} \qquad (2.45)$$

where d is a positive integer. As a binary number, the leading bits of d are a 1-bit followed by the trailing significand bits and then followed by zero or more 0-bits. Therefore, x is an integer and $\mathrm{round}_e(x) = x$.

Pseudocode for the rounding is presented next. The generic types Integer and UInteger represent signed and unsigned integers, respectively, with the same number of bits as the binary encoding for the floating-point number.

Listing 2.17 is an implementation of the default rounding mode: rounding with ties-to-even.

```
binaryN RoundToIntegralTiesToEven (binaryN x)
{
    UInteger sign, biased, trailing;
    GetEncoding(x, sign, biased, trailing);
    Integer exponent = biased - binaryN::EXPONENT_BIAS;

    if (exponent < -1)
    {
        // |x| < 1/2, round to +0 or -0.
        // Enable for RoundToIntegralExact:
        // if (!IsZero(x)) { RaiseFlags(SIGNAL_INEXACT); }
        return sign;
    }

    if (exponent == -1)
    {
        // |x| in [1/2,1)
        // Enable for RoundToIntegralExact:
        // RaiseFlags(SIGNAL_INEXACT);
        if (trailing == 0)
        {
            // |x| = 1/2, round to +0 or -0.
            return sign;
        }
        else
        {
            // |x| in (1/2,1), round to +1 or -1.
            return sign | binaryN::ONE;
        }
    }

    if (exponent < binaryN::NUM_TRAILING_BITS)
    {
        // Process the biased exponent and trailing simultaneously.
        UInteger nonnegative = abs(x);  // abs(x) sets sign bit to zero

        // Extract d.
        Integer dshift = binaryN::NUM_TRAILING_BITS - exponent;
        UInteger d = (nonnegative >> dshift);

        // Extract r.
        Integer rshift = binaryN::NUM_ENCODING_BITS - dshift;
        UInteger r = (nonnegative << rshift);
        // Enable for RoundToIntegralExact:
        // if (r > 0) { RaiseFlags(SIGNAL_INEXACT); }

        // Round up to d+1 according to the ties-to-even rule.
        // SIGN_MASK is the equivalent of "half" for r in its current
        // format, so HALF_PROXY = SIGN_MASK.
        if (r > binaryN::HALF_PROXY                    // 0.r > 1/2
        || (r == binaryN::HALF_PROXY && (d & 1)))   // 0.r = 1/2 and d odd
        {
            // In the event the trailing significand has all 1-bits, the
            // addition of 1 to d leads to a carry-overflow; that is, the
            // bit at index binaryN::NUM_TRAILING_BITS becomes a 1.
            // Therefore, the rounded result must be normalized (set
```

```
            // trailing  significand  to  zero,  increment  biased  exponent).
            // However,  this  is  handled  automatically  by  the  simple  logic
            // shown  here.
            ++d;
        }
        nonnegative = (d << dshift);
        return sign | nonnegative;
    }

    if (!IsSignalingNaN(x))
    {
        // Finite  floating−point  numbers  with
        //   exponent >= binaryN::NUM_TRAILING_BITS
        // are  themselves  integers.   Infinities  and  quiet  NaNs  are  mapped
        // to  themselves.
        return x;
    }

    // Quiet  a  signaling  NaN  on  invalid  operation.
    RaiseFlags(SIGNAL_INVALID_OPERATION);
    return x | binaryN::NAN_QUIET_MASK;
}
```

LISTING 2.17: An implementation of rounding with ties-to-even.

Rounding with Ties-to-Away. The rounding is nearly identical to that with ties-to-even. The discussion of the previous section applies to this case with two exceptions. Firstly, one-half is rounded to one instead of zero. Secondly, when $0.r = 1/2$, the floating-point value is rounded up. Listing 2.18 is an implementation.

```
binaryN RoundToIntegralTiesToAway (binaryN x)
{
    UInteger sign, biased, trailing;
    GetEncoding(x, sign, biased, trailing);
    Integer exponent = biased − binaryN::EXPONENT_BIAS;

    if (exponent < −1)
    {
        // |x| < 1/2,  round  to  +0  or  −0.
        // Enable  for  RoundToIntegralExact:
        // if (!IsZero(x)) { RaiseFlags(SIGNAL_INEXACT); }
        return sign;
    }

    if (exponent == −1)
    {
        // |x|  in  [1/2,1),  round  to  +1  or  −1.
        // Enable  for  RoundToIntegralExact:
        // RaiseFlags(SIGNAL_INEXACT);
        return sign | binaryN::ONE;
    }

    if (exponent < binaryN::NUM_TRAILING_BITS)
    {
        // Process  the  biased  exponent  and  trailing  simultaneously.
        UInteger nonnegative = abs(x);  // abs(x)  sets  sign  bit  to  zero.

        // Extract  d.
        Integer dshift = binaryN::NUM_TRAILING_BITS − exponent;
        UInteger d = (nonnegative >> dshift);

        // Extract  r.
        Integer rshift = binaryN::NUM_ENCODING_BITS − dshift;
```

```
        UInteger r = (nonnegative << rshift);
        // Enable for RoundToIntegralExact:
        // if (r > 0) { RaiseFlags(SIGNAL_INEXACT); }

        // Round up to d+1 according to the ties-to-away rule.
        // SIGN_MASK is the equivalent of "half" for r in its current
        // format, so HALF_PROXY = SIGN_MASK.
        if (r >= binaryN::HALF_PROXY)   // 0.r >= 1/2
        {
            ++d;
        }
        nonnegative = (d << dshift);
        return sign | nonnegative;
    }

    if (!IsSignalingNaN(x))
    {
        // Finite floating-point numbers with
        // exponent >= binaryN::NUM_TRAILING_BITS
        // are themselves integers.  Infinities and quiet NaNs are mapped
        // to themselves.
        return x;
    }

    // Quiet a signaling NaN on invalid operation.
    RaiseFlags(SIGNAL_INVALID_OPERATION);
    return x | binaryN::NAN_QUIET_MASK;
}
```

LISTING 2.18: An implementation of rounding with ties-to-away.

Rounding toward Zero. The pseudocode for this mode is slightly simpler than that for rounding with ties-to-even or ties-to-away. Listing 2.19 is an implementation.

```
binaryN RoundToIntegralTowardZero (binaryN x)
{
    UInteger sign, biased, trailing;
    GetEncoding(x, sign, biased, trailing);
    Integer exponent = biased - binaryN::EXPONENT_BIAS;

    if (exponent <= -1)
    {
        // |x| < 1, round to +0 or -0.
        // Enable for RoundToIntegralExact:
        // if (!IsZero(x)) { RaiseFlags(SIGNAL_INEXACT); }
        return sign;
    }

    if (exponent < binaryN::NUM_TRAILING_BITS)
    {
        // Process the biased exponent and trailing simultaneously.
        UInteger nonnegative = abs(x);   // abs(x) sets sign bit to zero.

        // Extract d.
        Integer dshift = binaryN::NUM_TRAILING_BITS - exponent;
        UInteger d = (nonnegative >> dshift);

        // Extract r.  Shifting d truncates the remainder r, which is
        // effectively rounding toward zero, so there is no need to
        // extract r other than for signaling.
        Integer rshift = binaryN::NUM_ENCODING_BITS - dshift;
        UInteger r = (nonnegative << rshift);
        // Enable for RoundToIntegralExact:
        // if (r > 0) { RaiseFlags(SIGNAL_INEXACT); }
```

```
            nonnegative = (d << dshift );
            return sign | nonnegative ;
    }

    if (! IsSignalingNaN (x))
    {
        // Finite floating-point numbers with
        // exponent >= binaryN :: NUM_TRAILING_BITS
        // are themselves integers . Infinities and quiet NaNs are mapped
        // to themselves .
        return x;
    }

    // Quiet a signaling NaN on invalid operation .
    RaiseFlags (SIGNAL_INVALID_OPERATION );
    return x | binaryN :: NAN_QUIET_MASK ;
}
```

LISTING 2.19: An implementation of rounding toward zero.

Rounding toward Positive. The pseudocode is once again similar to that of previous rounding modes. Despite the seemingly complicated Equation (2.42), the pseudocode is not that complicated. Listing 2.20 is an implementation.

```
binaryN RoundToIntegralTowardPositive (binaryN x)
{
    UInteger sign , biased , trailing ;
    GetEncoding (x, sign , biased , trailing );
    Integer exponent = biased - binaryN :: EXPONENT_BIAS ;

    if (IsZero (x))
    {
        // |x| = 0, round to +0 or -0.
        return x;
    }

    if (exponent < 0)
    {
        // x in (-1,1)
        // Enable for RoundToIntegralExact :
        // RaiseFlags (SIGNAL_INEXACT );
        if (sign == 0)
        {
            // x in (+0,1), round to 1.
            return binaryN :: ONE;
        }
        else
        {
            // x in (-1,-0), round to -0.
            return binaryN :: SIGN_MASK | binaryN :: ZERO;
        }
    }

    if (exponent < binaryN :: NUM_TRAILING_BITS)
    {
        // Process the biased exponent and trailing simultaneously .
        UInteger nonnegative = abs(x);  // abs(x) sets sign bit to zero.

        // Extract d.
        Integer dshift = binaryN :: NUM_TRAILING_BITS - exponent ;
        UInteger d = (nonnegative >> dshift );

        // Extract r.
        Integer rshift = binaryN :: NUM_ENCODING_BITS - dshift ;
```

```
        uint32_t  r  =  (nonnegative  <<  rshift );
        // Enable for RoundToIntegralExact:
        // if (r > 0) { RaiseFlags(SIGNAL_INEXACT); }

        // Round toward positive.  If the "else" clause were present,
        // it would simply truncate x, which means d may be used as is,
        // so the clause is not necessary.
        if (r > 0 && sign == 0)
        {
            ++d;
        }

        nonnegative = (d << dshift );
        return sign | nonnegative;
    }

    if  (! IsSignalingNaN (x))
    {
        // Finite floating-point numbers with
        // exponent >= binaryN::NUM_TRAILING_BITS
        // are themselves integers.  Infinities and quiet NaNs are mapped
        // to themselves.
        return x;
    }

    // Quiet a signaling NaN on invalid operation.
    RaiseFlags(SIGNAL_INVALID_OPERATION);
    return x | binaryN::NAN_QUIET_MASK;
}
```

LISTING 2.20: An implementation of rounding toward positive.

Rounding toward Negative. The pseudocode is similar to that for rounding toward positive. In the only case where d changes, the result is $\sigma d - 1 = -d - 1 = \sigma(d + 1)$, so the pseudocode correctly increments d. Listing 2.21 is an implementation.

```
binaryN RoundToIntegralTowardNegative (binaryN x)
{
    UInteger sign , biased , trailing;
    GetEncoding(x, sign, biased, trailing);
    Integer exponent = biased - binaryN::EXPONENT_BIAS;

    if (IsZero(x))
    {
        // |x| = 0, round to +0 or -0.
        return x;
    }

    if (exponent < 0)
    {
        // x in (-1,1)
        // Enable for RoundToIntegralExact:
        // RaiseFlags(SIGNAL_INEXACT);
        if (sign != 0)
        {
            // x in (-1,-0), round to -1.
            return binaryN::SIGN_MASK | binaryN::ONE;
        }
        else
        {
            // x in (+0,1), round to +0.
            return binary32::ZERO;
        }
    }
```

```
if (exponent < binaryN::NUM_TRAILING_BITS)
{
    // Process the biased exponent and trailing simultaneously.
    UInteger nonnegative = abs(x);  // abs(x) sets sign bit to zero.

    // Extract d.
    Integer dshift = binaryN::NUM_TRAILING_BITS - exponent;
    UInteger d = (nonnegative >> dshift);

    // Extract r.
    Integer rshift = binaryN::NUM_ENCODING_BITS - dshift;
    UInteger r = (nonnegative << rshift);
    // Enable for RoundToIntegralExact:
    // if (r > 0) { RaiseFlags(SIGNAL_INEXACT); }

    // Round toward negative. If the "else" clause were present,
    // it would simply truncate x, which means d may be used as is,
    // so the clause is not necessary.
    if (r > 0 && sign != 0)
    {
        ++d;
    }

    nonnegative = (d << dshift);
    return sign | nonnegative;
}

if (!IsSignalingNaN(x))
{
    // Finite floating-point numbers with
    // exponent >= binaryN::NUM_TRAILING_BITS
    // are themselves integers. Infinities and quiet NaNs are mapped
    // to themselves.
    return x;
}

// Quiet a signaling NaN on invalid operation.
RaiseFlags(SIGNAL_INVALID_OPERATION);
return x | binaryN::NAN_QUIET_MASK;
}
```

LISTING 2.21: An implementation of rounding toward negative.

The modes for rounding toward positive and rounding toward negative are useful for interval arithmetic.

2.5.2.7   Conversion from Integer to Floating-Point

Conversions from integers to floating-point numbers are common in applications. It is not always possible to represent an n-bit integer exactly as an n-bit floating-point number. This is easily seen with binary8. The 8-bit nonnegative integers represented by two's complement[2] are $\{-128, \ldots, 127\}$. The set of 8-bit integers exactly representable by binary8 are $\{-15, \ldots, 15\}$. The other 8-bit integers are converted to the corresponding signed infinities, in which case an invalid operation exception is generated.

The representable integers for binary8 are contiguous. The representable integers for floating-point types with more than eight bits are not necessar-

---

[2]The two's complement of an N-bit number is that number subtracted from 2^N.

ily contiguous, although there is always a subset that contains contiguous integers. In fact, the analysis in the previous section showed that when the exponent is at least equal to the number of bits of the trailing significand, *all* such floating-point numbers are integers.

For example, consider the type binary16. The trailing significand has ten bits. The integers i such that $|i| \leq 2^{11}$ are representable as binary16 numbers. For all exponents $e \geq 11$, all binary16 numbers are integers. Specifically, let $0 \leq e < 10$. The representable integers with exponent e are $2^e, \ldots, 2^{e+1} - 1$. The union over all such e is a contiguous set. When $e = 11$, the representable integers are $2^{11} + 2k$ for $0 \leq k < 1024$. Notice that 2^{11} (when $k = 0$) is adjacent to the largest element of the contiguous representable integers ($e < 11$). However, the next largest representable integer is $2^{11} + 2$, which means that $2^{11} + 1$ is not representable. Thus, gaps occur in the integers when trying to represent integers. The gap becomes larger as e increases. Generally, for $e \geq 11$, the representable integers are $2^e + 2^{e-10}k$ for $0 \leq k < 1024$.

Be careful when interpreting statements such as: "The largest representable integer in 32-bit floating-point is $2^{24} = 16{,}777{,}216$." What programmers mean is that this is the largest of a *contiguous set of integers* that are *all* exactly representable by 32-bit floating-point numbers. All 32-bit floating-point numbers larger than 2^{24} *exactly represent integers*, including FLT_MAX; some of them are representable as 32-bit integers and some of them are not. For example, FLT_MAX is the number $2^{127}(2 - 2^{-23}) = 2^{128} - 2^{104}$, which is an integer; however, it cannot be stored as a 32-bit integer.

Exercise 2.2 *The largest positive 16-bit signed integer is $2^{15} - 1 = 32{,}767$. Show that the largest positive 16-bit signed integer representable by a binary16 number is 32,752.*

Exercise 2.3 *The largest positive 32-bit signed integer is $2^{31} - 1 = 2{,}147{,}483{,}647$. What is the largest positive 32-bit signed integer representable by a binary32 number?*

Exercise 2.4 *Derive a formula for the largest positive signed 2^n-bit integer that is representable by a 2^n-bit floating-point number.*

The IEEE 754-2008 Standard specifies that an implementation must have functions to convert from all supported signed and unsigned integer formats to all supported arithmetic formats. The generic signature is: destinationFormat ConvertFromInt (sourceFormat), where the source format is a signed or unsigned integer and the destination format is an arithmetic format. The standard programming languages handle the cases when the arithmetic format is integral, but the floating-point system must handle the cases when the arithmetic format is a binaryN.

Let us derive the algorithm for converting a 32-bit signed integer to a binary32 number. As mentioned previously, the conversion is not always exact, so some rounding algorithm must be applied. The range of integers is

$-2147483648 = $ 0x80000000 to $2147483647 = $ 0x7fffffff. The pseudocode handles 0 and -2147483648 separately. For other inputs, it suffices to analyze the conversion for nonnegative integers and deal with the sign bit separately.

The integer $i = 0$ is mapped to $+0$, the positive zero of binary32 (an IEEE requirement). The integer $i = -2147483648 = -2^{31}$ is mapped to the binary encoding 0xcf000000; the sign bit is set and the biased exponent is $158 = 31 + 127$.

Now consider $i > 0$. Let ℓ be the index of the leading bit of i, so $0 \le \ell \le 30$. If $\ell < 23$, then

$$\begin{aligned} i &= 2^\ell + t_{\ell-1}2^{\ell-1} + \cdots + t_0 \\ &= 2^\ell \left(1 + t_{\ell-1}2^{-1} + \cdots + t_0 2^{-\ell} + 0\,2^{-\ell-1} + \cdots + 0\,2^{-23} \right) \\ &= 1.t * 2^\ell \end{aligned} \qquad (2.46)$$

where the leading ℓ bits of t are the ℓ trailing bits of i, and the remaining bits of t are zero. The binary scientific notation for i is exactly representable as a binary32. The biased exponent is $\bar{e} = \ell + 127$ and the trailing significand is $t = t_{\ell-1} \cdots t_0 0 \cdots 0$. If $\ell = 23$, then $i = 1.t * 2^{23}$, where $\bar{e} = 23 + 127 = 150$ and $t = t_{22} \cdots t_0$.

If $\ell \ge 24$, then i is not always exactly representable by a binary32, as we saw in a previous discussion. In this case,

$$\begin{aligned} i &= 2^\ell + t_{\ell-1}2^{\ell-1} + \cdots + t_{\ell-23}2^{\ell-23} + \cdots + t_0 \\ &= 2^\ell \left(1 + t_{\ell-1}2^{-1} + \cdots + t_{\ell-23}2^{-23} + \cdots + t_0 2^{-\ell} \right) \\ &= 2^\ell 1.t \\ &= 2^{\ell-23} \left(2^{23} + t_{\ell-1}2^{22} + \cdots + t_{\ell-23} + \cdots + t_0 2^{-\ell+23} \right) \\ &= 2^{\ell-23}d.r \end{aligned} \qquad (2.47)$$

The trailing significand t has $\ell \ge 24$ bits, which is too many to store in a binary32. Thus, we must round the result to twenty-three bits. The IEEE 754-2008 Standard requires the rounding to be according to the currently active rounding mode. To formulate this in terms of the material presented previously, i has been written as a power of two times $d.r$, where d is a positive integer and r is a nonnegative integer. Our rounding modes were stated as functions $\text{round}_c(\sigma d.r)$, where $c \in \{e, a, z, p, n\}$ is the current mode. If you have such supporting functions, you may call them for the rounding or you may simply hard-code the processing of t. Source code for the conversion that rounds to nearest with ties-to-even is shown in Listing 2.22.

```
binary32 ConvertFromInt (int32_t i)
{
    if (i == 0)
    {
        // Return +0.
        return 0u;
    }

    if (i == INT_MIN)
    {
        // Return -2^{31}, sign-bit 1, biased exponent 158 = 31+127.
```

```
        return 0xcf000000;
    }

    uint32_t sign;
    if (i >= 0)
    {
        sign = 0u;
    }
    else
    {
        i = -i;
        sign = binary32::SIGN_MASK;
    }

    int32_t leading = GetLeadingBit(i);
    uint32_t biased = (uint32_t)((leading + binary32::EXPONENT_BIAS)
        << binary32::NUM_TRAILING_BITS);
    uint32_t nonnegative = (uint32_t)i;
    if (leading <= binary32::NUM_TRAILING_BITS)
    {
        int32_t shift = binary32::NUM_TRAILING_BITS - leading;
        nonnegative = (nonnegative << shift) & binary32::TRAILING_MASK;
    }
    else
    {
        // Extract d.
        int32_t dshift = leading - binary32::NUM_TRAILING_BITS;
        uint32_t d = (nonnegative >> dshift) & binary32::TRAILING_MASK;

        // Extract r.
        int32_t rshift = binary32::NUM_ENCODING_BITS - dshift;
        uint32_t r = (nonnegative << rshift);
        if (r > 0)
        {
            RaiseFlags(SIGNAL_INEXACT);
        }

        // Round to nearest with ties-to-even.
        if (r > binary32::HALF_PROXY    // 0.r > 1/2
        || (r == binary32::HALF_PROXY && (d & 1)))   // 0.r = 1/2 and d odd
        {
            ++d;
        }

        nonnegative = d;
    }

    return sign | (biased + nonnegative);
}
```

LISTING 2.22: Conversion of a 32-bit signed integer to a 32-bit floating-point number.

Exercise 2.5 *Implement variations of* ConvertFromInt *that use the following rounding modes: round to nearest with ties-to-away, round toward zero, round toward positive, and round toward negative. Test your code for correctness. The mode for rounding to nearest with ties-to-away is not required by the IEEE 754-2008 Standard for binary formats, and in fact this mode is not supported by Intel floating-point hardware. Microsoft Visual Studio allows you to set the rounding mode via* _controlfp, *where the mask is* _MCW_RC *and the mode is one of* _RC_NEAR *(default, round to nearest with ties-to-even),* _RC_CHOP *(round toward zero),* _RC_UP *(round toward positive), or* _RC_DOWN *(round* *toward negative). Devise an experiment that verifies your implementation for rounding to nearest with ties-to-away is correct.*

Exercise 2.6 *Implement a function that converts a 16-bit signed integer (*int16_t*) to* binary32. *Include code that raises flags when exceptions occur.*

Exercise 2.7 *Implement a function that converts a 32-bit unsigned integer (*uint32_t*) to* binary32. *Include code that raises flags when exceptions occur.*

Exercise 2.8 *Implement a function that converts a 64-bit signed integer (*int64_t*) to* binary32. *Include code that raises flags when exceptions occur.*

Exercise 2.9 *Let* int256_t *represent 256-bit signed integers. Write pseudocode for a function that converts* int256_t *to* binary32. *This requires slightly more logic than converting smaller integer types, because now there is the potential for overflow—the input integer might be larger than the* binary32 *infinity.*

Exercise 2.10 *Given an arbitrary precision integer, say, class* Integer, *write pseudocode for a function that converts* Integer *to* binary32.

2.5.2.8　Conversion from Floating-Point to Rational

When computing using exact rational arithmetic, say, using a class Rational, the floating-point inputs first must be converted to Rational numbers. Assuming arbitrary precision rationals, the conversions are always exact—no rounding is necessary. If class Rational uses a fixed-size integer, then conversions are either exact or they overflow when the floating-point input is larger than the maximum rational represented by the class. The common conversions are presented here for binary32 and binary64.

Conversion from binary32 *to* Rational. Positive normal numbers are of the form

$$r = 2^{\bar{e}-127} \left(1 + \sum_{i=0}^{22} t_i \, 2^{i-23} \right) = 2^{\bar{e}-150} \left(2^{23} + t \right) \qquad (2.48)$$

where $\bar{e}$ is the biased exponent in $\{1, \ldots, 254\}$ and where t is an integer in the set $\{0, \ldots, 2^{23} - 1\}$. The rational number r is a product of the sum with a nonnegative power of two when $\bar{e} \geq 150$ or a ratio of the sum with a positive power of two when $\bar{e} < 150$. Positive subnormal numbers are of the form

$$r = 2^{-126} \sum_{i=0}^{22} t_i \, 2^{i-23} = 2^{-149} t \qquad (2.49)$$

where t is an integer in the set $\{1, \ldots, 2^{23} - 1\}$. Listing 2.23 is an implementation of the conversion.

```
Rational ConvertFrom (binary32 x)
{
    uint32_t sign, biased, trailing;
    GetEncoding(x, sign, biased, trailing);
    Integer numer, denom;

    if (biased == 0)
    {
        if (trailing == 0)
        {
            // x is +0 or -0.
            numer = 0;
            denom = 1;
        }
        else
        {
            // x is subnormal.
            numer = trailing;
            denom = (1 << 149);
        }
    }
    else if (biased <= 254)
    {
        // x is normal.
        numer = (1 << 23) + trailing;
        denom = 1;
        power = biased - 150;
        if (power > 0)
        {
            numer <<= power;
        }
        else if (power < 0)
        {
            denom <<= -power;
        }
    }
    else  // biased == 255.
    {
        if (trailing == 0)
        {
            // x is +infinity or -infinity.
            RaiseFlags(SIGNAL_OVERFLOW);
        }
        else
        {
            // x is a NaN.
            RaiseFlags(SIGNAL_INVALID_OPERATION);
        }

        // The number is infinite, a quiet NaN, or a signaling NaN.
        // In all cases, return the maximum normal binary32.
        numer = ((1 << 24) - 1) << 104;
        denom = 1;
    }

    if (sign ! 0)
    {
        numer = -numer;
    }

    return Rational(numer, denom);
}
```

LISTING 2.23: Conversion from a 32-bit floating-point number to a rational number.

Conversion from binary64 *to* Rational. Positive normal numbers are of the form

$$r = 2^{\bar{e}-1023}\left(1 + \sum_{i=0}^{51} t_i\, 2^{i-52}\right) = 2^{\bar{e}-1075}\left(2^{52} + t\right) \qquad (2.50)$$

where $\bar{e}$ is the biased exponent in $\{1, \dots, 2046\}$ and where t is an integer in the set $\{0, \dots, 2^{52} - 1\}$. The rational number r is a product of the sum with a nonnegative power of two when $\bar{e} \geq 1075$ or a ratio of the sum with a positive power of two when $\bar{e} < 1075$. Positive subnormal numbers are of the form

$$r = 2^{-1022}\sum_{i=0}^{51} b_i\, 2^{i-52} = 2^{-1074}t \qquad (2.51)$$

where t is an integer in the set $\{1, \dots, 2^{52} - 1\}$. Listing 2.24 is an implementation of the conversion.

```
Rational ConvertFrom ( binary64 x)
{
    uint64_t sign, biased, trailing;
    GetEncoding(x, sign, biased, trailing);
    Integer numer, denom;

    if (biased == 0)
    {
        if (trailing == 0)
        {
            // x is +0 or -0.
            numer = 0;
            denom = 1;
        }
        else
        {
            // x is subnormal.
            numer = trailing;
            denom = (1 << 1074);
        }
    }
    else if (biased <= 2046)
    {
        // x is normal.
        numer = (1 << 52) + trailing;
        denom = 1;
        power = biased - 1075;
        if (power > 0)
        {
            numer <<= power;
        }
        else if (power < 0)
        {
            denom <<= -power;
        }
    }
    else  // biased == 2047.
    {
        if (trailing == 0)
        {
            // x is +infinity or -infinity.
            RaiseFlags(SIGNAL_OVERFLOW);
        }
        else
```

```
    {
        // x is a NaN.
        RaiseFlags(SIGNAL_INVALID_OPERATION);
    }

        // The number is infinite, a quiet NaN, or a signaling NaN.
        // In all cases, return the maximum normal binary64.
        numer = ((1 << 53) − 1) << 971;
        denom = 1;
}

if (sign ! 0)
{
    numer = −numer;
}

    return Rational(numer, denom);
}
```

LISTING 2.24: Conversion from a 64-bit floating-point number to a rational number.

Exercise 2.11 *Write pseudocode that converts a* binaryN *number to a* Rational *number.*

2.5.2.9   Conversion from Rational to Floating-Point

When computing using exact rational arithmetic, the rational output must be converted to floating-point numbers. The conversion from a rational number to a floating-point number is not always exact. For example, as a binary number, $1/3 = 0.\overline{01}^{\infty}$, indicating the bit pattern 01 repeats ad infinitum. That is $1/3 = 1/4 + 1/16 + \cdots 1/4^p + \cdots$. To verify, let $S = 1/4 + 1/16 + \cdots$; then $4S = 1 + 1/4 + \cdots$. Subtracting, $3S = 4S − S = 1$, which implies $S = 1/3$. Because the bit pattern is infinitely repeating, conversion to a floating-point number with finite precision requires rounding. Another example is when the rational number is larger than the maximum floating-point number. The conversion is deemed to be the floating-point infinity, which is tagged as overflow and an inexact conversion. The common conversions are presented here for binary32 and binary64.

Conversion from Rational *to* binary32. Let r_s be a positive subnormal floating-point number and let r_n be a positive normal floating-point number. We know that

$$
\begin{aligned}
0 \;\;&<\;\; \frac{r_{\text{smin}}}{2} < r_{\text{smin}} \leq r_s \leq r_{\text{smax}} < \frac{r_{\text{smax}}+r_{\text{nmin}}}{2} \\
&<\;\; r_{\text{nmin}} \leq r_n \leq r_{\text{nmax}} < \frac{r_{\text{nmax}}+r_{\infty}}{2} < r_{\infty}
\end{aligned} \tag{2.52}
$$

where $r_{\text{smin}} = 0.\bar{0}^{22}1 * 2^{-126}$, $r_{\text{smax}} = 0.\bar{1}^{23} * 2^{-126}$, $r_{\text{nmin}} = 1.\bar{0}^{23} * 2^{-126}$, $r_{\text{nmax}} = 1.\bar{1}^{23} * 2^{127}$, and $r_{\infty} = 2^{128}$. The numbers of the form $0.t$ and $1.t$ are written in binary. The notation $\bar{b}^n$ indicates a block of n consecutive b-valued bits. Because rationals are not always representable exactly by binary32, we need to choose a rounding mode. To illustrate, the default mode of rounding with ties-to-even is chosen. The averages in Equation (2.52) are listed because they are the midpoints at which ties occur. Specifically, $r_{smin}/2 = 2^{-150}$, $(r_{smax} + r_{nmin})/2 = 0.\bar{1}^{24} * 2^{-126}$, and $(r_{nmax} + r_{\infty})/2 = 1.\bar{1}^{24} * 2^{127}$.

Listing 2.25 shows the conversion. The power handling and much of the bit manipulations are motivated by the discussion in Section 2.4. Note that in production code, you must handle the case when the denominator of input r is zero. The example here does not do so.

```
binary32 ConvertTo (Rational r)
{
    if (r == Rational(0))
    {
        // Return +0.
        return binary32::ZERO;
    }

    // Process the signs.
    Integer n = r.Numerator(), d = r.Denominator();
    int nSign = (n >= 0 ? 1 : -1);
    int dSign = (d >= 0 ? 1 : -1);
    int rSign = nSign*dSign;
    uint32_t sign = (rSign < 0 ? binary32::SIGN_MASK : binary32::ZERO);

    // Work with the positive rational number.  The comments refer
    // to the manipulation of the positive number, but the sign is
    // handled in the return statement.
    n = nSign*n;
    d = dSign*d;

    int leadingN = GetLeadingBit(n);
    int leadingD = GetLeadingBit(d);
    int p = leadingN - leadingD;
    if (p > 0) { d <<= p; } else if (p < 0) { n <<= -p; }
    if (n < d) { n <<= 1; --p; }

    if (p < -150)  // 0 < r < 2^{-150}
    {
        // Round to +0.
        RaiseFlags(SIGNAL_INEXACT);
        return sign | binary32::ZERO;
    }

    if (p == -150)  // r = (n/d)*2^{-150}
    {
        RaiseFlags(SIGNAL_INEXACT);
        if (n == d)
        {
            // r = 2^{-150}, round to +0 based on ties-to-even.
            return sign | binary32::ZERO;
        }
        else  //
        {
            // 2^{-150} < r < 2^{-149}, round to minimum subnormal.
            return sign | binary32::MIN_SUBNORMAL;
        }
    }

    if (p >= 128)  // r >= infinity.
    {
        RaiseFlags(SIGNAL_OVERFLOW | SIGNAL_INEXACT);
        return sign | binary32::INFINITY;
    }

    // 0.1^{23} * 2^{-126} <= r < 2^{128}.  Compute the trailing
    // significand to 23 bits and compute the remainder to determine
```

```
// how to round.
uint32_t biased;
int32_t c, rshift;
if (p < -126)
{
    // 2^{-149} <= r < 2^{-126} (subnormal); use r = 0.c * 2^{-126}.
    biased = 0;            // Number is subnormal.
    c = 0;                 // Leading bit is 0.
    d <<= 1;               // Prepare for 0.c format.
    rshift = -(p + 127);   // Right-shift of trailing significand.
}
else
{
    // 2^{-126} <= r < 2^{128} (normal); use r = 1.c * 2^{-126}.
    biased = p + 127;      // Number is normal.
    c = 1;                 // Leading bit is 1.
    rshift = 0;            // No right-shift of trailing significand.
}

uint32_t trailing = 0u;
for (uint32_t mask = ((1 << 22) >> rshift); mask > 0; mask >>= 1)
{
    if (c == 1)
    {
        n -= d;   // s = s - c;
    }
    n <<= 1;       // s = 2*s
    if (n >= d)    // s >= 1
    {
        c = 1;
        trailing |= mask;
    }
    else
    {
        c = 0;
    }
}

if (c == 1)
{
    n -= d;
}
// n/d = 0.r[0]r[1]...

if (n != 0)
{
    RaiseFlags(SIGNAL_INEXACT);
}

// Round up when n/d > 1/2 or (n/d = 1/2 and trailing is odd).
Integer test = 2*n - d;
if (test > 0 || (test == 0 && (trailing & 1)))
{
    ++trailing;
}

return sign | ((biased << 23) + trailing);
}
```

LISTING 2.25: Conversion from a rational number to a 32-bit floating-point number.

Exercise 2.12 *Modify the pseudocode of Listing 2.25 to use the other rounding modes: round with ties-to-away, round toward zero, round toward positive, and round toward negative.*

Exercise 2.13 *The pseudocode of Listing 2.25 does not handle an input rational with zero denominator. Modify the pseudocode to handle such a rational input.*

Conversion from Rational *to* binary64. In Equation (2.52), $r_{smin} = 0.\bar{0}^{51}1 * 2^{-1022}$, $r_{smax} = 0.\bar{1}^{52} * 2^{-1022}$, $r_{nmin} = 1.\bar{0}^{52} * 2^{-1022}$, $r_{nmax} = 1.\bar{1}^{52} * 2^{1023}$, $r_\infty = 2^{1024}$, $r_{smin}/2 = 2^{-1075}$, $(r_{smax} + r_{nmin})/2 = 0.\bar{1}^{53} * 2^{-1022}$, and $(r_{nmax} + r_\infty)/2 = 1.\bar{1}^{53} * 2^{1023}$.

The pseudocode for the conversion is a trivial modification of that for the conversion to binary32. Replace binary32 with binary64, uint32_t with uint64_t, int32_t with int64_t, −150 with −1075, −149 with −1074, −126 with −1022, 22 with 51, 23 with 52, 127 with 1023, and 128 with 1024.

Exercise 2.14 *Modify the pseudocode for converting a rational to a* binary64 *to use the other rounding modes: round with ties-to-away, round toward zero, round toward positive, and round toward negative.*

Exercise 2.15 *Write pseudocode that converts* Rational *to* binaryN *where* N *is a multiple of thirty-two and larger than sixty-four.*

2.5.2.10   Conversion to Wider Format

To illustrate, consider the conversion from binary8 to binary16. The conversion is exact for finite numbers. We consider it to be exact for all encodings in the sense that the 8-bit infinities are mapped to the corresponding 16-bit infinities. An 8-bit NaN with payload is mapped to a 16-bit NaN by copying the 8-bit payload to the most significant bits of the 16-bit payload, and the quiet bit is copied when set.

Normal 8-bit numbers are converted to normal 16-bit numbers in a trivial manner. The biased exponent for the 8-bit number is adjusted to become a biased exponent for the 16-bit number. The trailing bits for the 8-bit number are copied to the correct location in the trailing bits for the 16-bit number.

Subnormal 8-bit numbers are also converted to normal 16-bit numbers. The conversion is the following:

$$0.t * 2^{-2} = 0.t_3 \cdots t_0 * 2^{-2} = 1.\bar{t}_9 \cdots \bar{t}_0 * 2^{\bar{e}-15} = 1.\bar{t} * 2^{\bar{e}-15} \qquad (2.53)$$

Let ℓ be the index of the leading 1-bit of the integer t. It is necessary that $0 \leq \ell \leq 3$, because a subnormal number has $t \neq 0$. Consequently,

$$0.t_3 \cdots t_0 * 2^{-2} = 1.t_{\ell-1} \cdots t_0 * 2^{\ell-6} = 1.t_{\ell-1} \cdots t_0 * 2^{((\ell-6)+15)-15} \qquad (2.54)$$

which implies

$$\bar{t} = (t << (10 - \ell)), \ \ \bar{e} = \ell + 9 \qquad (2.55)$$

Listing 2.26 has source code for the conversion, where the input is the encoding for binary8 and the output is the encoding for binary16.

```
uint16_t Convert (uint8_t encoding)
{
    // Extract the channels for the binary8 number.
    uint8_t sign8 = (encoding & 0x80);
    uint8_t biased8 = ((encoding & 0x70) >> 4);
    uint8_t trailing8 = (encoding & 0x0f);

    // Generate the channels for the binary16 number.
    uint16_t sign16 = (sign8 << 8);
    uint16_t biased16, trailing16;

    if (biased8 == 0)
    {
        if (trailing8 == 0)
        {
            // The number is 8-zero.  Convert to 16-zero.
            return sign16;
        }
        else
        {
            // The number is 8-subnormal.  Convert to 16-normal.
            int32_t leading = GetLeadingBit(trailing16);
            int32_t shift = 10 - leading;
            biased16 = leading + 9;
            trailing16 = (trailing8 << shift) & 0x03ff;
            return sign16 | (biased16 << 10) | trailing16;
        }
    }

    if (biased8 < 7)
    {
        // The number is 8-normal.  Convert to 16-normal.
        biased16 = biased8 + 12;
        trailing16 = (trailing8 << 6);
        return sign16 | (biased16 << 10) | trailing16;
    }

    if (trailing8 == 0)
    {
        // The number is 8-infinite.  Convert to 16-infinite.
        return sign16 | 0x7c00;
    }

    // The number is 8-NaN.  Convert to 16-NaN with 8-payload embedded in
    // the high-order bits of the 16-payload.  The code also copies the
    // 8-quietNaN mask bit.
    uint16_t maskPayload = ((trailing8 & 0x0f) << 6);
    return sign16 | 0x7c00 | maskPayload;
}
```

LISTING 2.26: Conversion of an 8-bit floating-point number to a 16-bit floating-point number.

Exercise 2.16 *Write a program that implements the conversion from 8-bit encodings to 16-bit encodings. Write a test function to print to a file the conversions for all 256 inputs. By inspecting and testing several cases, verify that the conversions are correct.*

The pattern is general for conversion to a wider format. Let the narrow format have n_0 trailing bits and exponent bias β_0. Let the wide format have n_1 trailing bits and exponent bias β_1. The conversion from narrow subnormal to wide normal is

$$0.t * 2^{1-\beta_0} = 0.t_{n_0-1} \cdots t_0 * 2^{1-\beta_0} = 1.\bar{t}_{n_1-1} \cdots \bar{t}_0 * 2^{\bar{e}-\beta_1} = 1.\bar{t} * 2^{\bar{e}-\beta_1} \quad (2.56)$$

Let ℓ be the index of the leading 1-bit of the integer t. It is necessary that $0 \le \ell \le n_0 - 1$, because a subnormal number has $t \ne 0$. Consequently,

$$
\begin{aligned}
0.t_{n_0-1} \cdots t_0 * 2^{1-\beta_0} &= 1.t_{\ell-1} \cdots t_0 * 2^{1-\beta_0-n_0+\ell} \\
&= 1.t_{\ell-1} \cdots t_0 * 2^{(1-\beta_0-n_0+\ell+\beta_1)-\beta_1}
\end{aligned}
\quad (2.57)
$$

which implies

$$\bar{t} = (t << (n_1 - \ell)), \quad \bar{e} = 1 - \beta_0 - n_0 + \ell + \beta_1 \quad (2.58)$$

Listing 2.27 shows the general conversion, where NAR refers to the narrow format and WID refers to the wide format.

```
UInteger ConvertNarrowToWide (UInteger encoding)
{
    // Extract the channels for the narrow-format number.
    UInteger signNAR = (encoding & NAR_SIGN_MASK);
    UInteger biasedNAR =
        ((encoding & NAR_BIASED_EXPONENT_MASK) >> NAR_NUM_TRAILING_BITS);
    UInteger trailingNAR = (encoding & NAR_TRAILING_MASK);

    // Generate the channels for the wide-format number.
    UInteger signWID =
        (signNAR << (WID_NUM_ENCODING_BITS - NAR_NUM_ENCODING_BITS));
    UInteger biasedWID, trailingWID;

    if (biasedNAR == 0)
    {
        if (trailingNAR == 0)
        {
            // The number is NAR-zero.  Convert to WID-zero.
            return signWID;
        }
        else
        {
            // The number is NAR-subnormal.  Convert to WID-normal.
            Integer leading = GetLeadingBit(trailingNAR);
            biasedWID = leading + 1 + WID_EXPONENT_BIAS -
                NAR_EXPONENT_BIAS - NAR_NUM_TRAILING_BITS;
            trailingWID = (trailingNAR << (WID_NUM_TRAILING_BITS -
                leading)) & NAR_TRAILING_MASK;
            return signWID | (biasedWID << WID_NUM_TRAILING_BITS) |
                trailingWID;
        }
    }

    if (biasedNAR < NAR_MAX_BIASED_EXPONENT)
    {
        // The number is NAR-normal.  Convert to WID-normal.
        biasedWID = biasedNAR + WID_EXPONENT_BIAS - NAR_EXPONENT_BIAS;
        trailingWID = (trailingNAR << (WID_NUM_TRAILING_BITS -
            NAR_NUM_TRAILING_BITS));
        return signWID | (biasedWID << WID_NUM_TRAILING_BITS) |
            trailingWID;
    }

    if (trailingNAR == 0)
```

```
{
    // The number is NAR-infinite. Convert to WID-infinite.
    return signWID | WID_BIASED_EXPONENT_MASK;
}

// The number is NAR-NaN. Convert to WID-NaN with NAR-payload
// embedded in the high-order bits of the WID-payload. The code
// also copies the NAR-quietNaN mask bit.
UInteger maskPayload = ((trailingNAR & NAR_TRAILING_MASK)
    << (WID_NUM_TRAILING_BITS - NAR_NUM_TRAILING_BITS));
return signWID | WID_BIASED_EXPONENT_MASK | maskPayload;
}
```

LISTING 2.27: Conversion of a narrow floating-point format to a wide floating-point format.

2.5.2.11 Conversion to Narrower Format

The conversions from a wide format to a narrow format are not always exact for finite numbers, so rounding must be used. Round-to-nearest is used with ties-to-even. A wide-format NaN is mapped to a narrow-format NaN, but if the wide-format payload has more 1-valued bits than can be stored in the narrow-format payload, there will be a loss of information. The IEEE 754-2008 Standard requires the result to be a quiet NaN with (optional) diagnostic information in the payload.

Figure 2.16 illustrates two floating-point formats on the nonnegative number line with important values marked. The mapping from wider to narrower format is illustrated with grayscale bars and text indicating how to round. All labeled values are exactly representable in the wide format, but some are not exactly representable in the narrow format. For example, nar-avr-min-normal-zero is the average of nar-zero and nar-min-subnormal. Even though the two inputs are exactly representable in the narrow format, the average is not. This is not a problem, because the comparisons made during conversion are all in the wide-format number system.

Using encodings in the wide-format number system, let x_{zero} be the positive zero for the narrow format and let x_{sub0} be the minimum subnormal for the narrow format. The average of the two numbers is $\alpha_0 = x_{\text{sub0}}/2$. The half-open interval of numbers $[x_{\text{zero}}, \alpha_0)$ is nearest x_{zero}, so any wide-format number in this interval is converted to x_{zero}. All such conversions are *inexact* except for zero itself. The half-open interval of numbers $(\alpha_0, x_{\text{sub0}}]$ is nearest x_{sub0}, so any wide-format number in this interval is converted to x_{sub0}. Again, all such conversion are inexact except for x_{sub0} itself. The midpoint α_0 is converted to x_{zero} because of the ties-to-even rule: the last bit of the encoding for zero is 0 (even) and the last bit of the encoding for the minimum subnormal is 1 (odd), so the rounding is to the number with the even bit.

Similarly, let x_{nor1} be the maximum normal for the narrow format. Let x_{inf} be the positive infinity for the narrow format, but for the purpose of computing the average of the two numbers, the encoding of x_{inf} is treated as if it were for a finite number. The average of the numbers is $\alpha_1 = (x_{\text{nor1}} + x_{\text{inf}})/2$. The half-open interval $[x_{\text{nor1}}, \alpha_1)$ is nearest x_{nor0}, so any wide-format number in

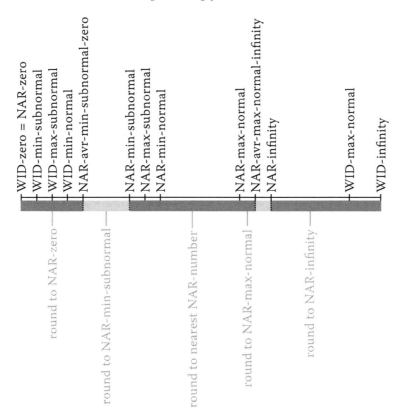

FIGURE 2.16: Two floating-point formats on the nonnegative number line. The labels with prefix wid are for the wider format and the labels with prefix nar are for the narrow format.

this interval is converted to x_{nor0}. All such conversions are inexact except for x_{nor1} itself. Let w_{inf} be the positive infinity for the wide format. The half-open interval $(\alpha_1, w_{inf}]$ is nearest to x_{inf}, so any wide-format number in this interval is converted to x_{inf}. The conversions are all inexact.

The wide-format numbers in the open interval (x_{sub0}, x_{nor1}) are converted to narrow-format numbers using round-to-nearest with ties-to-even. Many of the conversions are inexact, but some are exact. The algorithm for rounding a number to its nearest floating-point neighbor (Figure 2.16) depends on whether the nearest number is subnormal or normal. In the ensuing discussion, define x_{nor0} to be the wide-format number that represents the minimum normal for the narrow format.

Once again for illustration, consider the conversion from binary16 to binary8, in which case $x_{sub0} = 2^{-6}$ and $x_{nor0} = 2^{-2}$. The open interval in terms of wide-format numbers written as subnormals is the closed interval $[0.00010000000001 * 2^{-2}, 0.11111111111 * 2^{-2}]$. If $0.s_{13} \cdots s_0$ is the significand to a number in this interval, the corresponding narrow subnormal number is $0.s_{13}s_{12}s_{11}s_{10} + \varepsilon$, where ε is zero or one based on rounding. Define integers i and f by $i.f = s_{13} \cdots s_{10}.s_9 \cdots s_0$. Using round-to-nearest with ties-to-even, the value ε is one when $0.f > 1/2$ or when $0.f = 1/2$ and i is odd. If $i = 15$ (all s-bits are 1), then $\varepsilon = 1$ and the addition causes a carry out of s_{13}. The result is $i = 16$. When using bit-manipulation methods in the source code, the addition is to the trailing significand. The carry-out is to the low-order bit of the biased exponent. In the current case, the (left-shifted) biased exponent is zero (the target is a narrow subnormal), so OR-ing the trailing significand into the final encoding amounts to increasing the exponent by one. This is the correct behavior, because the trailing significand becomes zero, the exponent increases by one, and the output is the narrow maximum normal.

Regarding an implementation, it is convenient to generate i and f in a canonical format. If t is the trailing significand for the input wide-format number, then the significand is $1.t$. The integer $1t$ represents the t with a prepended 1, the result containing eleven bits. We may shift right to eliminate the fractional bits; that is, $i = (1t >> \sigma)$. The significand corresponding to the minimum of the subnormal interval is 1.0000000001 and has the corresponding exponent -6 and biased exponent $\bar{e} = 9 = -6 + 15$. The 11-bit integer is 10000000001, which when shifted right by $\sigma = 10$ produces binary $i = 0001$. The significand corresponding to the maximum of the subnormal interval is 1.1111111111 and has corresponding exponent -3 and biased exponent $\bar{e} = 12 = -3 + 15$. The 11-bit integer is 11111111111, which when shifted right by $\sigma = 7$ produces binary $i = 1111$. The right shift is $\sigma = 10 - (\bar{e} - 9) = 19 - \bar{e}$.

The generation of f is similar, using a left shift so that the first fraction bit occurs in the high-order bit of a 16-bit number. The full 16-bit encoding for the minimum interval endpoint is $000001000000001 = $ 0x0401. A left shift by six produces binary $\bar{f} = 0000000001000000 = $ 0x0040. The encoding for the maximum interval endpoint is $0000011111111111 = $ 0x07ff. A left shift by twelve produces binary $\bar{f} = 1111111000000000 = $ 0xfe00. The operation is $\bar{f} = 1t << \sigma$, where $\sigma = \bar{e} - 3$. The comparison of $0.f$ to one-half requires identifying which bit index contains the first bit of f and building a mask to represent one-half. In the modified formulation, the comparison is now between $\bar{f}$ and 0x8000.

The next case is when the input is in the half-open interval $[x_{\mathrm{nor0}}, x_{\mathrm{nor1}})$, where $x_{\mathrm{nor1}} = 1.1111 * 2^3$. The input is $1.t * 2^e = 1.t_9 \cdots t_0 * 2^e$ and the output is $1.s * 2^e = 1.s_3 \cdots s_0 * 2^e$. Let β_1 be the exponent bias for the wide format and let β_0 be the exponent bias for the narrow format. The biased exponent for the input is $\bar{e}_1 = e + \beta_1$ and the biased exponent for the output is $\bar{e}_0 = e + \beta_0 = \bar{e}_1 - \beta_1 + \beta_0$. Both input and output are in normal form, so there is no need to prepend one to t. Using the canonical form described in the previous two paragraphs, $i = (t >> 6)$ and $\bar{f} = (t << 10)$. The same issue arises about a carry-out to the exponent when rounding. In this case, the (left-shifted) biased exponent is not necessarily zero, so we must add the incremented trailing significand to the biased exponent rather than OR-ing it.

Listing 2.28 has source code for the conversion, where the input is the encoding for binary16 and the output is the encoding for binary8.

```
uint8_t Convert (uint16_t encoding)
{
    // Extract the channels for the binary16 number.
    uint16_t sign16 = (encoding & 0x8000);
    uint16_t biased16 = ((encoding & 0x7c00) >> 10);
    uint16_t trailing16 = (encoding & 0x03ff);
    uint16_t nonneg16 = (encoding & 0x7fff);

    // Generate the channels for the binary8 number.
    uint8_t sign8 = (sign16 >> 8);
    uint8_t biased8, trailing8;
    uint16_t frcpart;

    if (biased16 == 0)
    {
        // noneg16 is 16-zero or 16-subnormal; nearest is 8-zero.
        return sign8;
    }

    if (biased16 < 31)
    {
        // nonneg16 is 16-normal.
        if (nonneg16 <= 0x2000)    // <= nar-avrminsubnormal-zero = 2^{-7}
        {
            // nonneg16 <= 2^{-7}; nearest is 8-zero.
            return sign8;
        }

        if (nonneg16 <= 0x2400)    // <= nar-minsubnormal = 2^{-6}
        {
            // 2^{-7} < nonneg16 <= 2^{-6}; nearest is 8-min-subnormal.
            return sign8 | 0x01;   // represents nar-min-subnormal
        }

        if (nonneg16 < 0x3400)    // < nar-minnormal = 2^{-2}
        {
            // 2^{-6} < nonneg16 < 2^{-2}; round to nearest 8-subnormal
            // with ties-to-even.  Note that the biased8 value is
            // implicitly zero.
            trailing16 |= 0x0400;
            trailing8 = (trailing16 >> (19 - biased16));
            frcpart = (trailing16 << (biased16 - 3));
            if (frcpart > 0x8000
            || (frcpart == 0x8000 && (trailing8 & 1)))
            {
                // If there is a carry into the exponent, the nearest is
                // actually 8-min-normal 1.0*2^{-6}, so the high-order
                // bit of trailing8 makes biased8 equal to 1 and the
                // result is correct.
                ++trailing8;
            }
            return sign8 | trailing8;
        }

        if (nonneg16 < 0x4be0)    // < nar-maxnormal = 1.1111*2^{3}
        {
            // 2^{-2} <= nonneg16 < 1.1111*2^{3}; round to nearest
            // 8-normal with ties to even.
            biased8 = ((biased16 - 15 + 3) << 4);
            trailing8 = (trailing16 >> 6);
            frcpart = (trailing16 << 10);
            if (frcpart > 0x8000
            || (frcpart == 0x8000 && (trailing8 & 1)))
```

```
        {
            // If there is a carry into the exponent, the addition
            // of trailing8 to biased8 (rather than OR-ing) produces
            // the correct result.
            ++trailing8;
        }
        return sign8 | (biased8 + trailing8);
    }

    if (nonneg16 < 0x4bf0)  // < nar-avrmaxnor-inf = 1.11111*2^{3}
    {
        // 1.1111*2^{3} <= nonneg16 < 1.11111*2^{3}; the number is
        // closest to 8-max-normal.
        return sign8 | 0x6f;  // represents nar-max-normal
    }

    // nonneg16 >= 1.11111*2^{3}; convert to 8-infinite.
    return sign8 | 0x70;  // represents nar-infinity
}

if (trailing16 == 0)
{
    // The number is 16-infinite.  Convert to 8-infinite.
    return sign8 | 0x70;  // represents nar-infinity
}

// The number is 16-NaN.  Convert to 8-NaN with 8-payload the
// high-order 3 bits of the 16-payload.  The code also grabs the
// 16-quietNaN mask bit.
if ((trailing16 & 0x003f) == 0)
{
    // The 16-payload has only its first 3 bits set, so it can be
    // represented as an 8-payload without loss of information.
    uint8_t maskPayload = (uint8_t)((trailing16 & 0x03ff) >> 6);
    return sign8 | 0x70 | maskPayload;
}

// The 16-payload cannot be represented as an 8-payload without
// loss of information.  Make the NaN quiet (as required) and set
// the low-order bit to 1 (user-defined diagnostic information).
return sign8 | 0x79;
}
```

LISTING 2.28: Conversion from a wide floating-point format to a narrow floating-point format.

Exercise 2.17 *Write a program that implements the conversion from 16-bit encodings to 8-bit encodings. Write a test function to print to a file the conversions for all 65,536 inputs. By inspecting and testing several cases, verify that the conversions are correct.*

Exercise 2.18 *Suppose that your floating-point system has a status word whose bits represent the IEEE exceptions that can occur: inexact operation, underflow, overflow, division by zero, and invalid operation. Modify the source code for conversion from 16-bit encodings to 8-bit encodings by inserting statements that set the appropriate bits of the status words when exceptions occur. In particular, the inexact-operation bit must be set when a 16-bit number cannot be exactly represented as an 8-bit number.*

Exercise 2.19 *In the source code, when the 16-payload does not map exactly to the 8-payload, the returned value is a quiet NaN. The arbitrary choice was made to set the 8-payload to 1. You cannot rely on a 1-valued low-order payload bit to indicate the inexact payload conversion, because a 16-bit payload of 001000000 will map to an 8-bit payload of 001, and the 1-bit in the 16-bit payload does not correspond to an inexact payload conversion from 32-bit to 16-bit. In your floating-point system, let the low-order payload bit always correspond to the inexact representation of NaN payload during conversion. Modify the source code to support this choice.*

The pattern is general for conversion to a narrower format. Let the number of trailing significand bits be n_0 for the narrow format and n_1 for the wide format. Let the exponent biases be β_0 for the narrow format and β_1 for the wide format.

Consider the case when the output is in the narrow subnormal range,

$$\left(0.\bar{0}^{n_0-1}1 * 2^{1-\beta_0}, 0.\bar{1}^{n_0} * 2^{1-\beta_0}\right) \tag{2.59}$$

where $\bar{b}^p$ denotes the bit-value b repeated p times. The open interval in terms of wide-format numbers written as subnormals is the closed interval

$$\left[0.\bar{0}^{n_0-1}1\bar{0}^{n_1-1}1 * 2^{1-\beta_0}, 0.n_1\bar{+}1 * 2^{1-\beta_0}\right] \tag{2.60}$$

The significand to a number in this interval requires at most $n_0 + n_1$ bits, say,

$$0.s_{n_0+n_1-1} \cdots s_{n_1} \cdots s_{n_1-1} \cdots s_0 \tag{2.61}$$

The corresponding narrow subnormal number is $0.s_{n_0+n_1-1} \cdots s_{n_1} + \varepsilon$, where ε is zero or one based on rounding. As in the example for converting a 16-bit encoding to an 8-bit encoding, we may defined integers i and f such that $i.f = s_{n_1-1} \cdots s_{n_1}.s_{n_1-1} \cdots s_0$.

If the input is $1.t * 2^{e_1}$, the integer $1t$ contains $n_1 + 1$ bits. We may shift right to eliminate the fractional bits, $i = (1t >> \sigma_r)$, where

$$\sigma_r = (n_1 - n_0) + (\beta_1 - \beta_0) + 1 - \bar{e}_1 \tag{2.62}$$

where $\bar{e}_1 = e_1 + \beta_1$ is the biased exponent for the input. The reason for the right shift equation is motivated by the example provided previously. The minimum for the subnormal interval is

$$0.\bar{0}^{n_0-1}1\bar{0}^{n_1-1}1 * 2^{1-\beta_0} = 1.\bar{0}^{n_1-1} * 2^{1-\beta_0-n_0} \tag{2.63}$$

and the biased exponent is $\bar{e}_1 = 1 - \beta_0 - n_0 + \beta_1$. The right shift is exactly n_1, so if the general formula is $\sigma_r = n_1 - (\bar{e}_1 - v)$, we need $v = 1 - \beta_0 - n_0 + \beta_1$ to ensure the formula is correct at the interval minimum. Let $\bar{f}$ be the left-shifted value of f such that the high-order bit of f is in the high-order bit of the k_1-bit integer that stores the wide format. Think of of $1t$ embedded in a large set of bits so that shifting does not lose any bits. When you right shift the integer

$1t$ by σ_r, the fractional part is located just to the right of a block of k_1 bits whose low-order bit contains the least significant bit of $(1t >> \sigma_r)$. The right shift that moves the fractional part to the high-order bit of the k_1-bit block must be k_1. The total left shifting is therefore

$$\sigma_\ell = k_1 - \sigma_r \tag{2.64}$$

To verify using the previous example, $k_1 = 16$, $\sigma_r = 19 - \bar{e}_1$, and $\sigma_\ell = \bar{e}_1 - 3$.

Consider the case when the input and output are both normal numbers. The wide input is $1.t * 2^e$ and the narrow output is $1.s * 2^e$. The biased exponent for the input is $\bar{e}_1 = e + \beta_1$ and the biased exponent for the output is $\bar{e}_0 = e + \beta_0 = \bar{e}_1 - \beta_1 + \beta_0$. Both input and output are in normal form, so there is no need to prepend one to t. The integer part is $i = (t >> \sigma_r)$, where

$$\sigma_r = n_1 - n_0 \tag{2.65}$$

and the fractional part is $\bar{f} = (t << \sigma_\ell)$, where

$$\sigma_\ell = k_1 - (n_1 - n_0) \tag{2.66}$$

As before, if the rounding causes a carry-out into the biased exponent, we handle this by adding the trailing significand to the (left-shifted) biased exponent rather than OR-ing it.

The pseudocode is shown in Listing 2.29, where WID refers to the wide format and NAR refers to the narrow format. When the prefix WID_NAR is used, this indicates that the identifier represents the narrow-format number as a wide-format number. The mask WID_HALF_PROXY is the same as WID_SIGN_MASK, which is a k_1-bit unsigned integer with all zero bits except for the high-order bit.

```
UInteger ConvertWideToNarrow (UInteger encoding)
{
    // Extract the channels for the wide number.
    UInteger signWID = (encoding & WID_SIGN_MASK);
    UInteger biasedWID =
        ((encoding & WID_EXPONENT_MASK) >> WID_NUM_TRAILING_BITS);
    UInteger trailingWID = (encoding & WID_TRAILING_MASK);
    UInteger nonnegWID = (encoding & WID_NOT_SIGN_MASK);

    // Generate the channels for the narrow number.
    UInteger signNAR =
        (signWID >> (WID_NUM_ENCODING_BITS - NAR_NUM_ENCODING_BITS));
    UInteger biasedNAR, trailingNAR;
    UInteger rshift, lshift, frcpart;

    if (biasedWID == 0)
    {
        // nonnegWID is WID-zero or WID-subnormal; nearest is NAR-zero.
        return signNAR;
    }

    if (biasedWID < WID_MAX_BIASED_EXPONENT)
    {
        // nonnegWID is WID-normal.
        if (nonnegWID <= WID_NAR_AVR_MIN_SUBNORMAL_ZERO)
```

```
    {
        // Nearest is NAR-zero.
        return signNAR;
    }

    if (nonnegWID <= WID_NAR_MIN_SUBNORMAL)
    {
        // Nearest is NAR-min-subnormal.
        return signNAR | NAR_MIN_SUBNORMAL;
    }

    if (nonnegWID < WID_NAR_MIN_NORMAL)
    {
        // Round to nearest NAR-subnormal with ties-to-even. Note
        // that biasedNAR is implicitly zero.
        trailingWID |= WID_SUP_TRAILING_MASK;
        rshift = WID_NUM_TRAILING_BITS - NAR_NUM_TRAILING_BITS +
            WID_EXPONENT_BIAS - NAR_EXPONENT_BIAS + 1 - biasedWID;
        trailingNAR = (trailingWID >> rshift);
        lshift = WID_NUM_ENCODING_BITS - rshift;
        frcpart = (trailingWID << lshift);
        if (frcpart > WID_HALF_PROXY
        || (frcpart == WID_HALF_PROXY && (trailingNAR & 1)))
        {
            // If there is a carry into the exponent, the high-order
            // bit of trailingNAR makes biasedNAR equal to 1 and the
            // result is correct.
            ++trailingNAR;
        }
        return signNAR | trailingNAR;
    }

    if (nonnegWID < WID_NAR_MAX_NORMAL)
    {
        // Round to nearest NAR-normal with ties-to-even.
        biasedNAR = ((biasedWID - WID_EXPONENT_BIAS + NAR_EXPONENT_BIAS)
            << NAR_NUM_TRAILING_BITS);
        rshift = WID_NUM_TRAILING_BITS - NAR_NUM_TRAILING_BITS;
        trailingNAR = (trailingWID >> rshift);
        lshift = WID_NUM_ENCODING_BITS - rshift;
        frcpart = (trailingWID << lshift);
        if (frcpart > WID_HALF_PROXY
        || (frcpart == WID_HALF_PROXY && (trailingNAR & 1)))
        {
            // If there is a carry into the exponent, the addition of
            // trailingNAR to biasedNAR (rather than OR-ing) produces
            // the correct result.
            ++trailing8;
        }
        return signNAR | (biasedNAR + trailingNAR);
    }

    if (nonnegWID < WID_NAR_AVR_MAX_NORMAL_INFINITY)
    {
        // nonneg16 is closest to NAR-max-normal.
        return signNAR | NAR_MAX_NORMAL;
    }

    // nonnegWID >= WID_NAR_AVR_MAX_NORMAL_INFINITY; convert to
    // NAR-infinite.
    return signNAR | NAR_INFINITY;
}

if (trailingWID == 0)
{
    // The number is WID-infinite. Convert to NAR-infinite.
    return signNAR | NAR_BIASED_EXPONENT_MASK;
```

```
    }

    // The number is WID–NaN.  Convert to NAR–NaN with NAR–payload the
    // high–order $n_0−1$ bits of the WID–payload.  The code also grabs
    // the WID6–quietNaN mask bit.
    if ((trailingWID & WID_PAYLOAD_EXCESS) == 0)
    {
        // The WID–payload has only its first WID_NUM_TRAILING_BITS−1
        // bits set, so it can be represented as a NAR–payload without
        // loss of information.
        rshift = WID_NUM_TRAILING_BITS − NAR_NUM_TRAILING_BITS;
        UInteger maskPayload = ((trailingWID & WID_TRAILING_MASK)
            >> rshift);
        return signNAR | NAR_BIASED_EXPONENT_MASK | maskPayload;
    }

    // The WID–payload cannot be represented as a NAR–payload without
    // loss of information.  Make the NaN quiet (as required) and set
    // the low–order bit to 1 (user–defined diagnostic information).
    return signNAR | NAR_BIASED_EXPONENT_MASK | NAR_QUIET_MASK | 1;
}
```

LISTING 2.29: The conversion of a wide-format number to a narrower format.

The mask **WID_PAYLOAD_EXCESS** locates the bits of the wide payload that cannot be mapped to bits of the narrow payload. The trailing significand for the narrow number is $q p_{n_0-1} \cdots p_0$, where q is the bit to set for a quiet NaN. The trailing significand is $\bar{q}\bar{p}_{n_1-2} \cdots \bar{p}_{n_1-n_0}\bar{p}_{n_1-n_0-1} \cdots \bar{p}_0$ for the wide number, where $\bar{q}$ is the bit to set for a quiet NaN. The first n_0 bits $\bar{q}\bar{p}_{n_1-2} \cdots \bar{p}_{n_1-n_0}$ are shifted to occupy $q p_{n_0-1} \cdots p_0$. The other bits are lost. The payload-excess mask has 1-valued bits at the indices 0 through $n_1 - n_0 - 1$ and zeros at all other indices.

Exercise 2.20 *Using the pseudocode as a guide, write a program that* (1) *converts* 16-*bit encodings to* 32-*bit encodings and* (2) *converts* 32-*bit encodings to* 16-*bit encodings. Write a test program with a sufficient number of examples to verify that your implementations are correct. (Hint: Think about this in terms of* code *coverage.)*

2.5.3   Arithmetic Operations

The arithmetic operations of addition, subtraction, and multiplication are as described in Section 2.4.2, although the implementation in hardware will not look like the software algorithms I discussed. Division can be implemented as described previously, using a straightforward division of binary numbers similar to what you do for long division of integers. The floating-point hardware uses barrel shifters in the implementation.

Other division approaches are possible. To compute a reciprocal $1/x$ for a specified positive number x, we can use Newton's method to compute the root y of $f(y) = 1/y - x$ for a suitably chosen initial guess y_0. The iterates are

$$y_{i+1} = y_i - f(y_i)/f'(y_i) = y_i(2 - xy_i), \quad i \geq 0 \qquad (2.67)$$

Using binary scientific notation, we can factor out a power of two so that the number for which we actually compute the reciprocal is $x \in [1/2, 1)$. Using a minimax algorithm (see Section 3.3), we can fit $1/x$ on $[1/2, 1)$ with a linear polynomial $c_0 + c_1 x$ to minimize the maximum absolute value of the error $|E(x)|$ where $E(x) = x(c_0 + c_1 x) - 1$. The local minimum on $[1/2, 1]$ occurs when $E'(x) = 0$, in which case $x = -c_0/(2c_1)$. To balance the error according to the Chebyshev equioscillation theorem, we need $E(1/2) = E(1) = -E(-c_0/2c_1)$, which leads to two equations in the two unknowns c_0 and c_1. The solution is $c_0 = 48/17$ and $c_1 = -32/17$, and the maximum fitted error is approximately 0.0588235. The inital guess is chosen as $y_0 = (48 - 32x)/17$.

A more interesting implementation of division in hardware uses *multiplicative division* [15]. To compute the division x/y observe that

$$\frac{x}{y} = \frac{x f_0 f_1 \ldots f_{n-1}}{y f_0 f_1 \ldots f_{n-1}} \tag{2.68}$$

for any positive factors f_i. With carefully chosen factors, we can iteratively drive the denominator $y f_0 \ldots f_{n-1}$ to 1, in which case the numerator $x f_0 \ldots f_{n-1}$ is the result of the division. Factoring out powers of two for x and y so that $x \in [0, 1/2)$ and $y \in (1/2, 1]$, we can choose initial values $x_0 = x$, $y_0 = y$, and factors $f_i = 1 + x^{2^i}$. The iterates are

$$\frac{x_{i+1}}{y_{i+1}} = \frac{x_i f_i}{y_i f_i}, \quad i \geq 0 \tag{2.69}$$

After n iterations, the result has minimum precision of 2^n bits.

2.5.4   Mathematical Functions

The IEEE 754-2008 Standard has requirements about various operations and mathematical functions to support correctly rounded results. With the default mode of round-to-nearest, a function such as y = sqrt(x) for a (nonnegative) 32-bit floating-point input x must return a 32-bit floating-point input y that is the closest floating-point number to the theoretical square root. For example, Listing 2.30 shows the correctly rounded result for a square root operation.

```
float x = 1.25f;     // x.binary32 = 0x3fa00000 (exact representation)
float y = sqrt(x);   // y.binary32 = 0x3f8f1bbd
                     // y.binary64 = 0x3ff1e377a0000000
                     // y.binary = 1.1e377a
yTheoretical.binary = 1.1e3779b9 + remainder;
y = RoundToNearestFloat(yTheoretical);
```

LISTING 2.30: Correctly rounded result for square root.

The exact value is irrational but may be expanded to as many binary places as is shown. The closest 32-bit floating-point value to the theoretical answer is obtained in this case by rounding up. If the rounding mode of the FPU were set to round toward zero, the sqrt function would be required to return the 32-bit floating-point number with encoding 0x3ff1e377b.

Generally, deriving mathematical approximations to functions with correct rounding is a technical challenge. FPU hardware can provide fast computation by using registers with higher precision than that of the inputs to the functions. If the floating-point arithmetic were to be implemented in software, you might not obtain as fast a computation as you would like. However, you may consider trading accuracy for speed. This is a typical trade-off for computing with SIMD registers; see Chapter 3.

The standard mathematics library that ships with Microsoft Visual Studio has several functions supported by an FPU, shown in Listing 2.31. Variations are provided for float and double.

```
acos(x)      // inverse cosine
asin(x)      // inverse sine
atan(x)      // inverse tangent
atan2(y,x)   // inverse tangent with quadrant selection
ceil(x)      // round up to integer value
cos(x)       // cosine
cosh(x)      // hyperbolic cosine
exp(x)       // exponential base e
fabs(x)      // absolute value
floor(x)     // round down to integer
fmod(x,y)    // remainder of x/y
frexp(x,y)   // get trailing significand and exponent of a number
ldexp(x,y)   // compute number from trailing significand and exponent
log(x)       // logarithm base e
log10(x)     // logarithm base 10
modf(f,i)    // split f into fractional and integer parts
pow(x,y)     // raise x to power y
sin(x)       // sine
sinh(x)      // hyperbolic sine
sqrt(x)      // square root
tan(x)       // tangent
tanh(x)      // hyperbolic tangent
```

LISTING 2.31: The standard mathematics library functions.

2.5.5 Floating-Point Oddities

This section contains a small collection of problems whose solutions are unexpected.

2.5.5.1 Where Have My Digits Gone?

Compute the roots of a quadratic equation $a_2x^2 + a_1x + a_0 = 0$. The standard formula is

$$x = \frac{-a_1 \pm \sqrt{a_1^2 - 4a_0a_2}}{2a_2} \tag{2.70}$$

where the discriminant is $\Delta = a_1^2 - 4a_0a_2$. The equation has no real-valued roots when $\Delta < 0$, one repeated real-value root when $\Delta = 0$, and two distinct real-valued roots when $\Delta > 0$.

For the case $\Delta > 0$, when a_2 is nearly zero and $a_1 > 0$, the numerator for the larger root is $-a_1 + \sqrt{a_1^2 - 4a_0a_2}$. The argument of the square root function is approximately a_1^2, so the square root is approximately a_1, in which case you have a difference of two numbers of similar magnitude. This can lead to cancellation of many significant digits, producing a numerator that is nearly zero and effectively noise. The division by the nearly zero a_2 then magnifies the result. The recommended way to avoid this problem is to modify the equation,

$$
\begin{aligned}
\frac{-a_1+\sqrt{a_1^2-4a_0a_2}}{2a_2} &= \frac{-a_1+\sqrt{a_1^2-4a_0a_2}}{2a_2} \cdot \frac{-a_1-\sqrt{a_1^2-4a_0a_2}}{-a_1-\sqrt{a_1^2-4a_0a_2}} \\
&= \frac{a_1^2-(a_1^2-4a_0a_2)}{-2a_2(a_1+\sqrt{a_1^2-4a_0a_2})} \\
&= \frac{a_0}{(a_1+\sqrt{a_1^2-4a_0a_2})/2}
\end{aligned}
\tag{2.71}
$$

The new formula is mathematically equivalent to the old formula, but now the denominator has a sum of nearly equal values, which avoids the cancellation.

The basic illustration of subtractive cancellation is shown in Listing 2.32.

```
float  a0 = -0.01f;       // 0xbc23d70a
float  a1 = 0.001f;       // 0x3a83126f
float  a2 = 0.000001f;    // 0x358637bd
float  discriminant = a1*a1 - 4.0f*a0*a2;   // is positive
float  rootDiscriminant = sqrtf(discriminant);
float  root[2], rootPrev[2], rootNext[2];
float  poly[2], polyPrev[2], polyNext[2];
// Value(a0,a1,a2,r) = a0 + r*(a1 + r*a2)

// Original formula.
float  invTwoA2 = 0.5f/a2;
root[0] = (-a1 - rootDiscriminant)*invTwoA2;
root[1] = (-a1 + rootDiscriminant)*invTwoA2;
poly[0] = a0 + root[0]*(a1 + root[0]*a2);
poly[1] = a0 + root[1]*(a1 + root[1]*a2);

rootPrev[0] = NextDown(root[0]);               // -1009.9020 (0xc47c79bb)
rootCurr[0] = root[0];                         // -1009.9020 (0xc47c79ba)
rootNext[0] = NextUp(root[0]);                 // -1009.9019 (0xc47c79b9)
polyPrev[0] = Value(a0,a1,a2,rootPrev[0]);    // +3.8622883e-8 (0x3325e24f)
polyCurr[0] = Value(a0,a1,a2,rootCurr[0]);    // -2.3621011e-8 (0xb2cae727)
polyNext[0] = Value(a0,a1,a2,rootNext[0]);    // -8.5864897e-8 (0xb3b864ba)

rootPrev[1] = NextDown(root[1]);               // +9.9019375 (0x411e6e56)
rootCurr[1] = root[1];                         // +9.9019384 (0x411e6e57)
rootNext[1] = NextUp(root[1]);                 // +9.9019394 (0x411e6e58)
polyPrev[1] = Value(a0,a1,a2,rootPrev[1]);    // -1.3455720e-8 (0xb2672ae2)
polyCurr[1] = Value(a0,a1,a2,rootCurr[1]);    // -1.2483159e-8 (0xb2567584)
polyNext[1] = Value(a0,a1,a2,rootNext[1]);    // -1.1510599e-8 (0xb245c026)

// Modified formula.
float  temp = -0.5f*(a1 + rootDiscriminant);
root[0] = temp/a2;
root[1] = a0/temp;
poly[0] = a0 + root[0]*(a1 + root[0]*a2);
poly[1] = a0 + root[1]*(a1 + root[1]*a2);

// 0-indexed values same as for original formula.

rootPrev[1] = NextDown(root[1]);               // +9.9019499 (0x411e6e63)
rootCurr[1] = root[1];                         // +9.9019508 (0x411e6e64)
rootNext[1] = NextUp(root[1]);                 // +9.9019518 (0x411e6e65)
polyPrev[1] = Value(a0,a1,a2,rootPrev[1]);    // -8.1242973e-10 (0xb05f51a9)
polyCurr[1] = Value(a0,a1,a2,rootCurr[1]);    // +1.6013110e-10 (0x2f3010e6)
polyNext[1] = Value(a0,a1,a2,rootNext[1]);    // +1.1326919e-09 (0x309bad0e)
```

LISTING 2.32: Subtractive cancellation in floating-point arithmetic.

The 0-index roots are the same for the two methods but the 1-index roots differ. In fact, the roots have trailing significands that differ by seven, which amounts to a floating-point difference of $1/2^{21} + 1/2^{22} + 1/2^{23} \doteq 8.34465e{-}7$.

The pseudocode shows the two floating-point neighbors of the 0-index root, namely, rootPrev[0] and rootNext[0]. Observe that the polynomial values at those points have opposite signs, which means that zero lies between them (in terms of infinite precision). The polynomial value at the computed root is nearly zero and has a magnitude smaller than that of the polynomial value at the root's next-up neighbor. Thus, the floating-point value computed for the root is the best that you can do in terms of 32-bit float and polynomial evaluation defined as it is.

The pseudocode also shows the two floating-point neighbors of the 1-index root computed using the original quadratic formula. Observe that the polynomial value at that root is nearly zero. However, the two floating-point neighbors of the root have polynomial values of the same sign as that of the root, so the next-down and next-up values do not bound a root (in terms of infinite precision). The modified formula does lead to a floating-point approximation to the root whose next-down and next-up values do bound the infinite precision root. This is clear by observing that the polynomial values at the neighbors have opposite signs and the magnitude of the polynomial value at the estimated root is smaller than the magnitudes of the polynomial values at the neighbors.

Notice that the original formula uses one division but the modified formula uses two divisions. Thus, the modified formula is more expensive to compute, but it gives a better estimate of the root. If you polish the root from the original formula using one iteration of Newton's method, you obtain the root produced by the modified method.

```
//  root[1] = +9.9019384  (0x411e6e57)
//  poly[1] = -1.2483159e-008
root[1] -= poly[1]/(a1 + root[1]*(2.0f*a2));
poly[1] = a0 + root[1]*(a1 + root[1]*a2);
//  root[1] = +9.9019508  (0x411e6e64)
//  poly[1] = +1.6013110e-010
```

The root polishing involves a second division, so in effect the original formula plus one Newton iteration gets you to the same place. Here are several questions for investigation. The assumption is that the quadratic coefficients are chosen so that the root estimates involve only finite floating-point numbers—that is, NaNs and infinities are not generated.

Exercise 2.21 *Let r_0 be a root estimate from the original formula. Let $f(r) = a_0 + r(a_1 + ra_2)$ be the floating-point expression used to evaluate the quadratic polynomial. Let $r_1 = r_0 - f(r_0)/(a_1 + r_0(2a_2))$. Let r_2 be an estimate for the same root using the modified formula. Is it always true that $r_1 = r_2$?*

Exercise 2.22 *If the answer to the previous question is false, what is the maximum number of Newton iterations that leads to the root estimate of the* *modified formula? Is it ever possible for the Newton iterates to cycle, thus preventing convergence to an estimated root?*

Exercise 2.23 *Let r be a root estimate from the modified formula. Let r_d be the next-down neighbor of r and let r_u be the next-up neighbor of r. Let $f(r) = a_0 + r(a_1 + ra_2)$ be the floating-point expression used to evaluate the quadratic polynomial. Is it always true that $f(r_d)f(r_u) \leq 0$ and $|f(r)| = \min\{|f(r_d)|, |f(r)|, |f(r_u)|\}$?*

The leading coefficient is chosen to be very small. Listing 2.33 shows how bad the subtractive cancellation can be.

```
float  a0 = −0.01f;          // 0xbc23d70a
float  a1 = 0.001f;          // 0x3a83126f
float  a2 = 10.0f*FLT_MIN;   // 1.1754944e−37 (0x02200000)
float  discriminant = a1*a1 − 4.0f*a0*a2;   // is positive
float  rootDiscriminant = sqrtf(discriminant);
float  root[2], rootPrev[2], rootNext[2];
float  poly[2], polyPrev[2], polyNext[2];
// Value(a0,a1,a2,r) = a0 + r*(a1 + r*a2)

// Original formula.
float  invTwoA2 = 0.5f/a2;
root[0] = (−a1 − rootDiscriminant)*invTwoA2;
root[1] = (−a1 + rootDiscriminant)*invTwoA2;
poly[0] = a0 + root[0]*(a1 + root[0]*a2);
poly[1] = a0 + root[1]*(a1 + root[1]*a2);

rootPrev[0] = NextDown(root[0]);               // −8.5070602e+33 (0xf7d1b719)
rootCurr[0] = root[0];                         // −8.5070596e+33 (0xf7d1b718)
rootNext[0] = NextUp(root[0]);                 // −8.5070590e+33 (0xf7d1b717)
polyPrev[0] = Value(a0,a1,a2,rootPrev[0]);     // +6.1897012e+23 (0x67031270)
polyCurr[0] = Value(a0,a1,a2,rootCurr[0]);     // −0.0099999998  (0xbc23d70a)
polyNext[0] = Value(a0,a1,a2,rootNext[0]);     // −6.1896998e+23 (0xe703126e)

rootPrev[1] = NextDown(root[1]);               // −1.401e−45#DEN (0x80000001)
rootCurr[1] = root[1];                         // 0.00000000     (0x00000000)
rootNext[1] = NextUp(root[1]);                 // +1.401e−45#DEN (0x00000001)
polyPrev[1] = Value(a0,a1,a2,rootPrev[1]);     // −0.0099999998  (0xbc23d70a)
polyCurr[1] = Value(a0,a1,a2,rootCurr[1]);     // −0.0099999998  (0xbc23d70a)
polyNext[1] = Value(a0,a1,a2,rootNext[1]);     // −0.0099999998  (0xbc23d70a)

// Modified formula.
float  temp = −0.5f*(a1 + rootDiscriminant);
root[0] = temp/a2;
root[1] = a0/temp;
poly[0] = a0 + root[0]*(a1 + root[0]*a2);
poly[1] = a0 + root[1]*(a1 + root[1]*a2);

// 0−indexed values same as for original formula.

rootPrev[1] = NextDown(root[1]);               // +9.9999981 (0x411ffffe)
rootCurr[1] = root[1];                         // +9.9999990 (0x411fffff)
rootNext[1] = NextUp(root[1]);                 // +10.000000 (0x41200000)
polyPrev[1] = Value(a0,a1,a2,rootPrev[1]);     // −1.2088568e−09 (0xb0a624de)
polyCurr[1] = Value(a0,a1,a2,rootCurr[1]);     // −2.5518243e−10 (0xaf8c49bc)
polyNext[1] = Value(a0,a1,a2,rootNext[1]);     // +6.9849193e−10 (0x30400000)
```

LISTING 2.33: Another example of subtractive cancellation and how bad it can be.

The original formula estimates a root of 0.0 with corresponding polynomial value -0.0099999998. The coefficient $a_0 = 0.001$ cannot be exactly represented in floating point, so the polynomial value is a_0 as represented in floating point. The modified formula estimates a root of 9.9999990, which is much different from 0.0. The corresponding polynomial value is $-2.5518243e-010$, which is closer to zero than the polynomial value for the estimated root obtained by the original formula.

Once again observe that the next-down and next-up values for the estimated root using the modified formula produce polynomial values of opposite sign. Moreover, the magnitude of the polynomial value at the estimate root is smaller than the magnitudes of the polynomial values at the neighbors. The modified formula is the best you can do for estimating the root using 32-bit floats.

The estimated root from the original formula appears to be quite bad. How bad is it? Well, try polishing the root with one iteration of Newton's method.

```
// root[1] = 0.00000000      (0x00000000)
// poly[1] = -0.0099999998   (0xbc23d70a)
root[1] -= poly[1]/(a1 + root[1]*(2.0f*a2));
poly[1] = a0 + root[1]*(a1 + root[1]*a2);
// root[1] = +9.9999990 (0x411fffff)
// poly[1] = -2.5518243e-010 (0xaf8c49bc)
```

Once again we have obtained the estimated root of the modified formula with only a single iteration. Perhaps the estimated root of the original formula appeared to be inaccurate, but the root polishing appears to indicate that it was close enough to quickly refine it to a good estimate.

An issue to be aware of for the modified formula is when $a_1 = 0$. The quadratic equation is $a_2 x^2 + a_0 = 0$. When there are real-valued roots, they must be $x = \pm\sqrt{-a_0/a_2}$. One root is the negative of the other (when $a_0 \neq 0$). The modified formula, however, will estimate two roots that are not negatives of each other, as shown in Listing 2.34.

```
float  a0 = -0.01f;           // 0xbc23d70a
float  a1 = 0.0f;             // 0x00000000
float  a2 = 0.001f;           // 0x3a83126f
float  discriminant = a1*a1 - 4.0f*a0*a2;  // is positive
float  rootDiscriminant = sqrtf(discriminant);
float  root[2], rootPrev[2], rootNext[2];
float  poly[2], polyPrev[2], polyNext[2];
// Value(a0,a1,a2,r) = a0 + r*(a1 + r*a2)

// Original formula.
float  invTwoA2 = 0.5f/a2;
root[0] = (-a1 - rootDiscriminant)*invTwoA2;
root[1] = (-a1 + rootDiscriminant)*invTwoA2;
poly[0] = a0 + root[0]*(a1 + root[0]*a2);
poly[1] = a0 + root[1]*(a1 + root[1]*a2);

rootPrev[0] = NextDown(root[0]);          // -3.1622779 (0xc04a62c3)
rootCurr[0] = root[0];                    // -3.1622777 (0xc04a62c2)
rootNext[0] = NextUp(root[0]);            // -3.1622775 (0xc04a62c1)
polyPrev[0] = Value(a0,a1,a2,rootPrev[0]); // +2.4489206e-09 (0x312849de)
polyCurr[0] = Value(a0,a1,a2,rootCurr[0]); // +9.4102892e-10 (0x30815583)
polyNext[0] = Value(a0,a1,a2,rootNext[0]); // -5.6686256e-10 (0xb01bd168)
```

```
rootPrev[1] = NextDown(root[1]);             // +3.1622775 (0x404a62c1)
rootCurr[1] = root[1];                        // +3.1622777 (0x404a62c2)
rootNext[1] = NextUp(root[1]);                // +3.1622779 (0x404a62c3)
polyPrev[1] = Value(a0,a1,a2,rootPrev[1]);    // -5.6686256e-10 (0xb01bd168)
polyCurr[1] = Value(a0,a1,a2,rootCurr[1]);    // +9.4102892e-10 (0x30815583)
polyNext[1] = Value(a0,a1,a2,rootNext[1]);    // +2.4489206e-09 (0x312849de)

// Modified formula.
float temp = -0.5f*(a1 + rootDiscriminant);
root[0] = temp/a2;
root[1] = a0/temp;
poly[0] = a0 + root[0]*(a1 + root[0]*a2);
poly[1] = a0 + root[1]*(a1 + root[1]*a2);

// 0-indexed values same as for original formula.

rootPrev[1] = NextDown(root[1]);             // +3.1622772 (0x404a62c0)
rootCurr[1] = root[1];                        // +3.1622775 (0x404a62c1)
rootNext[1] = NextUp(root[1]);                // +3.1622777 (0x404a62c2)
polyPrev[1] = Value(a0,a1,a2,rootPrev[1]);    // -2.0747539e-09 (0xb10e9375)
polyCurr[1] = Value(a0,a1,a2,rootCurr[1]);    // -5.6686256e-10 (0xb01bd168)
polyNext[1] = Value(a0,a1,a2,rootNext[1]);    // +9.4102892e-10 (0x30815583)
```

LISTING 2.34: Numerically incorrect quadratic roots when using the modified quadratic formula.

The original formula estimates two roots, one the negative of the other. Notice that the next-down and next-up values for the 0-index root have opposite sign polynomial values, so next-down and next-up bound the root (as an infinite precision value). However, the magnitude of the polynomial value at the estimated root is larger than the magnitude of the polynomial value at the next-up neighbor.

The modified formula estimates two roots, one not the negative of the other, but they are sufficiently close in magnitude. The next-down and next-up values for the 1-index root have opposite-sign polynomial values and the magnitude of the polynomial value at the estimated root is smaller than the magnitudes of the polynomial values at the neighbors. But as in the other examples, one Newton iterate applied to the 1-index estimated root from the original formula will polish the root to be the 1-index estimated root from the modified formula.

One Newton iterate to polish the 0-index root produces an estimated root of -3.162775. The polished roots are negatives of each other.

2.5.5.2 Have a Nice Stay!

In the previous section, root polishing was used for the estimated roots obtained from the original formula. In each of the two examples, a single Newton iterate was sufficient to produce the estimated root obtained from the modified formula.

Generally, you might be tempted to polish roots regardless of the formula used. Naturally, you want an estimate for which the polynomial value is *close to zero*. Be very careful here. Suppose you chose a small threshold $\varepsilon > 0$ for which you want the estimated root r to satisfy $|f(r)| < \varepsilon$. Being mathematical, this is a natural thing to try.

```
float  a0 = <something >,  a1 = <something >,  a2 = <something >;
float  root = <estimated using original or modified formula >;
float  poly = a0 + root*(a1 + root*a2);
const float myPolyEpsilon = 1e-06f;
while (fabsf(poly) > myPolyEpsilon)
{
    float polyDerivative = a1 + root*(2.0f*a2);
    root -= poly/polyDerivative;
    poly = a0 + root*(a1 + root*a2);
}
```

In many cases, you will be waiting a very long time for your program to terminate—a very long time, as this is an infinite loop. It is better to limit the number of iterations by a user-specified loop maximum. Even better, use a std::set to store the visited root candidates. When a candidate already exists in the set, you have a cycle of numbers, in which case you can terminate the root finding and report the number whose corresponding function value is closest to zero.

2.5.5.3   The Best I Can Do Is That Bad?

Listing 2.35 is an example that shows the best you can do in finding roots but where one of the roots looks to be absolutely wrong.

```
float  a0 = 1.3852034e−27f;  // 0x12db7e87
float  a1 = 0.00013351663f;  // 0x390c0099
float  a2 = 3.0170867e−38f;  // 0x0124440d
float  discriminant = a1*a1 − 4.0f*a0*a2;  // is positive
float  rootDiscriminant = sqrtf(discriminant);
float  root[2], rootPrev[2], rootNext[2];
float  poly[2], polyPrev[2], polyNext[2];
// Value(a0,a1,a2,r) = a0 + r*(a1 + r*a2)

// Modified formula.
float  temp = −0.5f*(a1 + rootDiscriminant);
root[0] = temp/a2;
root[1] = a0/temp;
poly[0] = a0 + root[0]*(a1 + root[0]*a2);
poly[1] = a0 + root[1]*(a1 + root[1]*a2);

rootPrev[0] = NextDown(root[0]);             // −4.4253497e+33 (0xf75a2fc4)
rootCurr[0] = root[0];                       // −4.4253494e+33 (0xf75a2fc3)
rootNext[0] = NextUp(root[0]);               // −4.4253491e+33 (0xf75a2fc2)
polyPrev[0] = Value(a0,a1,a2,rootPrev[0]);   // +2.1253151e+22 (0x64900457)
polyCurr[0] = Value(a0,a1,a2,rootCurr[0]);   // −2.0068245e+22 (0xe487fcdb)
polyNext[0] = Value(a0,a1,a2,rootNext[0]);   // −6.1389634e+22 (0xe54fff05)

rootPrev[1] = NextDown(root[1]);             // −1.0374764e−23 (0x9948ad58)
rootCurr[1] = root[1];                       // −1.0374763e−23 (0x9948ad57)
rootNext[1] = NextUp(root[1]);               // −1.0374763e−23 (0x9948ad56)
polyPrev[1] = Value(a0,a1,a2,rootPrev[1]);   // −2.0747539e−09 (0x870f9998)
polyCurr[1] = Value(a0,a1,a2,rootCurr[1]);   // −5.6686256e−10 (0x84663fc0)
polyNext[1] = Value(a0,a1,a2,rootNext[1]);   // +9.4102892e−10 (0x0708679a)
```

LISTING 2.35: An example of correct root finding, although at first glance they look incorrect.

The 0-index root estimate is $-4.4253494e + 33$, which is quite large in magnitude, and the polynomial value at the root is $-2.0068245e + 22$, which is also quite large in magnitude. When you first see the result, you will probably tell yourself that there is a bug somewhere in your code. However, observe that the next-down and next-up values for the estimated root have opposite-sign polynomial values, so the infinite-precision root is bounded by next-up and next-down. Moreover, the magnitude of the polynomial value at the estimated root is smaller than the magnitudes of the polynomial values at the neighbors. *This is the best you can do.*

This example just emphasizes how sparse the floating-point numbers are on the real line when those numbers are large in magnitude.

If you repeat the experiment using 64-bit doubles, the results are more what you expect. The coefficients are the exact 64-bit representations of the 32-bit values of the last code block. Listing 2.36 shows the results.

```
double a0 = 1.3852034457886450e−27;
double a1 = 0.00013351663073990494;
double a2 = 3.0170866780915123e−38;
double discriminant = a1*a1 − 4.0*a0*a2;   // is positive
double rootDiscriminant = sqrt(discriminant);
double root[2], rootPrev[2], rootNext[2];
double poly[2], polyPrev[2], polyNext[2];
// Value(a0,a1,a2,r) = a0 + r*(a1 + r*a2)

// Modified formula.
double temp = −0.5*(a1 + rootDiscriminant);
root[0] = temp/a2;
root[1] = a0/temp;
poly[0] = a0 + root[0]*(a1 + root[0]*a2);
poly[1] = a0 + root[1]*(a1 + root[1]*a2);

rootPrev[0] = NextDown(root[0]);           // −4.4253495171163665e+33
rootCurr[0] = root[0];                      // −4.4253495171163659e+33
rootNext[0] = NextUp(root[0]);              // −4.4253495171163653e+33
polyPrev[0] = Value(a0,a1,a2,rootPrev[0]); // 119949339011631.06
polyCurr[0] = Value(a0,a1,a2,rootCurr[0]); // 1.3852034457886450e−27
polyNext[0] = Value(a0,a1,a2,rootNext[0]); // −119949339011631.03

rootPrev[1] = NextDown(root[1]);           // −1.0374763339310665e−23
rootCurr[1] = root[1];                      // −1.0374763339310664e−23
rootNext[1] = NextUp(root[1]);             // −1.0374763339310662e−23
polyPrev[1] = Value(a0,a1,a2,rootPrev[1]); // −1.7936620343357659e−43
polyCurr[1] = Value(a0,a1,a2,rootCurr[1]); // 0.00000000000000000
polyNext[1] = Value(a0,a1,a2,rootNext[1]); // 1.7936620343357659e−43
```

LISTING 2.36: The example of Listing 2.35 but computed using double-precision numbers. The hexadecimal encodings are omitted here.

This shows that having a very large number of 64-bit floating-point numbers between the 32-bit floating-point next-down and next-up of the previous code block allows you to produce a precise estimate of the 0-index root ($-4.4253495171163659e + 33$) with a polynomial value nearly zero ($1.3852034457886450e−27$).

2.5.5.4 You Have Been *More* Than Helpful

There is a tendency to think that you can help the compiler in its optimization by factoring out subexpressions, thus avoiding redundant computations. You do this by computing the subexpressions and storing in temporary local variables. For example,

```
float  x = <something >,  y = <something >,  z = <something >;

// Original  expressions.   Five  arithmetic  operations (when unoptimized ).
float  expression1 = x*y*z;
float  expression2 = x*y*(z + 1.0 f );

// Trying  to  be  helpful  to  the  compiler.   Three  arithmetic  operations (hand
// optimized ).
float  xyProduct  = x*y;
float  expression1 = xyProduct *z;
float  expression2 = expression1 + xyProduct ;
```

Be careful! If x and y are very large numbers, explicitly computing xyProduct can lead to problems, as the following example illustrates.

```
float  large1 = 1.1e+24f;   // 0x6768ef1f
float  large2 = 2.2e+24f;   // 0x67e8ef1f
float  small = 1e−12f;      // 0x2b8cbccc

// Internally ,  right−hand  side  is  computed  using  64−bit  double ,  avoiding  the
// 32− bit  float  overflow  in  the  product  large1*large2.   The  result  is
// in  the  normal  range  for  32−bit  float.   The  floating−point  processor
// signals  "inexact"  because  the  64−bit  result  is  not  exactly
// representable  as  a  32−bit  number ,  so  rounding−to−nearest  is  applied.
float  product1 = large1*large2*small;   // 2.4200001e+36 (0x7be9099c )

// Internally ,  right−hand  side  is  computed  using  64−bit  double ,  avoiding  the
// 32− bit  float  overflow.   However ,  the  64−bit  result  is  larger  than
// 32−bit  infinity ,  so  the  conversion  back  to  32−bit  float  fails.   The
// floating−point  processor  signals  "overflow"  and  "inexact"  and  assigns
// infinity  to  temp.
float  temp = large1*large2;   // 1.#INF000 (0x7f800000)

// Too  late.   temp  is  infinity  and  the  product  on  the  right−hand  side
// remains  infinity  (no  signal  generated  by  the  floating−point  processor).
// Mathematically ,  product1  and  product2  are  the  "same"  but  the
// floating−point  calculations  lead  to  different  values.
float  product2 = temp*small;   // 1.#INF000 (0x7f800000)

// The  right−hand  side  for  computing  product1  in  64−bit.
double  dlarge1 = (double)large1;
double  dlarge2 = (double)large2;
double  dsmall = (double)small;
double  dproduct1 = dlarge1*dlarge2*small;
// 2.4200001207672320e+036
// 0x477d21337c642a3d
// f = 2^{120} * 1.11010010000100110011100
// d = 2^{120} * 1.1101001000010011011111100011001000010101000111101
//
//                                       ^
//                                     first  mismatch
// Rounding  error  is  approximately  2^{120}*2^{−21} = 2^{99}.
```

The last part of the code shows that the rounding error in computing product1 is very large, but this is most likely preferable to having an indeterminate result of infinity.

2.5.5.5 Hardware and Optimizing Compiler Issues

Optimizing compilers can generate a different order of operations than what you might have specified (without parentheses), which can affect the final result. The optimizer interferes with carefully written code that deals with rounding and overflow. If you have carefully designed expressions to be evaluated in a certain order, use parentheses to force that order.

Subnormals can cause a switch from hardware to microcode, leading to slow execution.

As shown in the example for GPU root finding, the hardware/drivers might not be compliant with the IEEE 754-2008 standard.

Intermediate calculations in 80-bit registers might be temporary stored in a 32-bit register for later use. The programmer cannot control this because the compiler generates the code and (usually) does not provide the ability to give hints about what you want to happen. Until language groups agree on providing explicit control to programmers, such as /fp:precise for Microsoft Visual Studio regarding compiled code, you might have to resort to assembly instructions or platform- and compiler-specific solutions.

Attempts to compute functions such as fast inverse sqrt on CPUs such as the PowerPC might not work as you see on Intel CPUs. For example, fast invsqrt on the PowerPC has load-hit-store penalties when trying to access a union—the value is manipulated as an unsigned int but then as a float, so different registers must be read and written. This is particularly a problem on game consoles, so you might as well skip the fast method and use hardware-provided alternatives.

Chapter 3

SIMD Computing

3.1 Intel Streaming SIMD Extensions

Current CPUs have small-scale parallel support for 3D mathematics computations using *single-instruction-multiple-data* (SIMD) computing. The processors provide 128-bit registers, each register storing four 32-bit float values. The fundamental concepts are

- to provide addition and multiplication of four numbers simultaneously (a single instruction applied to multiple data) and

- to allow *shuffling*, sometimes called *swizzling*, of the four components.

Of course, such hardware has support for more than just these operations.

In this section I will briefly summarize the SIMD support for Intel CPUs, discuss a wrapper class that GTEngine has, and cover several approximations to standard mathematics functions. The latter topic is necessary because many SIMD implementations do not provide instructions for the standard functions. This is true for Intel's SIMD, and it is true for Direct3D 11 GPU hardware. You might very well find that you have to implement approximations for both the GPU and SIMD on the CPU.

The original SIMD support on Intel CPUs is called *Intel Streaming SIMD Extensions* (SSE). New features were added over the years, and with each the version number was appended to the acronym. Nearly everything I do with GTEngine requires the second version, SSE2. To access the support for programming, you simply need to include two header files,

```
#include <xmmintrin.h>
#include <emmintrin.h>
```

These give you access to data types for the registers and compiler intrinsics that allow you to use SIMD instructions within your C++ programs.

The main data type is the union __m128 whose definition is found in xmmintrin.h. It has a special declaration so that it is 16-byte aligned, a requirement to use SSE2 instructions. If you require dynamic allocation to create items of this type, you can use Microsoft's _aligned_malloc and _aligned_free. SSE2 provides also its own wrappers for aligned allocations, _mm_malloc and _mm_free.

The online MSDN documentation has many pages about the intrinsics available to you. I will not list them all here, but I will talk about the ones I use to illustrate the basic concepts. The instructions are prefixed with _mm. For example, to load two 128-bit registers and add them as 4-tuples,

```
__m128 v0 = _mm_set_ps(3.0f,2.0f,1.0f,0.0f);  // v0  = (0.0f,1.0f,2.0f,3.0f)
__m128 v1 = _mm_set_ps1(4.0f);                 // v1  = (4.0f,4.0f,4.0f,4.0f)
__m128 sum = _mm_add_ps(v0, v1);               // sum = (4.0f,5.0f,6.0f,7.0f)
```

Notice that the order of the numbers in the loading of v0 is reversed from what you are used to. You will need to be careful about this reversal when looking at a __m128 object in a debugger watch window. If you want to load them using the reversed order, you can use the _mm_setr_ps instruction.

3.1.1 Shuffling Components

Shuffling of components of __mm128 is supported by the instruction _mm_shuffle_ps and the _MM_SHUFFLE macro,

```
#define _MM_SHUFFLE(i3,i2,i1,i0)\
    (i0) | ((i1) << 2) | ((i2) << 4) | ((i3) << 6)
__m128 a;  // (a[0],a[1],a[2],a[3]) = _mm_set_ps(a[3],a[2],a[1],a[0])
__m128 b;  // (b[0],b[1],b[2],b[3]) = _mm_set_ps(b[3],b[2],b[1],b[0])
__m128 result = _mm_shuffle_ps(v0,v1,_MM_SHUFFLE(i3,i2,i1,i0));
// = (a[i0],a[i1],b[i2],b[i3]) = _mm_set_ps(b[i3],b[i2],a[i1],a[i0])
```

The _MM_SHUFFLE is defined in xmmintrin.h for convenience. Each input to the macro is a number from zero to three, so you need only two bits per number. The macro hides the shifting and OR-ing that builds a single 8-bit number that represents your selection.

Shuffling can be used to compute a dot product of 4-tuples, as shown in Listing 3.1.

```
__m128 Dot(__m128 const v0, __m128 const v1)
{
    // v0 = (x0, y0, z0, w0)
    // v1 = (x1, y1, z1, w1)
    // dot(v0, v1) = x0*x1 + y0*y1 + z0*z1 + w0*w1

    // (x0*x1, y0*y1, z0*z1, w0*w1)
    __m128 t0 = _mm_mul_ps(v0, v1);

    // (y0*y1, x0*x1, w0*w1, z0*z1)
    __m128 t1 = _mm_shuffle_ps(t0, t0, _MM_SHUFFLE(2, 3, 0, 1));

    // (x0*x1 + y0*y1, x0*x1 + y0*y1, z0*z1 + w0*w1, z0*z1 + w0*w1)
    __m128 t2 = _mm_add_ps(t0, t1);

    // (z0*z1 + w0*w1, z0*z1 + w0*w1, x0*x1 + y0*y1, x0*x1 + y0*y1)
    __m128 t3 = _mm_shuffle_ps(t2, t2, _MM_SHUFFLE(0, 0, 2, 2));

    // (dot, dot, dot, dot)
    __m128 dotSplat = _mm_add_ps(t2, t3);
    return dotSplat;
}
```

LISTING 3.1: Computing a dot product of 4-tuples using SSE2.

The parallel multiplication is the obvious first step to compute. The technical problem is to sum the components after the multiplication. To do so, you must shuffle the components and perform additions. The use of the word *splat* indicates that each channel of a 4-tuple is set to the same number. The dot product, which is a scalar, is splatted across all four components of the result.

Notice that the final result is itself stored in a 128-bit register. If you need to consume the scalar value of the dot product, you must extract it from the register,

```
__m128 dotSplat = Dot(v0, v1);
float dot = dotSplat.m128_f32[0];
```

The dot-product calculations are all performed in 128-bit registers. As soon as you extract a component, you *break the SIMD pipeline*, so to speak. This is a performance loss if you were to continue processing the data in the 128-bit registers for your final results. I discuss this concept later in the section.

3.1.2 Single-Component versus All-Component Access

In the dot-product code of Listing 3.1, the instructions worked in parallel on all four components. For example, _mm_add_ps adds two 4-tuples and returns a 4-tuple. The suffix _ps indicates that the operation applies to all components. It is possible to execute on the first component without extracting that single component to a CPU register. The instructions supporting this have suffix _ss. For example,

```
__m128 v0;  // (x0, y0, z0, w0)
__m128 v1;  // (x1, y1, z1, w1)
__m128 sumFirstKeepOthers = _mm_add_ss(v0, v1);  // (x0 + x1, y0, z0, w0)
```

The single-component instructions used with shuffling can lead to computations that have a heterogeneous flavor about them; that is, you can compute in the first channel, shuffle it to the fourth channel, compute in the first channel, shuffle it to the third channel, and so on until you have four channels filled with your desired computations. For example, you might build a 4-tuple $(f_0(x), f_1(x), f_2(x), f_3(x))$ in this manner for four different functions $f_i(x)$.

3.1.3 Load and Store Instructions

We already saw the initialization functions _mm_set_ps and _mm_setr_ps that set the four channels of a __m128 object. And we saw _mm_set_ps1 that sets the channels to the same scalar. You might need to *load* the channels of a __m128 from values in an array. You might also want to *store* the channels to an array.

```
// Load from CPU to __m128.  DO NOT USE THIS CODE.
float numbers[4] = { 0.0f, 1.0f, 2.0f, 3.0f };
__m128 v = _mm_load_ps(numbers);  // v = (0.0f,1.0f,2.0f,3.0f)
```

```
// Save from __m128 to CPU.  DO NOT USE THIS CODE.
v = _mm_shuffle_ps(v,v,_MM_SHUFFLE(0,1,2,3));   // Reverse component order.
float otherNumbers[4];
_mm_store_ps(otherNumbers, v);   // otherNumbers = {3.0f,2.0f,1.0f,0.0f}
```

I added comments about not using these code blocks for loading and storing. The problem is that both the load and store instructions require their arguments to be 16-byte aligned. With the compiler default settings for alignment, numbers or otherNumbers are guaranteed to be 4-byte aligned but not 16-byte aligned. If you execute the code in the debugger and, say, numbers is not 16-byte aligned, you will crash with an access violation. On my machine the messages in the output window were

```
First-chance exception at 0x009DFA4C in LoadStoreTest.exe: 0xC0000005: Access violation reading
location 0xFFFFFFFF.
Unhandled exception at 0x009DFA4C in LoadStoreTest.exe: 0xC0000005: Access violation reading
location 0xFFFFFFFF.
```

With no other information, a crash due to misalignment is difficult to diagnose.

To avoid the alignment problem it is not enough to typecast, say,

```
// Typecasting does not affect the byte alignment of "numbers."
float numbers[4] = { 0.0f, 1.0f, 2.0f, 3.0f };
__m128 value = *(__m128*)numbers;
```

Instead, you must use instructions that are designed to handle unaligned inputs, namely, _mm_loadu_ps and _mm_storeu_ps. The corrected examples for load and store are

```
// Load from CPU to __m128.  USE THIS CODE.
float numbers[4] = { 0.0f, 1.0f, 2.0f, 3.0f };
__m128 v = _mm_loadu_ps(numbers);   // v = (0.0f,1.0f,2.0f,3.0f)
```

```
// Save from __m128 to CPU.  USE THIS CODE.
v = _mm_shuffle_ps(v,v,_MM_SHUFFLE(0,1,2,3));   // reverse component order
float otherNumbers[4];
_mm_storeu_ps(otherNumbers, v);   // otherNumbers = {3.0f,2.0f,1.0f,0.0f}
```

The unaligned loads and stores can be a performance issue if they occur often. If you use the alignment macros provided by the runtime library to align your own data, you can avoid using the unaligned load and store instructions altogether. The compiler will generate code to load and store using the aligned instructions, so you will not pay the performance hit for the unaligned accesses.

Choosing aligned data has some additional details you must pay attention to. For example, consider the code

```
struct MyTuple4
{
    MyTuple4 () {}
    MyTuple4 (float x, float y, float z, float w)
    {
        number[0] = x;
        number[1] = y;
        number[2] = z;
        number[3] = w;
    }
```

```
    MyTuple4 operator+(MyTuple const& v) const
    {
        MyTuple4 sum;
        for (int i = 0; i < 4; ++i)
        {
            sum.number[0] = number[0] + v.number[0];
        }
        return sum;
    }

    float number[4];
};

MyTuple4 v0(1.0f, 2.0f, 3.0f, 4.0f);
MyTuple4 v1(5.0f, 6.0f, 7.0f, 8.0f);
MyTuple4 sum = v0 + v1;
```

To gain some performance by using SSE2, you might instead implement your addition operator as

```
MyTuple4 MyTuple4::operator+(MyTuple4 const& v)
{
    MyTuple4 sum;
    __m128 sseV0 = _mm_loadu_ps(&v0[0]);
    __m128 sseV1 = _mm_loadu_ps(&v1[0]);
    __m128 sseSum = _mm_add_ps(sseV0, sseV1);
    _mm_storeu_ps(&sum[0], sseSum);
    return sum;
};
```

As mentioned, the unaligned loads and stores can be a performance hit. An alternative to avoid the unaligned instructions is to align the struct itself,

```
struct __declspec(align(16)) MyTuple4
{
    // Same body as before.
};

MyTuple4 MyTuple4::operator+(MyCPUTuple4 const& v)
{
    MyTuple4 sum;
    __m128 sseV0 = _mm_load_ps(&v0[0]);
    __m128 sseV1 = _mm_load_ps(&v1[0]);
    __m128 sseSum = _mm_add_ps(sseV0, sseV1);
    _mm_store_ps(&sum[0], sseSum);
    return sum;
};
```

Yet another alternative is to declare the class as

```
struct MyTuple4
{
    MyTuple4 () {}
    MyTuple4 (float x, float y, float z, float w)
    {
        number = _mm_setr_ps(x, y, z, w);
    }

    MyTuple4 operator+(MyTuple4 const& v) const
    {
        MyTuple4 sum;
        sum.number = _mm_add_ps(number, v.number);
        return sum;
```

```
    }

    __m128 number;
};
```

The general rule for alignment of a struct is that it is equal to the largest alignment of its components. In this case, __m128 is 16-byte aligned which guarantees that MyTuple4 is 16-byte aligned.

The alignment of the struct is based on stack location. In the MyTuple4 version with __m128 number, a MyTuple4 object declared on the stack is 16-byte aligned; that is, its address is a multiple of 16 bytes. However, if you were to dynamically allocate the object using new or malloc, the address is not guaranteed to be 16-byte aligned. Fortunately with Microsoft Visual Studio 2013, warnings are generated when this is possible. Compiling for Win32, a 32-bit configuration,

```
// With the 16−byte aligned versions of MyTuple4, this line of code...
MyTuple4* v = new MyTuple4(1.0f, 2.0f, 3.0f, 4.0f);
// .. generates the warning.
// Warning C4316: 'MyTuple4' : object allocated on the heap may not
// be aligned 16.
```

The warning does not appear for x64, the 64-bit configuration. Memory allocations on x64 are guaranteed to be 8-byte aligned on 32-bit Windows and 16-byte aligned on 64-bit Windows. If you plan to support only 64-bit Windows, you need not worry about the heap alignment for data to be loaded directly to 128-bit registers. However, stack alignment on either 32-bit or 64-bit Windows by default is 8-byte, so you still need the special declaration for the struct.

Mixing C++ member function calls and SSE2 instructions can also be a performance issue. The problem is that the compiler will generate instructions for CPU registers that handle the implicit this pointer that is present in nonstatic member functions. When you look at the assembly instructions, you will see interleaved instructions for the CPU and for SSE2. This interleaving is part of breaking the SIMD pipeline. Although an object-oriented purist might like everything to be hidden behind a class interface, when it comes to performance sometimes it is better not to hide the complexity. This means making it clear that you are executing a contiguous sequence of SSE2 instructions, at most using an inline C-style function to wrap the sequence.

3.1.4   Logical Instructions

SSE2 instructions for logical operations of two bit patterns include __mm_and_ps for AND, __mm_or_ps for OR, and __mm_xor_ps for XOR. The NOT operation is achieved using XOR,

```
__m128 FFFF = _mm_set_ps1(0xFFFFFFFF); // A mask of all 1−bits.
__m128 value; // A 4−tuple of unsigned int.
__m128 notValue = _mm_xor_ps(FFFF, value); // Flip the bits in value.
```

TABLE 3.1: SIMD comparison operators

comparisions	negated comparisons
eq for equal	neq for not-equal
lt for less-than	nlt for not-less-than
le for less-than-or-equal	nle for not-less-than-or-equal
gt for greater-than	ngt for not-greater-than
ge for greater-than-or-equal	nge for not-greater-than-or-equal

SSE2 also has the instruction _mm_andnot_ps(x,y) that flips the bits of x then ANDs the result with y,

```
__m128 v0, v1;  // Two 4-tuples of unsigned int.
__m128 result = _mm_andnot_ps(v0, v1);  // ~v0 & v1
__m128 sameResult = _mm_and_ps(_mm_xor_ps(FFFF, v0), v1);
```

3.1.5 Comparison Instructions

A full suite of comparisons are available and shown in Table 3.1. The single-channel instructions are of the form _mm_cmp<operator>_ss and the all-channel types are of the form _mm_cmp<operator>_ps. These are not your typical comparisons! SSE2 neither has if-then and if-then-else branching constructs nor loop constructs. Instead, each comparison instruction has two inputs, each a 4-tuple of float. The return value is a 4-tuple of unsigned int. If two corresponding channels satisfy the comparison query, the returned channel for that pair is 0xFFFFFFFF; otherwise, the returned channel is 0x00000000. For example,

```
__m128 v0 = _mm_setr_ps(1.0f, 3.0f, 5.0f, 6.0f);
__m128 v1 = _mm_setr_ps(2.0f, 1.0f, 5.0f, 7.0f);
__m128 c0 = _mm_cmplt_ps(v0, v1);
// c0 = (0xFFFFFFFF, 0x00000000, 0x00000000, 0xFFFFFFFF)
__m128 c1 = _mm_cmpnlt_ps(v0, v1);
// c1 = (0x00000000, 0xFFFFFFFF, 0xFFFFFFFF, 0x00000000)
__m128 c2 = _mm_cmpeq_ps(v0, v1);
// c2 = (0x00000000, 0x00000000, 0xFFFFFFFF, 0x00000000)
```

Branching is an expensive thing to do on a processor, so SSE2 does not support it. In basic numerical computations using SIMD, it may be faster to compute the results of *both* branches and then select the result from those. The return value of the comparison instructions can be used for the selection. Consider computing the minimum components of two 4-tuples,

```
__m128 v0 = _mm_setr_ps(1.0f, 3.0f, 5.0f, 6.0f);
__m128 v1 = _mm_setr_ps(2.0f, 1.0f, 5.0f, 7.0f);
__m128 c = _mm_cmplt_ps(v0, v1);
// c = (0xFFFFFFFF, 0x00000000, 0x00000000, 0xFFFFFFFF)
__m128 minV0V1 = _mm_or_ps(_mm_and_ps(c, v0), _mm_andnot_ps(c, v1));
// minV0V1 = (1.0f, 1.0f, 5.0f, 6.0f)
```

SSE2 actually has instructions for minimum (_mm_min_ps) and maximum (_mm_max_ps), but the example is a good illustration of how you select rather

TABLE 3.2: SIMD arithmetic operators

operation	operation
add for addition	sqrt for the square root function
sub for subtraction	rcp for the reciprocal of a number
mul for multiplication	rsqrt for the reciprocal of a square root
div for division	

than branch. More examples of selection are provided later in the section on flattening branches.

3.1.6   Arithmetic Instructions

The basic arithmetic instructions are shown in Table 3.2. The single-channel instructions are of the form _mm_<operator>_ss and the all-channel types are of the form _mm_<operator>_ps.

3.1.7   Matrix Multiplication and Transpose

A motivator for SSE was vector and matrix algebra in computer graphics. The 4-tuples can represent vectors (last component zero) or points (last component one), both examples of homogeneous points in affine algebra. Homogeneous matrices are of size 4×4 and can represent linear, affine, and projective transformations. SSE2 can support matrices as a 4-tuple of _m128 objects. However, you will have to choose whether the objects are the rows of the matrix or the columns of the matrix. And you will have to implement either matrix-vector products, vector-matrix products, or both. I discuss these conventions in Section 6.2. GTEngine allows you to select the conventions using conditional compilation; the default is row-major order with matrix-vector as the natural order for a product.

Matrix-vector products are interesting in SSE2. The abstract formulation of the product is

$$MV = \begin{bmatrix} m_{00} & m_{01} & m_{02} & m_{03} \\ m_{10} & m_{11} & m_{12} & m_{13} \\ m_{20} & m_{21} & m_{22} & m_{23} \\ m_{30} & m_{31} & m_{32} & m_{33} \end{bmatrix} \begin{bmatrix} v_0 \\ v_1 \\ v_2 \\ v_3 \end{bmatrix} \tag{3.1}$$

On a CPU, your instinct is to compute the matrix-vector product as four dot products, each a dot of a matrix row and the vector:

$$MV = \begin{bmatrix} \mathbf{R}_0 \cdot \mathbf{V} \\ \mathbf{R}_1 \cdot \mathbf{V} \\ \mathbf{R}_2 \cdot \mathbf{V} \\ \mathbf{R}_3 \cdot \mathbf{V} \end{bmatrix} \tag{3.2}$$

where as a 4-tuple, $\mathbf{R}_i = (m_{i0}, m_{i1}, m_{i2}, m_{i3})$. This appears to have good cache coherence, although on a Windows machine the cache line size is sixty-four bytes, which is enough to store a 4×4 matrix of float. An alternative view of matrix-vector multiplication is

$$M\mathbf{V} = v_0\mathbf{C}_0 + v_1\mathbf{C}_1 + v_2\mathbf{C}_2 + v_3\mathbf{C}_3 \tag{3.3}$$

which is a linear combination of the columns of the matrix. As a 4-tuple, $\mathbf{C}_j = (m_{0j}, m_{1j}, m_{2j}, m_{3j})$.

Listing 3.2 shows how to compute Equation (3.2) using the SSE2 dot product of Listing 3.1.

```
__m128 M[4];   // matrix M stored as rows
__m128 V;   // the vector V
__m128 Product;   // M*V
__m128 t0, t1, t2, t3;   // temporary registers

// dot product of row 0 and vector
t0 = _mm_mul_ps(M[0], V);
t1 = _mm_shuffle_ps(t0, t0, _MM_SHUFFLE(2, 3, 0, 1));
t2 = _mm_add_ps(t0, t1);
t3 = _mm_shuffle_ps(t2, t2, _MM_SHUFFLE(0, 0, 2, 2));
__m128 p0splat = _mm_add_ps(t2, t3);

// dot product of row 1 and vector
t0 = _mm_mul_ps(M[1], V);
t1 = _mm_shuffle_ps(t0, t0, _MM_SHUFFLE(2, 3, 0, 1));
t2 = _mm_add_ps(t0, t1);
t3 = _mm_shuffle_ps(t2, t2, _MM_SHUFFLE(0, 0, 2, 2));
__m128 p1splat = _mm_add_ps(t2, t3);

// dot product of row 2 and vector
t0 = _mm_mul_ps(M[2], V);
t1 = _mm_shuffle_ps(t0, t0, _MM_SHUFFLE(2, 3, 0, 1));
t2 = _mm_add_ps(t0, t1);
t3 = _mm_shuffle_ps(t2, t2, _MM_SHUFFLE(0, 0, 2, 2));
__m128 p2splat = _mm_add_ps(t2, t3);

// dot product of row 3 and vector
t0 = _mm_mul_ps(M[3], V);
t1 = _mm_shuffle_ps(t0, t0, _MM_SHUFFLE(2, 3, 0, 1));
t2 = _mm_add_ps(t0, t1);
t3 = _mm_shuffle_ps(t2, t2, _MM_SHUFFLE(0, 0, 2, 2));
__m128 p3splat = _mm_add_ps(t2, t3);

// Shuffle to obtain P = (p0, p1, p2, p3).
t0 = _mm_shuffle_ps(p0splat, p1splat, _MM_SHUFFLE(0, 1, 0, 0));
t1 = _mm_shuffle_ps(p2splat, p3splat, _MM_SHUFFLE(0, 1, 0, 0));
Product = _mm_shuffle_ps(t0, t1, _MM_SHUFFLE(2, 0, 2, 0));
```

LISTING 3.2: Computing the matrix-vector product as four row-vector dot products in SSE2.

On the other hand, Equation (3.3) is computed as shown in Listing 3.3.

```
__m128 M[4];   // matrix M stored as columns
__m128 V;   // the vector V
__m128 Product;   // M*V
__m128 t0, t1, t2, t3;   // temporary registers

// Splat the coefficients V[i] for the matrix columns, setting up for
// parallel multiply.
__m128 v0splat = _mm_shuffle_ps(V, V, _MM_SHUFFLE(0, 0, 0, 0));
```

```
__m128 v1splat = _mm_shuffle_ps(V, V, _MM_SHUFFLE(1, 1, 1, 1));
__m128 v2splat = _mm_shuffle_ps(V, V, _MM_SHUFFLE(2, 2, 2, 2));
__m128 v3splat = _mm_shuffle_ps(V, V, _MM_SHUFFLE(3, 3, 3, 3));

t0 = _mm_mul_ps(M[0], t0);   // (m00*v0,  m10*v0,  m20*v0,  m30*v0)
t1 = _mm_mul_ps(M[1], t1);   // (m01*v1,  m11*v1,  m21*v1,  m31*v1)
t2 = _mm_mul_ps(M[2], t2);   // (m02*v2,  m12*v2,  m22*v2,  m32*v2)
t3 = _mm_mul_ps(M[3], t3);   // (m03*v3,  m13*v3,  m23*v3,  m33*v3)
t0 = _mm_add_ps(t0, t1);
// t0 = (m00*v0+m01*v1,  m10*v0+m11*v1,  m20*v0+m21*v1,  m30*v0+m31*v1)
t2 = _mm_add_ps(t2, t3);
// t2 = (m02*v2+m03*v3,  m12*v2+m13*v3,  m22*v2+m23*v3,  m32*v2+m33*v3)

Product = _mm_add_ps(t0, t2);
```

LISTING 3.3: Computing the matrix-vector product as a linear combination of columns in SSE2.

The lesson appears to be that to support matrix-vector products $M\mathbf{V}$, the matrix should be stored in column-major order rather than row-major order. The conclusion is based on the dot product requiring several instructions to implement, which is due to the use of SSE2. In fact, more SIMD features have been added over the years. SSE4.1 added a dot-product intrinsic, _mm_dp_ps(a,b,mask), where a and b are 4-tuples of floats. The mask is an integer whose low-order 8 bits have meaning. Bits four through seven indicate which components of the inputs should be multiplied: a 1-bit means multiply and a 0-bit means use a zero in the sum. Bits zero through three indicate which components of the output should be written. Listing 3.2 can then be modified to the code of Listing 3.4.

```
__m128 M[4];  // matrix M stored as rows
__m128 V;    // the vector V
__m128 p0 = _mm_dp_ps(M[0], V, 0x0F1);   // (p0, 0, 0, 0)
__m128 p1 = _mm_dp_ps(M[1], V, 0x0F2);   // (0, p1, 0, 0)
__m128 p2 = _mm_dp_ps(M[2], V, 0x0F4);   // (0, 0, p2, 0)
__m128 p3 = _mm_dp_ps(M[3], V, 0x0F8);   // (0, 0, 0, p3)
__m128 Product = _mm_or_ps(_mm_or_ps(p0, p1), _mm_or_ps(p2, p3));
```

LISTING 3.4: Computing the matrix-vector product as four row-vector dot products in SSE4.1.

With direct hardware support for dot product, now the row-major order storage for M is acceptable when computing $M\mathbf{V}$. On the GPU, hardware support is provided for dot products, so you will find that a GPU-based matrix-vector is compiled to assembly code similar to that of Listing 3.4.

Transposing a matrix is another common operation in linear algebra. For 4×4 matrices, the transpose is computed by shuffling components. The file xmmintrin.h defines a macro, _MM_TRANSPOSE4_PS, that takes as input the four rows (or columns) of a matrix, computes the transpose by shuffling, and stores the result in the original four rows. If you do not want an in-place transpose, you can easily implement your own function, as shown in Listing 3.5. This code works whether you have stored the matrix as rows or as columns. The comments indicate what the registers store after the operations following them, *rows* for row-major storage or *cols* for column-major storage.

```
void Transpose(__m128 const* mat, _m128* trn)
{
    // rows:(m00, m01, m10, m11), cols:(m00, m10, m01, m11)
    __m128 s0 = _mm_shuffle_ps(mat[0], mat[1], _MM_SHUFFLE(1, 0, 1, 0));
    // rows:(m20, m21, m30, m31), cols:(m02, m12, m03, m13)
    __m128 s1 = _mm_shuffle_ps(mat[2], mat[3], _MM_SHUFFLE(1, 0, 1, 0));
    // rows:(m02, m03, m12, m13), cols:(m20, m30, m21, m31)
    __m128 s2 = _mm_shuffle_ps(mat[0], mat[1], _MM_SHUFFLE(3, 2, 3, 2));
    // rows:(m22, m23, m32, m33), cols:(m22, m32, m23, m33)
    __m128 s3 = _mm_shuffle_ps(mat[2], mat[3], _MM_SHUFFLE(3, 2, 3, 2));
    // rows:(m00, m10, m20, m30), cols:(m00, m01, m02, m03)
    trn[0] = _mm_shuffle_ps(s0, s1, _MM_SHUFFLE(2, 0, 2, 0));
    // rows:(m01, m11, m21, m31), cols:(m10, m11, m12, m13)
    trn[1] = _mm_shuffle_ps(s0, s1, _MM_SHUFFLE(3, 1, 3, 1));
    // rows:(m02, m12, m22, m32), cols:(m20, m21, m22, m23)
    trn[2] = _mm_shuffle_ps(s2, s3, _MM_SHUFFLE(2, 0, 2, 0));
    // rows:(m03, m13, m23, m33), cols:(m30, m31, m32, m33)
    trn[3] = _mm_shuffle_ps(s2, s3, _MM_SHUFFLE(3, 1, 3, 1));
}
```

LISTING 3.5: Transpose of a 4×4 matrix using shuffling.

3.1.8 IEEE Floating-Point Support

Intel SSE provides the ability to control floating-point behavior by manipulating the *control register* for the SIMD floating-point hardware. You can set the register using _mm_setcsr or get the register using _mm_getcsr. File xmmintrin.h has several flags that can be used to control the exceptions that are raised, to control the rounding mode for arithmetic operations, and to decide whether or not to flush subnormals to the same-sign zero.

3.1.9 Keep the Pipeline Running

You should avoid breaking the pipeline during your sequence of instructions. Sometimes this leads to code that, at first glance, seems unnecessary or cryptic. For example, consider normalizing a 4-tuple vector. You might try to write SIMD code as shown in Listing 3.6.

```
__m128 NormalizeWithBreak(__m128 const v)
{
    // (sqrLength, sqrLength, sqrLength, sqrLength)
    __m128 sqrLength = Dot(v, v);

    // (length, length, length, length)
    __m128 length = _mm_sqrt_ps(sqrLength);

    if (length.m128_f32[0] > 0.0f)
    {
        // Divide by the length to normalize.
        __m128 normalized = _mm_div_ps(v, length);
        return normalized;
    }
    else
    {
        // If length is zero, v = (0,0,0,0).
        return v;
    }
}
```

LISTING 3.6: Normalizing a vector using SSE2 with a break in the pipeline.

The problem is that the SIMD register which stores length must have a component extracted and copied to a CPU register, and then the comparison is computed on the CPU. Transfers between CPU and SIMD registers will slow you down.

The code shown in Listing 3.7 is a better choice because it avoids the break in the pipeline.

```
__m128 Normalize(__m128 const v)
{
    // (sqrLength, sqrLength, sqrLength, sqrLength)
    __m128 sqrLength = Dot(v, v);

    // (length, length, length, length)
    __m128 length = _mm_sqrt_ps(sqrLength);

    // Divide by length to normalize; potentially produces a divide by zero.
    __m128 normalized = _mm_div_ps(v, length);

    // Set to zero when the original length is zero.
    __m128 zero = _mm_setzero_ps();  // = (0.0f, 0.0f, 0.0f, 0.0f)
    __m128 mask = _mm_cmpneq_ps(zero, length);
    normalized = _mm_and_ps(mask, normalized);
    return normalized;
}
```

LISTING 3.7: Normalizing a vector using SSE2 without a break in the pipeline.

Where did the if-else branch go in Listing 3.6? You will notice in Listing 3.7 the instruction _mm_cmpneq_ps. If length has positive components, the mask has components 0xFFFFFFFF. When you AND the mask with normalized, you obtain normalized, which is the desired output. If length has zero components, the comparisons are false and mask has zero components. When the mask is AND-ed with normalized, you obtain zero, which is the desired output. The code implements the selection mechanism mentioned previously. In the next section we will look at several possibilities for dealing with nested branching.

3.1.10   Flattening of Branches

Let us look at comparisons and how to write branchless code. Using the selection mechanism mentioned previously, Listing 3.8 defines a function for simplicity of presentation,

```
__m128 Select(__m128 cmp, __m128 v0, __m128 v1)
{
    return _mm_or_ps(_mm_and_ps(cmp, v0), _mm_andnot_ps(cmp, v1));
}
```

LISTING 3.8: The definition of the Select function for flattening branches.

where cmp is intended to be a result from a comparison, and v0 and v1 are the inputs whose components are to be selected. In most cases, cmp has components that are either 0xFFFFFFFF or 0x00000000, but the function is more general in that cmp can have any bit patterns of interest.

The term *flatten* means to replace branching code (if-then or if-then-else) with branchless code that evaluates both of the original branches and selects the correct result. The simplest form of flattening is shown in Listing 3.9. CPU code illustrates the original branching using single floating-point numbers, and the SIMD version is shown afterward using 4-tuples.

```
float v0, v1, v2, v3, r;
if (v0 > v1)
{
    r = v2;
}
else
{
    r = v3;
}

__m128 sv0, sv1, sv2, sv3, sr;
sr = Select(_mm_gt_ps(sv0, sv1), sv2, sv3);
```
LISTING 3.9: Flattening a single branch.

Listing 3.10 shows nested branching where only the outer-then clause contains a branch.

```
float v0, v1, v2, v3, v4, v5, v6, r;
if (v0 > v1)
{
    if (v2 > v3)
    {
        r = v4;
    }
    else
    {
        r = v5;
    }
}
else
{
    r = v6;
}

__m128 sv0, sv1, sv2, sv3, sv4, sv5, sv6, sr;
__m128 thenResult = Select(_mm_gt_ps(sv2, sv3), sv4, sv5);
sr = Select(_mm_gt_ps(sv0, sv1), thenResult, v6);
```
LISTING 3.10: Flattening a two-level branch where the outer-then clause has a nested branch.

Listing 3.11 shows nested branching where only the outer-else clause contains a branch.

```
float v0, v1, v2, v3, v4, v5, v6, r;
if (v0 > v1)
{
    r = v4;
}
else
{
    if (v2 > v3)
    {
        r = v5;
    }
```

```
        else
        {
            r = v6;
        }
}

__m128 sv0, sv1, sv2, sv3, sv4, sv5, sv6, sr;
__m128 elseResult = Select(_mm_gt_ps(sv2, sv3), sv5, sv6);
sr = Select(_mm_gt_ps(sv0, sv1), sv4, elseResult);
```

LISTING 3.11: Flattening a two-level branch where the outer-else clause has a nested branch.

Listing 3.12 shows nested branching where both outer clauses contain branches.

```
float v0, v1, v2, v3, v4, v5, v6, v7, v8, v9, r;
if (v0 > v1)
{
    if (v2 > v3)
    {
        r = v6;
    }
    else
    {
        r = v7;
    }
}
else
{
    if (v4 > v5)
    {
        r = v8;
    }
    else
    {
        r = v9;
    }
}

__m128 sv0, sv1, sv2, sv3, sv4, sv5, sv6, sv7, sv8, sv9, sr;
__m128 thenResult = Select(_mm_gt_ps(sv2, sv3), sv6, sv7);
__m128 elseResult = Select(_mm_gt_ps(sv4, sv5), sv8, sv9);
sr = Select(_mm_gt_ps(v0, v1), thenResult, elseResult);
```

LISTING 3.12: Flattening a two-level branch where the outer clauses have nested branches.

3.2 SIMD Wrappers

The SSE code can become quite lengthy for complicated operations. The dot-product code of Listing 3.1 was short, consisting of five instructions plus comments. The GTEngine SIMD code for computing the inverse of a 4×4 matrix is on the order of 330 lines of comments and code! Naturally, you will want to encapsulate many of your common operations with inline function wrappers.

Microsoft has SIMD wrappers now referred to as *DirectX Math*. You can find the top-level header files in the Windows Kits folder,

C:/Program Files (x86)/Windows Kits/8.1/Include/um/DirectXMath.h
C:/Program Files (x86)/Windows Kits/8.1/Include/um/DirectXMathConvert.inl
C:/Program Files (x86)/Windows Kits/8.1/Include/um/DirectXMathMatrix.inl
C:/Program Files (x86)/Windows Kits/8.1/Include/um/DirectXMathMisc.inl
C:/Program Files (x86)/Windows Kits/8.1/Include/um/DirectXMathVector.inl
C:/Program Files (x86)/Windows Kits/8.1/Include/um/DirectXPackedVector.h
C:/Program Files (x86)/Windows Kits/8.1/Include/um/DirectXPackedVector.inl
C:/Program Files (x86)/Windows Kits/8.1/Include/um/DirectXCollision.h
C:/Program Files (x86)/Windows Kits/8.1/Include/um/DirectXCollision.inl

You will find support for Intel SSE2, Microsoft Xbox 360 (VMX128), and Microsoft Xbox One (ARM-Neon). An online blog is maintained about topics related to DirectX and DirectX Math [56].

The GTEngine source code contains an implementation of various mathematical concepts using SSE2. I will be updating this to SSE4 over time. The current code is quite extensive and has conditional compilation to support row-major order (the _m128 array stores rows) or column-major order (the _m128 array stores columns). You can find the code at

GeometricTools/GTEngine/Source/Mathematics/SIMD/GteIntelSSE.{h,inl,cpp}

Generally, you want the SIMD instructions to be inlined, so the implementation is contained in the *.inl file. The reason for the existence of the *.cpp is to define SIMD constants that are useful throughout the code.

Many of the algorithms are simple, but some have significant mathematics behind them. The algorithms are discussed in Chapter 6.

3.3 Function Approximations

Several approximations to standard mathematics library functions are described in this section. These involve trading accuracy to obtain speed. These may be used in CPU, GPU, or SIMD code. Some of the approximations take advantage of binary representations of 32-bit IEEE floating-point numbers. Other approximations are mathematical in nature, usually applying minimax algorithms to obtain polynomial or rational function appproximations, whether 32-bit or 64-bit floating-point arithmetic is used.

The approximations are presented for floating-point on the CPU. It is straightforward to implement SSE2 versions.

3.3.1 Minimax Approximations

Many approximation problems tend to be formulated as *least-squares problems*. If $p(x) = \sum_{i=0}^{d} p_i x^i$, which is a polynomial of degree d with coefficients

p_0 through p_d, the least-squares approximation is obtained by minimizing

$$E(p_0, \ldots, p_d) = \int_a^b |f(x) - p(x)|^2 \, dx \tag{3.4}$$

The coefficients of the polynomial are determined by setting the first-order partial derivatives of E to zero,

$$0 = \frac{\partial E}{\partial p_j} = -2 \int_a^b (f(x) - p(x)))x^j \, dx \tag{3.5}$$

which simplifies to

$$\int_a^b x^j p(x) \, dx = \int_a^b x^j f(x) \, dx \tag{3.6}$$

and then to

$$\sum_{i=0}^d \left(\frac{b^{i+j+1} - a^{i+j+1}}{i+j+1} \right) p_i = \int_a^b x^j f(x) \, dx = c_j \tag{3.7}$$

where the last equality defines the values c_j. This is a linear system of $d+1$ equations in $d+1$ unknowns that may be solved numerically for the p_i. It is necessary to integrate $x^j f(x)$, either in closed form or through numerical quadrature methods, to obtain c_j.

The approximation error is $\sqrt{E(p_0, \ldots, p_d)/(b-a)}$, a root-mean-squared error that measures the average error over the domain $[a, b]$ of the function. When computing numerically, such an error is typically of little use. What we usually want to know is the maximum error between $p(x)$ and $f(x)$ for all inputs x. This leads us to a formulation of the approximation in the L^∞ sense (maximum absolute error for any input) rather than in the L^2 sense (root-mean-square error over an interval).

Unfortunately, the L^∞ formulation is rarely taught in undergraduate mathematics programs, because the proofs and constructions require mathematical machinery that is deeper than what the curriculum supports. In the following sections, the polynomials that approximate the function are constructed to minimize the maximum error for a polynomial of a specified degree. The proofs of why the polynomials attain the minimum are not provided here. However, a practicing computer scientist may easily understand the algorithms and implement or modify them accordingly.

Given a function $f(x)$ on an interval $[a, b]$, our goal is to construct a polynomial $p(x)$ of degree d that approximates $f(x)$ and minimizes the maximum absolute error between $f(x)$ and $p(x)$ on $[a, b]$. Such a polynomial generates the smallest *minimax error*

$$\varepsilon_d = \min \left\{ \max_{x \in [a,b]} |f(x) - p(x)| : p \text{ is a polynomial of degree } d \right\} \tag{3.8}$$

The choice of degree depends on your application's constraints. Generally, the larger the degree, the more time is required to evaluate $p(x)$. On the other hand, as the degree increases, we expect the error to decrease. This is a classical trade-off in computer science: Greater accuracy comes at the cost of increased computational time.

When I first started investigating fast function approximations to standard mathematics functions, I looked at formulas in [1]. As advertised, this is a handbook and unfortunately contains no mathematical derivations. Some of the approximations were credited to a technical report from Los Alamos Laboratory in 1955 [3]; I managed to obtain a PDF of a scanned, typewritten document. The Abramowitz book and the Carlson report both reference work by Hastings, and I managed to obtain a used copy [4]. All of these works were not satisfying in that the mathematical details are sketchy. In the end, though, I managed to piece together the concepts and algorithms and wrote code for many of the standard mathematics functions. The underlying principle is the *Chebyshev equioscillation theorem*, which states that the polynomial $p(x)$ of degree d that best fits $f(x)$ in the sense of Equation (3.8) has the property that there exist at least $d + 2$ values of x for which $|f(x) - p(x)| = \varepsilon_d$. The differences equioscillate: if x_i and x_{i+1} are two consecutive values for which $|f(x) - p(x)| = \varepsilon_d$, then $[f(x_{i+1}) - p(x_{i+1})] = -[f(x_i) - p(x_i)]$. Also, p is the unique polynomial with degree$(p) \leq d$ for which this equioscillation occurs. The set $\{x_i\}$ is referred to as an *alternating set*.

To read a detailed description of the mathematics and some algorithms to construct the polynomials, see [25]. The Remez algorithm I discuss here is described in [50, Section 17.6]. Let ε represent the minimax error (or the negative of the minimax error) and let p_0 through p_d be the polynomial coefficients.

1. Start with an alternating set $S_0 = \{x_i\}_{i=0}^{d+1}$ of points on the interval $[a, b]$, where $x_0 = a$ and $x_{d+1} = b$.

2. Solve the equations $p(x_i) + (-1)^i \varepsilon = f(x_i)$, a linear system of $d + 2$ equations in $d + 2$ unknowns p_0 through p_d and ε.

3. Compute the set S_1 of x-values for which $|f(x) - p(x)|$ attains its local maxima. One always keeps a and b in the set, so we need compute only the interior local maximum points.

4. If the local maxima have equal values and the $(f(x) - p(x))$ values alternate in sign, then $p(x)$ is the best-fit polynomial; otherwise replace S_0 with S_1 and repeat steps 2, 3, and 4.

In step 1, you need to choose S_0. Sources suggest choosing roots of Chebyshev polynomials; for example, see [50, Chapter 17] on Functional Approximation. For the functions to which I applied the minimax algorithm, I instead chose $p(x)$ equal to $f(x)$ on a uniformly spaced set of interior points of $[a, b]$. This gives you an initial polynomial approximation for which $f(x) - p(x)$ has oscillatory behavior.

In step 3, you may solve for the roots of $g(x) = f'(x) - p'(x)$ using a numerical method of your choice. Some sources of information state that you may start with $x \in S_0$ and use a Newton-Raphson iterate to obtain $\bar{x} = x - G(x)/G'(x)$ that is (hopefully) close to a root of $G(x)$, and then insert $\bar{x}$ in S_1. The key word here is *hopefully*; the idea might work in some cases, but it is possible in other cases that $\bar{x}$ is farther from a local maximum point than is x. When I tried this algorithm to approximate $\sin(x)$ on $[0, \pi/2]$ with a degree-5 polynomial, the single-iterate approach failed. My goal is to compute polynomial coefficients that will be used in a hard-coded function. The computational time required to accurately find the roots of $G(x)$ is unimportant, so I used bisection for root finding. Each pair of consecutive roots of $g(x)$ are used as a bounding interval for roots of $g'(x)$. Some of the functions have double roots at the endpoints of the domain of approximation, so I choose bounding interval endpoints slightly different from the domain endpoints.

As you increase the degree of the polynomial, the linear system solver for computing the initial polynomial coefficients can have enough numerical roundoff error that the polynomial is numerically suspect. If you need higher-degree approximations, you will have to resort to high-precision arithmetic to solve the system.

3.3.2 Inverse Square Root Function Using Root Finding

A fast inverse square root has been a popular topic for many years. Its history and discussion is found on the Wikipedia page entitled "Fast inverse square root." You can also read about it via the online document [21]. The algorithm described there is effectively Newton's method for root finding and includes a magic number whose origin spurred a lot of the discussion. I present the algorithm here but later provide an alternative using minimax approximations.

The root-finding algorithm uses Newton's method to estimate a root of $f(y) = 1/y^2 - x$. The iterates are

$$y_{i+1} = y_i - f(y_i)/f'(y_i) = y_i(3 - xy_i^2)/2, \ i \geq 0 \qquad (3.9)$$

for an initial estimate y_0. The algorithm is shown in Listing 3.13.

```
float FastInverseSqrt (float x)
{
    union Binary32 { float number; uint32_t encoding; };
    float xhalf = 0.5f*x;
    Binary32 y;
    y.number = x;
    y.encoding = 0x5f3759df - (y.encoding >> 1);
    y.number = y.number*(1.5f - xhalf*y.number*y.number); // Newton step
    return y.number;
}
```
LISTING 3.13: A fast approximation to 1/sqrt(x) for 32-bit floating-point.

The accuracy is reasonable as long as x is not too small (i.e., not a subnormal). To increase accuracy, you can repeat the Newton step one or more

TABLE 3.3: Inverse square root accuracy and performance

iterates	max rel error	max abs error	speed up over $1/\text{sqrt}(x)$
1	1.75238e-03	1.56142e+16	4.30
2	4.76837e-06	4.06819e+13	2.29
3	2.38419e-07	2.19902e+12	1.52
4	2.38419e-07	1.64927e+12	1.11

time. Table 3.3 shows the maximum relative and absolute errors for normal floating-point inputs for one through four Newton steps. It also shows the speedups when using the approximation. The accuracy is reported only for normal numbers. The accuracy for subnormals is not good. Although the absolute error looks atrocious, those values are for extremely small floating-point inputs. For numbers on the order of one, the absolute error is about 1e-03. As the numbers increase in magnitude, the absolute error decreases. For numbers on the order of the maximum normal, the absolute error is approximately 1e-22.

Listing 3.14 has a double-precision version of the approximation. This can be used on the GPU, because as of D3D11.1, there is no double-precision square root instruction available for HLSL.

```
double FastInverseSqrt (double x)
{
    union Binary64 { double number; uint64_t encoding; };
    double xhalf = 0.5*x;
    Binary64 y;
    y.number = x;
    y.encoding = 0x5fe6ec85e7de30daULL - (y.encoding >> 1);
    y.number = y.number*(1.5 - xhalf*y.number*y.number);
    return y.number;
}
```

LISTING 3.14: A fast approximation to 1/sqrt(x) for 64-bit floating-point.

3.3.3 Square Root Function

One fast approximation uses the fast inverse square root function; that is, you can use FastSqrt(x) = x * FastInvSqrt(x). Apply as many Newton steps as needed for the desired accuracy.

A range reduction and a polynomial approximation together lead to a fast approximation. In binary scientific notation, let $x = 1.t * 2^p$ where t is the trailing significand and p is the unbiased exponent. Thinking of t as a fraction in $[0, 1)$, we can write $x = (1+t) * 2^p$. If p is even, then $y = \sqrt{x} = \sqrt{1+t} * 2^{p/2}$. If p is odd, then $y = \sqrt{x} = \sqrt{2}\sqrt{1+t} * 2^{(p-1)/2}$. You may extract t and p from the floating-point encoding, so the approximation we need is for $\sqrt{1+t}$ for $t \in [0, 1)$. The logic for float numbers is

```
float const sqrt2 = sqrt(2.0f);   // Precomputed constant.
// Get t in [0,1).
int p;
float m = frexp(x, &p);   // m in [1/2,1)
```

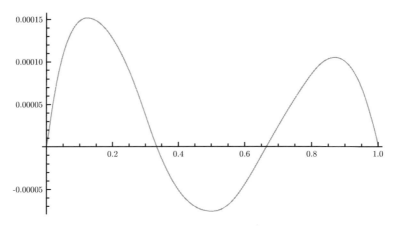

FIGURE 3.1: The plot of $g(x) = \sqrt{1+x} - p(x)$ for the initial polynomial of degree 3.

```
float  t = 2.0f*m − 1.0f;   // t in [0,1)
—p;
// Select sqrt(2) or 1; avoid branching for speed.
float  adjust = (1 & p)*sqrt2 + (1 & ~p)*1.0f;
int  halfP = (p − 1) / 2;
float  sqrtT = Polynomial(t);   // approximation for sqrt(1 + t), t in [0,1)
float  y = adjust*ldexp(sqrtT, halfP);   // approximation for sqrt(x)
```

The function to approximate is $f(x) = \sqrt{1+x}$ and the approximating polynomial is $p(x) = \sum_{i=0}^{d} p_i x^i$ of degree $d \geq 1$. I required that $p(0) = f(0) = 1$ and $p(1) = f(1) = \sqrt{2}$, so we need to compute coefficients p_i for $1 \leq i \leq d-1$. An initial guess for $p(x)$ is $p(i/d) = f(i/d)$ for $1 \leq i \leq d-1$, in which case $g(x) = f(x) - p(x)$ is oscillatory. For degree 3, the conditions are $p(0) = f(0)$, $p(1/3) = f(1/3)$, $p(2/3) = f(2/3)$, and $p(1) = f(1)$, which lead to the initial polynomial $p(x) = 1 + 0.497043x - 0.106823x^2 + 0.023993x^3$. The plot of $g(x)$ is shown in Figure 3.1. You can see that the roots of $g(x)$ are $\{0, 1/3, 2/3, 1\}$. Also, the function is oscillatory but the maximum and minimum values do not have the same magnitude; that is, the initial polynomial is not the minimax approximation.

The three local extrema are located using bisection applied to double-precision domain values. Listing 3.15 shows one step of the Remez iteration.

```
double root0[d + 1];   // The roots of g(x); d is the degree of p(x).
double root1[d];   // The roots of g'(x).
for (int i = 0, j = 0; i < d; ++i)
{
    // The bounding interval for a root of g'(x) is [x0,x1].
    double x0 = root0[i], x1 = root0[i + 1];

    // Bisect based on sign of g'(x), signs in {−1,0,1}.  Problem is
    // configured so that s0*s1 < 0.
    int s0 = Sign(g'(x0));
    int s1 = Sign(g'(x1));
    for (;;)
```

```
        {
            double xmid = 0.5*(x0 + x1);
            int smid = Sign(g'(xmid));
            if (x0 == xmid || x1 == xmid || smid == 0)
                { root1[j++] = xmid; break; }
            if (smid == s0) { x0 = xmid; } else { x1 = xmid; }
        }
    }
}

// Compute g(x) at the local extrema. In theory, the minimax polynomial
// causes these values to have same magnitude but oscillate in sign.
// You can use these to determine when to terminate Remez iterations.
double error[d];
for (int i = 0; i < d; ++i)
{
    error[i] = g(root1[i]);
}
// STOP when you have met your criteria for convergence.

// Solve p(root1[i]) + (-1)^{i}*e = f(root1[i]) for e and coefficients
// of p, a total of d+2 unknowns. We know p[0] = 1, so we need only
// solve a linear system of d+1 equations.
Matrix<d+1,d+1,double> A;  // (d+1)-by-(d+1) matrix
Vector<d+1,double> B;      // (d+1)-by-1 vector
double sign = 1.0;
for (int r = 0; r < d; ++r, sign = -sign)
{
    A(r, 0) = root1[r];
    for (int c = 1; c < d; ++c) { A(r, c) = root1[r] * A(r, c - 1); }
    A(r, d) = sign;
    B[r] = f(root1[r]) - 1.0;
}
for (int c = 0; c < d; ++c) { A(d, c) = 1.0; }
A(d, d) = 0.0;
B[d] = f(1.0) - 1.0;

Vector<d+1,double> solution = Inverse(A)*B;
for (int i = 0; i < d; ++i) { p[i + 1] = solution[i]; }
// After several iterations, e is the common magnitude of error[].
double e = solution[degree];

// Compute the roots of g(x) for the next Remez iteration.
for (int i = 0, j = 0; i < d - 1; ++i)
{
    // The bounding interval for a root of g(x) is [x0,x1], which is
    // reasonable for a good initial guess for p(x).
    double x0 = root1[i], x1 = root1[i + 1];

    // Bisect based on sign of g(x), signs in {-1,0,1}. Problem is
    // configured so that s0*s1 < 0.
    int s0 = Sign(g(x0));
    int s1 = Sign(g(x1));
    for (;;)
    {
        double xmid = 0.5*(x0 + x1);
        int smid = Sign(g(xmid));
        if (x0 == xmid || x1 == xmid || smid == 0)
            { root0[j++] = xmid; break; }
        if (smid == s0) { x0 = xmid; } else { x1 = xmid; }
    }
}
```

LISTING 3.15: One Remez iteration for updating the locations of the local extrema.

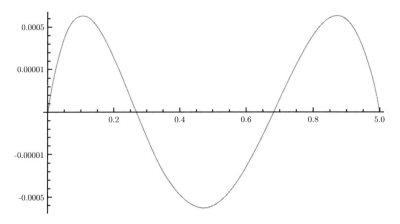

FIGURE 3.2: The plot of $g(x) = \sqrt{1+x} - p(x)$ for the final polynomial of degree 3.

Figure 3.2 shows the plot of $g(x)$ for degree 3 after several Remez iterations. The figure makes it clear that the values of $g(x)$ at the local extrema have the same magnitude and alternate in sign.

Table 3.4 shows the coefficients of the minimax polynomials of degrees one through seven for $f(x) = \sqrt{1+x}$ for $x \in [0, 1)$. The numbers are the coefficients p_i for the polynomial $p(x)$. The table shows the maximum error for the approximation. The tool GeometricTools/GTEngine/Tools/GenerateApproximations generated Table 3.4 using files FitSqrt.h and FitSqrt.inl.

3.3.4   Inverse Square Root Using a Minimax Algorithm

The application of the minimax algorithm is nearly identical to that for the square root function. In binary scientific notation, let $x = 1.t * 2^p$ where t is the trailing significand and p is the unbiased exponent. Thinking of t as a fraction in $[0, 1)$, we can write $x = (1 + t) * 2^p$. If p is even, then $1/\sqrt{x} = (1/\sqrt{1+t}) * 2^{-p/2}$. If p is odd, then $1/\sqrt{x} = (1/(\sqrt{2}\sqrt{1+t})) * 2^{-(p-1)/2}$. You may extract t and p from the floating-point encoding, so the approximation we need is for $1/\sqrt{1+t}$ for $t \in [0, 1)$.

The tool GeometricTools/GTEngine/Tools/GenerateApproximations has the minimax implementation in FitInvSqrt.h and FitInvSqrt.inl and is nearly identical to the code used for the square root function. This code generates Table 3.5, showing the coefficients of the minimax polynomials of degrees one through seven for $f(x) = 1/\sqrt{1+x}$ for $x \in [0, 1)$. The numbers are the coefficients p_i for the polynomial $p(x)$. The table shows the maximum error for the approximation.

TABLE 3.4: Minimax polynomial approximations to $\sqrt{1+x}$

d	coefficients			d	coefficients		
1	p_0	=	$+1$	2	p_0	=	$+1$
	p_1	=	$+4.1421356237309505 * 10^{-1}$		p_1	=	$+4.8563183076125260 * 10^{-1}$
	e	=	$+1.7766952966368793 * 10^{-2}$		p_2	=	$-7.1418268388157458 * 10^{-2}$
					e	=	$+1.1795695163108744 * 10^{-3}$
3	p_0	=	$+1$	4	p_0	=	$+1$
	p_1	=	$+4.9750045320242231 * 10^{-1}$		p_1	=	$+4.9955939832918816 * 10^{-1}$
	p_2	=	$-1.0787308044477850 * 10^{-1}$		p_2	=	$-1.2024066151943025 * 10^{-1}$
	p_3	=	$+2.4586189615451115 * 10^{-2}$		p_3	=	$+4.5461507257698486 * 10^{-2}$
	e	=	$+1.1309620116468910 * 10^{-4}$		p_4	=	$-1.0566681694362146 * 10^{-2}$
					e	=	$+1.2741170151556180 * 10^{-5}$
5	p_0	=	$+1$	6	p_0	=	$+1$
	p_1	=	$+4.9992197660031912 * 10^{-1}$		p_1	=	$+4.9998616695784914 * 10^{-1}$
	p_2	=	$-1.2378506719245053 * 10^{-1}$		p_2	=	$-1.2470733323278438 * 10^{-1}$
	p_3	=	$+5.6122776972699739 * 10^{-2}$		p_3	=	$+6.0388587356982271 * 10^{-2}$
	p_4	=	$-2.3128836281145482 * 10^{-2}$		p_4	=	$-3.1692053551807930 * 10^{-2}$
	p_5	=	$+5.0827122737047148 * 10^{-3}$		p_5	=	$+1.2856590305148075 * 10^{-2}$
	e	=	$+1.5725568940708201 * 10^{-6}$		p_6	=	$-2.6183954624343642 * 10^{-3}$
					e	=	$+2.0584155535630089 * 10^{-7}$
7	p_0	=	$+1$	8	p_0	=	$+1$
	p_1	=	$+4.9999754817809228 * 10^{-1}$		p_1	=	$+4.9999956583056759 * 10^{-1}$
	p_2	=	$-1.2493243476353655 * 10^{-1}$		p_2	=	$-1.2498490369914350 * 10^{-1}$
	p_3	=	$+6.1859954146370910 * 10^{-2}$		p_3	=	$+6.2318494667579216 * 10^{-2}$
	p_4	=	$-3.6091595023208356 * 10^{-2}$		p_4	=	$-3.7982961896432244 * 10^{-2}$
	p_5	=	$+1.9483946523450868 * 10^{-2}$		p_5	=	$+2.3642612312869460 * 10^{-2}$
	p_6	=	$-7.5166134568007692 * 10^{-3}$		p_6	=	$-1.2529377587270574 * 10^{-2}$
	p_7	=	$+1.4127567687864939 * 10^{-3}$		p_7	=	$+4.5382426960713929 * 10^{-3}$
	e	=	$+2.8072302919734948 * 10^{-8}$		p_8	=	$-7.8810995273670414 * 10^{-4}$
					e	=	$+3.9460605685825989 * 10^{-9}$

TABLE 3.5: Minimax polynomial approximations to $f(x) = 1/\sqrt{1+x}$

d	coefficients			d	coefficients		
1	p_0	=	$+1$	2	p_0	=	$+1$
	p_1	=	$-2.9289321881345254 * 10^{-1}$		p_1	=	$-4.4539812104566801 * 10^{-1}$
	e	=	$+3.7814314552701983 * 10^{-2}$		p_2	=	$+1.5250490223221547 * 10^{-1}$
					e	=	$+4.1953446330581234 * 10^{-3}$
3	p_0	=	$+1$	4	p_0	=	$+1$
	p_1	=	$-4.8703230993068791 * 10^{-1}$		p_1	=	$-4.9710061558048779 * 10^{-1}$
	p_2	=	$+2.8163710486669835 * 10^{-1}$		p_2	=	$+3.4266247597676802 * 10^{-1}$
	p_3	=	$-8.7498013749463421 * 10^{-2}$		p_3	=	$-1.9106356536293490 * 10^{-1}$
	e	=	$+5.6307702007266786 * 10^{-4}$		p_4	=	$+5.2608486153198797 * 10^{-2}$
					e	=	$+8.1513919987605266 * 10^{-5}$
5	p_0	=	$+1$	6	p_0	=	$+1$
	p_1	=	$-4.9937760586004143 * 10^{-1}$		p_1	=	$-4.9987029229547453 * 10^{-1}$
	p_2	=	$+3.6508741295133973 * 10^{-1}$		p_2	=	$+3.7220923604495226 * 10^{-1}$
	p_3	=	$-2.5884890281853501 * 10^{-1}$		p_3	=	$-2.9193067713256937 * 10^{-1}$
	p_4	=	$+1.3275782221320753 * 10^{-1}$		p_4	=	$+1.9937605991094642 * 10^{-1}$
	p_5	=	$-3.2511945299404488 * 10^{-2}$		p_5	=	$-9.3135712130901993 * 10^{-2}$
	e	=	$+1.2289367475583346 * 10^{-5}$		p_6	=	$+2.0458166789566690 * 10^{-2}$
					e	=	$+1.9001451223750465 * 10^{-6}$
7	p_0	=	$+1$	8	p_0	=	$+1$
	p_1	=	$-4.9997357250704977 * 10^{-1}$		p_1	=	$-4.9999471066120371 * 10^{-1}$
	p_2	=	$+3.7426216884998809 * 10^{-1}$		p_2	=	$+3.7481415745794067 * 10^{-1}$
	p_3	=	$-3.0539882498248971 * 10^{-1}$		p_3	=	$-3.1023804387422160 * 10^{-1}$
	p_4	=	$+2.3976005607005391 * 10^{-1}$		p_4	=	$+2.5977002682930106 * 10^{-1}$
	p_5	=	$-1.5410326351684489 * 10^{-1}$		p_5	=	$-1.9818790717727097 * 10^{-1}$
	p_6	=	$+6.5598809723041995 * 10^{-2}$		p_6	=	$+1.1882414252613671 * 10^{-1}$
	p_7	=	$-1.3038592450470787 * 10^{-2}$		p_7	=	$-4.6270038088550791 * 10^{-2}$
	e	=	$+2.9887724993168940 * 10^{-7}$		p_8	=	$+8.3891541755747312 * 10^{-3}$
					e	=	$+4.7596926146947771 * 10^{-8}$

3.3.5   Sine Function

To approximate the function $\sin(x)$, the Chebyshev equioscillation theorem may be used with or without additional constraints on the function. Without constraints, the sine function can be approximated on the interval $[0, \pi/2]$ with a polynomial having only odd-power terms, $p(x) = \sum_{i=0}^{n} p_i x^{2i+1}$ of degree $d = 2n + 1$. Choosing degree 5 and using the initial alternating set $S_0 = \{\pi/6, \pi/3, 1\}$, four Remez iterations led to

$$p(x) = 0.999698 - 0.165674x + 0.0075147x^3 \qquad (3.10)$$

with a global error bound $6.7277003513603606 * 10^{-5}$.

However, the slope of the polynomial at $x = 0$ is not one, which is the slope of the sine function at zero. Instead, I prefer approximations whose first term is x, say,

$$f(x) = \sin(x) \doteq x + \sum_{i=1}^{n} p_i x^{2i+1} = p(x) \qquad (3.11)$$

of degree $d = 2n + 1$. The first constraint is that $p'(0) = f'(0) = \cos(0) = 1$. I also impose the second constraint that the approximation should match the function at the other endpoint; that is, $p(\pi/2) = f(\pi/2) = \sin(\pi/2) = 1$. This constrained problem can be solved similar to how I fitted the square root function. The interval for the approximation is $[0, \pi/2]$.

The sine function is odd, $\sin(-x) = -\sin(x)$, in which case you automatically have an approximation on the interval $[-\pi/2, \pi/2]$. To compute an approximation for any real-valued input, you must use *range reduction* by applying trigonometric identities and appealing to the periodicity of the function. For example, if you want to estimate $\sin(x)$ for $x \in [\pi/2, \pi]$, observe that $\sin(x) = \sin(\pi - x)$. If $x \in [\pi/2, \pi]$, then $\pi - x \in [0, \pi/2]$. For $x \in [\pi, 2\pi]$, $\sin(x) = -\sin(x - \pi)$ where $x - \pi \in [0, \pi]$. Finally, for $x > 2\pi$, we can reduce to a value in $[0, 2\pi]$ and use the periodicity $\sin(x + 2\pi k) = \sin(x)$ for any integer k.

The tool GeometricTools/GTEngine/Tools/GenerateApproximations has the minimax implementation in FitSin.h and FitSin.inl. The implementation is slightly different from that of the square root function because we want only the odd-power terms. The code generates Table 3.6 for $f(x) = \sin(x)$ with $x \in [-\pi/2, \pi/2]$. The fitted polynomial is $p(x) = x \sum_{i=0}^{n} p_i x^{2i}$.

3.3.6   Cosine Function

The tool GeometricTools/GTEngine/Tools/GenerateApproximations has the minimax implementation in FitCos.h and FitCos.inl. The implementation is similar to that of the sine function except that we want only the even-power terms. The code generates Table 3.7 for $f(x) = \cos(x)$ with $x \in [-\pi/2, \pi/2]$. The fitted polynomial is $p(x) = \sum_{i=0}^{n} p_i x^{2i}$.

TABLE 3.6: Minimax polynomial approximations to $f(x) = \sin(x)$

d	coefficients			d	coefficients		
3	p_0	=	$+1$	5	p_0	=	$+1$
	p_1	=	$-1.4727245910375519 * 10^{-1}$		p_1	=	$-1.6600599923812209 * 10^{-1}$
	e	=	$+1.3481903639145865 * 10^{-2}$		p_2	=	$+7.5924178409012000 * 10^{-3}$
					e	=	$+1.4001209384639779 * 10^{-4}$
7	p_0	=	$+1$	9	p_0	=	$+1$
	p_1	=	$-1.6665578084732124 * 10^{-1}$		p_1	=	$-1.6666656235308897 * 10^{-1}$
	p_2	=	$+8.3109378830028557 * 10^{-3}$		p_2	=	$+8.3329962509886002 * 10^{-3}$
	p_3	=	$-1.8447486103462252 * 10^{-4}$		p_3	=	$-1.9805100675274190 * 10^{-4}$
	e	=	$+1.0205878936686563 * 10^{-6}$		p_4	=	$+2.5967200279475300 * 10^{-6}$
					e	=	$+5.2010746265374053 * 10^{-9}$
11	p_0	=	$+1$				
	p_1	=	$-1.6666666601721269 * 10^{-1}$				
	p_2	=	$+8.3333303183525942 * 10^{-3}$				
	p_3	=	$-1.9840782426250314 * 10^{-4}$				
	p_4	=	$+2.7521557770526783 * 10^{-6}$				
	p_5	=	$-2.3828544692960918 * 10^{-8}$				
	e	=	$+1.9295870457014530 * 10^{-11}$				

TABLE 3.7: Minimax polynomial approximations to $f(x) = \cos(x)$

d	coefficients			d	coefficients		
2	p_0	=	$+1$	4	p_0	=	$+1$
	p_1	=	$-4.0528473456935105 * 10^{-1}$		p_1	=	$-4.9607181958647262 * 10^{-1}$
	e	=	$+5.4870946878404048 * 10^{-2}$		p_2	=	$+3.6794619653489236 * 10^{-2}$
					e	=	$+9.1879932449712154 * 10^{-4}$
6	p_0	=	$+1$	8	p_0	=	$+1$
	p_1	=	$-4.9992746217057404 * 10^{-1}$		p_1	=	$-4.9999925121358291 * 10^{-1}$
	p_2	=	$+4.1493920348353308 * 10^{-2}$		p_2	=	$+4.1663780117805693 * 10^{-2}$
	p_3	=	$-1.2712435011987822 * 10^{-3}$		p_3	=	$-1.3854239405310942 * 10^{-3}$
	e	=	$+9.2028470133065365 * 10^{-6}$		p_4	=	$+2.3154171575501259 * 10^{-5}$
					e	=	$+5.9804533020235695 * 10^{-8}$
10	p_0	=	$+1$				
	p_1	=	$-4.9999999508695869 * 10^{-1}$				
	p_2	=	$+4.1666638865338612 * 10^{-2}$				
	p_3	=	$-1.3888377661039897 * 10^{-3}$				
	p_4	=	$+2.4760495088926859 * 10^{-5}$				
	p_5	=	$-2.6051615464872668 * 10^{-7}$				
	e	=	$+2.7006769043325107 * 10^{-10}$				

3.3.7 Tangent Function

The tool GeometricTools/GTEngine/Tools/GenerateApproximations has the minimax implementation in FitTan.h and FitTan.inl. The implementation is similar to that of the sine function. The code generates Table 3.8 for $f(x) = \tan(x)$ with $x \in [-\pi/4, \pi/4]$. The fitted polynomial is $p(x) = \sum_{i=0}^{n} p_i x^{2i+1}$.

3.3.8 Inverse Sine Function

The inverse of the sine function is not easily approximated with a polynomial. If the algorithm applied to the sine function is also applied to the inverse sine function, say, $\mathrm{asin}(x) \doteq \sum_{i=0}^{n} p_i x^{2i+1}$ for $x \in [0, 1]$, the coefficients and errors bounds produced by the algorithm are shown in Table 3.9.

TABLE 3.8: Minimax polynomial approximations to $f(x) = \tan(x)$

d	coefficients			d	coefficients		
3	p_0	=	1	5	p_0	=	1
	p_1	=	$4.4295926544736286 * 10^{-1}$		p_1	=	$3.1401320403542421 * 10^{-1}$
	e	=	$1.1661892256204731 * 10^{-2}$		p_2	=	$2.0903948109240345 * 10^{-1}$
					e	=	$5.8431854390143118 * 10^{-4}$
7	p_0	=	1	9	p_0	=	1
	p_1	=	$3.3607213284422555 * 10^{-1}$		p_1	=	$3.3299232843941784 * 10^{-1}$
	p_2	=	$1.1261037305184907 * 10^{-1}$		p_2	=	$1.3747843432474838 * 10^{-1}$
	p_3	=	$9.8352099470524479 * 10^{-2}$		p_3	=	$3.7696344813028304 * 10^{-2}$
	e	=	$3.5418688397723108 * 10^{-5}$		p_4	=	$4.6097377279281204 * 10^{-2}$
					e	=	$2.2988173242199927 * 10^{-6}$
11	p_0	=	1	13	p_0	=	1
	p_1	=	$3.3337224456224224 * 10^{-1}$		p_1	=	$3.3332916426394554 * 10^{-1}$
	p_2	=	$1.3264516053824593 * 10^{-1}$		p_2	=	$1.3343404625112498 * 10^{-1}$
	p_3	=	$5.8145237645931047 * 10^{-2}$		p_3	=	$5.3104565343119248 * 10^{-2}$
	p_4	=	$1.0732193237572574 * 10^{-2}$		p_4	=	$2.5355038312682154 * 10^{-2}$
	p_5	=	$2.1558456793513869 * 10^{-2}$		p_5	=	$1.8253255966556026 * 10^{-3}$
	e	=	$1.5426257940140409 * 10^{-7}$		p_6	=	$1.0069407176615641 * 10^{-2}$

TABLE 3.9: Minimax polynomial approximations to $f(x) = \operatorname{asin}(x)$

d	coefficients			d	coefficients		
3	p_0	=	$+1$	5	p_0	=	$+1$
	p_1	=	$+5.7079632679489661 * 10^{-1}$		p_1	=	$-6.8255938822453732 * 10^{-1}$
	e	=	$+1.9685342444004972 * 10^{-2}$		p_2	=	$+1.2533557150194339$
					e	=	$+1.0028055316328449 * 10^{-1}$
7	p_0	=	$+1$	9	p_0	=	$+1$
	p_1	=	$+1.6842448305091242$		p_1	=	-2.2428186249120721
	p_2	=	-4.7058687958517496		p_2	=	$+1.3291181223980431 * 10^{+1}$
	p_3	=	$+3.5924202921375237$		p_3	=	$-2.1822323710205467 * 10^{+1}$
	e	=	$+6.8107317352554375 * 10^{-2}$		p_4	=	$+1.1344757437932010 * 10^{+1}$
					e	=	$+5.1836906475086431 * 10^{-2}$

The coefficients increase significantly in magnitude and the global error bound does not decrease much. Plots of the error $f(x) - p(x)$ showed me that the equioscillatory behavior is present, but to reduce the error to a small value will lead to such large coefficients that the polynomial is simply not practical in numerical computations.

The problem with the coefficients has to do with the behavior of the derivative of $\operatorname{asin}(x)$ at $x = 1$; that is, $\lim_{x \to 1^-} \operatorname{asin}'(x) = \lim_{x \to 1^-} 1/\sqrt{1 - x^2} = +\infty$. We can remove the derivative singularity by consider instead the function $f(x)$ and its derivative $f'(x)$,

$$f(x) = \frac{\pi/2 - \operatorname{asin}(x)}{\sqrt{1 - x}}, \quad f'(x) = \frac{-1/\sqrt{1 + x} + f(x)/2}{1 - x} \tag{3.12}$$

It may be shown using L'Hôpital's rule that $f(1) = \lim_{x \to 1^-} f(x) = \sqrt{2}$ and $f'(1) = \lim_{x \to 1^-} f'(x) = -2^{-3/2}/3 \doteq -0.117851$. We can approximate $f(x) \doteq p(x)$ where $p(x) = \sum_{i=0}^{d} p_i x^i$, thereby obtaining

$$\operatorname{asin}(x) \doteq \pi/2 - \sqrt{1 - x}\, p(x) \tag{3.13}$$

TABLE 3.10: Minimax polynomial approximations to $f(x) = (\pi/2 - \text{asin}(x))/\sqrt{1-x}$

d	coefficients			d	coefficients		
1	p_0	=	$+1.5707963267948966$	2	p_0	=	$+1.5707963267948966$
	p_1	=	$-1.5658276442180141 * 10^{-1}$		p_1	=	$-2.0347053865798365 * 10^{-1}$
	e	=	$+1.1659002803738105 * 10^{-2}$		p_2	=	$+4.6887774236182234 * 10^{-2}$
					e	=	$+9.0311602490029258 * 10^{-4}$
3	p_0	=	$+1.5707963267948966$	4	p_0	=	$+1.5707963267948966$
	p_1	=	$-2.1253291899190285 * 10^{-1}$		p_1	=	$-2.1422258835275865 * 10^{-1}$
	p_2	=	$+7.4773789639484223 * 10^{-2}$		p_2	=	$+8.4936675142844198 * 10^{-2}$
	p_3	=	$-1.8823635069382449 * 10^{-2}$		p_3	=	$-3.5991475120957794 * 10^{-2}$
	e	=	$+9.3066396954288172 * 10^{-5}$		p_4	=	$+8.6946239090712751 * 10^{-3}$
					e	=	$+1.0930595804481413 * 10^{-5}$
5	p_0	=	$+1.5707963267948966$	6	p_0	=	$+1.5707963267948966$
	p_1	=	$-2.1453292139805524 * 10^{-1}$		p_1	=	$-2.1458939285677325 * 10^{-1}$
	p_2	=	$+8.7973089282889383 * 10^{-2}$		p_2	=	$+8.8784960563641491 * 10^{-2}$
	p_3	=	$-4.5130266382166440 * 10^{-2}$		p_3	=	$-4.8887131453156485 * 10^{-2}$
	p_4	=	$+1.9467466687281387 * 10^{-2}$		p_4	=	$+2.7011519960012720 * 10^{-2}$
	p_5	=	$-4.3601326117634898 * 10^{-3}$		p_5	=	$-1.1210537323478320 * 10^{-2}$
	e	=	$+1.3861070257241426 * 10^{-6}$		p_6	=	$+2.3078166879102469 * 10^{-3}$
					e	=	$+1.8491291330427484 * 10^{-7}$
7	p_0	=	$+1.5707963267948966$	8	p_0	=	$+1.5707963267948966$
	p_1	=	$-2.1459960076929829 * 10^{-1}$		p_1	=	$-2.1460143648688035 * 10^{-1}$
	p_2	=	$+8.8986946573346160 * 10^{-2}$		p_2	=	$+8.9034700107934128 * 10^{-2}$
	p_3	=	$-5.0207843052845647 * 10^{-2}$		p_3	=	$-5.0625279962389413 * 10^{-2}$
	p_4	=	$+3.0961594977611639 * 10^{-2}$		p_4	=	$+3.2683762943179318 * 10^{-2}$
	p_5	=	$-1.7162031184398074 * 10^{-2}$		p_5	=	$-2.0949278766238422 * 10^{-2}$
	p_6	=	$+6.7072304676685235 * 10^{-3}$		p_6	=	$+1.1272900916992512 * 10^{-2}$
	p_7	=	$-1.2690614339589956 * 10^{-3}$		p_7	=	$-4.1160981058965262 * 10^{-3}$
	e	=	$+2.5574620927948377 * 10^{-8}$		p_8	=	$+7.1796493341480527 * 10^{-4}$
					e	=	$+3.6340015129032732 * 10^{-9}$

Evaluating at $x = 0$, we obtain $p(0) = \pi/2$. The remainder of the coefficients are determined by the minimax algorithm. The tool GeometricTools/ GTEngine/Tools/GenerateApproximations generated Table 3.10 using files FitASin.h and FitASin.inl.

3.3.9 Inverse Cosine Function

The same problems with the inverse sine function occur with the inverse cosine function acos(x). Although a minimax algorithm can be applied to acos(x)/$\sqrt{1-x}$ similar to that for the inverse sine function, a simple trigonometric identity suffices: acos(x) + asin(x) = $\pi/2$. Thus, the approximation is acos(x) = $\pi/2$ − asin(x) $\doteq \sqrt{1-x}\,p(x)$ where $p(x)$ is a polynomial constructed for the inverse sine approximation.

3.3.10 Inverse Tangent Function

The tool GeometricTools/GTEngine/Tools/GenerateApproximations has the minimax implementation in FitATan.h and FitATan.inl. The implementation is similar to that of the sine function. The code generates Table 3.11 for $f(x) = $ atan(x) for $x \in [-1, 1]$. The fitted polynomial is $p(x) = \sum_{i=0}^{n} p_i x^{2i+1}$.

TABLE 3.11: Minimax polynomial approximations to $f(x) = \text{atan}(x)$

d	coefficients			d	coefficients		
3	p_0	=	$+1$	5	p_0	=	$+1$
	p_1	=	$-2.1460183660255172 * 10^{-1}$		p_1	=	$-3.0189478312144946 * 10^{-1}$
	e	=	$+1.5970326392614240 * 10^{-2}$		p_2	=	$+8.7292946518897740 * 10^{-2}$
					e	=	$+1.3509832247372636 * 10^{-3}$
7	p_0	=	$+1$	9	p_0	=	$+1$
	p_1	=	$-3.2570157599356531 * 10^{-1}$		p_1	=	$-3.3157878236439586 * 10^{-1}$
	p_2	=	$+1.5342994884206673 * 10^{-1}$		p_2	=	$+1.8383034738018011 * 10^{-1}$
	p_3	=	$-4.2330209451053591 * 10^{-2}$		p_3	=	$-8.9253037587244677 * 10^{-2}$
	e	=	$+1.5051227215514412 * 10^{-4}$		p_4	=	$+2.2399635968909593 * 10^{-2}$
					e	=	$+1.8921598624582064 * 10^{-5}$
11	p_0	=	$+1$	13	p_0	=	$+1$
	p_1	=	$-3.3294527685374087 * 10^{-1}$		p_1	=	$-3.3324998579202170 * 10^{-1}$
	p_2	=	$+1.9498657165383548 * 10^{-1}$		p_2	=	$+1.9856563505717162 * 10^{-1}$
	p_3	=	$-1.1921576270475498 * 10^{-1}$		p_3	=	$-1.3374657325451267 * 10^{-1}$
	p_4	=	$+5.5063351366968050 * 10^{-2}$		p_4	=	$+8.1675882859940430 * 10^{-2}$
	p_5	=	$-1.2490720064867844 * 10^{-2}$		p_5	=	$-3.5059680836411644 * 10^{-2}$
	e	=	$+2.5477724974187765 * 10^{-6}$		p_6	=	$+7.2128853633444123 * 10^{-3}$
					e	=	$+3.5859104691865484 * 10^{-7}$

3.3.11 Exponential Functions

Given a floating-point input y, we wish to compute 2^y. Range reduction is obtained by choosing $y = i + x$, where $i = \lfloor y \rfloor$ is the largest integer smaller than y and where $x \in [0, 1)$ is the fractional part. We can easily compute 2^i, so the problem reduces to computing $f(x) = 2^x$ for $x \in [0, 1)$. Once again a minimax polynomial approximation may be used, $2^x \doteq \sum_{i=0}^{d} p_i x^i$. The tool GeometricTools/GTEngine/Tools/GenerateApproximations has the minimax implementation in FitExp2.h and FitExp2.inl. The implementation is similar to that of the square root function. The code generates Table 3.12 for $f(x) = 2^x$ for $x \in [0, 1]$. The fitted polynomial is $p(x) = \sum_{i=0}^{n} p_i x^i$.

To compute the natural exponential e^x, use the identity $2^y = e^x$ where $y = x \log_2(e)$ and then apply the minimax approximation for 2^y.

3.3.12 Logarithmic Functions

Range reduction may be used for an input x to $f(x) = \log_2(x)$; that is, $x = (1 + t) * 2^p$ for some integer power p and for $t \in [0, 1)$. Of course, this information may be obtained from the binary representation for a floating-point number. Applying the logarithm, we obtain $\log_2(x) = \log_2(1 + t) + p$. We may focus our attention on computing $\log_2(1 + t)$ for $t \in [0, 1)$, a problem similar to that for the square root function. The minimax approximation is $\log_2(1 + x) \doteq \sum_{i=1}^{d} p_i x^i$. Observe that the constant term of the polynomial is zero. The tool GeometricTools/GTEngine/Tools/GenerateApproximations has the minimax implementation in FitLog2.h and FitLog2.inl. The code generates Table 3.13 for $f(x) = \log_2(1 + x)$ for $x \in [0, 1]$. The fitted polynomial is

TABLE 3.12: Minimax polynomial approximations to $f(x) = 2^x$

d	coefficients			d	coefficients		
1	p_0	=	1	2	p_0	=	1
	p_1	=	1		p_1	=	$6.5571332605741528 * 10^{-1}$
	e	=	$8.6071332055934313 * 10^{-2}$		p_2	=	$3.4428667394258472 * 10^{-1}$
					e	=	$3.8132476831060358 * 10^{-3}$
3	p_0	=	1	4	p_0	=	1
	p_1	=	$6.9589012084456225 * 10^{-1}$		p_1	=	$6.9300392358459195 * 10^{-1}$
	p_2	=	$2.2486494900110188 * 10^{-1}$		p_2	=	$2.4154981722455560 * 10^{-1}$
	p_3	=	$7.9244930154334980 * 10^{-2}$		p_3	=	$5.1744260331489045 * 10^{-2}$
	e	=	$1.4694877755186408 * 10^{-4}$		p_4	=	$1.3701998859367848 * 10^{-2}$
					e	=	$4.7617792624521371 * 10^{-6}$
5	p_0	=	1	6	p_0	=	1
	p_1	=	$6.9315298010274962 * 10^{-1}$		p_1	=	$6.9314698914837525 * 10^{-1}$
	p_2	=	$2.4014712313022102 * 10^{-1}$		p_2	=	$2.4023013440952923 * 10^{-1}$
	p_3	=	$5.5855296413199085 * 10^{-2}$		p_3	=	$5.5481276898206033 * 10^{-2}$
	p_4	=	$8.9477503096873079 * 10^{-3}$		p_4	=	$9.6838443037086108 * 10^{-3}$
	p_5	=	$1.8968500441332026 * 10^{-3}$		p_5	=	$1.2388324048515642 * 10^{-3}$
	e	=	$1.3162098333463490 * 10^{-7}$		p_6	=	$2.1892283501756538 * 10^{-4}$
					e	=	$3.1589168225654163 * 10^{-9}$
7	p_0	=	1				
	p_1	=	$6.9314718588750690 * 10^{-1}$				
	p_2	=	$2.4022637363165700 * 10^{-1}$				
	p_3	=	$5.5505235570535660 * 10^{-2}$				
	p_4	=	$9.6136265387940512 * 10^{-3}$				
	p_5	=	$1.3429234504656051 * 10^{-3}$				
	p_6	=	$1.4299202757683815 * 10^{-4}$				
	p_7	=	$2.1662892777385423 * 10^{-5}$				
	e	=	$6.6864513925679603 * 10^{-11}$				

TABLE 3.13: Minimax polynomial approximations to $f(x) = \log_2(1 + x)$

d	coefficients			d	coefficients		
1	p_1	=	$+1$	2	p_1	=	$+1.3465553856377803$
	e	=	$+8.6071332055934202 * 10^{-2}$		p_2	=	$-3.4655538563778032 * 10^{-1}$
					e	=	$+7.6362868906658110 * 10^{-3}$
3	p_1	=	$+1.4228653756681227$	4	p_1	=	$+1.4387257478171547$
	p_2	=	$-5.8208556916449616 * 10^{-1}$		p_2	=	$-6.7778401359918661 * 10^{-1}$
	p_3	=	$+1.5922019349637218 * 10^{-1}$		p_3	=	$+3.2118898377713379 * 10^{-1}$
	e	=	$+8.7902902652883808 * 10^{-4}$		p_4	=	$-8.2130717995088531 * 10^{-2}$
					e	=	$+1.1318551355360418 * 10^{-4}$
5	p_1	=	$+1.4419170408633741$	6	p_1	=	$+1.4425449435950917$
	p_2	=	$-7.0909645927612530 * 10^{-1}$		p_2	=	$-7.1814525675038965 * 10^{-1}$
	p_3	=	$+4.1560609399164150 * 10^{-1}$		p_3	=	$+4.5754919692564044 * 10^{-1}$
	p_4	=	$-1.9357573729558908 * 10^{-1}$		p_4	=	$-2.7790534462849337 * 10^{-1}$
	p_5	=	$+4.5149061716699634 * 10^{-2}$		p_5	=	$+1.2179791068763279 * 10^{-1}$
	e	=	$+1.5521274478735858 * 10^{-5}$		p_6	=	$-2.5841449829670182 * 10^{-2}$
					e	=	$+2.2162051216689793 * 10^{-6}$
7	p_1	=	$+1.4426664401536078$	8	p_1	=	$+1.4426896453621882$
	p_2	=	$-7.2055423726162360 * 10^{-1}$		p_2	=	$-7.2115893912535967 * 10^{-1}$
	p_3	=	$+4.7332419162501083 * 10^{-1}$		p_3	=	$+4.7861716616785088 * 10^{-1}$
	p_4	=	$-3.2514018752954144 * 10^{-1}$		p_4	=	$-3.4699935395019565 * 10^{-1}$
	p_5	=	$+1.9302965529095673 * 10^{-1}$		p_5	=	$+2.4114048765477492 * 10^{-1}$
	p_6	=	$-7.8534970641157997 * 10^{-2}$		p_6	=	$-1.3657398692885181 * 10^{-1}$
	p_7	=	$+1.5209108363023915 * 10^{-2}$		p_7	=	$+5.1421382871922106 * 10^{-2}$
	e	=	$+3.2546531700261561 * 10^{-7}$		p_8	=	$-9.1364020499895560 * 10^{-3}$
					e	=	$+4.8796219218050219 * 10^{-8}$

$p(x) = \sum_{i=1}^{n} p_i x^i$. To compute the natural logarithm $\log(x)$, use the identity $\log(x) = \log_2(x)/\log_2(e)$ where $e \doteq 2.7182818$ is the natural base and then apply the minimax approximation for $\log_2(x)$.

Chapter 4

GPU Computing

4.1 Drawing a 3D Object

The classical use of shader programming on GPUs involves drawing 3D geometric primitives within a 2D window using perspective projection. In order to motivate the parallelism that a GPU provides, let us review all the steps involved in drawing a 3D geometric object. The parallelism comes in two forms. The first form is the partitioning of the work due to the large number of pixels that can be processed independently—this is *massive parallelism* due to a large number of cores on the GPU. The second form is the vectorized work per vertex and per pixel—this is *SIMD parallelism* available on each core. A detailed discussion of the components of a shader-based rendering engine may be found in [8].

4.1.1 Model Space

Consider a 3D geometric object composed of vertices and triangles that connect the vertices. The vertices are defined in *model space*. In games, such objects are sometimes referred to as models, and artists usually create them with a modeling package. The model space is whatever coordinate system the artist chose to use when creating the objects.

4.1.2 World Space

The 3D game itself is given a coordinate system called *world space*, the name suggesting that the geometric objects live in a consistent world. Points in the world are located as 3-tuple Cartesian coordinates. An origin must be chosen as a common reference point for all objects; usually the origin is the 3-tuple $(0, 0, 0)$. A set of three orthogonal direction vectors are chosen as the Cartesian frame; usually these are chosen as the 3-tuples $(1, 0, 0)$, $(0, 1, 0)$, and $(0, 0, 1)$. Which of these is the up-vector is your choice.

A geometric object must be placed somewhere in the world. The object was created in a model space, so we must transform its vertices to world space. Let W be the *model-to-world transformation* that accomplishes this. As is typical in computer graphics with perspective cameras, the vertices are stored as homogeneous points that are 4-tuples of the form $(x, y, z, 1)$. The x-, y-, and z-values represent the distances from the origin along each of the Cartesian direction vectors, and the combination of the three numbers is the location of that point in the world. The last component is an algebraic convenience to allow us to handle affine and perspective transformations within the same mathematical framework. Let $\mathbf{P}_{\mathrm{model}}$ be the 3×1 column vector whose rows are the components of (x, y, z). A 4×4 homogeneous matrix H_{world} represents an affine transformation consisting of translation and rotation; however, an artist might also intend for some objects to be scaled, whether uniformly or nonuniformly. Generally, the matrix is of the block form

$$H_{\mathrm{world}} = \left[\begin{array}{c|c} M & \mathbf{T} \\ \hline \mathbf{0}^{\mathsf{T}} & 1 \end{array} \right] \tag{4.1}$$

where $\mathbf{T}$ is the 3×1 translation and M represents rotations, scalings, shearing, or other linear-algebraic operations. The 3×1 zero vector is $\mathbf{0}$. The lower-right element is the scalar 1. The world-space location of the model-space point is

$$\left[\begin{array}{c} \mathbf{P}_{\mathrm{world}} \\ \hline 1 \end{array} \right] = H_{\mathrm{world}} \left[\begin{array}{c} \mathbf{P}_{\mathrm{model}} \\ \hline 1 \end{array} \right] = \left[\begin{array}{c} M\mathbf{P}_{\mathrm{model}} + \mathbf{T} \\ \hline 1 \end{array} \right] \tag{4.2}$$

As shown, the matrix has last row $(0, 0, 0, 1)$ to represent an affine transformation. GTEngine allows you to choose different conventions for matrix storage and multiplication; see Chapter 6.

4.1.3   View Space

Observers in the world have their own coordinate systems by which they can specify object locations. Although we naturally use stereo vision, for simplicity the assumption of monocular vision is used. Objects are observed from a location called the eyepoint, say, $\mathbf{E}$. Assuming the observer is standing, the body axis is the natural up direction, say, $\mathbf{U}$. Looking straight ahead, we have the direction of view, say, $\mathbf{D}$. We may choose a third direction to be to the right, say, $\mathbf{R}$. Abstractly, these quantites are part of a *camera* and the coordinate system is $\{\mathbf{E}; \mathbf{D}, \mathbf{U}, \mathbf{R}\}$ where the first point is the origin. The last three vectors are ordered and form a *right-handed orthonormal basis*; that is, the vectors are unit length, mutually perpendicular, and $\mathbf{R} = \mathbf{D} \times \mathbf{U}$. The last vector in the ordered set is the cross product of the first two vectors. The origin and vectors in the coordinate system are specified *in world coordinates*; as 3-tuples, the components are measured in the Cartesian directions mentioned in the previous paragraph.

A 3-tuple may be used to describe the location of a point relative to the camera, say, (d, u, r), which corresponds to the world point $\mathbf{P}_{\mathrm{world}} = \mathbf{E} + d\mathbf{D} + u\mathbf{U} + r\mathbf{R}$. In the standard transformation pipeline of computer graphics, the convention has been to list the order of measurements as (r, u, d). The ordered set of vectors $\{\mathbf{R}, \mathbf{U}, \mathbf{D}\}$ is a *left-handed orthonormal basis*, where

$\mathbf{D} = -\mathbf{R} \times \mathbf{U}$. Once again using homogeneous points, we may compute the *view space* (or *camera space*) point $\mathbf{P}_{\mathrm{view}}$ whose rows are the components of (r, u, d). Let $Q = [\mathbf{R} \ \mathbf{U} \ \mathbf{D}]$ be the matrix whose columns are the camera directions considered as 3×1 vectors. The homogeneous transformation from world space to view space is of the block form

$$H_{\mathrm{view}} = \left[\begin{array}{c|c} Q^{\mathsf{T}} & -Q^{\mathsf{T}}\mathbf{E} \\ \hline \mathbf{0}^{\mathsf{T}} & 1 \end{array} \right] \tag{4.3}$$

The view-space location of the world-space point is

$$\left[\frac{\mathbf{P}_{\mathrm{view}}}{1} \right] = H_{\mathrm{view}} \left[\frac{\mathbf{P}_{\mathrm{world}}}{1} \right] = \left[\frac{Q^{\mathsf{T}}(\mathbf{P}_{\mathrm{world}} - \mathbf{E})}{1} \right] \tag{4.4}$$

In your code, you should be clear about the relationship between the geometry you have in mind for the camera directions and the algebra associated with it. GTEngine has a class Camera that stores the eyepoint and camera coordinate vectors. The interface allows you to write these individually, but you may only read the view matrix.

4.1.4 Projection Space

Let us consider a perspective camera, although it is simple to allow an orthographic camera when drawing 3D objects. A *view plane* is chosen in front of the eyepoint and perpendicular to the direction of view. The 3D objects are projected onto this plane by intersecting the plane with rays from the eyepoint through the object points. For the simplified geometric primitives that represent the boundaries of objects and that consist of vertices and triangles, the vertices are projected onto the plane. Points on the boundaries and inside the triangles do not have to be explicitly projected—the perspective projections are obtained by interpolation of the vertex projections.

The view plane has normal vector $-\mathbf{D}$ so that it is perpendicular to the direction of view. The plane is positioned $d_{\min} > 0$ units in front of the eyepoint; that is, a point on the plane is $\mathbf{E} + d_{\min}\mathbf{D}$. Therefore, the equation of the view plane is

$$0 = -\mathbf{D} \cdot [\mathbf{X} - (\mathbf{E} + d_{\min}\mathbf{D})] = -\mathbf{D} \cdot (\mathbf{X} - \mathbf{E}) + d_{\min} \tag{4.5}$$

The points $\mathbf{X}$ satisfying this equation are on the plane. For each vertex $\mathbf{P}_{\mathrm{world}}$, a ray is parameterized by $\mathbf{X}(t) = \mathbf{E} + t(\mathbf{P}_{\mathrm{world}} - \mathbf{E})$ for $t > 0$. The constraint on t says that we care only about points in front of the eyepoint. Substituting this into the plane equation, we may solve for the t-value, say, $\bar{t} = d_{\min}/(\mathbf{P}_{\mathrm{world}} - \mathbf{E})$. If $\mathbf{V}_{\mathrm{world}} = \mathbf{X}(\bar{t})$ is the projection point, some algebraic steps lead to

$$\mathbf{V}_{\mathrm{world}} = \frac{(\mathbf{E}\mathbf{D}^{\mathsf{T}} + d_{\min}I)(\mathbf{P}_{\mathrm{world}} - \mathbf{E})}{\mathbf{D}^{\mathsf{T}}(\mathbf{P}_{\mathrm{world}} - \mathbf{E})} = \frac{\mathbf{N}}{\delta} \tag{4.6}$$

where I is the 3×3 identity matrix and where the last equality defines the numerator and denominator of the computation. We may compute the numerator and denominator separately using homogeneous points and matrices,

$$
\left[\begin{array}{c} \mathbf{N} \\ \hline \delta \end{array} \right] = \left[\begin{array}{c|c} \mathbf{E}\mathbf{D}^{\mathsf{T}} + d_{\min}I & -(\mathbf{E}\mathbf{D}^{\mathsf{T}} + d_{\min}I)\mathbf{E} \\ \hline \mathbf{D}^{\mathsf{T}} & -\mathbf{D}^{\mathsf{T}}\mathbf{E} \end{array} \right] \left[\begin{array}{c} \mathbf{P}_{\text{world}} \\ \hline 1 \end{array} \right] \tag{4.7}
$$

where the left-hand side is defined by the product on the right-hand side.

It is more convenient to formulate the projection in view space itself. The final result is a homogeneous point said to be in *projection space* or *clip space*:

$$
\begin{aligned}
\mathbf{P}_{\text{proj}} &= \left[\begin{array}{c} \mathbf{N}' \\ \hline \delta' \end{array} \right] \\[2mm]
&= \left[\begin{array}{c|c} Q^{\mathsf{T}} & -Q^{\mathsf{T}}\mathbf{E} \\ \hline \mathbf{0}^{\mathsf{T}} & 1 \end{array} \right] \left[\begin{array}{c} \mathbf{N} \\ \hline \delta \end{array} \right] \\[2mm]
&= \left[\begin{array}{c|c} Q^{\mathsf{T}} & -Q^{\mathsf{T}}\mathbf{E} \\ \hline \mathbf{0}^{\mathsf{T}} & 1 \end{array} \right] \left[\begin{array}{c|c} \mathbf{E}\mathbf{D}^{\mathsf{T}} + d_{\min}I & -(\mathbf{E}\mathbf{D}^{\mathsf{T}} + d_{\min}I)\mathbf{E} \\ \hline \mathbf{D}^{\mathsf{T}} & -\mathbf{D}^{\mathsf{T}}\mathbf{E} \end{array} \right] \left[\begin{array}{c} \mathbf{P}_{\text{world}} \\ \hline 1 \end{array} \right] \\[2mm]
&= \left[\begin{array}{c|c} Q^{\mathsf{T}} & -Q^{\mathsf{T}}\mathbf{E} \\ \hline \mathbf{0}^{\mathsf{T}} & 1 \end{array} \right] \left[\begin{array}{c|c} \mathbf{E}\mathbf{D}^{\mathsf{T}} + d_{\min}I & -(\mathbf{E}\mathbf{D}^{\mathsf{T}} + d_{\min}I)\mathbf{E} \\ \hline \mathbf{D}^{\mathsf{T}} & -\mathbf{D}^{\mathsf{T}}\mathbf{E} \end{array} \right] \left[\begin{array}{c|c} Q & \mathbf{E} \\ \hline \mathbf{0}^{\mathsf{T}} & 1 \end{array} \right] \left[\begin{array}{c} \mathbf{P}_{\text{view}} \\ \hline 1 \end{array} \right] \\[2mm]
&= \left[\begin{array}{c|c} d_{\min}I & \mathbf{0} \\ \hline \mathbf{D}^{\mathsf{T}}Q & 0 \end{array} \right] \left[\begin{array}{c} \mathbf{P}_{\text{view}} \\ \hline 1 \end{array} \right] \\[2mm]
&= \left[\begin{array}{c} d_{\min}\mathbf{P}_{\text{view}} \\ \hline \mathbf{D}^{\mathsf{T}}Q \end{array} \right] \\[2mm]
&= \left[\begin{array}{c} d_{\min} \left[\begin{array}{c} r \\ u \\ d \end{array} \right] \\ \hline d \end{array} \right]
\end{aligned} \tag{4.8}
$$

The projected point itself requires the *perspective divide*. The numerator is a 3-tuple and must be divided by the denominator d, leading to the view-plane point $(rd_{\min}/d, ud_{\min}/d, d_{\min})$. As expected, the last component is the distance from the eyepoint to the view plane.

At first glance it appears that the homogeneous projection matrix we should use is

$$
\hat{H}_{\text{proj}} = \left[\begin{array}{c|c} d_{\min}I & \mathbf{0} \\ \hline \mathbf{D}^{\mathsf{T}}Q & 0 \end{array} \right] \tag{4.9}
$$

in which case the transformation pipeline from model space to projection space is

$$
\mathbf{P}_{\text{proj}} = \hat{H}_{\text{proj}} H_{\text{view}} H_{\text{world}} \left[\begin{array}{c} \mathbf{P}_{\text{model}} \\ \hline 1 \end{array} \right] \tag{4.10}
$$

where the final result is a 4×1 homogeneous point. As a tuple, this point is $\mathbf{P}_{\text{proj}} = (\mathbf{N}', \delta')$ and the projected point on the view plane (in view coordinates) is $\mathbf{V}_{\text{proj}} = \mathbf{N}'/\delta' = (rd_{\min}/d, ud_{\min}/d, d_{\min})$. However, the world is a

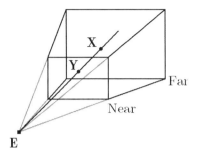

FIGURE 4.1: An eyepoint **E** and a view frustum. The point **X** in the view frustum is projected to the point **Y** on the view plane.

large place, so we can draw objects in only a small part of it, called the *view frustum*, a 6-sided convex polyhedron that is the frustum of a pyramid for perspective projection or a cube for an orthographic projection. The standard computer graphics transformation pipelines map the frustum into a cube. The D3D11 cube is $[-1,1]^2 \times [0,1]$. The actual homogeneous projection matrix used to obtain $\mathbf{P}_{\text{proj}}$ incorporates the view frustum bounds.

The view frustum is defined by selecting extreme values for the components of (r, u, d), say, $r_{\min} \le r \le r_{\max}$, $u_{\min} \le u \le u_{\max}$, and $d_{\min} \le d \le d_{\max}$. Figure 4.1 is a 3D rendering of the frustum as a wireframe. A symmetric view frustum has the property $r_{\min} = -r_{\max}$ and $u_{\min} = -u_{\max}$. Figure 4.2 shows a symmetric view frustum with its faces labeled. The horizontal field of view has half-angle θ_r that satisfies the equation $\tan(\theta_r) = r_{\max}/d_{\min}$ and the vertical field of view has half-angle θ_u that satisfies the equation $\tan(\theta_u) = u_{\max}/d_{\min}$.

In the general case, the *ru*-coordinates of points in the view frustum are mapped to $[-1,1]^2$ by

$$
\begin{aligned}
r' &= \frac{2}{r_{\max} - r_{\min}} \left(d_{\min} r - \frac{r_{\min} + r_{\max}}{2} d \right) \\
u' &= \frac{2}{u_{\max} - u_{\min}} \left(d_{\min} u - \frac{u_{\min} + u_{\max}}{2} d \right)
\end{aligned}
\tag{4.11}
$$

The perspective mapping of the interval $[d_{\min}, d_{\max}]$ to a target interval $[t_0, t_1]$ is of the form $t = a + b/d = (ad + b)/d = d'/d$, where the last equality defines the numerator d'. The coefficients a and b are determined from the linear system $a + b/d_{\min} = t_0$ and $a + b/d_{\max} = t_1$. The target interval for D3D11 is $[0, 1]$ and the numerator of the mapping is

$$
d' = \frac{d_{\max}(d - d_{\min})}{d_{\max} - d_{\min}}
\tag{4.12}
$$

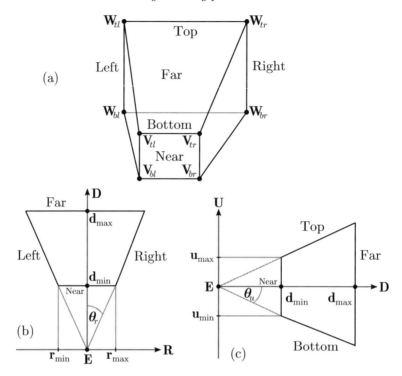

FIGURE 4.2: (a) A 3D drawing of the symmetric view frustum. The left, right, bottom, top, near, and far planes are labeled, as are the eight vertices of the frustum. (b) A 2D drawing of the frustum as seen from the top side. (c) A 2D drawing of the frustum as seen from the right side.

The corresponding homogeneous projection matrix is

$$H_{\text{proj}} = \left[\begin{array}{ccc|c} \frac{2d_{\min}}{r_{\max}-r_{\min}} & 0 & -\frac{r_{\max}+r_{\min}}{r_{\max}-r_{\min}} & 0 \\ 0 & \frac{2d_{\min}}{u_{\max}-u_{\min}} & -\frac{u_{\max}+u_{\min}}{u_{\max}-u_{\min}} & 0 \\ 0 & 0 & \frac{d_{\max}}{d_{\max}-d_{\min}} & -\frac{d_{\max}d_{\min}}{d_{\max}-d_{\min}} \\ 0 & 0 & 1 & 0 \end{array} \right] \quad (4.13)$$

The matrix of Equation (4.13) is indeed different from that in Equation (4.9). The projection-space point is not that of Equation (4.10); rather, it is

$$\mathbf{P}_{\text{proj}} = H_{\text{proj}} H_{\text{view}} H_{\text{world}} \left[\begin{array}{c} \mathbf{P}_{\text{model}} \\ 1 \end{array} \right] = \left[\begin{array}{c} r' \\ u' \\ d' \\ d \end{array} \right] \quad (4.14)$$

where r', u', and d' are defined in Equations (4.11) and (4.12). The view frustum is defined by the constraints $|r'| \le d$, $|u'| \le d$, $0 \le d' \le d_{\max}$, and $d_{\min} \le d \le d_{\max}$.

4.1.5 Window Space

The perspective divide is performed on the 4-tuples (r', u', d', d) to obtain

$$(r'', u'', d'') = (r'/d, u'/d, d'/d), \qquad (4.15)$$

called *normalized device coordinates*. They satisfy the constraints $|r''| \leq 1$, $|u''| \leq 1$, and $0 \leq d'' \leq 1$. The 2-tuples (r'', u'') are mapped to real-valued *window space* 2-tuples (x, y) in a window of width W and height H where $0 \leq x < W$ and $0 \leq y < H$. The (r'', u'') tuples are right handed but display windows are left handed, so the mapping involves a reflection. Specifically, the mapping is

$$x = \frac{W(1 + r'')}{2}, \quad y = \frac{H(1 - u'')}{2} \qquad (4.16)$$

Observe that the computations are real valued. The actual integer-valued pixels drawn are based on rules about real-valued pixel containment within triangles. The right edge $r'' = 1$ maps to $x = W$ and the bottom edge $u'' = -1$ maps to $y = H$. Both indices are out of range, but the containment rules lead to rejection of the corresponding pixels; see the next section on rasterization.

The mapping from (r'', u'') to (x, y) is based on using the entire window for drawing the objects. It is possible to draw the objects to a subrectangle of the window. This subrectangle is referred to as the *viewport*. In D3D11, the concept of viewport includes a subinterval of depth, so in fact the viewport is a subcube of the cube $[0, W) \times [0, H) \times [0, 1]$.

Viewport handling is definitely specific to the graphics API. Moreover, now that machines can have multiple monitors with extended displays, a window can occupy screen real estate on two monitors. The pixel indexing scheme in this case must support windows for which a dimension is larger than that of any single monitor. And it must support negative positions, especially if the secondary monitor is configured to be to the left of the primary monitor. The viewport APIs must allow for this. Even using only Direct3D on a Microsoft Windows computer, be aware that the viewport handling varies between D3D9, D3D10, and D3D11.

Let the viewport have upper-left corner (x_0, y_0), width $w_0 > 0$, and height $h_0 > 0$. The depth may be constrained to $[z_0, z_1] \subseteq [0, 1]$. The mapping from normalized device coordinates to the viewport is then

$$x = x_0 + \frac{w_0(1 + r'')}{2}, \quad y = y_0 + \frac{h_0(1 - u'')}{2}, \quad z = z_0 + (z_1 - z_0)d'' \quad (4.17)$$

If $\mathbf{P}_{\text{ndc}}$ is the 3×1 column vector whose rows are the normalized device coordinates (r'', u'', d'') and $\mathbf{P}_{\text{window}}$ is the 3×1 column vector whose rows are the window coordinates (x, y, z), then

$$\left[\frac{\mathbf{P}_{\text{window}}}{1} \right] \left[\begin{array}{ccc|c} w_0/2 & 0 & 0 & x_0 + w_0/2 \\ 0 & -h_0/2 & 0 & y_0 + h_0/2 \\ 0 & 0 & z_1 - z_0 & z_0 \\ \hline 0 & 0 & 0 & 1 \end{array} \right] \left[\frac{\mathbf{P}_{\text{ndc}}}{1} \right] \qquad (4.18)$$

TABLE 4.1: The transformation pipeline

point	transform name	matrix	equation
$\mathbf{P}_{\text{model}}$ $\downarrow$ $\mathbf{P}_{\text{world}}$ $\downarrow$ $\mathbf{P}_{\text{view}}$ $\downarrow$ $\mathbf{P}_{\text{proj}}$ $\downarrow$ $\mathbf{P}_{\text{ndc}}$ $\downarrow$ $\mathbf{P}_{\text{window}}$	world matrix, view matrix, projection matrix, perspective divide, window matrix,	$H_{\text{world}},$ $H_{\text{view}},$ $H_{\text{proj}},$ $H_{\text{window}},$	(4.1) (4.3) (4.13) (4.15) (4.19)

The final homogeneous matrix in the transformation pipeline is

$$H_{\text{window}} = \left[\begin{array}{ccc|c} w_0/2 & 0 & 0 & x_0 + w_0/2 \\ 0 & -h_0/2 & 0 & y_0 + h_0/2 \\ 0 & 0 & z_1 - z_0 & z_0 \\ \hline 0 & 0 & 0 & 1 \end{array} \right] \tag{4.19}$$

4.1.6   Summary of the Transformations

The previous sections show how to transform a point in a 3D model space to a point in window space. The sequence of steps is shown in Table 4.1. Software renderers implement the entire pipeline, both for vertices of the triangles and the interpolated points during rasterization of the triangles. When hardware-accelerated graphics for consumer machines first arrived, the application was still responsible for computing and multiplying the world, view, and projection matrices. The perspective divisions and mapping to window coordinates were performed in graphics hardware (*hardware rasterization*). On later graphics hardware, the entire transformation pipeline was handled by the hardware including computing texture coordinates and lighting data at vertices (*hardware texturing and lighting*). However, control of per-pixel attributes during rasterization was indirect and somewhat cryptic (*the fixed-function pipeline*). Finally, the graphics hardware evolved to allow detailed control over vertex and pixel attributes (*shader programming*).

The composition of the world, view, and projection homogeneous matrices is of importance to shader programs,

$$H_{\text{pvw}} = H_{\text{proj}} H_{\text{view}} H_{\text{world}} \tag{4.20}$$

Although each individual matrix may be used by shader programs, for standard drawing of 3D objects use the composition. It is convenient for the application to compute this matrix product and provide it to the shader.

4.1.7 Rasterization

We now get to the stage of drawing a 3D object that allows massive parallelism. Consider a 3D triangle that is fully in the view frustum and that is fully visible to the observer (the camera eyepoint). Let the model-space vertices be $\mathbf{V}_i$ for $0 \leq i \leq 2$. Each vertex has a set of attributes such as color, texture coordinate, or normal vector for lighting. Refer to these collectively as $\mathbf{A}_i$ for vertex $\mathbf{i}$. The vertices are transformed from model space to window space, leading to three real-valued pixels (x_i, y_i) for $0 \leq i \leq 2$. The vertex is assigned a color through some sequence of computations involving the vertex attributes. The triangle contains other pixels that we wish to assign colors. The standard approach is to *rasterize* the triangle into the pixel grid and perspectively interpolate the vertex attributes for the pixel colors.

Let $\mathbf{V}$ be a point in the triangle. We may write this point as a linear combination of the vertices: $\mathbf{V} = b_0\mathbf{V}_0 + b_1\mathbf{V}_1 + b_2\mathbf{V}_2$, where $b_i \geq 0$ and $b_0 + b_1 + b_2 = 1$. The coefficients b_i are called *barycentric coordinates* of $\mathbf{V}$ relative to the vertices. They are preserved by affine tranformations. We may interpolate the attributes $\mathbf{A}$ at $\mathbf{V}$ using barycentric coordinates and then applying the perspective divide. Let the projection-space coordinates of the vertices be (r_i', u_i', d_i', d_i). The perspectively interpolated attributes are

$$\mathbf{A} = \frac{b_0\mathbf{A}_0 + b_1\mathbf{A}_1 + b_2\mathbf{A}_2}{b_0d_0 + b_1d_1 + b_2d_2} \tag{4.21}$$

The standard approach to rasterization is to use the *top-left rule*. This is the extension of the one-dimensional concept of half-open intervals. The interval (x_0, x_1) consists of numbers x for which $x_0 < x < x_1$. Note that the endpoints are not included in the interval. In calculus, the interval is said to be *open*. The interval $[x_0, x_1]$ consists of numbers x for which $x_0 \leq x \leq x_1$. In this case, the endpoints are included in the interval and the interval is said to be *closed*. Define $[x_0, x_1)$ to be the set of numbers x for which $x_0 \leq x < x_1$. The interval is said to be *half open* in the sense that the number x_1 is not included in the set; however, x_0 is in the set. The interval is also said to be *half closed*.

Consider the set of real-valued numbers visualized as a line. Consider an ordered set of n real-valued numbers x_i for $0 \leq i < n$ and where $x_i < x_{i+1}$. Assign to each x_i a color c_i. We wish to assign colors to each integer in $[x_0, x_1)$ using linear interpolation of the colors at the x_i that bound the integer. Although we could iterate over the integers j in $[x_0, x_1)$, query for the interval $[x_i, x_{i+1}]$ that contains j, and interpolate a color $c = c_i + (j - x_i)/(x_{i+1} - x_i)(c_{i+1} - c_i)$, this is akin to the drawing objects in 2D by iterating over all the pixels and querying which geometric primitive contains it. However, in 2D we iterate over the geometric primitives and determine the pixels contained by each primitive. The natural specialization to 1D is to iterate over the intervals $[x_i, x_{i+1}]$ and determine which integers are contained by the interval. Moreover, we wish to "visit" each integer only once. This raises the question of ownership of integers by the intervals, something that can be determined

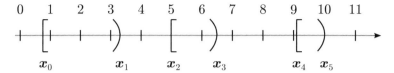

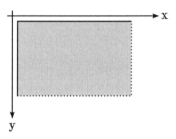

FIGURE 4.3: A one-dimensional illustration of pixel ownership using half-open intervals.

FIGURE 4.4: A set that is the Cartesian product of half-open intervals. The top and left edges of the rectangle are included in the set (drawn as solid black lines) but the right and bottom edges are not included (drawn as dotted black lines).

by using half-open intervals $[x_i, x_{i+1})$ to avoid the problem when an x_{i+1} is already an integer and shared by the intervals $[x_i, x_{i+1}]$ and $[x_{i+1}, x_{i+2}]$. Figure 4.3 illustrates the ownership for the 1D problem. Figure 4.3 shows a set of numbers x_0 through x_5 and integer points on the real line. The pixel ownerships are listed next.

- $[x_0, x_1)$ owns 1, 2, and 3.

- $[x_1, x_2)$ owns only 4 because $x_2 = 5$ and the right endpoint of the interval is excluded.

- $[x_2, x_3)$ owns 5 and 6.

- $[x_3, x_4)$ owns 7, 8, and 9.

- $[x_4, x_5)$ does not own any integers because $x_5 = 10$ and the right endpoint of the interval is excluded.

An extension of half-open intervals to 2D uses Cartesian products of 1D intervals. The rectangle $[x_0, x_1) \times [y_0, y_1)$ is the set of 2-tuples (x, y) for which $x_0 \leq x < x_1$ and $y_0 \leq y < y_1$. Figure 4.4 shows such a set drawn in a left-handed coordinate system with x increasing rightward and y increasing downward.

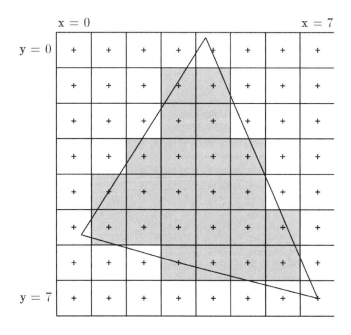

FIGURE 4.5: A two-dimensional illustration of pixel ownership using the top-left rasterization rule.

The concept of half-open interval may be extended to triangles in 2D. Edges are either horizontal (y is constant) or not horizontal. If a triangle edge is horizontal and all triangle points are on or below that edge, the edge is said to be a *top edge*. If a triangle edge is not horizontal and all triangle points in the rows spanned by the edge are on or right of that edge, the edge is said to be a *left edge*. A triangle has one or two left edges but does not necessarily have a top edge. Similar to the 1D rasterization shown in Figure 4.3, a 2D triangle with real-valued vertices may be drawn in the plane and covers various pixels (integer-valued points).

Top-Left Rasterization Rule *A pixel is owned by the triangle if it is*

- *strictly inside the triangle,*

- *on a top edge but not the rightmost point of that edge, or*

- *on a left edge but not the bottommost point of that edge.*

The rule guarantees a partitioning of the to-be-drawn pixels into disjoint sets of pixels, each set owned by a triangle. Figure 4.5 shows a triangle and its pixel ownership. The pixels are drawn as squares and the pixel centers are drawn as plus signs. The gray-colored pixels are those owned by the triangle. The pixels at $(1, 4)$ and $(3, 6)$ are exactly on left edges of the triangle, so they are owned by the triangle. The pixel at $(7, 7)$, although exactly a vertex, is not strictly inside the triangle and not on a top or left edge, so the triangle does not own it.

The disjoint partitioning of the pixels not only is relevant to guaranteeing a pixel is drawn once, it allows the pixel processing to be efficiently distributed across multiple cores, whether CPU cores in software rendering or GPU cores in hardware rendering. The partitioning of a rectangular array is a key observation to GPGPU computing, as we will see in the next section.

4.2   High Level Shading Language (HLSL)

In this section I will discuss shader programming using the D3D11 *high level shading language* (HLSL). Various shader types are examined without regard to how you actually hook up inputs, outputs, and execute them using a D3D11 engine.

4.2.1   Vertex and Pixel Shaders

Let us look at some simple shaders used for drawing. The discussion here builds on top of the presentation in Section 4.1. The first example involves vertex color attributes only. The sample application is

GeometricTools/GTEngine/Samples/Basics/VertexColoring

Listing 4.1 contains a vertex shader and a pixel shader. The shader uses the vector-on-the-right multiplication convention, although GTEngine has conditional compilation to support the vector-on-the-left convention.

```
cbuffer PVWMatrix
{
    float4x4 pvwMatrix;
};

struct VS_INPUT
{
    float3 modelPosition : POSITION;
    float4 modelColor : COLOR0;
};

struct VS_OUTPUT
{
    float4 vertexColor : COLOR0;
    float4 clipPosition : SV_POSITION;
};

VS_OUTPUT VSMain(VS_INPUT input)
{
    VS_OUTPUT output;
    output.vertexcolor = input.modelColor;
    output.clipPosition = mul(pvwMatrix, float4(modelPosition, 1.0f));
    return output;
}
```

```
struct PS_INPUT
{
    float4 vertexColor : COLOR0;
};

struct PS_OUTPUT
{
    float4 pixelColor0 : SV_TARGET0;
};

PS_OUTPUT PSMain(PS_INPUT input)
{
    PS_OUTPUT output;
    output.pixelColor0 = input.vertexColor;
    return output;
};
```

LISTING 4.1: A vertex shader and a pixel shader for simple vertex coloring of geometric primitives.

The vertex shader is the function named VSMain. The input to each invocation of the function is of type VS_INPUT, which has the model-space position of the vertex as a 3-tuple (modelPosition) and the color attribute (modelColor), which represents an RGBA color whose channels are floating-point numbers in the interval $[0, 1]$. The output of the function is of type VS_OUTPUT and simply passes through the model color as vertexColor. The other output parameter, clipPosition, is required and contains the projection-space coordinates of the incoming model-space position. The multiplication involves the *constant buffer* named PVWMatrix; specifically, the member pvwMatrix stores the matrix of Equation (4.20). If you choose the vector-on-the-left convention, the parameters in the mul operator are reversed; see the GteVertexColorEffect.cpp file to see how either convention is supported using conditional compilation within the HLSL shader itself. Constant buffers provide a mechanism for sharing parameters that are common to all invocations of a shader.

The pixel shader is the function PSMain. The input to each invocation of the function is of type PS_INPUT, which stores the color value that is perspectively interpolated by the rasterizer for the target pixel. The output of the function is of type PS_OUTPUT and simply passes through the interpolated color obtained from the rasterizer.

HLSL uses *semantics* to convey information about the use of input and output parameters. When rolling your own effects system, the vertex shader input semantics are not necessarily meaningful. The semantic name and the actual meaning of the data can be quite different; for example, you might pass in physical parameters through a TEXCOORD semantic even though the parameters are not used for texture lookups. However, the semantics are necessary to associate vertex shader outputs with pixel shader inputs.

Two of the semantics are prefixed with SV_. These are called *system value semantics*. The vertex shader must output the projection-space position using the semantic SV_POSITION, thereby letting the rasterizer know that clipPosition must be used to generate the window-space positions and for interpolation. A pixel shader input can also be labeled with the SV_POSITION semantic. This input stores the pixel center with a one-half offset in the xy components of that input member.

The pixel shader uses the semantic **SV_TARGET0**, indicating which output color buffer is written. In D3D11, the maximum number of such buffers is eight. In our example, we are writing to buffer zero. It is possible to write to multiple render targets. To do so, you add more members to **PS_OUTPUT** and label them with the semantics indicating which targets you want. The pixel shader then assigns values to each of the members.

Vertex and pixel shaders for basic 2D texturing of a square formed of two triangles are shown in Listing 4.2. The shader uses the vector-on-the-right multiplication convention, although GTEngine has conditional compilation to support the vector-on-the-left convention.

```
cbuffer PVWMatrix
{
    float4x4 pvwMatrix;
};

struct VS_INPUT
{
    float3 modelPosition : POSITION;
    float2 modelTCoord : TEXCOORD0;
};

struct VS_OUTPUT
{
    float2 vertexTCoord : TEXCOORD0;
    float4 clipPosition : SV_POSITION;
};

VS_OUTPUT VSMain(VS_INPUT input)
{
    VS_OUTPUT output;
    output.vertexTCoord = input.modelTCoord;
    output.clipPosition = mul(pvwMatrix, float4(modelPosition, 1.0f));
    return output;
}

struct PS_INPUT
{
    float2 vertexTCoord : TEXCOORD0;
};

struct PS_OUTPUT
{
    float4 pixelColor0 : SV_TARGET0;
};

Texture2D baseTexture;
SamplerState baseSampler;

PS_OUTPUT PSMain(PS_INPUT input)
{
    PS_OUTPUT output;
    output.pixelColor0 = baseTexture.Sample(baseSampler, input.vertexTCoord);
    return output;
};
```

LISTING 4.2: A vertex shader and a pixel shader for simple texturing of geometric primitives.

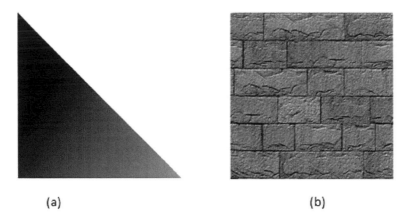

(a) (b)

FIGURE 4.6: (a) A rendering of a vertex-colored triangle. (b) A rendering of a textured square.

Sample applications to demonstrate vertex coloring of a single triangle and texturing of a square are

GeometricTools/GTEngine/Samples/Basics/VertexColoring
GeometricTools/GTEngine/Samples/Basics/Texturing

Figure 4.6 shows grayscale renderings. The application renderings are in color.

The shader programs are relatively easy to read without extensive knowledge of HLSL or D3D11. However, it is necessary to compile the shaders, whether offline or at runtime. At runtime, the shader inputs and outputs must be hooked up for execution. In the preceding examples, an application must create a constant buffer to store the 4×4 world-view-projection matrix of Equation (4.20). This buffer is hooked up to the shader at runtime using D3D11 API calls, and the name PVWMatrix is a convenience for identifying the input to hook up to. Although a programmer may look at an assembly listing of the compiled shader to determine the constant-buffer register assigned to PVWMatrix, *shader reflection* may be used to obtain that information, thus establishing a map of constant buffer names to registers.

The vertex shader is executed for vertices obtained from a user-constructed *vertex buffer*. This is a chunk of memory that you must let D3D11 know how it is to be interpreted. Moreover, you need to create an *input layout object* that establishes the relationship between members of the vertex buffer and the input format defined by VS_INPUT.

D3D11 will execute the vertex shader as needed, but it needs to know the type of geometric primitive you want drawn. The primitive topology is specified by the user: triangle mesh, triangle strip, line mesh, line strip, points, etc. The vertices are used in the order provided by the vertex buffer—an *indexless primitive*—or in an order specified by an *index buffer*. This buffer stores integer indices (16-bit or 32-bit) into the vertex buffer interpreted as an array of structures. When the corresponding D3D11 draw call is made, the vertices are processed by calls to VSMain. When an entire primitive is ready, say, the three vertices of a triangle have been processed by the vertex shader calls, the rasterizer identifies the pixels owned by the triangle and calls PSMain for each owned pixel.

In the texturing example, the model-space texture coordinates are passed through by the vertex shader. The rasterizer then interpolates these coordinates and passes them to the pixel shader so that the 2D texture can be sampled to obtain a color. The baseTexture object is a read-only texture that the programmer needs to create and hook up to the shader. The texture must be sampled. The standard methods are *nearest neighbor* or *linear interpolation*, and the programmer may specify these by creating baseSampler and hooking it up to the shader. The texture might also be created for mipmapping.

All in all, there are a *lot* of steps required to get D3D11 ready to draw something as simple as a vertex-colored or textured object! After I briefly discuss geometry shaders and compute shaders, the remainder of Section 4.2 is a discussion of the key steps, including how to create a D3D11 device and immediate context for drawing and how to create the aforementioned buffers. The daunting details of the self-contained low-level D3D11 commands in a single main program are discussed in Section 5.1. The source code for drawing a triangle that is both vertex colored and textured is provided using only low-level D3D11 commands. I guarantee that you do not want to keep repeating such low-level code for your applications. In that section, my intent is to motivate building a *D3D11 engine* that encapsulates as much of the work as possible. Consider GTEngine as a case study; you may find a brief discussion about its design and architecture in Section 5.1.

4.2.2   Geometry Shaders

One of the features introduced in Shader Model 4 (D3D10) that was not in Shader Model 3 (D3D9) is *geometry shaders*. These shaders give you the ability to generate geometric primitives from other primitives.

The prototypical example is generation of *billboards* that always face the camera. In particular, given a center point $\mathbf{C}$ in camera coordinates and a size $s > 0$, the four corners of the billboard are $(r, u, d) = \mathbf{C} \pm s(1, 0, 0) \pm s(0, 1, 0)$. In D3D9, you can generate billboards as an array of two-triangle quads, so for n billboards you need $4n$ vertices in the vertex buffer, each vertex position a 3-tuple. Thus, the vertex buffer has $12n$ floating-point values for the corner positions. However, we have only four degrees of freedom, three for the center point and one for the size. It would be convenient to have a vertex buffer for which the $12n$ floating-point positions are replaced by $4n$ floating-point values, three for center and one for size per vertex. Geometry shaders provide support to allow you to generate the corners on the GPU rather than on the CPU.

The sample application is

GeometricTools/GTEngine/Samples/Basics/GeometryShaders

Listing 4.3 contains the HLSL code for drawing square billboards that are axis aligned in window space. The vertex buffer is an array of structures, each structure containing the model-space location of the center of the billboard, a color for the billboard, and a size parameter that controls how large each square is. The geometry shader uses the vector-on-the-right multiplication convention, although GTEngine has conditional compilation to support the vector-on-the-left convention.

```
struct VS_STRUCT
{
    float3 position : POSITION;
    float3 color : COLOR0;
    float size : TEXCOORD0;
};

VS_STRUCT VSMain (VS_STRUCT input)
{
    return input;
}

struct GS_OUTPUT
{
    float3 color : COLOR0;
    float4 clipPosition : SV_POSITION;
};

cbuffer Matrices
{
    float4x4 vwMatrix;
    float4x4 pMatrix;
};

static float4 offset[4] =
{
    float4(-1.0f, -1.0f, 0.0f, 0.0f),
    float4(+1.0f, -1.0f, 0.0f, 0.0f),
    float4(-1.0f, +1.0f, 0.0f, 0.0f),
    float4(+1.0f, +1.0f, 0.0f, 0.0f)
};

[maxvertexcount(6)]
void GSMain (point VS_STRUCT input[1], inout TriangleStream<GS_OUTPUT> stream)
{
    GS_OUTPUT output[4];
    float4 viewPosition = mul(vwMatrix, float4(particle.position, 1.0f));
    for (int i = 0; i < 4; ++i)
    {
        float4 corner = viewPosition + input[0].size*offset[i];
        output[i].clipPosition = mul(pMatrix, corner);
        output[i].color = input[0].color;
    }

    stream.Append(output[0]);
    stream.Append(output[1]);
    stream.Append(output[3]);
    stream.RestartStrip();

    stream.Append(output[0]);
    stream.Append(output[3]);
```

```
    stream.Append(output[2]);
    stream.RestartStrip();
}

struct PS_OUTPUT
{
    float4 pixelColor0 : SV_TARGET0;
};

PS_OUTPUT PSMain(GS_OUTPUT input)
{
    PS_OUTPUT output;
    output.pixelColor0 = float4(input.color, 1.0f);
    return output;
}
```

LISTING 4.3: HLSL code to draw square billboards.

The vertex shader **VSMain** simply passes through its input, allowing the geometry shader to generate the billboards. The vertices are tagged by the application to be point primitives. The geometry shader **GSMain** is consistent with this, because its first parameter is labeled as **point** and is given a single vertex shader output structure. The incoming point is in model-space coordinates. It is transformed to view space using the product of the view matrix and the world matrix. The geometry shader generates the four corners of the billboard in view-space coordinates. Those corners are then transformed into projection space by application of the projection matrix. As with the previous vertex shader examples, the clip position must be returned so that the rasterizer can generate the pixels corresponding to the billboard squares. The billboard color is simply passed through.

The second parameter of the geometry shader specifies that the output of the shader is a list of triangles. These must be generated using the topology of a triangle strip. The **stream.Append** calls occur three at a time, placing a triangle into output stream. The indexing of the **output[]** array is that for a triangle strip. The call to **RestartStrip** indicates that an output primitive is complete. You have to specify the maximum number of output vertices—in this example, it is six.

The pixel shader now takes an input that is generated by the rasterizer when it processes the billboard triangles. The sample application uses a single color per billboard, so the billboard color value is the final result for the pixel.

Notice that **offset[]** is declared as a static array. The elements of the array are not accessible to the application code. The **[unroll]** directive in the geometry shader causes the loop to be unrolled. The assembly output listing verifies this; see Section 4.2.4 about generating the listing. The **offset[]** values are inlined accordingly. If the **static** keyword is omitted, a global constant buffer is created (called **$Global**) but the array values are still inlined.

Figure 4.7 shows grayscale renderings of the billboards for two different orientations of the virtual trackball. The application draws the billboards using color.

Geometry shaders have more sophisticated uses. The Marching Cubes surface extraction example uses geometry shaders to generate triangles within

FIGURE 4.7: Renderings of billboards generated by geometry shaders.

a voxel based on a table lookup of information. Geometry shaders are also useful for *splatting* point primitives; see [17].

4.2.3 Compute Shaders

To motivate compute shaders, let us look at small-scale Gaussian blurring of a 2D color image, a convolution of an image with a 3×3 kernel whose weights are nonnegative and sum to one. The sample application is

GeometricTools/GTEngine/Samples/Basics/GaussianBlurring

Listing 4.4 shows the HLSL file.

```
Texture2D<float4> input;
RWTexture2D<float4> output;

static float weight[3][3] =
{
    { 1.0f / 16.0f, 2.0f / 16.0f, 1.0f / 16.0f },
    { 2.0f / 16.0f, 4.0f / 16.0f, 2.0f / 16.0f },
    { 1.0f / 16.0f, 2.0f / 16.0f, 1.0f / 16.0f }
};

static int2 offset[3][3] =
{
    { int2(-1, -1), int2(0, -1), int2(+1, -1) },
    { int2(-1,  0), int2(0,  0), int2(+1,  0) },
    { int2(-1, +1), int2(0, +1), int2(+1, +1) }
};

[numthreads(NUM_X_THREADS, NUM_Y_THREADS, 1)]
void CSMain(int2 t : SV_DispatchThreadID)
{
    float4 result = 0.0f;
    for (int r = 0; r < 3; ++r)
    {
        for (int c = 0; c < 3; ++c)
```

```
    {
        result += weight[r][c] * input[t + offset[r][c]];
    }
  }
  output[t] = float4(result.rgb, 1.0f);
}
```

LISTING 4.4: A compute shader that implements small-scale Gaussian blurring.

The input and output images are 2D textures, each having 32-bit floating-point channels for red, green, blue, and alpha. For this example, the alpha channels are all one. The output at a pixel (x, y) is computed as the weighted average of the nine pixels in the 3×3 neighborhood of the input pixel at (x, y). By the way, the assignment of the scalar zero to a 4-tuple result appears to be an error. As it turns out, the HLSL compiler allows this, replicating (splatting) the scalar in all channels; thus, the initial value of result is $(0, 0, 0, 0)$.

A key difference between compute shaders and the other shaders we have looked at is that you need to handle the domain decomposition for the inputs. To be clear, for a single triangle the vertex shader is called by the graphics driver three times, once per vertex. Based on the output clip positions, the rasterizer identifies the pixels covered by the triangle, perspectively interpolates the vertex attributes at those pixels, and then calls the pixel shader for each pixel. You can access the (x, y) location of the pixel in the pixel shader using an input tagged as SV_POSITION.

On the other hand, a compute shader is responsible for processing a *group of threads*. These are provided via the attribute numthreads. Imagine the GPU threads partitioned into a 3D grid of dimensions N_x, N_y, and N_z with one thread per grid cell. Each cell is indexed by (x, y, z) with $0 \le x < N_x$, $0 \le y < N_y$, and $0 \le z < N_z$. The grid can be partition into a lower-resolution 3D grid of groups of dimensions G_x, G_y, and G_z with each group having T_x threads in the x-dimension, T_y threads in the y-dimension, and T_z threads in the z-dimension. T_x, T_y, and T_z are the parameters used in the numthreads attribute. In our example, T_x is NUM_X_THREADS, T_y is NUM_Y_THREADS, and T_z is 1. The counts are passed as macros to the compiler. In the sample application they are $T_x = 8$, $T_y = 8$, and $T_z = 1$. In normal usage, $N_x = G_x T_x$, $N_y = G_y T_y$, and $N_z = G_z T_z$. In the sample application, the image to be blurred has dimensions 1024×768, so $N_x = 1024$, $N_y = 768$, $N_z = 1$, $G_x = 1024/8 = 128$, $G_y = 768/8 = 96$, and $G_z = 1$. The group counts are passed to a function, ID3D11DeviceContext::Dispatch, that is called to execute the compute shader.

Observe that numthreads allows you to specify the T-counts; you need to specify the G-counts in your application code. But then how do you know which thread your program is actually using? This is the job of the system value semantic SV_DispatchThreadID passed to CSMain. Generally, you can pass in the ID t as an int3 or uint3; it is the tuple (x, y, z) for the grid cell (thread) that is calling CSMain. In the application, I know I am processing a 2D image and I partitioned the threads in a 2D manner, so I took the liberty to pass in

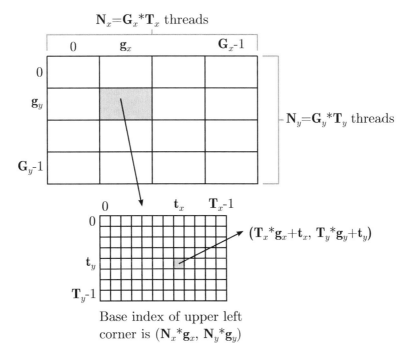

FIGURE 4.8: An illustration of Equation (4.22) that relates the dispatch thread ID to the group ID and the group thread ID.

t as an int2 for convenience. Notice that output is a 2D texture. This compute shader has no need for texture sampling, so we can look up the texture values directly without sampling. The operator[] provides the direct lookup and it expects a 2-tuple for the index. Because t is already a 2-tuple, I can use it as is. However, if I had declared int3 t, then I would need to perform the lookup as output[t.xy].

The indexing of cells is quite general and does not always have to be as simple as that shown in the sample application. Other system value semantics are supported for indexing: SV_GroupThreadID, SV_GroupID, and SV_GroupIndex. A detailed example with diagrams is presented at the MSDN page [38]. A *group thread ID* is a 3-tuple (t_x, t_y, t_z) with $0 \leq t_x < T_x$, $0 \leq t_y < T_y$, and $0 \leq t_z < T_z$; that is, the group thread ID gives you indexing relative to the group of threads that are currently executing and calling CSMain. A *group ID* is a 3-tuple (g_x, g_y, g_z) with $0 \leq g_x < G_x$, $0 \leq g_y < G_y$, and $0 \leq g_z < G_z$; that is, the group ID gives you indexing into the lower-resolution grid of groups of threads. The *dispatch thread ID* is the tuple

$$(d_x, d_y, d_z) = (T_x g_x + t_x, T_y g_y + t_y, T_z g_z + t_z) \qquad (4.22)$$

Figure 4.8 shows a 2D illustration of the dispatch thread ID.

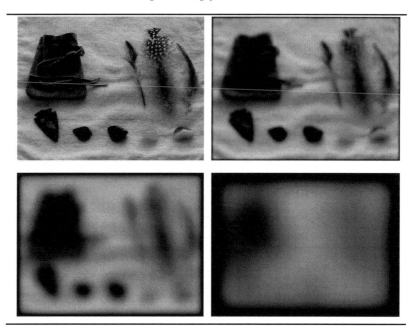

FIGURE 4.9: Upper left: the original image. Upper right: 100 blurring passes. Lower left: 1000 blurring passes. Lower right: 10,000 blurring passes.

The sample application creates a compute shader whose input is a color image and whose output is a blurred image of the same size. The roles of input and output are then swapped; as such, the input and output are called *ping-pong buffers*. The blurred image becomes the input and the output is a blur of the blurred image. Figure 4.9 shows the original image and several blurred copies. The borders of the blurred image become dark, nearly black, as the number of passes increases. This is the usual problem that occurs when filtering an image—how do you handle the pixels at the boundary? On the CPU, typically you handle the boundary pixels separately to avoid out-of-range accesses to the image pixels. The HLSL code in Listing 4.4 does not have explicit logic for handling the boundary. Instead, I rely on the out-of-range accesses to produce predictable values. Specifically, any access to the input[] that is out of range will return a 4-tuple with zero components. I will come back to this topic later when I discuss compiling the compute shader.

4.2.4   Compiling HLSL Shaders

Shader programs may be compiled using the command-line compiler FXC or they may be compiled at runtime using the D3DCompiler system. The MSDN documentation for the latter is available online, and the FXC compiler options are similar to those described for D3DCompile.

We will first look at FXC. Support for D3D11.0 is provided by Windows 8.0 in the Windows Kits folder, and support for D3D11.1 is provided by Windows 8.1 in the Windows Kits folder. I use Windows 8.1 on 64-bit machines; the FXC compiler path is

C:/Program Files (x86)/Windows Kits/8.1/bin/x64/fxc.exe

Assuming you have the containing folder in your environment path, you can run FXC from a command window. The list of options may be viewed by typing "fxc /?" in the window (without the quotes),

```
Microsoft (R) Direct3D Shader Compiler 6.3.9600.16384
Copyright (C) 2013 Microsoft. All rights reserved.

Usage: fxc <options> <files>

    /?, /help          print this message

    /T <profile>       target profile
    /E <name>          entrypoint name
    /I <include>       additional include path
    /Vi                display details about the include process

    /Od                disable optimizations
    /Op                disable preshaders
    /O{0,1,2,3}        optimization level; 1 is default
    /WX                treat warnings as errors
    /Vd                disable validation
    /Zi                enable debugging information
    /Zpr               pack matrices in row-major order
    /Zpc               pack matrices in column-major order

    /Gpp               force partial precision
    /Gfa               avoid flow control constructs
    /Gfp               prefer flow control constructs
    /Gdp               disable effect performance mode
    /Ges               enable strict mode
    /Gec               enable backwards compatibility mode
    /Gis               force IEEE strictness
    /Gch               compile as a child effect for FX 4.x targets

    /Fo <file>         output object file
    /Fl <file>         output a library
    /Fc <file>         output assembly code listing file
    /Fx <file>         output assembly code and hex listing file
    /Fh <file>         output header file containing object code
    /Fe <file>         output warnings and errors to a specific file
    /Fd <file>         extract shader PDB and write to given file
    /Vn <name>         use <name> as variable name in header file
    /Cc                output color coded assembly listings
    /Ni                output instruction numbers in assembly listings
    /No                output instruction byte offset in assembly listings
    /Lx                output hexadecimal literals

    /P <file>          preprocess to file (must be used alone)

    @<file>            options response file
    /dumpbin           load a binary file rather than compiling
    /Qstrip_reflect    strip reflection data from 4_0+ shader bytecode
    /Qstrip_debug      strip debug information from 4_0+ shader bytecode
    /Qstrip_priv       strip private data from 4_0+ shader bytecode

    /compress          compress DX10 shader bytecode from files
    /decompress        decompress bytecode from first file, output files should
                       be listed in the order they were in during compression
```

```
/shtemplate <file>    template shader file for merging/matching resources
/mergeUAVs            merge UAV slots of template shader and current shader
/matchUAVs            match template shader UAV slots in current shader
/res_may_alias        assume that UAVs/SRVs may alias for cs_5_0+

/setprivate <file>    private data to add to compiled shader blob
/getprivate <file>    save private data from shader blob

/D <id>=<text>        define macro
/nologo               suppress copyright message

<profile>: cs_4_0 cs_4_1 cs_5_0 ds_5_0 gs_4_0 gs_4_1 gs_5_0 hs_5_0 lib_4_0
    lib_4_1 lib_4_0_level_9_1 lib_4_0_level_9_3 lib_5_0 ps_2_0 ps_2_a ps_2_b
    ps_2_sw ps_3_0 ps_3_sw ps_4_0 ps_4_0_level_9_1 ps_4_0_level_9_3
    ps_4_0_level_9_0 ps_4_1 ps_5_0 tx_1_0 vs_1_1 vs_2_0 vs_2_a vs_2_sw
    vs_3_0 vs_3_sw vs_4_0 vs_4_0_level_9_1 vs_4_0_level_9_3 vs_4_0_level_9_0
    vs_4_1 vs_5_0
```

The options are extensive, but I will discuss the ones that I use most often.

- /T <profile>. The supported profiles are listed at the end of the command-line text. I use only Shader Model 5 on my machines, and this book does not discuss tessellation features. Thus, the only profiles I use in GTEngine are vs_5_0 (vertex shaders), ps_5_0 (pixel shaders), gs_5_0 (geometry shaders), and cs_5_0 (compute shaders).

- /E <name>. You can have multiple programs defined in a single HLSL file, so you must specify the name (*entry point*) of the shader program to be compiled. I tend to be consistent and use program names of the form XSMain, where X is one of V, P, G, or C, but at times it is convenient to group together related shaders and use names of a different format; see the Fluids2D shader EnforceStateBoundary.hlsl, for instance.

- /Fc <file>. I use FXC to ensure shaders compile before loading them in applications to be (re)compiled at runtime. Sometimes I want to see how constant buffers are laid out in memory or what bind points are associated with resources. This option allows you to write the assembly listing and other information to a text file.

- /Zi. Sometimes you want to look at the assembly output to understand whether your high-level code is inefficient and possibly needs rewriting. By default, the output is only a sequence of assembly instructions. This option requests that additional information be embedded in the output; for example, line numbers are printed followed by the corresponding blocks of assembly instructions.

- /Gis. This option forces strict compliance with IEEE standards for floating-point arithmetic. For 3D rendering, IEEE strictness is usually not necessary, but most likely you will want this for accurate (and predicatable) results using compute shaders.

- /Zpr and /Zpc. These specify the storage format for matrices; the default is column major. GTEngine is designed so that the default packing of matrices is consistent with your choice of packing on the CPU: row major if you have exposed the preprocessor symbol GTE_USE_ROW_MAJOR in the GTEngineDEF.h file or column major if you have hidden this symbol.

- /D <id>=<text>. You can define preprocessor symbols that are used by the shader programs.

Be aware that the option names are case sensitive! Let us look at the output of several experiments using FXC.

4.2.4.1 Compiling the Vertex Coloring Shaders

Copy Listing 4.1 to a file named VertexColoring.hlsl. Open a command window in the folder that contains this file. You can do so from Windows Explorer by navigating to that folder and selecting it using shift-right-click, which launches a pop-up dialog. One of the options is "Open command window here."

To compile the vertex shader, use

```
fxc /T vs_5_0 /E VSMain /Zpr /Fc VertexColoringR.vs5.txt VertexColoring.hlsl
```

I have selected row-major ordering for the matrices, so the application must attach a constant buffer with the pvwMatrix stored in row-major order. The contents of the output text file are shown in Listing 4.5.

```
//
// Generated by Microsoft (R) HLSL Shader Compiler 6.3.9600.16384
//
//
// Buffer Definitions:
//
// cbuffer PVWMatrix
// {
//
//    row_major float4x4 pvwMatrix;        // Offset:    0 Size:    64
//
// }
//
//
// Resource Bindings:
//
// Name                          Type  Format          Dim Slot Elements
// ------------------------------ ---- ------- ----------- ---- --------
// PVWMatrix                     cbuffer     NA          NA    0        1
//
//
//
// Input signature:
//
// Name                 Index   Mask Register SysValue  Format   Used
// -------------------- ----- ------ -------- -------- -------- ------
// POSITION                 0    xyz        0     NONE    float    xyz
// COLOR                    0   xyzw        1     NONE    float   xyzw
//
//
// Output signature:
//
// Name                 Index   Mask Register SysValue  Format   Used
// -------------------- ----- ------ -------- -------- -------- ------
// COLOR                    0   xyzw        0     NONE    float   xyzw
// SV_POSITION              0   xyzw        1      POS    float   xyzw
//
```

```
vs_5_0
dcl_globalFlags refactoringAllowed
dcl_constantbuffer cb0[4], immediateIndexed
dcl_input v0.xyz
dcl_input v1.xyzw
dcl_output o0.xyzw
dcl_output_siv o1.xyzw, position
dcl_temps 1
mov o0.xyzw, v1.xyzw
mov r0.xyz, v0.xyzx
mov r0.w, l(1.000000)
dp4 o1.x, cb0[0].xyzw, r0.xyzw
dp4 o1.y, cb0[1].xyzw, r0.xyzw
dp4 o1.z, cb0[2].xyzw, r0.xyzw
dp4 o1.w, cb0[3].xyzw, r0.xyzw
ret
// Approximately 8 instruction slots used
```

LISTING 4.5: The output assembly listing for the vertex shader of
VertexColoring.hlsl for row-major matrix storage.

The constant buffer information is displayed first. The default matrix storage for HLSL is column major, so when you select row major, the matrix member is tagged with row_major. The type is float4x4, denoting a 4×4 matrix. The offset is measured in bytes from the beginning of the buffer memory. In this case, the constant buffer has only one member, making it first in the memory with offset zero. The size sixty-four is the total number of bytes used by the buffer. The resource binding stores the buffer name (not the member name) and indicates that the buffer is associated with slot zero and has one element. This information is related to assigning constant buffer registers to hold the matrix values; see the discussion later in this section.

The signatures have the semantic names and the indices associated with them. The HLSL file declares the modelPosition member of VS_INPUT to be semantic POSITION, where the absence of a numeric suffix is assumed to mean zero; that is, the semantic is interpreted as POSITION0. The modelColor is tagged with COLOR0, indicating it is semantic COLOR at index zero. The masks indicate the total number of vector channels available. The member modelPosition is declared as float3, so only three channels are available as indicated by the mask xyz. The member modelColor is declared as float4, so all four channels are available. The last column of the table indicates which of these channels are actually used. In the current example, all available channels are used. The format specifies the scalar type, which is float for all channels of the inputs. It is possible for applications to specify vertex input members using other scalar types such as integers.

The register numbers refer to the input and output registers for the shader. The assembly statement dcl_input v0.xyz declares the input register v0 and that three channels are used. In the input signature comment, POSITION0 shows its register number to be zero, which indicates the position 3-tuple will be stored in register v0. The COLOR0 input uses register one; dcl_input v1.xyzw declares that register v1 will store the color. The SysValue column of the table indicates whether the semantic is a regular one or a system value one. The member vertexColor of VS_OUTPUT has regular semantic and is stored in register o0. The member clipPosition uses a system value semantic and is stored in register o1.

The initial comments are followed by a block of HLSL assembly instructions. These will be provided to the graphics driver at runtime, and the driver will make an additional pass, compiling to byte code for optimization. For all practical purposes, the optimization pass is a black box and invariably proprietary information. The first assembly line contains the shader profile, in our case vs_5_0. The instructions prefixed with dcl_ are declarations. I already mentioned that the input and output registers are declared. The statement with dcl_constantbuffer cb0[4] declares an array of four constant buffer registers with array name cb0. Each register holds a 4-tuple of 32-bit numbers, so cb0[4] stores the rows of pvwMatrix. In the resource bindings, the constant buffer named PVWMatrix is assigned to slot zero; the zero refers to cb0. The dcl_temps 1 instruction declares that one temporary register is used in the assembly, namely, register r0.

The instruction mov o0.xyzw, v1.xyzw copies the input modelColor to the output vertexColor. The instruction mov r0.xyz, v0.xyzx copies the input modelPosition to the temporary register r0. A 4-tuple is required for the rightmost argument of mov. Because v0 is declared as a 3-tuple, the compiler has *swizzled* the channels by replicating the x-channel into the w-channel. This w-channel is not used, so it does not matter which channel is swizzled into it. The w-channel of r0 is assigned using mov r0.w, l(1.000000). This instruction copies the literal constant 1 into that channel, after which r0 contains float4(modelPosition,1.0f).

The next four instructions dp4 are dot products of the rows of pvwMatrix with r0. This is equivalent to the matrix-vector product

$$
\begin{bmatrix} m_{00} & m_{01} & m_{02} & m_{03} \\ \hline m_{10} & m_{11} & m_{12} & m_{13} \\ \hline m_{20} & m_{21} & m_{22} & m_{23} \\ \hline m_{30} & m_{31} & m_{32} & m_{33} \end{bmatrix} \begin{bmatrix} v_0 \\ v_1 \\ v_2 \\ 1 \end{bmatrix} = \begin{bmatrix} \mathbf{R}_0^\mathsf{T} \\ \hline \mathbf{R}_1^\mathsf{T} \\ \hline \mathbf{R}_2^\mathsf{T} \\ \hline \mathbf{R}_3^\mathsf{T} \end{bmatrix} \mathbf{V}
$$

$$
= \begin{bmatrix} \mathbf{R}_0 \cdot \mathbf{V} \\ \mathbf{R}_1 \cdot \mathbf{V} \\ \mathbf{R}_2 \cdot \mathbf{V} \\ \mathbf{R}_3 \cdot \mathbf{V} \end{bmatrix}
$$

(4.23)

If you compile the vertex shader for column-major matrix storage,

fxc /T vs_5_0 /E VSMain /Zpc /Fc VertexColoringR.vs5.txt VertexColoring.hlsl

the matrix-vector assembly instructions are different, as shown in Listing 4.6. You may also omit /Zpc, because the FXC default is column-major storage.

```
mul  r0.xyzw,  v0.yyyy,  cb0[1].xyzw
mad  r0.xyzw,  cb0[0].xyzw,  v0.xxxx,  r0.xyzw
mad  r0.xyzw,  cb0[2].xyzw,  v0.zzzz,  r0.xyzw
add  o1.xyzw,  r0.xyzw,  cb0[3].xyzw
```

LISTING 4.6: The output assembly listing for the matrix-vector product of the vertex shader of VertexColoring.hlsl for column-major matrix storage.

This is equivalent to the matrix-vector product

$$
\begin{bmatrix}
m_{00} & m_{01} & m_{02} & m_{03} \\
m_{10} & m_{11} & m_{12} & m_{13} \\
m_{20} & m_{21} & m_{22} & m_{23} \\
m_{30} & m_{31} & m_{32} & m_{33}
\end{bmatrix}
\begin{bmatrix}
v_0 \\
v_1 \\
v_2 \\
1
\end{bmatrix}
= \begin{bmatrix} \mathbf{C}_0 & \mathbf{C}_1 & \mathbf{C}_2 & \mathbf{C}_3 \end{bmatrix} \mathbf{V}
$$

$$
= v_0 \mathbf{C}_0 + v_1 \mathbf{C}_1 + v_2 \mathbf{C}_2 + \mathbf{C}_3
$$

(4.24)

In the row-major format, the number of instructions is eight. In the column-major format, the number of instructions is six. You might be tempted to conclude that the column-major format with vector-on-the-right multiplication convention is faster. This is not the case for my AMD 7970 graphics card based on profiling experiments. The row-major code runs 1.5 times faster than the column-major code. See Section 5.3 for more details about the profiling.

Compile the pixel shader using

fxc /T ps_5_0 /E PSMain /Fc VertexColoringR.ps5.txt VertexColoring.hlsl

to obtain the output in Listing 4.7. No matrix multiplications are used in the pixel shader, so it does not matter what you specify for the matrix storage convention.

```
//
// Generated by Microsoft (R) HLSL Shader Compiler 6.3.9600.16384
//
//
//
// Input signature:
//
// Name                    Index  Mask  Register  SysValue   Format    Used
// ----------------------  -----  ----  --------  --------   ------    ----
// COLOR                     0     xyzw      0      NONE     float     xyzw
//
//
// Output signature:
//
// Name                    Index  Mask  Register  SysValue   Format    Used
// ----------------------  -----  ----  --------  --------   ------    ----
// SV_TARGET                 0     xyzw      0     TARGET    float     xyzw
//
ps_5_0
dcl_globalFlags refactoringAllowed
dcl_input_ps linear v0.xyzw
dcl_output o0.xyzw
mov o0.xyzw, v0.xyzw
ret
// Approximately 2 instruction slots used
```

LISTING 4.7: The output assembly listing for the pixel shader of VertexColoring.hlsl.

The assembly instructions are trivial, because the pixel shader is a pass through for the incoming color.

4.2.4.2   Compiling the Texturing Shaders

Copy Listing 4.2 to a file named Texturing.hlsl. The sample application is

GeometricTools/GTEngine/Samples/Basics/Texturing

Open a command window in the folder and compile the vertex shader. The only difference between the output listing for this shader and for the vertex color shader is that the vertex input has a 2-tuple texture coordinate rather than a 4-tuple color. The semantic is TEXCOORD0. When you compile the pixel shader, you get the output shown in Listing 4.8. The indexable command was manually split so that the listing fits within the width of the book.

```
//
// Generated by Microsoft (R) HLSL Shader Compiler 6.3.9600.16384
//
//
// Resource Bindings:
//
// Name                          Type  Format       Dim Slot Elements
// -------------------------------------------------------------------
// baseSampler                   sampler    NA        NA   0        1
// baseTexture                   texture float4       2d   0        1
//
//
//
// Input signature:
//
// Name              Index   Mask Register SysValue  Format   Used
// ------------------------------------------------------------------
// TEXCOORD            0      xy       0      NONE    float    xy
//
//
// Output signature:
//
// Name              Index   Mask Register SysValue  Format   Used
// ------------------------------------------------------------------
// SV_TARGET           0     xyzw      0     TARGET   float    xyzw
//
ps_5_0
dcl_globalFlags refactoringAllowed
dcl_sampler s0, mode_default
dcl_resource_texture2d (float,float,float,float) t0
dcl_input_ps linear v0.xy
dcl_output o0.xyzw
sample_indexable(texture2d)(float,float,float,float)
    o0.xyzw, v0.xyxx, t0.xyzw, s0
ret
// Approximately 2 instruction slots used
```

LISTING 4.8: The output assembly listing for the pixel shader of Texturing.hlsl.

This shows two new register types, a sampler register s0 and a texture register t0. The sampler is tagged mode_default, which means that you can use it as inputs to texture-object methods Sample (the function will select the appropriate mipmap level when the attached texture has mipmaps), SampleLevel (the function will use the specified mipmap level), and SampleGrad (the function uses a gradient to affect the sample location). The assembly instruction sample_indexable has four arguments. From right to left, these are the sampler state, the texture to sample (all four channels are requested), the texture coordinate (only the first two channels matter; the rest are swizzled), and the register for the output. The output in this case is an output register for the pixel shader. If you instead swizzled the sampling call, say,

```
output.pixelColor0 =
    baseTexture.Sample(baseSample, input.vertexTCoord).xxxx;
```

the assembly instructions are

```
sample_indexable(texture2d)(float, float, float, float)
    r0.x, v0.xyxx, t0.xyzw, s0
mov o0.xyzw, r0.xxxx
```

The sampled value is written to a temporary register and then that register is swizzled and assigned to the shader output register.

4.2.4.3   Compiling the Billboard Shaders

Copy Listing 4.3 to a file named Billboards.hlsl. Open a command window in the folder and compile the vertex shader. Because the vertex shader is just a pass-through of inputs, it does not matter which matrix storage option is specified. The output is shown in Listing 4.9.

```
//
// Generated by Microsoft (R) HLSL Shader Compiler 6.3.9600.16384
//
//
//
// Input signature:
//
// Name              Index   Mask  Register SysValue  Format   Used
// ----------------- ------  ----- -------- --------- -------- ------
// POSITION            0      xyz      0       NONE     float    xyz
// COLOR               0      xyz      1       NONE     float    xyz
// TEXCOORD            0      x        2       NONE     float    x
//
//
// Output signature:
//
// Name              Index   Mask  Register SysValue  Format   Used
// ----------------- ------  ----- -------- --------- -------- ------
// POSITION            0      xyz      0       NONE     float    xyz
// TEXCOORD            0        w      0       NONE     float      w
// COLOR               0      xyz      1       NONE     float    xyz
//
vs_5_0
dcl_globalFlags refactoringAllowed
dcl_input v0.xyz
dcl_input v1.xyz
dcl_input v2.x
dcl_output o0.xyz
dcl_output o0.w
dcl_output o1.xyz
mov o0.xyz, v0.xyzx
```

```
mov o0.w, v2.x
mov o1.xyz, v1.xyzx
ret
// Approximately 4 instruction slots used
```

LISTING 4.9: The output assembly listing for the vertex shader of Billboards.hlsl.

The input and output signatures are similar to what we have seen before, except that the HLSL compiler has taken the liberty to optimize the output. The POSITION0 and TEXCOORD0 outputs are stored in the same register, the position in the first three components (xyz) and the billboard size in the last component (w). When the geometry shader consumes the vertex shader output, only two registers per vertex are fetched rather than three if the compiler had decided not to optimize.

Compile the geometry shader now. This shader does access the matrix of the constant buffer, so it matters about matrix storage. For this example, I have selected option /Zpc for column-major storage. The output is shown in Listing 4.10. Some of the instructions were manually split to fit within the width of the book.

```
//
// Generated by Microsoft (R) HLSL Shader Compiler 6.3.9600.16384
//
//
// Buffer Definitions:
//
// cbuffer Matrices
// {
//
//    float4x4 vwMatrix;              // Offset:    0 Size:    64
//    float4x4 pMatrix;               // Offset:   64 Size:    64
//
// }
//
//
// Resource Bindings:
//
// Name                         Type  Format          Dim Slot Elements
// ───────────────────────────  ────  ──────          ─── ──── ────────
// Matrices                     cbuffer  NA              NA    0        1
//
//
//
// Input signature:
//
// Name                 Index   Mask Register SysValue  Format   Used
// ───────────────────  ─────   ──── ──────── ────────  ──────   ────
// POSITION                 0    xyz        0     NONE   float    xyz
// TEXCOORD                 0      w        0     NONE   float      w
// COLOR                    0    xyz        1     NONE   float    xyz
//
//
// Output signature:
//
// Name                 Index   Mask Register SysValue  Format   Used
// ───────────────────  ─────   ──── ──────── ────────  ──────   ────
// COLOR                    0    xyz        0     NONE   float    xyz
// SV_POSITION              0   xyzw        1      POS   float   xyzw
//
```

```
gs_5_0
dcl_globalFlags refactoringAllowed
dcl_constantbuffer cb0[8], immediateIndexed
dcl_input v[1][0].xyz
dcl_input v[1][0].w
dcl_input v[1][1].xyz
dcl_temps 4
dcl_inputprimitive point
dcl_stream m0
dcl_outputtopology trianglestrip
dcl_output o0.xyz
dcl_output_siv o1.xyzw, position
dcl_maxout 6
mov o0.xyz, v[0][1].xyzx
mul r0.xyzw, cb0[1].xyzw, v[0][0].yyyy
mad r0.xyzw, cb0[0].xyzw, v[0][0].xxxx, r0.xyzw
mad r0.xyzw, cb0[2].xyzw, v[0][0].zzzz, r0.xyzw
add r0.xyzw, r0.xyzw, cb0[3].xyzw
mad r1.xyzw, v[0][0].wwww, l(-1.000000, -1.000000, 0.000000, 0.000000),
     r0.xyzw
mul r2.xyzw, r1.yyyy, cb0[5].xyzw
mad r2.xyzw, cb0[4].xyzw, r1.xxxx, r2.xyzw
mad r2.xyzw, cb0[6].xyzw, r1.zzzz, r2.xyzw
mad r1.xyzw, cb0[7].xyzw, r1.wwww, r2.xyzw
mov o1.xyzw, r1.xyzw
emit_stream m0
mov o0.xyz, v[0][1].xyzx
mad r2.xyzw, v[0][0].wwww, l(1.000000, -1.000000, 0.000000, 0.000000),
     r0.xyzw
mul r3.xyzw, r2.yyyy, cb0[5].xyzw
mad r3.xyzw, cb0[4].xyzw, r2.xxxx, r3.xyzw
mad r3.xyzw, cb0[6].xyzw, r2.zzzz, r3.xyzw
mad r2.xyzw, cb0[7].xyzw, r2.wwww, r3.xyzw
mov o1.xyzw, r2.xyzw
emit_stream m0
mov o0.xyz, v[0][1].xyzx
mad r2.xyzw, v[0][0].wwww, l(1.000000, 1.000000, 0.000000, 0.000000),
     r0.xyzw
mad r0.xyzw, v[0][0].wwww, l(-1.000000, 1.000000, 0.000000, 0.000000),
     r0.xyzw
mul r3.xyzw, r2.yyyy, cb0[5].xyzw
mad r3.xyzw, cb0[4].xyzw, r2.xxxx, r3.xyzw
mad r3.xyzw, cb0[6].xyzw, r2.zzzz, r3.xyzw
mad r2.xyzw, cb0[7].xyzw, r2.wwww, r3.xyzw
mov o1.xyzw, r2.xyzw
emit_stream m0
cut_stream m0
mov o0.xyz, v[0][1].xyzx
mov o1.xyzw, r1.xyzw
emit_stream m0
mov o0.xyz, v[0][1].xyzx
mov o1.xyzw, r2.xyzw
emit_stream m0
mov o0.xyz, v[0][1].xyzx
mul r1.xyzw, r0.yyyy, cb0[5].xyzw
mad r1.xyzw, cb0[4].xyzw, r0.xxxx, r1.xyzw
mad r1.xyzw, cb0[6].xyzw, r0.zzzz, r1.xyzw
mad r0.xyzw, cb0[7].xyzw, r0.wwww, r1.xyzw
mov o1.xyzw, r0.xyzw
emit_stream m0
cut_stream m0
ret
// Approximately 45 instruction slots used
```

LISTING 4.10: The output assembly listing for the geometry shader of Billboards.hlsl.

The dcl_ instructions indicate that the constant buffer is stored as an array of registers, cb0[8], which is sufficient to store the two 4×4 matrices. The input registers are doubly indexed, which is different from what we saw in the previous examples. The first index n of V[n][i] represents the number of inputs to the geometry shader, which in our example is one because the input is a point. Generally, the input can also be line VS_STRUCT input[2] or triangle VS_STRUCT input[3]. The second index i represents the register number. The declarations indicate that register V[0][0] stores the position (xyz) and size (w), and register V[0][1] stores the color (xyz). Four temporary registers are used, r0 through r3. The input primitive is a point and the output topology is a triangle. The maximum number of vertices generated by the geometry shader is six. The output stream of triangles is managed by register m0. The color is returned in output register o0 and the clip position is returned in output register o1.

The mov and mad instructions are what we saw in the previous examples to compute the matrix-vector products when using column-major storage for the matrix and vector-on-the-right multiplication convention. The emit_stream instruction corresponds to the Append calls and the cut_stream instruction corresponds to the RestartStrip calls.

Compile the pixel shader to obtain the output shown in Listing 4.11.

```
//
// Generated by Microsoft (R) HLSL Shader Compiler 6.3.9600.16384
//
//
//
// Input signature:
//
// Name                  Index   Mask  Register SysValue  Format   Used
// ------------------------------------------------------------------------
// COLOR                   0      xyz       0      NONE     float    xyz
// SV_POSITION             0      xyzw      1      POS      float
//
//
// Output signature:
//
// Name                  Index   Mask  Register SysValue  Format   Used
// ------------------------------------------------------------------------
// SV_TARGET               0      xyzw      0      TARGET   float    xyzw
//
ps_5_0
dcl_globalFlags refactoringAllowed
dcl_input_ps linear v0.xyz
dcl_output o0.xyzw
mov o0.xyz, v0.xyzx
mov o0.w, l(1.000000)
ret
// Approximately 3 instruction slots used
```

LISTING 4.11: The output assembly listing for the pixel shader of Billboards.hlsl.

There are no surprises here. The shader input is a 3-tuple color and the shader output is the same color (xyz) with an alpha channel (w) set to one. The swizzle channels are named xyzw in the assembly listings, but in your HLSL code you may use rgba as alternate names.

4.2.4.4   Compiling the Gaussian Blurring Shaders

Copy Listing 4.4 to a file named GaussianBlurring.hlsl. The sample application is

GeometricTools/GTEngine/Samples/Basics/GaussianBlurring

Compile the compute shader using the command line

fxc /T cs_5_0 /E CSMain /D NUM_X_THREADS=8 /D NUM_Y_THREADS=8
/Fc GaussianBlurring.txt GaussianBlurring.hlsl

to obtain the output shown in Listing 4.12. The indexable instruction was manually split to fit within the width of the book.

```
//
// Generated by Microsoft (R) HLSL Shader Compiler 6.3.9600.16384
//
//
// Resource Bindings:
//
// Name                          Type  Format      Dim Slot Elements
// _____ _____ _____ ____ ____ _____
// input                      texture  float4       2d    0        1
// output                         UAV  float4       2d    0        1
//
//
//
// Input signature:
//
// Name                   Index   Mask Register SysValue  Format   Used
// _____ _____ _____ _____ _____ _____ _____
// no Input
//
// Output signature:
//
// Name                   Index   Mask Register SysValue  Format   Used
// _____ _____ _____ _____ _____ _____ _____
// no Output
cs_5_0
dcl_globalFlags refactoringAllowed
dcl_resource_texture2d (float,float,float,float) t0
dcl_uav_typed_texture2d (float,float,float,float) u0
dcl_input vThreadID.xy
dcl_temps 3
dcl_indexableTemp x0[9], 4
dcl_indexableTemp x1[9], 4
dcl_thread_group 8, 8, 1
mov x0[0].x, l(0.062500)
mov x0[1].x, l(0.125000)
mov x0[2].x, l(0.062500)
mov x0[3].x, l(0.125000)
mov x0[4].x, l(0.250000)
mov x0[5].x, l(0.125000)
mov x0[6].x, l(0.062500)
mov x0[7].x, l(0.125000)
mov x0[8].x, l(0.062500)
mov x1[0].xy, l(-1,-1,0,0)
mov x1[1].xy, l(0,-1,0,0)
```

```
mov x1 [2]. xy, l(1,−1,0,0)
mov x1 [3]. xy, l(−1,0,0,0)
mov x1 [4]. xy, l(0,0,0,0)
mov x1 [5]. xy, l(1,0,0,0)
mov x1 [6]. xy, l(−1,1,0,0)
mov x1 [7]. xy, l(0,1,0,0)
mov x1 [8]. xy, l(1,1,0,0)
mov r0.zw, l(0,0,0,0)
mov r1.xy, l(0,0,0,0)
loop
    ige r1.z, r1.y, l(3)
    breakc_nz r1.z
    mov r1.z, r1.x
    mov r1.w, l(0)
    loop
        ige r2.x, r1.w, l(3)
        breakc_nz r2.x
        imad r2.x, r1.y, l(3), r1.w
        mov r2.y, x0[r2.x + 0].x
        mov r2.xz, x1[r2.x + 0].xxyx
        iadd r0.xy, r2.xzxx, vThreadID.xyxx
        ld_indexable(texture2d)(float, float, float, float)
            r0.x, r0.xyzw, t0.xyzw
        mad r1.z, r2.y, r0.x, r1.z
        iadd r1.w, r1.w, l(1)
    endloop
    mov r1.x, r1.z
    iadd r1.y, r1.y, l(1)
endloop
store_uav_typed u0.xyzw, vThreadID.xyyy, r1.xxxx
ret
// Approximately 41 instruction slots used
```

LISTING 4.12: The output assembly listing for the compute shader of GaussianBlurring.hlsl.

This listing shows several register types we have not seen yet. Firstly, the input texture is declared as Texture2D<float4> and is assigned to register t0, which makes it a read-only texture. The input is processed in the application by attaching a *shader resource view* (SRV). The output texture is declared as RWTexture2D<float4>, which makes it writable and is assigned to register u0. The output is processed in the application by attaching an *unordered access view* (UAV). Although the RW prefix indicates read-write access, there are some restrictions on the data type for performing both reads and writes to a resource in the same call of the compute shader.

Secondly, there are registers named x0 and x1. These are referred to as *temporary indexable registers*. Their purpose is so we can index into the static arrays weight[][] and offset[][] when in the inner loop of the shader. The array values are loaded into the temporary indexable registers first, then the double loop is executed. You can see the nontrivial indexing x0[r2.x + 0].x and x1[r2.x + 0].xxyx inside the inner loop of the assembly code. Excessive use of temporary indexable registers can lead to a performance degradation because of the large number of mov instructions that are used to load the registers.

Looping itself can be a performance problem. Shader programs are most efficient when no branching is present. This a rule of thumb, but as always you need to profile to be sure. HLSL allows you to provide a hint that a loop should be unrolled by the compiler.. Modify the compute shader as shown next:

```
[unroll]
for (int r = 0; r < 3; ++r)
{
    [unroll]
    for (int c = 0; c < 3; ++c)
    {
        result += weight[r][c] * input[t + offset[r][c]];
    }
}
```

which tells the compiler to unroll both loops, if possible. In this case, the number of loop iterations is known at compile time, and we expect to obtain nine occurrences of the inner-loop body, say,

```
result += 0.0625f * input[int2(t.x − 1, t.y − 1)];
result += 0.1250f * input[int2(t.x    , t.y − 1)];
result += 0.0625f * input[int2(t.x + 1, t.y − 1)];
result += 0.1250f * input[int2(t.x − 1, t.y    )];
result += 0.2500f * input[int2(t.x    , t.y    )];
result += 0.1250f * input[int2(t.x + 1, t.y    )];
result += 0.0625f * input[int2(t.x − 1, t.y + 1)];
result += 0.1250f * input[int2(t.x    , t.y + 1)];
result += 0.0625f * input[int2(t.x + 1, t.y + 1)];
```

When you now compile the shader, you get the output of Listing 4.13.

```
//
// Generated by Microsoft (R) HLSL Shader Compiler 6.3.9600.16384
//
//
// Resource Bindings:
//
// Name                          Type   Format          Dim  Slot  Elements
// _____  _____  _____          ___  ____  _____
// input                         texture  float4          2d    0         1
// output                         UAV    float4          2d    0         1
//
//
//
// Input signature:
//
// Name              Index   Mask  Register  SysValue  Format   Used
// _____    _____   ____  _____  _____  _____   ____
// no Input
//
// Output signature:
//
// Name              Index   Mask  Register  SysValue  Format   Used
// _____    _____   ____  _____  _____  _____   ____
// no Output
cs_5_0
dcl_globalFlags refactoringAllowed
dcl_resource_texture2d (float, float, float, float) t0
dcl_uav_typed_texture2d (float, float, float, float) u0
dcl_input vThreadID.xy
dcl_temps 3
dcl_thread_group 8, 8, 1
mov r0.zw, l(0,0,0,0)
iadd r1.xyzw, vThreadID.xyxy, l(−1, −1, 0, −1)
mov r0.xy, r1.zwzz
```

```
ld_indexable(texture2d)(float,float,float,float) r0.xyz, r0.xyzw, t0.xyzw
mul r0.xyz, r0.xyzx, l(0.125000, 0.125000, 0.125000, 0.000000)
mov r1.zw, l(0,0,0,0)
ld_indexable(texture2d)(float,float,float,float) r1.xyz, r1.xyzw, t0.xyzw
mad r0.xyz, r1.xyzx, l(0.062500, 0.062500, 0.062500, 0.000000), r0.xyzx
mov r1.zw, l(0,0,0,0)
iadd r2.xyzw, vThreadID.xyxy, l(-1, 0, 1, -1)
mov r1.xy, r2.zwzz
ld_indexable(texture2d)(float,float,float,float) r1.xyz, r1.xyzw, t0.xyzw
mad r0.xyz, r1.xyzx, l(0.062500, 0.062500, 0.062500, 0.000000), r0.xyzx
mov r2.zw, l(0,0,0,0)
ld_indexable(texture2d)(float,float,float,float) r1.xyz, r2.xyzw, t0.xyzw
mad r0.xyz, r1.xyzx, l(0.125000, 0.125000, 0.125000, 0.000000), r0.xyzx
mov r1.xy, vThreadID.xyxx
mov r1.zw, l(0,0,0,0)
ld_indexable(texture2d)(float,float,float,float) r1.xyz, r1.xyzw, t0.xyzw
mad r0.xyz, r1.xyzx, l(0.250000, 0.250000, 0.250000, 0.000000), r0.xyzx
mov r1.zw, l(0,0,0,0)
iadd r2.xyzw, vThreadID.xyxy, l(-1, 1, 1, 0)
mov r1.xy, r2.zwzz
ld_indexable(texture2d)(float,float,float,float) r1.xyz, r1.xyzw, t0.xyzw
mad r0.xyz, r1.xyzx, l(0.125000, 0.125000, 0.125000, 0.000000), r0.xyzx
mov r2.zw, l(0,0,0,0)
ld_indexable(texture2d)(float,float,float,float) r1.xyz, r2.xyzw, t0.xyzw
mad r0.xyz, r1.xyzx, l(0.062500, 0.062500, 0.062500, 0.000000), r0.xyzx
mov r1.zw, l(0,0,0,0)
iadd r2.xyzw, vThreadID.xyxy, l(1, 1, 0, 1)
mov r1.xy, r2.zwzz
ld_indexable(texture2d)(float,float,float,float) r1.xyz, r1.xyzw, t0.xyzw
mad r0.xyz, r1.xyzx, l(0.125000, 0.125000, 0.125000, 0.000000), r0.xyzx
mov r2.zw, l(0,0,0,0)
ld_indexable(texture2d)(float,float,float,float) r1.xyz, r2.xyzw, t0.xyzw
mad r0.xyz, r1.xyzx, l(0.062500, 0.062500, 0.062500, 0.000000), r0.xyzx
mov r0.w, l(1.000000)
store_uav_typed u0.xyzw, vThreadID.xyyy, r0.xyzw
ret
// Approximately 39 instruction slots used
```

LISTING 4.13: The output assembly listing for the compute shader of GaussianBlurring.hlsl with loop unrolling.

The temporary indexable registers no longer occur. The static array values are used in literal values in the mul and mad instructions. How much faster can this be? On my AMD 7970, the sample application—without loop unrolling—runs at approximately 2200 frames per second. With loop unrolling, the application runs at approximately 3100 frames per second, which is a speedup of 1.4!

By the way, about the black borders in the images of Figure 4.9, this is due to out-of-range indexing in the compute shader when the pixel you process has neighbors outside of the image. On a CPU, you would test for boundary pixels and process accordingly. You can do the same on the GPU, either explicitly or by using the HLSL Sample instruction if the resource is a texture; however, you can also rely on the GPU to be consistent about fetching resources out of range. In particular, the ld_indexable instruction is guaranteed to return zero components for out-of-range indices in certain circumstances. The information is available through the online MSDN documentation, but there is no explicit entry for ld_indexable for either Shader Model 4 or Shader Model 5. You have to look at the Shader Model 4 documentation for the ld instruction [44].

4.2.5 Reflecting HLSL Shaders

So far the shader compiling has been illustrated using FXC; however, the shaders can be compiled at runtime using the D3DCompile function. Its signature is shown in Listing 4.14.

```
HRESULT D3DCompile(
    LPCVOID pSrcData,    // HLSL code as a string
    SIZE_T SrcDataSize,  // length of the string
    LPCSTR pSourceName,  // name for the string (optional)
    CONST D3D_SHADER_MACRO* pDefines,  // preprocessor (/D options in FXC)
    ID3DInclude* pInclude,  // specify an include file handler
    LPCSTR pEntrypoint,  // function to compile (the /E option in FXC)
    LPCSTR pTarget,  // profile to use (the /T option in FXC)
    UINT Flags1,  // options (such as /Zpr and /Gis in FXC)
    UINT Flags2,  // options for the DX11 effect system
    ID3DBlob** ppCode,  // output: byte code and other information
    ID3DBlob** ppErrorMsgs  // output: buffer of errors/warnings (if any)
);
```

LISTING 4.14: The signature for the D3DCompile function.

In previous versions of Direct3D, a compiler call was provided to compile the code in a file. This no longer exists, so the simplest thing to do is to load the file as text, build a string from the lines of text, and pass this to D3DCompile. The ID3DInclude* parameter is for advanced use, but the default used by GTEngine is D3D_COMPILE_STANDARD_FILE_INCLUDE. GTEngine also does not use the D3D11 effect system, so zero is passed for this parameter.

Assuming the compilation succeeded, the ID3DBlob* object returned in the next-to-last parameter stores the compiled code and information about it. In particular, the blob has the information we have been discussing that occurs in the text output from FXC. The blob may be queried for relevant information needed to know structure and buffer packing, to attach resources, and to execute the shaders at runtime. The query process is called *shader reflection*. The reflection function signature is shown in Listing 4.15.

```
HRESULT D3DReflect(
    LPCVOID pSrcData,    // compiled blob memory
    SIZE_T SrcDataSize,  // number of bytes in compiled blob memory
    REFIID pInterface,   // set to IID_ID3D11ShaderReflection for GTEngine
    void** ppReflector   // output: reflection interface
);
```

LISTING 4.15: The signature for the D3DReflect function.

Listing 4.16 shows how to compile the shader and perform reflection for some basic information. The reflection system has more features than are discussed here. In the code presented next, all calls are assumed to succeed, so the logic for handling HRESULT values is omitted for simplicity.

```
void CompileAndReflect(
    std::string hlsl,  // HLSL shader as a single string
    std::string name,  // string for ease of identification
    D3D_SHADER_MACRO defines[],  // macros provided by user
    ID3DINCLUDE* include,  // D3D_COMPILE_STANDARD_FILE_INCLUDE
    std::string entry,  // name of function; for example, "VSMain"
```

```
        std :: string target , // one of "vs_5_0", "ps_5_0", "gs_5_0", "cs_5_0"
        unsigned int compileFlags // bit flags that mimic options such as /Zpr
)
{
    // Compile the HLSL shader.
    ID3DBlob* compiledCode = nullptr;
    ID3DBlob* errors = nullptr;
    D3DCompile( hlsl.c_str(), hlsl.length(), name.c_str(),
        defines, include, entry.c_str(), target.c_str(), compileFlags, 0,
        &compiledCode, &errors );
    // On success, 'compiledCode' is not null and 'errors' is null.

    // Create the shader reflection interface.
    ID3D11ShaderReflection* reflector = nullptr;
    D3DReflect( compiledCode->GetBufferPointer(),
        compiledCode->GetBufferSize(), IID_ID3D11ShaderReflection,
        (void**)&reflector );
    // On success, 'reflector' is not null.

    // Get the top-level information about the shader.
    D3D11_SHADER_DESC shaderDesc;
    reflector->GetDesc(&shaderDesc);

    // Get the shader inputs (if any).
    for (UINT i = 0; i < shaderDesc.InputParameters; ++i)
    {
        D3D11_SIGNATURE_PARAMETER_DESC inputDesc;
        reflector->GetInputParameterDesc(i, &inputDesc);
    }

    // Get the shader outputs (if any).
    for (UINT i = 0; i < shaderDesc.InputParameters; ++i)
    {
        D3D11_SIGNATURE_PARAMETER_DESC outputDesc;
        reflector->GetOutputParameterDesc(i, &outputDesc);
    }

    // Get the "constant buffers", which includes constant buffers,
    // texture buffers, structs defined in shaders, and interface
    // pointers.
    for (UINT i = 0; i < shaderDesc.ConstantBuffers; ++i)
    {
        ID3D11ShaderReflectionConstantBuffer* cb =
            reflector->GetConstantBufferByIndex(i);
        D3D11_SHADER_BUFFER_DESC cbDesc;
        cb->GetDesc(&cbDesc);
        D3D11_SHADER_INPUT_BIND_DESC rbDesc;
        reflector->GetResourceBindingDescByName(cbDesc.Name, &rbDesc);
        GetVariables(cb, cbDesc.Variables);
    }

    // Get the resources bound to the shader.
    for (UINT i = 0; i < shaderDesc.BoundResources; ++i)
    {
        D3D11_SHADER_INPUT_BIND_DESC rbDesc;
        reflector->GetResourceBindingDesc(i, &rbDesc);
        if (rbDesc.Type == D3D_SIT_CBUFFER
        || rbDesc.Type == D3D_SIT_TBUFFER)
        {
            // These were processed in the last loop.
        }
        else if (rbDesc.Type == D3D_SIT_TEXTURE
        ||       rbDesc.Type == D3D_SIT_UAV_RWTYPED)
        {
            // number of channels [1 through 4]: 1 + (rbDesc.uFlags >> 2)
            // dimensions: determined by D3D_SRV_DIMENSION_* values
            // single or array: determined by D3D_SRV_DIMENSION_* values
```

```
                // writable in shader:  rbDesc.Type is D3D_SIT_UAV_RWTYPED
        }
        else if (rbDesc.Type == D3D_SIT_SAMPLER)
        {
            // no specialized information
        }
        else  // Other D3D_SIT_* values are for structured buffer types.
        {
            // writable in shader:  rbDesc.Type has UAV in its name
        }
    }
}

void GetVariables(ID3D11ShaderReflectionConstantBuffer* cb,
    UINT numVariables)
{
    for (UINT i = 0; i < numVariables; ++i)
    {
        ID3D11ShaderReflectionVariable* v = cb->GetVariableByIndex(i);
        ID3D11ShaderReflectionType* vType = v->GetType();
        D3D11_SHADER_VARIABLE_DESC vDesc;
        v->GetDesc(&vDesc);
        D3D11_SHADER_TYPE_DESC vtDesc;
        vType->GetDesc(&vtDesc);
        GetTypes(vType, vtDesc.Members);  // Recurse on nested structs.
    }
}

void GetTypes(ID3D11ShaderReflectionType* pType, unsigned int numChildren)
{
    for (UINT i = 0; i < numChildren; ++i)
    {
        ID3D11ShaderReflectionType* cType = pType->GetMemberTypeByIndex(i);
        char const* cName = pType->GetMemberTypeName(i);
        D3D11_SHADER_TYPE_DESC ctDesc;
        cType->GetDesc(&ctDesc);
        GetTypes(cType, ctDesc.Members);
    }
}
```

LISTING 4.16: Compile an HLSL program at runtime and start the shader reflection system.

The **HLSLFactory** library that ships with GTEngine is a wrapper around compilation and reflection. The error handling does exist in that code. The tool does not currently support reflection of dynamic linkage (the constant buffer case D3D_CT_INTERFACE_POINTERS).

A contrived HLSL compute shader that shows how to obtain member layouts for nested structures is provided in Listing 4.17. The point of the example is that a struct can have different member layouts depending on whether it is used in a constant buffer or as a structured buffer resource.

```
struct A { float fvalue[4]; int2 i2value; };
struct B { int ivalue; A avalue; };
cbuffer MyCBuffer { B input; };
StructuredBuffer<B> sbuffer[2];
Texture2D<float4> mytexture;
RWTexture1D<float> output;

[numthreads(1, 1, 1)]
void CSMain(int t : SV_DispatchThreadID)
{
```

```
float result = (float)input.ivalue;
for (int i = 0; i < 4; ++i)
{
    result += input.avalue.fvalue[i];
}
result += (float)input.avalue.i2value.x;
result += (float)input.avalue.i2value.y;
for (int j = 0; j < 2; ++j)
{
    B mybvalue = sbuffer[j][0];
    result += (float)mybvalue.ivalue;
    for (int k = 0; k < 4; ++k)
    {
        result += mybvalue.avalue.fvalue[k];
    }
    result += (float)mybvalue.avalue.i2value.x;
    result += (float)mybvalue.avalue.i2value.y;
}
result += mytexture[int2(0,0)].x;
output[0] = result;
}
```

LISTING 4.17: An example of nested structs for which constant buffers have one member layout but structured buffers have another member layout.

The output of **FXC** is shown in Listing 4.18. The generator comment was removed, white space was removed, the sbuffer layouts are the same for the two array members, the signatures were removed, and the ld_structured_indexable commands were split across multiple lines to fit in the width of the page.

```
// cbuffer MyCBuffer
// {
//    struct B
//    {
//        int ivalue;                // Offset:    0
//        struct A
//        {
//            float fvalue[4];       // Offset:   16
//            int2 i2value;          // Offset:   68
//        } avalue;                  // Offset:   16
//    } input;                       // Offset:    0 Size:    76
// }
//
// Resource bind info for sbuffer[0] and sbuffer[1]
// {
//    struct B
//    {
//        int ivalue;                // Offset:    0
//        struct A
//        {
//            float fvalue[4];       // Offset:    4
//            int2 i2value;          // Offset:   20
//        } avalue;                  // Offset:    4
//    } $Element;                    // Offset:    0 Size:    28
// }
//
// Resource Bindings:
//
// Name                     Type  Format     Dim Slot Elements
// ------------------------ ----- ---------- --- ---- --------
// sbuffer[0]               texture struct    r/o    0        1
// sbuffer[1]               texture struct    r/o    1        1
// mytexture                texture float4     2d    2        1
// output                      UAV  float      1d    0        1
// MyCBuffer                cbuffer   NA       NA    0        1
```

```
cs_5_0
dcl_globalFlags refactoringAllowed
dcl_constantbuffer cb0[5], immediateIndexed
dcl_resource_structured t0, 28
dcl_resource_structured t1, 28
dcl_resource_texture2d (float,float,float,float) t2
dcl_uav_typed_texture1d (float,float,float,float) u0
dcl_temps 2
dcl_thread_group 1, 1, 1
itof r0.x, cb0[0].x
add r0.x, r0.x, cb0[1].x
add r0.x, r0.x, cb0[2].x
add r0.x, r0.x, cb0[3].x
add r0.x, r0.x, cb0[4].x
itof r0.yz, cb0[4].yyzy
add r0.x, r0.y, r0.x
add r0.x, r0.z, r0.x
ld_structured_indexable(structured_buffer, stride=28)
    (mixed,mixed,mixed,mixed) r1.xyzw, l(0), l(0), t0.xyzw
itof r0.y, r1.x
add r0.x, r0.y, r0.x
add r0.x, r1.y, r0.x
add r0.x, r1.z, r0.x
add r0.x, r1.w, r0.x
ld_structured_indexable(structured_buffer, stride=28)
    (mixed,mixed,mixed,mixed) r0.yzw, l(0), l(16), t0.xxyz
add r0.x, r0.y, r0.x
itof r0.yz, r0.zzwz
add r0.x, r0.y, r0.x
add r0.x, r0.z, r0.x
ld_structured_indexable(structured_buffer, stride=28)
    (mixed,mixed,mixed,mixed) r1.xyzw, l(0), l(0), t1.xyzw
itof r0.y, r1.x
add r0.x, r0.y, r0.x
add r0.x, r1.y, r0.x
add r0.x, r1.z, r0.x
add r0.x, r1.w, r0.x
ld_structured_indexable(structured_buffer, stride=28)
    (mixed,mixed,mixed,mixed) r0.yzw, l(0), l(16), t1.xxyz
add r0.x, r0.y, r0.x
itof r0.yz, r0.zzwz
add r0.x, r0.y, r0.x
add r0.x, r0.z, r0.x
ld_indexable(texture2d)(float,float,float,float) r0.y, l(0, 0, 0, 0),
    t2.yxzw
add r0.x, r0.y, r0.x
store_uav_typed u0.xyzw, l(0,0,0,0), r0.xxxx
ret
// Approximately 34 instruction slots used
```

LISTING 4.18: A modified listing of the FXC output from the compute shader of Listing 4.17.

Notice that the constant buffer version of struct B uses 76 bytes but the structured buffer version uses 28 bytes. The latter is what you expect in a C-style struct that has seven members, each requiring 4 bytes. The constant buffer version is adhering to the HLSL packing rules. What still caught my attention, though, is the number 76. Given that each register uses 16 bytes, why not 80 bytes? I also thought at first that the constant buffer would use six registers requiring 96 bytes, because ivalue is stored in one register, each of the four fvalue array elements is stored in a register, and i2value uses one register. My thinking was incorrect. In fact, i2value is stored in the yz-channels of the register that stores fvalue[3] in its *x*-channel. This explains the size 76 rather than 80, because the 4-byte *w*-channel is unused. The layout is verified by the assembly instructions. The last typecast of float to int is the instruction itof r0.yz, cb0[4].yyzy that effectively copies the *yz*-channels of cb0[4] into the *yz*-channels of temporary register r0.

The shader reflection system produces a description whose non-default-value members are shown in Listing 4.19 with some comments added.

```
desc.Creator = "Microsoft (R) HLSL Shader Compiler 6.3.9600.16384"
desc.Version = 0x00050050      // vs_5_0
desc.Flags = 0x0000a908        // D3DCOMPILE_* flags
desc.ConstantBuffers = 3       // MyCBuffer, sbuffer[0,1]
desc.BoundResources = 5        // MyCBuffer, sbuffer[0,1], mytexture, output
desc.InstructionCount = 34     // start is first 'itof', final is 'ret'
desc.TempRegisterCount = 2     // 'dcl_temps 2''
desc.TextureLoadInstructions = 5    // 'ld_*' instructions
desc.FloatInstructionCount = 21     // 'add' instructions
desc.StaticFlowControlCount = 1     // 'ret' instruction
desc.cTextureStoreInstructions = 1  // 'store_uav_typed' instruction
```

LISTING 4.19: The non-default-value members of D3D11_SHADER_DESC for the compute shader of Listing 4.17.

The constant buffer loop produces the information shown in Listing 4.20. The one- and two-letter prefixes are from the D3D description member names, used here for the descriptions to fit the width of the page. The descriptions for sbuffer[0] and sbuffer[1] are the same, so only one block is written here.

```
cbDesc[0] {n="MyCBuffer", t=D3D_CT_CBUFFER, v=1, s=80, f=0}
rbDesc[0] {n="MyCBuffer", t=D3D_SIT_CBUFFER, bp=0, bc=1, f=0, rt=0,
            d=D3D_SRV_DIMENSION_UNKNOWN, ns=0}
  vDesc[0] {n="input", o=0, s=76, f=2, dv=null, stex=-1, texs=0, ssam=-1,
            sams=0}
  vtDesc[0] {cl=D3D_SVC_STRUCT, t=D3D_SVT_VOID, r=1, c=7, e=0, m=2, o=0,
            n="B"}
    cName="ivalue"
    ctDesc[0] {cl=D3D_SVC_SCALAR, t=D3D_SVT_INT, r=1, c=1, e=0, m=0, o=0,
            n="int"}
    cName="avalue"
    ctDesc[1] {cl=D3D_SVC_STRUCT, t=D3D_SVT_VOID, r=1, c=6, e=0, m=2, o=16,
            n="A"}
      ctDesc[0] {cl=D3D_SVC_SCALAR, t=D3D_SVT_FLOAT, r=1, c=1, e=4, m=0,
            o=0, n="float"}
      ctDesc[1] {cl=D3D_SVC_VECTOR, t=D3D_SVT_INT, r=1, c=2, e=0, m=0,
            o=52, n="int2"}

cbDesc[1,2] {n="sbuffer[0]", t=D3D_CT_RESOURCE_BIND_INFO, v=1, s=28, f=0}
rbDesc[1,2] {n="sbuffer[0]", t=D3D_SIT_STRUCTURED, bp=[0,1], bc=1, f=0,
            rt=D3D_RETURN_TYPE_MIXED, d=D3D_SRV_DIMENSION_BUFFER, ns=28}
  vDesc[0] {n="$Element", o=0, s=28, f=2, dv=null, stex=-1, texs=0,
            ssam=-1, sams=0}
  vtDesc[0] {cl=D3D_SVC_STRUCT, t=D3D_SVT_VOID, r=1, c=7, e=0, m=2, o=0,
            n="B"}
    cName="ivalue"
    ctDesc[0] {cl=D3D_SVC_SCALAR, t=D3D_SVT_INT, r=1, c=1, e=0, m=0, o=0,
            n="int"}
    cName="avalue"
    ctDesc[1] {cl=D3D_SVC_STRUCT, t=D3D_SVT_VOID, r=1, c=6, e=0, m=2, o=4,
            n="A"}
      cName="fvalue"
      ctDesc[0] {cl=D3D_SVC_SCALAR, t=D3D_SVT_FLOAT, r=1, c=1, e=4, m=0,
```

```
                              o=0, n="float"}
        cName="i2value"
        ctDesc[1] { cl=D3D_SVC_VECTOR, t=D3D_SVT_INT, r=1, c=2, e=0, m=0,
                              o=16, n="int2"}
```

LISTING 4.20: Descriptions about the constant buffers in the compute shader of Listing 4.17.

The descriptions for MyCBuffer indicate that the size is 80 bytes, the bind point is 0, and the bind count is 1. This information is needed by an application to create a DX11 buffer and to attach the resource to the shader program for execution. The variable and variable type descriptions provide the layout of the constant buffer. The vDesc[0] item says the constant buffer name used in the HLSL code is input and uses 76 of the 80 bytes of storage. The flag value two comes from bit flags in D3D_SHADER_VARIABLE_FLAGS, in this case a single flag D3D_SVF_USED that indicates the constant buffers is used in the shader.

The corresponding vtDesc[0] item describes the type of the variable. The type has name B and is a struct type (D3D_SVC_STRUCT and D3D_SVT_VOID). The r and c values are for rows and columns of a matrix type, but these are filled even when the type is not of matrix form. You must also look at the e value (number of elements). In the example at hand, $e = 0$, which indicates that the type is not of matrix form; rather, it is viewed as a single row ($r = 1$) of seven ($c = 7$) 4-byte quantities: ivalue (one 4-byte value), avalue.fvalue[0,1,2,3] (four 4-byte quantities), and avalue.i2value (two 4-byte quantities). The offset $o = 0$ is measured relative to the beginning of the constant buffer storage. The number of members (or children) is $m = 2$, indicating that struct B has two members: ivalue and avalue.

The recursive function GetTypes in Listing 4.16 produces the cName and ctDesc items in Listing 4.20. The first visited child (of B) has name ivalue and has type name int. Thus, it is a integer scalar type (D3D_SVC_SCALAR and D3D_SVT_INT). It is not of matrix form, so $e = 0$. As a scalar, it is viewed as a single row ($r = 1$) with one column ($c = 1$). Its offset is $o = 0$ and is measured relative to the base address of its parent. The parent is MyCBuffer, and we saw that input has offset zero. The absolute offset of ivalue is obtained by adding its relative offset zero to the parent offset zero (of input), which is zero; that is, ivalue fills the first four bytes of the constant buffer memory.

The second visited child of B has name avalue and has type name A. This member is itself a struct (D3D_SVC_STRUCT and D3D_SVT_VOID). The number of elements is $e = 0$, so A is not of matrix form but it is viewed as a single row ($r = 1$) of six ($c = 6$) 4-byte values: fvalue[0,1,2,3] (four 4-byte quantities) and i2value (two 4-byte quantities). The offset is $o = 16$, relative to the parent B, so the absolute offset in the constant buffer is sixteen. The number is sixteen because the packing rules for constant buffers requires ivalue to be stored in a 16-byte register, in which case A is stored starting in the next available register. The number of members is $m = 2$, indicating that struct A has two members: fvalue and i2value.

The first visited child of A has name fvalue and has type name float. It is a float scalar type (D3D_SVC_SCALAR and D3D_SVT_FLOAT). The number of elements is $e = 4$; because this number is not zero, this is of matrix form. The number of rows is $r = 1$, so the matrix is really a one-dimensional array that has $e = 4$ elements and each element has $c = 1$ columns. This is a fancy way of saying that the fvalue is an array of four float values, but the bookkeeping allows for handling general arrays of general elements. The relative offset from the base address of A is $o = 0$, so the absolute address from the base address of MyCBuffer is sixteen.

The second visited child of A has name i2value and has type name int2, indicating it is a 2-tuple of integers. This is a vector type as compared to a scalar type (D3D_SVC_VECTOR and D3D_SVT_INT). The number of elements is zero, so it is not of matrix form. It has $r = 1$ rows and $c = 2$ columns, the latter indicating that i2value is a 2-tuple. This member is not a struct so it has no children ($m = 0$). The relative offset from the base address of A is $o = 52$. As described previously, fvalue[3] is stored in the x-component of a register and i2value is stored in the yz-components, which leads to the offset value of 52. The absolute offset from the base address of MyCBuffer is $16 + 52 = 68$. This is the number displayed next to i2value in the MyCBuffer comments of Listing 4.18.

The descriptions of B for sbuffer[0] and sbuffer[1] are identical *except for the offset values*. As a structured buffer type, B is packed just as you would expect for a C-struct using 32-bit alignment, in this case seven 4-byte values are packed into a 28-byte chunk of memory.

The loop over the resources bound to the shader leads to a visit of MyCBuffer, which is ignored in this loop because it was processed in the previous loop, and visits to sbuffer[0,1], mytexture, and output. The resource binding description for sbuffer[0] shows it is of type D3D_SIT_STRUCTURED (read-only structured buffer) and has bind point zero. The bind point for sbuffer[1] is one. The bind points must be known by the application for attaching the resources to the shader for execution.

The resource binding description for mytexture shows it is of type D3D_SIT_TEXTURE (read-only texture). The bind point is two, which is the next available bind point for read-only inputs after the structured buffers are assigned bind points; these are assigned in the order the resources occur in the HLSL code. The return type is D3D_RETURN_TYPE_FLOAT, which is a consequence of using float4 in the template Texture2D<float4>. The number of components is obtained from the flags value $f = 12$ by the formula $4 = 1 + (f >> 2)$. Thus, the return type and the flags can be used to determine the template type, something that might be useful for a tool that generates C++ source code from an HLSL program in order to wrap all the resource management of that program. The dimension of this texture is reported as D3D_SRV_DIMENSION_TEXTURE2D.

The resource binding description for output shows it is of type D3D_SIT_UAV_RWTYPED (read-write texture). The fact that it is an *unordered access view* (UAV) means that the shader writes to the resource. In some cases you can read and write the resource, but this is limited to resources with a native 32-bit template type; for example, RWTexture2D<float>. The bind point is zero, which is needed by the application for attaching the resource for shader execution. The return type is also D3D_RETURN_TYPE_FLOAT, but the flag's value is $f = 0$ which implies there is $1 = 1 + (f >> 2)$ component. Thus, the reflection indicates that output was declared as RWTexture1D<float>. The dimension is reported as D3D_SRV_DIMENSION_TEXTURE1D.

4.3   Devices, Contexts, and Swap Chains

The top-level objects required for accessing the capabilities of a GPU are *devices and immediate contexts*. The immediate context is used to queue up GPU commands that are to be executed immediately (as soon as possible) on the GPU. D3D11 also has the concept of a *deferred context* where GPU command lists are inserted for execution at a later time. Deferred contexts are useful for coarse-level management of the GPU in multithreaded applications. Although useful, this book does not contain a discussion about deferred contexts. The GTEngine code is based on immediate contexts and takes advantage of the thread-safe device for creating resources to be used by the GPU at the appropriate times.

Compute shaders may be executed using only the services of a device and an immediate context. Drawing to a window using vertex, geometry, and pixel shaders requires additional D3D11 objects. Specifically, you need a *swap chain* and one or more pairs of color and depth-stencil buffers. The classical case, designed for performance, is to have two pairs for *double buffering*. The graphics system can draw to the *back buffer* while the *front buffer* is displayed to the monitor. Once complete, the two buffers are *swapped*, which is the responsibility of the swap chain object.

4.3.1   Creating a Device and an Immediate Context

A device and a corresponding immediate context are created by the D3D11 function

```
HRESULT D3D11CreateDevice (
    IDXGIAdapter* pAdapter ,
    D3D_DRIVER_TYPE DriverType ,
    HMODULE Software ,
    UINT Flags ,
    CONST D3D_FEATURE_LEVEL* pFeatureLevels ,
    UINT FeatureLevels ,
    UINT SDKVersion ,
    ID3D11Device** ppDevice ,
    D3D_FEATURE_LEVEL* pFeatureLevel ,
    ID3D11DeviceContext** ppImmediateContext );
```

where the last three parameters are the outputs of the creation. The standard use of this call is to obtain access to hardware acceleration on a machine with a single GPU. The function call is

```
UINT const numFeatureLevels = 7;
D3D_FEATURE_LEVEL const featureLevels[numFeatureLevels] =
{
    D3D_FEATURE_LEVEL_11_1,
    D3D_FEATURE_LEVEL_11_0,
    D3D_FEATURE_LEVEL_10_1,
    D3D_FEATURE_LEVEL_10_0,
    D3D_FEATURE_LEVEL_9_3,
    D3D_FEATURE_LEVEL_9_2,
    D3D_FEATURE_LEVEL_9_1
};

ID3D11Device* device;
D3D_FEATURE_LEVEL selectedFeatureLevel
ID3D11DeviceContext* immediateContext;
HRESULT hr = D3D11CreateDevice(nullptr, D3D_DRIVER_TYPE_HARDWARE,
    nullptr, 0, featureLevels, numFeatureLevels, D3D11_SDK_VERSION,
    &device, &selectedFeatureLevel, &immediateContext);
```

The featureLevels are listed in order of the feature set you want for the device. If Direct3D 11.1 is available on the machine, that feature will be selected. If it is not available but Direct3D 11.0 is available, that feature will be selected. The output selectedFeatureLevel indicates which feature level the device is. On success, hr is S_OK and both device and immediateContext are not null.

When the adapter input is null, the default adapter is requested and is the one associated with the GPU. If you have multiple GPUs, you can obtain nonnull adapter pointers by enumeration; see Section 4.8 for details on how to create devices and contexts when multiple GPUs are present.

The driver type is usually hardware, but other options are available. These include the ability to use software rendering and to create a *reference device.* The latter supports the D3D11 SDK in software and is mainly useful for debugging. Drivers shipped by graphics card manufacturers can have bugs in them. A comparison of outputs for the hardware-accelerated device and reference device might lead to proof that a driver has a bug. The HMODULE input must be null for hardware acceleration. If you happen to have written a software rasterizer you want to test, you can do so in a DLL, load that DLL, and use its module handle as the input to device creation. I do not discuss this capability in the book.

The Flags input is typically zero; otherwise, it may be a combination of D3D11_CREATE_DEVICE_FLAGS bit flags. Two bit flags that are useful for debugging are

D3D11_CREATE_DEVICE_DEBUG, D3D11_CREATE_DEVICE_SINGLETHREADED

I use the debug flag regularly and add the application to the list of executables monitored by the DirectX Control Panel; see Section 5.2 for details. The single-threading flag is useful if you believe your multithreaded application might have threading problems regarding the graphics system and you want to verify by showing that the single-threaded version runs correctly.

The feature levels of interest to you are provided via an array. You are not required to list all available levels. For example, if you know you are running on a machine with Direct3D 11.0 and want only a device of that type, you can define a featureLevels array with the single element D3D_FEATURE_LEVEL_11_0. The device creation does allow you to pass a null pointer, but at the present time the call will not create a D3D11.1 device when on a machine with D3D11.1.

The device and immediate context are reference counted, so when you are finished with them you must call their Release() functions.

4.3.2 Creating Swap Chains

Assuming you have created a window with an associated handle and whose client rectangle has a specified width and height, you can create a swap chain for a device as shown in Listing 4.21. For simplicity of presentation, no HRESULT error handling is included. The actual engine code does include this.

```
void CreateSwapChain(HWND handle, UINT width, UINT height,
    ID3D11Device* device, IDXGISwapChain*& swapChain)
{
    // Get a DXGI device and factory that will be used for creating the
    // swap chain.
    IDXGIDevice* dxgiDevice = nullptr;
    device->QueryInterface(__uuidof(IDXGIDevice), (void**)&dxgiDevice);
    IDXGIAdapter* dxgiAdapter = nullptr;
    dxgiDevice->GetAdapter(&dxgiAdapter);
    IDXGIFactory1* dxgiFactory = nullptr;
    dxgiAdapter->GetParent(__uuidof(IDXGIFactory1), (void**)&dxgiFactory);

    // Create the swap chain.
    DXGI_SWAP_CHAIN_DESC desc;
    desc.BufferDesc.Width = width;
    desc.BufferDesc.Height = height;
    desc.BufferDesc.RefreshRate.Numerator = 0;
    desc.BufferDesc.RefreshRate.Denominator = 1;
    desc.BufferDesc.Format = DXGI_FORMAT_R8G8B8A8_UNORM;
    desc.BufferDesc.ScanlineOrdering =
        DXGI_MODE_SCANLINE_ORDER_UNSPECIFIED;
    desc.BufferDesc.Scaling = DXGI_MODE_SCALING_UNSPECIFIED;
    desc.SampleDesc.Count = 1;
    desc.SampleDesc.Quality = 0;
    desc.BufferUsage =
        DXGI_USAGE_BACK_BUFFER | DXGI_USAGE_RENDER_TARGET_OUTPUT;
    desc.BufferCount = 2;
    desc.OutputWindow = handle;
    desc.Windowed = TRUE;
    desc.SwapEffect = DXGI_SWAP_EFFECT_DISCARD;
    desc.Flags = 0;
    IDXGISwapChain* swapChain = nullptr;
    dxgiFactory->CreateSwapChain(dxgiDevice, &desc, &swapChain);

    // Clean up and return.
    dxgiFactory->Release();
    dxgiAdapter->Release();
    dxgiDevice->Release();
    return swapChain;
}
```

LISTING 4.21: Creating a swap chain for displaying graphics data to a window.

The refresh rate is specified as a rational number in units of hertz. The rational number 0/1 indicates that the default refresh rate of the monitor should be used. The scanline ordering and scaling parameters are listed as unspecified, allowing the display system to use its defaults. The sample description is for multisampling; the default values are specified (no multisampling).

The buffer usage flag DXGI_USAGE_RENDER_TARGET indicates that you intend to write to the back buffer for output. It is possible to use back buffers as inputs to shaders and as unordered access views. The buffer count is two, indicating that you want a back buffer and a front buffer.

For classical drawing, the color output format is 8-bit RGBA. DXGI_FORMAT_R8G8B8A8_UNORM represents such a format; the UNORM prefix indicates that floating-point color channel values in $[0, 1]$ are interpreted as 8-bit values in $\{0, \ldots, 255\}$. It is possible to specify 16-bit RGBA or 10-10-10-2 RGBA format, which is useful when the back buffer is set up to be used as an input to a shader.

A window can be created to be full screen, but the advice is to create a windowed swap chain and use IDXGISwapChain::SetFullscreenState to toggle between windowed mode and full-screen mode.

The swap effect parameter indicates that the back buffer contents are discarded after the swap. Other parameters allow the back buffer contents to persist. In particular, for a Window Store application the swap effect must be DXGI_SWAP_EFFECT_FLIP_SEQUENTIAL. The creation of swap chains with advanced features is not described in this book. You can obtain more information from the MSDN online documentation about such features.

Once you are finished using a swap chain, remember to call its Release() function in order to decrement its reference count.

In GTEngine for the purpose of this book, swap chains are created as shown in Listing 4.21. You are welcome to explore other choices for the parameters. It is possible to create the device, the immediate context, and the swap chain all in one interface call: D3D11CreateDeviceAndSwapChain. In GTEngine, I have chosen to keep the creation calls separate.

In addition to a swap chain, you need to create a back buffer that consists typically of a color buffer and a depth-stencil buffer. For drawing, you also need various state information related to rasterization and blending operations. The creation of these are discussed in Section 4.4.

4.3.3 Creating the Back Buffer

Once the swap chain has been created, we need to associate with it the color and depth-stencil buffers that make up the back buffer. Listing 4.22 shows the creation, requiring both the device and its immediate context. For simplicity of presentation, no HRESULT error handling is included. The actual engine code does include the handling.

```
void CreateBackBuffer (UINT width, UINT height, ID3D11Device* device,
    ID3D11DeviceContext* immediateContext, IDXGISwapChain* swapChain,
```

```
ID3D11Texture2D*& colorBuffer , ID3D11RenderTargetView*& colorView ,
ID3D11Texture2D*& depthStencilBuffer ,
ID3D11DepthStencilView*& depthStencilView )
{
    // Create the color buffer and color view.
    swapChain->GetBuffer(0, __uuidof(ID3D11Texture2D),
        (void**)&colorBuffer);
    device->CreateRenderTargetView(colorBuffer , nullptr , &colorView );

    // Create the depth-stencil buffer and depth-stencil view.
    D3D11_TEXTURE2D_DESC desc;
    desc.Width = width;
    desc.Height = height;
    desc.MipLevels = 1;
    desc.ArraySize = 1;
    desc.Format = DXGI_FORMAT_D24_UNORM_S8_UINT;
    desc.SampleDesc.Count = 1;
    desc.SampleDesc.Quality = 0;
    desc.Usage = D3D11_USAGE_DEFAULT;
    desc.BindFlags = D3D11_BIND_DEPTH_STENCIL;
    desc.CPUAccessFlags = 0;
    desc.MiscFlags = 0;
    device->CreateTexture2D(&desc, nullptr , &depthStencilBuffer );
    device->CreateDepthStencilView(depthStencilBuffer , nullptr ,
        &depthStencilView );

    // Set the viewport to cover the entire window and the entire
    // depth range.
    D3D11_VIEWPORT viewport;
    viewport.Width = static_cast<float>(width);
    viewport.Height = static_cast<float>(height);
    viewport.TopLeftX = 0.0f;
    viewport.TopLeftY = 0.0f;
    viewport.MinDepth = 0.0f;
    viewport.MaxDepth = 1.0f;
    immediateContext->RSSetViewports(1, &viewport);

    // Set the color view and depth-stencil view to be active.
    immediateContext->OMSetRenderTargets(1, &colorView , depthStencilView );
}
```

LISTING 4.22: Creating a back buffer.

At various times during execution, you might want to set the color buffer or depth-stencil buffer to constant values via *clearing*. This can be done using a context; for example,

```
// clear color
float clearColor[4] = { 0.0f, 0.1f, 0.5f, 0.7f };   // RGBA
context->ClearRenderTargetView(colorView , clearColor)

// clear depth, stencil value ignored
float clearDepth = 0.5f;
context->ClearDepthStencilView(depthStencilView , D3D11_CLEAR_DEPTH,
    clearDepth , 0);

// clear stencil, depth value ignored
unsigned char clearStencil = 16;
context->ClearDepthStencilView(depthStencilView , D3D11_CLEAR_STENCIL, 0.0f,
    clearStencil );

// clear depth and stencil
context->ClearDepthStencilView(depthStencilView ,
    D3D11_CLEAR_DEPTH | D3D11_CLEAR_STENCIL, clearDepth , clearStencil );
```

The views determine which portions of the buffers are set to the constant values. The color and depth-stencil views created for the back buffer have views that cover the entire buffer, so all buffer values are set. It is possible to have multiple views for a single buffer, so if you want to clear only a subrectangle of a buffer, you must create a view of that size and pass that to the clear calls.

Once you are finished using the color buffer, color view, depth-stencil buffer, and depth-stencil view, remember to call their Release() functions so that their reference counts are decremented. If you plan on resizing the window during runtime, you will need to destroy the current back buffer objects and create new ones for the modified width and height. This is accomplished using IDXGISwapChain::ResizeBuffers. You must release the old objects first, call the ResizeBuffers function, and then create the new objects.

4.4   Resources

The HLSL shader programs discussed previously had various resources that needed to be attached for input and output, explicitly declared as constant buffers, structured buffers, textures, and sampler state. For drawing, we also had the implicit occurrence of vertex buffers (input to vertex shaders) and index buffers (geometric primitives that determine input to pixel shaders during rasterization). Other types of resources are available for more advanced computing and drawing.

D3D11 uses a hierarchy of COM interfaces with base IUnknown. The ID3D11Device interface inherits from IUnknown and the ID3D11DeviceContext interface inherits from ID3D11DeviceChild. A subhierarchy of interfaces related to the resources that may be attached to shaders for execution is shown next:

```
ID3D11DeviceChild
    ID3D11Resource
        ID3D11Buffer
        ID3D11Texture1D
        ID3D11Texture2D
        ID3D11Texture3D
    ID3D11BlendState
    ID3D11DepthStencilState
    ID3D11RasterizerState
    ID3D11SamplerState
    ID3D11VertexShader
    ID3D11GeometryShader
    ID3D11PixelShader
    ID3D11ComputeShader
```

The number of flavors of resources is more than the four listed under ID3D11Resource; for example, cube maps and texture-array resources are created as part of the aforementioned interfaces. The desired resource is selected via parameters to a description structure. For the purpose of object-oriented design using C++ virtual functions, it would have been convenient to have interfaces such as ID3D11Texture, ID3D11State, and ID3D11Shader from which the appropriate interfaces inherit. GTEngine deals with this by having a richer hierarchy of C++ classes that are tied to D3D11 objects via the *bridge pattern* but with some similarities to the *adapter pattern* [12]. See Section 5.1 for the GTEngine hierarchy and how those classes avoid accessing D3D11-specific information in order to hide the implementation details in the graphics engine. This abstraction is necessary when the time comes to provide a graphics engine for OpenGL and GLSL shader programming.

The main resource categories are *buffers*, *textures*, and *texture arrays*. The D3D11 mechanism for creating textures allows you to specify a singleton or an array, but the texture arrays require the concept of *subresource* to access elements of the array. The idea of subresource also applies to mipmaps of textures. In the presentation, I have separated out the texture-array resource discussion in order to emphasize the slightly different creation semantics compared to singleton textures.

Another category I call *draw targets*, which are containers that encapsulate render targets and depth-stencil textures for drawing to offscreen memory. The back buffer discussed in Section 4.3.3 is essentially a draw target that encapsulates a render target and a depth-stencil texture for direct display to the screen. Although a draw target is not a D3D11 construct, it is in GTEngine and simplifies working with offscreen drawing.

4.4.1   Resource Usage and CPU Access

The various description structures used to create resources have a member of type D3D11_USAGE and flags for CPU access related to copying,

```
enum D3D11_USAGE
{
    D3D11_USAGE_DEFAULT ,
    D3D11_USAGE_IMMUTABLE,
    D3D11_USAGE_DYNAMIC ,
    D3D11_USAGE_STAGING
};

enum D3D11_CPU_ACCESS_FLAG
{
    D3D11_CPU_ACCESS_WRITE = 0x10000L ,
    D3D11_CPU_ACCESS_READ  = 0x20000L
};
```

The default usage flag indicates the resource requires both read and write access by the GPU. The immutable usage flag indicates that the resource may be read by the GPU but not written to by the GPU; such a resource must have its memory initialized on creation. The dynamic usage flag declares that the resource may be read by the GPU and written by the CPU. Typical examples are constant buffers that store the transformations for positioning and orienting 3D objects or vertex buffers for deformable geometry. A dynamic resource is modified frequently by mapping the memory and providing a pointer to the data so the CPU can write to it. The staging usage is designed to support the transfer of video memory from the GPU to the CPU, which I refer to as *read-back from the GPU*, although the transfer can be in the other direction as well; see Section 4.7 for the details of how staging buffers are used.

The usage and CPU access are not independent concepts. In all the description structures discussed later (except for staging resources), a description desc has members desc.Usage and desc.CPUAccessFlags. Assuming an abstract input object that has requests input.wantImmutable, input.wantDynamic, and input.wantShaderOutput, the description members are set as shown in Listing 4.23.

```
void SetUsageAccess(desc, input)
{
    if (input.wantImmutable)
    {
        desc.Usage = D3D11_USAGE_IMMUTABLE;
        desc.CPUAccessFlags = 0;
    }
    else if (input.wantDynamic)
    {
        desc.Usage = D3D11_USAGE_DYNAMIC;
        desc.CPUAccessFlags = D3D11_CPU_ACCESS_WRITE;
    }
    else // input.wantShaderOutput
    {
        desc.Usage = D3D11_USAGE_DEFAULT;
        desc.CPUAccessFlags = 0;
    }
}
```

LISTING 4.23: Common code for setting the usage and CPU access for a description structure.

The usage and access might be modified additionally depending on the specific resource at hand. In particular, if a resource is declared as a render target, the usage must be D3D11_USAGE_DEFAULT. Staging resources are handled separately. The various code blocks will call this function and make it clear if usage and access must be modified.

4.4.2 Resource Views

Resources are created, but they are not accessed directly during graphics processing. Instead you need to create *views* of the resources. Think of an analogy with databases. The resource is the database and you can have multiple views of that database. The two common categories are *shader resource views* that are applied to shader inputs (read-only resources) and *unordered access views* that are applied to shader outputs (read-write resources). You can also create *render-target views* and *depth-stencil views* for working with frame buffers. In fact, these were used in the creation of the back buffer; see Section 4.3.3 for the details.

Listing 4.24 shows the description structure for a shader resource view and how to create such a view. Specific assignment of members of the description for each resource type is discussed in later sections.

```
struct D3D11_SHADER_RESOURCE_VIEW_DESC
{
    DXGI_FORMAT Format;
    D3D11_SRV_DIMENSION ViewDimension;
    union {
        D3D11_BUFFER_SRV  Buffer;
        D3D11_TEX1D_SRV  Texture1D;
        D3D11_TEX1D_ARRAY_SRV  Texture1DArray;
        D3D11_TEX2D_SRV  Texture2D;
        D3D11_TEX2D_ARRAY_SRV  Texture2DArray;
        D3D11_TEX2DMS_SRV  Texture2DMS;
        D3D11_TEX2DMS_ARRAY_SRV  Texture2DMSArray;
        D3D11_TEX3D_SRV  Texture3D;
        D3D11_TEXCUBE_SRV  TextureCube;
        D3D11_TEXCUBE_ARRAY_SRV  TextureCubeArray;
        D3D11_BUFFEREX_SRV  BufferEx;
    };
};

ID3D11Resource* resource = // The resource to be viewed for reading.
D3D11_SHADER_RESOURCE_VIEW_DESC srDesc;  // Set members as desired.
ID3D11ShaderResourceView* srView;
HRESULT hr = device->CreateShaderResourceView(resource, &srDesc, &srView);
```

LISTING 4.24: The description for a shader resource view and the code to create the view.

The ViewDimension member is set to a flag that indicates which of the union cases the view represents. Each case has its own structure of values that must be set according to the desired view capabilities.

Listing 4.25 shows the description structure for an unordered access view and how to create such a view. Specific assignment of members of the description for each resource type is discussed in later sections.

```
struct D3D11_UNORDERED_ACCESS_VIEW_DESC
{
    DXGI_FORMAT Format;
    D3D11_UAV_DIMENSION ViewDimension;
    union {
        D3D11_BUFFER_UAV  Buffer;
        D3D11_TEX1D_UAV  Texture1D;
        D3D11_TEX1D_ARRAY_UAV  Texture1DArray;
        D3D11_TEX2D_UAV  Texture2D;
        D3D11_TEX2D_ARRAY_UAV  Texture2DArray;
        D3D11_TEX3D_UAV  Texture3D;
    };
};

ID3D11Resource* resource = // The resource to be viewed for writing.
D3D11_UNORDERED_ACCESS_VIEW_DESC uaDesc;  // Set members as desired.
ID3D11UnorderedAccessView* uaView;
HRESULT hr = device->CreateUnorderedAccessView(resource, &uaDesc, &uaView);
```

LISTING 4.25: The description for an unordered access view and the code to create the view.

The ViewDimension member is set to a flag that indicates which of the union cases the view represents. Each case has its own structure of values that must be set according to the desired view capabilities.

Although render targets and depth-stencils are created as 2D textures, they need separate interfaces for creating views for writing. Listing 4.26 shows the description structures for these objects and how to create views.

```
struct D3D11_RENDER_TARGET_VIEW_DESC
{
    DXGI_FORMAT Format;
    D3D11_RTV_DIMENSION ViewDimension;
    union {
        D3D11_BUFFER_RTV Buffer;
        D3D11_TEX1D_RTV Texture1D;
        D3D11_TEX1D_ARRAY_RTV Texture1DArray;
        D3D11_TEX2D_RTV Texture2D;
        D3D11_TEX2D_ARRAY_RTV Texture2DArray;
        D3D11_TEX2DMS_RTV Texture2DMS;
        D3D11_TEX2DMS_ARRAY_RTV Texture2DMSArray;
        D3D11_TEX3D_RTV Texture3D;
    };
};

struct D3D11_DEPTH_STENCIL_VIEW_DESC
{
    DXGI_FORMAT Format;
    D3D11_DSV_DIMENSION ViewDimension;
    UINT Flags;
    union {
        D3D11_TEX1D_DSV Texture1D;
        D3D11_TEX1D_ARRAY_DSV Texture1DArray;
        D3D11_TEX2D_DSV Texture2D;
        D3D11_TEX2D_ARRAY_DSV Texture2DArray;
        D3D11_TEX2DMS_DSV Texture2DMS;
        D3D11_TEX2DMS_ARRAY_DSV Texture2DMSArray;
    };
};

ID3D11Texture2D* renderTarget = // The resource to be viewed for writing.
D3D11_RENDER_TARGET_VIEW_DESC rtDesc;   // Set members as desired.
ID3D11RenderTargetView* rtView;
HRESULT hr = device->CreateUnorderedAccessView(renderTarget, &rtDesc,
                                               &rtView);

ID3D11Texture2D* depthStencil = // The resource to be viewed for writing.
D3D11_DEPTH_STENCIL_VIEW_DESC dsDesc;   // Set members as desired.
ID3D11DepthStencilView* dsView;
HRESULT hr = device->CreateUnorderedAccessView(depthStencil, &dsDesc,
                                               &dsView);
```

LISTING 4.26: The descriptions for render target and depth-stencil views and the code to create the views.

The ViewDimension member is set to a flag that indicates which of the union cases the view represents. Each case has its own structure of values that must be set according to the desired view capabilities. The depth-stencil Flags member is used to specify read-only depth and/or stencil to allow multiple views of the same resource.

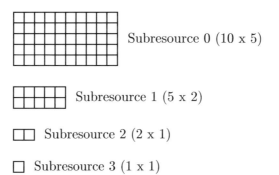

FIGURE 4.10: The mipmaps for a 10×5 texture, labeled with the subresource indices.

4.4.3 Subresources

You are likely familiar with textures and the *mipmaps* associated with them. Classical mipmapping is about generating a pyramid of textures, the original texture having the highest resolution and living at the base of the pyramid, and the tip of the pyramid having the lowest resolution. It is possible to create a texture in D3D11 and declare that it should have mipmaps. The texture and mipmaps are said to be *subresources* [48]. D3D11 has a numbering scheme for subresources that allows you to select them by an index. The original texture is subresource zero. The first mipmap generated from the texture is subresource one. If the texture has L mipmap levels, they are identified with subresource indices from 0 through $L - 1$. For example, Figure 4.10 shows the abstraction of a sequence of mipmaps for a 10×5 texture.

D3D11 has the concept of a texture-array resource. This is created as a single resource. All textures in the array are of the same dimensions and format, and each texture in the array is considered to be a subresource. If the array has N textures, you will guess that the subresource indices vary from 0 to $N - 1$. This is true when in fact the textures do not have mipmaps. However, when mipmaps exist, the indexing is by mipmap level first and array item second. For example, Figure 4.11 shows the abstraction of an array of 3 textures, each 10×5, each having mipmaps. The subresource index sri is a one-dimensional equivalent to the two-dimensional table location (item,level). The relationships between subresource indices and the levels are

```
// Convert table location (item, level) to a subresource index. The
// table location has constraints 0 <= item < numArrayItems and
// 0 <= level < numMipmapLevels.
sri = numMipmapLevels * item + level;

// Convert a subresource index to a table location (item, level). The index
// has constraints 0 <= sri < numArrayItems*numMipmapLevels.
item = sri / numMipmapLevels;
level = sri % numMipmapLevels;
```

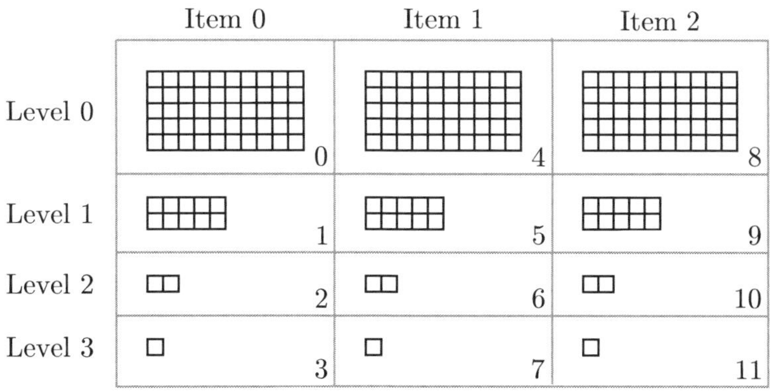

FIGURE 4.11: An array of three textures of size 10×5, each having mipmaps. The subresources are organized as a two-dimensional table. The subresource indices are listed inside the table entries.

The sizes of the mipmaps are according to the rules D3D11 imposes. The following formulas are the rules for a 3D texture with dimensions (width,height,depth), but they also apply to a 1D texture whose dimensions may be thought of as (width,1,1) or a 2D texture whose dimensions may be thought of as (width,height,1). Let $\lfloor t \rfloor$ denote the largest integer smaller than t (the floor function). If (W_ℓ, H_ℓ, D_ℓ) are the dimensions of the mipmap at level ℓ, then the dimensions of the next smallest mipmap at $\ell + 1$ are

$$
\begin{aligned}
&(W_{\ell+1}, H_{\ell+1}, D_{\ell+1}) \\
&= \left(\max\left(\lfloor W_\ell/2 \rfloor, 1\right), \max\left(\lfloor H_\ell/2 \rfloor, 1\right), \max\left(\lfloor D_\ell/2 \rfloor, 1\right)\right)
\end{aligned}
\quad (4.25)
$$

The number of mipmap levels is

$$
L = 1 + \max\left(\lfloor \log_2(W_0) \rfloor, \lfloor \log_2(H_0) \rfloor, \lfloor \log_2(D_0) \rfloor\right) \quad (4.26)
$$

where $\log_2(t)$ is the logarithm base 2 of t. In GTEngine code, L is computed using only integer operations.

4.4.4 Buffers

The buffer types available are constant buffers, texture buffers, vertex buffers, index buffers, structured buffers, append-consume buffers, byte-address buffers, indirect-arguments buffers, and staging buffers. All are created by filling in the members of the D3D11_BUFFER_DESC, defined by

```
struct D3D11_BUFFER_DESC
{
    UINT ByteWidth;
    D3D11_USAGE Usage;
    UINT BindFlags;        // bit flags in D3D11_BIND_FLAG
```

```
    UINT CPUAccessFlags;    // bit flags in D3D11_CPU_ACCESS_FLAG or 0
    UINT MiscFlags;         // bit flags in D3D11_RESOURCE_MISC_FLAG or 0
    UINT StructureByteStride;
};
```

ByteWidth is the number of bytes required to store the buffer. The Usage flags were described previously. The BindFlags member specifies how the buffer is bound to the graphics pipeline. The CPUAccessFlags member indicates how the CPU can access the buffer memory (if at all). With the MiscFlags member, we can select from the variations of structured buffers. It also supports advanced features including automatic mipmap generation, texture sharing between devices, and thread-safe access to shared resources. Staging buffers are used for copying between the CPU and GPU, the topic of Section 4.7.

The members of the buffer description are not independent. For example, if default usage is selected and the CPU-access is set for read, D3D11 will fail the buffer creation call. The examples of buffer creation shown next are all structured similarly in order to avoid (or at least minimize) the chances of an invalid description. In GTEngine, the application programmer must specify the usage for most buffer types, although some types require default usage. For buffers other than staging, the CPU access is set for write only in the dynamic usage case. The CPU access for read in GTEngine is restricted to staging buffers.

In the buffer creation code, I assume an ID3D11Device* device is available. I assume an input object that stores all the information necessary to create the buffer. Such objects are part of the front end of GTEngine (base class Buffer). I also assume an output object that stores the created D3D11 objects. Such objects are part of the back end of GTEngine (classes prefixed as DX11*, managed by class DX11Engine that encapsulates device). This design decouples the application code from D3D11-specific details to allow porting to OpenGL. For simplicity, the code listed here does not handle HRESULT errors, but the GTEngine code does.

The set up and call to create an ID3D11Buffer object is common to all buffers. The creation is conditional on whether or not you want to have the buffer initialized from CPU memory. Listing 4.27 defines a helper function that is used in all the sample creation code. It uses the abstract input object described previously.

```
ID3D11Buffer* CreateFrom(desc, input)
{
    ID3D11Buffer* buffer;
    if (input.data)
    {
        // Create the GPU version of the buffer and initialize it with
        // CPU data.  Initialization is required for D3D11_USAGE_IMMUTABLE.
        D3D11_SUBRESOURCE_DATA data;
        data.pSysMem = input.data;
        data.SysMemPitch = 0;
        data.SysMemSlicePitch = 0;
        device->CreateBuffer(&desc, &data, &buffer);
    }
    else
```

```
    {
        // Create an uninitialized GPU version of the buffer. The call
        // will fail if you have chosen D3D11_USAGE_IMMUTABLE.
        device->CreateBuffer(&desc, nullptr, &buffer);
    }
    return buffer;
}
```

LISTING 4.27: Common code for creating an ID3D11Buffer object.

4.4.4.1 Constant Buffers

A constant buffer is created as shown in Listing 4.28. See Listing 4.23 for information about SetUsageAccess and Listing 4.27 for information about CreateFrom.

```
D3D11_BUFFER_DESC desc;
desc.ByteWidth = input.numBytes;  // Must be a multiple of 16.
desc.BindFlags = D3D11_BIND_CONSTANT_BUFFER;
desc.MiscFlags = 0;
desc.StructureByteStride = 0;
SetUsageAccess(desc, input);
output.buffer = Createfrom(desc, input);
```

LISTING 4.28: Creating a constant buffer.

The bind flag indicates that a constant buffer should be created. If the constant buffer does not change during runtime, it is created to be immutable and its CPU access flag is set to zero. If you plan on modifying the constant buffer at runtime via memory mapping, you declare it to be dynamic and the CPU access flag must be set for writing. The miscelleaneous flags and the structure size (StructureByteStride) are irrelevant for this resource, so they are set to zero. The number of bytes can be determined from shader reflection.

4.4.4.2 Texture Buffers

Texture buffers were apparently designed to provide more efficient memory access compared to constant buffers. The online MSDN documentation [47] states that a texture buffer is a specialized resource that is accessed like a texture and can have better performance. You can bind up to 128 texture buffers per pipeline stage. I ran some experiments on my AMD 7970 graphics card to determine what the difference in memory performance is. I did not see an improvement, but perhaps there would be on a lower-end graphics card. As always, you should profile before making a design decision about which to use. If you choose to use a texture buffer, use the tbuffer declaration in the HLSL code just as you would use a cbuffer declaration. Listing 4.29 shows how to create a texture buffer. See Listing 4.23 for information about SetUsageAccess and Listing 4.27 for information about CreateFrom.

```
D3D11_BUFFER_DESC desc;
desc.ByteWidth = input.numBytes;
desc.BindFlags = D3D11_BIND_SHADER_RESOURCE;
desc.MiscFlags = 0;
desc.StructureByteStride = 0;
SetUsageAccess(desc, input);
```

```
output.buffer = CreateFrom(desc, input);

D3D11_SHADER_RESOURCE_VIEW_DESC srDesc;
srDesc.Format = input.srvFormat;
srDesc.ViewDimension = D3D11_SRV_DIMENSION_BUFFER;
srDesc.Buffer.FirstElement = 0;
srDesc.Buffer.NumElements = input.numElements;
device->CreateShaderResourceView(output.buffer, &srDesc, &output.srView);
```

LISTING 4.29: Creating a texture buffer.

Because the texture buffer is accessed like a texture, the bind flag must specify the buffer is a shader resource so that you can create a shader resource view for it. A texture buffer is not intended as a shader output, so there is no reason to create an unordered access view for it.

4.4.4.3   Vertex Buffers

A vertex buffer is created as shown in Listing 4.30. See Listing 4.23 for information about SetUsageAccess and Listing 4.27 for information about CreateFrom.

```
D3D11_BUFFER_DESC desc;
desc.ByteWidth = input.numBytes;
desc.BindFlags = D3D11_BIND_VERTEX_BUFFER;
desc.MiscFlags = 0;
desc.StructureByteStride = 0;
SetUsageAccess(desc, input);
output.buffer = CreateFrom(desc, input);
if (input.wantBindStreamOutput)
{
    // Generate vertices in geometry shaders.
    desc.Usage = D3D11_USAGE_DEFAULT;
    desc.BindFlags |= D3D11_BIND_STREAM_OUTPUT;
    desc.CPUAccessFlags = 0;
}
```

LISTING 4.30: Creating a vertex buffer.

The description members have no information for D3D11 about vertex buffer organization regarding position, colors, texture coordinates, and so on. This information is provided by the description structure,

```
struct D3D11_INPUT_ELEMENT_DESC
{
    LPCSTR SemanticName;
    UINT SemanticIndex;
    DXGI_FORMAT Format;
    UINT InputSlot;
    UINT AlignedByteOffset;
    D3D11_INPUT_CLASSIFICATION InputSlotClass;
    UINT InstanceDataStepRate;
};
```

For an example, see Listing 4.31.

```
struct MyVertex { float position[3], color[4], tcoord0[2], tcoord1; };

UINT const numElements = 4;  // position, color, tcoord0, tcoord1
D3D11_INPUT_ELEMENT_DESC desc[numElements];
```

```
// HLSL semantic is POSITION0
desc[0].SemanticName = "POSITION";
desc[0].SemanticIndex = 0;
desc[0].Format = DXGI_FORMAT_R32G32B32_FLOAT;   // position has 3 channels
desc[0].InputSlot = 0;
desc[0].AlignedByteOffset = 0;
desc[0].InputSlotClass = D3D11_INPUT_PER_VERTEX_DATA;
desc[0].InstanceDataStepRate = 0;

// HLSL semantic is COLOR0
desc[1].SemanticName = "COLOR";
desc[1].SemanticIndex = 0;
desc[1].Format = DXGI_FORMAT_R32G32B32A32_FLOAT;   // color has 4 channels
desc[1].InputSlot = 0;
desc[1].AlignedByteOffset = 12;   // offset after position[3]
desc[1].InputSlotClass = D3D11_INPUT_PER_VERTEX_DATA;
desc[1].InstanceDataStepRate = 0;

// HLSL semantic is TEXCOORD0
desc[2].SemanticName = "TEXCOORD";
desc[2].SemanticIndex = 0;
desc[2].Format = DXGI_FORMAT_R32G32_FLOAT;   // tcoord0 has 2 channels
desc[2].InputSlot = 0;
desc[2].AlignedByteOffset = 28;   // offset after color[4]
desc[2].InputSlotClass = D3D11_INPUT_PER_VERTEX_DATA;
desc[2].InstanceDataStepRate = 0;

// HLSL semantic is TEXCOORD1
desc[3].SemanticName = "TEXCOORD";
desc[3].SemanticIndex = 1;
desc[3].Format = DXGI_FORMAT_R32_FLOAT;   // tcoord1 has 1 channels
desc[3].InputSlot = 0;
desc[3].AlignedByteOffset = 36;   // offset after tcoord0[2]
desc[3].InputSlotClass = D3D11_INPUT_PER_VERTEX_DATA;
desc[3].InstanceDataStepRate = 0;
```

LISTING 4.31: Creating a vertex format via a D3D11_INPUT_ELEMENT
_DESC structure.

The element descriptions are needed to establish the connection between the vertex buffer data and the inputs required by a vertex shader; the connection uses the semantic names and indices. The interface object that does this is an *input layout* (ID3D11InputLayout) and the function ID3D11Device::CreateInputLayout creates one using the element description, the number of elements, a pointer to the CPU vertex buffer data, and the vertex shader blob produced by the D3DCompile function.

This graphics subsystem is one of the more complicated to manage. In GTEngine I have hidden the input layout management details by providing a VertexFormat class that allows you to provide the input element description in a manner independent of the D3D11 interfaces. In the previous example, the front end will have the following, where the Bind function has inputs: semantic name, component type, and semantic index.

```
VertexFormat vf;
vf.Bind(VA_POSITION, DF_R32G32B32_FLOAT, 0); // float3 position : POSITION0
vf.Bind(VA_COLOR, DF_R32G32B3A322_FLOAT, 0); // float4 color    : COLOR0
vf.Bind(VA_TEXCOORD, DF_R32G32_FLOAT, 0);    // float2 tcoord0  : TEXCOORD0
vf.Bind(VA_TEXCOORD, DF_R32_FLOAT, 1);       // float  tcoord1  : TEXCOORD1
```

The assumption is that the order of the elements in the description is the same as the order of the Bind calls. In the back end, the class DX11InputLayout contains the D3D11-specific details for creation of an input layout.

4.4.4.4   Index Buffers

An index buffer is created as shown in Listing 4.32. See Listing 4.23 for information about SetUsageAccess and Listing 4.27 for information about CreateFrom.

```
D3D11_BUFFER_DESC desc;
desc.ByteWidth = input.numBytes;
desc.BindFlags = D3D11_BIND_INDEX_BUFFER;
desc.MiscFlags = 0;
desc.StructureByteStride = 0;
SetUsageAccess(desc, input);
output.buffer = CreateFrom(desc, input);
```

LISTING 4.32: Creating an index buffer.

The type of primitive the index buffer represents is also not specified. This information is provided to the drawing system via the *input assembly* function ID3D11DeviceContext::IASetPrimitiveTopology. See Section 4.6.2 for details.

4.4.4.5   Structured Buffers

Creation of a structured buffer, declared in the HLSL code as StructuredBuffer or RWStructuredBuffer, is more complicated than that for constant, vertex, or index buffers. Listing 4.33 shows the details. See Listing 4.23 for information about SetUsageAccess and Listing 4.27 for information about CreateFrom.

```
D3D11_BUFFER_DESC desc;
desc.ByteWidth = input.numBytes;
desc.BindFlags = D3D11_SHADER_RESOURCE;
desc.MiscFlags = D3D11_RESOURCE_MISC_BUFFER_STRUCTURED;
desc.StructureByteStride = input.numBytesPerStruct;
SetUsageAccess(desc, input);
output.buffer = CreateFrom(desc, input);

D3D11_SHADER_RESOURCE_VIEW_DESC srDesc;
srDesc.Format = DXGI_FORMAT_UNKNOWN;
srDesc.ViewDimension = D3D11_SRV_DIMENSION_BUFFER;
srDesc.Buffer.FirstElement = 0;
srDesc.Buffer.NumElements = input.numElements;
device->CreateShaderResourceView(output.buffer, &srDesc, &output.srView);
if (input.wantShaderOutput)
{
    D3D11_UNORDERED_ACCESS_VIEW_DESC uaDesc;
    uaDesc.Format = DXGI_FORMAT_UNKNOWN;
    uaDesc.ViewDimension = D3D11_UAV_DIMENSION_BUFFER;
    uaDesc.Buffer.FirstElement = 0;
    uaDesc.Buffer.NumElements = input.numElements;
    uaDesc.Buffer.Flags = input.structuredBufferType;
    device->CreateUnorderedAccessView(output.buffer, &uaDesc,
        &output.uaView);
}
```

LISTING 4.33: Creating a structured buffer.

The ability to set a structured buffer to be writable in the shaders leads to some constraints on how the description members are set. Initially, the bind flag is set to D3D11_SHADER_RESOURCE because the structured buffer can be read by the shader. The miscellaneous flag is set to indicate that the buffer is indeed a structured buffer. Texture formats are explicitly defined in the D3D11 interface but structured buffer formats are defined by the user; thus, we need to tell the graphics system how large a struct is via the StructureByteStride member. If the structured buffer is an output of a shader, declared as RWStructuredBuffer, then it must have an unordered access view. Such a buffer must be declared with default usage.

A shader resource view must be created so that the structured buffer can be used as an input to a shader. The structure format is unknown to D3D11 internally, so you must specify it as DXGI_FORMAT_UNKNOWN. The ViewDimension parameter indicates the view is for a buffer type. The srDesc.Buffer.FirstElement and srDesc.Buffer.NumElements are set to values that imply the entire buffer is available in the view. However, it is possible to allow a view only for a subset determined by the starting offset into the buffer (FirstElement) and how many contiguous elements you want to allow access to (NumElements).

For a writable structured buffer that is declared in HLSL code as RWStructuredBuffer, an unordered access view must be created. The description structure is similar to that for a shader resource view, except that the ViewDimension parameter has UAV instead of SRV.

Structured buffers can have *internal counters*. The Buffer.Flags member is specific to UAVs and has value zero when you want a structured buffer without a counter. The other two choices are D3D11_BUFFER_UAV_FLAG_APPEND for an *append-consume buffer* or D3D11_BUFFER_UAV_FLAG_COUNTER for a *structured buffer with counter*. In Listing 4.33, input.structuredBufferType is one of these UAV flags.

Append buffers, declared in HLSL as AppendStructuredBuffer, are useful for compute shaders where an output occurs only under restricted conditions; that is, the compute shader does not output a value for each thread calling it. Output values are inserted into the append buffer as needed, and nothing prevents a single compute shader call from appending more than one value. Consume buffers, declared in HLSL as ConsumeStructuredBuffer, are also useful for compute shaders as inputs that are used only under restricted conditions. To create either type of buffer, create a structured buffer with an unordered access view whose UAV flag is D3D11_BUFFER_UAV_FLAG_APPEND.

A simple illustration is provided in the sample

GeometricTools/GTEngine/Samples/Basics/AppendConsumeBuffers

Listing 4.34 shows the HLSL file for this sample.

```
struct Particle { int2 location; };
ConsumeStructuredBuffer<Particle> currentState;
AppendStructuredBuffer<Particle> nextState;
// The test code uses Dispatch(1,1,1), so 'id' is (x,0,0) with 0 <= x < 32.
[numthreads(32, 1, 1)]
```

```
void CSMain(uint3 id : SV_GroupThreadID)
{
    // Append only half the current state (the even-indexed ones).
    Particle p = currentState.Consume();
    if ((p.location[0] & 1) == 0)
    {
        nextState.Append(p);
    }
}
```

LISTING 4.34: The HLSL file for the AppendConsumeBuffers sample application.

The main pitfall in using append buffers is knowing how large a buffer you need to create to store your results. A sample application where this is an issue is with exhaustive GPU-based root-finding, where the solutions of $F(x) = 0$ are located by evaluating F at all finite 32-bit floating-point numbers. See

GeometricTools/GTEngine/Samples/Numerics/RootFinding

As roots are found, they are stored in an append buffer. Care must be taken to ensure the append buffer has enough storage; otherwise, if the buffer becomes full, roots are potentially not recorded.

I was curious what the behavior is for the HLSL Append call when the buffer is full. The brief documentation [27] does not say anything about the behavior. As I have learned, when the documentation is insufficient for a high-level function, compile the shader, look at the assembly instructions generated by the compiler, and then look at the documentation for the assembly. In this case the Append call is compiled to imm_atomic_alloc and has documentation [43]. The instruction is an atomic increment of the interal counter, returning the previous value to be used for indexing (in our case, into the nextState buffer). The online documentation states, "There is no clamping of the count, so it wraps on overflow." I thought I found what I was looking for. When you create the D3D11 unordered access view for the append buffer, the maximum number of elements is specified, so D3D11 therefore knows the maximum number of elements in the buffer. If an attempt is made in the shader to append past the maximum number, the counter will wrap around and the element at index zero is overwritten. I performed an experiment to verify this, but the results were not in agreement with my interpretation of the quote. GTEngine maintains a staging buffer to which I can read back the value of the internal counter using the function ID3D11DeviceContext::CopyStructureCount. I created a consume buffer of four elements and an append buffer of two elements, and I executed a shader that consumed each of the four inputs and appended *all* of them to the output. After the read back, the internal counter was reported as four. I tried to read back four elements from the append buffer, but fortunately the Map call generated an error that the number of bytes requested exceeded that maximum size of the buffer. I ignored the error and checked the staging buffer's memory contents to see that in fact only two elements were copied. What this suggests is that when the internal counter is read back, it needs to be clamped to the maximum number of elements. You can look at the difference between the counter and the maximum number to determine how many Append calls were made during a full buffer (if this information is important to you).

Section 4.7 has the details of copying data between the CPU and GPU, including how to read back the internal counter and the appended elements. The buffer is typically not full, so you do not want to read back the entire buffer just to access a small subset.

A *structured buffer with counter* is intended to be written in the HLSL code, so you must create an unordered access view and the UAV flag must be set to D3D11_BUFFER_UAV_FLAG_COUNTER. You manage the counter yourself in the shader code by using uint IncrementCounter() and uint DecrementCounter(), which are atomic operations on the GPU.

4.4.4.6   Raw Buffers

Raw buffers, also called *byte-address buffers*, are supported by D3D11. The buffer is effectively an array of 4-byte values that can be read from and/or written to in the HLSL shader, but the data is presented as unsigned integers. You must reinterpret these bits according to how you designed the data layout of the raw buffers. A simple illustration is provided in the sample

GeometricTools/GTEngine/Samples/Basics/RawBuffers

Listing 4.35 shows the HLSL file for this sample.

```
// 16 bytes packed as: 'a', pi<double>, pi<float>, −1, 'b'
ByteAddressBuffer input;

// 16 bytes repackaged as: pi<double>, pi<float>, −1, 'a', 'b'
RWByteAddressBuffer output;

[numthreads(1, 1, 1)]
void CSMain(int3 t : SV_DispatchThreadID)
{
    uint4 inValue = input.Load4(0);

    // Extract character 'a'.
    uint a = inValue.x & 0x000000FF;

    // Extract double−precision pi.
    uint pidLoEncoding =
        (inValue.x >> 8) | ((inValue.y & 0x000000FF) << 24);
    uint pidHiEncoding =
        (inValue.y >> 8) | ((inValue.z & 0x000000FF) << 24);
    double pid = asdouble(pidLoEncoding, pidHiEncoding);

    // Extract single−precision pi.
    uint pifEncoding =
        (inValue.z >> 8) | ((inValue.w & 0x000000FF) << 24);
    float pif = asfloat(pifEncoding);

    // Extract short −1.
    uint minusOneEncoding = (inValue.w >> 8) & 0x0000FFFF;
    int minusOne = asint(minusOneEncoding) >> 16;

    // Extract character 'b'.
    uint b = (inValue.w >> 24);
```

```
// Return the repackaged input.  Although we already know the uint
// values are the same as extracted, this code shows how to
// reinterpret 'float' and 'double' values.
asuint(pid, pidLoEncoding, pidHiEncoding);
pifEncoding = asuint(pif);
uint4 outValue;
outValue.x = pidLoEncoding;
outValue.y = pidHiEncoding;
outValue.z = pifEncoding;
outValue.w = minusOneEncoding | (a << 16) | (b << 24);

output.Store4(0, outValue);
}
```

LISTING 4.35: The HLSL file for the RawBuffers sample application.

The byte-address buffer HLSL objects have Load* functions to read data from the buffer. The Load4(i) function call returns four 4-byte quantities starting at *byte address i*. This address must be a multiple of four. From experiments, it appears that if you pass in an index not a multiple of four, the largest multiple of four smaller than i is used instead. The writable byte-address buffer HLSL object also has Store* functions to write data to the buffer. The Store4(i,value) call stores four 4-byte quantities at byte address i. The address restrictions are the same as for Load.

Creation of a raw buffer is shown in Listing 4.36. See Listing 4.23 for information about SetUsageAccess and Listing 4.27 for information about CreateFrom.

```
D3D11_BUFFER_DESC desc;
desc.ByteWidth = input.numBytes;
desc.BindFlags = D3D11_BIND_SHADER_RESOURCE;
desc.MiscFlags = D3D11_RESOURCE_MISC_BUFFER_ALLOW_RAW_VIEWS;
desc.StructureByteStride = 0;
SetUsageAccess(desc, input);
output.buffer = CreateFrom(desc, input);

D3D11_SHADER_RESOURCE_VIEW_DESC srDesc;
srDesc.Format = DXGI_FORMAT_R32_TYPELESS;
srDesc.ViewDimension = D3D11_SRV_DIMENSION_BUFFEREX;
srDesc.BufferEx.FirstElement = 0;
srDesc.BufferEx.NumElements = input.numElements;
srDesc.BufferEx.Flags = D3D11_BUFFEREX_SRV_FLAG_RAW;
device->CreateShaderResourceView(output.buffer, &srDesc, &output.srView);
if (input.wantShaderOutput)
{
    D3D11_UNORDERED_ACCESS_VIEW_DESC uaDesc;
    uaDesc.Format = DXGI_FORMAT_R32_TYPELESS;
    uaDesc.ViewDimension = D3D11_UAV_DIMENSION_BUFFER;
    uaDesc.Buffer.FirstElement = 0;
    uaDesc.Buffer.NumElements = input.numElements;
    uaDesc.Buffer.Flags = D3D11_BUFFER_UAV_FLAG_RAW;
    hr = device->CreateUnorderedAccessView(output.buffer, &uaDesc,
        &output.uaView);
}
```

LISTING 4.36: Creation of a raw buffer.

Observe that the buffer description has a miscellaneous flag different from that of a structured buffer, so byte-address buffers are not consider structured. Also observe that the formats for the views are *typeless*, indicating that the byte layout is unknown to D3D11 internals other than the memory comes in

32-bit chunks (the R32 part of the flag). It is the programmer's responsibility to interpret the data as needed. The shader resource view description also needs to use the BufferEx variation in order to specify a raw buffer.

4.4.4.7 Indirect-Argument Buffers

The last type of buffer involves drawing *instances* of geometry. A vertex buffer may be used to provide per-vertex data for use by the vertex shader, but D3D11 also allows you to provide per-instance data when you want to have a world populated with lots of similar objects but each with minor variations compared to the others. The D3D11 functions DrawInstanced and DrawIndexedInstance are used for drawing instances, the first using the vertex ordering as it naturally occurs and the second using an index buffer to control the vertex ordering. Each of these functions has input parameters that are specified programatically; that is, the parameters are stored in variables that are reference in the code. D3D11 provides functions DrawInstancedIndirect and DrawIndexedInstanceIndirect that take *indirect-argument buffers*. The input parameters are stored in this buffer. This gives you a lot of flexibility to control drawing via the GPU rather than by CPU code.

Creation of an indirect-arguments buffer is shown in Listing 4.37. See Listing 4.23 for information about SetUsageAccess and Listing 4.27 for information about CreateFrom.

```
D3D11_BUFFER_DESC desc;
desc.ByteWidth = // number of bytes in the indirect-arguments buffer
desc.Usage = D3D11_USAGE_DEFAULT;
desc.BindFlags = 0;
desc.CPUAccessFlags = 0;
desc.MiscFlags = D3D11_RESOURCE_MISC_DRAWINDIRECT_ARGS;
desc.StructureByteStride = 0;
SetUsageAccess(desc, input);
output.buffer = CreateFrom(desc, input);
```
LISTING 4.37: Creation of an indirect-arguments buffer.

The description's miscellaneous flag has a special value that must be set.

None of the samples in this book use instancing. For more details on how to use instancing, directly or indirectly, see [57].

4.4.5 Textures

Unlike buffers where one description structure fits all, the description structures for textures are partitioned by dimension. The 1D and 2D descriptions support texture array resources in that you can specify the number of elements in the array. I will discuss these separately, because an array of textures in an HLSL program and a texture array are not the same thing. Suppose you have N 2D textures that you want accessed by the program, all the same size and format. Your options for accessing them are

```
// Shader reflection will show that these generate N bind points,
// one per texture, with names "arrayOfTextures[0]" through
```

```
//  " arrayOfTextures [N− 1]".
Texture2D<float4> arrayOfTextures [N];

// Shader reflection will show that this generates one bind point.
Texture2DArray<float4> textureArray ;
```

The form you choose might simply be a matter of taste when the total number
of resources for the shader is small. The limit on input resource bind points is
128 [46], so you might be hard pressed to reach that limit if you use an array
of textures.

The texture creations are set up so that mipmaps can be generated automatically if the application programmer so desires. This is acceptable when
textures are used for drawing and the artists are content with the standard
filtering algorithms used to generate the mipmap levels. If you want to generate the mipmaps procedurally, the mipmap parameters in creation must be
set differently. For GPGPU computing, the mipmap levels might have nothing
to do with the science of texturing, and switching among them can be tied
to some algorithmic behavior that you have invented. For the purpose of this
book, GTEngine currently uses mipmapping only for drawing.

In the texture creation code as in the buffer creation code, I assume there
is an input object with all the information necessary to create the texture, and
there is an output object to store the results. And I assume the existence of
an ID3D11Device* device to handle the creation.

The setup and call to create an ID3D11Texture<N>D object is common
to all textures of dimension N. The creation is conditional on whether or
not you want to have the texture initialized from CPU memory. Listing 4.38
defines helper functions that are used in all the sample creation code, one for
each dimension one, two, or three. It uses the abstract input object described
previously. Also, the automatic mipmap settings are common to all texture
types, so we have a helper function for the setting.

```
ID3D11Texture1D∗ Create1From (desc , input )
{
    ID3D11Texture1D∗ texture ;
    if ( input . data )
    {
        // Create the GPU version of the texture and initialize it with
        // CPU data .   Initialization is required for D3D11_USAGE_IMMUTABLE.
        D3D11_SUBRESOURCE_DATA∗ data =
            new D3D11_SUBRESOURCE_DATA[ input . numSubresources ];
        for ( sri = 0; sri < numSubresources ; ++sri )
        {
            data [ sri ]. pSysMem = input . subresource ( sri ). data ;
            data [ sri ]. SysMemPitch = 0;
            data [ sri ]. SysMemSlicePitch = 0;
        }
        device −>CreateTexture1D (&desc , data , &texture );
        delete [] data ;
    }
    else
    {
        // Create an uninitialized GPU version of the texture .   The call
        // will fail if you have chosen D3D11_USAGE_IMMUTABLE.
        device −>CreateTexture1D (&desc , nullptr , &texture );
    }
    return texture ;
}
```

```
ID3D11Texture2D* Create2From(desc, input)
{
    ID3D11Texture2D* texture;
    if (input.data)
    {
        // Create the GPU version of the texture and initialize it with
        // CPU data.  Initialization is required for D3D11_USAGE_IMMUTABLE.
        D3D11_SUBRESOURCE_DATA* data =
            new D3D11_SUBRESOURCE_DATA[input.numSubresources];
        for (sri = 0; sri < numSubresources; ++sri)
        {
            data[sri].pSysMem = input.subresource(sri).data;
            data[sri].SysMemPitch = input.subresource(sri).rowPitch;
            data[sri].SysMemSlicePitch = 0;
        }
        device->CreateTexture2D(&desc, data, &texture);
        delete[] data;
    }
    else
    {
        // Create an uninitialized GPU version of the texture.  The call
        // will fail if you have chosen D3D11_USAGE_IMMUTABLE.
        device->CreateTexture2D(&desc, nullptr, &texture);
    }
    return texture;
}

ID3D11Texture3D* Create3From(desc, input)
{
    ID3D11Texture3D* texture;
    if (input.data)
    {
        // Create the GPU version of the texture and initialize it with
        // CPU data.  Initialization is required for D3D11_USAGE_IMMUTABLE.
        D3D11_SUBRESOURCE_DATA* data =
            new D3D11_SUBRESOURCE_DATA[input.numSubresources];
        for (sri = 0; sri < numSubresources; ++sri)
        {
            data[sri].pSysMem = input.subresource(sri).data;
            data[sri].SysMemPitch = input.subresource(sri).rowPitch;
            data[sri].SysMemSlicePitch = input.subresource(sri).slicePitch;
        }
        device->CreateTexture3D(&desc, data, &texture);
        delete[] data;
    }
    else
    {
        // Create an uninitialized GPU version of the texture.  The call
        // will fail if you have chosen D3D11_USAGE_IMMUTABLE.
        device->CreateTexture3D(&desc, nullptr, &texture);
    }
    return texture;
}

void SetAutogenerateMipmaps(desc, input)
{
    if (input.wantAutogeneratedMipmaps && !input.wantSharing)
    {
        desc.Usage = D3D11_USAGE_DEFAULT;
        desc.BindFlags |= D3D11_BIND_RENDER_TARGET;
        desc.CPUAccessFlags = 0;
        desc.MiscFlags |= D3D11_RESOURCE_MISC_GENERATE_MIPS;
    }
}
```

LISTING 4.38: Common code for creating an ID3D11Texture<N>D object.

4.4.5.1   1D Textures

Listing 4.39 shows the creation of a 1D texture, including creation of views. See Listing 4.23 for information about SetUsageAccess and Listing 4.38 for information about Create1From and SetAutogenerateMipmaps.

```
D3D11_TEXTURE1D_DESC desc;
desc.Width = input.width;
desc.MipLevels = input.numMipmapLevels;
desc.ArraySize = 1;   // single texture, not a texture array
desc.Format = input.format;   // constrained to DXGI_FORMAT choices
desc.BindFlags = D3D11_BIND_SHADER_RESOURCE;
desc.MiscFlags = 0;
SetUsageAccess(desc, input);
SetAutogenerateMipmaps(desc, input);
output.texture = Create1From(desc, input);

D3D11_SHADER_RESOURCE_VIEW_DESC srDesc;
srDesc.Format = input.format;
srDesc.ViewDimension = D3D11_SRV_DIMENSION_TEXTURE1D;
srDesc.Texture1D.MostDetailedMip = 0;
srDesc.Texture1D.MipLevels = input.numMipmapLevels;
device->CreateShaderResourceView(output.texture, &srDesc, &output.srView);
if (input.wantShaderOutput)
{
    D3D11_UNORDERED_ACCESS_VIEW_DESC uaDesc;
    uaDesc.Format = desc.Format;
    uaDesc.ViewDimension = D3D11_UAV_DIMENSION_TEXTURE1D;
    uaDesc.Texture1D.MipSlice = 0;
    device->CreateUnorderedAccessView(output.texture, &uaDesc,
        &output.uaView);
}
```

LISTING 4.39: Creation of a 1D texture.

D3D11 expects that you have as many D3D11_SUBRESOURCE_DATA objects as there are subresources when you pass input.data to CreateTexture1D. If you have fewer than expected, the call will crash due to a memory access exception. Although the description guarantees that D3D11 can compute for itself the number of subresources, it simply cannot know how much memory you have allocated for input.data.

Automatic generation of mipmaps requires that the resource be a render target. It does not have to be an unordered access view. The latter can be specified additionally if you want to write to the render target textures in a shader.

The request for automatic generation of mipmaps does not actually lead to computation behind the scenes. You actually have to make a context call, as shown in Listing 4.40.

```
// device and associated immediate context
ID3D11Device* device;
ID3D11DeviceContext* context;
MyTexture input;   // All information is set before calling next function.
output = CreateMyDX11Texture(device, input);
if (input.wantAutogeneratedMipmaps)
{
    context->GenerateMips(output.srView);
}
```

```
// Modify the level−0 mipmap of output, either by mapped writes or by
// staging textures. Then make the next call to have the other levels
// computed.
if (input.wantAutogeneratedMipmaps)
{
    context−>GenerateMips(output.srView);
}
```

LISTING 4.40: Pseudocode for telling D3D11 to compute mipmap levels after the level-0 mipmap is initialized or (later) modified.

Because the generation requires a context, you cannot have them computed by the device (during the CreateMyDX11Texture) call. If you really want them computed at texture creation time, you will need to do so on the CPU at runtime or precomputed and loaded from disk, using your own code for mipmap computations. The input.data must have all subresources computed ahead of time in order to fill in all levels during the CreateTexture1D call. In GTEngine, I use the context call immediately after creation.

4.4.5.2 2D Textures

The texture creation shown here is for HLSL objects of type Texture2D and RWTexture2D. Creation for render targets and depth-stencil textures is discussed later in the section on draw targets.

Listing 4.41 shows the creation of a 2D texture that does not use multisampling. However, if you wish to share this texture with another device (from the same GPU), the construction allows this. The texture is created without multisampling but does allow sharing. See Listing 4.23 for information about SetUsageAccess and Listing 4.38 for information about Create2From and SetAutogenerateMipmaps.

```
D3D11_TEXTURE2D_DESC desc;
desc.Width = input.width;
desc.Height = input.height;
desc.MipLevels = input.numMipmapLevels;
desc.ArraySize = 1;  // single texture, not a texture array
desc.Format = input.format;  // constrained to DXGI_FORMAT choices
desc.SampleDesc.Count = 1;  // no multisampling
desc.SampleDesc.Quality = 0;  // no multisampling
desc.BindFlags = D3D11_BIND_SHADER_RESOURCE;
desc.MiscFlags = (input.wantSharing ? D3D11_RESOURCE_MISC_SHARED : 0);
SetUsageAccess(desc, input);
SetAutogenerateMipmaps(desc, input);
output.texture = Create2From(desc, input);

D3D11_SHADER_RESOURCE_VIEW_DESC srDesc;
srDesc.Format = input.format;
srDesc.ViewDimension = D3D11_SRV_DIMENSION_TEXTURE2D;
srDesc.Texture2D.MostDetailedMip = 0;
srDesc.Texture2D.MipLevels = input.numMipmapLevels;
device−>CreateShaderResourceView(output.texture, &srDesc, &output.srView);
if (input.wantShaderOutput)
{
    D3D11_UNORDERED_ACCESS_VIEW_DESC uaDesc;
    uaDesc.Format = input.format;
    uaDesc.ViewDimension = D3D11_UAV_DIMENSION_TEXTURE2D;
    uaDesc.Texture2D.MipSlice = 0;
```

```
    hr = device->CreateUnorderedAccessView(output.texture, &uaDesc,
        &output.uaView);
}
```

LISTING 4.41: Creation of a 2D texture for shader input and/or output but not for render targets or depth-stencil textures.

See Listing 4.40 for generating mipmaps automatically.

If you requested that the 2D texture be shared by another device, you have to do some COM programming to create the sharing ID3D11Texture2D object and you have to create views to go with it. Listing 4.42 shows the details. The HRESULT error handling is omitted for simplicity, but you really do need this in case you have tried to share a texture that cannot be shared. The GTEngine code handles the errors.

```
// a device and a 2D texture created with it
ID3D11Device* ownerDevice = // some device
ID3D11Texture2* ownertexture = // texture created with ownerDevice
ID3D11Device* sharingDevice = // the device that wants to share the texture
ID3D11Texture2* sharedTexture = // the texture shared with ownerDevice

// Get access to the DXGI resource for ownerTexture and obtain a handle
// from it to be used for sharing.
IDXGIResource* ownerResource = nullptr;
ownertexture->QueryInterface(__uuidof(IDXGIResource),
    (void**)&ownerResource);
HANDLE handle = nullptr;
ownerResource->GetSharedHandle(&handle);
ownerResource->Release();

// Create the shared texture for the sharing device.
sharingDevice->OpenSharedResource(handle, __uuidof(ID3D11Texture2D),
    (void**)&sharedTexture);
```

LISTING 4.42: Code that shows how to share an ID3D11Texture2D object created on one device with another device.

The sharing mechanism works as long as the two devices were created by the same *adapter*; see Section 4.8 for a discussion about adapters. If you have two devices, each created on a separate adapter, say, when you have two independent GPUs working, you cannot share textures between them.

4.4.5.3   3D Textures

Listing 4.43 shows the creation of a 3D texture, including creation of views. See Listing 4.23 for information about SetUsageAccess and Listing 4.38 for information about Create3From and SetAutogenerateMipmaps.

```
D3D11_TEXTURE3D_DESC desc;
desc.Width = input.width;
desc.Height = input.height;
desc.Depth = input.depth;
desc.MipLevels = input.numMipmapLevels;
desc.Format = input.format;
desc.BindFlags = D3D11_BIND_SHADER_RESOURCE;
desc.MiscFlags = 0;
SetUsageAccess(desc, input);
SetAutogenerateMipmaps(desc, input);
```

```
output.texture = Create3From(desc, input);

D3D11_SHADER_RESOURCE_VIEW_DESC srDesc;
srDesc.Format = input.format;
srDesc.ViewDimension = D3D11_SRV_DIMENSION_TEXTURE3D;
srDesc.Texture3D.MostDetailedMip = 0;
srDesc.Texture3D.MipLevels = input.numMipmapLevels;
device->CreateShaderResourceView(output.texture, &srDesc, &output.srView);
if (input.wantShaderOutput)
{
    D3D11_UNORDERED_ACCESS_VIEW_DESC uaDesc;
    uaDesc.Format = input.format;
    uaDesc.ViewDimension = D3D11_UAV_DIMENSION_TEXTURE3D;
    uaDesc.Texture3D.MipSlice = 0;
    uaDesc.Texture3D.FirstWSlice = 0;
    uaDesc.Texture3D.WSize = input.depth;
    device->CreateUnorderedAccessView(output.texture, &uaDesc,
        &output.uaView);
}
```

LISTING 4.43: Creation of a 3D texture.

See Listing 4.40 for generating mipmaps automatically.

4.4.6 Texture Arrays

As mentioned previously, HLSL supports texture-array resources that use a single bind point in a shader. Such resources exist for arrays of 1D textures and for arrays of 2D textures but not for arrays of 3D textures. A *cube map*, which consists of six textures covering the faces of a cube, has been used classically for environment mapping and then later as table lookups for normal vectors. Although a cube map might be thought of as a single texture, it is represented in D3D11 as a 2D texture array consisting of six items.

4.4.6.1 1D Texture Arrays

Listing 4.44 shows the creation of a 1D texture array, including creation of views. See Listing 4.23 for information about SetUsageAccess and Listing 4.38 for information about Create1From and SetAutogenerateMipmaps.

```
D3D11_TEXTURE1D_DESC desc;
desc.Width = input.width;
desc.MipLevels = input.numMipmapLevels;
desc.ArraySize = input.numArrayItems;
desc.Format = input.format;
desc.BindFlags = D3D11_BIND_SHADER_RESOURCE;
desc.MiscFlags = 0;
SetUsageAccess(desc, input);
SetAutogenerateMipmaps(desc, input);
output.texture = Create1From(desc, input);

D3D11_SHADER_RESOURCE_VIEW_DESC srDesc;
srDesc.Format = input.format;
srDesc.ViewDimension = D3D11_SRV_DIMENSION_TEXTURE1DARRAY;
srDesc.Texture1DArray.MostDetailedMip = 0;
srDesc.Texture1DArray.MipLevels = input.numMipmapLevels;
srDesc.Texture1DArray.FirstArraySlice = 0;
srDesc.Texture1DArray.ArraySize = input.numArrayItems;
device->CreateShaderResourceView(output.texture, &srDesc, &output.srView);
```

```
if (input.wantShaderOutput)
{
    D3D11_UNORDERED_ACCESS_VIEW_DESC uaDesc;
    uaDesc.Format = desc.Format;
    uaDesc.ViewDimension = D3D11_UAV_DIMENSION_TEXTURE1DARRAY;
    uaDesc.Texture1DArray.MipSlice = 0;
    uaDesc.Texture1DArray.FirstArraySlice = 0;
    uaDesc.Texture1DArray.ArraySize = input.numArrayItems;
    device->CreateUnorderedAccessView(output.texture, &uaDesc,
        &output.uaView);
}
```

LISTING 4.44: Creation of a 1D texture array.

One difference between creation of 1D texture arrays and 1D textures (Listing 4.39) is that desc.ArraySize is set to a number presumably larger than one. Another difference is that the abstract input object must know how many subresources there are and must deliver the subresource data pointers and pitches correctly to the D3D11_SUBRESOURCE_DATA objects. The views, however, have different ViewDimension values and additional members to set.

4.4.6.2   2D Texture Arrays

Listing 4.45 shows the creation of a 2D texture array, including creation of views. See Listing 4.23 for information about SetUsageAccess and Listing 4.38 for information about Create2From and SetAutogenerateMipmaps.

```
D3D11_TEXTURE2D_DESC desc;
desc.Width = input.width;
desc.MipLevels = input.numMipmapLevels;
desc.ArraySize = input.numArrayItems;
desc.Format = input.format;
desc.BindFlags = D3D11_BIND_SHADER_RESOURCE;
desc.MiscFlags = 0;
SetUsageAccess(desc, input);
SetAutogenerateMipmaps(desc, input);
output.texture = Create2From(desc, input);

D3D11_SHADER_RESOURCE_VIEW_DESC srDesc;
srDesc.Format = input.format;
srDesc.ViewDimension = D3D11_SRV_DIMENSION_TEXTURE2DARRAY;
srDesc.Texture2DArray.MostDetailedMip = 0;
srDesc.Texture2DArray.MipLevels = input.numMipmapLevels;
srDesc.Texture2DArray.FirstArraySlice = 0;
srDesc.Texture2DArray.ArraySize = input.numArrayItems;
device->CreateShaderResourceView(output.texture, &srDesc, &output.srView);
if (input.wantShaderOutput)
{
    D3D11_UNORDERED_ACCESS_VIEW_DESC uaDesc;
    uaDesc.Format = desc.Format;
    uaDesc.ViewDimension = D3D11_UAV_DIMENSION_TEXTURE2DARRAY;
    uaDesc.Texture2DArray.MipSlice = 0;
    uaDesc.Texture2DArray.FirstArraySlice = 0;
    uaDesc.Texture2DArray.ArraySize = input.numArrayItems;
    device->CreateUnorderedAccessView(output.texture, &uaDesc,
        &output.uaView);
}
```

LISTING 4.45: Creation of a 2D texture array.

One difference between creation of 2D texture arrays and 2D textures (Listing 4.41) is that desc.ArraySize is set to a number presumably larger than one. Another difference is that the abstract input object must know how many subresources there are and must deliver the subresource data pointers and pitches correctly to the D3D11_SUBRESOURCE_DATA objects. The views, however, have different ViewDimension values and additional members to set.

4.4.6.3 Cubemap Textures

Listing 4.46 shows the creation of a cubemap texture, including creation of views. See Listing 4.23 for information about SetUsageAccess and Listing 4.38 for information about Create2From and SetAutogenerateMipmaps.

```
D3D11_TEXTURE2D_DESC desc;
desc.Width = input.width;
desc.MipLevels = input.numMipmapLevels;
desc.ArraySize = 6;
desc.Format = input.format;
desc.BindFlags = D3D11_BIND_SHADER_RESOURCE;
desc.MiscFlags = D3D11_RESOURCE_MISC_TEXTURECUBE;
SetUsageAccess(desc, input);
SetAutogenerateMipmaps(desc, input);
output.texture = Create2From(desc, input);

D3D11_SHADER_RESOURCE_VIEW_DESC srDesc;
srDesc.Format = input.format;
srDesc.ViewDimension = D3D11_SRV_DIMENSION_TEXTURECUBE;
srDesc.TextureCube.MostDetailedMip = 0;
srDesc.TextureCube.MipLevels = input.numMipmapLevels;
device->CreateShaderResourceView(output.texture, &srDesc, &output.srView);
if (input.wantShaderOutput)
{
    D3D11_UNORDERED_ACCESS_VIEW_DESC uaDesc;
    uaDesc.Format = desc.Format;
    uaDesc.ViewDimension = D3D11_UAV_DIMENSION_TEXTURE2DARRAY;
    uaDesc.Texture2DArray.MipSlice = 0;
    uaDesc.Texture2DArray.FirstArraySlice = 0;
    uaDesc.Texture2DArray.ArraySize = input.numArrayItems;
    device->CreateUnorderedAccessView(output.texture, &uaDesc,
        &output.uaView);
}
```

LISTING 4.46: Creation of a cubemap texture.

Two differences between creation of a texture cube and a 2D texture array (Listing 4.45) are that desc.ArraySize is set explicitly to six and desc.MiscFlags is set to D3D11_RESOURCE_MISC_TEXTURECUBE. Another difference is that the abstract input object must know how many subresources there are and must deliver the subresource data pointers and pitches correctly to the D3D11_SUBRESOURCE_DATA objects. The shader resource views have different members but the unordered access views are the same; there is no UAV dimension for cube maps.

4.4.6.4   Cubemap Texture Arrays

Listing 4.47 shows the creation of a cubemap texture array, including creation of views. See Listing 4.23 for information about SetUsageAccess and Listing 4.38 for information about Create2From and SetAutogenerateMipmaps.

```
D3D11_TEXTURE2D_DESC desc;
desc.Width = input.width;
desc.MipLevels = input.numMipmapLevels;
desc.ArraySize = 6*input.numCubes;
desc.Format = input.format;
desc.BindFlags = D3D11_BIND_SHADER_RESOURCE;
desc.MiscFlags = D3D11_RESOURCE_MISC_TEXTURECUBE;
SetUsageAccess(desc, input);
SetAutogenerateMipmaps(desc, input);
output.texture = Create2From(desc, input);

D3D11_SHADER_RESOURCE_VIEW_DESC srDesc;
srDesc.Format = input.format;
srDesc.ViewDimension = D3D11_SRV_DIMENSION_TEXTURECUBEARRAY;
srDesc.TextureCubeArray.MostDetailedMip = 0;
srDesc.TextureCubeArray.MipLevels = input.numMipmapLevels;
srDesc.TextureCubeArray.First2DArrayFace = 0;
srDesc.TextureCubeArray.NumCubes = input.numCubes;
device->CreateShaderResourceView(output.texture, &srDesc, &output.srView);
if (input.wantShaderOutput)
{
    D3D11_UNORDERED_ACCESS_VIEW_DESC uaDesc;
    uaDesc.Format = desc.Format;
    uaDesc.ViewDimension = D3D11_UAV_DIMENSION_TEXTURE2DARRAY;
    uaDesc.Texture2DArray.MipSlice = 0;
    uaDesc.Texture2DArray.FirstArraySlice = 0;
    uaDesc.Texture2DArray.ArraySize = input.numArrayItems;
    device->CreateUnorderedAccessView(output.texture, &uaDesc,
        &output.uaView);
}
```

LISTING 4.47: Creation of a cubemap texture array.

Two differences between creation of a texture cube array and a 2D texture array (Listing 4.45) are that desc.ArraySize is set explicitly to six times the number of cubes and desc.MiscFlags is set to D3D11_RESOURCE_MISC_TEXTURECUBE. Another difference is that the abstract input object must know how many subresources there are and must deliver the subresource data pointers and pitches correctly to the D3D11_SUBRESOURCE_DATA objects. The shader resource views have different members but the unordered access views are the same; there is no UAV dimension for cube map arrays.

4.4.7   Draw Targets

Draw targets are a construct I use in GTEngine to encapsulate one or more render targets and optionally a depth-stencil texture for the purpose of offscreen rendering or computing within a pixel shader. In D3D11, all render targets must be enabled at the same time, so the encapsulation makes sense.

Using the same pattern of creation as for single textures, Listing 4.48 shows the creation of a render target, including creation of views. See Listing 4.38 for information about Create2From.

```
D3D11_TEXTURE2D_DESC desc;
desc.Width = input.width;
desc.Height = input.height;
desc.MipLevels = input.numMipmapLevels;
desc.ArraySize = 1;
desc.Format = input.format;
desc.SampleDesc.Count = 1;
desc.SampleDesc.Quality = 0;
desc.Usage = D3D11_USAGE_DEFAULT;
desc.BindFlags = D3D11_BIND_SHADER_RESOURCE | D3D11_BIND_RENDER_TARGET;
desc.CPUAccessFlags = D3D11_CPU_ACCESS_NONE;
desc.MiscFlags = (input.wantShared ?
    D3D11_RESOURCE_MISC_SHARED : D3D11_RESOURCE_MISC_NONE);
if (input.wantShaderOutput)
{
    desc.BindFlags |= D3D11_BIND_UNORDERED_ACCESS;
}
if (input.wantAutogeneratedMipmaps && !input.wantShared)
{
    desc.MiscFlags |= D3D11_RESOURCE_MISC_GENERATE_MIPS;
}
output.texture = Create2From(input);

D3D11_SHADER_RESOURCE_VIEW_DESC srDesc;
srDesc.Format = input.format;
srDesc.ViewDimension = D3D11_SRV_DIMENSION_TEXTURE2D;
srDesc.Texture2D.MostDetailedMip = 0;
srDesc.Texture2D.MipLevels = input.numMipmapLevels;
device->CreateShaderResourceView(output.texture, &srDesc, &output.srView);

D3D11_RENDER_TARGET_VIEW_DESC rtDesc;
rtDesc.Format = input.format;
rtDesc.ViewDimension = D3D11_RTV_DIMENSION_TEXTURE2D;
rtDesc.Texture2D.MipSlice = 0;
device->CreateRenderTargetView(output.texture, &rtDesc, &output.rtView);

if (input.wantShaderOutput)
{
    D3D11_UNORDERED_ACCESS_VIEW_DESC uaDesc;
    uaDesc.Format = input.format;
    uaDesc.ViewDimension = D3D11_UAV_DIMENSION_TEXTURE2D;
    uaDesc.Texture2D.MipSlice = 0;
    hr = device->CreateUnorderedAccessView(output.texture, &uaDesc,
        &output.uaView);
}
```

LISTING 4.48: Creation of a render target.

Listing 4.49 shows the creation of a depth-stencil texture, including creation of views. Such a texture cannot be a shader input; you cannot set the D3D11_BIND_SHADER_RESOURCE flag. There is also no reason to initialize the texture. You can initialize values to a constant using clearing, just as is done for the depth-stencil texture of the back buffer. Mipmapping is not supported. You cannot use this texture as a shader output.

```
D3D11_TEXTURE2D_DESC desc;
desc.Width = input.width;
desc.Height = input.height;
desc.MipLevels = 1;
desc.ArraySize = 1;
desc.Format = static_cast<DXGI_FORMAT>(texture->GetFormat());
desc.SampleDesc.Count = 1;
desc.SampleDesc.Quality = 0;
desc.Usage = D3D11_USAGE_DEFAULT;
```

```
desc.BindFlags = D3D11_BIND_DEPTH_STENCIL;
desc.CPUAccessFlags = D3D11_CPU_ACCESS_NONE;
desc.MiscFlags = (input.wantShared ?
    D3D11_RESOURCE_MISC_SHARED : D3D11_RESOURCE_MISC_NONE);

device->CreateTexture2D(&desc, nullptr, &output.texture);

// Create a view of the texture.
CreateDSView(device, desc);
```

LISTING 4.49: Creation of a depth-stencil texture.

The depth-stencil textures are quite restrictive. If you need to consume depth output from a draw target, you can read it back from the GPU and copy it to a 2D texture. Of course, you will need to interpret the depth-stencil data when consuming it. For example, if the depth format is 24-bits of depth and 8-bits of stencil, the 2D texture you copy to can be a 32-bit unsigned integer. The 8 high-order bits contain the stencil and the 24 low-order bits contain the depth. However, if you really want the depth information, it is easier to pass the perspective depth as an output of the vertex shader (clipPosition.z/clipPosition.w), set it as an input to the pixel shader, and write it to a render target. The render-target texture can be either a shader input or a shader output for another shader.

An example to demonstrate various features of draw targets is

GeometricTools/GTEngine/Samples/Basics/MultipleRenderTargets

A DrawTarget object is created with two render targets and a depth-stencil texture. The application renders a textured square to the draw target. To make it interesting, the first render target, say, renderTarget0, stores the pixel texture color and the second render target, say, renderTarget1, stores the SV_POSITION value that is generated by the vertex shader. The xy-coordinates of this value are the location of the pixel where the drawing is to occur, but with one-half added to each. The vertex shader also has an output that is the perspective depth, a value $z \in [0, 1]$. The pixel shader converts this to linearized depth $z' \in [0, 1]$ using

$$z' = \frac{d_{\min} z}{d_{\max}(1 - z) + d_{\min} z}$$

where $d_{\min}$ is the near distance of the view frustum and $d_{\max}$ is the far distance of the view frustum. The linearized depth is written to the depth-stencil texture because the semantic of the output is SV_DEPTH. This means your depth buffer no longer stores information about perspective depth. However, only a single square is in the scene, so there is no side effect regarding occlusion.

In half of the application window, the renderTarget0 is drawn to the screen, so you see what appears to be the 3D rendering of the square. You can move the camera and rotate the square via the virtual trackball.

After drawing the render target, the depth-stencil texture is read back from the GPU and copied to a 32-bit single-channel float texture, say, linearDepth.

The render targets are created with shader resource views, so they can both be used as shader inputs. The first render target is created so that it is a shader output—it has an unordered access view associated with it. This is *in addition to the texture being bound as a render target*. The application has another shader whose inputs are renderTarget0, renderTarget1, and linearDepth. Moreover, renderTarget0 is a shader output. The shader draws to the other half of the window grayscale values corresponding to the linearized depth, not sampled from the incoming window location; rather, they are sampled using the screen positions stored in renderTarget1 that were generated by the 3D rendering of the square. At the same time, the color values stored in renderTarget0 are set to a constant color.

Finally, renderTarget0 is set for automatic mipmap generation. The application has verification code that reads back level one of the mipmap and writes it to a PNG file. The render target is 1024^2 and the PNG file has an image of size 512^2. After drawing to the window, the render target is read back again to verify that the second shader has set it to a constant color. Level zero is written to a PNG file to show it indeed is constant.

4.5 States

The state objects related to drawing are blending control (ID3D11BlendState), depth-stencil control (ID3D11DepthStencilState), and rasterization control (ID3D11RasterizerState). The sampler state has a similar creation interface, although it probably should be thought of more as an object to be bound to a shader rather than as a controller of global drawing state.

States are created similar to the buffer and texture resources: a description structure is assigned the desired state values and passed to a creation function, producing an interface pointer for the corresponding state. For example,

```
D3D11_BLEND_DESC bDesc;  // Fill in the description fields.
ID3D11BlendState* bState;
HRESULT hr = device->CreateBlendState(&bDesc, &bState);

D3D11_DEPTH_STENCIL_DESC dsDesc;  // Fill in the description fields.
ID3D11DepthStencilState* dsState;
HRESULT hr = device->CreateDepthStencilState(&dsDesc, &dsState);

D3D11_RASTERIZER_DESC rDesc;  // Fill in the description fields.
ID3D11RasterizerState* rState;
HRESULT hr = device->CreateRasterizerState(&rDesc, &rState);

D3D11_SAMPLER_DESC sDesc;  // Fill in the description fields.
ID3D11SamplerState* sState;
HRESULT hr = device->CreateSamplerState(&sDesc, &sState);
```

The blend state description structure has an array of eight descriptor structures of type D3D11_RENDER_TARGET_BLEND_DESC. A context may have up to eight render targets attached, each whose blending is controlled by one of these descriptors.

Despite the usage differences between sampler state and the other states, GTEngine groups together the four states as derived classes from a base class named DX11DrawingState.

4.6   Shaders

The creation and basic use of vertex, geometry, pixel, and compute shaders are presented in this section.

4.6.1   Creating Shaders

Section 4.2.4 contains an in-depth discussion about compiling HLSL code, either offline using FXC or at runtime using the D3DCompile function. The output of D3DCompile is an ID3DBlob* interface that effectively wraps a chunk of memory that contains the compiled code and the information necessary for shader reflection. Creation of shaders simply requires access to this blob, as shown in Listing 4.50. The ID3D11ClassLinkage capabilities are not used here.

```
// The blob associated with compiling a shader.
ID3DBlob* blob = <D3DCompile output>;
void const* buffer = blob->GetBufferPointer();
size_t numBytes = blob->GetBufferSize();
HRESULT hr;

ID3D11VertexShader* vshader = nullptr;
hr = device->CreateVertexShader(buffer, numBytes, nullptr, &vshader);

ID3D11GeometryShader* gshader = nullptr;
hr = device->CreateGeometryShader(buffer, numBytes, nullptr, &gshader);

ID3D11PixelShader* pshader = nullptr;
hr = device->CreatePixelShader(buffer, numBytes, nullptr, &pshader);

ID3D11ComputeShader* cshader = nullptr;
hr = device->CreateComputeShader(buffer, numBytes, nullptr, &cshader);
```

LISTING 4.50: Creation of vertex, geometry, pixel, and compute shaders.

4.6.2   Vertex, Geometry, and Pixel Shader Execution

During application runtime, you will be executing various instructions through the immediate context related to drawing. When finished, you need to initiate the buffer swapping. Effectively, this tells the graphics system to commit to executing whatever drawing commands have been queued up. For real-time drawing in a single-threaded application, the drawing is performed during application idle time. A typical loop is shown next in pseudocode:

```
while (application_has_idle_time)
{
    clear_color_and_depth_stencil_buffers;
    issue_drawing_commands;
    swapChain->Present(syncInterval, flags);   // Swap buffers.
}
```

The Present call is for D3D11.0. When the syncInterval is set to zero, the buffers are presented to the display immediately without synchronization to vertical blanking. A value of 1, 2, 3, or 4 allows you to wait for vertical blanking the specified number of times. For example, if you have a 60 Hz monitor—and assuming you can draw your scene at 60 Hz, a syncInterval value of 1 will present the back buffer at 60 Hz. If the drawing takes less than 1/60 of a second, the Present call will block until 1/60 of a second has elapsed (and the display is ready for a refresh draw). A syncInterval of 2 will present the back buffer at 30 Hz (2 times 1/60 of a second).

The flags parameter is a combination of bit flags of type DXGI_PRESENT. The common flag is 0, indicating that the current buffer should simply be presented. Other flags are used for advanced features including restricting output (not all monitors display the results), stereo rendering, testing, and for allowing custom presentation, among other options. The MSDN documentation suggests that for D3D11.1 you use Present1 [42], which has an additional parameter of type DXGI_PRESENT_PARAMETERS. The parameter allows you to work with dirty rectangles and scrolling, useful for limiting drawing on devices for which you want to minimize power consumption.

To illustrate the basic sequence of drawing commands, consider a geometric primitive with a vertex buffer and optionally an index buffer. Suppose that we have a vertex shader, optionally a geometry shader, and a pixel shader to execute and that none of the shaders has UAV outputs. The pixel shader output goes to the back buffer; that is, no draw targets are enabled. Listing 4.51 shows one way to draw the primitive. This is pseudocode to avoid repetition of code that varies for each shader type only by the D3D11 interface names. In GTEngine, a shader type and its various interfaces are encapsulated into a class to hide the dependency of interface names on shader type.

```
// the D3D11 objects required for drawing the primitive
ID3D11DeviceContext* context;  // the active immediate context
ID3D11Buffer* vbuffer;  // vertex buffer
ID3D11Buffer* ibuffer;  // index buffer
ID3D11VertexShader* Vshader;
ID3D11GeometryShader* Gshader;
ID3D11PixelShader* Pshader;
ID3D11InputLayout* layout; // connects vbuffer elements and Vshader inputs

// Enable the vertex buffer.
UINT vbindpoint;  // get from shader reflection
UINT vbindcount = 1;  // get from shader reflection, using 1 for simplicity
ID3D11Buffer* vbuffers[vbindcount] = { vbuffer };
UINT vstrides[vbindcount] = { size_of_vertex };
UINT voffsets[vbindcount] = { starting_offset_in_vbuffer };
context->IASetVertexBuffers(vbindpoint, vbindcount, vbuffers, vstrides,
    voffsets);
```

```
// Enable the index buffer.
DXGI_FORMAT iformat;   // DXGI_FORMAT_R32_UINT or DXGI_FORMAT_R16_UINT
UINT ioffset = { starting_offset_in_ibuffer };
context->IASetIndexBuffer(ibuffer, iformat, ioffset);

// Enable the input layout.
context->IASetInputLayout(layout);

// Enable the shaders.
for (each shader type $ in {V, G, P})
{
    // Attach constant buffers.
    UINT cbindpoint;   // get from shader reflection
    UINT cbindcount;   // get from shader reflection
    ID3D11Buffer* cbuffers[cbindcount];
    context->$SSetConstantBuffers(cbindpoint, cbindcount, cbuffers);

    // Attach the input resources.
    UINT rbindpoint;   // get from shader reflection
    UINT rbindcount;   // get from shader reflection
    ID3D11ShaderResourceView* srViews[rbindcount];
    context->$SSetShaderResources(rbindpoint, rbindcount, srViews);

    // Attach the samplers (if any) for use by textures.
    UINT sbindpoint;   // get from shader reflection
    UINT sbindcount;   // get from shader reflection
    ID3D11SamplerState* samplerStates[sbindcount];
    context->$SSetSamplers(sbindpoint, sbindcount, samplerStates);

    // Enable the shader for execution.
    UINT numInstances;   // currently not used in GTEngine
    ID3D11ClassInstance* instances[numInstances];
    context->$SSetShader($shader, instances, numInstances);
}

// These are obtained from the client-side vertex buffer and index buffer.
UINT vertexOffset;
UINT numActiveIndices;
UINT firstIndex;
D3D11_PRIMITIVE_TOPOLOGY topology;   // what the indices represent
context->IASetPrimitiveTopology(topology);
context->DrawIndexed(numActiveIndices, firstIndex, vertexOffset);
```

LISTING 4.51: Typical setup for executing vertex, geometry, and pixel shaders.

If the vertex ordering in the buffer represents the primitives you want to draw, you do not need an index buffer but you do need the topology information. The enabling of the index buffer is therefore conditional. In GTEngine, I designed a class IndexBuffer to store indices and topology. In the case that the vertex buffer ordering does not require indices, IndexBuffer is still used but it stores only the topology. The drawing call for the non-indexed case is

```
// These are obtained from the client-side vertex buffer and index buffer.
UINT numActiveVertices;
UINT vertexOffset;
D3D11_PRIMITIVE_TOPOLOGY topology;   // what the vertices represent
context->IASetPrimitiveTopology(topology);
context->Draw(numActiveVertices, vertexOffset);
```

It is possible to query for the number of drawn pixels. This is sometimes useful for debugging. Listing 4.52 shows the details.

```
uint64_t numPixelsDrawn = 0;
D3D11_QUERY_DESC desc;
desc.Query = D3D11_QUERY_OCCLUSION;
desc.MiscFlags = D3D11_QUERY_MISC_NONE;
ID3D11Query* query;
device->CreateQuery(&desc, &query);
context->Begin(query);

context->Draw*(...);

context->End(query);
while (S_OK != context->GetData(query,&numPixelsDrawn, sizeof(UINT64),0))
{
    // Wait for end of query.
}
query->Release();
```

LISTING 4.52: Using a query to count the number of drawn pixels.

Compute shaders typically have unordered access views for shader output. There is an interface call ID3D11DeviceContext::CSSetUnorderedAccessViews that allows you to enable these before compute-shader execution. D3D11.0 allows pixel shaders to use unordered access views. However, there is no interface named ID3D11DeviceContext::PSSetUnorderedAccessViews. The output of pixel shaders are normally render targets, and the render targets must be enabled so you can write to them. If the pixel shader has unordered access views, the render targets and the unordered access views must be set simultaneously with a single call to ID3D11DeviceContext::OMSetRenderTargetsAndUnorderedAccessViews, which is part of the *output merger (OM)* stage. The technical difficulty is that you might already have bound render targets, even if only the back buffer. To avoid the complicated flow of logic to have everything enabled and ready to draw, the OMSet* call has a special parameter that tells D3D11 to keep the currently bound render targets but to set the incoming unordered access views. Specifically,

```
// the unordered access views of a pixel shader output resource
UINT ubindpoint;   // get from shader reflection
UINT ubindcount;   // get from shader reflection
ID3D11UnorderedAccessView* uaviews[ubindcount];
UINT initialCounts[ubindcount];   // used by buffers with counters
context->OMSetRenderTargetsAndUnorderedAccessViews(
    D3D11_KEEP_RENDER_TARGETS_AND_DEPTH_STENCIL, nullptr, nullptr,
    ubindpoint, ubindcount, uaviews, initialCounts);
```

D3D11.1 allows all the shader types to have unordered access views.

4.6.3   Compute Shader Execution

Setting up for the execution of a compute shader is relatively simple and uses the consistent approach that was discussed for drawing in Section 4.6.2. Resources are attached to the shader as constant buffers and as views: shader resource views (SRVs) for inputs and unordered access views (UAVs) for output. Listing 4.53 shows the typical set up and execution.

```
// Attach constant buffers.
UINT cbindpoint;   // get from shader reflection
UINT cbindcount;   // get from shader reflection
ID3D11Buffer* cbuffers[cbindcount];
context->CSSetConstantBuffers(cbindpoint, cbindcount, cbuffers);

// Attach the input resources.
UINT rbindpoint;   // get from shader reflection
UINT rbindcount;   // get from shader reflection
ID3D11ShaderResourceView* srViews[rbindcount];
context->CSSetShaderResources(rbindpoint, rbindcount, srViews);

// Attach the output resources.
UINT ubindpoint;   // get from shader reflection
UINT ubindcount;   // get from shader reflection
ID3D11UnorderedAccessView* uaviews[ubindcount];
unsigned int initialcounts[ubindCount];   // used by buffers with counters;
context->CSSetUnorderedAccessViews(ubindPoint, ubindcount, uaviews,
    initialcounts);

// Attach the samplers (if any) for use by textures.
UINT sbindpoint;   // get from shader reflection
UINT sbindcount;   // get from shader reflection
ID3D11SamplerState* samplerStates[sbindcount];
context->CSSetSamplers(sbindpoint, sbindcount, samplerStates);

// Enable the compute shader for execution.
ID3D11ComputeShader* cshader;   // compute shader to execute
UINT numInstances;   // currently not used in GTEngine
ID3D11ClassInstance* instances[numInstances];
context->CSSetShader(cshader, instances, numInstances);

// Execute the compute shader.
context->Dispatch(numXGroups, numYGroups, numZGroups);
```

LISTING 4.53: Typical setup for executing a compute shader.

The Dispatch call is not blocking, so it is asynchronous in the sense that the GPU can execute the shader while the CPU continues to execute other instructions. If you need to read back the shader output from GPU to CPU immediately after the dispatch, a stall will occur because the CPU must wait for the GPU to finish.

Sometimes you might want the GPU to finish anyway before continuing CPU execution. In my experience, this was sometimes necessary because the display driver would shut down and restart due to the GPU taking too long on the queued command lists. In D3D11.0, the timeout when executing a GPU packet is two seconds. D3D11.1 gives you the ability to disable the timeout, although you should be cautious about doing so. See the MSDN documentation on the device creation flag D3D11_CREATE_DEVICE_DISABLE_GPU_TIMEOUT [28]. If you want to wait for the GPU to finish, you can launch a D3D11 query after the Dispatch call. The query is shown in Listing 4.54.

```
D3D11_QUERY_DESC desc;
desc.Query = D3D11_QUERY_EVENT;
desc.MiscFlags = 0;
ID3D11Query* query = nullptr;
if (SUCCEEDED(device->CreateQuery(&desc, &query)))
{
    immediateContext->End(query);
    BOOL data = 0;
```

```
    while (S_OK != immediateContext->GetData(query,&data, sizeof(data),0))
    {
        // Wait for the GPU to finish.
    }
    query->Release();
}
```

LISTING 4.54: A query that causes the CPU to wait for the GPU to finish executing its current command list.

4.7 Copying Data between CPU and GPU

As powerful as GPUs are for computing, you have to upload data from the CPU to the GPU in order to compute. And you might have to download computed results from the GPU to the CPU. For data-heavy processing, the memory copies are a major bottleneck.

In this section, I will discuss several ways for copying data between the CPU and GPU. These are all single-threaded operations, occurring on the thread in which the device was created. Similar to the discussions in Section 4.4 on the creation of resources, this discussion assumes the existence of an immediate context and a client-side input that stores all necessary information for the copy to succeed.

Applications that generate a lot of texture data can be multithreaded for performance regarding memory copies. The processing of the textures occurs on the thread in which the device and immediate context were created. The GPU resource creation depends only on the device, and the device calls are thread safe, assuming you did not create the device to be single threaded. If the texture processing is fast enough to exceed the rate of texture generation, a producer-consumer model may be used to parallelize the creation and the processing. See Section 7.1 about the sample application

GeometricTools/GTEngine/Samples/Graphics/VideoStreams

that implements this concept.

The various mechanisms to copy data between processors are shown in Figure 4.12.

4.7.1 Mapped Writes for Dynamic Update

For resources that were created with the D3D11_USAGE_DYNAMIC flag, the mechanism to update the GPU memory uses *memory mapping*. Update of a buffer resource is shown in Listing 4.55. The abstract input object stores an offset into the data. The number of active bytes must be selected to ensure that the copied block of memory is a subblock of input.data. The output.buffer was created using the code of Section 4.4.

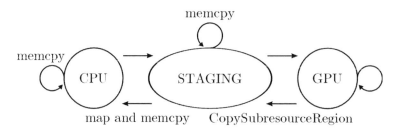

FIGURE 4.12: Copying data between processors.

```
D3D11_MAPPED_SUBRESOURCE sub;
context−>Map( output . buffer , 0, D3D11_MAP_WRITE_DISCARD, 0, &sub );
memcpy( sub . pData , input . data + input . offset , input . numActiveBytes );
context−>Unmap( output . buffer , 0);
```

LISTING 4.55: Updating an ID3D11Buffer object using mapped writes.

The ID3D11DeviceContext::Map function [39] takes as input the buffer object, the subresource index zero because buffers have only one subresource, a D3D11_MAP value [29], and a D3D11_MAP_FLAG value [30]; the function then fills in a D3D11_MAPPED_SUBRESOURCE subresource data structure [31]. The returned HRESULT is not tested in the example for simplicity, but your code should test it; the GTEngine code does. The memory is *locked* for exclusive access while the mapping is in effect. This subresource structure has a pointer sub.pData to the mapped memory. After you have written to it, you need to *unlock* the memory with the ID3D11DeviceContext::Unmap function [40]. The map flag D3D11_MAP_WRITE_DISCARD tells D3D11 that the previous buffer contents can be discarded and are considered to be undefined.

Updating a texture resource using memory mapping requires more work. In particular, 2D and 3D textures might not be stored in contiguous GPU memory. When the textures are created and initialized, a row pitch for 2D and 3D textures and a slice pitch for 3D textures are provided for the *source* data (your CPU data). The GPU versions might have to adhere to requirements of byte alignment different from those on the CPU—this is akin to Intel SSE data requiring 16-byte alignment when CPU data only needs 4-byte alignment. When the D3D11_MAPPED_SUBRESOURCE members are filled in, you have to copy rows and slices one-by-one when the pitches do not match your CPU version of the texture. Update of a texture resource is shown in Listing 4.56. The output.texture was created using the code of Section 4.4.

```
unsigned int sri; // the index for the subresource to be updated
D3D11_MAPPED_SUBRESOURCE sub;
context−>Map( output . texture , sri , D3D11_MAP_WRITE_DISCARD, 0, &sub );

// the client−side subresource information
Subresource csub = input . subresource ( sri );
if ( input . numDimensions == 1)
```

```
{
    // Mipmap levels for 1D textures and texture arrays are in contiguous
    // memory.
    memcpy(sub.pData, csub.data, csub.GetNumBytesFor(csub.level));
}
else if (input.numDimensions == 2)
{
    unsigned int numRows = csub.GetNumRowsFor(csub.level);
    CopyPitched2(numRows, csub.rowPitch, csub.data,
        sub.RowPitch, sub.pData);
}
else  // input.numDimensions == 3
{
    unsigned int numRows = csub.GetNumRowsFor(csub.level);
    unsigned int numSlices = csub.GetNumSlicesFor(csub.level);
    CopyPitched3(numRows, numSlices, csub.rowPitch, csub.slicePitch,
        csub.data, sub.RowPitch, sub.DepthPitch, sub.pData);
}
context->Unmap(texture, sri);
```

LISTING 4.56: Updating an ID3D11Texture object using mapped writes.

The client-side subresource information includes the texture element format, the number of texture array items, the number of mipmap levels, and mipmap image sizes. The **csub.Get*** calls access that information. Again for simplicity, the HRESULT value for the Map function is not handled but should be in real code. The dimension-specific copies are shown in Listing 4.57.

```
void CopyPitched2(
    unsigned int numRows,
    unsigned int srcRowPitch, void const* srcData,
    unsigned int trgRowPitch, void* trgData)
{
    if (srcRowPitch == trgRowPitch)
    {
        // The memory is contiguous.
        memcpy(trgData, srcData, trgRowPitch*numRows);
    }
    else
    {
        // Padding was added to each row of the texture, so we must
        // copy a row at a time to compensate for differing pitches.
        unsigned int numRowBytes = std::min(srcRowPitch, trgRowPitch);
        char const* srcRow = static_cast<char const*>(srcData);
        char* trgRow = static_cast<char*>(trgData);
        for (unsigned int row = 0; row < numRows; ++row)
        {
            memcpy(trgRow, srcRow, numRowBytes);
            srcRow += srcRowPitch;
            trgRow += trgRowPitch;
        }
    }
}

void CopyPitched3(unsigned int numRows, unsigned int numSlices,
    unsigned int srcRowPitch, unsigned int srcSlicePitch,
    void const* srcData, unsigned int trgRowPitch,
    unsigned int trgSlicePitch, void* trgData)
{
    if (srcRowPitch == trgRowPitch && srcSlicePitch == trgSlicePitch)
    {
        // The memory is contiguous.
        memcpy(trgData, srcData, trgSlicePitch*numSlices);
    }
```

```
    else
    {
        // Padding was added to each row and/or slice of the texture, so
        // we must copy the data to compensate for differing pitches.
        unsigned int numRowBytes = std::min(srcRowPitch, trgRowPitch);
        char const* srcSlice = static_cast<char const*>(srcData);
        char* trgSlice = static_cast<char*>(trgData);
        for (unsigned int slice = 0; slice < numSlices; ++slice)
        {
            char const* srcRow = srcSlice;
            char* trgRow = trgSlice;
            for (unsigned int row = 0; row < numRows; ++row)
            {
                memcpy(trgRow, srcRow, numRowBytes);
                srcRow += srcRowPitch;
                trgRow += trgRowPitch;
            }
            srcSlice += srcSlicePitch;
            trgSlice += trgSlicePitch;
        }
    }
}
```

LISTING 4.57: Memory copies used by dynamic updates of textures.

D3D11 also has an update function, ID3D11DeviceContext::UpdateSubresource, for copying CPU data to a subresource that was created in nonmappable memory [41].

4.7.2 Staging Resources

The dynamic writes using memory mapping are one way to copy CPU data to the GPU resource. However, you cannot use memory-mapped reads to copy GPU resource data directly to CPU memory. D3D11 requires copying from the GPU to a *staging resource* first and then copying from the staging resource to CPU memory. The double hop invariably makes copying from the GPU to the CPU expensive.

Staging resources are created using the same description structures that were used for the original resources. I will not present all the variations here; you can look at the GTEngine source code. To illustrate one of these, Listing 4.58 shows the creation of a staging texture for a 2D texture without multisampling.

```
D3D11_TEXTURE2D_DESC desc;
desc.Width = input.width;
desc.Height = input.height;
desc.MipLevels = input.numMipmapLevels;
desc.ArraySize = input.numArrayItems;
desc.Format = input.format;
desc.SampleDesc.Count = 1;
desc.SampleDesc.Quality = 0;
desc.Usage = D3D11_USAGE_STAGING;
desc.BindFlags = 0;
desc.CPUAccessFlags = // D3D11_CPU_ACCESS_WRITE, D3D11_CPU_ACCESS_READ
desc.MiscFlags = 0;
device->CreateTexture2D(&desc, nullptr, &output.staging);
```

LISTING 4.58: Creation of a 2D staging texture without multisampling.

The desc.CPUAccessFlags is set for read or write or both. You can have bidirectional support by OR-ing the two flags together. The output.staging object is of type ID3D11Texture2D*.

4.7.3 Copy from CPU to GPU

The copy from CPU to GPU for a buffer resource is shown in Listing 4.59. The abstract input object stores an offset into the data. The number of active bytes must be selected to ensure that the copied block of memory is a subblock of input.data. The output.buffer was created using the code of Section 4.4.

```
// Copy from CPU to staging resource.
D3D11_MAPPED_SUBRESOURCE sub;
context->Map(output.staging, 0, D3D11_MAP_WRITE, 0, &sub);
memcpy(sub.pData, input.data + input.offset, input.numActiveBytes);
context->Unmap(mStaging, 0);

// Copy from staging resource to GPU memory.
D3D11_BOX box = { input.offset, 0, 0, input.numActiveBytes, 1, 1 };
context->CopySubresourceRegion(output.buffer, 0, input.offset, 0, 0,
    output.staging, 0, &box);
```

LISTING 4.59: Copy from CPU to GPU for a buffer resource. The subresource index is zero because buffers have only one subresource.

The staging resource was created to have the same size as the buffer. The box and the destination x, y, and z parameters to the copy call specify the source and destination regions for the copy.

The copy from CPU to GPU for a texture resource is shown in Listing 4.60. The output.texture was created using the code of Section 4.4.

```
// Copy from CPU to staging resource.
unsigned int sri;  // the index for the subresource to be copied
D3D11_MAPPED_SUBRESOURCE sub;
context->Map(output.staging, sri, D3D11_MAP_WRITE, 0, &sub);

// Copy from CPU memory to staging texture. This is identical to the
// dynamic update copy except that the destination is the staging texture.

// the client-side subresource information
Subresource csub = input.subresource(sri);
if (input.numDimensions == 1)
{
    // Mipmap levels for 1D textures and texture arrays are in contiguous
    // memory.
    memcpy(sub.pData, csub.data, csub.GetNumBytesFor(csub.level));
}
else if (input.numDimensions == 2)
{
    unsigned int numRows = csub.GetNumRowsFor(csub.level);
    CopyPitched2(numRows, csub.rowPitch, csub.data,
        sub.RowPitch, sub.pData);
}
else  // input.numDimensions == 3
{
    unsigned int numRows = csub.GetNumRowsFor(csub.level);
    unsigned int numSlices = csub.GetNumSlicesFor(csub.level);
    CopyPitched3(numRows, numSlices, csub.rowPitch, csub.slicePitch,
        csub.data, sub.RowPitch, sub.DepthPitch, sub.pData);
```

```
}
context—>Unmap( output . staging ,  sri );

// Copy from staging texture to GPU memory .  The entire subresource is
// copied .
context—>CopySubresourceRegion ( output . texture ,  sri ,  0 ,  0 ,  0 ,
    output . staging ,  sri ,  nullptr );
```

LISTING 4.60: Copy from CPU to GPU for a texture resource.

4.7.4   Copy from GPU to CPU

The copy from GPU to CPU for a buffer resource is shown in Listing 4.61. The abstract input object stores an offset into the data. The number of active bytes must be selected to ensure that the copied block of memory is a subblock of input.data. The output.buffer was created using the code of Section 4.4.

```
// Copy from GPU to staging resource .
D3D11_BOX box = { input . offset ,  0 ,  0 ,  input . numActiveBytes ,  1 ,  1 };
context—>CopySubresourceRegion ( output . staging ,  0 ,  input . offset ,  0 ,  0 ,
    output . buffer ,  0 ,  &box );

// Copy from staging resource to CPU .
D3D11_MAPPED_SUBRESOURCE sub ;
context—>Map( outupt . staging ,  0 ,  D3D11_MAP_READ ,  0 ,  &sub );
memcpy( input . data + input . offset ,  sub . pData ,  input . numActiveBytes );
context—>Unmap( mStaging ,  0 );
```

LISTING 4.61: Copy from GPU to CPU for a buffer resource. The subresource index is zero because buffers have only one subresource.

The staging resource was created to have the same size as the buffer. The box and the destination x, y, and z parameters to the copy call specify the source and destination regions for the copy.

The copy from GPU to CPU for a texture resource is shown in Listing 4.62. The output.texture was created using the code of Section 4.4.

```
// Copy from GPU to staging resource .
ID3D11Resource* dxTexture = GetDXResource ();
context—>CopySubresourceRegion ( output . staging ,  sri ,  0 ,  0 ,  0 ,
    output . Texture ,  sri ,  nullptr );

// Copy from staging texture to CPU memory .
D3D11_MAPPED_SUBRESOURCE sub ;
context—>Map( output . staging ,  sri ,  D3D11_MAP_READ ,  0 ,  &sub );

// the client—side subresource information
Subresource csub = input . subresource ( sri );
if ( input . numDimensions == 1)
{
    memcpy( sr . data ,  sub . pData ,  texture—>GetNumBytesFor( sr . level ));
}
else if ( input . numDimensions == 2)
{
    unsigned int numRows = csub . GetNumRowsFor( csub . level );
    CopyPitched2 (numRows,  sub . RowPitch ,  sub . pData ,
        csub . rowPitch ,  csub . data );
}
else  // input . numDimensions == 3
{
    unsigned int numRows = csub . GetNumRowsFor( csub . level );
```

```
        unsigned int numSlices = csub.GetNumSlicesFor(csub.level);
        CopyPitched3(numRows, numSlices, sub.RowPitch, sub.DepthPitch,
            sub.pData, csub.rowPitch, csub.slicePitch, csub.data);
}
context->Unmap(output.staging, sri);
```

LISTING 4.62: Copy from GPU to CPU for a texture resource.

4.7.5 Copy from GPU to GPU

D3D11 has functions for GPU-to-GPU copy via the ID3D11DeviceContext interfaces, CopyResource [36] and CopySubresourceRegion [37]. The main technical problem is that you cannot copy between arbitrary formats. I had mentioned previously in Section 4.4.7 about trying to copy from a depth-stencil texture with format DXGI_FORMAT_D24_UNORM_S8_UINT to a regular texture with format DXGI_R32_UINT. The textures are of the same dimensions and the texture elements are 32-bit integers. An attempt to call CopyResource for these textures generates an error in the D3D11 debug layer. The function itself does not have a returned HRESULT for you to detect the error and handle it accordingly. This means you have to be careful when attempting to copy between resources.

It is possible to use the copy functions already discussed to avoid the formatting issues, assuming you are careful and know what you are doing will work; for example,

```
ClientInput depthStencilInput;    // CPU version of depth-stencil texture
ClientOutput depthStencilOutput;  // GPU version of depth-stencil texture
ClientInput regularInput;         // CPU version of R32_UINT 2D texture
ClientOutput regularOutput;       // GPU version of R32_UINT 2D texture
CopyGpuToCpu(depthStencilOutput.texture, depthStencilInput.texture);
memcpy(depthStencilInput.texture, regularInput.texture);
CopyCpuToGpu(regularInput.texture, regularOutput.texture);
```

The problem with this approach is that there are four copies: GPU-to-staging, staging-to-CPU, CPU-to-staging, and staging-to-GPU. The design of CopyCpuToGpu and CopyGpuToCpu involves transferring the memory into and out of the CPU-version of the resource. For a GPU-to-GPU copy, you can skip this transferring.

```
ClientInput depthStencilInput;    // CPU version of depth-stencil texture
ClientOutput depthStencilOutput;  // GPU version of depth-stencil texture
ClientInput regularInput;         // CPU version of R32_UINT 2D texture
ClientOutput regularOutput;       // GPU version of R32_UINT 2D texture
CopyGpuToStaging(depthStencilOutput.texture, depthStencilOutput.staging);
CopyStagingToStaging(depthStencilOutput.staging, regularOutput.staging);
CopyStagingToGpu(regularOutput.staging, regularOutput.texture);

// The actual DX11 code:
ID3D11DeviceContext* context;     // the active immediate context
unsigned int numBytes;            // total bytes, same for both textures
ID3D11Texture2* dsTexture;        // depth-stencil texture
ID3D11Texture2* dsStaging;        // depth-stencil staging
ID3D11Texture2* rgTexture;        // regular texture
ID3D11Texture2* rgStaging;        // regular staging
context->CopySubresourceRegion(dsStaging, 0, 0, 0, 0, dsTexture, 0,
    nullptr);
```

```
D3D11_MAPPED_SUBRESOURCE dsSub, rgSub;
context->Map(dsStaging, 0, D3D11_MAP_READ, 0, &dsSub);
context->Map(rgStaging, 0, D3D11_MAP_WRITE, 0, &rgSub);
memcpy(rgSub.pData, dsSub.pData, numBytes);
context->Unmap(dsStaging, 0);
context->Unmap(rgStaging, 0);
context->CopySubresourceRegion(rgTexture, 0, 0, 0, 0, rgStaging, 0,
    nullptr);
```

We now have three copies: GPU-to-staging, staging-to-staging, and staging-to-GPU. In exchange, the CPU memory of the regular texture no longer matches that of the GPU memory. This would be an issue only if you have to consume the CPU memory. Generally for real-time applications, one of your main performance goals is to avoid having to copy from GPU all the way back to CPU memory, so it is usually not necessary for CPU and GPU versions of memory to match.

4.8   Multiple GPUs

Computers may have multiple graphics cards installed whose GPUs can work together through a cable that connects them. AMD Radeon cards do this through their CrossFireX technology. NVIDIA cards do this through their SLI technology. In fact, it is possible to build a machine with more than two graphics cards. The motherboards must support this, you need a hefty power supply, and the operating system drivers must support this.

4.8.1   Enumerating the Adapters

The GPUs are referred to as *adapters* and D3D11 allows you to enumerate them, as shown in Listing 4.63. Each graphics card can have monitors attached to it; these are called *outputs* and also may be enumerated for each adapter. For simplicity of presentation, the HRESULT error processing is omitted; you should check the return values in real code.

```
IDXGIFactory1* factory = nullptr;
CreateDXGIFactory1(__uuidof(IDXGIFactory1), (void**)&factory);

struct AdapterInfo { IDXGIAdapter1* adapter; DXGI_ADAPTER_DESC1 desc; };
std::vector<AdapterInfo> aiArray;
for (unsigned int i = 0; /**/; ++i)
{
    AdapterInfo ai;
    if (factory->EnumAdapters1(i, &ai.adapter) != DXGI_ERROR_NOT_FOUND)
    {
        ai.adapter->GetDesc1(&ai.desc);
        aiArray.push_back(ai);
    }
    else // All adapters have been found.
    {
        break;
    }
}
```

```cpp
struct OutputInfo { IDXGIOutput* output; DXGI_OUTPUT_DESC desc; };
struct AOInfo { AdapterInfo ai;  std::vector<OutputInfo> oiArray; };
std::vector<AOInfo> aoArray;
for (auto const& ai : aiArray)
{
    AOInfo ao;
    ao.ai = ai;
    for (unsigned int j = 0; /**/; ++j)
    {
        OutputInfo oi;
        if (ai.adapter->EnumOutputs(j, &oi.output)
            != DXGI_ERROR_NOT_FOUND)
        {
            oi.output->GetDesc(&oi.desc);
            ao.oiArray.push_back(oi);
        }
        else  // All outputs for this adapter have been found.
        {
            break;
        }
    }
    aoArray.push_back(ao);
}

factory->Release();
```

LISTING 4.63: Enumeration of adapters and outputs attached to the adapters.

When the application is finished using the adapters and outputs, they must be released because the enumeration calls increased their internal reference counts. GTEngine provides class wrappers to handle the reference counting for you.

As discussed in Section 4.3, the first device creation is an IDXGIAdapter* interface pointer. When null, the device is created for the default adapter, which is a GPU if you have one attached. However, you can specify an adapter that was produced by the enumeration. For dual-GPU machines, two scenarios exist. If the GPUs are configured to use CrossFireX for AMD or SLI for NVIDIA, the enumeration reports only one GPU adapter. If CrossFireX or SLI are disabled, the enumeration reports two GPU adapters. You may create a DX11Engine object for each adapter and use them independently.

On my Windows 8.1 machine with dual AMD 7970 machine and Cross-FireX disabled, the enumeration reports three adapters. The first two are for the GPUs. The first GPU adapter reports two outputs because I have two monitors attached. The second GPU adapter reports no outputs (no monitors attached). Starting with Windows 8, the enumeration reports another adapter called the *Microsoft Basic Render Driver*. This is effectively a software renderer that you can use. An overview of DXGI is found online [33]. This page describes enumeration of adapters and how you can access the basic render driver if so desired.

4.8.2 Copying Data between Multiple GPUs

Dual GPUs can be a double-edged sword. If you have independent computing pipelines, you can get good parallelism from the two GPUs. However, if you have UAV outputs computed on one GPU that must be consumed by the other GPU, you have to transfer the data between the GPUs. Unfortunately, the mechanism for sharing textures between two devices works only when those devices are created from a single adapter. Thus, you need to design carefully how the pipelines are laid out. Ideally, if you have to transfer data from one GPU to another, you should try to do so without stalling both GPUs. While you are reading back data on one GPU, you should do so by copying it to a staging buffer. The other GPU should be kept busy computing during this phase. When the read-back of the first GPU is complete and the second GPU is ready, copy the memory from the staging buffer of the first GPU to a staging buffer for the second GPU and then upload the results to GPU memory.

Listing 4.64 shows a complete example of copying a one-dimensional texture from the video memory of one GPU to that of another. The HRESULT error checking is omitted for simplicity.

```cpp
// Enumerate the adapters but not the outputs attached to the
// adapters. The test machine is known to have two adapters
// that are not configured to work in unison.
IDXGIFactory1* factory = nullptr;
CreateDXGIFactory1(__uuidof(IDXGIFactory1), (void**)&factory);
IDXGIAdapter1* adapter[2];
factory->EnumAdapters1(0, &adapter[0]);
factory->EnumAdapters1(1, &adapter[1]);
factory->Release();

// Create D3D11.0 devices, one from each adapter. The driver type must be
// D3D_DRIVER_TYPE_UNKNOWN when you pass a non-null pointer for adapter.
D3D_FEATURE_LEVEL featureLevels[1] = { D3D_FEATURE_LEVEL_11_0 };
D3D_FEATURE_LEVEL featureLevel;

ID3D11Device* device0 = nullptr;
ID3D11DeviceContext* context0 = nullptr;
D3D11CreateDevice(adapter[0], D3D_DRIVER_TYPE_UNKNOWN, nullptr, 0,
    featureLevels, 1, D3D11_SDK_VERSION, &device0, &featureLevel,
    &context0);

ID3D11Device* device1 = nullptr;
ID3D11DeviceContext* context1 = nullptr;
D3D11CreateDevice(adapter[1], D3D_DRIVER_TYPE_UNKNOWN, nullptr, 0,
    featureLevels, 1, D3D11_SDK_VERSION, &device1, &featureLevel,
    &context1);

// Create texture0 on GPU0 and initialize it to { 0, 1, 2, 3 }.
unsigned int const width = 4;
D3D11_TEXTURE1D_DESC desc;
desc.Width = width;
desc.MipLevels = 1;
desc.ArraySize = 1;
desc.Format = DXGI_FORMAT_R8G8B8A8_UNORM;
desc.Usage = D3D11_USAGE_DEFAULT;
desc.BindFlags = 0;
desc.CPUAccessFlags = 0;
desc.MiscFlags = 0;
unsigned char initial0[width] = { 0, 1, 2, 3 };
D3D11_SUBRESOURCE_DATA srData;
srData.pSysMem = initial0;
srData.SysMemPitch = 4*width;
srData.SysMemSlicePitch = 0;
ID3D11Texture1D* texture0 = nullptr;
    device0->CreateTexture1D(&desc, &srData, &texture0);
```

```
// Create texture1 on GPU1 and initialize it to { 0, 0, 0, 0 }.
unsigned char initial1[width] = { 0, 0, 0, 0 };
srData.pSysMem = initial1;
ID3D11Texture1D* texture1 = nullptr;
device1->CreateTexture1D(&desc, &srData, &texture1);

// Create staging0 on GPU0 so that it can be mapped for reading.
desc.Usage = D3D11_USAGE_STAGING;
desc.CPUAccessFlags = D3D11_CPU_ACCESS_READ;
ID3D11Texture1D* staging0 = nullptr;
device0->CreateTexture1D(&stDesc, nullptr, &staging0);

// Create staging1 on GPU1 so that it can be mapped for writing and
// reading.  The latter is required so we can verify by a read-back
// that the video memory copy actually occurred.
desc.CPUAccessFlags |= D3D11_CPU_ACCESS_WRITE;
ID3D11Texture1D* staging1 = nullptr;
device1->CreateTexture1D(&desc, nullptr, &staging1);

// Copy from GPU0 video memory to GPU0 staging buffer.
context0->CopyResource(staging0, texture0);

// Map the GPU0 staging buffer for reading.
D3D11_MAPPED_SUBRESOURCE sub0;
context0->Map(staging0, 0, D3D11_MAP_READ, 0, &sub0);

// Map the GPU1 staging buffer for writing.
D3D11_MAPPED_SUBRESOURCE sub1;
context1->Map(staging1, 0, D3D11_MAP_WRITE, 0, &sub1);

// Copy from staging buffer of GPU0 to staging buffer of GPU1.
memcpy(sub1.pData, sub0.pData, 4*width);

// Unmap the staging buffers.
context0->Unmap(staging0, 0);
context1->Unmap(staging1, 0);

// Copy from GPU1 staging buffer to GPU1 video memory.
context1->CopyResource(texture1, staging1);

// Read back from GPU1 video memory to verify the copy actually occurred.
context1->CopyResource(staging1, texture1);
context1->Map(staging1, 0, D3D11_MAP_READ, 0, &sub1);
unsigned char* data = (unsigned char*)sub1.pData;  // data = { 0, 1, 2, 3 }
context1->Unmap(staging1, 0);

// Destroy all the D3D11.0 objects.
staging0->Release();    staging1->Release();
texture0->Release();    texture1->Release();
context0->Release();    context1->Release();
device0->Release();     device1->Release();
```

LISTING 4.64: An example of copying a texture from the video memory of one GPU to that of another.

4.9   IEEE Floating-Point on the GPU

D3D11 supports various floating-point formats, some of them with deviations from the IEEE 754-2008 standard. A summary of the formats and rules is found at [34].

For 32-bit floating-point numbers, some of the deviations from the rules are about the handling of quiet or signaling NaNs. Two variations that potentially have more impact when comparing the results from the GPU and from an FPU associated with the CPU are the following.

- The default rounding rule for IEEE 754-2008 is *round-to-nearest ties-to-even*. This rule is discussed in Section 2.5.2.1. The idea is that a floating-point operation produces the floating-point number nearest to the theoretical result. When the theoretical result has a fractional part that is one-half, you round down if the integer part is even or round up if the integer part is odd. D3D11 does not require the hardware to adhere to this rule; that is, the hardware can truncate the result rather than rounding to nearest.

- Subnormal numbers are flushed to sign-preserved zero on input and output of floating-point mathematical operations. If the numbers are simply copied and not mathematically manipulated, the flushing does not occur.

The hardware can support 64-bit floating-point numbers. According to [34], the double precision hardware is compliant with the IEEE 754-2008 Standard. However, the standard has many requirements. Section 5.4.1 of the Standard document is about arithmetic operations; it states that implementations shall provide a square root operation. As of D3D11.1, no such operation exists.

Surprisingly, at least to me, is that 64-bit subnormals are not flushed to zero during arithmetic operations. I would have expected the opposite to be true—that single precision would not flush to zero and double precision does. I tried an experiment to verify this,

GeometricTools/GTEngine/Samples/Basics/IEEEFloatingPoint

Listing 4.65 shows a compute shader for adding two float numbers read from an input structured buffer with the result returned in an output structured buffer. The application code is listed below the HLSL code; the application creates the input structured buffer with two subnormal floating-point numbers. Reading back the output buffer, the result is zero which shows that the 32-bit flush-to-zero semantics were applied.

```
// code in TestSubnormals.hlsl, macro REAL is float or double
StructuredBuffer<REAL> input;    // two subnormal numbers
RWStructuredBuffer<REAL> output;    // sum of inputs that is subnormal
[numthreads(1,1,1)]
void CSMain(int3 t : SV_DispatchThreadID)
{
    output[0] = input[0] + input[1];
}

template <typename Real, typename Binary>
class TestSubnormals
{
```

```cpp
public:
    TestSubnormals(std::string const& hlslfile, std::string const& realname,
        Binary& result)
    {
        DX11Engine engine;

        std::shared_ptr<StructuredBuffer> inputBuffer(
            new StructuredBuffer(2, sizeof(Real)));
        Real* input = inputBuffer->Get<Real>();
        Binary v0, v1;
        v0.encoding = 1;
        v1.encoding = 1;
        input[0] = v0.number;  // smallest positive subnormal
        input[1] = v1.number;  // same as v0

        // Compute v0+v1 and store in this buffer.
        std::shared_ptr<StructuredBuffer> outputBuffer(
            new StructuredBuffer(1, sizeof(Real)));
        outputBuffer->SetUsage(Resource::SHADER_OUTPUT);
        outputBuffer->SetCopyType(Resource::COPY_STAGING_TO_CPU);
        Real* output = outputBuffer->Get<Real>();
        output[0] = (Real)0;

        HLSLDefiner definer;
        definer.SetString("REAL", realname);
        std::shared_ptr<ComputeShader> cshader(
            ShaderFactory::CreateCompute(hlslfile, definer));
        cshader->Set("input", inputBuffer);
        cshader->Set("output", outputBuffer);

        engine.Execute(cshader, 1, 1, 1);
        engine.CopyGpuToCpu(outputBuffer);

        result.number = output[0];

        inputBuffer = nullptr;
        outputBuffer = nullptr;
        cshader = nullptr;
    }
};

void main()
{
    union Float
    {
        float number;
        uint32_t encoding;
    };
    Float result;
    TestSubnormals<float,Float> test("TestSubnormals.hlsl", "float",
        result);
    // With IEEE 754-2008 behavior that preserves subnormals, the output
    // result should have encoding 2 (number is 2^{-148}). Instead,
    // result.encoding = 0, which means that the GPU has flushed the
    // subnormal result to zero.
}
```

LISTING 4.65: Verification that float subnormals are flushed to zero when used in arithmetic operations.

I ran the same experiment with 64-bit floating-point numbers. Listing 4.66 shows the application code.

```cpp
void main()
{
    union Double
```

```
{
    double number;
    uint64_t encoding;
};
Double result;
TestSubnormals<double,Double> dtest("TestSubnormals.hls!", "double",
    result);
// With IEEE 754-2008 behavior that preserves subnormals, the output
// result should have encoding 2 (number is 2^{-1073}). Indeed,
// dresult.encoding = 2, so the subnormal result was not flushed.
}
```

LISTING 4.66: Verification that double subnormals are not flushed to zero when used in arithmetic operations.

What this argues is that if you need the full range of 32-bit floating-point numbers, including subnormals, in your GPGPU computations, you can use double precision instead—recall that all 32-bit subnormal numbers convert to 64-bit normal numbers. You can do the conversion on the FPU associated with the CPU and then upload those double-precision numbers to the GPU for consumption.

The amount of work to compute with double instead of float might take more effort. For example, the exhaustive float-based root finder

GeometricTools/GTEngine/Samples/Numerics/RootFinding

uses the dispatch thread ID to generate the 23-bit trailing significand embedded in a 32-bit uint, loops over the biased exponents, and builds the float values using asfloat to be used as the function inputs. The question is whether a float-to-double conversion will produce the correct double-precison value. On my AMD 7970, the answer is *no*. For example,

```
StructuredBuffer<float> input;    // subnormal 2^{-149}
RWStructuredBuffer<double> output;
[numthreads(1,1,1)]
void CSMain(int3 t : SV_DispatchThreadID)
{
    output[0] = (double)input[0];
}
```

I looked at the assembly output to see there was a ftod instruction for the conversion of float to double. Reading back the output, the result was the double-precision number 0.0, so the hardware flushed the subnormal float to zero during the assignment. The MSDN documentation for the assembly instruction ftod [35] states that implementations may either honor subnormals or flush them to zero. This means you are not guaranteed that the hardware will convert the 32-bit numbers properly. Instead, you need to implement in HLSL the narrow-to-wide conversion code of Section 2.5.2.10, at least the case when the narrow value is subnormal.

In terms of HLSL assembly instructions, D3D11.0 supports addition dadd; multiplication dmul; comparisons deq, dge dlt, dne; extremes dmin, dmax; assignment dmov; and conversions between 32-bit and 64-bit floating-point dtof, ftod. D3D11.1 additionally supports division ddiv, reciprocal drcp, and fused multiply-add dfma.

The assembly instructions do not include any common mathematical functions such as square root, exponential and logarithm, or trigonometric functions. If you need these, you will have to roll your own function approximations, much like what was done for Intel SSE2 in Section 3.3.

Chapter 5

Practical Matters

5.1 Engine Design and Architecture

I mentioned previously that the low-level D3D11 code for a simple application can be enormous. You definitely want to wrap much of the execution code that is common to applications. In this section, I discuss a simple application that uses the Windows API for window creation, event handling, and window destruction. The application also uses the DirectX API for D3D11 object creation, handling, and destruction. The idea is to show how everything fits together without hiding the internal mechanics. Although the argument is for the encapsulation of the components in a *graphics engine*, this simple application provides a test bed where everything is exposed. You can easily modify this to experiment with D3D11 features that interest you.

5.1.1 A Simple Low-Level D3D11 Application

The sample application

GeometricTools/GTEngine/Samples/Basics/LowLevelD3D11

creates a window and a large collection of D3D11 objects in order to draw a single triangle that is vertex colored and textured. Additionally, a virtual trackball is provided so that you can left-click-and-drag the mouse in order to rotate the triangle in real time. The total number of lines of source code in Application.{h,cpp} files is approximately 1350. This is a significant amount of code just to draw a single triangle! The file LowLevelD3D11.cpp contains a simple main function that creates an application object, runs it, and then deletes it:

```
void main()
{
    TheApplication = new Application();
    if (TheApplication->Create(64, 64, 512, 512, D3D_FEATURE_LEVEL_11_1,
        D3D11_CREATE_DEVICE_DEBUG))
    {
        TheApplication->Run();
    }
    delete TheApplication;
}
```

The Create function has inputs for the upper-left corner of the window, the window width and height, the desired version of D3D11, and flags for device creation.

Listing 5.1 shows the header file for the application class. The first three header files are those for D3D11. The math header is used to access sqrt and acos in the virtual trackball code. The file streaming header is used to load compiled shaders from disk.

```cpp
#include <D3D11.h>
#include <D3Dcompiler.h>
#include <DXGI.h>
#include <cmath>
#include <fstream>

class Application
{
public:
    ~Application();
    Application();

    bool Create(int xOrigin, int yOrigin, int xSize, int ySize,
        D3D_FEATURE_LEVEL featureLevel, UINT flags);
    void Run();

private:
    static LRESULT CALLBACK WindowProcedure(HWND handle, UINT message,
        WPARAM wParam, LPARAM lParam);

    // support for creation
    bool CreateAppWindow(int xOrigin, int yOrigin, int xSize, int ySize);
    bool CreateGraphics(D3D_FEATURE_LEVEL featureLevel, UINT flags);
    bool CreateShaders();
    ID3DBlob* LoadShaderBlob(std::wstring const& filename);
    bool CreateVertexBuffer();
    bool CreateInputLayout();
    bool CreateConstantBuffer();
    bool CreateTexture();
    bool CreateShaderResourceView();
    bool CreateBlendState();
    bool CreateDepthStencilState();
    bool CreateRasterizerState();
    bool CreateSamplerState();

    // support for drawing
    void ClearBuffers();
    void Draw();
    void SwapBuffers(unsigned int syncInterval);

    // support for virtual trackball
    void OnLeftMouseDown(int x, int y);
    void OnLeftMouseDrag(int x, int y);
    void OnLeftMouseUp(int x, int y);
    void RotateTrackball(float x0, float y0, float x1, float y1);
    void ComputeProjectionMatrix();
    void ComputeViewMatrix();
    void ComputeWorldMatrix();
    void UpdateConstantBuffer();

    // window parameters
    ATOM mAtom;
    HWND mHandle;
    int mXOrigin, mYOrigin, mXSize, mYSize;
```

```
// D3D11 objects and parameters
ID3D11Device* mDevice;
ID3D11DeviceContext* mImmediate;
D3D_FEATURE_LEVEL mFeatureLevel;
IDXGISwapChain* mSwapChain;
ID3D11Texture2D* mColorBuffer;
ID3D11RenderTargetView* mColorView;
ID3D11Texture2D* mDepthStencilBuffer;
ID3D11DepthStencilView* mDepthStencilView;
D3D11_VIEWPORT mViewport;

// application-specific D3D11 objects
ID3D11VertexShader* mVertexShader;
ID3DBlob* mVertexShaderBlob;
ID3D11PixelShader* mPixelShader;
ID3D11Buffer* mVertexBuffer;
ID3D11InputLayout* mInputLayout;
ID3D11Buffer* mConstantBuffer;
ID3D11Texture2D* mTexture;
ID3D11ShaderResourceView* mShaderResourceView;
ID3D11SamplerState* mSamplerState;
ID3D11BlendState* mBlendState;
ID3D11DepthStencilState* mDepthStencilState;
ID3D11RasterizerState* mRasterizerState;

struct Vertex
{
    float position[3];
    float color[4];
    float tcoord[2];
};

int mNumVertices;
int mVertexOffset;

// camera parameters
float mUpFOVDegrees;
float mAspectRatio;
float mDMin, mDMax, mUMin, mUMax, mRMin, mRMax;
float mEye[3], mDVector[3], mUVector[3], mRVector[3];
float mViewMatrix[4][4];
float mProjectionMatrix[4][4];
float mWorldMatrix[4][4];

// data for a virtual trackball
float mTrackballMatrix[4][4];
float mXTrack0, mYTrack0, mXTrack1, mYTrack1;
float mSaveTrackballMatrix[4][4];
bool mTrackBallDown;
};

extern Application* TheApplication;
```

LISTING 5.1: The Application class header file.

As you can see, the Application class has a small public interface but the private interface manages a lot of objects. The public Create function is a simple call to all the private creation functions. The CreateAppWindow function uses the Windows API to create an application window that has a message pump and function for processing the messages. The CreateGraphics function creates the D3D11 device, the immediate context, the swap chain, the color buffer and its shader resource view, and the depth-stencil buffer and its shader resource view. The creation functions for blend state, depth-stencil state, and rasterization state are designed to give you the default states for most applications. Some applications have a need for multiple states, switching them based on the current drawing needs. For example, some objects might require alpha blending enabled to be drawn properly.

The remaining creation functions are related to the geometric primitive to be drawn. The triangle is a non-indexed primitive, so no index buffer is created. The constant buffer stores the world-view-projection matrix of Equation (4.20), which is needed to transform the triangle vertices into the view frustum so that the rasterizer can project and draw the correct pixels. The various D3D11 objects needed for drawing were discussed in Chapter 4, so the source code will look familiar to you.

The application Run function contains the standard message pump for a Windows application. The window is displayed and the message pump is started. This is a loop that checks for pending events such as key presses or mouse clicks and then calls the window's event handler to process them. When no events are pending, you have idle time to consume. The D3D11 code for real-time rendering occurs here: updating the constant buffer, clearing the color and depth-stencil buffers, drawing the geometric primitive, and swapping the front and back buffers.

5.1.2   HLSL Compilation in Microsoft Visual Studio

The sample application also shows off a feature of Microsoft Visual Studio 2013 that is convenient for development. When you add HLSL files to your project, they are automatically set up to be compiled by FXC. Initiating a build, HLSL files are compiled first followed by CPP files. The *compiled shader output* (*.cso) files are generated in the appropriate output folders (Debug and Release). The format is binary and may be loaded as ID3DBlob* objects, which is what you need to create D3D11 shader objects; for example, you would load a compiled vertex shader output to an ID3DBlob* and pass it to ID3D11Device::CreateVertexShader to create a ID3D11VertexShader object.

Although it is usually convenient to package together a vertex shader and a pixel shader for a single effect, the automatic HLSL compilation cannot process both shaders in a single HLSL build step. Therefore, the advice is to keep separate HLSL files for the shaders. For each such file, you must set the file properties accordingly. For example, in the sample application you can launch the property page for SimpleVShader.hlsl. Under the General configuration properties, you will see that the Item Type is HLSL Compiler. Under the configuration properties, select the HLSL Compiler drop-down list. The dialog pane on the right shows some properties that I set. The Entrypoint Name is set to VSMain; the default name when you first include an HLSL file is main, so I changed this to what I want. Optimizations are disabled for a Debug build and debugging information is enabled. For a Release build, optimizations are enabled and debugging information is disabled.

The default ShaderType is blank, so I changed this to VertexShader /vs using the provided drop-down list. The default shader model is the minimum feature level Shader Model 4 Level 9_1 (/4_0_level_9_1), so I changed this to Shader Model 5 (/5_0). If you have defines that need to be set, you can add those to the Preprocessor Definitions section.

I selected the Advanced item on the left. The dialog pane on the right has a field Additional Options. I added command-line options requesting row-major storage for shader matrices (/Zpr) because that is how I set up matrices in the sample; GTEngine uses row-major storage by default. I also requested to enable strict mode (/Ges) and force IEEE strictness (/Gis).

Finally, select the Command Line item on the left. The dialog pane on the right shows you the FXC command line that is generated by your choices. In the case at hand, it is

```
/Zi /E"VSMain" /Od /Fo"<MyPath>\LowLevelD3D11\Debug\SimpleVShader.cso" /vs"_5_0" /nologo
```

If you want the compiled shader output embedded in your application, you can instead compile to a header file that contains a character representation of the ID3DBlob*. The header file is then included in your application and you do not have to ship *.cso files separately.

I do not use the automatic compilation of HLSL in GTEngine applications, preferring instead to keep the shaders bundled together. This also supports my tool for generating C++ code from HLSL and using that tool in a custom build step for the HLSL file.

5.1.3 Design Goals for the Geometric Tools Engine

I will describe briefly the high-level design goals for the Geometric Tools engine, named GTEngine. A more detailed discussion of the design could be a book on its own.

5.1.3.1 An HLSL Factory

The driving force for the engine design is the HLSL shader file. High-performance algorithm development invariably involves thinking how you can write shaders to accomplish your goals. Once those shaders are written and correctly compile, an application needs to create corresponding objects at runtime, to create input and output resources to attach to the shaders and to execute the shaders. Consequently, I wrote the library HLSLFactory as a stand-alone system that compiles HLSL shaders and uses the D3D11 reflection system to obtain information about the various resources, such as the type of resource and bind points. As a stand-alone system, you can use this within your own engine code; that is, you do not have to use GTEngine at all if you so choose.

The top-level class in the library is HLSLShaderFactory and has only two public static functions: CreateFromFile and CreateFromString. The inputs for the former include the name of the HLSL file, the entry function name, the target profile, an HLSLDefiner object that stores the preprocessor defines necessary to compile the HLSL shader, and a bit flag for compiler options. The inputs for the latter are similar except that you provide a string for the shader and a name that plays the role of the file name. The output of each call is a HLSLShader object that stores all the information necessary to create and manipulate D3D11 shaders at runtime. The subsystems in HLSLShaderFactory were described in to some extent in Section 4.2.

The GTEngine interface to an HLSLShader object is provided by the class ShaderFactory. This class also has only public static functions, creators with names specific to the shader type. For example, there is a function CreateVertex that passes its inputs to the HLSL factory system and takes the resulting HLSLShader object and produces a GTEngine VertexShader object. The GTEngine shader classes such as VertexShader are shims to introduce runtime-type information and are derived from class Shader. This base class is the GTEngine analogy to HLSLShader and stores the relevant information need to create and manipulate D3D11 objects at runtime.

5.1.3.2 Resource Bridges

The Geometric Tools source code named Wild Magic 5 has a large graphics component that supports D3D9 and OpenGL on Microsoft Windows, and supports OpenGL on Linux and Macintosh OS X. In order to hide the platform dependencies, I use a *bridge pattern* [12] so I can manipulate graphics objects in a platform-independent manner within the application code. The back-end graphics objects specific to D3D9 or OpenGL have separate implementations that hide the platform dependencies. You can actually write an application once, yet it compiles and runs for each supported platform. My goal for GTEngine is similar, although for the purpose of this book I am shipping only a D3D11 version first. Knowing that later I will support OpenGL on Linux and Macintosh OS X, I chose once again to use a bridge pattern.

The relevant COM interface hierarchy for D3D11 resources is shown next.

```
ID3D11DeviceChild
    ID3D11Resource
        ID3D11Buffer
        ID3D11Texture1D
        ID3D11Texture2D
        ID3D11Texture3D
    ID3D11BlendState
    ID3D11DepthStencilState
    ID3D11RasterizerState
    ID3D11SamplerState
    ID3D11VertexShader
    ID3D11GeometryShader
    ID3D11PixelShader
    ID3D11ComputeShader
```

Although it would have been convenient for object-oriented wrappers and factoring out common code, interfaces ID3D11Texture, ID3D11State, or

ID3D11Shader do not exist. The ID3D11Buffer interface supports a variety of types, including constant buffers, vertex buffers, index buffers, and so on. I introduced a slightly richer hierarchy by wrapping these resources in classes whose names are prefixed with DX11; for example, there is an abstract class wrapper DX11Texture and a concrete class wrapper DX11Texture1. I also have an abstract class wrapper DX11Buffer and a concrete class wrapper DX11ConstantBuffer.

For the bridge pattern, I have similar classes for the platform-independent front end whose names do not have the DX11 prefix. The hierarchy is shown next for the front end. The back-end classes have the same name except with the DX11 prefix.

```
GraphicsObject
    Resource
        Buffer
            ConstantBuffer
            TextureBuffer
            VertexBuffer
            IndexBuffer
            StructuredBuffer
            TypedBuffer
            RawBuffer
            IndirectArgumentsBuffer
        Texture
            TextureSingle
                Texture1
                Texture2
                    TextureRT
                    TextureDS
                Texture3
            TextureArray
                Texture1Array
                Texture2Array
                TextureCube
                TextureCubeArray
    Shader
        VertexShader
        GeometryShader
        PixelShader
        ComputeShader
    DrawingState
        SamplerState
        BlendState
        DepthStencilState
        RasterizerState
```

I have broken out the special types for buffers and for textures. The textures are factored further into TextureSingle and TextureArray. The former is intended to represent a single texture (an array of one item) but the latter is intended for an array of multiple textures. TextureRT represents render targets and TextureDS represents depth-stencil textures, both handled different from regular textures used for geometric primitives. Although sampler state is grouped together with the other global states, keep in mind that it is handled as a resource to be attached to shaders.

The D3D11 back end has some additional classes that do not need exposure on the front end. The class DX11InputLayout encapsulates the creation and manipulation of ID3D11InputLayout objects; however, these can be built from a front-end vertex buffer and vertex shader without the front end having to generate the layout. GPU adapter and output support is encapsulated in the engine classes DXGIAdapter and DXGIOutput, both requiring only the lower-level DXGI support provided by DirectX.

The workhorse of GTEngine graphics is the class DX11Engine. This class is a manager of the creation, destruction, and manipulation of objects and resources. You can think of DX11Engine as an encapulation of a device (ID3D11Device*) and an immediate context (ID3D11DeviceContext*). The class also acts as the bridge manager using member functions Bind and Unbind. Given a front-end resource, say, Texture2, you can call Bind on that texture. DX11Engine determines whether this is the first time it has seen that texture. If so, it creates a back-end DX11Texture2 and stores the front-end and back-end pair in a map container. Each time the Texture2 object is used in a graphics operation, the engine has the responsibility for setting up the drawing or computing pipeline accordingly. At any time you can call Unbind on a resource so that its D3D11 equivalent is destroyed.

The front-end base class GraphicsObject has a *listener* system whose interface is a nested class ListenerForDestruction. Any listener derived from this interface is notified during a GraphicsObject destructor call that the object is about to be destroyed. The listener can take action before the destruction occurs. DX11Engine has a listener for such objects; for example, when the Texture2 object is destroyed, the engine listener destroys the corresponding DX11Texture2 object via an Unbind call. You can explicitly call Unbind on a resource if you want the D3D11 resource destroyed even though the front-end resource is not being destroyed.

All bridges are handled in a thread-safe manner; that is, if you are creating and destroying resources in threads different from the one on which the drawing or computing is occurring, the bridge maps are accessed using critical sections.

5.1.3.3 Visual Effects

The front end has a class VisualEffect that is a container for a vertex shader, a pixel shader, and an optional geometry shader. The class is convenient because typically you draw using a pair of vertex and pixel shaders with the vertex shader optionally feeding a geometry shader.

Some common but simple effects are derived from VisualEffect and provided for your convenience: Texture2Effect and Texture3Effect support pixel shaders that access a single 2D or 3D texture, VertexColorEffect supports geometric primitives whose vertices are assigned RGBA vertex colors, and ConstantColorEffect supports geometric primitives for which all vertices have the same vertex color (constant diffuse material color).

TextEffect supports drawing text overlaid on the application window. I use bitmapped fonts for this; in particular, I have a font class that stores the information, namely, FontArialW400H18. It is derived from a base class Font, so you can have more than one font active in an application. The tool

GeometricTools/GTEngine/Tools/BitmapFontCreator

allows you to use the Windows API to process a font and generate the Font-derived class. However, please be aware that some fonts are licensed, so you should not ship such fonts even when converted to bitmaps using this tool. If you must, you should contact the owners of the font and purchase a license.

The class OverlayEffect is not derived from VisualEffect, but it has the same flavor. This class is used mainly for drawing 2D rectangular GUI widgets overlaid on the application window. For example, if you want to write an application with your own custom-designed buttons, sliders, and other controls solely within the realm of the 3D graphics engine (i.e., no Windows API calls), you can do so with an overlay. Of course you are responsible for processing mouse clicks, key strokes, and any other GUI logic necessary to accomplish your goals.

5.1.3.4 Visual Objects and Scene Graphs

The geometric primitives you plan on drawing require geometry, optional indexing, and a visual effect. For convenience, the front end has a class Visual that is a container for these. Additionally, 3D primitives are built so that you need to use a transform from model space to world space, so I have factored out a base class called Spatial that stores transforms. Even this class is fairly general in that it supports a hierarchical data structure called a *scene graph*. The leaf nodes of the hierarchy are Spatial objects; for this book, they are Visual objects but you can also add sound-related objects, like Audial, that support 3D sound via emitters and listeners. The interior nodes of the hierarchy are defined by class Node. The Spatial class stores a pointer to a unique parent; that is, trees are supported but not directed acyclic graphs. The Node class stores child pointers. The scene graph system has support for hierarchical transforms and bounding spheres used for high-level object culling. Thus, the Spatial class stores a *local transform* that determines how its represented object is positioned and oriented within the coordinate space of its parent. It also stores a *world transform* that determines how its represented object is positioned and oriented within the coordinate system of the world, which corresponds to the root of the hierarchy. A goal of this book does not include discussing scene graph management. For much more detail on this topic, see [8].

5.1.3.5 Cameras

The Camera class is really a transformation manager for drawing 3D primitives. Section 4.1 has a detailed presentation of the various matrices involved. The concept of a camera is convenient in most applications, so you will find in the GTEngine Window class an instance of a camera. This camera is initialized with the desired parameters and it is accessed and used to update constant buffers used by vertex shaders that require a world-view-projection matrix of Equation (4.20) to transform model-space vertices to projection space for use by the rasterizer.

5.2   Debugging

Debugging is an important part of the development process for GPGPU, just as it is for CPU programming. CPU debuggers have evolved significantly over the years; GPU debuggers are younger and still evolving. Regardless, the art of debugging is more about your skills in formulating good hypotheses and testing them than it is about having the appropriate tools available.

5.2.1   Debugging on the CPU

GPU debugging support within Microsoft Visual Studio 2013 comes in the form of the *DirectX Control Panel*. You can access this by selecting the Debug option on the menu bar. Select the second item on the menu, which is labeled Graphics, and you will see a pop-up menu with an option labeled DirectX Control Panel. You have to run this with administrator privileges, so you will get the usual darkened screen and a dialog asking you whether you want to run the tool.

A dialog box appears with the title DirectX Properties. I always choose the Debug Layer radio button to be Force On. You must add executables you want monitored via the Scope option by selecting the Edit List button and browsing for the desired executables. In Message Settings, I checked the Info box. In Break Settings I checked the Enable break on functionality box. I can then check boxes in the Break on Severity part of the dialog. Of these I checked Corruption, Error, and Warning. With these options and device creation flag chosen to be D3D11_CREATE_DEVICE_DEBUG, DirectX will display messages in the output window of Microsoft Visual Studio. If your code generates a DirectX corruption, error, or warning, the debugger will break—typically because of an exception—and you will have access to a call stack. Moreover, the DirectX debug output will usually have suggestions about what the problem is and what you need to do to avoid it.

Various objects that are created, used, and destroyed have information displayed in the output window, but the default is to use memory addresses to identify them. This is not particularly helpful. You can, however, provide names for such objects via the device context. Specifically, you can use

```
const char* myName = <some name>;
UINT length = strlen(myName);
HRESULT hr = context->SetPrivateData(WKPDID_D3DDebugObjectName,
    length, myName);
```

When an object with a name causes the DirectX debug layer to emit information about the object, you will see the object's name appear with that information. I have wrapped the naming in GTEngine to allow you to conditionally turn the names of objects on or off.

5.2.2 Debugging on the GPU

Microsoft Visual Studio 2013 allows you to debug HLSL shaders. You can actually have HLSL shaders in your project files. If you drag an HLSL file into the project, its file properties show that it will be built by the "HLSL Compiler." If you choose to use this mechanism, you must set compiler options via the properties dialog. Currently, you must have one shader type per file, because the custom build mechanism cannot be set up to compile two different shaders from the same file.

I prefer not to use this mechanism, because in my production environment I have custom build steps that generate C++ source code from HLSL using my own tools that use the shader factory tool mentioned in Section 4.2. However, I can still use the HLSL debugging capabilities that Microsoft Visual Studio 2013 provides, and I am not limited by the one-shader-per-file constraint.

For example, look at the sample application

GeometricTools/GTEngine/Samples/Graphics/BlendedTerrain

The file BlendedTerrain.hlsl file contains both a vertex shader and a pixel shader. The source file BlendedTerrainEffect.cpp has the function

```
bool BlendedTerrainEffect::LoadShader(Environment const& environment,
    std::string const& name)
```

The compiler flags include

D3DCOMPILE_DEBUG   and   D3DCOMPILE_SKIP_OPTIMIZATION

in order to support the debugging from within Microsoft Visual Studio 2013.

Assuming the application compiles and runs, you can select from the menu bar the Debug option, then Graphics, and then Start Diagnostics. The application will launch and the screen will have text that asks you to capture a frame using the Print Screen key. After doing so, you will see a new window in the IDE with a captured frame. In this application, the frame is a colored rendering of a mountain and sky. After capturing, you can terminate the application. The HLSL debugger effectively runs as a simulation using the captured data. You cannot toggle between CPU debugging and HLSL debugging.

Select a mountain pixel in the scene. You will see a new window displayed entitled Graphics Pixel History. A tree control is available for the instruction ID3D11DeviceContext::DrawIndexed. If you expand the tree control, expand the item that says Triangle, you will see buttons to start debugging either the vertex shader or the pixel shader. Pressing one of these, the BlendedTerrain.hlsl file will appear in the IDE with the familiar debugger icon for the current line to be executed. Just as with the CPU debugger, you can step through the lines of HLSL code and watch variables and registers.

Debugging compute shaders is similar, although you still have to capture frames even though the compute shader is usually not frame based. For example, look at the sample application

GeometricTools/GTEngine/Samples/Basics/GaussianBlurring

This application uses the compute shader GaussianBlurring.hlsl to blur an image repeatedly. The resulting images are displayed on the screen, so you can capture frames as described previously. The compute shader is compiled with debugging information:

```
HLSLDefiner definer;
definer.SetInt("NUM_X_THREADS", mNumXThreads);
definer.SetInt("NUM_Y_THREADS", mNumYThreads);
path = env.GetPath("GaussianBlur3x3.hlsl");
unsigned int flags =
    D3DCOMPILE_ENABLE_STRICTNESS |
    D3DCOMPILE_IEEE_STRICTNESS |
    D3DCOMPILE_DEBUG |
    D3DCOMPILE_SKIP_OPTIMIZATION;
mGaussianBlurShader.reset(ShaderFactory::CreateCompute(path, definer,
    "CSMain", "cs_5_0", flags));
```

Capture a frame and terminate the application. Select a pixel in the frame. When the graphics debugger is active, a tool bar appears on the menu that has an option Pipeline Stages. Select that option and a new window will appear that has a thumbnail of the frame, information about the compute shader Dispatch call, and a button that allows you to start debugging the compute shader. Press the button and the HLSL file will appear in the IDE with the usual debugging capabilities.

In some applications, you might not have frames to capture. You can try mixing the compute shaders into the application so that during idle time, you call the compute shader, draw a rectangle that covers the application window, capture a frame, and then use the HLSL debugger. Alternatively, you can use the old-fashioned printf debugging in GPU style. Include writable textures or structured buffers in your compute shader that can store intermediate computations. You can read these back from GPU to CPU and analyze the results. For example,

```
Texture2D<float> input;
RWTexture2D<float> output;
RWTexture2D<float2> debugInfo;
[numthreads(NUMX, NUMY, 1)]
void CSMain(int2 t : SV_DispatchThreadID)
{
    float temp0 = SomeFunction(input[t]);
    float temp1 = SomeOtherFunction(input[t]);
    output = temp0 + temp1;
    debugInfo[t] = float2(temp0, temp1);
}
```

After readback, you can examine the values of `temp0` and `temp1` in case they appear not to be correct because the output appears not to be correct.

More detailed information about using graphics debugging and HLSL debugging is available online [32].

5.2.3 Be Mindful of Your Surroundings

When writing complicated computer shaders, I occasionally came across apparent bugs in the HLSL compiler; in the D3D11 runtime when executing a shader; and in the graphics drivers, whether AMD or NVIDIA. These are usually difficult to diagnose. I always assume first that I have made an error or that I misunderstand something about the graphics system. In many cases the assumption is correct. In other cases—well—all software has bugs.

When shaders do not behave the way you expect and you are certain the problem is not of your doing, you have to be diligent in your investigations. You have to formulate hypotheses and test them. I have lost count of the number of times I have heard professional developers try guessing at the causes, whether software failures or performance problems. If only you could be so lucky to guess right. My rules of thumb for shader problems are the following:

1. Figure out what **I** did wrong.

2. Try to write a simple program that reproduces the problem.

3. If successful in Rule 2, try running the program using a different version of the driver or using a different manufacturer's graphics card or using the D3D11 reference driver to see whether the problem persists.

4. Look at the HLSL assembly code to get some clues about the source of error.

I have applied Rule 3 successfully in one such problem when using an AMD graphics card. I was trying to build a pyramid of textures that was not a standard mipmap of box averages. The textures were incorrect from a certain level on. The reference driver produced the correct textures as did the same shader program running on an NVIDIA graphics card. I have had problems on NVIDIA cards where complicated shaders were not running correctly, acting almost as if there were too many instructions for the driver to handle. In these situations, I was able to run the shaders successfully on AMD cards. I have also seen a deadlock in an NVIDIA driver, occurring when the texture resource system was trying to delete a texture in one thread and create a texture in another thread—a D3D11 device is supposedly thread-safe, so this deadlock should not happen. After poring through call stacks on various threads and looking at timelines with a concurrency visualizer, I decided the problem was not of my doing. An upgrade to a newer NVIDIA driver fixed the problem.

5.2.3.1 An Example of an HLSL Compiler Bug

As an example, consider the discussion of Section 4.2.4.1 regarding the storage convention for matrices. The FXC output differs depending on whether you use option /Zpr for row-major storage or /Zpc for column-major storage. Although the standard way to pass the world-view-projection matrix of Equation (4.20) to a shader is via a constant buffer, I thought I would experiment and pass the matrix to the shader via a structured buffer. The results were unexpected. Consider the HLSL code in Listing 5.2, where I used a compute shader for the experiment.

```
StructuredBuffer<float4x4> input;   // 1 element
RWTexture1D<float> output;   // 16 elements
[numthreads(1,1,1)]
void CSMain(int3 t : SV_DispatchThreadID)
{
    for (int j = 0, k = 0; j < 4; ++j)
    {
        for (int i = 0; i < 4; ++i, ++k)
        {
            output[k] = input[0][j][i];
        }
    }
}
```

LISTING 5.2: A compute shader program that fetches a matrix from a structured buffer with native type float4x4.

The FXC output is shown in Listing 5.3 regardless of whether the option is specified for row-major or column-major order! The ld_structured_indexable instruction was manually split across lines to fit in the width of the page.

```
//
// Generated by Microsoft (R) HLSL Shader Compiler 6.3.9600.16384
//
//
// Buffer Definitions:
//
// Resource bind info for input
// {
//
//    float4x4 $Element;                 // Offset:    0 Size:    64
//
// }
//
//
// Resource Bindings:
//
// Name                          Type  Format      Dim Slot Elements
// ------------------------------ ------- -------- ----- ---- --------
// input                         texture struct     r/o   0        1
// output                            UAV  float      1d   0        1
//
//
//
// Input signature:
//
// Name                 Index   Mask Register SysValue  Format    Used
// -------------------- -----  ----- -------- --------  --------  ----
// no Input
//
```

```
// Output signature:
//
// Name                         Index    Mask  Register  SysValue  Format  Used
//  ──────────────────────────  ───────  ────  ────────  ────────  ──────  ────
// no Output
cs_5_0
dcl_globalFlags refactoringAllowed
dcl_resource_structured t0, 64
dcl_uav_typed_texture1d (float, float, float, float) u0
dcl_temps 2
dcl_thread_group 1, 1, 1
mov r0.xy, I(0,0,0,0)
loop
    ige r0.z, r0.x, I(4)
    breakc_nz r0.z
    ishl r0.z, r0.x, I(2)
    mov r1.x, r0.y
    mov r1.y, I(0)
    loop
        ige r0.w, r1.y, I(4)
        breakc_nz r0.w
        ishl r0.w, r1.y, I(4)
        iadd r0.w, r0.w, r0.z
        ld_structured_indexable(structured_buffer, stride=64)
            (mixed, mixed, mixed, mixed) r0.w, I(0), r0.w, t0.xxxx
        store_uav_typed u0.xyzw, r1.xxxx, r0.wwww
        iadd r1.xy, r1.xyxx, I(1, 1, 0, 0)
    endloop
    mov r0.y, r1.x
    iadd r0.x, r0.x, I(1)
endloop
ret
// Approximately 20 instruction slots used
```

LISTING 5.3: The FXC output from the compute shader of Listing 5.2 is the same whether you use /Zpr or /Zpc.

I compiled with the two different options and ran Beyond Compare to view the file differences—the files were identical. When using /Zpr, what caught my attention was the absence of the row_major tag on the float 4x4 $Element in the resource binding information. The input matrix A was set to a known pattern and the output array B is expected to be an increasing sequence, as shown in Equation (5.1).

$$A = \begin{bmatrix} 0 & 1 & 2 & 3 \\ 4 & 5 & 6 & 7 \\ 8 & 9 & 10 & 11 \\ 12 & 13 & 14 & 15 \end{bmatrix} \tag{5.1}$$

$$B = \{0, 1, 2, 3, 4, 5, 6, 7, 8, 9, 10, 11, 12, 13, 14, 15\}$$

However, when /Zpr is set, the input A is still interpreted as column major even though the test application passed the matrix through the structured buffer in row-major order. The output was the incorrect $\{0, 4, 8, 12, 1, 5, 9, 13, 2, 6, 10, 14, 3, 7, 11, 15\}$.

As an experiment, I modified the HLSL file slightly as shown in Listing 5.4. This program should be equivalent to that of Listing 5.2.

```
struct MyMatrix { float4x4 A; };
StructuredBuffer<MyMatrix> input;  // 1 element
RWTexture1D<float> output;  // 16 elements
[numthreads(1,1,1)]
void CSMain(int3 t : SV_DispatchThreadID)
{
    for (int j = 0, k = 0; j < 4; ++j)
    {
        for (int i = 0; i < 4; ++i, ++k)
        {
            output[k] = input[0].A[j][i];
        }
    }
}
```

LISTING 5.4: A compute shader program that fetches a matrix from a structured buffer with a struct that has a single member float4x4.

The output from FXC using /Zpr is shown in Listing 5.5. The ld_structured_indexable instruction was manually split across lines to fit in the width of the page.

```
//
// Generated by Microsoft (R) HLSL Shader Compiler 6.3.9600.16384
//
//
// Buffer Definitions:
//
// Resource bind info for input1
// {
//
//    struct MyMatrix
//    {
//
//        row_major float4x4 A;          // Offset:    0
//
//    } $Element;                        // Offset:    0 Size:    64
//
// }
//
//
// Resource Bindings:
//
// Name                        Type  Format         Dim Slot Elements
// ------------------------------ ---------- ------------ ----- -------- --------
// input1                     texture  struct         r/o   0        1
// output                        UAV  float          1d    0        1
//
//
//
// Input signature:
//
// Name                    Index   Mask Register SysValue  Format   Used
// ------------------- ----- ------ -------- -------- ------- ------
// no Input
//
// Output signature:
//
// Name                    Index   Mask Register SysValue  Format   Used
// ------------------- ----- ------ -------- -------- ------- ------
// no Output
cs_5_0
dcl_globalFlags refactoringAllowed
dcl_resource_structured t0, 64
dcl_uav_typed_texture1d (float, float, float, float) u0
dcl_temps 2
```

```
dcl_thread_group 1, 1, 1
mov r0.xy, l(0,0,0,0)
loop
    ige  r0.z, r0.x, l(4)
    breakc_nz r0.z
    ishl r0.z, r0.x, l(4)
    mov r1.x, r0.y
    mov r1.y, l(0)
    loop
        ige  r0.w, r1.y, l(4)
        breakc_nz r0.w
        ishl r0.w, r1.y, l(2)
        iadd r0.w, r0.w, r0.z
        ld_structured_indexable(structured_buffer, stride=64)
            (mixed,mixed,mixed,mixed) r0.w, l(0), r0.w, t0.xxxx
        store_uav_typed u0.xyzw, r1.xxxx, r0.wwww
        iadd r1.xy, r1.xyxx, l(1, 1, 0, 0)
    endloop
    mov r0.y, r1.x
    iadd r0.x, r0.x, l(1)
endloop
ret
// Approximately 20 instruction slots used
```

LISTING 5.5: The FXC output from the compute shader of Listing 5.4 using /Zpr.

Now we see the row_major tag on the matrix in the resource binding information. The only other differences in output are the lines with the ishl instructions. This compute shader, whether compiled with /Zpr or /Zpc, produces the same correct output.

5.2.3.2   An Example of a Programmer Bug

The compute shader program shown in Listing 5.6 is a greatly simplified example of what I was actually working on, but it is sufficient to demonstrate the problem.

```
cbuffer MyCBuffer { float input[4]; };
RWTexture1D<float> output;  // four elements
[numthreads(1,1,1)]
void CSMain(int t : SV_DispatchThreadID)
{
    for (int i = 0; i < 4; ++i)
    {
        output[i] = input[i];  // pass through the input values
    }
}
```

LISTING 5.6: An example of a programmer bug.

The constant buffer has four floating-point numbers, so I created a buffer of 16 bytes and and initialized the values to $\{0, 1, 2, 3\}$. The output texture values are $\{0, 0, 0, 0\}$, which is not what I expected. I modified the inputs to $\{1, 2, 3, 4\}$ and obtained the output values $\{1, 0, 0, 0\}$, which is still not what I expected. Surely this is a bug in the HLSL compiler? I stuck to my rules of thumb. In this case I posted a question on www.gamedev.net and mentioned the problem. A responder provided the link [45]. The webpage mentions the

HLSL packing rules for constant buffers. Arrays in constant buffers are not packed by default. This avoids offset computations if you have four array elements per register. If you want to incur the ALU overhead, you can always pack the arrays yourself. The problem, though, is you cannot loop over the array in your HLSL code, so that code must unpack manually. In the previous code sample, the problem really was mine—my lack of understanding of the HLSL packing rules. According to the rules, there should be four registers assigned to MyCBuffer.

The output of FXC is shown in Listing 5.7.

```
//
// Generated by Microsoft (R) HLSL Shader Compiler 6.3.9600.16384
//
//
// Buffer Definitions:
//
// cbuffer MyCBuffer
// {
//
//    float input[4];                        // Offset:    0 Size:    52
//
// }
//
//
// Resource Bindings:
//
// Name                         Type  Format         Dim Slot Elements
// ------------------------ ---------- ------- ----------- ---- --------
// output                        UAV   float          1d   0         1
// MyCBuffer                 cbuffer     NA          NA   0         1
//
//
//
// Input signature:
//
// Name                  Index   Mask Register SysValue  Format   Used
// ------------------ -------- ------ -------- -------- -------- ------
// no Input
//
// Output signature:
//
// Name                  Index   Mask Register SysValue  Format   Used
// ------------------ -------- ------ -------- -------- -------- ------
// no Output
cs_5_0
dcl_globalFlags refactoringAllowed
dcl_constantbuffer cb0[4], dynamicIndexed
dcl_uav_typed_texture1d (float,float,float,float) u0
dcl_temps 1
dcl_thread_group 1, 1, 1
mov r0.x, l(0)
loop
    ige r0.y, r0.x, l(4)
    breakc_nz r0.y
    store_uav_typed u0.xyzw, r0.xxxx, cb0[r0.x + 0].xxxx
    iadd r0.x, r0.x, l(1)
endloop
ret
// Approximately 8 instruction slots used
```

LISTING 5.7: The output of FXC applied to the code of Listing 5.6.

The first hint the output provides is the size of 52 for the constant buffer. If the packing had been as I assumed, the size should be 16. Even knowing the packing rules, should the size be 64 (four registers at 16 bytes each)? Yes, there are four registers assigned—you can see this in the instruction dcl_constantbuffer cb0[4]. However, the FXC compiler is reporting that you are only "using" 52 of these bytes. This count includes the forty-eight bytes for the first three registers, but the program uses only the first component of the fourth register (4 more bytes). Well, be careful about interpreting the comments in the human-readable output. In the shader reflection that GTEngine uses to compile shaders at runtime, the number of bytes for MyCBuffer is queried from a D3D11_SHADER_BUFFER_DESC and the size is reported as 64 bytes.

So in fact the problem is mine. I modified the constant buffer creation to use a buffer of 64 bytes, typecast it as an array of four Vector4<float> objects, and set the zeroth components of the vectors to be 0, 1, 2, and 3. The output was then exactly these input values.

5.3 Performance

GPGPU is very much about high performance. Despite the availability of embarrassingly parallel hardware, you have the responsibility of ensuring the end-to-end performance of your applications. In turn, you must understand what tools are available to you to accomplish your performance goals.

5.3.1 Performance on the CPU

On a CPU, the standard tool for measuring performance is a *profiler*. Microsoft Visual Studio 2013 has a profiler you may use. This is accessible throught the main menu by choosing the Analyze option. In the pop-up menu, you then choose the Profiler option. For fastest access to the capabilities, you can run an uninstrumented version of your application and *attach* a profiler to it. You cannot profile an application with a debugger attached. Thus, you should run your application from the menu option Debug and then select the suboption Start Without Debugging. After the application launches, select menu option Analyze, suboption Profiler, and then select the Attach/Detach item. You need to run the tool in administrator mode to access the high-performance counters, so the first time you run this during a Microsoft Visual Studio session, you will be prompted with the usual dialog box about running as administrator.

Once the tool starts up, you will see a dialog box containing a list of applications that are running. Select the application you want to profile; that is the one the profiler will be attached to. A window will appear in the IDE showing that the profiler is running. You can either terminate the application or select an option that says to stop profiling. In either case, the profiler will display output telling you that it is collecting the data. Finally, a window is displayed with the results. A simple summary is displayed, but the most useful is listed under Related Views, specifically the Functions link.

When you visit the functions link, you will see a list of functions and DLLs, and you can sort by *exclusive* (count time in that function) or by *inclusive* (count time in that function and in the functions it calls). For real-time graphics, I prefer the inclusive view, because it gives me a quick idea about where I am spending the time in the call stack. You can double-click a function to display a window of the source code for that function with lines highlighted that are taking the majority of the time to execute. Of course, there are many other options you can explore. I suggest playing with this tool for a while and explore the information available to you.

Another tool that is available as a plugin to Microsoft Visual Studio 2013 is the Concurrency Visualizer. You can obtain this for free through the IDE by selecting the menu option

Tools | Extensions and Updates | Online | Visual Studio Gallery | Tools | Performance |
    Concurrency Visualizer for Visual Studio 2013

An installation button is available. Once installed, the menu option Analyze now has a new suboption Concurrency Visualizer. Just as with the profiler, start your application without a debugger attached. Attach the Concurrency Visualizer to your application process. Once again you need to run this in administrator mode, so you might be prompted with a dialog box. A window appears in the IDE that tells you to terminate the application when desired, or you can select a link that says to stop the data collection (but the application continues to run). The amount of information this tool generates is quite large, so you do not want to run it for long.

A window appears with a summary of information. The most important link to select is the Threads link. You get a collection of timelines for threads. A slider allows you to zoom in and see various color-coded blocks; the legend for coloring is shown. Selecting the green blocks in the main thread, you can see what code is being executed. Having the thread timelines adjacent to each other can give you information, for example, when one thread is stalling another. The tool itself can detect this and show you which thread's callstack is blocking your thread (and vice versa). The DirectX GPU threads are also displayed; these are the DLL threads, not individual GPU compute shader execution threads. Again, I suggest you play with this tool to see what information is available.

If you want a larger suite of tools with more capabilities, but one that is not free, I suggest *Intel Parallel Studio XE 2013*. The profiling tool is *Intel VTune Amplifier XE 2013*. You can obtain profiling information at the assembly level and customize what you want to measure. Filtering by thread is a nice capability, and you can view timelines for the threads. The suite also comes with a tool called *Intel Inspector XE 2013* that helps you track down memory errors, leaks, and threading problems.

5.3.2 Performance on the GPU

Performance measurements on the GPU are possible at a high level using only D3D11 support. Firstly, you can always measure frame rate during idle loop time to give you a coarse idea of how long something takes to compute or how much faster something is after you have made shader changes. The GTEngine sample applications show how to do this. Secondly, the ID3D11Device interface allows queries related to timing. Listing 5.8 shows the basic code. The HRESULT processing is omitted for simplicity, but the GTEngine code handles the return values.

```
// ——— initialization code
ID3D11Device* device;    // the device of interest
ID3D11DeviceContext* immediate;   // the associated context

D3D11_QUERY_DATA_TIMESTAMP_DISJOINT timeStamp;
ID3D11Query* frequencyQuery;
ID3D11Query* startTimeQuery;
ID3D11Query* finalTimeQuery;

D3D11_QUERY_DESC desc;
desc.Query = D3D11_QUERY_TIMESTAMP_DISJOINT;
desc.MiscFlags = D3D11_QUERY_MISC_NONE;
device->CreateQuery(&desc, &frequencyQuery);

desc.Query = D3D11_QUERY_TIMESTAMP;
desc.MiscFlags = D3D11_QUERY_MISC_NONE;
device->CreateQuery(&desc, &startTimeQuery);
device->CreateQuery(&desc, &finalTimeQuery);

// ——— runtime code
// Begin timer.
immediate->Begin(frequencyQuery);
immediate->End(startTimeQuery);
int64_t startTime;
while (S_OK != immediate->GetData(startTimeQuery, &startTime,
    sizeof(startTime), 0))
{
    // Wait for end of query.
}

// CPU code that calls into the GPU goes here.

// End timer.
immediate->End(finalTimeQuery);
int64_t finalTime;
while (S_OK != immediate->GetData(finalTimeQuery, &finalTime,
    sizeof(finalTime), 0))
{
    // Wait for end of query.
}
immediate->End(frequencyQuery);
while (S_OK != immediate->GetData(frequencyQuery, &timeStamp,
    sizeof(timeStamp), 0))
{
    // Wait for end of query.
}
```

```
// number of ticks for GPU execution
int64_t numTicks = finalTime − startTime;
// number of seconds for GPU execution
double numSeconds = ((double)numTicks)/((double)timeStamp.Frequency);
```

LISTING 5.8: D3D11 code to support timing of execution on the GPU.

GTEngine encapsulates this system in class DX11PerformanceCounter and the engine functions DX11Engine::BeginTimer and DX11Engine::EndTimer. The typical usage is

```
DX11Engine engine;
DX11PerformanceCounter performance(engine.GetDevice());
engine.BeginTimer(performance);
// CPU code that calls into the GPU goes here.
engine.EndTimer(performance);
double seconds = performance.GetSeconds();
```

The D3D11 timing query is at best a quick measurement of performance. However, it says nothing about what is actually happening on the GPU regarding computation (arithmetic logic units, both scalar and vector) or memory bandwidth (cache behavior). Graphics chip manufacturers provide their own performance tools. NVIDIA has its Nsight tool so you can work within Microsoft Visual Studio; it is available for download from NVIDIA's website. You can debug shaders as well as profile with this tool.

AMD has performance tools you may download from their website. I have had mixed success with the stand-alone tools. I have had better success with their GPU Performance API that you can load dynamically loaded and use directly within an application. The version I am using is 2.11.739.0. Although I have a class wrapper that encapsulates their DLL, I cannot redistribute the library. To use my class wrapper, you must download the API yourself and agree to the license. I can, however, show you how the wrapper works. I have installed the AMD GPU Performance API to the following folders:

GeometricTools/GTEngine/Tools/GPUPerfAPI-2.11.739.0/Bin
GeometricTools/GTEngine/Tools/GPUPerfAPI-2.11.739.0/Include
GeometricTools/GTEngine/Tools/GPUPerfAPI-2.11.739.0/Source

The Include and Source folders also contain my class-based wrapper AMDPerformance. You can add the wrapper header and source file to any project for which you want GPU profiling on an AMD graphics card. The API is loaded dynamically, so the DLLs must be found at runtime. To support this in any Geometric Tools development, I have created folders

C:/Program Files (x86)/GeometricTools/x86
C:/Program Files (x86)/GeometricTools/x64

and copied the AMD performance DLLs to these folders. The same folders will be used for DLL versions of GTEngine. Of course, you need administrative privileges to do this, and you will need to do this manually because the software does not come with an installer. I also have these folders as part of the system PATH environment variable, which is searched when an application requires DLLs.

The AMD GPU Performance API has various counters it can measure depending on the model of your graphics card. The API allows you to enumerate these. For an AMD 7970, the enumeration shows 62 counters I can measure. For example, there is a counter named GPUTime that I can request and have the API report its value. A sample application shows how to use the counters,

GeometricTools/GTEngine/Basics/PerformanceAMD

The application draws 1024 triangles with random vertices in the cube $[-1, 1]^3$ and with random texture coordinates in $[0, 1]^2$. Back-face culling is disabled. The texture for the triangles is loaded from the hard disk but each frame is blurred using a compute shader. The PerformanceAMDWindow header file declares

```
private:
    static void Listener(GPA_Logging_Type type, char const* message);
    AMDPerformance mPerformance;
```

The Listener function is a callback provided to the performance library to be called when events are generated by the library during the measurements. I have these messages written to the output window of the IDE. The constructor of the application window object is

```
PerformanceAMDWindow::PerformanceAMDWindow(Parameters& parameters)
    :
    Window(parameters),
    mTextColor(0.0f, 0.0f, 0.0f, 1.0f),
    mPerformance(mEngine->GetDevice())
{
    CreateCamera();
    CreateTextureGenerator();
    CreateScene();

    // Disable back-face culling.
    mNoCullingState.reset(new RasterizerState());
    mNoCullingState->cullMode = RasterizerState::CULL_NONE;
    mEngine->SetRasterizerState(mNoCullingState);

    mPerformance.SaveCounterInformation("AMD7970Counters.txt");
    mPerformance.Register(Listener);
    mPerformance.SetAllCounters();
}
```

The mPerformance object is constructed by giving it the ID3D11Device object associated with the window. At the end of the constructor, a description of the counters is written to a file. You need do this only once for a specific graphics card. The Listener callback is provided to the performance system and all counters enumerated by the system are enabled for measurement.

The idle-time function for the real-time behavior is

```
void PerformanceAMDWindow::OnIdle()
{
    MeasureTime();
```

```
MoveCamera ();
UpdateConstants ();

mEngine->ClearBuffers ();

mPerformance . Profile ([ this ]()
{
    mEngine->Execute (mGenerateTexture , mNumXGroups, mNumYGroups, 1);
    mEngine->Draw (mTriangles );
});

// Compute the average measurements. GetAverage allows you to access
// the measurements during application runtime. SaveAverage calls
// GetAverage and writes the results to a spreadsheet.
std :: vector <std :: vector <AMDPerformance :: Measurement>> measurements ;
if (mPerformance . GetNumProfileCalls() == 16)
{
    mPerformance . GetAverage (measurements );
    mPerformance . SaveAverage (" ProfileResults .csv" );
}

DrawFrameRate (8, mYSize − 8, mTextColor );
mEngine->DisplayColorBuffer (0);

UpdateFrameCount ();
}
```

The CPU-based frame rate counter is part of the GTEngine window class; it is measured using MeasureTime and UpdateFrameCount, and the frame rate is displayed (in frames per second) in the application window (lower-left corner). The GPU operations I want to measure are bounded by the lambda function passed to mPerformance.Profile. The capture clause specifies the variable this because I need to access class members of PerformanceAMDWindow.

The sample is designed to measure the GPU performance during the first sixteen calls of OnIdle, after which it computes the average of the measurements and saves the results to a comma-separated-value file. This format allows you to open the file with Microsoft Excel or other spreadsheet tool. At the highest level, the counter GPUTime has a measurement of 0.49 milliseconds of execution on the GPU. The counter GPUBusy was measured at 100 percent. Table 5.1 shows measurements related to the vertex and pixel shaders.

TABLE 5.1: Vertex and pixel shader performance measurements

counter	measurement	description
VSBusy	1.27	percentage of time the shader unit has vertex shader work to do
VSVerticesIn	3072	number of vertices processed by vertex shader
PSBusy	11.76	percentage of time the shader unit has pixel shader work to do
PrimitivesIn	1024	number of primitives received by the hardware
PSPixelsOut	258247	color buffer writes by the pixel shader
PSExportStalls	0.03	percentage of GPUBusy (positive means bottleneck in late depth testing or in color buffer)
TexUnitBusy	85.61	percentage of GPUTime the texture unit is active
CBMemWritten	1228420	bytes written to the color buffer

TABLE 5.2: Compute shader performance measurements

counter	measurement	description
CSThreadGroups	12288	number of thread groups
CSThreads	1048130	number of threads
CSWavefronts	12288	number of wavefronts
CSBusy	86.24	percentage time the shader unit has compute shader work to do
CSMemUnitBusy	87.15	percentage of GPUTime the memory unit is active
CSMemUnitStalled	0.47	percentage of GPUTime the memory unit is stalled
CSFetchSize	5220.28	total kilobytes fetched from video memory
CSWriteSize	3072	kilobytes written to video memory
CSWriteUnitStalled	0.14	percentage of GPUTime the write unit is stalled
CSCacheHit	67.23	percentage of instructions that hit the data cache
CSSALUBusy	0.09	percentage of GPUTime scalar ALU instructions are processed
CSSALUInsts	0.32	average number of scalar ALU instructions per work item
CSSFetchInsts	0.09	average number of scalar fetch instructions from video memory executed per work item
CSVALUBusy	4.16	percentage of GPUTime vector ALU instructions are processed
CSVALUInsts	28.48	average number of vector ALU instructions per work item
CSVFetchInsts	4.49	average number of vector fetch instructions from video memory executed per work item
CSVWriteInsts	0.09	average number of vector write instructions to video memory executed per work item
CSVALUUtilization	99.97	percentage of active vector ALU threads in a wave

Table 5.2 shows the measurements related to the compute shader. The first category of measurements involve thread counting. An AMD wavefront consists of sixty-four threads. I chose the compute shader to use $8 \times 8 \times 1$ threads, which is one wavefront per thread group. Thus, the reported numbers of thread groups and wavefronts are the same. The second category of measurements are about memory accesses. The third category is about the arithmetic logic units (ALUs), both scalar (single-channel operations) and vector (multichannel operations in the SIMD sense).

Table 5.3 shows the measurements related to depth, stencil, and culling state (including clipping). The application disabled back-face culling and all triangles are visible during the performance testing, so culling primitives and clipped primitives are both zero.

5.3.3 Performance Guidelines

Here is a brief list of guidelines to follow in order to obtain high performance when writing GPGPU-based applications.

- Choose thread group sizes properly. On AMD hardware, a *wavefront* consists of sixty-four GPU threads. On NVIDIA, a *warp* consists of

TABLE 5.3: Depth, stencil, and culling state performance measurements

counter	measurement	description
PrimitiveAssemblyBusy	9.42	percentage of GPUTime that clipping and culling is busy
CulledPrims	0	number of culled primitives
ClippedPrims	0	number of primitives requiring at least one clipping operation
DepthStencilBusy	10.24	percentage of time GPU spent performing depth and stencil tests
ZUnitStalled	0.10	percentage of GPUTime depth buffer waits for color buffer to be ready for writes
HiZQuadsCulled	95.93	percentage of quads not continuing in the pipeline after HiZ test (written directly to depth buffer or culled)
PostZQuads	1.74	percentage of quads for which pixel shader will run and may be PostZ tested
PreZQuadsCulled	2.33	percentage of quads rejected based on detailZ and earlyZ tests
PreZSamplesFailingZ	383368	number of samples tested for Z before shading and failed Z test
PreZSamplesPassing	258247	number of samples tested for Z after shading and passed
PreZTilesDetailCulled	0.03	percentage of tiles rejected because the primitive had no contributing area

thirty-two GPU threads. You should choose the numthreads parameters to have a product that is a multiple of these numbers; otherwise, the excess threads will be executed anyway yet their work is rejected. You should prefer to keep all the threads busy doing work that is accepted.

- Prefer to avoid branching and the associated stalls whenever possible; if necessary, use SIMD-style flattening, manually or via the flatten directive.

- Use group-shared memory to avoid redundant memory accesses when computing in neighborhoods of a point and to store shared computations that are expensive. Be sure to determine the break-even point for when group-shared memory outperforms the naive look-up-everything-in-the-neighborhood approach.

- Prefer loop unrolling via the unroll directive, but profile the shader because sometimes loop unrolling might lead to slower code. I had this happen on occasion but not frequently.

- Avoid loops controlled by variables associated with unordered access views. Such control is usually a performance problem. If your algorithm requires this and you have designed this in a sequential manner, you can analyze the algorithm to see whether you can make it a multipass algorithm that avoids the UAV loop control. For example, I had to do this when writing a GPU-based connected component labeler that used a union-find algorithm.

- Try to keep data on GPU; that is, avoid uploads to the GPU and read-backs from the GPU in the middle of an end-to-end algorithm. The memory transfer is a serious bottleneck.

- When creating a lot of D3D11 resources, try to do so in a thread that is separate from the consumer of the resources. This takes advantage of the thread safety of the ID3D11Device object. In the producer-consumer model, you will have to thread the CPU code for the consumption.

- If you have a sequence of GPU stages that must be performed in order, and if one of them performs worse than the CPU algorithm, that is not a reason to avoid porting to the GPU. The goal is a speedup for the entire sequence. It is not necessary to have each GPU stage outperform the corresponding CPU stage.

- Use GPU performance counters for hardware information such as memory and texture cache misses; memory reads, write, and stalls; scalar ALU usage; vector ALU usage; etc.

- Use multiple tools, because one alone is usually not sufficient to give you enough information to diagnose. You should definitely use a CPU profiler for end-to-end performance measurements, a GPU profiler to understand what is happening on the GPU, and a tool such as Microsoft's Concurrency Visualizer to see how the application threads are laid out over time in order to determine where stalls are in the end-to-end execution.

- *Do not follow the guidelines as if they are absolute rules.* For example, if you have branching and the profiler shows that branching is not a bottleneck, there is no reason to remove the branching—especially if it makes the algorithm more complicated. As another example, just because you access shader resources in a neighborhood of the location specified by the dispatch thread ID does not mean you should immediately use group-shared memory. Such sharing has some fixed costs associated with it. Try writing the shaders both way, with and without group-shared memory, and measure the performance in order to make your final decision.

5.4   Code Testing

In an industrial software engineering development environment, you invariably have test teams to support what you do. One of those tasks is to verify that (most of) your code has been exercised so that you have some assurance that what you wrote is actually used during application runtime. This falls in the realm of *code testing*. To illustrate some of the testing topics, consider the contrived function of Listing 5.9.

```
enum ErrorCode { INSERTED, NO_MATCH, INVALID_INPUT };

ErrorCode Insert(char const* name, Database& db)
{
    ErrorCode code = INSERTED;
    if (name != nullptr)
    {
        if (name[0] == 'A')
        {
            db.InsertARecord(name);
        }
        else if (name[0] == 'B' && name[1] == 'a')
        {
            db.InsertBCRecord(name);
        }
        else if (name[0] == 'D')
        {
            db.InsertERecord(name);
        }
        else
        {
            code = NO_MATCH;
        }
    }
    else
    {
        code = INVALID_INPUT;
    }
    return code;
}
```

LISTING 5.9: A simple example to illustrate testing concepts.

5.4.1   Topics in Code Testing

Code testing is a large topic, and I do not plan on going into detail about it in this book. But I do want to mention several topics because they should be on your mind during development. Some high-level questions you must ask yourself are:

1. Does the code do what it is designed to do?

2. Will the code perform robustly for the inputs it is intended to process?

3. What are the conditions under which the code will fail? If any, what safeguards does the code have to prevent failure?

In the example at hand, I assume the existence of an object db that allows you to insert character strings into a database. The code is designed to allow insertion of strings starting with "A", "Ba", or "D"; other strings are not inserted. Given this limited description, I would say that the code does what it is designed to do. You can test the code with

```
ErrorCode code;
code = Insert("Alligator", db);  // code = INSERTED
code = Insert("Bat", db);        // code = INSERTED
code = Insert("Dog", db);        // code = INSERTED
```

```
code = Insert("Cat", db);         // code = NO_MATCH
code = Insert(nullptr, db);       // code = INVALID_INPUT
```

However, without a formal requirements list, do you really know whether the code does what it is designed to do? For example, is the name matching supposed to be case sensitive?

```
code = InsertName("BAt");  // code = NO_MATCH, is this what you want?
```

Checking your code against a requirements list is not something for which tools are readily available. You will need to be diligent about this topic. In my industrial experience, getting a well-written requirements list from your clients or coworkers is as painful as pulling teeth.

Regarding robustness, the code at least tests whether the input pointer is not null. However, the code is not as robust as it could be. For example,

```
char const* name0 = "B";
code = InsertName(name0, db);  // code = NO_MATCH, which is okay
char const* name1 = new char[1];
name1[0] = 'B';
// What should the returned code be?  Dereferencing name1[1] is a memory
// access violation.
code = InsertName(name1, db);
```

Most likely the programmer intended the input name to be a null-terminated string, but string handling is problematic, because you have no idea of the length of the string and strlen measures the length by searching for a null character. Thus, the caller of Insert has the responsibility for meeting the *precondition* that name is a null-terminated string. A better design might be to pass in the length:

```
ErrorCode InsertAlt1(unsigned int length, char const* name, Database& db)
{
    ErrorCode code = NO_MATCH;
    if (name != nullptr && length > 0)
    {
        if (length >= 1)
        {
            if (name[0] == 'A' || name[0] == 'D')
            {
                db.InsertARecord(name);
                code = INSERTED;
            }
        }
        else if (length >= 2)
        {
            if (name[0] == 'B' && name[1] == 'a')
            {
                db.InsertBCRecord(name);
                code = INSERTED;
            }
        }
    }
    else
    {
        code = INVALID_MATCH;
    }
    return code;
}
```

However, there is no guarantee that the caller has ensured that the length is correct for the specified name. Alternatively, you can use a different data structure for the string:

```
ErrorCode InsertAlt2(std::string const& name, Database& db)
{
    ErrorCode code = NO_MATCH;
    if (name != "")
    {
        if (name.length() >= 1)
        {
            if (name[0] == 'A' || name[0] == 'D')
            {
                db.InsertARecord(name.c_str());
                code = INSERTED;
            }
        }
        else if (name.length() >= 2)
        {
            if (name[0] == 'B' && name[1] == 'a')
            {
                db.InsertBCRecord(name.c_str());
                code = INSERTED;
            }
        }
    }
    else
    {
        code = INVALID_MATCH;
    }
    return code;
}
```

This alternative is attractive in that the caller must properly formulate the name string, although an accidental memory overwrite can be painful. This gives you fewer responsibilities. The db object is still expecting a native pointer, but at least you are passing a pointer to a well-formed string, relying on std::string to be implemented and tested properly.

Regardless of how you design the algorithm for insertion, it is your responsibility to test the code, even before passing it off to a formal team of testers. Concepts you should be familiar with are *unit testing, regression testing*, and *code coverage*. Unit testing has two goals. The first goal is to verify that your code correctly solves the problems you intended. Because you are most likely not the only person working on the code base, others might change the code. The code might have been deemed correct but later changes make it incorrect. Unit tests tend to be executed on a regular basis in order to trap problems introduced during code maintenance; thus, the second goal of unit testing is to find regressions in behavior. As always, do not wait for a test team to find any regressions or bugs you have introduced. *The best time to diagnose and find bugs is as soon as you have introduced them.* If you wait, you might forget what you were thinking when you made the code changes.

The unit tests should be designed to exercise as much of the code as possible, including any error conditions that your code tries to trap. Code coverage generally comes in a few flavors. You can measure which functions in your code are entered during execution, which blocks of code are executed, or which lines of code are executed. Function coverage is useful mainly for high-level measurements of what parts of your code base are actually being used. Line coverage is, perhaps, too fine a measurement—if you have n lines without branching, all lines will be executed.

In my experience at Microsoft, the automated code coverage tools used block counting where the blocks are determined from the generated assembly code. One block is a sequence of assembly instructions without branching. Although this makes sense at a high level, there are some low-level consequences that you must keep in mind. Firstly, the assembly code generated for debug configurations and release configurations are different, especially when code is inlined. Secondly, the tools will count function call entry and function call exit blocks, and sometimes branching is handled in a manner you did not expect. For example, a simple function of the form

```
bool IsDepthTexture (Texture texture)
{
    return texture.type == DEPTH_TEXTURE_ENUMERATION;
}

Texture mytexture;
if (IsDepthTexture(mytexture))
{
    DoSomething;
}
```

shows up as four blocks. Two of those blocks are the call entry and call exit handling, usually stack manipulation to push and pop input parameters. Two other blocks are generated because of the implied branching due to the operator== comparison. The small code stub most likely generates 75 percent code coverage, because the *calling code* does not have an else clause, and the code coverage tool thinks you have not tested the case of the texture not being a depth texture. The code coverage tools typically come with a user interface that allows you to see coverage information at the source-code level, even though the blocks are counted at the assembly level.

You should certainly strive for full code coverage, but in practice you cannot expect to reach 100 percent because you invariably will have fault conditions that are difficult to test. This is in the realm of *fault injection*, which is difficult to implement. For example, if your code creates a D3D11 device and context, and that code works fine on your machine, you might not have ever tested your code to see what happens if the device creation fails, say, on a machine that has only D3D9 hardware. To test the failure, you could step through with a debugger and set the return HRESULT to something other than S_OK, then let the program continue running to see whether it terminates properly. Unfortunately, manual fault injection of this type is not suitable for a production environment where you want to automate the testing.

Unit tests that lead to 100 percent code coverage do not necessarily guarantee that your code works correctly. If your algorithm is implemented incorrectly, no amount of code coverage measurement will help you. Thus, code coverage is necessary for your development environment but it is not entirely sufficient for a quality product. And unit testing is not always enough. Such tests tend to be for low-level components of your code. For an entire application, you tend to have *end-to-end testing*. Each component might be unit tested and deemed correct, but do the components all work together correctly to produce the desired application results? End-to-end test design is specific to the application at hand, so there are no general guidelines for how to do this within your environment.

5.4.2   Code Coverage and Unit Testing on the GPU

Because of the highly parallel nature of a GPU, tool support that you normally find for CPU computing is not as evolved for GPU computing. As mentioned previously, you can copy intermediate computations into structured buffers, read them back from GPU to CPU, and analyze them for any problems in the shader code. The same idea applies to obtaining code coverage. You can provide a structured buffer or texture that has unsigned integers used as bit flags, set for each block of code in the shader. For example, consider Listing 5.10.

```
Texture2D<float4> input;
RWTexture2D<float4> output;
RWTexture2D<uint> codeCoverage;   // initially all zero values
[numthreads(NUMX, NUMY, 1)]
void CSMain(int2 t : SV_DispatchThreadID)
{
    if (input[t].r > 0.0f)
    {
        output[t] = input[t].rrrr;
        codeCoverage[t] |= 1;
    }
    else if (input[t].g > 0.0f)
    {
        output[t] = input[t].gggg;
        codeCoverage[t] |= 2;
    }
    else if (input[t].b > 0.0f)
    {
        output[t] = input[t].bbbb;
        codeCoverage[t] |= 4;
    }
    else
    {
        output[t] = input[t].aaaa;
        codeCoverage[t] |= 8;
    }
}
```

LISTING 5.10: An example of measuring code coverage on the GPU.

The codeCoverage output sets a bit in the bit flag based on which block of code is executed. Moreover, in this example you additionally get information about the block for each thread with ID t.

If you care only about the generic block regardless of thread, you could easily have a single-element 2D texture and set only bits of codeCoverage[0]. However, keep in mind that the current code guarantees no concurrent access to codeCoverage[t]. Using a single element, you want to guard against concurrent access. This is particularly true if you want to count how many times you executed a block. For example, consider Listing 5.11.

```
Texture2D<float4> input;
RWTexture2D<float4> output;
RWStructuredBuffer<uint> codeCoverage;  // four values, all initially zero
[numthreads(8, 8, 1)]
void CSMain(int2 t : SV_DispatchThreadID)
{
    if (input[t].r > 0.0f)
    {
        output[t] = input[t].rrrr;
        uint oldValue0;
        InterlockedAdd(codeCoverage[0], 1, oldValue0);
    }
    else if (input[t].g > 0.0f)
    {
        output[t] = input[t].gggg;
        uint oldValue1;
        InterlockedAdd(codeCoverage[1], 1, oldValue1);
    }
    else if (input[t].b > 0.0f)
    {
        output[t] = input[t].bbbb;
        uint oldValue2;
        InterlockedAdd(codeCoverage[2], 1, oldValue2);
    }
    else
    {
        output[t] = input[t].aaaa;
        uint oldValue3;
        InterlockedAdd(codeCoverage[3], 1, oldValue3);
    }
}
```

LISTING 5.11: An example of code coverage on the GPU where you count how many times each block is visited.

As always, a measurement taken during an experiment affects the experiment itself. The HLSL compiler does a good job of optimizing code. If you insert instructions for measuring code coverage, it is possible that the optimizer cannot do what it did before the insertion. Thus, the code coverage measurements change the actual code whose coverage you are trying to measure. Also, if the shader is extremely lengthy and complicated, you can spend a lot of time adding the code coverage instructions. Moreover, if your shader is bordering on the limit of number of instructions, the additional code coverage instructions could push you over the limit and the shader will not compile.

One thing you should do if you plan on measuring the code coverage on a regular basis—wrap the code coverage instructions with preprocessor macros that you can turn on or off. Within GTEngine, you can do this using the HLSLDefiner class.

Regarding unit testing, my general rule of thumb is to write C++ code that is designed to do the same thing the HLSL code is designed to do. You can read back the HLSL outputs and compare them to the C++ outputs. If the outputs are dependent on the IEEE floating-point behavior, say, you expect some subnormals in the C++ code, your unit tests will have to account for this and compare properly. If your shader output is from the image processing domain, you can write unit tests and do regression testing by reading back the image outputs and compare them to a database of images generated from previous runs of the code.

Chapter 6

Linear and Affine Algebra

6.1 Vectors

Vectors and matrices are the most common entities manipulated in real-time applications. I assume you are familiar with the algebra and geometry of these. Although it is important to understand the abstract concepts one normally encounters in courses on linear or affine algebra, the focus here is on the concrete computational aspects and on the geometric relationships associated with these entities. We will work only with real-valued computations, so there is no need to have a data type or support for complex numbers.

In practice, vectors are represented as one-dimensional arrays of scalars; typically, the data type is floating-point, either 32-bit float or 64-bit double. GTEngine supports both by implementing its mathematics library using templates. Matrices are represented as two-dimensional arrays of scalars.

Mathematics engines for real-time applications provide vector implementations that support basic arithmetic: sum and difference of vectors, multiplication of a vector by a scalar, dot product of vectors, and length of a vector. Usually, support is included for normalizing a vector, where you compute a unit-length vector in the same direction as the original, assuming it is not zero. GTEngine does so and also includes support for computing extreme values from a set of vectors, the result an axis-aligned bounding box. The engine provides geometric operations related to orthogonality, namely, computing orthogonal vectors or bases; cross products in 3D are part of this support. Affine operations include computing barycentric coordinates and determining within a user-specified tolerance the dimensionality of a set of vectors. Finally, comparison operators are provided to support standard C++ sorted containers.

GTEngine has a base template class Vector<int,Real> whose first parameter is the dimension (number of components) and whose second parameter is the floating-point type (float or double). Derived classes Vector2<Real>, Vector3<Real>, and Vector4<Real> provide additional dimension-specific constructors and operations.

6.1.1   Robust Length and Normalization Computations

A common operation for vectors is computing the length. If $\mathbf{V}$ has components x_i for $0 \le i < n$, the length is mathematically defined as

$$|\mathbf{V}| = \sqrt{\sum_{i=0}^{n-1} x_i^2} \tag{6.1}$$

The most frequently encountered implementation is the obvious one, shown in Listing 6.1, where components of the vector V can be accessed by the bracket operator. The data type Real is either float or double.

```
Real Length (Vector V)
{
    Real length = 0;
    for (int i = 0; i < n; ++i)
    {
        length += V[i]*V[i];
    }
    length = sqrt(length);
    return length;
}
```

LISTING 6.1: Computing the length of a vector.

For small-magnitude components, this implementation is reasonable, but if the components are large in magnitude, the floating-point computations for the sum of squares can overflow, leading to a return value of floating-point infinity. For example, let M be the maximum finite floating-point number for Real. The vector $\mathbf{V} = (M/2, M/2, M/2)$ has theoretical length $\sqrt{3}M/2$, which should have a finite floating-point number that approximates it. However, using floating-point arithmetic, the term V[0]*V[0] will overflow to become the floating-point infinity. The same is true for the other squares, and accumulating them will still produce floating-point infinity. The sqrt function returns floating-point infinity when its input is infinite.

A mathematically equivalent algorithm that leads to a robust implementation is the following. Let j be the index for the vector's component of largest magnitude; thus, $|x_i| \le |x_j|$ for all i. If $x_j = 0$, then the vector is the zero vector and its length is zero. If $x_j \ne 0$, factor the vector to $\mathbf{V} = |x_j|(\mathbf{V}/|x_j|)$. The vector $\mathbf{W} = \mathbf{V}/|x_j|$ has components all smaller or equal to one in magnitude, so the obvious length computation for it does not overflow. Listing 6.2 has pseudocode for this algorithm.

```
Real LengthRobust (Vector V)
{
    Real maxAbsComponent = |V[0]|;
    for (int i = 1; i < n; ++i)
    {
        Real absComponent = |V[i]|;
        if (absComponent > maxAbsComponent)
        {
            maxAbsComponent = absComponent;
        }
```

```
    }
    Real  length ;
    if  (maxAbsComponent > 0)
    {
        Vector  W = V/maxAbsComponent;
        length  =  maxAbsComponent*sqrt(Length(W));
    }
    else
    {
        length  =  0;
    }
    return  length ;
}
```

LISTING 6.2: Computing the length of a vector robustly.

Normalization of a vector requires computing the length of the vector and dividing the vector by it when not zero. The obvious implementation suffers from the same numerical problems that length computations do. The algorithm replaces the vector by its normalization and returns the computed length. Listing 6.3 has pseudocode for the algorithm. The ampersand indicates that the input V will be modified as a side effect of the function.

```
Real  Normalize (Vector& V)
{
    Real  length = Length(V);   // The computation can overflow.
    if (length > 0)
    {
        V = V/length ;
    }
    return  length ;
}
```

LISTING 6.3: Normalizing a vector.

A robust implementation that uses the idea of factoring out the largest magnitude component is shown in Listing 6.4.

```
Real  NormalizeRobust (Vector& V)
{
    Real  maxAbsComponent = |V[0]|;
    for (int  i = 1; i < n; ++i)
    {
        Real  absComponent = |V[i]|;
        if (absComponent > maxAbsComponent)
        {
            maxAbsComponent = absComponent;
        }
    }

    Real  length ;
    if (maxAbsComponent > 0)
    {
        V = V/maxAbsComponent;
        length  = Length(V);
        V = V/length ;
        length  *= maxAbsComponent;
    }
    return  length ;
}
```

LISTING 6.4: Normalizing a vector robustly.

Sometimes the length of a vector might be computed from a dot product that was previously computed: length = sqrt(Dot(V,V)). The dot product itself can overflow, and there is no protection against that. If you expect large-magnitude components in your computations, you will want to avoid computing the length from a dot product.

The base class for vectors has the interface to support the various functions described here, shown in Listing 6.5.

```
template <int N, typename Real>
Real Dot (Vector<N,Real> const& v0, Vector<N,Real> const& v1);

template <int N, typename Real>
Real Length (Vector<N,Real> const& v);

template <int N, typename Real>
Real LengthRobust (Vector<N,Real> const& v);

template <int N, typename Real>
Real Normalize (Vector<N,Real>& v);

template <int N, typename Real>
Real NormalizeRobust (Vector<N,Real>& v);
```

LISTING 6.5: The vector class interface for dot products, length, and normalization.

6.1.2 Orthogonality

Two nonzero vectors $\mathbf{U}$ and $\mathbf{V}$ are said to be *orthogonal* or *perpendicular* when their dot product is zero: $\mathbf{U} \cdot \mathbf{V} = 0$. Geometrically, the angle between the vectors is 90 degrees.[1] Observe that the vectors $s\mathbf{U}$ for nonzero scalars s are also orthogonal to $\mathbf{V}$.

6.1.2.1 Orthogonality in 2D

In 2D, it is easy to compute an orthogonal vector corresponding to a nonzero vector $\mathbf{V} = (x_0, y_0)$, namely, $\mathbf{V}^{\perp} = (y_0, -x_0)$. The superscript symbol on the orthogonal vector is standard mathematical notation for a vector perpendicular to the one named in the expression. As mentioned, $s(y_0, -x_0)$ for nonzero s are all perpendicular to $\mathbf{V}$. If $\mathbf{V}$ is unit length, there are exactly two unit-length vectors perpendicular to it: $(y_0, -x_0)$ and $(-y_0, x_0)$.

GTEngine has functions to support orthogonality in 2D, as shown in Listing 6.6.

```
template <typename Real>
Vector2<Real> Perp (Vector2<Real> const& v);

template <typename Real>
```

---

[1] The concept of orthogonal is more general. The vectors are orthogonal with respect to a positive definite matrix A when $\mathbf{U}^{\mathrm{T}} A \mathbf{V} = 0$. The matrix is referred to as a *metric* and the left-hand side of the equation is referred to as an *inner product*. When A is the identity matrix, the test is $\mathbf{U}^{\mathrm{T}} \mathbf{V} = 0$, where the left-hand side of the equation is the dot product of vectors.

```
Vector2<Real> UnitPerp (Vector2<Real> const& v);

template <typename Real>
Real DotPerp (Vector2<Real> const& v0, Vector2<Real> const& v1);
```

LISTING 6.6: The 2D vector interface for perpendicular vectors and dot-perp.

The function Perp computes $(y_0, -x_0)$ for input (x_0, y_0). The components of the input are swapped and the second one is negated. The choice for negating the first component rather than the second component is based on generating the perpendicular vector via a formal determinant,

$$\det \begin{bmatrix} \mathbf{E}_0 & \mathbf{E}_1 \\ x_0 & y_0 \end{bmatrix} = y_0 \mathbf{E}_0 - x_0 \mathbf{E}_1 \tag{6.2}$$

where $\mathbf{E}_0 = (1, 0)$ and $\mathbf{E}_1 = (0, 1)$. The determinant idea is useful for computing perpendicular vectors in higher dimensions. The function UnitPerp computes the unit-length vector $(y_0, -x_0)/\sqrt{x_0^2 + y_0^2}$ when the input is nonzero. The zero vector is returned when the input is the zero vector. Sometimes 2D geometric algorithms involve dot products of the form

$$\begin{aligned} (x_0, y_0) \cdot (x_1, y_1)^\perp &= (x_0, y_0) \cdot (y_1, -x_1) \\ &= x_0 y_1 - x_1 y_0 \\ &= \det \begin{bmatrix} x_0 & y_0 \\ x_1 & y_1 \end{bmatrix} \end{aligned} \tag{6.3}$$

The computation is referred to as the *dot-perp* of the vectors. A useful identity is $\mathbf{U} \cdot \mathbf{V}^\perp = -\mathbf{V} \cdot \mathbf{U}^\perp$. The function DotPerp returns the dot-perp of the inputs.

6.1.2.2 Orthogonality in 3D

In 3D, an orthogonal vector $\mathbf{V}_2 = (x_2, y_2, z_2)$ may be computed corresponding to two linearly independent vectors $\mathbf{V}_0 = (x_0, y_0, z_0)$ and $\mathbf{V}_1 = (x_1, y_1, z_1)$ using the cross-product operator,

$$\mathbf{V}_2 = \mathbf{V}_0 \times \mathbf{V}_1 = \det \begin{bmatrix} \mathbf{E}_0 & \mathbf{E}_1 & \mathbf{E}_2 \\ x_0 & y_0 & z_0 \\ x_1 & y_1 & z_1 \end{bmatrix} \tag{6.4}$$

$$= (y_0 z_1 - y_1 z_0, z_0 x_1 - x_0 z_1, x_0 y_1 - x_1 y_0)$$

GTEngine has functions to support orthogonality in 3D, as shown in Listing 6.7. The functions have a template integer parameter N that should be three or four. The latter case allows you to use the functions when you choose to represent affine points and vectors with 4-tuples. The last component of affine points is one and the last component of affine vectors is zero. The cross product of two affine vector 4-tuples will produce an affine vector 4-tuple whose last component is zero.

```
template <int N, typename Real>
Vector<N,Real> Cross (Vector<N,Real> const& v0, Vector<N,Real> const& v1);

template <int N, typename Real>
Vector<N,Real> UnitCross (Vector<N,Real> const& v0,
    Vector<N,Real> const& v1);

template <int N, typename Real>
Real DotCross (Vector<N,Real> const& v0, Vector<N,Real> const& v1,
    Vector<N,Real> const& v2);
```

LISTING 6.7: The vector interface for cross products and dot-cross, where N is three or four.

The function Cross computes the cross product of the inputs. If you require a unit-length orthogonal vector, the cross product can be normalized, a result returned by function UnitCross. If the cross product is zero, the function returns the zero vector. Similar to the dot-perp operation in 2D, the dot-cross operation is useful and is more commonly referred to as the *triple scalar product* of three vectors defined by $\mathbf{V}_0 \cdot \mathbf{V}_1 \times \mathbf{V}_2$. The function DotCross computes the triple scalar product.

$$\mathbf{V}_0 \cdot \mathbf{V}_1 \times \mathbf{V}_2 = \det \begin{bmatrix} x_0 & y_0 & z_0 \\ x_1 & y_1 & z_1 \\ x_2 & y_2 & z_2 \end{bmatrix} \tag{6.5}$$
$$= x_2(y_0 z_1 - y_1 z_0) + y_2(z_0 x_1 - x_0 z_1) + z_2(x_0 y_1 - x_1 y_0)$$

6.1.2.3 Orthogonality in 4D

In 4D, an orthogonal vector $\mathbf{V}_3 = (x_3, y_3, z_3, w_3)$ may be computed corresponding to three linearly independent vectors $\mathbf{V}_0 = (x_0, y_0, z_0, w_0)$, $\mathbf{V}_1 = (x_1, y_1, z_1, w_1)$, and $\mathbf{V}_2 = (x_2, y_2, z_2, w_2)$ using an extension of the determinant idea to 4D. I call this the *hypercross product*:

$$
\begin{aligned}
\mathbf{V}_3 &= \text{Hypercross}(\mathbf{V}_0, \mathbf{V}_1, \mathbf{V}_2) \\
&= \det \begin{bmatrix} \mathbf{E}_0 & \mathbf{E}_1 & \mathbf{E}_2 & \mathbf{E}_3 \\ x_0 & y_0 & z_0 & w_0 \\ x_1 & y_1 & z_1 & w_1 \\ x_2 & y_2 & z_2 & w_2 \end{bmatrix} \\
&= \det \begin{bmatrix} y_0 & z_0 & w_0 \\ y_1 & z_1 & w_1 \\ y_2 & z_2 & w_2 \end{bmatrix} \mathbf{E}_0 - \det \begin{bmatrix} x_0 & z_0 & w_0 \\ x_1 & z_1 & w_1 \\ x_2 & z_2 & w_2 \end{bmatrix} \mathbf{E}_1 \\
&\quad + \det \begin{bmatrix} x_0 & y_0 & w_0 \\ x_1 & y_1 & w_1 \\ x_2 & y_2 & w_2 \end{bmatrix} \mathbf{E}_2 - \det \begin{bmatrix} x_0 & y_0 & z_0 \\ x_1 & y_1 & z_1 \\ x_2 & y_2 & z_2 \end{bmatrix} \mathbf{E}_3
\end{aligned}
\tag{6.6}
$$

GTEngine has functions to support orthogonality in 4D, as shown in Listing 6.8.

```
template <typename Real>
Vector4<Real> HyperCross (Vector4<Real> const& v0,
    Vector4<Real> const& v1, Vector4<Real> const& v2);
```

```
template <typename Real>
Vector4<Real> UnitHyperCross (Vector4<Real> const& v0,
    Vector4<Real> const& v1, Vector4<Real> const& v2);

template <typename Real>
Real DotHyperCross (Vector4<Real> const& v0, Vector4<Real> const& v1,
    Vector4<Real> const& v2, Vector4<Real> const& v3);
```

LISTING 6.8: The vector interface for hypercross products and dot-hypercross.

The function HyperCross computes the hypercross product of the inputs. If you require a unit-length orthogonal vector, the hypercross product can be normalized, a result returned by function UnitHyperCross. If the hypercross product is zero, the function returns the zero vector. Similar to the dot-cross operation in 3D, the dot-hypercross operation is

$$\mathrm{DotHyperCross}(\mathbf{V}_0, \mathbf{V}_1, \mathbf{V}_2, \mathbf{V}_3) = \det \begin{bmatrix} x_0 & y_0 & z_0 & w_0 \\ x_1 & y_1 & z_1 & w_1 \\ x_2 & y_2 & z_2 & w_2 \\ x_3 & y_3 & z_3 & w_3 \end{bmatrix} \quad (6.7)$$

6.1.2.4 Gram-Schmidt Orthonormalization

In d-dimensional space, let $\{\mathbf{V}_i\}_{i=0}^{n-1}$ be a linearly independent set of vectors; necessarily $n \leq d$. An algorithm for modifying these to construct a set $\{\mathbf{U}_i\}_{i=0}^{n-1}$ whose elements are unit length and mutually perpendicular is called *Gram-Schmidt orthonormalization*. The construction is iterative:

$$\mathbf{U}_0 = \frac{\mathbf{V}_0}{|\mathbf{V}_0|}; \quad \mathbf{U}_i = \frac{\mathbf{V}_i - \sum_{j=0}^{i-1}(\mathbf{U}_j \cdot \mathbf{V}_i)\mathbf{U}_j}{|\mathbf{V}_i - \sum_{j=0}^{i-1}(\mathbf{U}_j \cdot \mathbf{V}_i)\mathbf{U}_j|}, \; i \geq 1 \quad (6.8)$$

The idea is to compute the first vector $\mathbf{U}_0$ by normalizing $\mathbf{V}_0$. The second vector $\mathbf{U}_1$ is obtained by projecting out the $\mathbf{U}_0$ component from $\mathbf{V}_1$ and then normalizing. The resulting vector is necessarily orthogonal to the first. The next vector is projected by removing components from the previous orthogonal vectors, followed by normalization. Theoretically, this is a correct algorithm, but in practice using floating-point arithmetic, when d is large, the numerical roundoff errors can be problematic. Other numerical methods are typically used to avoid this [16].

The resulting set of vectors is referred to as an *orthonormal set of vectors*, a topic explored in the next section. GTEngine has a single templated function for computing the algorithm as stated here. The interface is defined in the base vector class; see Listing 6.9.

```
template <int N, typename Real>
Real Orthonormalize (int numElements, Vector<N,Real>* v);
```

LISTING 6.9: The vector interface for Gram-Schmidt orthonormalization.

The number of elements is specified, and this must be no larger than the parameter N. The vectors are orthonormalized in place, so v is an input-output array.

6.1.3   Orthonormal Sets

A frequently asked question in computer graphics is how, given a unit-length vector $\mathbf{N} = (x, y, z)$, one computes two unit-length vectors $\mathbf{U}$ and $\mathbf{V}$ so that the three vectors are mutually perpendicular. For example, $\mathbf{N}$ might be a normal vector to a plane, and you want to define a coordinate system in the plane, which requires computing $\mathbf{U}$ and $\mathbf{V}$. There are many choices for the vectors, but for numerical robustness, I have always recommended the following algorithm.

Locate the component of maximum absolute value. To illustrate, suppose that x is this value, so $|x| \geq |y|$ and $|x| \geq |z|$. Swap the first two components, changing the sign on the second, and set the third component to 0, obtaining $(y, -x, 0)$. Normalize this to obtain

$$\mathbf{U} = \frac{(y, -x, 0)}{\sqrt{x^2 + y^2}} \tag{6.9}$$

Now compute a cross product to obtain the other vector,

$$\mathbf{V} = \mathbf{N} \times \mathbf{U} = \frac{(xz, yz, -x^2 - y^2)}{\sqrt{x^2 + y^2}} \tag{6.10}$$

As you can see, a division by $\sqrt{x^2 + y^2}$ is required, so it is necessary that the divisor not be zero. In fact it is not, because of how we choose x. For a unit-length vector (x, y, z) where $|x| \geq |y|$ and $|x| \geq |z|$, it is necessary that $|x| \geq 1/\sqrt{3}$. The division by $\sqrt{x^2 + y^2}$ is therefore numerically robust—you are not dividing by a number close to zero.

In linear algebra, we refer to the set $\{\mathbf{U}, \mathbf{V}, \mathbf{N}\}$ as an *orthonormal set*. By definition, the vectors are unit length and mutually perpendicular. Let $\langle \mathbf{N} \rangle$ denote the *span* of $\mathbf{N}$. Formally, this is the set

$$\langle \mathbf{N} \rangle = \{t\mathbf{N} : t \in \mathbb{R}\} \tag{6.11}$$

where $\mathbb{R}$ is the set of real numbers. The span is the line that contains the origin $\mathbf{0}$ with direction $\mathbf{N}$. We may define the span of any number of vectors. For example, the span of $\mathbf{U}$ and $\mathbf{V}$ is

$$\langle \mathbf{U}, \mathbf{V} \rangle = \{s\mathbf{U} + t\mathbf{V} : s \in \mathbb{R}, t \in \mathbb{R}\} \tag{6.12}$$

This is the plane that contains the origin and has unit-length normal $\mathbf{N}$; that is, any vector in $\langle \mathbf{U}, \mathbf{V} \rangle$ is perpendicular to $\mathbf{N}$. The span of $\mathbf{U}$ and $\mathbf{V}$ is said to be the *orthogonal complement* of the span of $\mathbf{N}$. Equivalently, the span of $\mathbf{N}$ is said to be the orthogonal complement of the span of $\mathbf{U}$ and $\mathbf{V}$. The notation for orthogonal complement is to add a superscript "perp" symbol. $\langle \mathbf{N} \rangle^{\perp}$ is the orthogonal complement of the span of $\mathbf{N}$ and $\langle \mathbf{U}, \mathbf{V} \rangle^{\perp}$ is the orthogonal complement of the span of $\mathbf{U}$ and $\mathbf{V}$. Moreover,

$$\langle \mathbf{U}, \mathbf{V} \rangle^{\perp} = \langle \mathbf{N} \rangle, \quad \langle \mathbf{N} \rangle^{\perp} = \langle \mathbf{U}, \mathbf{V} \rangle \tag{6.13}$$

6.1.3.1 Orthonormal Sets in 2D

The ideas in the introduction specialize to two dimensions. Given a unit-length vector $\mathbf{U}_0 = (x_0, y_0)$, a unit-length vector perpendicular to it is $\mathbf{U}_1 = (x_1, y_1) = (y_0, -x_0)$. The span of each vector is a line and the two lines are perpendicular; therefore,

$$\langle \mathbf{U}_0 \rangle^{\perp} = \langle \mathbf{U}_1 \rangle, \quad \langle \mathbf{U}_1 \rangle^{\perp} = \langle \mathbf{U}_0 \rangle \tag{6.14}$$

The set $\{\mathbf{U}_0, \mathbf{U}_1\}$ is an orthonormal set.

The set $\{\mathbf{U}_0, \mathbf{U}_1\}$ is a *left-handed orthonormal set*. The vectors are unit length and perpendicular, and the matrix $M = [\mathbf{U}_0 \, \mathbf{U}_1]$ whose columns are the two vectors is orthogonal with $\det(M) = -1$. To obtain a *right-handed orthonormal set*, negate the last vector: $\{\mathbf{U}_0, -\mathbf{U}_1\}$.

The Vector2<Real> interface for computing orthogonal complements is shown in Listing 6.10.

```
template <typename Real>
Real ComputeOrthogonalComplement (int numInputs, Vector2<Real>* v);
```

LISTING 6.10: The 2D vector interface for computing orthogonal complements.

The return values of the functions is the minimum length of the unnormalized vectors constructed during the Gram-Schmidt algorithm. It is possible the inputs are nearly linearly dependent, in a numerical sense, in which case the return value is nearly zero. The function provides a consistent signature across dimensions. The numInputs must be one and v[] must have one vector.

6.1.3.2 Orthonormal Sets in 3D

The ideas in the preamble to the section on orthonormal sets were for 3D. This subsection formalizes the ideas.

One Vector from Two Inputs. Given two vectors $\mathbf{V}_0$ and $\mathbf{V}_1$, the cross product is obtained from Equation (6.4). If either of the input vectors is the zero vector or if the input vectors are nonzero and parallel, the cross product is the zero vector. If the input vectors are unit length and perpendicular, then the cross product is guaranteed to be unit length and $\{\mathbf{V}_0, \mathbf{V}_1, \mathbf{V}_2\}$ is an orthonormal set.

If the input vectors are linearly independent, we may use Equation (6.8) to obtain a pair of unit-length vectors, $\mathbf{U}_0$ and $\mathbf{U}_1$. We may then compute the cross product to obtain another unit-length vector, $\mathbf{U}_2 = \mathbf{U}_0 \times \mathbf{U}_1$, which is perpendicular to the input vectors; that is,

$$\langle \mathbf{U}_2 \rangle = \langle \mathbf{U}_0, \mathbf{U}_1 \rangle^{\perp} \tag{6.15}$$

Two Vectors from One Input. If we start with only one unit-length vector $\mathbf{U}_2$, we wish to find two unit-length vectors $\mathbf{U}_0$ and $\mathbf{U}_1$ such that $\{\mathbf{U}_0, \mathbf{U}_1, \mathbf{U}_2\}$

is an orthonormal set, in which case

$$\langle \mathbf{U}_0, \mathbf{U}_1 \rangle = \langle \mathbf{U}_2 \rangle^{\perp} \tag{6.16}$$

But we have already seen how to do this—in the introduction section. Let us be slightly more formal and use the symbolic determinant idea. This idea allows us to generalize to four dimensions.

Let $\mathbf{U}_2 = (x, y, z)$ be a unit-length vector. Suppose that x has the largest absolute value of the three components. We may construct a determinant whose last row is one of the basis vectors $\mathbf{E}_i$ that does not have a zero in its first component—the one corresponding to the location of x. Let us choose $(0, 0, 1)$ as this vector; then

$$\det \begin{bmatrix} \mathbf{E}_0 & \mathbf{E}_1 & \mathbf{E}_2 \\ x & y & z \\ 0 & 0 & 1 \end{bmatrix} = y\mathbf{E}_0 - x\mathbf{E}_1 + 0\mathbf{E}_2 = (y, -x, 0) \tag{6.17}$$

which matches the construction in the introduction. This vector cannot be the zero vector, because we know that x has largest absolute magnitude and so cannot be zero because the initial vector is not the zero vector. Normalizing the vector, we have $\mathbf{U}_0 = (y, -x, 0)/\sqrt{x^2 + y^2}$. We may then compute $\mathbf{U}_1 = \mathbf{U}_2 \times \mathbf{U}_0$.

If y has the largest absolute magnitude, then the last row of the determinant can be either $(1, 0, 0)$ or $(0, 0, 1)$; that is, we may not choose the Euclidean basis vector with a one in the same component that corresponds to y. For example,

$$\det \begin{bmatrix} \mathbf{E}_0 & \mathbf{E}_1 & \mathbf{E}_2 \\ x & y & z \\ 1 & 0 & 0 \end{bmatrix} = 0\mathbf{E}_0 + z\mathbf{E}_1 - y\mathbf{E}_2 = (0, z, -y) \tag{6.18}$$

Once again the result cannot be the zero vector, so we may robustly compute $\mathbf{U}_0 = (0, z, -y)/\sqrt{y^2 + z^2}$ and $\mathbf{U}_1 = \mathbf{U}_2 \times \mathbf{U}_0$.

And finally, let z have the largest absolute magnitude. We may compute

$$\det \begin{bmatrix} \mathbf{E}_0 & \mathbf{E}_1 & \mathbf{E}_2 \\ x & y & z \\ 0 & 1 & 0 \end{bmatrix} = -z\mathbf{E}_0 + 0\mathbf{E}_1 + x\mathbf{E}_2 = (-z, 0, x) \tag{6.19}$$

which cannot be the zero vector. Thus, $\mathbf{U}_0 = (-z, 0, x)/\sqrt{x^2 + z^2}$ and $\mathbf{U}_1 = \mathbf{U}_2 \times \mathbf{U}_0$. Of course, we could have also chosen the last row to be $(1, 0, 0)$.

The set $\{\mathbf{U}_0, \mathbf{U}_1, \mathbf{U}_2\}$ is a *right-handed orthonormal set*. The vectors are unit length and mutually perpendicular, and the matrix $M = [\mathbf{U}_0 \ \mathbf{U}_1 \ \mathbf{U}_2]$, whose columns are the three vectors, is orthogonal with $\det(M) = +1$. To obtain a *left-handed orthonormal set*, negate the last vector: $\{\mathbf{U}_0, \mathbf{U}_1, -\mathbf{U}_2\}$.

The 3D interface for computing orthogonal complements is shown in Listing 6.11.

```
template <typename Real>
Real ComputeOrthogonalComplement (int numInputs,  Vector3<Real>* v);
```

LISTING 6.11: The 3D vector interface for computing orthogonal complements.

The return values of the functions is the minimum length of the unnormalized vectors constructed during the Gram-Schmidt algorithm. It is possible the inputs are nearly linearly dependent, in a numerical sense, in which case the return value is nearly zero. The function provides a consistent signature across dimensions. The numInputs must be one or two and v[] must have numInputs vectors.

6.1.3.3   Orthonormal Sets in 4D

This section shows how the concepts in three dimensions extend to four dimensions.

One Vector from Three Inputs. Consider three vectors $\mathbf{V}_i$ for $i = 0, 1, 2$ that are linearly independent. We may compute a fourth vector $\mathbf{V}_3$ that is perpendicular to the three inputs using the hypercross formula in Equation (6.6). Gram-Schmidt orthonormalization of Equation (6.8) may be applied to the four vectors to obtain an orthonormal set.

Two Vectors from Two Inputs. Let us consider two unit-length and perpendicular vectors $\mathbf{U}_i = (x_i, y_i, z_i, w_i)$ for $i = 0, 1$. If the inputs are only linearly independent, we may use Gram-Schmidt orthonormalization to obtain the unit-length and perpendicular vectors. The inputs have six associated 2×2 determinants: $x_0 y_1 - x_1 y_0$, $x_0 z_1 - x_1 z_0$, $x_0 w_1 - x_1 w_0$, $y_0 z_1 - y_1 z_0$, $y_0 w_1 - y_1 w_0$, and $z_0 w_1 - z_1 w_0$. It is guaranteed that not all of these determinants are zero when the input vectors are linearly independent. We may search for the determinant of largest absolute magnitude, which is equivalent to searching for the largest absolute magnitude component in the three-dimensional setting.

For simplicity, assume that $x_0 y_1 - x_1 y_0$ has the largest absolute magnitude. The handling of other cases is similar. We may construct a symbolic determinant whose last row is either $(0, 0, 1, 0)$ or $(0, 0, 0, 1)$. The idea is that we need a Euclidean basis vector whose components corresponding to the x and y locations are zero. We used a similar approach in three dimensions. To illustrate, let us choose $(0, 0, 0, 1)$. The determinant is

$$
\det \begin{bmatrix} \mathbf{E}_0 & \mathbf{E}_1 & \mathbf{E}_2 & \mathbf{E}_3 \\ x_0 & y_0 & z_0 & w_0 \\ x_1 & y_1 & z_1 & w_1 \\ 0 & 0 & 0 & 1 \end{bmatrix} \tag{6.20}
$$

$$
= (y_0 z_1 - y_1 z_0)\mathbf{E}_0 - (x_0 z_1 - x_1 z_0)\mathbf{E}_1 + (x_0 y_1 - x_1 y_0)\mathbf{E}_2 + 0\mathbf{E}_3
$$

This vector cannot be the zero vector, because we know that $x_0 y_1 - x_1 y_0$ has the largest absolute magnitude and is not zero. Moreover, we know that this vector is perpendicular to the first two row vectors in the determinant. We can choose the unit-length vector

$$\mathbf{U}_2 = (x_2, y_2, z_2, w_2) = \frac{(y_0 z_1 - y_1 z_0, x_1 z_0 - x_0 z_1, x_0 y_1 - x_1 y_0, 0)}{|(y_0 z_1 - y_1 z_0, x_1 z_0 - x_0 z_1, x_0 y_1 - x_1 y_0, 0)|} \quad (6.21)$$

Observe that (x_2, y_2, z_2) is the normalized cross product of (x_0, y_0, z_0) and (x_1, y_1, z_1), and $w_2 = 0$.

We may now compute

$$\mathbf{U}_3 = \det \begin{bmatrix} \mathbf{E}_0 & \mathbf{E}_1 & \mathbf{E}_2 & \mathbf{E}_3 \\ x_0 & y_0 & z_0 & w_0 \\ x_1 & y_1 & z_1 & w_1 \\ x_2 & y_2 & z_2 & 0 \end{bmatrix} \quad (6.22)$$

which is guaranteed to be unit length. Moreover,

$$\langle \mathbf{U}_2, \mathbf{U}_3 \rangle = \langle \mathbf{U}_0, \mathbf{U}_1 \rangle^{\perp} \quad (6.23)$$

That is, the span of the output vectors is the orthogonal complement of the span of the input vectors.

The same idea applies to each of the six cases that arise when locating the maximum of the 2×2 determinants.

Three Vectors from One Input. Let $\mathbf{U}_0 = (x_0, y_0, z_0, w_0)$ be a unit-length vector. Similar to the construction in three dimensions, search for the component of largest absolute magnitude. For simplicity, assume it is x_0. The other cases are handled similarly.

Choose $\mathbf{U}_1 = (y_0, -x_0, 0, 0)/\sqrt{x_0^2 + y_0^2}$, which is not the zero vector. $\mathbf{U}_1$ is unit length and perpendicular to $\mathbf{U}_1$. Now apply the construction of the previous section to obtain $\mathbf{U}_2$ and $\mathbf{U}_3$.

The set $\{\mathbf{U}_0, \mathbf{U}_1, \mathbf{U}_2, \mathbf{U}_3\}$ is a *left-handed orthonormal set*. The vectors are unit length and mutually perpendicular, and the matrix $M = [\mathbf{U}_0 \ \mathbf{U}_1 \ \mathbf{U}_2 \ \mathbf{U}_3]$, whose columns are the four vectors, is orthogonal with $\det(M) = -1$. To obtain a *right-handed orthonormal set*, negate the last vector: $\{\mathbf{U}_0, \mathbf{U}_1, \mathbf{U}_2, -\mathbf{U}_3\}$.

The Vector4<Real> interface for computing orthogonal complements is shown in Listing 6.12.

```
template <typename Real>
Real ComputeOrthogonalComplement (int numInputs, Vector4<Real>* v);
```

LISTING 6.12: The 4D vector interface for computing orthogonal complements.

The return values of the functions is the minimum length of the unnormalized vectors constructed during the Gram-Schmidt algorithm. It is possible the inputs are nearly linearly dependent, in a numerical sense, in which case the return value is nearly zero. The function provides a consistent signature across dimensions. The numInputs must be one, two, or three and inputs[] must have numInputs vectors. The implementation was carefully written to ensure that if the number of inputs is one or two and the inputs are 3D vectors written as 4D affine vectors ($w = 0$), the output is the same as if you had passed the 3D vectors to the 3D version of the function with last component $w = 0$.

6.1.4 Barycentric Coordinates

Let $\mathbf{P}_0$, $\mathbf{P}_1$, and $\mathbf{P}_2$ be the vertices of a triangle in 2D. The triangle is assumed to be nondegenerate; mathematically, the vectors $\mathbf{P}_0 - \mathbf{P}_2$ and $\mathbf{P}_1 - \mathbf{P}_2$ must be linearly independent. Another point $\mathbf{P}$ can be represented as a linear combination of the triangle vertices,

$$\mathbf{P} = b_0\mathbf{P}_0 + b_1\mathbf{P}_1 + b_2\mathbf{P}_2 \tag{6.24}$$

where $b_0 + b_1 + b_2 = 1$. The coefficients are referred to as the *barycentric coordinates* of $\mathbf{P}$ relative to the triangle. The coordinates may be computed as follows. Subtract $\mathbf{P}_2$ from the linear combination,

$$\begin{aligned} \mathbf{P} - \mathbf{P}_2 &= b_0\mathbf{P}_0 + b_1\mathbf{P}_1 + (b_2 - 1)\mathbf{P}_2 \\ &= b_0(\mathbf{P}_0 - \mathbf{P}_2) + b_1(\mathbf{P}_1 - \mathbf{P}_2) \end{aligned} \tag{6.25}$$

Dotting the equation with perpendicular vectors of point differences, we obtain

$$\begin{aligned} b_0 &= (\mathbf{P} - \mathbf{P}_2) \cdot (\mathbf{P}_1 - \mathbf{P}_2)^\perp / (\mathbf{P}_0 - \mathbf{P}_2) \cdot (\mathbf{P}_1 - \mathbf{P}_2)^\perp \\ b_1 &= (\mathbf{P}_0 - \mathbf{P}_2) \cdot (\mathbf{P} - \mathbf{P}_2)^\perp / (\mathbf{P}_0 - \mathbf{P}_2) \cdot (\mathbf{P}_1 - \mathbf{P}_2)^\perp \\ b_2 &= 1 - b_0 - b_1 \end{aligned} \tag{6.26}$$

The formula for b_1 was constructed using the identity $\mathbf{U} \cdot \mathbf{V}^\perp = -\mathbf{V} \cdot \mathbf{U}^\perp$.

The Vector2<Real> class has the interface function shown in Listing 6.13.

```
template <typename Real>
bool ComputeBarycentrics (Vector2<Real> const& p, Vector2<Real> const& v0,
    Vector2<Real> const& v1, Vector2<Real> const& v2, Real bary[3],
    Real epsilon = (Real)0);
```

LISTING 6.13: The 2D vector interface for barycentric coordinates.

The denominators for the b_0 and b_1 expressions can be nearly zero, which might generate enough numerical error to be of concern. Geometrically, the triangle is needlelike (nearly a line segment). The functions allow you to specify a floating-point tolerance for which a denominator smaller than the tolerance implies a degenerate triangle. The Boolean return is true if and only if the denominators are larger than the tolerance. The barycentric coordinates are considered to be valid only when the function returns true; they are actually set to zero when the function returns false.

Let $\mathbf{P}_0$, $\mathbf{P}_1$, $\mathbf{P}_2$, and $\mathbf{P}_3$ be the vertices of a tetrahedron in 3D. The tetrahedron is assumed to be nondegenerate; mathematically, the vectors $\mathbf{P}_0 - \mathbf{P}_3$,

$\mathbf{P}_1 - \mathbf{P}_3$, and $\mathbf{P}_2 - \mathbf{P}_3$ must be linearly independent. Another point $\mathbf{P}$ can be represented as a linear combination of the tetrahedron vertices,

$$\mathbf{P} = b_0\mathbf{P}_0 + b_1\mathbf{P}_1 + b_2\mathbf{P}_2 + b_3\mathbf{P}_3 \tag{6.27}$$

where $b_0 + b_1 + b_2 + b_3 = 1$. The coefficients are referred to as the *barycentric coordinates* of $\mathbf{P}$ relative to the tetrahedron. The coordinates may be computed as follows. Subtract $\mathbf{P}_3$ from the linear combination,

$$\begin{aligned} \mathbf{P} - \mathbf{P}_3 &= b_0\mathbf{P}_0 + b_1\mathbf{P}_1 + b_2\mathbf{P}_2 + (b_3 - 1)\mathbf{P}_3 \\ &= b_0(\mathbf{P}_0 - \mathbf{P}_3) + b_1(\mathbf{P}_1 - \mathbf{P}_3) + b_2(\mathbf{P}_2 - \mathbf{P}_3) \\ \mathbf{E} &= b_0\mathbf{E}_0 + b_1\mathbf{E}_1 + b_2\mathbf{E}_2 \end{aligned} \tag{6.28}$$

where the last equation defines the vectors $\mathbf{E}$ and $\mathbf{E}_i$ for $i = 0, 1, 2$. Applying cross products and dot products, we obtain

$$\begin{aligned} b_0 &= \mathbf{E} \cdot \mathbf{E}_1 \times \mathbf{E}_2 / \mathbf{E}_0 \cdot \mathbf{E}_1 \times \mathbf{E}_2 \\ b_1 &= \mathbf{E} \cdot \mathbf{E}_2 \times \mathbf{E}_0 / \mathbf{E}_0 \cdot \mathbf{E}_1 \times \mathbf{E}_2 \\ b_2 &= \mathbf{E} \cdot \mathbf{E}_0 \times \mathbf{E}_1 / \mathbf{E}_0 \cdot \mathbf{E}_1 \times \mathbf{E}_2 \\ b_3 &= 1 - b_0 - b_1 - b_2 \end{aligned} \tag{6.29}$$

The Vector3<Real> class has the interface function shown in Listing 6.14.

```
template <typename Real>
bool ComputeBarycentrics (Vector3<Real> const& p, Vector3<Real> const& v0,
    Vector3<Real> const& v1, Vector3<Real> const& v2,
    Vector3<Real> const& v3, Real bary[4], Real epsilon = (Real)0);
```

LISTING 6.14: The 3D vector interface for barycentric coordinates.

The denominators for the b_0, b_1, and b_2 expressions can be nearly zero, which might generate enough numerical error to be of concern. Geometrically, the tetrahedron is nearly flat or needlelike (nearly degenerate). The functions allow you to specify a floating-point tolerance for which a denominator smaller than the tolerance implies a degenerate triangle. The Boolean return is true if and only if the denominators are larger than the tolerance. The barycentric coordinates are considered to be valid only when the function returns true; they are actually set to zero when the function returns false.

6.1.5   Intrinsic Dimensionality

In several applications it might be of use to know the *intrinsic dimensionality* of a collection of n-dimensional vectors. For example, if the collection contains all the same vector, the intrinsic dimensionality is zero. If the vectors all lie on the same line, the intrinsic dimensionality is one. It is possible the vectors all lie in a k-dimensional subspace, in which case the intrinsic dimensionality is k. The concept is more general. For example, if a collection of 3D vectors all lie on a sphere, the intrinsic dimensionality is two. However, identifying a k-dimensional manifold that contains a collection of points in n dimensions is a complicated problem; see the literature on generating surfaces from unordered points.

GTEngine provides support for determining numerically the intrinsic dimensionality in terms of points, lines, and planes as the approximating objects. A typical application is computation of the convex hull of a set of 3D points. Books describing convex hull algorithms for three dimensions assume that the set of points is not degenerate; that is, the points are not all the same, do not lie on a line, and do not line in a plane. In practice, you most likely do not have this knowledge about your set of points. An implementation of convex hull for 3D points must decide when to switch to convex hull for 2D points (intrinsic dimensionality is two) or to convex hull for 1D points (intrinsic dimensionality is one). The implementation for determining intrinsic dimensionality uses floating-point tolerances that are user controlled to decide whether the points are sufficiently close to lying in a plane or sufficiently close to lying on a line. The actual plane or line is computed, allowing you to project the points onto the object to reduce the dimension and call a lower-dimension convex hull finder.

The class for 2D intrinsic dimensionality is shown in Listing 6.15.

```
template <typename Real>
class IntrinsicsVector2
{
public:
    IntrinsicsVector2 (int numVectors, Vector2<Real> const* v,
        Real inEpsilon);

    Real epsilon;
    int dimension;
    Real min[2], max[2];
    Real maxRange;
    Vector2<Real> origin;
    Vector2<Real> direction[2];
    int extreme[3];
    bool extremeCCW;
};
```

LISTING 6.15: The 2D vector interface for intrinsic dimensionality.

All work is performed in the constructor, storing inEpsilon in class member epsilon and computing the remaining class members according to the following algorithm.

The axis-aligned bounding box of the input points is computed and stored in min[] and max[]. The member maxRange stores the maximum difference of max[0]-min[0] and max[1]-min[1]. The indices into v[] for the points that support the bounding box in the direction of maximum range are stored in extreme[0] and extreme[1]. The origin is chosen to be v[extreme[0]].

If the maximum range is less than or equal to epsilon, the point set is assumed to degenerate to a single point, namely, origin. The equality to epsilon allows the input tolerance to be exactly zero. The dimension is set to zero. The member extremeCCW is not meaningful in this case.

If the maximum range is greater than epsilon, the length of the vector connecting the two extreme points must have length greater than or equal to epsilon. The member direction[0] is computed as the unit-length vector connecting the extreme points. The member direction[1] is a perpendicular unit-length vector, computed using the *negative* of the function Vector2<Real>::Perp so that direction[1] is a counterclockwise rotation of direction[0]. The idea is that the points have intrinsic dimensionality of at least one with significant components in the direction of the line origin+t*direction[0].

The maximum distance from the input points to the line origin+t*direction[0] is computed, a quantity measured in the direction[1]. In fact, signed distances are computed to support orientation information about the extreme set. We know the point of maximum distance from the line and on which side of the line it lives. The index into v[] for the point of maximum distance is stored in extreme[2]. We are effectively building an oriented bounding box for the points with axes direction[].

If the maximum distance is less than or equal to epsilon*maxRange, the point set is assumed to degenerate to a line segment. The dimension is set to one. The member extremeCCW is not meaningful in this case. The use of epsilon*maxRange instead of epsilon alone is to be invariant to scaling; that is, epsilon is a relative error tolerance rather than an absolute error tolerance.

If the maximum is larger than epsilon*maxRange, the dimension is set to two and the points have full intrinsic dimensionality. The points indexed by extreme[] form a triangle. The ordering of the extreme points is stored in extremeCCW. Observe that knowing which side of the line v[extreme[2]] lives on is essential to know ordering.

The geometric ideas for class IntrinsicsVector2 extend naturally to 3D. The class for 3D intrinsic dimensionality is shown in Listing 6.16.

```
template <typename Real>
class IntrinsicsVector2
{
public:
    IntrinsicsVector3 (int numVectors, Vector3<Real> const* v,
        Real inEpsilon );

    Real epsilon;
    int dimension;
    Real min[3], max[3];
    Real maxRange;
    Vector3<Real> origin;
    Vector3<Real> direction[3];
    int extreme[4];
    bool extremeCCW;
};
```

LISTING 6.16: The 3D vector interface for intrinsic dimensionality.

All work is performed in the constructor, storing inEpsilon in class member epsilon and computing the remaining class members according to the following algorithm.

The axis-aligned bounding box of the input points is computed and stored in min[] and max[]. The member maxRange stores the maximum difference of the max[i]-min[i]. The indices into v[] for the points that support the bounding box in the direction of maximum range are stored in extreme[0] and extreme[1]. The origin is chosen to be v[extreme[0]].

If the maximum range is less than or equal to epsilon, the point set is assumed to degenerate to a single point, namely, origin. The equality to epsilon allows the input tolerance to be exactly zero. The dimension is set to zero. The member extremeCCW is not meaningful in this case.

If the maximum range is greater than epsilon, the length of the vector connecting the two extreme points must have length greater than or equal to epsilon. The member direction[0] is computed as the unit-length vector connecting the extreme points.

The maximum distance from the input points to the line origin+t*direction[0] is computed, a quantity measured in the orthogonal complement of direction[0]. We do not actually need to know a basis for the orthogonal complement, because we can project out the direction[0] component from v[i]-origin and measure the length of the projection. The index into v[] for the point of maximum distance is stored in extreme[2].

If the maximum distance is less than or equal to epsilon*maxRange, the point set is assumed to degenerate to a line segment. The dimension is set to one. The member extremeCCW is not meaningful in this case. The use of epsilon*maxRange instead of epsilon alone is to be invariant to scaling; that is, epsilon is a relative error tolerance rather than an absolute error tolerance.

If the maximum is larger than epsilon*maxRange, we now know that the intrinsic dimensionality is two or three. We compute the orthogonal complement of direction[0] and store the basis vectors in direction[1] and direction[2]. The maximum distance from the input points to the plane origin+s*direction[0]+t*direction[1] is computed. We can do so by computing the component in the direction[0] from v[i]-origin. The sign of the distance is important for computing orientation, so that information is tracked. The index into v[] of the point of maximum distance is stored in extreme[3].

If the maximum distance is less than or equal to epsilon*maxRange, the point set is assumed to degenerate to a planar polygon. The dimension is set to two. The member extremeCCW is not meaningful in this case.

If the maximum distance is larger than epsilon*maxRange, the dimension is set to three and the points have full intrinsic dimensionality. The points indexed by extreme[] form a tetrahedron. The ordering of the extreme points is stored in extremeCCW. Observe that knowing which side of the plane v[extreme[3]] lives on is essential to know ordering.

6.2 Matrices

Mathematics engines provide matrix implementations that are focused on the tranformational aspects, namely, matrix-vector multiplication, matrix-

matrix multiplication, transposes, determinants, and inverses. Rotation matrices are a special classes of matrices that are also supported. The extent of the support can vary and might include the ability to generate and convert among many representations: axis-angle, Euler angles, and quaternions. GTEngine provides a full suite of classes and functions for rotation support. Although not used often in the applications, support exists for sums and differences of matrices, for product of a matrix with a scalar, and for L^p norms where $p \in \{1, 2, \infty\}$. As with vectors, comparison operators are provided to support sorted containers.

GTEngine has a base template class Matrix<int,int,Real> whose first parameter is the number of rows, second parameter is the number of columns, and third parameter is the floating-point type. Derived classes Matrix2x2<Real>, Matrix3x3<Real>, and Matrix4x4<Real> provide additional dimension-specific constructors and operations for the commonly occurring square matrices of low dimension.

6.2.1   Matrix Storage and Transfom Conventions

One source of pain when using mathematics engines, especially when you already have your own code that duplicates functionality, is figuring out the engines' conventions and how they relate to yours. I doubt any of us have been immune to dealing with interoperability concerns. Two major conventions to deal with are the *matrix storage convention* and the *matrix transform convention*.

The first convention refers to whether you store your matrices in *row-major order* or *column-major order*. Effectively, this is a choice for mapping a two-dimensional array into a one-dimensional array. Let $A = [a_{rc}]$ be an $n \times m$ matrix whose first index refers to row r with $0 \le r < n$ and whose second index refers to column c with $0 \le c < m$. We visualize this as a table, shown next for $n = 2$ and $m = 3$:

$$A = \left[\begin{array}{ccc} a_{00} & a_{01} & a_{02} \\ a_{10} & a_{11} & a_{12} \end{array} \right] \tag{6.30}$$

Row-major order stores the elements as $(a_{00}, a_{01}, a_{02}, a_{10}, a_{11}, a_{12})$, whereas column-major order stores the elements as $(a_{00}, a_{10}, a_{01}, a_{11}, a_{02}, a_{12})$. Generally, the one-dimensional array is $B = [b_i]$ and has nm elements. For row-major order, the index mapping from A to B is $i = c + mr$. The inverse mapping is $(c, r) = (i\%m, i/m)$, where $\%$ is the integer modulo operator and $/$ is integer division. For column-major order, the index mapping from A to B is $i = r + nc$. The inverse mapping is $(c, r) = (i\%n, i/n)$.

The second convention refers to which side of the matrix you envision a vector when multiplying. If A is a square matrix and $\mathbf{V}$ is a vector of the appropriate size, do you choose the product to be $A\mathbf{V}$ or $\mathbf{V}^\mathsf{T} A$? I refer to the former product as *vector-on-the-right convention* and the latter product as *vector-on-the-left convention*. If A is not a square matrix, then the side of the matrix on which a vector lives depends solely on the dimensions of the matrix and vector; that is, there is no ambiguity about the product.

GTEngine allows you to select these conventions by conditional compilation of the libraries. The file

GeometricTools/GTEngine/Source/GTEngineDEF.h

contains preprocessor macros that you can enable or disable as you desire. The macros enabled by default are GTE_USE_ROW_MAJOR, indicating that matrices are stored in row-major-order, and GTE_USE_MAT_VEC, indicating that vector-on-the-right is used. Flexibility on your part has its consequences. Firstly, whenever algorithms in the engine depend on either convention, the implementations have conditionally compiled code. This requires me to provide multiple versions of the implementation, and I need to ensure that the sample applications do the same. Secondly, the HLSL compiler for D3D11 has similar conventions, so you need to ensure that your shaders are set up properly to match your conventions. In the sample applications with shaders, I have included conditional compilation in the HLSL files themselves—controlled by the very same preprocessor macros in the C++ code. The HLSL compiler provides the ability to enable or disable macros via arguments to the compiler function call.

Other engine conventions related to coordinate system handling are necessary. I will go into detail about those conventions in the section on coordinate systems.

6.2.2 Base Class Matrix Operations

The base class is template <int NumRows, int NumCols, typename Real> Matrix, which supports general matrices with user-specified sizes. The storage itself is protected, because the details cannot be exposed to the public based on the user-selectable convention for row-major or column-major storage. Listing 6.17 shows the data representation.

```
template <int NumRows, int NumCols, typename Real>
class Matrix
{
protected:
    // The data structures take advantage of the built-in operator[],
    // range checking, and visualizers in MSVS.

    class Table
    {
    public:
        // operator() provides storage-order-independent element access.
#if defined(GTE_USE_ROW_MAJOR)
        Real const& operator() (int r, int c) const
            { return mStorage[r][c]; }
        Real& operator() (int r, int c) { return mStorage[r][c]; }
        std::array<std::array<Real,NumCols>,NumRows> mStorage;
#else
        Real const& operator() (int r, int c) const
            { return mStorage[c][r]; }
        Real& operator() (int r, int c) { return mStorage[c][r]; }
        std::array<std::array<Real,NumRows>,NumCols> mStorage;
```

```
#endif
    };

    union
    {
        // Access as a one-dimensional array.
        std::array<Real,NumRows*NumCols> mTuple;

        // Access as a two-dimensional array.
        Table mTable;
    };
};
```

LISTING 6.17: Storage for the matrix class.

The data structures take advantage of the built-in operator[] for std::array, including range checking and visualizers in Microsoft Visual Studio 2013. The union allows internal manipulation of the matrix entries either as a one-dimensional or two-dimensional array. As the comments indicate, access via operator() hides the storage convention.

The class has the default constructor, a copy constructor, and an assignment operator. Constructors that are dependent on dimension are declared in derived classes.

Listing 6.18 shows the accessor interface for the class.

```
template <int NumRows, int NumCols, typename Real>
class Matrix
{
public:
    // The storage representation for the members is transparent to the
    // user. The matrix entry in row r and column c is A(r,c).  The first
    // operator() returns a const reference rather than a Real value.
    // This supports writing via standard file operations that require a
    // const pointer to data.
    inline Real const& operator() (int r, int c) const;
    inline Real& operator() (int r, int c);

    // Member access is by rows or by columns.
    void SetRow (int r, Vector<NumCols,Real> const& vec);
    void SetCol (int c, Vector<NumRows,Real> const& vec);
    Vector<NumCols,Real> GetRow (int r) const;
    Vector<NumRows,Real> GetCol (int c) const;

    // Member access is by one-dimensional index.  NOTE: These accessors
    // are useful for the manipulation of matrix entries when it does not
    // matter whether storage is row-major or column-major.  Do not use
    // constructs such as M(c+NumCols*r) or M(r+NumRows*c) that expose
    // the storage convention.
    inline Real const& operator() (int i) const;
    inline Real& operator() (int i);
};
```

LISTING 6.18: Member accessors for the matrix class.

The first two functions allow you to access individual matrix entries by specifying the row and column. The next four functions allow you to access a row or a column as a whole. The last two functions allow you to access the matrix as a one-dimensional array, but the intent is to support simple operations such as memory copying and streaming to and from disk.

Finally, the class implements the standard six comparison operators to support sorted container classes; see Listing 6.19.

```
template <int NumRows, int NumCols, typename Real>
class Matrix
{
public:
    // comparisons for sorted containers and geometric ordering
    bool operator== (Matrix const& mat) const;
    bool operator!= (Matrix const& mat) const;
    bool operator<  (Matrix const& mat) const;
    bool operator<= (Matrix const& mat) const;
    bool operator>  (Matrix const& mat) const;
    bool operator>= (Matrix const& mat) const;
};
```

LISTING 6.19: Comparison operators for the matrix class.

A large number of functions are defined outside the class, a practice suggested in [55, Rule 44]. Included are unary operators so that you can write expressions +M and −M for matrices. Also included are the linear-algebraic operations for matrix addition, subtraction, scalar multiplication and division, and the usual arithemtic update operators such as operator+=.

Three L^p matrix norms are implemented, for $p \in \{1, 2, \infty\}$. The L^1 norm is the sum of the absolute values of the matrix entries; see function L1Norm. The L^2 norm is the sum of the squared matrix entries, the most commonly used matrix norm; see function L2Norm. The L^∞ norm is the maximum of the absolute values of the matrix entries; see function LInfinityNorm.

Inversion of square matrices is provided by the function Inverse. The algorithm involves Gaussian elimination with full pivoting. When the inverse does not exist as determined numerically, the zero matrix is returned. Inversion for square matrices of sizes two, three, and four are specialized by the derived classes for these sizes; the algorithms use cofactor expansions. If M is an invertible matrix, M^{-1} denotes the inverse.

The matrix transpose is provided by the function Transpose. The transpose is denoted by M^{T}.

Two matrix-vector products are supported; see Listing 6.20 for the interfaces.

```
// M*V
template <int NumRows, int NumCols, typename Real>
Vector<NumRows, Real>
operator* (
    Matrix<NumRows, NumCols, Real> const& M,
    Vector<NumCols, Real> const& V);

// V^T*M
template <int NumRows, int NumCols, typename Real>
Vector<NumCols, Real>
operator* (
    Vector<NumRows, Real> const& V,
    Matrix<NumRows, NumCols, Real> const& M);
```

LISTING 6.20: Matrix-vector products.

The operators make it clear which product you get based on the order of the inputs. The template declarations ensure at compile time the enforcement of the rules for products. The product $M\mathbf{V}$ is defined only when the number of columns of M is equal to the number of rows of $\mathbf{V}$. The product $\mathbf{V}^{\mathsf{T}}M$ is defined only when the number of rows of M is equal to the number of columns of $\mathbf{V}^{\mathsf{T}}$ (equivalently, the number of rows of $\mathbf{V}$).

A collection of matrix-matrix products are provided: AB, AB^{T}, $A^{\mathsf{T}}B$, and $A^{\mathsf{T}}B^{\mathsf{T}}$, where A and B are the appropriate size matrices. Once again, the template declartions ensure that at compile time the row-column count equalities are enforced. For a diagonal matrix D, there are functions to compute MD and DM as long as the row-column sizes are valid. However, the diagonal matrix is represented as a vector that stores the diagonal entries.

6.2.3 Square Matrix Operations in 2D

Square matrices of size two are built by derivation from the base class. Listing 6.21 shows the minimal interface.

```
template <typename Real>
class Matrix2x2 : public Matrix<2,2,Real>
{
public:
    // Construction and destruction. The destructor hides the base-class
    // destructor, but the latter has no side effects. Matrix2x2 is
    // designed to provide specialized constructors and geometric
    // operations. The default constructor does not initialize its data.
    ~Matrix2x2 ();
    Matrix2x2 ();
    Matrix2x2 (Matrix2x2 const& mat);
    Matrix2x2 (Matrix<2,2,Real> const& mat);
    Matrix2x2 (Real m00, Real m01, Real m10, Real m11);

    // Create a diagonal matrix. Pass zeros to create the zero matrix.
    // Pass ones to create the identity matrix.
    Matrix2x2 (Real m00, Real m11);

    // Create a rotation matrix from an angle (in radians). The matrix is
    // [GTE_USE_MAT_VEC]
    //     R(t) = {{c,-s},{s,c}}
    // [GTE_USE_VEC_MAT]
    //     R(t) = {{c,s},{-s,c}}
    // where c = cos(t), s = sin(t), and the inner-brace pairs are rows of
    // the matrix.
    Matrix2x2 (Real angle);

    // Create special matrices.
    void MakeZero ();
    void MakeIdentity ();
    void MakeDiagonal (Real m00, Real m11);
    void MakeRotation (Real angle);

    // Get the angle (radians) from a rotation matrix. The caller is
    // responsible for ensuring the matrix is a rotation.
    void Get (Real& angle) const;

    // assignment
    Matrix2x2& operator= (Matrix2x2 const& mat);
    Matrix2x2& operator= (Matrix<2,2,Real> const& mat);
```

```
        // special matrices
        static Matrix2x2 Zero ();
        static Matrix2x2 Identity ();
};
```

LISTING 6.21: The class interface for 2×2 matrices.

The constructors are for the specific size two. The constructor and assignment operator for the base class are provided to allow implicit conversions. Static functions are implemented to return the zero matrix and the identity matrix. We use functions to avoid the standard template dilemma of declaring static members that might be instantiated in multiple modules.

Geometric operations are implemented outside the class; see Listing 6.22.

```
template <typename Real>
Matrix2x2<Real> Inverse (Matrix2x2<Real> const& M);

template <typename Real>
Matrix2x2<Real> Adjoint (Matrix2x2<Real> const& M);

template <typename Real>
Real Determinant (Matrix2x2<Real> const& M);

template <typename Real>
Real Trace (Matrix2x2<Real> const& M);
```

LISTING 6.22: Geometric operations for 2×2 matrices.

The matrix and the quantities these functions compute are shown next.

$$M = \begin{bmatrix} m_{00} & m_{01} \\ m_{10} & m_{11} \end{bmatrix}, \ \ \text{trace}(M) = m_{00} + m_{11},$$

$$\det(M) = m_{00}m_{11} - m_{01}m_{10}, \ \ \text{adjoint}(M) = \begin{bmatrix} m_{11} & -m_{01} \\ -m_{10} & m_{00} \end{bmatrix}, \qquad (6.31)$$

$$M^{-1} = \text{adjoint}(M)/\det(M)$$

The inverse exists only when $\det(M) \neq 0$. As in the base class inversion, if the matrix is not invertible, the Inverse function returns the zero matrix. The adjoint matrix is the transpose of the matrix of *cofactors* for M.

In the implementations, you will notice that there is no conditional compilation for code depending on the matrix storage convention. The base class hides the conditional compilation, so derived classes can manipulate the matrix entries via operator()(int,int) without regard to the storage convention.

6.2.4 Square Matrix Operations in 3D

Square matrices of size three are built by derivation from the base class. Listing 6.23 shows the minimal interface.

```
template <typename Real>
class Matrix3x3 : public Matrix<3,3,Real>
{
public:
    // Construction and destruction.  The destructor hides the base-class
    // destructor, but the latter has no side effects.  Matrix3x3 is
    // designed to provide specialized constructors and geometric
    // operations.  The default constructor does not initialize its data.
    ~Matrix3x3 ();
    Matrix3x3 ();
    Matrix3x3 (Matrix3x3 const& mat);
    Matrix3x3 (Matrix<3,3,Real> const& mat);
    Matrix3x3 (
        Real m00, Real m01, Real m02,
        Real m10, Real m11, Real m12,
        Real m20, Real m21, Real m22);

    // Create a diagonal matrix.  Pass zeros to create the zero matrix.
    // Pass ones to create the identity matrix.
    Matrix3x3 (Real m00, Real m11, Real m22);

    // Create special matrices.
    void MakeZero ();
    void MakeIdentity ();
    void MakeDiagonal (Real m00, Real m11, Real m22);

    // assignment
    Matrix3x3& operator= (Matrix3x3 const& mat);
    Matrix3x3& operator= (Matrix<3,3,Real> const& mat);

    // special matrices
    static Matrix3x3 Zero ();
    static Matrix3x3 Identity ();
};
```

LISTING 6.23: The class interface for 3×3 matrices.

The constructors are for the specific size three. The constructor and assignment operator for the base class are provided to allow implicit conversions. Static functions are implemented to return the zero matrix and the identity matrix. We use functions to avoid the standard template dilemma of declaring static members that might be instantiated in multiple modules.

Geometric operations are implemented outside the class; see Listing 6.24.

```
template <typename Real>
Matrix3x3<Real> Inverse (Matrix3x3<Real> const& M);

template <typename Real>
Matrix3x3<Real> Adjoint (Matrix3x3<Real> const& M);

template <typename Real>
Real Determinant (Matrix3x3<Real> const& M);

template <typename Real>
Real Trace (Matrix3x3<Real> const& M);
```

LISTING 6.24: Geometric operations for 3×3 matrices.

The matrix and the quantities these functions compute are shown next.

$$
M = \begin{bmatrix} m_{00} & m_{01} & m_{02} \\ m_{10} & m_{11} & m_{12} \\ m_{20} & m_{21} & m_{22} \end{bmatrix},
$$

$$\operatorname{trace}(M) = m_{00} + m_{11} + m_{22},$$

$$\det(M) = m_{00}(m_{11}m_{22} - m_{12}m_{21}) + m_{01}(m_{12}m_{20} - m_{10}m_{22})$$
$$+ m_{02}(m_{10}m_{21} - m_{11}m_{20}),$$

$$\operatorname{adjoint}(M) =$$

(6.32)

$$\begin{bmatrix} m_{11}m_{22} - m_{12}m_{21} & m_{02}m_{21} - m_{01}m_{22} & m_{01}m_{12} - m_{02}m_{11} \\ m_{12}m_{20} - m_{10}m_{22} & m_{00}m_{22} - m_{02}m_{20} & m_{02}m_{10} - m_{00}m_{12} \\ m_{10}m_{21} - m_{11}m_{20} & m_{01}m_{20} - m_{00}m_{21} & m_{00}m_{11} - m_{01}m_{10} \end{bmatrix},$$

$$M^{-1} = \operatorname{adjoint}(M)/\det(M)$$

The inverse exists only when $\det(M) \neq 0$. As in the base class inversion, if the matrix is not invertible, the Inverse function returns the zero matrix. In the implementations, you will notice that there is no conditional compilation for code depending on the matrix storage convention. The base class hides the conditional compilation, so derived classes can manipulate the matrix entries via operator() without regard to the storage convention.

6.2.5 Square Matrix Operations in 4D

Square matrices of size four are built by derivation from the base class. Listing 6.25 shows the minimal interface.

```
template <typename Real>
class Matrix4x4 : public Matrix<4,4,Real>
{
public:
    // Construction and destruction.  The destructor hides the base-class
    // destructor, but the latter has no side effects.  Matrix4x4 is
    // designed to provide specialized constructors and geometric
    // operations.  The default constructor does not initialize its data.
    ~Matrix4x4 ();
    Matrix4x4 ();
    Matrix4x4 (Matrix4x4 const& mat);
    Matrix4x4 (Matrix<4,4,Real> const& mat);
    Matrix4x4 (
        Real m00, Real m01, Real m02, Real m03,
        Real m10, Real m11, Real m12, Real m13,
        Real m20, Real m21, Real m22, Real m23,
        Real m30, Real m31, Real m32, Real m33);

    // Create a diagonal matrix.  Pass zeros to create the zero matrix.
    // Pass ones to create the identity matrix.
    Matrix4x4 (Real m00, Real m11, Real m22, Real m33);

    // Create special matrices.
    void MakeZero ();
    void MakeIdentity ();
    void MakeDiagonal (Real m00, Real m11, Real m22, Real m33);

    // assignment
    Matrix4x4& operator= (Matrix4x4 const& mat);
    Matrix4x4& operator= (Matrix<4,4,Real> const& mat);
```

```
// special matrices
static Matrix4x4 Zero ();
static Matrix4x4 Identity ();
};
```

LISTING 6.25: The class interface for 4×4 matrices.

The constructors are for the specific size four. The constructor and assignment operator for the base class are provided to allow implicit conversions. Static functions are implemented to return the zero matrix and the identity matrix. We use functions to avoid the standard template dilemma of declaring static members that might be instantiated in multiple modules.

Geometric operations are implemented outside the class; see Listing 6.26.

```
template <typename Real>
Matrix4x4<Real> Inverse (Matrix4x4<Real> const& M);

template <typename Real>
Matrix4x4<Real> Adjoint (Matrix4x4<Real> const& M);

template <typename Real>
Real Determinant (Matrix4x4<Real> const& M);

template <typename Real>
Real Trace (Matrix4x4<Real> const& M);
```

LISTING 6.26: Geometric operations for 4×4 matrices.

Let $M = [m_{rc}]$ be a 4×4 matrix. The trace of the matrix is $\text{trace}(M) = m_{00} + m_{11} + m_{22} + m_{33}$. The adjoint matrix, determinant, and inverse may be computed in a manner similar to what was done for 3×3 matrices—expansion across a row using cofactors. This is what is typically taught in a linear algebra class. The expression for the determinant is a product of the first row of M and the first column of $\text{adjoint}(M)$. The column entries are effectively 3×3 determinants. Construction of M^{-1} requires computing all the adjoint entries, so you have twelve 3×3 determinants to compute. These in turn can be computed by cofactor expansions, a recursive process. As it turns out, a more efficient procedure may be used to compute $\text{adjoint}(M)$, $\det(M)$, and M^{-1}; it is discussed in the next section.

6.2.6   The Laplace Expansion Theorem

Let us revisit the computation of the determinant of a 3×3 matrix $A = [a_{rc}]$, where the row index satisfies $0 \le r \le 2$ and the column index satisfies $0 \le c \le 2$. The matrix is

$$A = \begin{bmatrix} a_{00} & a_{01} & a_{02} \\ a_{10} & a_{11} & a_{12} \\ a_{20} & a_{21} & a_{22} \end{bmatrix} \tag{6.33}$$

Expanding by the first row,

$$\det(A) = +a_{00} \cdot \det \begin{bmatrix} a_{11} & a_{12} \\ a_{21} & a_{22} \end{bmatrix} - a_{01} \cdot \det \begin{bmatrix} a_{10} & a_{12} \\ a_{20} & a_{22} \end{bmatrix}$$
$$+ a_{02} \cdot \det \begin{bmatrix} a_{10} & a_{11} \\ a_{20} & a_{21} \end{bmatrix}$$
$$= +a_{00}(a_{11}a_{22} - a_{12}a_{21}) - a_{01}(a_{10}a_{22} - a_{12}a_{20})$$
$$+ a_{02}(a_{10}a_{21} - a_{11}a_{20})$$
$$= +a_{00}a_{11}a_{22} + a_{01}a_{12}a_{20} + a_{02}a_{10}a_{21} - a_{00}a_{12}a_{21}$$
$$- a_{01}a_{10}a_{22} - a_{02}a_{11}a_{20} \tag{6.34}$$

Each term in the first line of Equation (6.34) involves a sign, an entry from row 0 of A, and a determinant of a submatrix of A. If a_{0c} is an entry in row 0, then the sign is $(-1)^{0+c}$ and the submatrix is obtained by removing row 0 and column c from A.

Five other expansions produce the same determinant formula: by row 1, by row 2, by column 0, by column 1, or by column 2. In all six formulas, each term involves a matrix entry a_{rc}, an associated sign $(-1)^{r+c}$, and a submatrix M_{rc} that is obtained from A by removing row r and column c. The cofactor associated with the term is

$$\gamma_{rc} = (-1)^{r+c} \det M_{rc} \tag{6.35}$$

The matrix of cofactors is $\text{adjoint}(A) = [\gamma_{rc}]$ for rows $0 \leq r \leq 2$ and for columns $0 \leq c \leq 2$, specifically,

$$\text{adjoint}(A) = \begin{bmatrix} +(a_{11}a_{22} - a_{12}a_{21}) & -(a_{01}a_{22} - a_{02}a_{21}) & +(a_{01}a_{12} - a_{02}a_{11}) \\ -(a_{10}a_{22} - a_{12}a_{20}) & +(a_{00}a_{22} - a_{02}a_{20}) & -(a_{00}a_{12} - a_{02}a_{10}) \\ +(a_{10}a_{21} - a_{11}a_{20}) & -(a_{00}a_{21} - a_{01}a_{20}) & +(a_{00}a_{11} - a_{01}a_{10}) \end{bmatrix} \tag{6.36}$$

The first line of Equation (6.34) may be written also as

$$\det(A) = + \det[a_{00}] \cdot \det \begin{bmatrix} a_{11} & a_{12} \\ a_{21} & a_{22} \end{bmatrix}$$
$$- \det[a_{01}] \cdot \det \begin{bmatrix} a_{10} & a_{12} \\ a_{20} & a_{22} \end{bmatrix} + \det[a_{02}] \cdot \det \begin{bmatrix} a_{10} & a_{11} \\ a_{20} & a_{21} \end{bmatrix} \tag{6.37}$$

which is a sum of the products of the determinants of the submatrices of A, with alternating signs for the terms. A visual way to look at this is shown in Figure 6.1. Each 3×3 grid represents the matrix entries. The dark-colored cells represent the 1×1 submatrices in the determinant formula and the light-colored cells represent the 2×2 submatrices in the determinant formula.

In the left 3×3 grid of the figure, the dark-colored cell represents the submatrix $[a_{00}]$ from the first term in the determinant formula. The light-colored cells are the *complementary submatrix* of $[a_{00}]$, namely, the 2×2 submatrix that is part of the first term of the formula; the first row has a_{11}

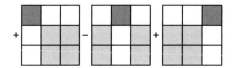

FIGURE 6.1: A visualization of the determinant of a 3×3 matrix.

and a_{12} and the second row has a_{21} and a_{22}. The submatrix is obtained from A by removing row 0 and column 0.

In the middle 3×3 grid of the figure, the dark-colored cell represents the submatrix $[a_{01}]$ from the second term in the determinant formula. The light-colored cells are the complementary submatrix of $[a_{01}]$, namely, the 2×2 submatrix that is part of the second term of the formula; the first row has a_{10} and a_{12} and the second row has a_{20} and a_{22}. The submatrix is obtained from A by removing row 0 and column 1.

In the right 3×3 grid of the figure, the dark-colored cell represents the submatrix $[a_{02}]$ from the third term in the determinant formula. The light-colored cells are the complementary submatrix of $[a_{02}]$, namely, the 2×2 matrix that is part of the third term of the formula; the first row has a_{10} and a_{11} and the second row has a_{20} and a_{21}. The submatrix is obtained from A by removing row 0 and column 2.

The *Laplace expansion theorem* is a general formula for computing the determinant of an $n \times n$ matrix A. Let $\mathbf{r} = (r_1, r_2, \ldots, r_k)$ be a list of k row indices for A, where $1 \le k < n$ and $0 \le r_1 < r_2 < \cdots < r_k < n$. Let $\mathbf{c} = (c_1, c_2, \ldots, c_k)$ be a list of k column indices for A, where $1 \le k < n$ and $0 \le c_1 < c_2 < \cdots < c_k < n$. The submatrix obtained by *keeping* the entries in the intersection of any row and column that are in the lists is denoted

$$S(A; \mathbf{r}, \mathbf{c}) \tag{6.38}$$

The submatrix obtained by *removing* the entries in the rows and columns that are in the list is denoted

$$S'(A; \mathbf{r}, \mathbf{c}) \tag{6.39}$$

and is the *complementary submatrix* for $S(A; \mathbf{r}, \mathbf{c})$. For example, let A be a 3×3 matrix. Let $\mathbf{r} = (0)$ and $\mathbf{c} = (1)$. Then

$$S(A; \mathbf{r}, \mathbf{c}) = [a_{01}], \quad S'(A; \mathbf{r}, \mathbf{c}) = \begin{bmatrix} a_{10} & a_{12} \\ a_{20} & a_{22} \end{bmatrix} \tag{6.40}$$

In the middle 3×3 grid of Figure 6.1, $S(A; (0), (1))$ is formed from the dark-colored cell and $S'(A; (0), (1))$ is formed from the light-colored cells.

The Laplace expansion theorem is as follows. Let A be an $n \times n$ matrix. Let $\mathbf{r} = (r_1, r_2, \ldots, r_k)$ be a list of k row indices, where $1 \le k < n$ and $0 \le r_1 < r_2 < \cdots r_k < n$. The determinant of A is

$$\det(A) = (-1)^{|\mathbf{r}|} \sum_{\mathbf{c}} (-1)^{|\mathbf{c}|} \det S(A; \mathbf{r}, \mathbf{c}) \det S'(A; \mathbf{r}, \mathbf{c}) \tag{6.41}$$

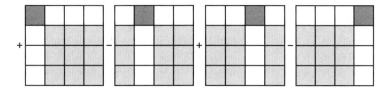

FIGURE 6.2: A visualization of the expansion by row zero of a 4×4 matrix in order to compute the determinant.

where $|\mathbf{r}| = r_1 + r_2 + \cdots + r_k$, $|\mathbf{c}| = c_1 + c_2 + \cdots + c_k$, and the summation is over all k-tuples $\mathbf{c} = (c_1, c_2, \ldots, c_k)$ for which $1 \le c_1 < c_2 < \cdots < c_k < n$.

For example, consider a 3×3 matrix with $\mathbf{r} = (0)$ (that is, $k = 1$). Then $|\mathbf{r}| = 0$, $\mathbf{c} = (c_0)$, and the determinant is

$$
\begin{aligned}
\det(A) &= \sum_{c_0=0}^{2} (-1)^{c_0} \det S(A; (0), (c_0)) \det S'(A; (0), (c_0)) \\[2mm]
&= (-1)^0 \det S(A; (0), (0)) \det S'(A; (0), (0)) \\
&\quad + (-1)^1 \det S(A; (0), (1)) \det S'(A; (0), (1)) \\
&\quad + (-1)^2 \det S(A; (0), (2)) \det S'(A; (0), (2)) \\[2mm]
&= + \det[a_{00}] \cdot \det \begin{bmatrix} a_{11} & a_{12} \\ a_{21} & a_{22} \end{bmatrix} - \det[a_{01}] \cdot \det \begin{bmatrix} a_{10} & a_{12} \\ a_{20} & a_{22} \end{bmatrix} \\[2mm]
&\quad + \det[a_{02}] \cdot \det \begin{bmatrix} a_{10} & a_{11} \\ a_{20} & a_{21} \end{bmatrix}
\end{aligned}
\tag{6.42}
$$

which is Equation (6.37).

The Laplace expansion theorem may be applied to 4×4 matrices in a couple of ways. The first way uses an expansion by a row or by a column, which is the most common approach. The matrix is

$$
A = \begin{bmatrix} a_{00} & a_{01} & a_{02} & a_{03} \\ a_{10} & a_{11} & a_{12} & a_{13} \\ a_{20} & a_{21} & a_{22} & a_{23} \\ a_{30} & a_{31} & a_{32} & a_{33} \end{bmatrix}
\tag{6.43}
$$

Using the visualization as motivated by Figure 6.1, an expansion by row zero is visualized in Figure 6.2: The algebraic equivalent is

$$
\begin{aligned}
\det(A) &= + \det[a_{00}] \cdot \det \begin{bmatrix} a_{11} & a_{12} & a_{13} \\ a_{21} & a_{22} & a_{23} \\ a_{31} & a_{32} & a_{33} \end{bmatrix} - \det[a_{01}] \cdot \det \begin{bmatrix} a_{10} & a_{12} & a_{13} \\ a_{20} & a_{22} & a_{23} \\ a_{30} & a_{32} & a_{33} \end{bmatrix} \\[2mm]
&\quad + \det[a_{02}] \cdot \det \begin{bmatrix} a_{10} & a_{11} & a_{13} \\ a_{20} & a_{21} & a_{23} \\ a_{30} & a_{31} & a_{33} \end{bmatrix} - \det[a_{03}] \cdot \det \begin{bmatrix} a_{10} & a_{11} & a_{12} \\ a_{20} & a_{21} & a_{22} \\ a_{30} & a_{31} & a_{32} \end{bmatrix}
\end{aligned}
\tag{6.44}
$$

It is possible, however, to use the Laplace expansion theorem in a different manner. Choose $\mathbf{r} = (0, 1)$, an expansion by rows zero and one, so to speak; then $|\mathbf{r}| = 0 + 1 = 1$, $\mathbf{c} = (c_0, c_1)$, and

$$
\begin{aligned}
\det(A) &= -\sum_{\mathbf{c}}(-1)^{c_0+c_1} \det S(A; (0,1), \mathbf{c}) \det S'(A; (0,1), \mathbf{c}) \\[1em]
&= + \det S(A; (0,1), (0,1)) \det S'(A; (0,1), (0,1)) \\
&\quad - \det S(A; (0,1), (0,2)) \det S'(A; (0,1), (0,2)) \\
&\quad + \det S(A; (0,1), (0,3)) \det S'(A; (0,1), (0,3)) \\
&\quad + \det S(A; (0,1), (1,2)) \det S'(A; (0,1), (1,2)) \\
&\quad - \det S(A; (0,1), (1,3)) \det S'(A; (0,1), (1,3)) \\
&\quad + \det S(A; (0,1), (2,3)) \det S'(A; (0,1), (2,3))
\end{aligned}
$$

$$
\begin{aligned}
&= \; + \det \begin{bmatrix} a_{00} & a_{01} \\ a_{10} & a_{11} \end{bmatrix} \det \begin{bmatrix} a_{22} & a_{23} \\ a_{32} & a_{33} \end{bmatrix} \\[1em]
&\quad - \det \begin{bmatrix} a_{00} & a_{02} \\ a_{10} & a_{12} \end{bmatrix} \det \begin{bmatrix} a_{21} & a_{23} \\ a_{31} & a_{33} \end{bmatrix} \\[1em]
&\quad + \det \begin{bmatrix} a_{00} & a_{03} \\ a_{10} & a_{13} \end{bmatrix} \det \begin{bmatrix} a_{21} & a_{22} \\ a_{31} & a_{32} \end{bmatrix} \\[1em]
&\quad + \det \begin{bmatrix} a_{01} & a_{02} \\ a_{11} & a_{12} \end{bmatrix} \det \begin{bmatrix} a_{20} & a_{23} \\ a_{30} & a_{33} \end{bmatrix} \\[1em]
&\quad - \det \begin{bmatrix} a_{01} & a_{03} \\ a_{11} & a_{13} \end{bmatrix} \det \begin{bmatrix} a_{20} & a_{22} \\ a_{30} & a_{32} \end{bmatrix} \\[1em]
&\quad + \det \begin{bmatrix} a_{02} & a_{03} \\ a_{12} & a_{13} \end{bmatrix} \det \begin{bmatrix} a_{20} & a_{21} \\ a_{30} & a_{31} \end{bmatrix}
\end{aligned}
\tag{6.45}
$$

The visualization for this approach, similar to that of Figure 6.2, is shown in Figure 6.3.

Computing the determinant of a 2×2 matrix requires one multiplication and one addition (or subtraction). The operation count is listed as a 2-tuple, the first component the number of multiplications and the second component the number of additions: $\Theta_2 = (2, 1)$. Computing the determinant of a 3×3 matrix, when expanded by the first row according to Equation (6.34), requires the following number of operations: $\Theta_3 = 3\Theta_2 + (3, 2) = (9, 5)$. Using the row expansion of Equation (6.44) to compute the determinant of a 4×4 matrix, the operation count is $\Theta_4 = 4\Theta_3 + (4, 3) = (40, 23)$. However, if you use Equation (6.45) to compute the determinant, the operation count is $\Theta'_4 = 12\Theta_2 + (6, 5) = (30, 17)$. The total number of operations using Equation (6.44) is sixty-three and the total number of operation using Equation (6.45) is forty-seven, so the latter equation is more efficient in terms of operation count.

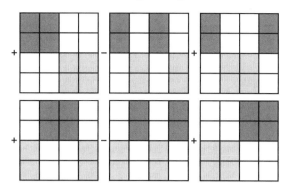

FIGURE 6.3: A visualization of the expansion by rows zero and one of a 4×4 matrix in order to compute the determinant.

To compute the inverse of a 4×4 matrix A, first construct the adjoint matrix. The cofactors involve 3×3 determinants. For example, the entry in row zero and column zero of $\text{adjoint}(A)$ is

$$
+\det \begin{bmatrix} a_{11} & a_{12} & a_{13} \\ a_{21} & a_{22} & a_{23} \\ a_{31} & a_{32} & a_{33} \end{bmatrix} = +a_{11} \cdot \det \begin{bmatrix} a_{22} & a_{23} \\ a_{32} & a_{33} \end{bmatrix}
$$

$$
- a_{12} \cdot \det \begin{bmatrix} a_{21} & a_{23} \\ a_{31} & a_{33} \end{bmatrix} + a_{13} \cdot \det \begin{bmatrix} a_{21} & a_{22} \\ a_{31} & a_{32} \end{bmatrix}
$$

(6.46)

This equation involves determinants of 2×2 submatrices that also occur in the equation for the determinant of the 4×4 matrix. This suggests computing all of the entries of $\text{adjoint}(A)$ using only 2×2 submatrices.

Specifically, define

$$
\begin{aligned}
s_0 &= \det \begin{bmatrix} a_{00} & a_{01} \\ a_{10} & a_{11} \end{bmatrix}, & c_5 &= \det \begin{bmatrix} a_{22} & a_{23} \\ a_{32} & a_{33} \end{bmatrix} \\
s_1 &= \det \begin{bmatrix} a_{00} & a_{02} \\ a_{10} & a_{12} \end{bmatrix}, & c_4 &= \det \begin{bmatrix} a_{21} & a_{23} \\ a_{31} & a_{33} \end{bmatrix} \\
s_2 &= \det \begin{bmatrix} a_{00} & a_{03} \\ a_{10} & a_{13} \end{bmatrix}, & c_3 &= \det \begin{bmatrix} a_{21} & a_{22} \\ a_{31} & a_{32} \end{bmatrix} \\
s_3 &= \det \begin{bmatrix} a_{01} & a_{02} \\ a_{11} & a_{12} \end{bmatrix}, & c_2 &= \det \begin{bmatrix} a_{20} & a_{23} \\ a_{30} & a_{33} \end{bmatrix} \\
s_4 &= \det \begin{bmatrix} a_{01} & a_{03} \\ a_{11} & a_{13} \end{bmatrix}, & c_1 &= \det \begin{bmatrix} a_{20} & a_{22} \\ a_{30} & a_{32} \end{bmatrix} \\
s_5 &= \det \begin{bmatrix} a_{02} & a_{03} \\ a_{12} & a_{13} \end{bmatrix}, & c_0 &= \det \begin{bmatrix} a_{20} & a_{21} \\ a_{30} & a_{31} \end{bmatrix}
\end{aligned}
$$

(6.47)

then

$$
\det(A) = s_0 c_5 - s_1 c_4 + s_2 c_3 + s_3 c_2 - s_4 c_1 + s_5 c_0 \tag{6.48}
$$

and adjoint$(A) = [m_{ij}]$ has the following entries:

$$
\begin{aligned}
m_{00} &= +a_{11}c_5 - a_{12}c_4 + a_{13}c_3 \\
m_{01} &= -a_{01}c_5 + a_{02}c_4 - a_{03}c_3 \\
m_{02} &= +a_{31}s_5 - a_{32}s_4 + a_{33}s_3 \\
m_{03} &= -a_{21}s_5 + a_{22}s_4 - a_{23}s_3 \\
m_{10} &= -a_{10}c_5 + a_{12}c_2 - a_{13}c_1 \\
m_{11} &= +a_{00}c_5 - a_{02}c_2 + a_{03}c_1 \\
m_{12} &= -a_{30}s_5 + a_{32}s_2 - a_{33}s_1 \\
m_{13} &= +a_{20}s_5 - a_{22}s_2 + a_{23}s_1 \\
m_{20} &= +a_{10}c_4 - a_{11}c_2 + a_{13}c_0 \\
m_{21} &= -a_{00}c_4 + a_{01}c_2 - a_{03}c_0 \\
m_{22} &= +a_{30}s_4 - a_{31}s_2 + a_{33}s_0 \\
m_{23} &= -a_{20}s_4 + a_{21}s_2 - a_{23}s_0 \\
m_{30} &= -a_{10}c_3 + a_{11}c_1 - a_{12}c_0 \\
m_{31} &= +a_{00}c_3 - a_{01}c_1 + a_{02}c_0 \\
m_{32} &= -a_{30}s_3 + a_{31}s_1 - a_{32}s_0 \\
m_{33} &= +a_{20}s_3 - a_{21}s_1 + a_{22}s_0
\end{aligned}
\tag{6.49}
$$

If the determinant is not zero, then the inverse of A is computed using $A^{-1} = $ adjoint$(A)/\det(A)$.

The implementations of adjoint, determinant, and inverse for the Matrix4x4<Real> class uses this approach.

6.3 Rotations

Rotations are a common operation that occur in 3D applications. This section describes the basic concepts and various representations of rotations, namely, by matrix, by quaternion, by axis-angle, and by Euler angles.

6.3.1 Rotation in 2D

The rotation of the vector (x, y) about the origin by an angle $\theta > 0$ is the vector (x', y') specified by $x' = x\cos\theta - y\sin\theta$ and and $y' = x\sin\theta + y\cos\theta$. The formula is derived using a standard trigonometric construction. The direction of rotation is counterclockwise about the origin. In vector-matrix form the equation is

$$
\begin{bmatrix} x' \\ y' \end{bmatrix} = \begin{bmatrix} \cos\theta & -\sin\theta \\ \sin\theta & \cos\theta \end{bmatrix} \begin{bmatrix} x \\ y \end{bmatrix}
\tag{6.50}
$$

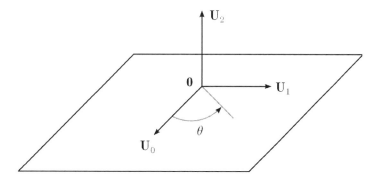

FIGURE 6.4: $\{\mathbf{U}_0, \mathbf{U}_1, \mathbf{U}_2\}$ is a right-handed orthonormal set. A rotation is desired about $\mathbf{U}_2$ by the angle $\theta > 0$.

6.3.2 Rotation in 3D

If we add a third dimension, the rotation of the vector (x, y, z) about the z-axis by an angle $\theta > 0$ is just a rotation of the (x, y) portion about the origin in the xy-plane. The rotated vector (x', y', z') is specified by

$$
\begin{bmatrix} x' \\ y' \\ z' \end{bmatrix} = \begin{bmatrix} \cos\theta & -\sin\theta & 0 \\ \sin\theta & \cos\theta & 0 \\ 0 & 0 & 1 \end{bmatrix} \begin{bmatrix} x \\ y \\ z \end{bmatrix}
\tag{6.51}
$$

Setting $\mathbf{V} = [x\,y\,z]^{\mathsf{T}}$, $\mathbf{V}' = [x'\,y'\,z']^{\mathsf{T}}$, $\sigma = \sin\theta$, and $\gamma = \cos\theta$, the rotation is $\mathbf{V}' = R_0\mathbf{V}$, where R_0 is the rotation matrix,

$$
R_0 = \begin{bmatrix} \gamma & -\sigma & 0 \\ \sigma & \gamma & 0 \\ 0 & 0 & 1 \end{bmatrix}
\tag{6.52}
$$

The standard coordinate axis directions (standard basis), represented as 3×1 vectors, are $\mathbf{E}_0 = [1\,0\,0]^{\mathsf{T}}$, $\mathbf{E}_1 = [0\,1\,0]^{\mathsf{T}}$, and $\mathbf{E}_2 = [0\,0\,1]^{\mathsf{T}}$. Observe that

$$
R_0\mathbf{E}_0 = \gamma\mathbf{E}_0 + \sigma\mathbf{E}_1, \quad R_0\mathbf{E}_1 = -\sigma\mathbf{E}_0 + \gamma\mathbf{E}_1, \quad R_0\mathbf{E}_2 = \mathbf{E}_2
\tag{6.53}
$$

The vectors $R_0\mathbf{E}_0$, $R_0\mathbf{E}_1$, and $R_0\mathbf{E}_2$ are the columns of R_0. The vectors $\mathbf{E}_0^{\mathsf{T}}R_0$, $\mathbf{E}_1^{\mathsf{T}}R_0$, and $\mathbf{E}_2^{\mathsf{T}}R_0$ are the rows of R_0.

The equation for rotation of a 3D vector $\mathbf{V}$ by an angle $\theta > 0$ about an axis with unit-length direction $\mathbf{U}_2$ is derived next. Let $\mathbf{U}_0$ and $\mathbf{U}_1$ be unit-length and perpendicular vectors in the plane containing the origin and having normal $\mathbf{U}_2 = \mathbf{U}_0 \times \mathbf{U}_1$; thus, $\{\mathbf{U}_0, \mathbf{U}_1, \mathbf{U}_2\}$ is a right-handed orthonormal set. Figure 6.4 is an illustration. The orthonormal set of vectors may be used as a basis, both as domain and range of the rotational transformation. The matrix R_0 in Equation (6.52) represents the rotation in this basis. A matrix R_1 that represents the rotation in the standard basis $\{\mathbf{E}_0, \mathbf{E}_1, \mathbf{E}_2\}$ will transform $\mathbf{U}_0$, $\mathbf{U}_1$, and $\mathbf{U}_2$ as

$$R_1\mathbf{U}_0 = \gamma\mathbf{U}_0 + \sigma\mathbf{U}_1, \quad R_1\mathbf{U}_1 = -\sigma\mathbf{U}_0 + \gamma\mathbf{U}_1, \quad R_1\mathbf{U}_2 = \mathbf{U}_2 \qquad (6.54)$$

The similarity between Equation (6.54) and Equation (6.53) is no coincidence. The equations in (6.53) may be collected into block-matrix form,

$$R_1 \begin{bmatrix} \mathbf{U}_0 & \mathbf{U}_1 & \mathbf{U}_2 \end{bmatrix} = \begin{bmatrix} \gamma\mathbf{U}_0 + \sigma\mathbf{U}_1 & -\sigma\mathbf{U}_0 + \gamma\mathbf{U}_1 & \mathbf{U}_2 \end{bmatrix}$$

$$= \begin{bmatrix} \mathbf{U}_0 & \mathbf{U}_1 & \mathbf{U}_2 \end{bmatrix} \begin{bmatrix} \gamma & -\sigma & 0 \\ \sigma & \gamma & 0 \\ 0 & 0 & 1 \end{bmatrix} \qquad (6.55)$$

The matrix $P = [\mathbf{U}_0\,\mathbf{U}_1\,\mathbf{U}_2]$, whose columns are the specified vectors, is itself a rotation matrix because $\{\mathbf{U}_0, \mathbf{U}_1, \mathbf{U}_2\}$ is a right-handed orthonormal set; its inverse is just its transpose. Equation (6.55) is $R_1 P = P R_0$. Solving for $R_1 = P R_0 P^{\mathsf{T}}$, we have

$$\begin{aligned} R_1 &= \begin{bmatrix} \mathbf{U}_0 & \mathbf{U}_1 & \mathbf{U}_2 \end{bmatrix} \begin{bmatrix} \gamma & -\sigma & 0 \\ \sigma & \gamma & 0 \\ 0 & 0 & 1 \end{bmatrix} \begin{bmatrix} \mathbf{U}_0 & \mathbf{U}_1 & \mathbf{U}_2 \end{bmatrix}^{\mathsf{T}} \\[2mm] &= \begin{bmatrix} \mathbf{U}_0 & \mathbf{U}_1 & \mathbf{U}_2 \end{bmatrix} \begin{bmatrix} \gamma & -\sigma & 0 \\ \sigma & \gamma & 0 \\ 0 & 0 & 1 \end{bmatrix} \begin{bmatrix} \mathbf{U}_0^{\mathsf{T}} \\ \mathbf{U}_1^{\mathsf{T}} \\ \mathbf{U}_2^{\mathsf{T}} \end{bmatrix} \\[2mm] &= \begin{bmatrix} \mathbf{U}_0 & \mathbf{U}_1 & \mathbf{U}_2 \end{bmatrix} \begin{bmatrix} \gamma\mathbf{U}_0^{\mathsf{T}} - \sigma\mathbf{U}_1^{\mathsf{T}} \\ \sigma\mathbf{U}_0^{\mathsf{T}} + \gamma\mathbf{U}_1^{\mathsf{T}} \\ \mathbf{U}_2^{\mathsf{T}} \end{bmatrix} \\[2mm] &= \mathbf{U}_0\left(\gamma\mathbf{U}_0^{\mathsf{T}} - \sigma\mathbf{U}_1^{\mathsf{T}}\right) + \mathbf{U}_1\left(\sigma\mathbf{U}_0^{\mathsf{T}} + \gamma\mathbf{U}_1^{\mathsf{T}}\right) + \mathbf{U}_2\mathbf{U}_2^{\mathsf{T}} \\[1mm] &= c\left(\mathbf{U}_0\mathbf{U}_0^{\mathsf{T}} + \mathbf{U}_1\mathbf{U}_1^{\mathsf{T}}\right) + s\left(\mathbf{U}_1\mathbf{U}_0^{\mathsf{T}} - \mathbf{U}_0\mathbf{U}_1^{\mathsf{T}}\right) + \mathbf{U}_2\mathbf{U}_2^{\mathsf{T}} \end{aligned} \qquad (6.56)$$

Keep in mind that $\mathbf{U}_0\mathbf{U}_0^{\mathsf{T}}$ is the product of a 3×1 matrix and a 1×3 matrix, the result a 3×3 matrix. This is not the same as $\mathbf{U}_0^{\mathsf{T}}\mathbf{U}_0$, a product of a 1×3 matrix and a 3×1 matrix, the result a 1×1 matrix (a scalar). Similarly, $\mathbf{U}_1\mathbf{U}_1^{\mathsf{T}}$, $\mathbf{U}_2\mathbf{U}_2^{\mathsf{T}}$, $\mathbf{U}_1\mathbf{U}_0^{\mathsf{T}}$, and $\mathbf{U}_0\mathbf{U}_1^{\mathsf{T}}$ are 3×3 matrices. From a computational perspective, R_1 is easily computed from Equation (6.56), but requires selecting $\mathbf{U}_0$ and $\mathbf{U}_1$ for the specified axis direction $\mathbf{U}_2$. Your intuition, though, should tell you that the rotation about the axis is independent of which pair of orthonormal vectors you choose in the plane. The following construction shows how to remove the dependence.

The representation of $\mathbf{V}$ in the basis $\{\mathbf{U}_0, \mathbf{U}_1, \mathbf{U}_2\}$ is

$$\begin{aligned} \mathbf{V} &= (\mathbf{U}_0 \cdot \mathbf{V})\,\mathbf{U}_0 + (\mathbf{U}_1 \cdot \mathbf{V})\,\mathbf{U}_1 + (\mathbf{U}_2 \cdot \mathbf{V})\,\mathbf{U}_2 \\ &= a_0\mathbf{U}_0 + a_1\mathbf{U}_1 + a_2\mathbf{U}_2 \end{aligned} \qquad (6.57)$$

where the last equality defines a_0, a_1, and a_2 as the dot products of the basis vectors with $\mathbf{V}$. This renaming is done for simplicity of notation in the constructions. A couple of vector quantities of interest are

$$
\begin{aligned}
\mathbf{U}_2 \times \mathbf{V} &= \mathbf{U}_2 \times (a_0\mathbf{U}_0 + a_1\mathbf{U}_1 + a_2\mathbf{U}_2) \\
&= a_0\mathbf{U}_2 \times \mathbf{U}_0 + a_1\mathbf{U}_2 \times \mathbf{U}_1 + a_2\mathbf{U}_2 \times \mathbf{U}_2 \\
&= -a_1\mathbf{U}_0 + a_0\mathbf{U}_1
\end{aligned}
\tag{6.58}
$$

and

$$
\begin{aligned}
\mathbf{U}_2 \times (\mathbf{U}_2 \times \mathbf{V})) &= \mathbf{U}_2 \times (a_0\mathbf{U}_1 - a_1\mathbf{U}_0) \\
&= a_0\mathbf{U}_2 \times \mathbf{U}_1 - a_1\mathbf{U}_2 \times \mathbf{U}_0 \\
&= -a_0\mathbf{U}_0 - a_1\mathbf{U}_1
\end{aligned}
\tag{6.59}
$$

The cross product $\mathbf{U}_2 \times \mathbf{V}$ can be written as a matrix multiplied by a vector. Let $\mathbf{U}_2 = (s_0, s_1, s_2)$ and $\mathbf{V} = (v_0, v_1, v_2)$; then

$$
\begin{aligned}
\mathbf{U}_2 \times \mathbf{V} &= \begin{bmatrix} s_1v_2 - s_2v_1 \\ s_2v_0 - s_0v_2 \\ s_0v_1 - s_1v_0 \end{bmatrix} \\
&= \begin{bmatrix} 0 & -s_2 & s_1 \\ s_2 & 0 & -s_0 \\ -s_1 & s_0 & 0 \end{bmatrix} \begin{bmatrix} v_1 \\ v_2 \\ v_3 \end{bmatrix} \\
&= S\mathbf{V}
\end{aligned}
\tag{6.60}
$$

where the last equality defines the 3×3 matrix S. This matrix is skew-symmetric because $S^{\mathsf{T}} = -S$. The cross product $\mathbf{U}_2 \times (\mathbf{U}_2 \times \mathbf{V})$ is written as a matrix multiplied by a vector by applying Equation (6.60) twice:

$$
\mathbf{U}_2 \times (\mathbf{U}_2 \times \mathbf{V}) = S(\mathbf{U}_2 \times \mathbf{V}) = S(S\mathbf{V}) = S^2\mathbf{V}
\tag{6.61}
$$

We now look closer at the vectors $\mathbf{V} = I\mathbf{V}$, where I is the identity matrix; $\mathbf{U}_2 \times \mathbf{V} = S\mathbf{V}$; and $\mathbf{U}_2 \times (\mathbf{U}_2 \times \mathbf{V}) = S^2\mathbf{V}$ to determine how $\mathbf{U}_0$, $\mathbf{U}_1$, and their various products are related to the matrices I, S, and S^2.

Firstly, observe that Equation (6.57) may be manipulated as

$$
\begin{aligned}
I\mathbf{V} &= \mathbf{V} \\
&= (\mathbf{U}_0 \cdot \mathbf{V})\mathbf{U}_0 + (\mathbf{U}_1 \cdot \mathbf{V})\mathbf{U}_1 + (\mathbf{U}_2 \cdot \mathbf{V})\mathbf{U}_2 \\
&= \mathbf{U}_0(\mathbf{U}_0^{\mathsf{T}}\mathbf{V}) + \mathbf{U}_1(\mathbf{U}_1^{\mathsf{T}}\mathbf{V}) + \mathbf{U}_2(\mathbf{U}_2^{\mathsf{T}}\mathbf{V}) \\
&= (\mathbf{U}_0\mathbf{U}_0^{\mathsf{T}} + \mathbf{U}_1\mathbf{U}_1^{\mathsf{T}} + \mathbf{U}_2\mathbf{U}_2^{\mathsf{T}})\mathbf{V}
\end{aligned}
\tag{6.62}
$$

The equation is true for all vectors $\mathbf{V}$, so

$$
I = \mathbf{U}_0\mathbf{U}_0^{\mathsf{T}} + \mathbf{U}_1\mathbf{U}_1^{\mathsf{T}} + \mathbf{U}_2\mathbf{U}_2^{\mathsf{T}}
\tag{6.63}
$$

Secondly, Equations (6.57), (6.58), and (6.60) imply

$$
\begin{aligned}
S\mathbf{V} &= \mathbf{U}_2 \times \mathbf{V} \\
&= a_0\mathbf{U}_1 - a_1\mathbf{U}_0 \\
&= (\mathbf{U}_0 \cdot \mathbf{V})\mathbf{U}_1 - (\mathbf{U}_1 \cdot \mathbf{V})\mathbf{U}_0 \\
&= \mathbf{U}_1(\mathbf{U}_0^\mathsf{T}\mathbf{V}) - \mathbf{U}_0(\mathbf{U}_1^\mathsf{T}\mathbf{V}) \\
&= (\mathbf{U}_1\mathbf{U}_0^\mathsf{T} - \mathbf{U}_0\mathbf{U}_1^\mathsf{T})\mathbf{V}
\end{aligned} \tag{6.64}
$$

This equation is true for all vectors $\mathbf{V}$, so

$$
S = \mathbf{U}_1\mathbf{U}_0^\mathsf{T} - \mathbf{U}_0\mathbf{U}_1^\mathsf{T} \tag{6.65}
$$

Thirdly, Equations (6.57), (6.59), and (6.61) imply the relationship

$$
\begin{aligned}
S^2\mathbf{V} &= \mathbf{U}_2 \times (\mathbf{U}_2 \times \mathbf{V}) \\
&= -a_0\mathbf{U}_0 - a_1\mathbf{U}_1 \\
&= (\mathbf{U}_2 \cdot \mathbf{V})\mathbf{U}_2 - \mathbf{V} \\
&= \mathbf{U}_2(\mathbf{U}_2^\mathsf{T}\mathbf{V}) - \mathbf{V} \\
&= (\mathbf{U}_2\mathbf{U}_2^\mathsf{T} - I)\mathbf{V}
\end{aligned} \tag{6.66}
$$

This equation is true for all vectors $\mathbf{V}$, so

$$
S^2 = \mathbf{U}_2\mathbf{U}_2^\mathsf{T} - I \tag{6.67}
$$

Combining these relationships with Equation (6.56),

$$
\begin{aligned}
R_1 &= \gamma(\mathbf{U}_0\mathbf{U}_0^\mathsf{T} + \mathbf{U}_1\mathbf{U}_1^\mathsf{T}) + \sigma(\mathbf{U}_1\mathbf{U}_0^\mathsf{T} - \mathbf{U}_0\mathbf{U}_1^\mathsf{T}) + \mathbf{U}_2\mathbf{U}_2^\mathsf{T} && \text{Equation (6.56)} \\
&= \gamma(I - \mathbf{U}_2\mathbf{U}_2^\mathsf{T}) + \sigma(\mathbf{U}_1\mathbf{U}_0^\mathsf{T} - \mathbf{U}_0\mathbf{U}_1^\mathsf{T}) + \mathbf{U}_2\mathbf{U}_2^\mathsf{T} && \text{by Equation (6.63)} \\
&= \gamma(I - \mathbf{U}_2\mathbf{U}_2^\mathsf{T}) + \sigma S + \mathbf{U}_2\mathbf{U}_2^\mathsf{T} && \text{by Equation (6.65)} \\
&= I + \sigma S + (1 - \gamma)(\mathbf{U}_2\mathbf{U}_2^\mathsf{T} - I) \\
&= I + (\sin\theta)S + (1 - \cos\theta)S^2 && \text{by Equation (6.67)}
\end{aligned}
$$
$$\tag{6.68}$$

This equation provides the rotation matrix R_1 in terms of the unit-length axis direction $\mathbf{U}_2$ stored as the matrix S and the angle θ occurring in $\sigma = \sin\theta$ and $\gamma = \cos\theta$. The application of the rotation matrix to a vector is

$$
\begin{aligned}
R_1\mathbf{V} &= (I + \sigma S + (1 - \gamma)S^2)\mathbf{V} \\
&= I\mathbf{V} + \sigma S\mathbf{V} + (1 - \gamma)S^2\mathbf{V} \\
&= \mathbf{V} + \sigma\mathbf{U}_2 \times \mathbf{V} + (1 - \gamma)\mathbf{U}_2 \times (\mathbf{U}_2 \times \mathbf{V})
\end{aligned} \tag{6.69}
$$

Make sure you understand the constructions used to obtain Equations (6.56) and (6.68). The same idea is used later to motivate how a quaternion is related to a rotation matrix in four dimensions.

6.3.3   Rotation in 4D

Equation (6.69) is referred to as the *Rodrigues rotation formula*. The formula allows you to rotate a vector knowing the angle of rotation and unit-length axis direction without explicitly constructing the rotation matrix. Computing the rotation matrix via the skew-symmetric decomposition in Equation (6.68) is standard in practice because it is not expensive computationally.

Rotation matrices in 2D may be similarly decomposed,

$$
\begin{aligned}
R &= \begin{bmatrix} \cos\theta & -\sin\theta \\ \sin\theta & \cos\theta \end{bmatrix} \\[2mm]
&= \cos\theta \begin{bmatrix} 1 & 0 \\ 0 & 1 \end{bmatrix} + \sin\theta \begin{bmatrix} 0 & -1 \\ 1 & 0 \end{bmatrix} \\[2mm]
&= (\cos\theta)I + (\sin\theta)S
\end{aligned}
\tag{6.70}
$$

where the last equality defines the skew-symmetric matrix S. The matrix S of Equation (6.68) has three distinctly labeled entries: s_0, s_1, and s_2. In the 2D case, S has one distinctly labeled entry (the upper-right entry): $s_0 = -1$.

Generally, rotation matrices R in n dimensions have skew-symmetric decompositions

$$
R = \sum_{k=0}^{n-1} c_k \theta^k S^k
\tag{6.71}
$$

that may be constructed by exponentiating the $n \times n$ skew-symmetric matrix $R = \exp(\theta S)$. The power series for the exponential function is $\exp(x) = \sum_{k=0}^{\infty} x^k/k!$. Formally replacing the matrix S in the expression, we have a power series of matrices. The series is actually finite, using the Cayley-Hamilton theorem from linear algebra. The *characteristic polynomial* of S is $p(t) = \det(tI - S)$, a polynomial of degree n. The theorem states that when you substitute the matrix S formally into the polynomial, it must be that $p(S) = 0$, where the right-hand side is the zero matrix. If the polynomial is $p(t) = \sum_{k=0}^{n} p_k t^k$, where $p_n = 1$, then

$$
p(S) = \sum_{k=0}^{n} p_k S^k = 0
\tag{6.72}
$$

which provides an expression for S^n in terms of lower-degree powers of S. The power series $\exp(S)$ may be reduced modulo $p(S)$ to produce a finite sum whose largest-degree term is S^{n-1}.

The power series construction for 4D rotation matrices is tedious. The details are not presented here but the summary is. Following the patterns for S in 2D and 3D, define

$$
S = \begin{bmatrix}
0 & -s_5 & +s_4 & -s_2 \\
+s_5 & 0 & -s_3 & +s_1 \\
-s_4 & +s_3 & 0 & -s_0 \\
+s_2 & -s_1 & +s_0 & 0
\end{bmatrix}
\tag{6.73}
$$

where $s_0^2 + s_1^2 + s_2^2 + s_3^2 + s_4^2 + s_5^2 = 1$. Define $d = s_0 s_5 - s_1 s_4 + s_2 s_3$, $r = \sqrt{1 - 4d^2}$, $\omega_0 = \sqrt{(1-r)/2}$, and $\omega_1 = \sqrt{(1+r)/2}$. The argument for the square root in the definition for r can be shown to be nonnegative, so r is real-valued and in the interval $[0, 1]$. Consequently, $0 \leq \omega_0 \leq \omega_1 \leq 1$. The skew-symmetric decomposition for $R = \exp(S)$ is listed next, where $\sigma_i = \sin(\omega_i \theta)$ and $\gamma_i = \cos(\omega_i \theta)$,

$$
R = \begin{cases}
c_0 I + c_1 S + c_2 S^2 + c_3 S^3, & 0 < r < 1 \\
I + (\sin\theta)S + (1 - \cos\theta)S^2, & r = 1 \\
\cos(\theta/\sqrt{2})I + \sqrt{2}\sin(\theta/\sqrt{2})S, & r = 0
\end{cases} \tag{6.74}
$$

where

$$
\begin{aligned}
c_0 &= \left(\omega_1^2 \gamma_0 - \omega_0^2 \gamma_1\right) / \left(\omega_1^2 - \omega_0^2\right) \\
c_1 &= \left(\omega_1^2 (\sigma_0/\omega_0) - \omega_0^2 (\sigma_1/\omega_1)\right) / \left(\omega_1^2 - \omega_0^2\right) \\
c_2 &= (\gamma_0 - \gamma_1) / \left(\omega_1^2 - \omega_0^2\right) \\
c_3 &= ((\sigma_0/\omega_0) - (\sigma_1/\omega_1)) / \left(\omega_1^2 - \omega_0^2\right)
\end{aligned} \tag{6.75}
$$

The first case in Equation (6.74) is referred to as a *double rotation* and corresponds to a rotation occurring in a two-dimensional plane and a rotation occurring in the orthogonal complement (also a two-dimensional plane), each rotation occurring with different angles.

The second case in Equation (6.74) is referred to as a *simple rotation*, because it is the type of rotation in 3D that we are familiar with. The rotation is within one two-dimensional plane in 4D. The decomposition can be derived symbolically from the double-rotation case by setting $\omega_0 = 0$. The result has an S^3 term. The characteristic polynomial $p(t)$ has degree 4, but the *minimal polynomial* is $m(t) = t^3 + t$ and $m(S) = S^3 + S = 0$, which allows us to replace $S^3 = -S$.

The third case in Equation (6.74) is referred to as an *equiangular rotation*, a double rotation but with both rotation angles the same. In fact, $\omega_0 = \omega_1 = 1/\sqrt{2}$. The decomposition can be obtained symbolically from the double-rotation case by taking a limit as ω_1 approaches ω_0 and using l'Hôpital's Rule. The result has S^3 and S^4 terms. The characteristic polynomial has degree 4, but the minimal polynomial is $m(t) = t^2 + 1/2$ and $m(S) = S^2 + I/2$, which allows us to replace $S^2 = -I/2$ and $S^3 = -S/2$.

6.3.4   Quaternions

A *quaternion* is specified by the abstract quantity $q = xi + yj + zk + w$, where x, y, z, and w are real numbers. This quantity can be thought of as a vector $(x, y, z, w) \in \mathbb{R}^4$. A quaternion is unit length when $x^2 + y^2 + z^2 + w^2 = 1$, which is a point on a hypersphere in 4D with radius one. The unit-length quaternions are related to rotations when an algebraic structure is imposed on them, the topic of this section.

Practitioners sometimes use the term quaternion in place of unit-length quaternion when dealing with rotations. It is important to keep in mind the context. For example, in physical simulations orientation can be represented by a unit-length quaternion but angular velocity is represented by a quaternion that is not necessarily unit length. Another issue to be aware of is the ordering of the components. Some programmers might implement quaternions with order (w, x, y, z). In GTEngine, the order is (x, y, z, w).

6.3.4.1 Algebraic Operations

The symbols i, j, and k in $q = xi + yj + zk + w$ can be endowed with a product operation, $i^2 = j^2 = k^2 = ijk = -1$. In abstract algebra, the set $\{\pm 1, \pm i, \pm j, \pm k\}$ is a *group* with the specified operation. In fact, it is a *noncommutative* group because the operation is not generally commutative. For example, $ij = k$ and $ji = -1 \cdot k = -k$, so $ij \neq ji$. Generally, $ij = k$, $jk = i$, $ki = j$, $ji = -k$, $kj = -i$, and $ik = -j$.

The quaternion q allows formal linear combinations of 1, i, j, and k, where the coefficients are real numbers. In abstract algebra, the set of all such combinations is a *group algebra* when it is endowed with addition and scalar multiplication and when it inherits the multiplication of the underlying group.

Addition of two quaternions is defined by

$$
\begin{aligned}
q_0 + q_1 &= (x_0 i + y_0 j + z_0 k + w_0) + (x_1 i + y_1 j + z_1 k + w_1) \\
&= (x_0 + x_1)i + (y_0 + y_1)j + (z_0 + z_1)k + (w_0 + w_1)
\end{aligned}
\tag{6.76}
$$

Scalar multiplication of a quaternion by a real number c is defined by

$$
cq = c(xi + yj + zk + w) = (cx)i + (cy)j + (cz)k + (cw)
\tag{6.77}
$$

The *subtraction* operation is defined as a consequence of these two definitions, $q_0 - q_1 = q_0 + (-1)q_1$.

Multiplication is allowed for quaternions. The product of quaternions is defined by allowing the distributive law to apply and by using the various product formulas for the i, j, and k terms:

$$
\begin{aligned}
q_0 q_1 &= (x_0 i + y_0 j + z_0 k + w_0)(x_1 i + y_1 j + z_1 k + w_1) \\
&= (w_0 x_1 + w_1 x_0 + y_0 z_1 - z_0 y_1)i + \\
&\quad (w_0 y_1 + w_1 y_0 + z_0 x_1 - x_0 z_1)j + \\
&\quad (w_0 z_1 + w_1 z_0 + x_0 y_1 - y_0 x_1)k + \\
&\quad (w_0 w_1 - x_0 x_1 - y_0 y_1 - z_0 z_1)
\end{aligned}
\tag{6.78}
$$

As noted, multiplication is not generally commutative. The product in the other order obtained from Equation (6.78) by interchanging the zero and one subscripts is

$$
\begin{aligned}
q_1 q_0 &= (x_1 i + y_1 j + z_1 k + w_1)(x_0 i + y_0 j + z_0 k + w_0) \\
&= (w_0 x_1 + w_1 x_0 + y_1 z_0 - y_0 z_1)i + \\
&\quad (w_0 y_1 + w_1 y_0 + z_1 x_0 - z_0 x_1)j + \\
&\quad (w_0 z_1 + w_1 z_0 + x_1 y_0 - x_0 y_1)k + \\
&\quad (w_0 w_1 - x_0 x_1 - y_0 y_1 - z_0 z_1)
\end{aligned}
\tag{6.79}
$$

The w-components of $q_0 q_1$ and $q_1 q_0$ are the same. On the other hand, the last two terms in each of the i-, j-, and k-components in Equation 6.79 are opposite in sign to their counterparts in Equation 6.78. Symbolically, Equations (6.78) and (6.79) are different, but for *some* quaternions (but not all), it is possible that $q_0 q_1 = q_1 q_0$ (the product commutes). For this to happen we need

$$
\begin{aligned}
(x_0, y_0, z_0) \times (x_1, y_1, z_1) &= (y_0 z_1 - y_1 z_0, z_0 x_1 - z_1 x_0, x_0 y_1 - y_0 x_1) \\
&= (y_1 z_0 - y_0 z_1, z_1 x_0 - z_0 x_1, x_1 y_0 - x_0 y_1) \\
&= (x_1, y_1, z_1) \times (x_0, y_0, z_0)
\end{aligned}
$$

(6.80)

which says that the cross product of two vectors is the same. The only way this can happen is if the cross product is zero: $(x_0, y_0, z_0) \times (x_1, y_1, z_1) = (0, 0, 0)$.

The fact that squares of i, j, and k are -1 shows that there are some similarities to the complex numbers. The complex number $c = w + ix$ has *real part* w and *imaginary part* x. The *conjugate* of the numbers is $\bar{c} = w - ix$. The *norm* of the complex number is $N(c) = w^2 + x^2$ and the *length* is $|c| = \sqrt{N(c)}$. Observe that the squared length is $|c|^2 = c\hat{c} = \hat{c}c$. If the length is not zero, the *inverse* of the complex number is $c^{-1} = \bar{c}/N(c)$. The *polar form* of a unit-length complex number is $c = \cos\phi + i\sin\phi$.

Similar definitions may be formulated for quaternions. Define $\hat{v} = xi + yj + zk$ so that $q = \hat{v} + w$. The w-component is referred to as the *real part* of q and $\hat{v}$ is referred to as the *imaginary portion* of q (not *part* because there are multiple terms in the expression). The *conjugate* of q is denoted $q^* = -\hat{v} + w$; for historical reasons, the conjugate notation uses a superscript asterisk rather than an overline bar. Because quaternion multiplication is not commutative but complex multiplication is, there is a difference between the two algebras regarding conjugates. If p and q are quaternions, $(pq)^* = q^* p^*$; that is, the order is reversed after taking the conjugate. This has a similarity to transpose of two matrices. The *norm* of q is $N(q) = x^2 + y^2 + z^2 + w^2$ and the *length* is $|q| = \sqrt{N(q)}$. The squared length is $|q|^2 = qq^* = q^*q$. If the length is not zero, the *inverse* of the quaternion is $q^{-1} = q^*/N(q)$. The *polar form* of a unit-length quaternion is $q = \cos\phi + \hat{d}\sin\phi$, where $\hat{d} = xi + yj + zk$ is the unit-length portion; that is, $x^2 + y^2 + z^2 = 1$. It is easily shown that $\hat{d}^2 = -1$.

The representation $q = w + \hat{v}$ is a coordinate-free description. We may identify $\hat{v} = xi + yj + zk$ with the vector $\mathbf{v} = (x, y, z)$. This allows us to define two operations on the imaginary portions based on how those operations apply to vectors. The *dot product* of $\hat{v}_0$ and $\hat{v}_1$ is denoted $\hat{v}_0 \cdot \hat{v}_1$ and defined to be the real-valued vector dot product $\mathbf{v}_0 \cdot \mathbf{v}_1$. The *cross product* of $\hat{v}_0$ and $\hat{v}_1$ is denoted $\hat{v}_0 \times \hat{v}_1$, another quaternion with zero w component. Its x, y, and z values are the components of the vector cross product $\mathbf{v}_0 \times \mathbf{v}_1$. In this formulation, the product of two quaternions is

$$
(w_0 + \hat{v}_0)(w_1 + \hat{v}_1) = (w_0 w_1 - \hat{v}_0 \cdot \hat{v}_1) + w_0 \hat{v}_1 + w_1 \hat{v}_0 + \hat{v}_0 \times \hat{v}_1 \qquad (6.81)
$$

As we showed previously, the product commutes if and only if $\hat{v}_0 \times \hat{v}_1 = 0$.

A straightforward implementation of quaternions and the associated algebra is provided by the interface shown in Listing 6.27. The Rotate and Slerp functions are discussed later in this section.

```
template <typename Real>
class Quaternion : public Vector <4,Real>
{
public :
    // The quaternions are of the form q = x*i + y*j + z*k + w.  In tuple
    // form , q = (x,y,z,w).

    // Construction and destruction .  The default constructor does not
    // initialize the members.
    ~Quaternion ();
    Quaternion ();
    Quaternion (Quaternion const& q);
    Quaternion (Vector <4,Real> const& q);
    Quaternion (Real x, Real y, Real z, Real w);

    // assignment
    Quaternion& operator= (Quaternion const& q);
    Quaternion& operator= (Vector <4,Real> const& q);

    // special quaternions
    static Quaternion Zero ();        // z = 0*i + 0*j + 0*k + 0
    static Quaternion I ();           // i = 1*i + 0*j + 0*k + 0
    static Quaternion J ();           // j = 0*i + 1*j + 0*k + 0
    static Quaternion K ();           // k = 0*i + 0*j + 1*k + 0
    static Quaternion Identity();     // 1 = 0*i + 0*j + 0*k + 1
};

template <typename Real>
Quaternion<Real> operator* (Quaternion<Real> const& q0,
    Quaternion<Real> const& q1);

template <typename Real>
Quaternion<Real> Inverse (Quaternion<Real> const& q);

template <typename Real>
Quaternion<Real> Conjugate (Quaternion<Real> const& q);

template <typename Real>
Vector <4,Real> Rotate (Quaternion<Real> const& q, Vector <4,Real> const& v);

template <typename Real>
Quaternion<Real> Slerp (Real t, Quaternion<Real> const& q0,
    Quaternion<Real> const& q1);
```

LISTING 6.27: The Quaternion<Real> interface for the quaternions and algebra associated with them.

6.3.4.2 Relationship of Quaternions to Rotations

Consider rotating a vector $\mathbf{v}$ about an axis with unit-length direction $\mathbf{d}$ by an angle θ to obtain a vector $\mathbf{u}$. The sense of the rotation is counterclockwise, as shown in Figure 6.4.

The quaternions $\hat{d}$, $\hat{v}$, and $\hat{u}$ are those identified with the vectors $\mathbf{d}$, $\mathbf{v}$, and $\mathbf{u}$. Define the quaternion $q = \gamma + \sigma\hat{d}$, where $\gamma = \cos(\theta/2)$ and $\sigma = \sin(\theta/2)$. The quaternion $\hat{u} = q\hat{v}q^*$ has a zero w-component; the left-hand side is written as if there is no w-component, but we do need to verify this. The vector $\mathbf{u}$

turns out to be the rotation of **v**. The formal calculations are listed next:

$$
\begin{aligned}
q\hat{v}q^* &= (\gamma + \sigma\hat{d})(0 + \hat{v})(\gamma - \sigma\hat{d}) \\
&= (-\sigma\hat{d}\cdot\hat{v} + \gamma\hat{v} + \sigma\hat{d}\times\hat{v})(\gamma - \sigma\hat{d}) \\
&= [(-\sigma\hat{d}\cdot\hat{v})(\gamma) - (\gamma\hat{v} + \sigma\hat{d}\times\hat{v})(-\sigma\hat{d})] + \\
&\quad (\gamma)(\gamma\hat{v} + \sigma\hat{d}\times\hat{v}) + (-\sigma\hat{d}\cdot\hat{v})(-\sigma\hat{d}) + \\
&\quad (\gamma\hat{v} + \sigma\hat{d}\times\hat{v})\times(-\sigma\hat{d}) \\
&= \gamma^2\hat{v} + \sigma^2(\hat{d}\cdot\hat{v})\hat{d} + 2\sigma\gamma\hat{d}\times\hat{v} + \sigma^2\hat{d}\times(\hat{d}\times\hat{v})
\end{aligned} \tag{6.82}
$$

The second equality uses Equation (6.81), the third equality uses Equation (6.81), and the last equality uses the identities $(\hat{d}\times\hat{v})\cdot\hat{d} = 0$, $\hat{v}\times\hat{d} = -\hat{d}\times\hat{v}$ and $\hat{d}\times(\hat{d}\times\hat{v}) = -(\hat{d}\times\hat{v})\times\hat{d}$, the same identities that the vector counterparts **d** and **v** satisfy. Continuing with the calculations,

$$
\begin{aligned}
q\hat{v}q^* &= (1 - \sigma^2)\hat{v} + 2\sigma\gamma\hat{d}\times\hat{v} + \sigma^2[(\hat{d}\cdot\hat{v})\hat{d} + \hat{d}\times(\hat{d}\times\hat{v})] \\
&= \hat{v} + 2\sigma\gamma\hat{d}\times\hat{v} + \sigma^2[(\hat{d}\cdot\hat{v})\hat{d} - \hat{v} + \hat{d}\times(\hat{d}\times\hat{v})]
\end{aligned} \tag{6.83}
$$

An identity from vector algebra is $\mathbf{d}\times(\mathbf{d}\times\mathbf{v}) = (\mathbf{d}\cdot\mathbf{v})\mathbf{d} - (\mathbf{d}\cdot\mathbf{d})\mathbf{v} = (\mathbf{d}\cdot\mathbf{v})\mathbf{d} - \mathbf{v}$, the last equality a consequence of **d** being unit length. The quaternion counterpart satisfies the same identity, so

$$
q\hat{v}q^* = \hat{v} + 2\sigma\gamma\hat{d}\times\hat{v} + 2\sigma^2\hat{d}\times(\hat{d}\times\hat{v}) \tag{6.84}
$$

Recall also the trigonometric identities $\sin\theta = 2\sin(\theta/2)\cos(\theta/2) = 2\sigma\gamma$ and $1 - \cos\theta = 2\sin^2(\theta/2) = 2\sigma^2$, so we finally arrive at

$$
q\hat{v}q^* = \hat{v} + (\sin\theta)\hat{d}\times\hat{v} + (1 - \cos\theta)\hat{d}\times(\hat{d}\times\hat{v}) \tag{6.85}
$$

This is the quaternion counterpart of Equation (6.69), the general rotation of **v** about an axis **d** by an angle θ. The vector **u** corresponding to $\hat{u} = q\hat{v}q^*$ is therefore the rotation of **v**.

The GTEngine function that implements this operation is shown in Listing 6.28.

```
template <typename Real>
Vector <4,Real> Rotate (Quaternion<Real> const& q, Vector <4,Real> const& v)
{
    Vector <4,Real> u = q*Quaternion<Real>(v)*Conjugate(q);
    // Zero-out the w-component to avoid numerical roundoff error.
    u[3] = (Real)0;
    return u;
}
```

LISTING 6.28: Source code for the rotation of a vector directly by quaternion operations.

The rotation matrix R corresponding to the quaternion q may be obtained by computing symbolically the right-hand side of $\hat{u} = q\hat{v}q^*$ and factoring the coefficients of the i-, j-, and k-terms to obtain $\mathbf{u} = R\mathbf{v}$, where

$$
R = \begin{bmatrix} 1 - 2y^2 - 2z^2 & 2xy - 2wz & 2xz + 2wy \\ 2xy + 2wz & 1 - 2x^2 - 2z^2 & 2yz - 2wx \\ 2xz - 2wy & 2yz + 2wx & 1 - 2x^2 - 2y^2 \end{bmatrix} \tag{6.86}
$$

The GTEngine source code for this and other conversions is described later. Take note that the rotation matrix here is for the vector-on-the-right multiplication convention.

Composition of rotations is stated easily in terms of quaternion algebra. If p and q are unit-length quaternions that represent rotations, and if $\hat{v}$ is the quaternion identified with vector $\mathbf{v}$, then the rotation represented by q is accomplished by $\hat{u} = q\hat{v}q^*$ as shown earlier. The vector $\mathbf{u}$ identified with $\hat{u}$ is further modified by the rotation represented by p:

$$
\begin{aligned}
p\hat{u}p^* &= p(q\hat{v}q^*)p^* \\
&= (pq)\hat{v}(q^*p^*) \quad \text{quaternion multiplication is associative} \\
&= (pq)\hat{v}(pq)^* \quad \text{property of conjugation}
\end{aligned}
\tag{6.87}
$$

This equation shows that the composite rotation is represented by the quaternion product pq.

6.3.4.3 Spherical Linear Interpolation of Quaternions

As we have seen, unit-length quaternions represent rotations. Orientation of an object is represented by a rotation matrix, where the columns (or rows) of the matrix are the axes associated with the orientation. Keyframe animation is an application in which positions and orientations are chosen for an object at specific times. The intermediate positions and orientations between the specific times are computed via interpolation. The simplest algorithm for handling positions is linear interpolation, sometimes reduced to the acronym *LERP*. If $\mathbf{P}_0$ and $\mathbf{P}_1$ are positions at specified times s_0 and s_1, the in-between positions are

$$
\mathbf{P}(s) = \frac{(s_1 - s)}{s_1 - s_0}\mathbf{P}_0 + \frac{s - s_0}{s_1 - s_0}\mathbf{P}_1
\tag{6.88}
$$

for $s \in [s_0, s_1]$. When s is normalized to $t = (s - s_0)/(s_1 - s_0) \in [0, 1]$, the linear interpolation is

$$
\mathbf{P}(t) = (1 - t)\mathbf{P}_0 + t\mathbf{P}_1
\tag{6.89}
$$

Uniform sampling of $t \in [0, 1]$ leads to uniform spacing of points along the line segment connecting $\mathbf{P}_0$ and $\mathbf{P}_1$. In mathematical terms, this property is implied by the derivative of the parameterized curve having constant length. For LERP the length of the derivative is $|\mathbf{P}'(t)| = |\mathbf{P}_1 - \mathbf{P}_0|$, which is a constant.

The quaternion counterpart for linear interpolation is referred to as *spherical linear interpolation* or *SLERP* for short. This was made popular in computer graphics by [52]. The motivation for the definition comes from unit-length vectors in 2D, which live on a circle of radius one. Figure 6.5 illustrates the idea. On the unit hypersphere in 4D, we choose the great circle arc connecting the two quaternions. We want an interpolation of the form $q(t) = c_0(t)q_0 + c_1(t)q_1$ for to-be-determined coefficient functions $c_0(t)$ and $c_1(t)$. The angle between q_0 and q_1 is $\theta \in [0, \pi)$, the angle between q_0 and $q(t)$

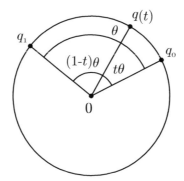

FIGURE 6.5: Interpolation of quaternions q_0 and q_1 on a circle of radius 1. The parameter t is in $[0, 1]$.

is $t\theta$, and the angle between q_1 and $q(t)$ is $(1-t)\theta$. The dot product of vectors gives us the cosine of the angle between them,

$$\cos(t\theta) = q_0 \cdot q(t) = c_0(t) + \cos(\theta)c_1(t)$$
$$\cos((1-t)\theta) = q_1 \cdot q(t) = \cos(\theta)c_0(t) + c_1(t) \tag{6.90}$$

These are two equations in two unknowns; the solution is

$$c_0(t) = \frac{\cos(t\theta) - \cos(\theta)\cos((1-t)\theta)}{1 - \cos^2(\theta)} = \frac{\sin((1-t)\theta)}{\sin(\theta)} \tag{6.91}$$

$$c_1(t) = \frac{\cos((1-t)\theta) - \cos(\theta)\cos(t\theta)}{1 - \cos^2(\theta)} = \frac{\sin(t\theta)}{\sin(\theta)}$$

Spherical linear interpolation is therefore

$$\text{slerp}(t; q_0, q_1)) = q(t) = \frac{\sin((1-t)\theta)q_0 + \sin(t\theta)q_1}{\sin(\theta)} \tag{6.92}$$

Uniform sampling of $t \in [0, 1]$ leads to uniform spacing of quaternions along the circular arc connection q_0 and q_1. The length of the derivative is

$$|q'(t)| = \left| \frac{-\theta\cos((1-t)\theta)q_0 + \theta\cos(t\theta)q_1}{\sin(\theta)} \right| = \theta \tag{6.93}$$

where the right-hand side is expanded as a dot product and the computations use $q_0 \cdot q_0 = 1$, $q_0 \cdot q_1 = \cos(\theta)$, $q_1 \cdot q_1 = 1$, and some trigonometric identities are applied. The derivative has constant length, so in fact the uniform spacing is guaranteed for uniform t-samples. Observe that SLERP is not defined for antipodal points $q_1 = -q_0$, because there are infinitely many great circle arcs that connect them.

An implementation of Equation (6.92) requires dealing with three issues. Firstly, if the quaternions are equal, the angle between them is zero, in which case SLERP has a divide by zero. The same divide-by-zero problem occurs when the quaternions are antipodal, but this is not a problem because SLERP is not defined for antipodal points. Secondly, quaternions represent rotations but provide a double covering: q and $-q$ represent the same rotation. An implementation will avoid the antipodal points and the double-covering issue by requiring the angle between the quaternions to be acute. If desired, this can be accomplished by preprocessing the sequence of quaternions in an animation sequence, negating quaternions in the sequence as needed to guarantee that consecutive quaternions have a nonnegative dot product. Thirdly, the function acos is applied to compute θ from $q_0 \cdot q_1 = \cos\theta$. When using floating-point arithmetic, roundoff errors can lead to a dot product slightly larger than one. This condition must be trapped and handled, because the acos function returns a quiet NaN for arguments larger than one. A typical implementation of SLERP is shown in Listing 6.29

```
Quaternion Slerp (Real t, Quaternion q0, Quaternion q1)
{
    Real cosTheta = Dot(q0,q1);
    if (cosTheta < 0)
    {
        q1 = -q1;
        cosTheta = -cosTheta;
    }

    if (cosTheta < 1)
    {
        // Angle theta is in the interval (0,pi/2].
        Real theta = acos(cosTheta);
        Real invSinTheta = 1/sin(theta);
        Real c0 = sin((1-t)*theta)*invSinTheta;
        Real c1 = sin(t*theta)*invSinTheta;
        return c0*q0 + c1*q1;
    }
    else
    {
        // Angle theta is zero, so just return one of the inputs.
        return q0;
    }
}
```

LISTING 6.29: A direct implementation of SLERP.

SLERP is an expensive function to compute because of one call to acos, three calls to sin, and one division. Moreover, branching is potentially expensive, although on modern CPUs, branching tables for branch prediction eliminate much of that expense. On SIMD hardware, the if-then-else processing is replaced by selection, which adds some overhead cost, although the gain from parallelism offsets this.

One way to avoid the expensive function calls is to approximate sin by a polynomial and acos by a square root and a polynomial [1]. However, a simple observation about the coefficients used in SLERP and some basic ideas from linear differential equations lead to a faster SLERP evaluation, one that uses only multiplications and additions and has no branching. For applications that make heavy use of SLERP, the approximation provides a decent approximation with a significant speedup.

An alternative that is faster and more robust is presented in [10], which involves a two-variable polynomial approximation. The algorithm uses only multiplication, addition, and subtraction and does not require division, branching, or testing for special conditions. It is also friendly to SIMD.

The coefficient $\sin(t\theta)/\sin(\theta)$ in Equation (6.92) is evaluated for $t \in [0, 1]$. It has the same form as $\sin(n\theta)/\sin(\theta)$ for nonnegative integers n, an expression that is related to *Chebyshev polynomials of the second kind*, $u_n(x)$, defined for $|x| \leq 1$; see [50, Section 7.6] on orthogonal polynomials. The polynomials are defined recursively by $u_0(x) = 1$, $u_1(x) = 2x$, $u_n(x) = 2xu_{n-1}(x) - u_{n-2}(x)$ for $n \geq 2$ and have the property $u_{n-1}(\cos(\theta)) = \sin(n\theta)/\sin(\theta)$. They are solutions to the second-order linear differential equation

$$\left(x^2 - 1\right) u''_{n-1}(x) + 3xu'_{n-1}(x) + \left(1 - n^2\right) u_{n-1}(x) = 0 \qquad (6.94)$$

where $x = \cos(\theta) \in [0, 1]$ for angles $\theta \in [0, \pi/2]$. Equation (6.94) allows for a continuous variable t rather than the discrete variable n, so if we define $u_{t-1}(\cos(\theta)) = \sin(t\theta)/\sin(\theta)$ for real-valued $t \in [0, 1]$, the SLERP equation is rewritten as

$$\mathrm{slerp}(t; q_0, q_1) = u_{-t}(\cos(\theta))\, q_0 + u_{t-1}(\cos(\theta))\, q_1 \qquad (6.95)$$

Equation (6.95) suggests that we can construct formulas for u_{-t} and u_{1-t} that depend only on $\cos(\theta) = q_0 \cdot q_1$, thereby avoiding the explicit computation of θ and the calls to the sine function.

Define $f(x; t) = u_{t-1}(x)$, which is viewed as a function of x for a specified real-valued parameter t. It is a solution to Equation (6.94) with n formally replaced by t,

$$\left(x^2 - 1\right) f''(x; t) + 3xf'(x; t) + \left(1 - t^2\right) f(x; t) = 0 \qquad (6.96)$$

The prime symbols denote differentiation with respect to x.

We may specify an initial value for $f(1; t)$ at the endpoint $x = 1$. Obtaining a unique solution to a linear second-order differential equation normally requires specifying the derivative value at $x = 1$; however, the equation is singular at $x = 1$, because the coefficient of f'' is 0 at $x = 1$. The uniqueness is guaranteed by specifying only the value of f at the endpoint. When x is one, θ is zero and evaluation of $u_{t-1}(0)$ is in the limiting sense,

$$u_{t-1}(1) = \lim_{\theta \to 0} u_{t-1}(\cos(\theta)) = \lim_{\theta \to 0} \frac{\sin(t\theta)}{\sin(\theta)} = \lim_{\theta \to 0} \frac{t \cos(t\theta)}{\cos(\theta)} = t \qquad (6.97)$$

The next-to-last equality of Equation (6.97) uses an application of l'Hôpital's Rule. The initial condition is therefore $f(1; t) = t$.

A standard undergraduate course on differential equations shows how to solve the differential equation using power series [2]. Because we want an expansion at $x = 1$, the powers are $(x - 1)^i$. The next equation lists power series for f and its first- and second-order derivatives with respect to x:

$$f = \sum_{i=0}^{\infty} a_i(x-1)^i, \quad f' = \sum_{i=0}^{\infty} i a_i(x-1)^{i-1}, \quad f'' = \sum_{i=0}^{\infty} i(i-1)a_i(x-1)^{i-2} \quad (6.98)$$

The coefficients of the powers of $(x - 1)$ are written to show their functional dependence on t. Substituting these into Equation (6.96),

$$
\begin{aligned}
0 &= \left(x^2 - 1\right) f'' + 3xf' + \left(1 - t^2\right) f \\
&= \left[(x-1)^2 + 2(x-1)\right] f'' + 3\left[(x-1) + 1\right] f' + \left(1 - t^2\right) f \qquad (6.99) \\
&= \sum_{i=0}^{\infty} \left[(i+1)(2i+3)a_{i+1} + ((i+1)^2 - t^2))a_i\right](x-1)^i
\end{aligned}
$$

For the power series to be identically zero for all x, it is necessary that the coefficients are all zero. The condition $f(1;t) = t$ implies $a_0 = t$. These lead to a recurrence equation with initial condition,

$$a_0 = t, \quad a_i = \frac{t^2 - i^2}{i(2i+1)} a_{i-1}, \quad i \geq 1 \qquad (6.100)$$

It is apparent from Equation (6.100) that $a_i(t)$ is a polynomial in t with degree $2i + 1$. Observe that $a_0(0) = 0$, which implies $a_i(0) = 0$ for $i \geq 0$; this is equivalent to $f(x;0) = 0$. Similarly, $a_0(1) = 1$ and $a_1(1) = 0$, which implies $a_i(1) = 0$ for $i \geq 1$; this is equivalent to $f(x;1) = 1$.

We now have a power series for $f(x;t)$ using powers of $(x - 1)$ and whose coefficients are polynomials in t that may be generated iteratively. The power series may be truncated and given an error term,

$$
\begin{aligned}
f(x;t) &= \sum_{i=0}^{n} a_i(t)(x-1)^i + \sum_{i=n+1}^{\infty} a_i(t)(x-1)^i \\
&= \sum_{i=0}^{n} a_i(t)(x-1)^i + \varepsilon(x;t,n) \\
&\doteq \sum_{i=0}^{n} a_i(t)(x-1)^i + \mu_n a_n(t)(x-1)^n \\
&= \hat{f}(x;t)
\end{aligned}
\qquad (6.101)
$$

where $\varepsilon(x;t,n)$ is the error of truncation. The approximation is $\hat{f}(x;t)$, where μ_n is a constant that is chosen to provide a global error bound. A large part of [10] is about how to choose μ and delves into the Chebyshev equioscillation theorem and the Remez algorithm; the details are skipped here. The global error bound is $|f(x;t) - \hat{f}(x;t)| \leq e_n$. Table 6.1 summarizes the error bounds and how many terms are used in the approximation. You may select the desired error bound e_n, look up the corresponding μ, and choose the n terms of the polynomial to be evaluated. Equation (6.100) is evaluated as many times as is required for the choice of n.

TABLE 6.1: Error balancing for several n in the Remez algorithm

n	μ_n	e_n	n	μ_n	e_n
1	0.62943436108234530	$5.745259 * 10^{-3}$	9	0.91015881189952352	$5.277561 * 10^{-7}$
2	0.73965850021313961	$1.092666 * 10^{-3}$	10	0.91767344933047190	$2.110597 * 10^{-7}$
3	0.79701067629566813	$2.809387 * 10^{-4}$	11	0.92401541194159076	$8.600881 * 10^{-8}$
4	0.83291820510335812	$8.409177 * 10^{-5}$	12	0.92944142668012797	$3.560875 * 10^{-8}$
5	0.85772477879039977	$2.763477 * 10^{-5}$	13	0.93413793373091059	$1.494321 * 10^{-8}$
6	0.87596835698904785	$9.678992 * 10^{-6}$	14	0.93824371262559758	$6.344653 * 10^{-9}$
7	0.88998444919711206	$3.551215 * 10^{-6}$	15	0.94186426368404708	$2.721482 * 10^{-9}$
8	0.90110745351730037	$1.349968 * 10^{-6}$	16	0.94508125972497303	$1.177902 * 10^{-9}$

GTEngine implements this algorithm on the CPU/FPU for $n = 8$. The implementation is shown in Listing 6.30.

```cpp
template <typename Real> Quaternion<Real> Slerp (Real t,
    Quaternion<Real> const& q0, Quaternion<Real> const& q1)
{
    Real const onePlusMuFPU = (Real)1.90110745351730037;

    Real const a[9] =
    {
        (Real)1/((Real)1*(Real)3),   (Real)1/((Real)2*(Real)5),
        (Real)1/((Real)3*(Real)7),   (Real)1/((Real)4*(Real)9),
        (Real)1/((Real)5*(Real)11),  (Real)1/((Real)6*(Real)13),
        (Real)1/((Real)7*(Real)15),  (Real)1/((Real)8*(Real)17),
        onePlusMuFPU*(Real)1/((Real)9*(Real)19)
    };

    Real const b[9] =
    {
        (Real)1/(Real)3,    (Real)2/(Real)5,
        (Real)3/(Real)7,    (Real)4/(Real)9,
        (Real)5/(Real)11,   (Real)6/(Real)13,
        (Real)7/(Real)15,   (Real)8/(Real)17,
        onePlusMuFPU*(Real)9/(Real)19
    };

    Real cs = Dot(q0, q1);
    Real sign;
    if (cs >= (Real)0)
    {
        sign = (Real)1;
    }
    else
    {
        cs = -cs;
        sign = (Real)-1;
    }

    Real csm1 = cs - (Real)1;
    Real term0 = (Real)1 - t, term1 = t;
    Real sqr0 = term0*term0, sqr1 = term1*term1;
    Real u0 = term0, u1 = term1;
    for (int i = 0; i <= 8; ++i)
    {
        term0 *= (a[i]*sqr0 - b[i])*csm1;
        term1 *= (a[i]*sqr1 - b[i])*csm1;
        u0 += term0;
        u1 += term1;
    }
    u1 *= sign;
```

```
Quaternion<Real> slerp = q0*u0 + q1*u1;
    return slerp;
}
```

LISTING 6.30: A fast, accurate, and robust implementation of SLERP.

On the CPU/FPU, the speed-up over the code in Listing 6.29 is more than two-fold for 32-bit floating-point numbers. A SIMD implementation, described in a later section, provides for parallel SLERP operations for additional speed ups.

6.3.5 Euler Angles

Rotations about the coordinate axes are easy to define and work with. My convention is that a positive angle θ corresponds to a counterclockwise rotation in the plane when viewed by an observer on the positive side of the axis looking at the origin. In order to conform to this convention, the rotation matrix depends on the matrix-vector multiplication convention in effect.

name	vector-on-the-right	vector-on-the-left	name
$R_0(\theta_0)$	$\begin{bmatrix} 1 & 0 & 0 \\ 0 & \cos\theta_0 & -\sin\theta_0 \\ 0 & \sin\theta_0 & \cos\theta_0 \end{bmatrix}$	$\begin{bmatrix} 1 & 0 & 0 \\ 0 & \cos\theta_0 & \sin\theta_0 \\ 0 & -\sin\theta_0 & \cos\theta_0 \end{bmatrix}$	$\hat{R}_0(\theta_0)$
$R_1(\theta_1)$	$\begin{bmatrix} \cos\theta_1 & 0 & \sin\theta_1 \\ 0 & 1 & 0 \\ -\sin\theta_1 & 0 & \cos\theta_1 \end{bmatrix}$	$\begin{bmatrix} \cos\theta_1 & 0 & -\sin\theta_1 \\ 0 & 1 & 0 \\ \sin\theta_1 & 0 & \cos\theta_1 \end{bmatrix}$	$\hat{R}_1(\theta_1)$
$R_2(\theta_2)$	$\begin{bmatrix} \cos\theta_2 & -\sin\theta_2 & 0 \\ \sin\theta_2 & \cos\theta_2 & 0 \\ 0 & 0 & 1 \end{bmatrix}$	$\begin{bmatrix} \cos\theta_2 & \sin\theta_2 & 0 \\ -\sin\theta_2 & \cos\theta_2 & 0 \\ 0 & 0 & 1 \end{bmatrix}$	$\hat{R}_2(\theta_2)$

$$(6.102)$$

Index zero indicates a rotation about the x-axis, index one indicates a rotation about the y-axis, and index 2 indicates a rotation about the z-axis. The angles are referred to as *Euler angles*.

For example, using vector-on-the-right convention, consider a rotation matrix that is a composition of coordinate rotation matrices, $R = R_0(\theta_0)R_1(\theta_1)R_2(\theta_2)$. The ordering is said to be xyz. Five other possible combinations are xzy, yxz, yzx, zxy, and zyx. Another type of composition involves three angles but only two coordinate axes; for example, $R = R_0(\theta_0)R_1(\theta_1)R_0(\theta_2)$. The ordering is said to be xyx. Five other possible combinations are xzx, yxy, yzy, zxz, and zyz. In total, we have twelve possible combinations of coordinate axis rotation matrices.

The term "xyz ordering" is confusing when you allow for different multiplication conventions. In the previous paragraph, xyz ordering is a composition for which the z-axis rotation is applied first, the y-axis rotation second, and the x-axis rotation third:

$$R\mathbf{V} = R_0(\theta_0)[R_1(\theta_1)[R_2(\theta_2)\mathbf{V}]] \tag{6.103}$$

Using vector-on-the-left convention, the rotation $\hat{R} = R^\mathsf{T}$ leads to equal 3-tuples $R\mathbf{V}$ and $\mathbf{V}^\mathsf{T}\hat{R}$. It is convenient to implement Euler angles in a manner that hides the underlying matrix-vector multiplication convention. For the current example, we want a composition for $\hat{R}$ that applies the z-axis rotation first, the y-axis rotation second, and the x-axis rotation third. Specifically, $\hat{R} = \hat{R}_2(\theta_2)\hat{R}_1(\theta_1)\hat{R}_0(\theta_0)$, which is a "$zyx$ ordering." The application to a vector is

$$\mathbf{V}^\mathsf{T}\hat{R} = \left[\left[\mathbf{V}^\mathsf{T}\hat{R}_2(\theta_2)\right]\hat{R}_1(\theta_1)\right]\hat{R}_0(\theta_0) \tag{6.104}$$

which is the same 3-tuple as $R\mathbf{V}$. In terms of matrix operations, all we are doing is applying tranposes,

$$
\begin{aligned}
\hat{R} &= R^\mathsf{T} \\
&= (R_0(\theta_0)R_1(\theta_1)R_0(\theta_2))^\mathsf{T} \\
&= R_2(\theta_2)^\mathsf{T} R_1(\theta_1)^\mathsf{T} R_0(\theta_2)^\mathsf{T} \\
&= \hat{R}_2(\theta_2)\hat{R}_1(\theta_1)\hat{R}_0(\theta_0)
\end{aligned} \tag{6.105}
$$

GTEngine hides the matrix-vector multiplication convention as described previously. The Euler angle composition is presented through an interface that implements the function W,

$$
\begin{aligned}
&W(\mathbf{E}_{i_0}, \phi_0, \mathbf{E}_{i_1}, \phi_1, \mathbf{E}_{i_2}, \phi_2) = \\
&\begin{cases} R(\mathbf{E}_{i_2}, \phi_2)R(\mathbf{E}_{i_1}, \phi_1)R(\mathbf{E}_{i_0}, \phi_0), & \text{vector-on-the-right convention} \\ \hat{R}(\mathbf{E}_{i_0}, \phi_0)\hat{R}(\mathbf{E}_{i_1}, \phi_1)\hat{R}(\mathbf{E}_{i_2}, \phi_2), & \text{vector-on-the-left convention} \end{cases}
\end{aligned} \tag{6.106}
$$

For three distinct axes, (i_0, i_1, i_2) is one of $(0, 1, 2)$, $(0, 2, 1)$, $(1, 2, 0)$, $(1, 0, 2)$, $(2, 0, 1)$, or $(2, 1, 0)$. For two distinct axes, (i_0, i_1, i_2) is one of $(0, 1, 0)$, $(0, 2, 0)$, $(1, 0, 1)$, $(1, 2, 1)$, $(2, 0, 2)$, or $(2, 1, 2)$. The indexing of axes is such that regardless of multiplication convention, the rotation about axis i_0 is applied first, the rotation about axis i_1 is applied second, and the rotation about axis i_2 is applied third. The angles are $\phi_j = \theta_{i_j}$ for $0 \leq j \leq 2$.

6.3.5.1   World Coordinates versus Body Coordinates

I refer to the twelve factorizations of the last section as *Euler angles in world coordinates*. The coordinate axis rotations are specified for the original coordinate axes, and the rotations are applied one at a time in the world coordinate system. It is also possible to define *Euler angles in body coordinates*. In this scenario, the coordinate axes themselves are rotated. In my opinion, specifying Euler angles in body coordinates is more intuitive than specifying them in world coordinates, because you can imagine the actual motion of the object for each selected body-axis rotation.

Let the initial body axes be the orthonormal right-handed basis $\{\mathbf{U}_0, \mathbf{U}_1, \mathbf{U}_2\}$. The vectors are unit-length, mutually perpendicular, and $\mathbf{U}_0 \times \mathbf{U}_1 = \mathbf{U}_2$. Let the rotation angles be θ_i for $0 \le i \le 2$ and define $s_i = \sin\theta_i$ and $c_i = \cos\theta_i$. The rotation matrix by an angle θ corresponding to an axis with unit-length direction $\mathbf{V}$ is $R(\mathbf{V}, \theta)$.

The illustration assumes the vector-on-the-right multiplication convention. The first rotation is by angle θ_0 about the body axis $\mathbf{U}_0$; let the rotation matrix be denoted $R_0 = R(\mathbf{U}_0, \theta_0)$. The second rotation is by angle θ_1 about the rotated body axis $R_0 \mathbf{U}_0$; the rotation matrix is $R_1 = R(R_0 \mathbf{U}_0, \theta_1)$. The third rotation is by angle θ_2 about the twice-rotated body axis $R_1 R_0 \mathbf{U}_2$; the rotation matrix is $R_2 = R(R_1 R_0 \mathbf{U}_2, \theta_2)$. The composition of the three rotations is $R_2 R_1 R_0$, say,

$$
\begin{aligned}
B(&\mathbf{U}_0, \theta_0, \mathbf{U}_1, \theta_1, \mathbf{U}_2, \theta_2) \\
&= R(R(R(\mathbf{U}_0, \theta_0)\mathbf{U}_1, \theta_1)\mathbf{U}_2, \theta_2)R(R(\mathbf{U}_0, \theta_0)\mathbf{U}_1, \theta_1)R(\mathbf{U}_0, \theta_0) \\
&= R(s_1\mathbf{U}_0 - s_0 c_1 \mathbf{U}_1 - s_0 c_0 \mathbf{U}_2, \theta_2)R(c_0\mathbf{U}_1 + s_0\mathbf{U}_2, \theta_1)R(\mathbf{U}_0, \theta_0) \\
&= UB(\mathbf{E}_0, \theta_0, \mathbf{E}_1, \theta_1, \mathbf{E}_2, \theta_2)U^{\mathsf{T}}
\end{aligned}
\tag{6.107}
$$

where $\mathbf{E}_0 = (1,0,0)$, $\mathbf{E}_1 = (0,1,0)$, $\mathbf{E}_2 = (0,0,1)$, and $U = [\mathbf{U}_0\ \mathbf{U}_1\ \mathbf{U}_2]$ is the rotation matrix whose columns are the specified vectors. I leave it as an exercise to prove the following relationship between Euler angles in world coordinates and Euler angles in body coordinates,

$$
B(\mathbf{E}_0, \theta_0, \mathbf{E}_1, \theta_1, \mathbf{E}_2, \theta_2) = W(\mathbf{E}_0, \theta_0, \mathbf{E}_1, \theta_1, \mathbf{E}_0, \theta_2)
\tag{6.108}
$$

Observe that the world-coordinate function corresponds to a three-axis rotation where one of the axes is repeated.

We may also compose three body-axis rotations when one of the axes is repeated. The general composition formula in Equation (6.107) is overloaded to cover this case. For example, the xyx composition using the standard Euclidean basis is

$$
\begin{aligned}
B(&\mathbf{U}_0, \theta_0, \mathbf{U}_1, \theta_1, \mathbf{U}_0, \theta_2) \\
&= R(R(R(\mathbf{U}_0, \theta_0)\mathbf{U}_1, \theta_1)\mathbf{U}_0, \theta_2)R(R(\mathbf{U}_0, \theta_0)\mathbf{U}_1, \theta_1)R(\mathbf{U}_0, \theta_0) \\
&= R(c_1\mathbf{U}_0 + s_0 s_1 \mathbf{U}_1 - c_0 s_1 \mathbf{U}_2, \theta_2)R(c_0\mathbf{U}_1 + s_0\mathbf{U}_2, \theta_1)R(\mathbf{U}_0, \theta_0) \\
&= UB(\mathbf{E}_0, \theta_0, \mathbf{E}_1, \theta_1, \mathbf{E}_0, \theta_2)U^{\mathsf{T}} \\
&= UB(\mathbf{E}_0, \theta_0 + \theta_2, \mathbf{E}_1, \theta_1, \mathbf{E}_0, 0)U^{\mathsf{T}}
\end{aligned}
\tag{6.109}
$$

The last equality appeals to your intuition that—with body coordinates—if you rotate around a body axis two separate times, you might as well rotate around it once by the sum of the angles. This reduction is not valid when using xyx Euler angles in world coordinates.

The body-axis composition when using the vector-on-the-left convention is

$$
\begin{aligned}
B(&\mathbf{U}_0, \theta_0, \mathbf{U}_1, \theta_1, \mathbf{U}_2, \theta_2) \\
&= \hat{R}(\mathbf{U}_0, \theta_0)\hat{R}(\mathbf{U}_1^{\mathsf{T}}\hat{R}(\mathbf{U}_0, \theta_0), \theta_1)\hat{R}(\mathbf{U}_2^{\mathsf{T}}\hat{R}(\mathbf{U}_1^{\mathsf{T}}\hat{R}(\mathbf{U}_0, \theta_0), \theta_1), \theta_2)
\end{aligned}
\tag{6.110}
$$

The matrix-vector convention is hidden by using the same interface for both conventions.

6.3.6   Conversion between Representations

GTEngine supports four different representations for rotations: matrices, axis-angle pairs, quaternions, and Euler angles in world coordinates. In most applications, invariably you want to convert from one representation to another. There are twelve such conversions—a 4×4 table where the off-diagonal entries correspond to the conversion functions.

The conversions are encapsulated by a templated class, Rotation<N,Real>, where N is three or four and Real is float or double. The idea of parameter N is to support conversions for 3D rotations embedded in 4D when using affine algebra. I also wanted a consistent interface for any-to-any conversions, but as is well known, the return type of C++ functions is not part of the signature when generating decorated names. It is convenient to have compact code as shown in Listing 6.31.

```
// Error:  The compiler complains that the Convert functions are ambiguous,
// because the return type is not part of the function signature.
template <int N, typename Real> Matrix<N,N,Real>
Convert (Quaternion<Real const&);

template <int N, typename Real> Matrix<N,N,Real>
Convert (AxisAngle<Real> const&);

Quaternion<float> q = <some quaternion>;
AxisAngle <3,float> aa = <some angle−axis pair>;
Matrix3x3<float> r0 = Convert(q);
Matrix3x3<float> r1 = Convert(aa);
```

LISTING 6.31: An attempt to have compact conversion code. The compiler does not allow this.

The usual way to deal with this is to return the result via a function parameter, as shown in Listing 6.32.

```
template <int N, typename Real>
void Convert (Quaternion<Real const&, Matrix<N,N,Real>&);

template <int N, typename Real>
void Convert (AxisAngle<Real> const&, Matrix<N,N,Real>&);

Quaternion<float> q = <some quaternion>;
AxisAngle <3,float> aa = <some angle−axis pair>;
Matrix3x3<float> r0, r1;
Convert(q, r0);
Convert(aa, r1);
```

LISTING 6.32: A workaround for the compiler complaints of Listing 6.31.

I prefer the compact code. To circumvent the compiler complaints, I implemented the Rotation class so that its constructors act as the input consumers of the conversion and implicit operators act as the output producers of the conversion, as shown in Listing 6.33.

```
template <int N, typename Real>
class Rotation
{
public:
```

```
// Create rotations from various representations.
Rotation (Matrix<N,N,Real> const& matrix);
Rotation (Quaternion<Real> const& quaternion);
Rotation (AxisAngle<N,Real> const& axisAngle);
Rotation (EulerAngles<Real> const& eulerAngles);

// Convert one representation to another.
operator Matrix<N,N,Real> () const;
operator Quaternion<Real> () const;
operator AxisAngle<N,Real> () const;
operator EulerAngles<Real> () const;
};

Quaternion<float> q = <some quaternion>;
AxisAngle<3,float> aa = <some angle-axis pair>;
Matrix3x3<float> r0 = Rotation <3,Real>(q);
Matrix3x3<float> r1 = Rotation <3,Real>(aa);

Rotation <3,Real> rotation(q);
Matrix3x3 matrix = rotation;
EulerAngles<float> euler = rotation;
```

LISTING 6.33: The final conversion code that provides compact code but no compiler warnings.

The conversions themselves are implemented as private class member functions. In fact, you can have a persistant Rotation object that can be used to convert to different representations, as shown by the final block of code in the listing. In a sense, Rotation is an abstraction of the concept of a rotation. To apply a rotation, you need an instantiation as some algebraic entity, which is what the implicit operator conversions give you.

6.3.6.1 Quaternion to Matrix

The conversion from a quaternion to a rotation matrix for the vector-on-the-right convention was provided by Equation (6.86). The rotation matrix for the vector-on-the-left convention is the transpose of the matrix of that equation.

6.3.6.2 Matrix to Quaternion

The rotation matrices corresponding to quaternions contain quadratic terms involving the quaternion components x, y, z, and w. Let the entries of the rotation matrix be r_{ij} for $0 \le i \le 2$ and $0 \le j \le 2$.

$$4x^2 = (+r_{00} - r_{11} - r_{22} + 1), \quad 4y^2 = (-r_{00} + r_{11} - r_{22} + 1),$$
$$4z^2 = (-r_{00} - r_{11} + r_{22} + 1), \quad 4w^2 = (+r_{00} + r_{11} + r_{22} + 1),$$
$$4xy = r_{01} + r_{10}, \quad 4xz = r_{02} + r_{20}, \quad 4yz = r_{12} + r_{21},$$
$$4xw = r_{21} - r_{12}, \quad 4yw = r_{02} - r_{20}, \quad 4zw = r_{10} - r_{01}, \quad \text{(vector-on-right)} \quad (6.111)$$
$$4xw = r_{12} - r_{21}, \quad 4yw = r_{20} - r_{02}, \quad 4zw = r_{01} - r_{10}, \quad \text{(vector-on-left)}$$
$$2(x^2 + y^2) = 1 - r_{22}, \quad 2(z^2 + w^2) = 1 + r_{22},$$
$$2(y^2 - x^2) = r_{11} - r_{00}, \quad 2(w^2 - z^2) = r_{11} + r_{00}$$

If **Q** is the 4×1 vector corresponding to the 4-tuple (x, y, z, w), the previous equations give us a matrix

$$4\mathbf{QQ}^{\mathsf{T}} = \begin{bmatrix} 4x^2 & 4xy & 4xz & 4zw \\ 4yx & 4y^2 & 4yz & 4yw \\ 4zx & 4zy & 4z^2 & 4zw \\ 4wx & 4wy & 4wz & 4w^2 \end{bmatrix} \qquad (6.112)$$

Theoretically, any nonzero row of the matrix can be normalized to obtain a quaternion q. To be numerically robust, the code determines the row of maximum length and normalizes it to obtain q.

The row of maximum length corresponds to the quaternion component of largest magnitude, but this begs the question because we do not know yet what the quaternion components are. Instead, we must infer the largest-magnitude component. The quaternion is obtained by normalizing the corresponding row. The pseudocode in Listing 6.34 does the job.

```
Real sign = (vector-on-right-convention ? +1 : -1);
if (r22 <= 0)  // 2(x^2 + y^2) >= 1
{
    omr22 = 1 - r22;  dif10 = r11 - r00;
    if (dif10 <= 0)  // x^2 >= y^2, 4x^2 >= 1, x >= 1/2, |x| is maximum
    {
        fourxsqr = omr22 - dif10;  invfourx = 0.5/sqrt(fourxsqr);
        q.x = fourxsqr*invfourx;
        q.y = (r01+r10)*invfourx;
        q.z = (r02+r20)*invfourx;
        q.w = sign*(r21-r12)*invfourx;
    }
    else  // y^2 >= x^2, 4y^2 >= 1, y >= 1/2, |y| is maximum
    {
        fourysqr = om22 + dif10;  invfoury = 0.5/sqrt(fourysqr);
        q.x = (r01+r10)*invfoury;
        q.y = fourysqr*inv4y;
        q.z = (r12+r21)*invfoury;
        q.w = sign*(r02-r20)*invfoury;
    }
}
else  // 2(z^2 + w^2) >= 1
{
    opr22 = 1 + r22;  sum10 = r11 + r00;
    if (sum10 <= 0)  // z^2 >= w^2, 4z^2 >= 1, z >= 1/2, |z| is maximum
    {
        fourzsqr = opr22 - sum10;  invfourz = 0.5/sqrt(fourzsqr);
        q.x = (r02+r20)*invfourz;
        q.y = (r12+r21)*invfourz;
        q.z = fourzsqr*invfourz;
        q.w = sign*(r10-r01)*invfourz;
    }
    else  // w^2 >= z^2, 4w^2 >= 1, w >= 1/2, |w| is maximum
    {
        fourwsqr = opr22 + sum10;  invfourw = 0.5/sqrt(fourwsqr);
        q.x = sign*(r21-r12)*invfourw;
        q.y = sign*(r02-r20)*invfourw;
        q.z = sign*(r10-r01)*invfourw;
        q.w = fourwsqr*inv4w;
    }
}
```

LISTING 6.34: Determining the largest-magnitude component of q from the products of components.

6.3.6.3 Axis-Angle to Matrix

The conversion from an axis-angle pair to a matrix is provided by Equation (6.68). The equation was derived for the vector-on-the-right convention. The implementation for vector-on-the-left just computes the transpose of the matrix of this equation.

6.3.6.4 Matrix to Axis-Angle

For the vector-on-the-right convention, the rotation matrix is $R = I + (\sin\theta)S + (1 - \cos\theta)S^2$, where $S = [s_{ij}]$ is the skew-symmetric matrix whose components determine the unit-length direction of the axis of rotation. If that direction is $\mathbf{U} = (u_0, u_1, u_2)$, then $s_{01} = -u_2$, $s_{02} = u_1$, and $s_{12} = -u_0$. The trace of R is the sum of the diagonal entries, and it can be determined from the matrix equation: $\text{trace}(R) = 1 + 2\cos\theta$. Solving for the angle, $\theta = \mathsf{acos}((\text{trace}(R) - 1)/2) \in [0, \pi]$.

If $\theta = 0$, the rotation matrix is the identity I. Any axis serves as the rotation axis, so the source code uses (arbitrarily) $\mathbf{U} = (1, 0, 0)$.

If $\theta \in (0, \pi)$, the axis direction is extracted from $S = (R - R^\mathsf{T})/(2\sin\theta)$. To be numerically robust, the 3-tuple extracted is normalized to minimize the effects of numerical roundoff errors when θ is nearly 0 or nearly π. To avoid bias from previous roundoff errors and guarantee the result is the same whether we extract from R or R^T, set $u_0 = r_{21} - r_{12}$, $u_1 = r_{02} - r_{20}$, and $u_2 = r_{10} - r_{01}$. The resulting 3-tuple is the normalized. For the vector-on-the-left convention, the axis direction is extracted from $S = (R^\mathsf{T} - R)/(2\sin\theta)$ using $u_0 = r_{12} - r_{21}$, $u_1 = r_{20} - r_{02}$, and $u_2 = r_{01} - r_{10}$ followed by normalization.

If $\theta = \pi$, then

$$R + I = 2(I + S^2) = 2\mathbf{U}\mathbf{U}^\mathsf{T} = \begin{bmatrix} 2u_0^2 & 2u_0u_1 & 2u_0u_2 \\ 2u_0u_1 & 2u_1^2 & 2u_1u_2 \\ 2u_0u_2 & 2u_1u_2 & 2u_2^2 \end{bmatrix} \qquad (6.113)$$

which is a symmetric matrix regardless of choice of multiplication convention. The source code does not need to use conditional defines to handle separate cases. Extracting $\mathbf{U}$ in a numerically robust manner is similar to how we computed a quaternion from a matrix. In this case, we simply compute the maximum diagonal entry of $R + I$ to determine the largest-magnitude component of $\mathbf{U}$ and select the corresponding row of the matrix to normalize. The axis direction is obtained by normalizing the corresponding row. The pseudocode in Listing 6.35 illustrates.

```
if (r00 >= r11)
{
    if (r00 >= r22)   // u0^2 largest-magnitude
    {
        U = (r00 + 1, (r01 + r10)/2, (r02 + r20)/2);
    }
    else   // u2^2 largest-magnitude
    {
        U = ((r20 + r02)/2, (r21 + r12)/2, r22 + 1);
```

```
        }
    }
    else
    {
        if (r11 >= r22)  // u1^2 largest-magnitude
        {
            U = ((r10 + r01)/2, r11 + 1, (r12 + r21)/2);
        }
        else  // u2^2 largest-magnitude
        {
            U = ((r20 + r02)/2, (r21 + r12)/2, r22 + 1);
        }
    }
}
Normalize(U);
```

LISTING 6.35: Determining the largest-magnitude component of **U** from the products of components.

Numerical bias is avoided by averaging the off-diagonal terms, ensuring the results are the same for R or R^{T}. It does not matter that the normalization computes a positive entry in **U** corresponding to the specially computed diagonal entry. For a rotation by π radians, $R(\mathbf{U}, \pi)$ and $R(-\mathbf{U}, \pi)$ are the same rotation matrix.

6.3.6.5 Axis-Angle to Quaternion

This conversion is simple. The quaternion angle is half the rotation angle and the imaginary portion of the quaternion is a multiple of the rotation axis. Listing 6.36 has the pseudocode for converting an axis-angle pair (axis,angle) to a quaternion q.

```
Real sign = (vector-on-the-right-convention ? +1 : -1);
Real halfAngle = 0.5*sign*angle;
Real sn = sin(halfAngle);
q[0] = sn*axis[0];
q[1] = sn*axis[1];
q[2] = sn*axis[2];
q[3] = cos(halfAngle);
```

LISTING 6.36: Conversion of an axis-angle pair (axis,angle) to a quaternion q.

6.3.6.6 Quaternion to Axis-Angle

This conversion is as simple as that for axis-angle to quaternion, as shown in Listing 6.37.

```
Real sign = (vector-on-the-right-convention ? +1 : -1);
Real axisSqrLen = q[0]*q[0] + q[1]*q[1] + q[2]*q[2];
if (axisSqrLen > 0)
{
    Real adjust = sign/sqrt(axisSqrLen);
    axis[0] = q[0]*adjust;
    axis[1] = q[1]*adjust;
    axis[2] = q[2]*adjust;
    angle = acos(q[3]);
}
else
{
```

```
    // The angle is 0 (modulo 2*pi). Any axis will work, so choose (1,0,0).
    a.axis[0] = 1;
    a.angle = 0;
}
```

LISTING 6.37: Conversion of a quaternion q to an axis-angle pair (axis,angle).

6.3.6.7 Euler Angles to Matrix

The conversion involves a simple composition of coordinate-axis rotations, as shown in Listing 6.38. The pseudocode assumes that the indices are correctly formed; all are distinct, or the first and last indices are the same and different from the middle.

```
struct EulerAngles
{
    int axis[3];    // in {0,1,2}
    Real angle[3];  // in radians
}

Vector3 Unit[3] = { (1,0,0), (0,1,0), (0,0,1) };

Matrix3x3 r0 = Rotation(AxisAngle(Unit(e.axis[0]), e.angle[0]));
Matrix3x3 r1 = Rotation(AxisAngle(Unit(e.axis[1]), e.angle[1]));
Matrix3x3 r2 = Rotation(AxisAngle(Unit(e.axis[2]), e.angle[2]));
Matrix3x3 r = (vector-on-right-convention ? r2*r1*r0 : r0*r1*r2);
```

LISTING 6.38: Conversion of Euler angles e to a rotation matrix r.

6.3.6.8 Matrix to Euler Angles

Define $c_i = \cos(\theta_i)$ and $s_i = \sin(\theta_i)$ for $0 \le i \le 2$. Let the rotation matrix be $R = [r_{ij}]$ for $0 \le i \le 2$ and $0 \le j \le 2$.

The product $R = R_0(\theta_0)R_1(\theta_1)R_2(\theta_1)$ serves as the pattern for six factorizations with three distinct coordinate axes. Formally multiplying the three coordinate rotation matrices and equating yields

$$\begin{bmatrix} r_{00} & r_{01} & r_{02} \\ r_{10} & r_{11} & r_{12} \\ r_{20} & r_{21} & r_{22} \end{bmatrix} = \begin{bmatrix} c_1 c_2 & -c_1 s_2 & s_1 \\ c_0 s_2 + s_0 s_1 c_2 & c_0 c_2 - s_0 s_1 s_2 & -s_0 c_1 \\ s_0 s_2 - c_0 s_1 c_2 & s_0 c_2 + c_0 s_1 s_2 & c_0 c_1 \end{bmatrix} \quad (6.114)$$

The simplest term to work with is $s_1 = r_{02}$, so $\theta_1 = \mathsf{asin}(r_{02})$. There are three cases to consider.

1. If $\theta_1 \in (-\pi/2, \pi/2)$, then $c_1 \ne 0$ and $c_1(s_0, c_0) = (-r_{12}, r_{22})$, in which case $\theta_0 = \mathsf{atan2}(-r_{12}, r_{22})$, and $c_1(s_2, c_2) = (-r_{01}, r_{00})$, in which case $\theta_2 = \mathsf{atan2}(-r_{01}, r_{00})$. In the source code, this case is tagged as UNIQUE.

2. If $\theta_1 = \pi/2$, then $s_1 = 1$ and $c_1 = 0$. In this case,

$$\begin{bmatrix} r_{10} & r_{11} \\ r_{20} & r_{21} \end{bmatrix} = \begin{bmatrix} s_0 c_2 + c_0 s_2 & c_0 c_2 - s_0 s_2 \\ s_0 s_2 - c_0 c_2 & s_0 c_2 + c_0 s_2 \end{bmatrix}$$

$$= \begin{bmatrix} \sin(\theta_0 + \theta_2) & \cos(\theta_0 + \theta_2) \\ -\cos(\theta_0 + \theta_2) & \sin(\theta_0 + \theta_2) \end{bmatrix}$$

Therefore, $\theta_0 + \theta_2 = \text{atan2}(r_{10}, r_{11})$. There is one degree of freedom, so the factorization is not unique. In the source code, this case is tagged as NOT_UNIQUE_SUM.

3. If $\theta_1 = -\pi/2$, then $s_1 = -1$ and $c_1 = 0$. In this case,

$$
\begin{bmatrix} r_{10} & r_{11} \\ r_{20} & r_{21} \end{bmatrix} = \begin{bmatrix} c_0 s_2 - s_0 c_2 & c_0 c_2 + s_0 s_2 \\ c_0 c_2 + s_0 s_2 & s_0 c_2 - c_0 s_2 \end{bmatrix}
$$

$$
= \begin{bmatrix} \sin(\theta_2 - \theta_0) & \cos(\theta_2 - \theta_0) \\ \cos(\theta_2 - \theta_0) & -\sin(\theta_2 - \theta_0) \end{bmatrix}
$$

Therefore, $\theta_2 - \theta_0 = \text{atan2}(r_{10}, r_{11})$. There is one degree of freedom, so the factorization is not unique. In the source code, this case is tagged as NOT_UNIQUE_DIF.

The factorization $R = R_0(\theta_0) R_1(\theta_1) R_0(\theta_2)$ serves as the pattern for six factorizations with two distinct coordinate axes, one repeated. Formally multiplying the three coordinate rotation matrices and equating yields

$$
\begin{bmatrix} r_{00} & r_{01} & r_{02} \\ r_{10} & r_{11} & r_{12} \\ r_{20} & r_{21} & r_{22} \end{bmatrix} = \begin{bmatrix} c_1 & s_1 s_2 & s_1 c_2 \\ s_0 s_1 & c_0 c_2 - s_0 c_1 s_2 & -s_0 c_1 c_2 - c_0 s_2 \\ -c_0 s_1 & s_0 c_2 + c_0 c_1 s_2 & c_0 c_1 c_2 - s_0 s_2 \end{bmatrix} \quad (6.115)
$$

The simplest term to work with is $c_1 = r_{00}$, so $\theta_1 = \text{acos}(r_{00})$. There are three cases to consider.

1. If $\theta_1 \in (0, \pi)$, then $s_1 \neq 0$ and $s_1(s_0, c_0) = (r_{10}, -r_{20})$, in which case $\theta_0 = \text{atan2}(r_{10}, -r_{20})$, and $s_1(s_2, c_2) = (r_{01}, r_{02})$, in which case $\theta_2 = \text{atan2}(r_{01}, r_{02})$. In the source code, this case is tagged as UNIQUE.

2. If $\theta_1 = 0$, then $c_1 = 1$ and $s_1 = 0$. In this case,

$$
\begin{bmatrix} r_{11} & r_{12} \\ r_{21} & r_{22} \end{bmatrix} = \begin{bmatrix} c_0 c_1 - s_0 s_1 & -s_0 c_1 - c_0 s_1 \\ s_0 c_1 + c_0 s_1 & c_0 c_1 - s_0 s_1 \end{bmatrix}
$$

$$
= \begin{bmatrix} \cos(\theta_1 + \theta_0) & -\sin(\theta_1 + \theta_0) \\ \sin(\theta_1 + \theta_0) & \cos(\theta_1 + \theta_0) \end{bmatrix}
$$

Therefore, $\theta_1 + \theta_0 = \text{atan2}(-r_{12}, r_{11})$. There is one degree of freedom, so the factorization is not unique. In the source code, this case is tagged as NOT_UNIQUE_SUM.

3. If $\theta_1 = \pi$, then $c_1 = -1$ and $s_1 = 0$. In this case,

$$
\begin{bmatrix} r_{11} & r_{12} \\ r_{21} & r_{22} \end{bmatrix} = \begin{bmatrix} c_0 c_1 + s_0 s_1 & s_0 c_1 - c_0 s_1 \\ s_0 c_1 - c_0 s_1 & -c_0 c_1 - s_0 s_1 \end{bmatrix}
$$

$$
= \begin{bmatrix} \cos(\theta_1 - \theta_0) & -\sin(\theta_1 - \theta_0) \\ -\sin(\theta_1 - \theta_0) & -\cos(\theta_1 - \theta_0) \end{bmatrix}
$$

Therefore, $\theta_1 - \theta_0 = \mathsf{atan2}(-r_{12}, r_{11})$. There is one degree of freedom, so the factorization is not unique. In the source code, this case is tagged as NOT_UNIQUE_DIF.

All twelve cases of Euler angles can be analyzed as shown previously. A simple implementation involves setting up a switch statement to select among these cases. However, it is possible to establish patterns in all the code fragments to eliminate the switch in favor of a couple of comparisons. Listing 6.39 shows the compact code for the vector-on-the-right convention. The pseudocode assumes that the indices are correctly formed; all are distinct, or the first and last indices are the same and different from the middle. The Euler angle structure is the same as that of Listing 6.38.

```
if (e.axis[0] != e.axis[2])
{
    // Map (0,1,2), (1,2,0), and (2,0,1) to +1.  Map (0,2,1), (2,1,0),
    // and (1,0,2) to -1.
    int parity = (((e.axis[2] | (e.axis[1] << 2)) >> e.axis[0]) & 1);
    Real const sign = (parity & 1 ? -1 : +1);

    if (r(e.axis[2],e.axis[0]) < 1)
    {
        if (r(e.axis[2],e.axis[0]) > -1)
        {
            e.angle[2] = atan2(sign*r(e.axis[1],e.axis[0]),
                r(e.axis[0],e.axis[0]));
            e.angle[1] = asin(-sign*r(e.axis[2],e.axis[0]));
            e.angle[0] = atan2(sign*r(e.axis[2],e.axis[1]),
                r(e.axis[2],e.axis[2]));
            result = UNIQUE;
        }
        else
        {
            e.angle[2] = 0;
            e.angle[1] = sign*pi/2;
            e.angle[0] = atan2(-sign*r(e.axis[1],e.axis[2]),
                r(e.axis[1],e.axis[1]));
            result = NOT_UNIQUE_DIF;
        }
    }
    else
    {
        e.angle[2] = 0;
        e.angle[1] = -sign*pi/2;
        e.angle[0] = atan2(-sign*r(e.axis[1],e.axis[2]),
            r(e.axis[1],e.axis[1]));
        result = NOT_UNIQUE_SUM;
    }
}
else
{
    // Map (0,2,0), (1,0,1), and (2,1,2) to +1.  Map (0,1,0), (1,2,1),
    // and (2,0,2) to -1.
    int b0 = 3 - e.axis[1] - e.axis[2];
    int parity = (((b0 | (e.axis[1] << 2)) >> e.axis[2]) & 1);
    Real const sign = (parity & 1 ? +1 : -1);

    if (r(e.axis[2],e.axis[2]) < 1)
    {
        if (r(e.axis[2],e.axis[2]) > -1)
        {
            e.angle[2] = atan2(r(e.axis[1],e.axis[2]),
```

```
                sign*r(b0,e.axis[2]));
        e.angle[1] = acos(r(e.axis[2],e.axis[2]));
        e.angle[0] = atan2(r(e.axis[2],e.axis[1]),
            -sign*r(e.axis[2],b0));
        e.result = UNIQUE;
    }
    else
    {
        e.angle[2] = 0;
        e.angle[1] = pi;
        e.angle[0] = atan2(sign*r(e.axis[1],b0),
            r(e.axis[1],e.axis[1]));
        e.result = NOT_UNIQUE_DIF;
    }
    }
    else
    {
        e.angle[2] = 0;
        e.angle[1] = 0;
        e.angle[0] = atan2(sign*r(e.axis[1],b0),
            r(e.axis[1],e.axis[1]));
        e.result = NOT_UNIQUE_SUM;
    }
}
```

LISTING 6.39: Conversion of a rotation matrix r to Euler angles e when using the vector-on-the-right convention.

The main difficulty in establishing the pattern is in discovering the need for the parity, sign, and b0 variables.

The pseudocode for the vector-on-the-left convention is shown in Listing 6.40.

```
if (e.axis[0] != e.axis[2])
{
    // Map (0,1,2), (1,2,0), and (2,0,1) to +1. Map (0,2,1), (2,1,0),
    // and (1,0,2) to -1.
    int parity = (((e.axis[0] | (e.axis[1] << 2)) >> e.axis[2]) & 1);
    Real const sign = (parity & 1 ? +1 : -1);

    if (r(e.axis[0],e.axis[2]) < 1)
    {
        if (r(e.axis[0],e.axis[2]) > -1)
        {
            e.angle[0] = atan2(sign*r(e.axis[1],e.axis[2]),
                r(e.axis[2],e.axis[2]));
            e.angle[1] = asin(-sign*r(e.axis[0],e.axis[2]));
            e.angle[2] = atan2(sign*r(e.axis[0],e.axis[1]),
                r(e.axis[0],e.axis[0]));
            e.result = UNIQUE;
        }
        else
        {
            e.angle[0] = 0;
            e.angle[1] = sign*pi/2;
            e.angle[2] = atan2(-sign*r(e.axis[1],e.axis[0]),
                r(e.axis[1],e.axis[1]));
            e.result = NOT_UNIQUE_DIF;
        }
    }
    else
    {
```

```
            e.angle[0] = 0;
            e.angle[1] = -sign*pi/2;
            e.angle[2] = atan2(-sign*r(e.axis[1],e.axis[0]),
                r(e.axis[1],e.axis[1]));
            e.result = NOT_UNIQUE_SUM;
        }
    }
}
else
{
    // Map (0,2,0), (1,0,1), and (2,1,2) to -1.  Map (0,1,0), (1,2,1),
    // and (2,0,2) to +1.
    int b2 = 3 - e.axis[0] - e.axis[1];
    int parity = (((b2 | (e.axis[1] << 2)) >> e.axis[0]) & 1);
    Real const sign = (parity & 1 ? -1 : +1);

    if (r(e.axis[0],e.axis[0]) < 1)
    {
        if (r(e.axis[0],e.axis[0]) > -1)
        {
            e.angle[0] = atan2(r(e.axis[1],e.axis[0]),
                sign*r(b2,e.axis[0]));
            e.angle[1] = acos(r(e.axis[0],e.axis[0]));
            e.angle[2] = atan2(r(e.axis[0],e.axis[1]),
                -sign*r(e.axis[0],b2));
            e.result = UNIQUE;
        }
        else
        {
            e.angle[0] = 0;
            e.angle[1] = pi;
            e.angle[2] = atan2(sign*r(e.axis[1],b2),
                r(e.axis[1],e.axis[1]));
            e.result = NOT_UNIQUE_DIF;
        }
    }
    else
    {
        e.angle[0] = 0;
        e.angle[1] = 0;
        e.angle[2] = atan2(sign*r(e.axis[1],b2),
            r(e.axis[1],e.axis[1]));
        e.result = NOT_UNIQUE_SUM;
    }
}
```

LISTING 6.40: Conversion of a rotation matrix r to Euler angles e when using the vector-on-the-left convention.

The main difficulty in establishing the pattern is in discovering the need for the parity, sign, and b2 variables.

6.3.6.9   Euler Angles to and from Quaternion or Axis-Angle

The conversions use those developed previously. For conversion of Euler angles to quaternion or axis-angle, the Euler angles are first converted to a matrix representation. The matrix is then converted to quaternion or axis-angle. For the conversion of quaternion or axis-angle to Euler angles, the quaternion or axis-angle is first converted to a matrix representation. The matrix is then converted to Euler angles.

6.4   Coordinate Systems

Coordinate systems in the 3D world are a convenient way for describing where objects are located and how they move. We each might have our own systems, but as always it is generally difficult to get two people to agree!

We have three degrees of freedom in our world for specifying locations and directions. In the abstract, we will talk about those degrees of freedom as scalar measurements and list them as a 3-tuple, (x, y, z). Invariably there is a reference point from which the measurements are made. In the abstract, this is called the *origin* and is denoted $(0, 0, 0)$. The directions at the origin along which we make the measurements are denoted $(1, 0, 0)$ for the x-measurement, $(0, 1, 0)$ for the y-measurement, and $(0, 0, 1)$ for the z-measurement. Clearly, if two people observe the same object in the world, that object is located *somewhere*. How the people measure where that location is depends on their choices for the origin and the directions of measurement. No matter how we make those measurements based on our conventions, the object exists in the world in a fixed location. What is required to avoid the ambiguity of multiple measurement systems is a *common frame of reference*.

The common frame of reference is an abstraction that allows you to do *bookkeeping*, so to speak. Choosing a common frame of reference and setting up coordinate systems appears to be a chicken-and-egg problem. To choose a common frame, do we not get back to the same ambiguity when two people define the frame differently? The ambiguity is in the bookkeeping. Your brain gives you the ability to visualize the world and its *geometric relationships*, and the geometry has no ambiguities. When attempting to work with two coordinate systems, you must visualize how one system is overlaid on the other so that the geometric relationships are the same.

The common frame of reference is called the *Cartesian frame*. The 3-tuples to identify the origin and directions of measurement are referred to as the *Cartesian coordinate system*. I like to think of these as the *world* and *world coordinate system*. Naturally, I can have my world and you can have yours. But if you want to play in my world, you must accept my world coordinate system, and you must understand how your bookkeeping relates to mine.

One of the problems in understanding coordinate systems is the use of (x, y, z) when teaching people 3D mathematics. The meanings of the coordinate values and how they relate to the geometry of the world are typically implicit in the lectures and depend on the choices of the lecturer. As a mathematician, I am guilty of using (x, y, z) in different contexts with different meanings. In my writings about computer graphics, I prefer to talk in terms of the visually meaningful degrees of freedom. For example, I might use more meaningful symbols, say, the 3-tuple (f, r, u), to indicate locations relative to a stationary observer at an origin $(0, 0, 0)$. The observer measures distances if he were to move forward or backward, left or right, and up or down. The measurement f is made in the forward direction where a positive value implies forward motion and a negative value implies backward motion. Similarly, the measurement r is made in the right direction and the measurement u is made in the up direction. Even so, someone else writing about computer graphics might instead choose to use bookkeeping in the order (f, u, r). The swapping of the last two components is effectively a *change in handedness*, and all bookkeeping depends on your choice of ordering. In the end, you must make clear what your conventions are, what the variables measure, and how you are doing your bookkeeping.

In this section I will describe the basics for setting up a coordinate system and communicating your conventions to someone else in case they have to convert between their coordinate system and yours. In particular, a frequently asked question in 3D applications is how to convert between right-handed coordinate systems and left-handed coordinate systems. I will introduce some example conversions and then describe the general mathematical process for conversions.

6.4.1 Geometry and Affine Algebra

The mathematical framework for dealing with the algebra of coordinate systems as related to the geometry is referred to as *affine algebra*. The Cartesian frame represents *points* as 3-tuples (x, y, z), and the origin $(0, 0, 0)$ is a special point. The directions of measurements are also 3-tuples and are called *vectors*. Points are measurements of absolute location whereas vectors are measurements of relative locations.

Vectors are the central focus in a course on *linear algebra*. Sets of vectors endowed with an addition operator and a scalar multiplication operator are called *vector spaces*. The introduction of points, distinct from vectors, are the focus of affine algebra. Such an algebra involves a vector space L and a set of points A. The following conditions are the definition for affine algebra:

1. For each ordered pair of points $\mathcal{P}, \mathcal{Q} \in A$, there is a unique vector in L called the *difference vector* and denoted by $\Delta(\mathcal{P}, \mathcal{Q})$.

2. For each point $\mathcal{P} \in A$ and $\mathbf{V} \in L$, there is a unique point $\mathcal{Q} \in A$ such that $\mathbf{V} = \Delta(\mathcal{P}, \mathcal{Q})$.

3. For any three points $\mathcal{P}, \mathcal{Q}, \mathcal{R} \in A$, it must be that $\Delta(\mathcal{P}, \mathcal{Q}) + \Delta(\mathcal{Q}, \mathcal{R}) = \Delta(\mathcal{P}, \mathcal{R})$.

Figure 6.6 illustrates these three items. If $\mathcal{P}$ and $\mathcal{Q}$ are specified, $\mathbf{V}$ is uniquely determined (item 1). If $\mathcal{P}$ and $\mathbf{V}$ are specified, $\mathcal{Q}$ is uniquely determined (item 2). Figure 6.6(b) illustrates item 3.

The formal definition for an affine space introduced the difference vector $\Delta(\mathcal{P}, \mathcal{Q})$. Figure 6.6 gives you the geometric intuition about the difference, specifically that it appears to be a subtraction operation for two points. How-

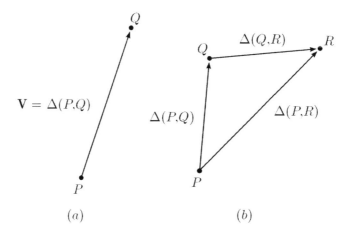

FIGURE 6.6: (a) A vector $\mathbf{V}$ connecting two points $\mathcal{P}$ and $\mathcal{Q}$. (b) The sum of vectors, each vector determined by two points.

ever, certain consequences of the definition may be proved directly without having a concrete formulation for an actual subtraction of points.

A few consequences of the definition for an affine algebra follow.

1. $\Delta(\mathcal{P}, \mathcal{P}) = \mathbf{0}$.

2. $\Delta(\mathcal{Q}, \mathcal{P}) = -\Delta(\mathcal{P}, \mathcal{Q})$.

3. If $\Delta(\mathcal{P}_1, \mathcal{Q}_1) = \Delta(\mathcal{P}_2, \mathcal{Q}_2)$, then $\Delta(\mathcal{P}_1, \mathcal{P}_2) = \Delta(\mathcal{Q}_1, \mathcal{Q}_2)$.

The first consequence follows immediately from item 3 in the definition where $\mathcal{Q}$ is replaced by $\mathcal{P}$, $\Delta(\mathcal{P}, \mathcal{P}) + \Delta(\mathcal{P}, \mathcal{R}) = \Delta(\mathcal{P}, \mathcal{R})$. The vector $\Delta(\mathcal{P}, \mathcal{R})$ is subtracted from both sides to obtain $\Delta(\mathcal{P}, \mathcal{P}) = \mathbf{0}$.

The second consequence also follows from item 3 in the definition where $\mathcal{R}$ is replaced by $\mathcal{P}$, $\Delta(\mathcal{P}, \mathcal{Q}) + \Delta(\mathcal{Q}, \mathcal{P}) = \Delta(\mathcal{P}, \mathcal{P}) = \mathbf{0}$. The last equality is what we just proved in the previous paragraph. The first vector is subtracted from both sides to obtain $\Delta(\mathcal{Q}, \mathcal{P}) = -\Delta(\mathcal{P}, \mathcal{Q})$.

The third consequence is called the *parallelogram law*. Figure 6.7 illustrates this law. Item 3 in the definition can be applied in two ways:

$$
\begin{aligned}
\Delta(\mathcal{P}_1, \mathcal{P}_2) + \Delta(\mathcal{P}_2, \mathcal{Q}_2) &= \Delta(\mathcal{P}_1, \mathcal{Q}_2) \quad \text{and} \\
\Delta(\mathcal{P}_1, \mathcal{Q}_1) + \Delta(\mathcal{Q}_1, \mathcal{Q}_2) &= \Delta(\mathcal{P}_1, \mathcal{Q}_2)
\end{aligned}
\tag{6.116}
$$

Subtracting these leads to

$$
\begin{aligned}
\mathbf{0} &= \Delta(\mathcal{P}_1, \mathcal{P}_2) + \Delta(\mathcal{P}_2, \mathcal{Q}_2) - \Delta(\mathcal{P}_1, \mathcal{Q}_1) - \Delta(\mathcal{Q}_1, \mathcal{Q}_2) \\
&= \Delta(\mathcal{P}_1, \mathcal{P}_2) - \Delta(\mathcal{Q}_1, \mathcal{Q}_2)
\end{aligned}
\tag{6.117}
$$

where the last equality is valid because we assumed $\Delta(\mathcal{P}_1, \mathcal{Q}_1) = \Delta(\mathcal{P}_2, \mathcal{Q}_2)$. Therefore, $\Delta(\mathcal{P}_1, \mathcal{P}_2) = \Delta(\mathcal{Q}_1, \mathcal{Q}_2)$.

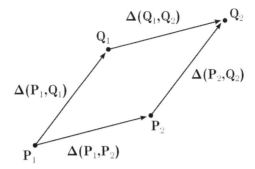

FIGURE 6.7: The parallelogram law for affine algebra.

In the formal sense of affine algebra, points and vectors are distinct entities. We have already used two different fonts to help distinguish between them: $\mathcal{P}$ is a point, $\mathbf{V}$ is a vector. To be suggestive of the standard implementation of difference of points, we may use $\mathbf{V} = \mathcal{Q} - \mathcal{P}$ instead of $\mathbf{V} = \Delta(\mathcal{P}, \mathcal{Q})$, and we may reorganize the expression as $\mathcal{Q} = \mathcal{P} + \mathbf{V}$.

When implementing the concepts of points and vectors in an object-oriented mathematics, you have the choice of creating separate classes, say, Point and Vector. It is common to use 4-tuples (x, y, z, w) for both, choosing points as $(x, y, z, 1)$ and vectors as $(x, y, z, 0)$. In this way, the difference of points is a vector, and the sum of a point and a vector is a point. However, if you attempt to add two points, you obtain a w-component of two, which should not be allowed. You can rely on the compiler to enforce some of the rules that distinguish points from vectors. For example, your Point class will define an operator for subtracting two points but not an operator to add two points. If a user tries to add points, the compiler complains. However, as you add more functionality to the class, you will find that you have to enforce some of the rules at runtime, say, by generating exceptions. This is particularly true when computing an *affine sum of points*, a weighted sum of points where the weights sum to one, in which case the result is a point. This type of operation is what barycentric coordinates is about. Similarly, you can have an *affine difference of points*, a weighted sum of points where the weights sum to zero, in which case the result is a vector. This type of operation occurs when estimating derivatives of point-valued functions—the derivatives are vector quantities. Finally, if you then allow homogeneous points in general, where w can be any real-valued number, and you allow homogeneous transformations that include affine matrices and projection matrices, the rule enforcement becomes more complicated.

Over the years I have flip-flopped between enforcement of the distinction between points and vectors or simply having a single vector class. In the former case, the enforcement is complicated. In the latter case, the programmer is responsible for keeping the distinction in his head and enforcing the rules accordingly. In my last commercial endeavor I attempted to build a very general homogeneous algebra system, supporting linear algebra, affine algebra, and homogeneous operations, while at the same time having as much compiler support and runtime support for enforcing the rules. In the end, the programmers using the system still found ways to violate the point-vector distinction although not intentionally. My conclusion was that the effort spent trying to protect a programmer from inadvertently making errors was not justified by the maintenance costs. The bottom line is: You must understand and be adept at the mathematical abstractions, and you are responsible for getting it right in code. In GTEngine, I have implemented only the Vector class; there is no support for Point. The Matrix4x4 class allows you to use affine algebra, as shown in the next section.

6.4.2   Transformations

Affine transformations are the most frequent type of transformation encountered in 3D applications. Less frequent are projections, but these are necessary for 3D graphics applications, whether the drawing uses perspective or orthographic projection. Having to manipulate 4×4 matrices directly is sometimes error prone, whereby a programmer forgets to distinguish between a point and a vector. If there is no strong type checking, one might very well compute a difference of 4-tuple points (w-components are 1), the result a 4-tuple vector (w-component is 0), but assign the result to a point, thus overlooking the fact that the point now (incorrectly) has a w-component of 0. This is particularly a problem when the tuples and matrices are designed for SIMD support.

Additionally, programmers tend to think geometrically rather than algebraically when it comes to transformations. We have geometric intuition what it means to translate, scale, rotate, and shear. The algebraic details are once again part of the bookkeeping process. It is natural and convenient to provide a *transformation factory* for programmers to use. Such a factory allows one to specify the natural *channels* of translation, scaling, rotation, and shearing. Projection transformations represented as homogeneous 4×4 matrices are less intuitive geometrically than affine transformations, but these also may be created by a transformation factory.

In this section I am assuming the vector-on-the-right convention when using matrices and vectors. The actual convention can be hidden by the interface for the transformation factory.

6.4.2.1   Composition of Affine Transformations

The natural channels of an affine transformation include translation, scaling, rotation, and shearing. Composing these channels is a straightforward process, as shown next. As a reminder, we are using the right-handed coordinate system with origin $(0, 0, 0)$ and ordered axis direction vectors $(1, 0, 0)$, $(0, 1, 0)$, and $(0, 0, 1)$. We use the vector-on-the-right convention for matrix-vector multiplication.

Translation. The simplest of transformations is translation. In tuple form, if (t_0, t_1, t_2) is the specified translation, a tuple (x_0, x_1, x_2) is translated to $(y_0, y_1, y_2) = (x_0 + t_0, x_1 + t_1, x_2 + t_2)$. In affine form using 3×3 matrices,

$$\mathbf{Y} = \begin{bmatrix} y_0 \\ y_1 \\ y_2 \end{bmatrix} = \begin{bmatrix} x_0 + t_0 \\ x_1 + t_1 \\ x_2 + t_2 \end{bmatrix} = \begin{bmatrix} x_0 \\ x_1 \\ x_2 \end{bmatrix} + \begin{bmatrix} t_0 \\ t_1 \\ t_2 \end{bmatrix} = I\mathbf{X} + \mathbf{T} = \mathbf{X} + \mathbf{T} \quad (6.118)$$

where I is the 3×3 identity matrix. Linear transformations are of the form $\mathbf{Y} = A\mathbf{X}$, where A is a 3×3 matrix of constants, and where $\mathbf{X}$ and $\mathbf{Y}$ are vectors. The translation equation is of the form $\mathbf{Y} = I\mathbf{X} + \mathbf{T}$, where I is the 3×3 identity matrix. This is not a linear transformation because of the addition of the translation vector $\mathbf{T}$. It is an affine transformation.

This representation clouds the distinction between a point and a vector. If you noticed, I referred to $\mathbf{X}$, $\mathbf{Y}$, and $\mathbf{T}$ as vectors. No mention is made about points, yet translation is an affine transformation. Because $\mathbf{T}$ is the term that prevents the translation from being a linear one, we could say that $\mathbf{T}$ is a point rather than a vector. The consequence is that $\mathbf{X} + \mathbf{T}$ is the sum of a vector and a point. Our axioms of affine algebra state that the result must be a point, yet we have called $\mathbf{Y}$ a vector.

The problem lies in trying to think of $\mathbf{T}$ as either a point or a vector. The resolution is to use 4×4 matrices and the convention of the w-component of 0 for vectors and 1 for points. The affine form of translation is then

$$\left[\frac{\mathbf{Y}}{1} \right] = \begin{bmatrix} y_0 \\ y_1 \\ y_2 \\ 1 \end{bmatrix} = \begin{bmatrix} x_0 + t_0 \\ x_1 + t_1 \\ x_2 + t_2 \\ 1 \end{bmatrix} = \left[\begin{array}{ccc|c} 1 & 0 & 0 & t_0 \\ 0 & 1 & 0 & t_1 \\ 0 & 0 & 1 & t_2 \\ \hline 0 & 0 & 0 & 1 \end{array} \right] \begin{bmatrix} x_0 \\ x_1 \\ x_2 \\ 1 \end{bmatrix} \quad (6.119)$$

$$= H_T \left[\frac{\mathbf{X}}{1} \right] = \left[\frac{\mathbf{X} + \mathbf{T}}{1} \right]$$

The translation components are part of the homogeneous matrix H_T, so in this sense the translation is neither a point nor a vector. However, the difference of input and output points is

$$\left[\frac{\mathbf{Y}}{1} \right] - \left[\frac{\mathbf{X}}{1} \right] = \left[\frac{\mathbf{T}}{0} \right] \quad (6.120)$$

so the translation may be thought of a 4-tuple $(\mathbf{T}, 0)$ that is a vector, not a point.

We may summarize the block-matrix form of H_T, namely,

$$H_T = \left[\begin{array}{ccc|c} 1 & 0 & 0 & t_0 \\ 0 & 1 & 0 & t_1 \\ 0 & 0 & 1 & t_2 \\ \hline 0 & 0 & 0 & 1 \end{array}\right] = \left[\begin{array}{c|c} I & \mathbf{T} \\ \hline \mathbf{0}^\mathsf{T} & 1 \end{array}\right] \tag{6.121}$$

The inverse of the translation is $\mathbf{X} = \mathbf{Y} - \mathbf{T}$. The corresponding homogeneous inverse matrix is

$$H_T^{-1} = \left[\begin{array}{ccc|c} 1 & 0 & 0 & -t_0 \\ 0 & 1 & 0 & -t_1 \\ 0 & 0 & 1 & -t_2 \\ \hline 0 & 0 & 0 & 1 \end{array}\right] = \left[\begin{array}{c|c} I & -\mathbf{T} \\ \hline \mathbf{0}^\mathsf{T} & 1 \end{array}\right] \tag{6.122}$$

when applied to the 4-tuple $(\mathbf{Y}, 1)$, we obtain the 4-tuple $(\mathbf{X}, 1) = (\mathbf{Y} - \mathbf{T}, 1)$.

Scaling. Let s_0, s_1, and s_2 be nonzero scaling parameters. Although a scaling can be zero, typically we do not see this in a 3D application. Also, the scales are usually positive. A negative scale acts like a reflection and a positive scale in the corresponding axis direction. A tuple (x_0, x_1, x_2) is scaled by $(y_0, y_1, y_2) = (s_0 x_0, s_1 x_1, s_2 x_2)$. In affine form using 3×3 matrices,

$$\mathbf{Y} = \left[\begin{array}{c} y_0 \\ y_1 \\ y_2 \end{array}\right] = \left[\begin{array}{c} s_0 x_0 \\ s_1 x_1 \\ s_2 x_2 \end{array}\right] = \left[\begin{array}{ccc} s_0 & 0 & 0 \\ 0 & s_1 & 0 \\ 0 & 0 & s_2 \end{array}\right] \left[\begin{array}{c} x_0 \\ x_1 \\ x_2 \end{array}\right] = S\mathbf{X} \tag{6.123}$$

where S is the diagonal matrix of scales.

In affine form using 4×4 matrices,

$$\left[\begin{array}{c} \mathbf{Y} \\ \hline 1 \end{array}\right] = \left[\begin{array}{c} y_0 \\ y_1 \\ y_2 \\ \hline 1 \end{array}\right] = \left[\begin{array}{c} s_0 x_0 \\ s_1 x_1 \\ s_2 x_2 \\ \hline 1 \end{array}\right] = \left[\begin{array}{ccc|c} s_0 & 0 & 0 & 0 \\ 0 & s_1 & 0 & 0 \\ 0 & 0 & s_2 & 0 \\ \hline 0 & 0 & 0 & 1 \end{array}\right] \left[\begin{array}{c} x_0 \\ x_1 \\ x_2 \\ \hline 1 \end{array}\right]$$

$$= H_S \left[\begin{array}{c} \mathbf{X} \\ \hline 1 \end{array}\right] = \left[\begin{array}{c} S\mathbf{X} \\ \hline 1 \end{array}\right] \tag{6.124}$$

The scale components are part of the homogeneous matrix H_S.

We may summarize the block-matrix form of H_S, namely,

$$H_S = \left[\begin{array}{ccc|c} s_0 & 0 & 0 & 0 \\ 0 & s_1 & 0 & 0 \\ 0 & 0 & s_2 & 0 \\ \hline 0 & 0 & 0 & 1 \end{array}\right] = \left[\begin{array}{c|c} S & \mathbf{0} \\ \hline \mathbf{0}^\mathsf{T} & 1 \end{array}\right] \tag{6.125}$$

When the scales are nonzero, the inverse of the translation is $\mathbf{X} = S^{-1}\mathbf{Y}$. The corresponding homogeneous inverse matrix is

$$H_S^{-1} = \left[\begin{array}{ccc|c} \frac{1}{s_0} & 0 & 0 & 0 \\ 0 & \frac{1}{s_1} & 0 & 0 \\ 0 & 0 & \frac{1}{s_2} & 0 \\ \hline 0 & 0 & 0 & 1 \end{array}\right] = \left[\begin{array}{c|c} S^{-1} & \mathbf{0} \\ \hline \mathbf{0}^\mathsf{T} & 1 \end{array}\right] \tag{6.126}$$

when applied to the 4-tuple $(\mathbf{Y}, 1)$, we obtain the 4-tuple $(\mathbf{X}, 1) = (S^{-1}\mathbf{Y}, 1)$.

A special case of interest is *uniform scaling*, where the scales are all the same: $s_0 = s_1 = s_2$.

Rotation. The 3D rotation matrices were discussed previously, where positive angles correspond to counterclockwise rotations assuming the observer is looking at the rotation plane in the direction opposite that of the rotation axis. Let the rotation axis direction be the unit-length vector $\mathbf{U} = (u_0, u_1, u_2)$ and let the rotation angle be θ. Using the Rodrigues formula $R = I + (\sin\theta)S + (1 - \cos\theta)S^2$, where S is the skew symmetric matrix such that $S\mathbf{V} = \mathbf{U} \times \mathbf{V}$, a vector $\mathbf{X}$ is rotated to $\mathbf{Y} = R\mathbf{X}$. In affine form using 4×4 matrices,

$$\left[\begin{array}{c} \mathbf{Y} \\ \hline 1 \end{array}\right] = \left[\begin{array}{c|c} R & \mathbf{0} \\ \hline \mathbf{0}^\mathsf{T} & 1 \end{array}\right] \left[\begin{array}{c} \mathbf{X} \\ \hline 1 \end{array}\right] = H_R \left[\begin{array}{c} \mathbf{X} \\ \hline 1 \end{array}\right] \tag{6.127}$$

The inverse transformation is

$$\left[\begin{array}{c} \mathbf{X} \\ \hline 1 \end{array}\right] = \left[\begin{array}{c|c} R^\mathsf{T} & \mathbf{0} \\ \hline \mathbf{0}^\mathsf{T} & 1 \end{array}\right] \left[\begin{array}{c} \mathbf{Y} \\ \hline 1 \end{array}\right] = H_R^{-1} \left[\begin{array}{c} \mathbf{Y} \\ \hline 1 \end{array}\right] \tag{6.128}$$

The inverse transformation uses the fact that a rotation matrix is orthogonal, $R^\mathsf{T} R = I$.

Shearing. In 2D, shearing matrices are of the form

$$A = \left[\begin{array}{cc} 1 & a \\ 0 & 1 \end{array}\right], \quad B = \left[\begin{array}{cc} 1 & 0 \\ b & 1 \end{array}\right] \tag{6.129}$$

The matrix A represents a shear in the x_0-direction. The shearing of tuple (x_0, x_1) is $(y_0, y_1) = (x_0 + ax_1, x_1)$. Observe that the x_1-component are unchanged, so each tuple is moved along lines parallel to the x_0-axis. The matrix B represents a shear in the x_1-direction. The shearing of tuple (x_0, x_1) is $(y_0, y_1) = (x_0, x_1 + bx_0)$. Observe that the x_0-components is unchanged, so each tuple is moved along lines parallel to the x_1-axis.

In 3D, shearing matrices are

$$A = \left[\begin{array}{ccc} 1 & a_0 & a_1 \\ 0 & 1 & a_2 \\ 0 & 0 & 1 \end{array}\right], \quad B = \left[\begin{array}{ccc} 1 & 0 & 0 \\ b_0 & 1 & 0 \\ b_1 & b_2 & 1 \end{array}\right] \tag{6.130}$$

The corresponding 4×4 affine matrices are

$$H_A = \begin{bmatrix} 1 & a_0 & a_1 & 0 \\ 0 & 1 & a_2 & 0 \\ 0 & 0 & 1 & 0 \\ \hline 0 & 0 & 0 & 1 \end{bmatrix} = \left[\begin{array}{c|c} A & \mathbf{0} \\ \hline \mathbf{0}^\mathsf{T} & 1 \end{array} \right]$$

$$H_B = \begin{bmatrix} 1 & 0 & 0 & 0 \\ b_0 & 1 & 0 & 0 \\ b_1 & b_2 & 1 & 0 \\ \hline 0 & 0 & 0 & 1 \end{bmatrix} = \left[\begin{array}{c|c} B & \mathbf{0} \\ \hline \mathbf{0}^\mathsf{T} & 1 \end{array} \right]$$

(6.131)

The inverses are

$$H_A^{-1} = \begin{bmatrix} 1 & -a_0 & a_0 a_2 - a_1 & 0 \\ 0 & 1 & -a_2 & 0 \\ 0 & 0 & 1 & 0 \\ \hline 0 & 0 & 0 & 1 \end{bmatrix} = \left[\begin{array}{c|c} A^{-1} & \mathbf{0} \\ \hline \mathbf{0}^\mathsf{T} & 1 \end{array} \right]$$

$$H_B^{-1} = \begin{bmatrix} 1 & 0 & 0 & 0 \\ -b_0 & 1 & 0 & 0 \\ b_0 b_2 - b_1 & -b_2 & 1 & 0 \\ \hline 0 & 0 & 0 & 1 \end{bmatrix} = \left[\begin{array}{c|c} B^{-1} & \mathbf{0} \\ \hline \mathbf{0}^\mathsf{T} & 1 \end{array} \right]$$

(6.132)

The inverses are themselves shearing matrices. In the transform factory implementation using our vector-on-the-right convention, we use only shears for which the matrices are upper triangular.

Exercise 6.1 *Consider shearing matrices*

$$A_0 = \begin{bmatrix} 1 & a_0 \\ 0 & 1 \end{bmatrix}, \quad A_1 = \begin{bmatrix} 1 & 0 \\ a_1 & 1 \end{bmatrix}, \quad A_2 = \begin{bmatrix} 1 & a_2 \\ 0 & 1 \end{bmatrix}$$

Determine a_0, a_1, and a_2 so that the product $A_0 A_1 A_2$ is a rotation matrix. Show that every rotation matrix can be factored into a product of three shearing matrices.

Exercise 6.2 *Is it possible to factor a 3D rotation into a product of shearing matrices? If so, how many shearing matrices are needed and what is the formula?*

Composition of the Homogeneous Matrices. We may multiply any combination of translations, scalings, rotations, and shears, the end result an affine matrix. Generally, the product of two affine matrices is an affine matrix,

$$\left[\begin{array}{c|c} M_0 & \mathbf{T}_0 \\ \hline \mathbf{0}^\mathsf{T} & 1 \end{array} \right] \left[\begin{array}{c|c} M_1 & \mathbf{T}_1 \\ \hline \mathbf{0}^\mathsf{T} & 1 \end{array} \right] = \left[\begin{array}{c|c} M_0 M_1 & M_0 \mathbf{T}_1 + \mathbf{T}_0 \\ \hline \mathbf{0}^\mathsf{T} & 1 \end{array} \right]$$

(6.133)

Thus, it is simple enough to compose matrices as a product. The more difficult problem is how to decompose a matrix into translations, rotations, scalings, and shearings. That is the topic of the next section.

A special set of transformations is the set of *rigid transformations*. These consist of products of translations and rotations. An object for which all its points are transformed by translations and rotations retains its shape—only its location and orientation vary. A rigid transformation is of the form

$$H = \left[\begin{array}{c|c} R & \mathbf{T} \\ \hline \mathbf{0}^{\mathsf{T}} & 1 \end{array} \right] \tag{6.134}$$

Another special set of transformations involve only translations, uniform scalings, and rotations. I will call these *scaled rigid transformations*. Such a transformation is of the form

$$H = \left[\begin{array}{c|c} sR & \mathbf{T} \\ \hline \mathbf{0}^{\mathsf{T}} & 1 \end{array} \right] \tag{6.135}$$

for some scale $s \neq 0$.

Exercise 6.3 *Show that the product of rigid transformations is a rigid transformation. Show the inverse of a rigid transformation is a rigid transformation.*

Exercise 6.4 *Show that the product of scaled rigid transformations is a scaled rigid transformation. Show that the inverse of a scaled rigid transformation is a scaled rigid transformation.*

Exercise 6.5 *Consider the set of transformations consisting of shearings and translations. Show that the product of shear-translation transformations is a shear-translation transformation. Show that the inverse of a shear-translation transformation is a shear-translation transformation.*

Exercise 6.6 *What do translations, scalings, rotations, and shearings look like as 4×4 matrices using the vector-on-the-left convention?*

Exercise 6.7 *Equation (6.133) shows that the product of two affine matrices is an affine matrix. Therefore, the product of three affine matrices is an affine matrix. What is the final matrix resulting from a product of three affine matrices? What is the final matrix resulting from a product of four affine matrices? Generalize this to a closed-form equation for the product of n affine matrices.*

6.4.2.2 Decomposition of Affine Transformations

It is not always possible to factor a matrix M into a product of a rotation matrix, a scale matrix and a translation matrix. The translation part is always trivial to factor out, so consider M without translation. Generally, the best you can do is factor $M = LSR$ where L and R are rotation matrices and S is a diagonal matrix of nonnegative entries. This is referred to as a *singular value decomposition*. Related to this is the *polar decomposition*, $M = RS$, where R is a rotation matrix and S is a symmetric matrix. These factorizations are advanced topics; for example, see [18].

Any 3×3 invertible matrix M may be decomposed uniquely into the product of an orthogonal matrix, a scaling matrix with positive scales, and a shearing matrix. The first step in showing this involves the *QR decomposition*, which may be computed using Gram-Schmidt orthonormalization. Let $M = [\mathbf{M}_0 \, \mathbf{M}_1 \, \mathbf{M}_2]$, where the three vectors are the columns of M. Because M is invertible, $\mathbf{M}_0$ is not the zero vector and may be normalized:

$$\mathbf{Q}_0 = \frac{\mathbf{M}_0}{|\mathbf{M}_0|} \tag{6.136}$$

Because M is invertible, $\mathbf{M}_0$ and $\mathbf{M}_1$ cannot be parallel. Thus, projecting $\mathbf{M}_0$ onto the plane perpendicular to $\mathbf{Q}_0$ must produce a nonzero vector that is perpendicular to $\mathbf{Q}_0$ and may be normalized:

$$\mathbf{Q}_1 = \frac{\mathbf{M}_1 - (\mathbf{M}_1 \cdot \mathbf{Q}_0)\mathbf{Q}_0}{|\mathbf{M}_1 - (\mathbf{M}_1 \cdot \mathbf{Q}_0)\mathbf{Q}_0|} \tag{6.137}$$

Because M is invertible, $\mathbf{M}_2$ cannot lie in the plane spanned by $\mathbf{M}_0$ and $\mathbf{M}_1$, so projecting $\mathbf{M}_2$ onto the line perpendicular to that plane must produce a nonzero vector that is perpendicular to both $\mathbf{Q}_0$ and $\mathbf{Q}_1$ and may be normalized:

$$\mathbf{Q}_2 = \frac{\mathbf{M}_2 - (\mathbf{M}_2 \cdot \mathbf{Q}_0)\mathbf{Q}_0 - (\mathbf{M}_2 \cdot \mathbf{Q}_1)\mathbf{Q}_1}{|\mathbf{M}_2 - (\mathbf{M}_2 \cdot \mathbf{Q}_0)\mathbf{Q}_0 - (\mathbf{M}_2 \cdot \mathbf{Q}_1)\mathbf{Q}_1|} \tag{6.138}$$

By the construction of the $\mathbf{Q}_i$ vectors, the matrix $Q = [\mathbf{Q}_0 \, \mathbf{Q}_1 \, \mathbf{Q}_2]$ is orthogonal. It is a rotation matrix when the determinant of M is positive; it is a reflection matrix when the determinant of M is negative. We will see why in a moment.

The columns of Q are linearly independent vectors, so we may represent the columns of M in terms of those vectors. Moreover, some of the terms in the representation are not present because of how we constructed the columns of Q from the columns of M:

$$
\begin{aligned}
\mathbf{M}_0 &= (\mathbf{Q}_0 \cdot \mathbf{M}_0)\mathbf{Q}_0 + (0)\mathbf{Q}_1 + (0)\mathbf{Q}_1 \\
\mathbf{M}_1 &= (\mathbf{Q}_0 \cdot \mathbf{M}_1)\mathbf{Q}_0 + (\mathbf{Q}_1 \cdot \mathbf{M}_1)\mathbf{Q}_1 + (0)\mathbf{Q}_2 \\
\mathbf{M}_2 &= (\mathbf{Q}_0 \cdot \mathbf{M}_2)\mathbf{Q}_0 + (\mathbf{Q}_1 \cdot \mathbf{M}_2)\mathbf{Q}_1 + (\mathbf{Q}_2 \cdot \mathbf{M}_2)\mathbf{Q}_2
\end{aligned}
\tag{6.139}
$$

This is written in matrix form as

$$
\begin{aligned}
M &= [\mathbf{M}_0 \, \mathbf{M}_1 \, \mathbf{M}_2] \\
&= [\mathbf{Q}_0 \, \mathbf{Q}_1 \, \mathbf{Q}_2]
\begin{bmatrix}
\mathbf{Q}_0 \cdot \mathbf{M}_0 & \mathbf{Q}_0 \cdot \mathbf{M}_1 & \mathbf{Q}_0 \cdot \mathbf{M}_2 \\
0 & \mathbf{Q}_1 \cdot \mathbf{M}_1 & \mathbf{Q}_1 \cdot \mathbf{M}_2 \\
0 & 0 & \mathbf{Q}_2 \cdot \mathbf{M}_2
\end{bmatrix}
= QR
\end{aligned}
\tag{6.140}
$$

where the matrix R is upper triangular, but sometimes called right triangular, which is why R is used in the name of the decomposition.

The determinant may be computed as

$$\det(M) = \det(Q)\det(R) = \det(Q)(\mathbf{Q}_0 \cdot \mathbf{M}_0)(\mathbf{Q}_1 \cdot \mathbf{M}_1)(\mathbf{Q}_2 \cdot \mathbf{M}_2) \quad (6.141)$$

where $\det(Q) = +1$ when Q represents a rotation or $\det(Q) = -1$ when Q represents a reflection. The remaining terms on the right-hand side of the determinant equation turn out to be positive. Dotting equation (6.136) with $\mathbf{M}_0$ leads to

$$\mathbf{Q}_0 \cdot \mathbf{M}_0 = |\mathbf{M}_0| > 0 \qquad (6.142)$$

Dotting equation (6.137) with $\mathbf{M}_1$ and the orthonormality of the $\mathbf{Q}_i$ lead to

$$
\begin{aligned}
\mathbf{Q}_1 \cdot \mathbf{M}_1 &= \mathbf{Q}_1 \cdot [\mathbf{M}_1 - (\mathbf{Q}_0 \cdot \mathbf{M}_1)\mathbf{Q}_0] \\
&= |\mathbf{M}_1 - (\mathbf{Q}_0 \cdot \mathbf{M}_1)\mathbf{Q}_0| > 0
\end{aligned}
\qquad (6.143)
$$

Dotting equation (6.138) with $\mathbf{M}_2$ and using the orthonormality of the $\mathbf{Q}_i$ lead to

$$
\begin{aligned}
\mathbf{Q}_2 \cdot \mathbf{M}_2 &= \mathbf{Q}_2 \cdot [\mathbf{M}_2 - (\mathbf{Q}_0 \cdot \mathbf{M}_2)\mathbf{Q}_0 - (\mathbf{Q}_1 \cdot \mathbf{M}_2)\mathbf{Q}_1] \\
&= |\mathbf{M}_1 - (\mathbf{Q}_0 \cdot \mathbf{M}_1)\mathbf{Q}_0 - (\mathbf{Q}_0 \cdot \mathbf{M}_2)\mathbf{Q}_1| > 0
\end{aligned}
\qquad (6.144)
$$

Therefore, the Q is a rotation when $\det(M) > 0$ or Q is a reflection when $\det(M) < 0$.

The decomposition is unique when all we require is that M is invertible and Q is orthogonal. The diagonal entries of R are positive. If we define those diagonal entries by $s_i = \mathbf{Q}_i \cdot \mathbf{M}_i$ and define the scale matrix $S = \text{diagonal}(s_0, s_1, s_2)$, then the decomposition is $M = QCS$, where $C = RS^{-1}$ is an upper triangular matrix whose diagonal entries are all one. Thus, Q is orthogonal, C is a shearing matrix, and S is a scaling matrix.

If we always wish to have a decomposition where Q is a rotation matrix, then the uniqueness of the decomposition is not possible. To see this, suppose Q is a reflection matrix. We can negate one of its columns to obtain a rotation matrix. To preserve the equality in the decomposition, we in turn must negate the diagonal entry of R in that same column. This gives us three possibilities for factoring M into a rotation, a shearing, and a scaling. Eliminating the reflection means introducing a negative scale.

The construction here should make it clear why reflections and negative scales are both undesirable in most 3D applications. If we *require* that any 3×3 matrix M used in an affine transformation have positive determinant, then we will have a unique decomposition $M = RCS$, where R is a rotation matrix (notice the switch in notation from Q to R), C is an upper-triangular shearing matrix, and S is a scaling matrix of positive scales. This *requirement* is the foundation for the transformation factory whose implementation is provided later. The factory allows us to create transformations by manipulating only translations, rotations, upper-triangular shearings, and positive scalings.

6.4.2.3 A Simple Transformation Factory

Let us first consider 4×4 affine transformations,

$$H = \left[\begin{array}{c|c} M & \mathbf{T} \\ \hline \mathbf{0}^{\mathsf{T}} & 1 \end{array} \right] \tag{6.145}$$

A programmer can manipulate the twelve entries of M and $\mathbf{T}$ directly, choosing them to represent the desired translation, scaling, rotation, and shearing. If M is known to be a composition of rotation and uniform scale, we might wish to update only the scale or only the rotation. This requires decomposing $M = Rs$, where R is the rotation matrix and s is the scale. Knowing M is of this form, the scale is the length of the first column of M and, in fact, the length of any column of M. The rotation matrix is extracted by normalizing the columns of M:

$$M = [\mathbf{M}_0 \ \mathbf{M}_1 \ \mathbf{M}_2] \rightarrow s = |\mathbf{M}_0|, \quad R = M/s \tag{6.146}$$

The scale and/or rotation may be updated and composed to form the new matrix M.

Similarly, if M is known to be a composition of rotation and shearing, we might wish to update only the rotation or only the shearing. The programmer must use Gram-Schmidt orthonormalization to decompose $M = RC$, where R is a rotation and C is a shear. In this case, though, knowing the order of composition is important. We might have built $M = CR$, in which case the decomposition is different. Having the programmer remember the order of composition and the process of decomposing matrix is typically cumbersome, repetitive, and error prone. It makes sense to specify the order of composition of the individual components and to provide a factory that encapsulates the details of the composition and decomposition.

As discussed previously, if we require $\det(M) > 0$, we can factor $M = RCS$ uniquely, where R is a rotation matrix, C is an upper-triangular shearing matrix, and S is a scaling matrix of positive scales. The affine matrix has twelve independent components; the last row is always $(0, 0, 0, 1)$. We wish to store the translation, scale, rotation, and shear and allow the programmer to set and get these as desired. When the programmer requests the composition of these as an affine matrix, the factory will do so at that time.

The translation has three components, (t_0, t_1, t_2). The scales are (s_0, s_1, s_2) with the understanding that all three scales are equal when we want uniform scaling. The rotation matrix has nine elements, but we can store it instead as a quaternion with components $q = q_0 i + q_1 j + q_2 k + q_3$. We know that $-q$ also represents the rotation, so if we require $q_3 \geq 0$ and take advantage of the unit length of q as a 4-tuple, we can reduce the storage to (q_0, q_1, q_2). The factory is responsible for computing $q_3 = \sqrt{1 - q_0^2 - q_1^2 - q_2^2}$ at the time the affine matrix is requested. The shearing matrix has 3 unknown components, (c_0, c_1, c_2). In total, the factory must only store twelve numbers for the channels used to build the affine matrix, so the memory requirements are the same as those for storing M and $\mathbf{T}$ generally. The advantage of the separate channels, though, is that the programmer can manipulate them in a geometrically intuitive manner and not have to worry about the mathematical details of the composition or decomposition.

The simple transformation factory may be extended to support projection matrices, including those for a symmetric view frustum, for a nonsymmetric view frustum, and for a convex quadrilateral viewport.

In GTEngine, we have provided a transformation factory for the most commonly used channels: translation, rotation (with multiple representations), and nonzero uniform scaling. The class interface is shown in Listing 6.41.

```cpp
template <typename Real>
class Transform : public Matrix4x4<Real>
{
public:
    // Construction and destruction. The default constructor generates the
    // identity transformation.
    ~Transform ();
    Transform ();
    Transform (Transform const& transform);

    // Assignment.
    Transform& operator= (Transform const& transform);

    // Set the transformation to the identity.
    void SetIdentity ();

    // The quaternion is unit length.
    void SetQuaternion (Quaternion<Real> const& q);
    Quaternion<Real> GetQuaternion () const;

    // The axis is unit length and the angle is in radians.
    void SetAxisAngle (AxisAngle <4,Real> const& axisAngle);
    AxisAngle <4,Real> GetAxisAngle () const;

    // The Euler angles are in radians. The GetEulerAngles function
    // expects the eulerAngles.axis[] values to be set to the axis order
    // you want.
    void SetEulerAngles (EulerAngles<Real> const& eulerAngles);
    void GetEulerAngles (EulerAngles<Real>& eulerAngles) const;

    // The caller must ensure that the input to SetRotation is a rotation
    // matrix.
    void SetRotation (Matrix4x4<Real> const& rotation);
    Matrix4x4<Real> GetRotation () const;

    // The scale is a nonzero number.
    void SetScale (Real scale);
    Real GetScale () const;

    // No constraints exist for the translation components. The second
    // Set* function uses only the first three components of
    // 'translation'. The Get*W* functions store the translation in the
    // first three components of the output. The fourth component is w=0
    // or w=1 depending on which function you call.
    void SetTranslation (Real x0, Real x1, Real x2);
    Vector3<Real> GetTranslation () const;
    void SetTranslation (Vector4<Real> const& translation);
    Vector4<Real> GetTranslationW0 () const;
    Vector4<Real> GetTranslationW1 () const;
```

```
// Multiplication of transforms.   M0 is 'this', M1 is 'transform',
// and the function returns M0*M1.
Transform<Real> operator* (Transform<Real> const& transform ) const;

private :
    // Compute the base−class Matrix4x4<Real> from the channels.
    void UpdateMatrix ();

    Quaternion<Real> mQuaternion;
    Real mTranslation[3] , mScale;
};
```

LISTING 6.41: The Transform class in GTEngine.

The Transform class stores the individual channels for rotation, translation, and uniform scale. Each Set* operation invokes the private UpdateMatrix that computes the actual 4×4 affine representation and stores it in the Matrix4x4 base-class member.

The class works for either matrix-vector multiplication conventions. The translation handling allows you to set the w-component when using affine algebra, which allows you to manipulate a translation as either a point or a vector. The multiplication operator is convenient for products of transforms, especially for scene graph transformation hierarchies; see classes Spatial and Node.

6.4.3   Coordinate System Conventions

I will focus on the most common coordinate systems, those where the axis directions form an orthonormal set. This naturally ties coordinate systems to the concepts of rotation. Let us review briefly rotation in the xy-plane. The classical view is to select the (x, y) coordinates so that the positive x-axis is directed rightward and the positive y-axis is directed upward, as is shown in Figure 6.8.

The length of the vector (x_0, y_0) is $r = \sqrt{x_0^2 + y_0^2}$. From basic trigonometry, $x_0 = r \cos \phi$ and $y_0 = r \sin \phi$. Because (x_1, y_1) is obtained by rotating (x_0, y_0), its length is also r. Also from basic trignometry, $x_1 = r \cos(\theta + \phi)$ and $y_1 = r \sin(\theta + \phi)$. Therefore,

$$x_1 = r \cos(\theta + \phi) = r \cos \theta \cos \phi - r \sin \theta \sin \phi = x_0 \cos \theta - y_0 \sin \theta$$
$$y_1 = r \sin(\theta + \phi) = r \sin \theta \cos \phi + r \cos \theta \sin \phi = x_0 \sin \theta + y_0 \cos \theta$$

The visualization of the problem is an appeal to geometry. The construction uses trigonometry. The final aspect is bookkeeping, where we algebraically write the equations in tabular form as a matrix-vector product.

$$\begin{bmatrix} x_1 \\ y_1 \end{bmatrix} = \begin{bmatrix} \cos \theta & -\sin \theta \\ \sin \theta & \cos \theta \end{bmatrix} \begin{bmatrix} x_0 \\ y_0 \end{bmatrix} \tag{6.147}$$

This should be a familiar formula that you have used for rotating vectors in the plane.

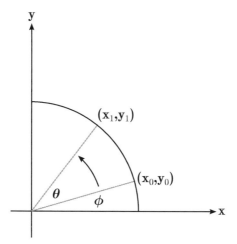

FIGURE 6.8: Illustration of a counterclockwise rotation of (x_0, y_0) to (x_1, y_1) by a positive angle θ measured from the positive x-axis. The positive angle ϕ is the angle between the x-axis and the initial point (x_0, y_0). The positive angle $\theta + \phi$ is the angle between the x-axis and the final point (x_1, y_1).

A substantial amount of terminology was introduced for constructing Equation (6.147), which represents a rotation in the xy-plane. Most of us would construct the equation without thinking twice about our conventions, but indeed we have several issues that need addressing. It is important to document the conventions you are using for your coordinate systems.

- *Clearly Defined Coordinate System.* The origin is the point $(0,0)$. Although this is not specifically stated in the chapter introduction, you probably assumed this to be the case based on Figure 6.8. The figure also clearly defines the coordinate axis directions, which numerically you would intuitively choose as $(1,0)$ for the x-axis direction and $(0,1)$ for the y-axis direction.

- *Points or Vectors?* It is not clear whether the 2-tuple (x, y) refers to a point in the plane or is a vector measured relative to the origin $(0,0)$. Equation (6.147) intends for the 2-tuples to be vectors.

- *Which Handedness?* The coordinate system is defined to be *right handed*. This is an arbitrary convention in 2D, without appeal to the right-hand rule for cross products in 3D. However, right handedness is the standard choice for the geometry shown in Figure 6.8. When processing 2D images, it is typical to use *left-handed coordinates*, where the origin is the upper-left corner of the image, the x-axis is directed rightward, and the y-axis is directed downward.

- *Angle Measurement and Rotation Direction.* The caption of Figure 6.8 specifies that the angles are measured from the positive x-axis, and that a *positive angle* corresponds to a *counterclockwise rotation.* Although the use of the terms clockwise and counterclockwise rotation are standard, not all clocks have hands that move the way you expect![2] I will assume that we all agree what clockwise and counterclockwise refer to.

- *Column or Row Vectors?* Equation (6.147) has a tabular form that represents the 2-tuples as 2×1 column vectors. The matrix-vector product uses what I refer to as the *vector-on-the-right* convention. I could have easily used a *vector-on-the-left* convention, whereby the 2-tuples are represented as 1×2 row vectors. This changes the tabular format of the equation.

- *Matrix Data Storage.* Although this is a concept that is irrelevant mathematically, it is important when implementing vector and matrix algebra on a computer. The two standard choices are to store the 2D-array data in 1D-memory either in row-major or column-major order. At first glance this might be viewed as an arbitrary choice, but there are performance consequences to consider (discussed later in this chapter).

Is this much ado about nothing? In my experience, no. The most annoying aspect of working with someone else's mathematics library is when the conventions are not clearly stated. You have to rely on code samples that use that library in order to reverse engineer the conventions, either by reading those samples or by writing your own and executing the code to see the relationships among inputs and outputs. Moreover, the conventions stated here have dependencies. It is absolutely essential that you make clear what your conventions are. To stress the importance, let us further look at the 2D rotation problem.

Suppose that you are using a mathematics library that supports 2D rotation and the comment in the source code is that of Listing 6.42.

```
// The 2D rotation matrix for the library is of the form
//    +-              -+
// R = | cos(t)  -sin(t) |
//    | sin(t)   cos(t) |
//    +-              -+
```

LISTING 6.42: Incomplete comments describing the form of a 2D rotation matrix.

At least the code has some comments, but they are not sufficient for you to understand the conventions. If R is intended to be used according to the conventions described previously in this chapter, then you need to be told

---

[2]When I was in 9th grade, my homeroom was the Electric Shop. We salvaged useable components from Army Surplus equipment, such as transistors the size of your little fingertip. We were entertained by an odd piece of equipment—a clock whose numbers were the opposite order you are used to and whose hands moved in the opposite direction you are used to. That throws a wrench into a consistent definition of clockwise and counterclockwise.

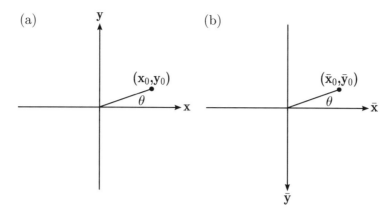

FIGURE 6.9: A point in the world located with different coordinates systems. (a) The coordinate system (x, y) is right handed. (b) The coordinate system $(\bar{x}, \bar{y})$ is left handed.

this. What if the library provider uses the vector-on-the-left and positive-angle-counterclockwise conventions? In this case, R represents a rotation in the opposite direction from that with vector-on-the-right and positive-angle-counterclockwise. What if the library provider uses the vector-on-the-left and positive-angle-clockwise conventions? Now R represents the rotation we discussed when using vector-on-the-right and positive-angle-counterclockwise.

Wait! The analysis of the previous paragraph is based on the assumptions that the coordinate system is right handed and that angles are measured from the positive x-axis. Figure 6.9 compares the two systems with different handedness. If (x_0, y_0) is a specific point in the right-handed system, its representation in the left-handed system is $(\bar{x}_0, \bar{y}_0) = (x_0, -y_0)$. Let r be the length of the tuples as vectors. Assuming the right-handed system uses the vector-on-the-right and positive-angle-counterclockwise conventions, (x_0, y_0) is obtained by rotating $(r, 0)$ counterclockwise by the angle $\theta > 0$. The matrix R represents the rotation. The same matrix represents the rotation when using vector-on-the-left and positive-angle-clockwise conventions. In fact, R represents the rotation in the left-handed system as long as that system uses the vector-on-the-right and positive-angle-clockwise conventions or if it uses the vector-on-the-left and positive-angle-counterclockwise conventions. In all four cases, the angle is measured from the positive rightward axis.

For notation's sake, let us use the acronyms RHS for right-handed system, LHS for left-handed system, VOR for vector-on-the-right, VOL for vector-on-the-left, CW for positive-angle-clockwise, and CCW for positive-angle-counterclockwise. Table 6.2 shows the combination of conventions for which R is the rotation matrix and for which R^{T} is the rotation matrix. As is apparent, the handedness, the vector-multiplication convention, and the direction of rotation are interdependent. In fact, if you change one of these three attributes, the matrix you should choose is the transpose of the one chosen before the

TABLE 6.2: Rotation conventions

R is the rotation matrix			R^{T} is the rotation matrix		
RHS	VOR	CCW	RHS	VOR	CW
RHS	VOL	CW	RHS	VOL	CCW
LHS	VOR	CW	LHS	VOR	CCW
LHS	VOL	CCW	LHS	VOL	CW

change. Three attributes, each having two choices, leads to eight possibilities, as Table 6.2 shows. It is important to make clear how you have chosen these conventions.

6.4.4 Converting between Coordinate Systems

Consider a simple case of converting between two coordinate systems, one a right-handed system and one a left-handed system, both based at their natural origins. Figure 6.10 illustrates. Both coordinate system origins are at the Cartesian frame origin $(0,0,0)$. The Cartesian coordinate axis directions are $(1,0,0)$ in the right direction, $(0,1,0)$ into the plane of the page, and $(0,0,1)$ in the up direction. The coordinate axis directions for the first system are the same as those for the Cartesian frame. Observe that $(1,0,0) \times (0,1,0) = (0,0,1)$, so the last vector is the cross product of the first two. Geometrically, these conform to the *right-hand rule* for cross products, so the coordinate system is *right handed*. The coordinate axis directions for the second system in the order specified by (x'_0, x'_1, x'_2) *and in terms of the same common Cartesian frame as the first system* are $(1,0,0)$, $(0,0,1)$, and $(0,1,0)$. Observe that $(1,0,0) \times (0,0,1) = (0,-1,0)$, so the last vector is the negative cross product of the first two. These conform to the *left-hand rule* for cross products, so the coordinate system is *left handed*.

The conversion details are driven by the geometry of the images in the figure. The axes are all aligned but their names are different. The x_i coordinate of the first system and the x'_i coordinate correspond to the same measurement along their common axis. We can set up a matrix equation that relates the measurements,

$$\mathbf{X}' = \begin{bmatrix} x'_0 \\ x'_1 \\ x'_2 \end{bmatrix} = \begin{bmatrix} 1 & 0 & 0 \\ 0 & 0 & 1 \\ 0 & 1 & 0 \end{bmatrix} \begin{bmatrix} x_0 \\ x_1 \\ x_2 \end{bmatrix} = C\mathbf{X} \tag{6.148}$$

where the last equation defines the 3×3 matrix C. The matrix C swaps the last two components of a vector. The matrix is orthogonal, because $C^{\mathsf{T}}C = I$, and $\det(C) = -1$, which makes the matrix a reflection. The conversion in the other direction is

$$\begin{bmatrix} x_0 \\ x_1 \\ x_2 \end{bmatrix} \begin{bmatrix} 1 & 0 & 0 \\ 0 & 0 & 1 \\ 0 & 1 & 0 \end{bmatrix} \begin{bmatrix} x'_0 \\ x'_1 \\ x'_2 \end{bmatrix} = C^{-1} \begin{bmatrix} x'_0 \\ x'_1 \\ x'_2 \end{bmatrix} \tag{6.149}$$

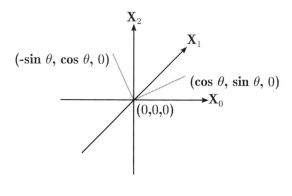

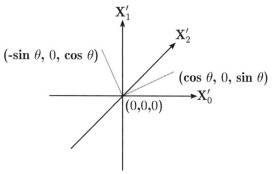

FIGURE 6.10: Conversion from (x_0, x_1, x_2) in a right-handed coordinate system to (x_0', x_1', x_2') in a left-handed coordinate system.

It so happens that $C^{-1} = C^{\mathsf{T}} = C$. For orthonormal coordinate axes, generally $C^{-1} = C^{\mathsf{T}}$.

Equations (6.148) and (6.149) are easy enough to set up based on a visual inspection of the coordinate axes. Now suppose that we have a rotation in the first coordinate system, and that rotation is represented by a rotation matrix R. We want to determine the rotation matrix R' in the second coordinate system that produces the same rotation. For example, suppose we rotate points about the z-axis by a small angle θ. The left image of Figure 6.10 shows the action of the rotation for inputs $(1, 0, 0)$ and $(0, 1, 0)$. The right image shows the same action, which is a rotation in the $x'z'$-plane. The transformations are

$$
\mathbf{U} = \begin{bmatrix} u_0 \\ u_1 \\ u_2 \end{bmatrix} = \begin{bmatrix} c & -s & 0 \\ s & c & 0 \\ 0 & 0 & 1 \end{bmatrix} \begin{bmatrix} x_0 \\ x_1 \\ x_2 \end{bmatrix} = R\mathbf{X}
$$

$$
\mathbf{U}' = \begin{bmatrix} u_0' \\ u_1' \\ u_2' \end{bmatrix} = \begin{bmatrix} c & 0 & -s \\ 0 & 1 & 0 \\ s & 0 & c \end{bmatrix} \begin{bmatrix} x_0' \\ x_1' \\ x_2' \end{bmatrix} = R'\mathbf{X}'
$$

(6.150)

where $c = \cos\theta$ and $s = \sin\theta$. The linear-algebraic relationship between R and R' is obtained by substituting Equations (6.148) and (6.149) for both inputs and outputs into the last equation, $R'\mathbf{X} = \mathbf{U}' = C\mathbf{U} = CR\mathbf{X} = CRC^{-1}\mathbf{X}'$, in which case

$$R' = CRC^{-1}, \quad R = C^{-1}R'C \tag{6.151}$$

This is known in linear algebra as a *change of basis*. We can represent the same geometric action in two different coordinate systems. In our case, the domain and range of the transformation have the same basis. Change of basis is more general in that you can have different bases for the domain and range.

Let us generalize for a more complicated setting. Suppose that the right-handed coordinate system has origin at a point $\mathbf{P}$ and the left-handed coordinate system has an origin at a point $\mathbf{P}'$. To determine the conversion between systems, we can reduce this case to the one discussed previously by subtracting the origins from our points to form vectors. Equation (6.148) is compactly written as $\mathbf{X}' = C\mathbf{X}$. In our current scenario, the equation becomes

$$\mathbf{X}' - \mathbf{P}' = C\left(\mathbf{X} - \mathbf{P}\right) \tag{6.152}$$

Equation (6.149) is compactly written as $\mathbf{X} = C^{-1}\mathbf{X}'$. In our current scenario, the equation becomes

$$\mathbf{X} - \mathbf{P} = C^{-1}\left(\mathbf{X}' - \mathbf{P}'\right) \tag{6.153}$$

Equation (6.152) may be written using points and affine matrices,

$$\begin{bmatrix} I & -\mathbf{P}' \\ \mathbf{0}^\mathsf{T} & 1 \end{bmatrix} \begin{bmatrix} \mathbf{X}' \\ 1 \end{bmatrix} = \begin{bmatrix} C & \mathbf{0} \\ \mathbf{0}^\mathsf{T} & 1 \end{bmatrix} \begin{bmatrix} I & -\mathbf{P} \\ \mathbf{0}^\mathsf{T} & 1 \end{bmatrix} \begin{bmatrix} \mathbf{X} \\ 1 \end{bmatrix} \tag{6.154}$$

and then inverting the matrix on the left and multiplying both sides of the equation and composing products:

$$\begin{bmatrix} \mathbf{X}' \\ 1 \end{bmatrix} = \begin{bmatrix} C & \mathbf{P}' - C\mathbf{P} \\ \mathbf{0}^\mathsf{T} & 1 \end{bmatrix} \begin{bmatrix} \mathbf{X} \\ 1 \end{bmatrix} = A \begin{bmatrix} \mathbf{X} \\ 1 \end{bmatrix} \tag{6.155}$$

where the last equality defines the 4×4 matrix A. Similarly, Equation (6.153) becomes

$$\begin{bmatrix} \mathbf{X} \\ 1 \end{bmatrix} = \begin{bmatrix} C^{-1} & \mathbf{P} - C^{-1}\mathbf{P}' \\ \mathbf{0}^\mathsf{T} & 1 \end{bmatrix} \begin{bmatrix} \mathbf{X} \\ 1 \end{bmatrix} = A^{-1} \begin{bmatrix} \mathbf{X}' \\ 1 \end{bmatrix} \tag{6.156}$$

This is referred to as an *affine change of basis*.

The conversion of matrices is similar to the original example. Geometrically, the rotation in the right-handed coordinate system is about the axis containing the origin $\mathbf{P}$ with x_2-axis direction. The same rotation in the left-handed coordinate system is about the axis containing the origin $\mathbf{P}'$ with x_1'-axis direction. We may subtract the origins to obtain vectors that are rotated as shown previously,

$$\mathbf{U} - \mathbf{P} = R(\mathbf{X} - \mathbf{P}), \quad \mathbf{U}' - \mathbf{P}' = R'(\mathbf{X}' - \mathbf{P}') \tag{6.157}$$

$$
\begin{array}{ccc}
 & M' & \\
H & \longrightarrow & H \\
A \uparrow\downarrow A^{-1} & & A \uparrow\downarrow A^{-1} \\
H & \longrightarrow & H \\
 & M &
\end{array}
$$

FIGURE 6.11: The commutative diagram that shows how transformations are related via a change of basis.

Applying the change of basis for both inputs and outputs,

$$
R'(\mathbf{X}' - \mathbf{P}') = \mathbf{U}' - \mathbf{P}' = C(\mathbf{U} - \mathbf{P}) = CR(\mathbf{X} - \mathbf{P}) = CRC^{-1}(\mathbf{X}' - \mathbf{P}') \quad (6.158)
$$

Of course we already know that $R' = CRC^{-1}$, but the equation allows us to represent the relationship between the rotations using affine matrices. The transformation for the right-handed coordinate system involves translating the coordinate system origin $\mathbf{P}$ to the Cartesian origin, rotating about the up axis, then translating back to $\mathbf{P}$. The transformation is

$$
\begin{aligned}
\begin{bmatrix} \mathbf{U} \\ 1 \end{bmatrix} &= \begin{bmatrix} I & \mathbf{P} \\ \mathbf{0}^\mathsf{T} & 1 \end{bmatrix} \begin{bmatrix} R & \mathbf{0} \\ \mathbf{0}^\mathsf{T} & 1 \end{bmatrix} \begin{bmatrix} I & -\mathbf{P} \\ \mathbf{0}^\mathsf{T} & 1 \end{bmatrix} \begin{bmatrix} \mathbf{X} \\ 1 \end{bmatrix} \\
&= \begin{bmatrix} R & \mathbf{P} - R\mathbf{P} \\ \mathbf{0}^\mathsf{T} & 1 \end{bmatrix} \begin{bmatrix} \mathbf{X} \\ 1 \end{bmatrix} = M \begin{bmatrix} \mathbf{X} \\ 1 \end{bmatrix}
\end{aligned}
\quad (6.159)
$$

where the last equality defines the 4×4 matrix M. The transformation for the left-handed coordinate system is

$$
\begin{aligned}
\begin{bmatrix} \mathbf{U}' \\ 1 \end{bmatrix} &= \begin{bmatrix} I & \mathbf{P}' \\ \mathbf{0}^\mathsf{T} & 1 \end{bmatrix} \begin{bmatrix} R' & \mathbf{0} \\ \mathbf{0}^\mathsf{T} & 1 \end{bmatrix} \begin{bmatrix} I & -\mathbf{P}' \\ \mathbf{0}^\mathsf{T} & 1 \end{bmatrix} \begin{bmatrix} \mathbf{X}' \\ 1 \end{bmatrix} \\
&= \begin{bmatrix} R' & \mathbf{P}' - R'\mathbf{P}' \\ \mathbf{0}^\mathsf{T} & 1 \end{bmatrix} \begin{bmatrix} \mathbf{X}' \\ 1 \end{bmatrix} = M' \begin{bmatrix} \mathbf{X}' \\ 1 \end{bmatrix}
\end{aligned}
\quad (6.160)
$$

where the last equality defines the 4×4 matrix M'. The transformations M and M' are related by

$$
M' = AMA^{-1}, \quad M = A^{-1}M'A \quad (6.161)
$$

The relationship is summarized by the *commutative diagram* shown in Figure 6.11. In fact, this diagram is valid for any affine transformation M and any change of basis, even if the bases are nonorthogonal sets. The symbol H denotes the space of 4-tuple points. In the bottom row, the domain of the transformation is the leftmost H, and M maps the domain to the range, which is the rightmost H. Alternatively, you can follow the path from lower-left H to upper-left H (apply A), to upper-right H (apply M'), and then to lower-right H (apply A^{-1}). That is, M and $A^{-1}M'A$ produce the same result, where application of matrices is from right to left (vector-on-the-right convention). Similarly, you can apply M' from upper-left H to upper-right H or you can equivalently traverse from upper-left to lower-left to lower-right to upper-right using AMA^{-1}.

For orthonormal bases, the process is automated for you except the very first step: You must visualize how the coordinate axes are overlayed and you must then construct the matrix C. That's geometry. The rest is algebra.

The process applies even for general bases but creating the change of basis matrix is slightly more complicated. Let the basis for the first coordinate system be $\{\mathbf{V}_0, \mathbf{V}_1, \mathbf{V}_2\}$ and the basis for the second coordinate system be $\{\mathbf{V}'_0, \mathbf{V}'_1, \mathbf{V}'_2\}$. The change of basis matrix C has the property that $\mathbf{V}'_i = C\mathbf{V}_i$ for all i. If V is the matrix whose columns are the $\mathbf{V}_i$ and V' is the matrix whose columns are the $\mathbf{V}'_i$, then $V' = CV$. We can invert V to obtain $C = V'V^{-1}$.

The conversions of transformations assumed both coordinate systems use the vector-on-the-right multiplication convention. If either or both coordinate systems use the vector-on-the-left convention, you can still use the conversion here but you must transpose each matrix that uses the vector-on-the-left convention, apply the conversion, then transpose the result. For example, if the first coordinate system uses vector-on-the-right and the second coordinate system uses vector-on-the-left, the transformation M' for the second coordinate system is $(M')^{\mathsf{T}} = AMA^{-1}$. If the first coordinate system uses vector-on-the-left and the second coordinate system uses vector-on-the-right, the relationship is $M' = AM^{\mathsf{T}}A^{-1}$. If both use vector-on-the-right, then $(M')^{\mathsf{T}} = AM^{\mathsf{T}}A^{-1}$.

Chapter 7

Sample Applications

7.1 Video Streams

The video stream sample illustrates the parallel copying that was mentioned in Section 4.7. The application is located at

GeometricTools/GTEngine/Samples/Graphics/VideoStreams

A video stream is a collection of images through time. Some application domains have multiple video streams, presumably synchronized in time. Stereo vision is one such domain where you have two streams, one per camera. The goal is to process the images as they arrive from their producer, whether live camera feeds or recordings on disk.

Although it would be nice to demonstrate the concept with real video data, that is a lot of data to download from the Geometric Tools website. For the sake of reducing bandwidth, four video streams are generated randomly by the sample and written to disk. Later, the streams are loaded from disk and are processed using a producer-consumer model. The producer is the file loader, which runs in its own thread, and the consumer is the main thread that displays the images in the application window. Because the randomly generated images are not interesting, I have not provided any screen captures for this book.

7.1.1 The VideoStream Class

The abstract base class VideoStream encapsulates the behavior for processing a stream of images. It provides a frame capturing system that calls a virtual function, GetImage, to access a single image in the stream. Each derived class overrides GetImage; in our case, the class is FileVideoStream that loads the next available image from disk. If you were building a system driven by live cameras, a class CameraVideoSystem can be implemented whose GetImage obtains the next available image from the camera.

The image is stored in a GTEngine Texture2 object of the appropriate format and size so that it can be processed by the GPU. A frame is defined as a structure that contains a Texture2 image, a unique frame number, and the time (in ticks) required to acquire the image from the producer and copy it to

GPU memory. The latter value is simply for performance measurements and might not be necessary for other applications. Listing 7.1 shows the code for acquiring the image and creating the texture.

```
void VideoStream :: CaptureFrame ()
{
    int64_t startTicks = mProductionTimer.GetTicks ();
    char* data = GetImage ();
    if (data)
    {
        mFrame.image.reset (
            new Texture2 (mType, mWidth, mHeight, false, false ));
        mFrame.image->SetData (data);
        mEngine->Bind (mFrame.image);
        mFrame.image->SetData (nullptr);
    }
    int64_t finalTicks = mProductionTimer.GetTicks ();
    mFrame.ticks = finalTicks - startTicks;
    mPerformanceTicks = mPerformanceTimer.GetTicks ();
    ++mPerformanceFrames;
}
```

LISTING 7.1: Acquiring an image and creating a texture from it.

The timer is started and a call is made to acquire the image. In our case, the call leads to a load of the image from disk. For typical images, the size is large enough that in a single-threaded program, the disk load can cause a noticeable stall. If the producer cannot provide an image when requested, it has the option of returning a null pointer as a signal that the consumer the data is not available—a dropped frame, so to speak.

When the data is available, a Texture2 object is created from the known format mType with the known sizes mWidth and mHeight. The first false parameter says we do not want mipmaps for this texture, which is a message to the engine to create the GPU version without mipmaps. The second false parameter says we do *not* want a system memory copy in which to store the texture. We could have used the default creation using the default-initialized inputs and then copied the image data to the system memory, using

```
mFrame.image.reset (new Texture2 (mType, mWidth, mHeight ));
memcpy (mFrame.image->GetData (), data, mFrame.image->GetNumBytes ());
mEngine->Bind (mFrame.image);
```

but this leads to an extra copy—from CPU to CPU—that is inefficient. Instead, the GTEngine Resource base class (for Texture2) allows you to specify a pointer to data that is used as the data source when the Bind call creates the GPU version of the resource.

After the capture and creation of the GPU version of the texture, the timer is stopped. The application displays the performance statistics overlaid on top of the application window.

7.1.2   The VideoStreamManager Class

It is convenient to have a manager class for multiple video streams, especially when the streams need to be synchronized (as they do in stereo vision).

The class VideoStreamManager provides the necessary mananagement, and it also has summary statistics for the performance for all the video streams. In this sample, the number of video streams is four.

The class has support for various methods of capturing, both in serial and in parallel, to demonstrate the performance characteristics of each approach. You can change the method by exposing one of four conditional defines in the VideoStreamsWindow.h file. Their names involve MANUAL or TRIGGERED. The former means that the frame capture is explicitly launched by calls in the main thread. The latter means that the frame capture is implicitly launched by a separate thread using a timer that is designed to deliver frames at a fixed rate. The names also involve SERIAL or PARALLEL. The former means that the video streams are captured one at a time. The latter means the frames are captured by launching threads for all the streams and waiting for them all to finish.

Regardless of the capture method, once all video frames are available they must be assembled into an aggregrate frame. The frame data structure for VideoStreamManager consists of an array of Texture2 images—one per video stream and presumably synchronized to be images captured of the same scene, a unique frame number, and the time (in ticks) required to acquire all the images and copying them to GPU memory. The latter value is for performance measurements and might not be necessary for other applications. To support parallelism and concurrent access, the frames are placed in a thread-safe queue. Thus, the video stream manager acts as the producer for frames, depositing frames on the queue. When the consumer is ready to process a frame, it accesses the same queue and removes the frame it will process. The function for assembling frames is named AssembleFullFrame.

Listing 7.2 is the function for capturing the video streams serially.

```
void VideoStreamManager :: CaptureFrameSerial ()
{
    int64_t startTicks = mProductionTimer . GetTicks ();
    size_t const numVideoStreams = mVideoStreams . size ();
    for (size_t i = 0; i < numVideoStreams; ++i)
    {
        mVideoStreams[i]->CaptureFrame ();
    }
    AssembleFullFrame (startTicks);
}
```

LISTING 7.2: Capturing video streams serially.

Listing 7.3 is the function for capturing the video streams in parallel.

```
void VideoStreamManager :: CaptureFrameParallel ()
{
    int64_t startTicks = mProductionTimer . GetTicks ();
    size_t const numVideoStreams = mVideoStreams . size ();
    std :: vector<std :: thread> captureThread (numVideoStreams);
    for (size_t i = 0; i < numVideoStreams; ++i)
    {
        captureThread[i] = std :: thread
        (
            [this , i]()
```

```
                  {
                      mVideoStreams[i]−>CaptureFrame ();
                  }
              );
          }
          for (size_t i = 0; i < numVideoStreams; ++i)
          {
              captureThread[i]. join ();
          }

          AssembleFullFrame (startTicks );
      }
```

LISTING 7.3: Capturing video streams in parallel.

The first loop launches threads to capture frames, one per video stream. The second loop waits for the threads to finish. The application must explicitly call one or the other when capture is initiated in the main thread, say, in the OnIdle function call,

```
mVideoStreamManager−>CaptureFrameSerial ();
// or mVideoStreamManager−>CaptureFrameParallel();
if (mVideoStreamManager−>GetFrame(mCurrent ))
{
    for (int i = 0; i < 4; ++i)
    {
        mOverlay[i]−>SetTexture (mCurrent . frames[i] .image );
        mEngine−>Draw(mOverlay[i ]);
    }
    DrawStatistics ();
    mEngine−>DisplayColorBuffer(0);
}
```

The consumer is the main thread, which sets the overlay effects to use the textures and draws them to the application window. Control of the frame rate can be accomplished by setting the input parameter to DisplayColorBuffer to 1 for 60 frames per second, 2 for 30 frames per second, etc. In the sample, the input 0 says not to wait for the vertical retrace. The GetFrame call determines whether the queue of frames has elements. If it does, one is removed from the queue and returned in the mCurrent object. The capture is occurring in the same frame, so the queue should always have a frame for consumption as long as the producer has created one. The file loading always blocks until the image is loaded, so indeed the producer always inserts an image into the queue.

For triggered capturing, the application must launch a thread that calls either the serial or parallel capture function. Listing 7.4 shows the implementation.

```
void VideoStreamManager :: StartTriggeredCapture (double fps , bool parallel )
{
    if (nullptr == mTrigger && fps > 0.0)
    {
        void (VideoStreamManager ::∗ Capture )(void );
        if (parallel )
        {
            Capture = &VideoStreamManager :: CaptureFrameParallel;
        }
        else
        {
```

```
            Capture = &VideoStreamManager :: CaptureFrameSerial ;
    }

    mTrigger = new Trigger ( ) ;
    mTrigger−>ticksPerFrame = mTrigger−>timer . GetTicks (1.0/ fps );
    mTrigger−>running = true ;

    mTrigger−>triggerThread = new std :: thread
    (
        [this , Capture ]()
        {
            int64_t startTime = mTrigger−>timer . GetTicks ( ) ;
            while (mTrigger−>running )
            {
                int64_t finalTime = startTime + mTrigger−>ticksPerFrame ;
                do
                {
                    startTime = mTrigger−>timer . GetTicks ( ) ;
                }
                while (startTime < finalTime );
                (this −>∗Capture )( ) ;
            }
        }
    );
    }
}
```

LISTING 7.4: Launching a thread to handle image capturing.

The frame rate in frames per second and the choice of serial or parallel capture are provided as inputs. The Trigger object is a structure that has a 64-bit timer, a pointer to the thread object, a Boolean that may be set to enable or disable capturing, and a counter for the number of ticks per frame. The latter is used so that we can call Capture using the 64-bit counter rather than always converting ticks to seconds and using floating-point numbers instead. The thread function is specified as a lambda, which is simple to read and encapsulates the thread creation in a single code block.

The application calls this function once it is ready to start the message pump, which is usually at the end of the constructor. Once the message pump starts, OnIdle is called frequently. The function has the code block

```
if (mVideoStreamManager−>GetFrame(mCurrent ))
{
    for (int i = 0; i < 4; ++i)
    {
        mOverlay[i]−>SetTexture(mCurrent . frames [ i ]. image );
        mEngine−>Draw(mOverlay[ i ]) ;
    }
    DrawStatistics ( ) ;
    mEngine−>DisplayColorBuffer(0);
}
```

As before, GetFrame queries the queue of frames to determine whether there is a frame available. Because the image capture is running in a separate thread and occurs at a specified rate, most of the time GetFrame finds there is no image available. When there is one, it is removed from the thread-safe queue and the images are drawn.

Generally, disk loading is slow, so it might not be possible to run at 60 or 30 frames per second. If you have a solid state drive, you might get the impression it is. Also, disk caching might give the illusion you are running fast. But when the video streams are on the order of gigabytes of data, you will probably notice the drop in frame rate. For live camera capture, as long as the camera hardware can deliver at 60 or 30 frames per second, the drawing can easily keep up with that rate and there are no stalls in the application. However, any extensive image processing that occurs in OnIdle might take long enough that you cannot meet the desired frame rate. For example, in stereo vision where you are trying to match corresponding points to obtain depth values, the computations will be extensive. You might have to balance image size, camera frame rate, and CPU/GPU frame rate in order to accomplish your goals.

7.2   Root Finding

Several methods are discussed for computing roots to functions when you are in a single-threaded CPU environment. As an alternative, the GPU may allow you to find roots using an exhaustive search when computing with 32-bit floating-point numbers, but you will need to interpret properly the output depending on the function.

7.2.1   Root Bounding

The general problem is this: given a continuous real-valued function $f(x)$ with domain $D \subseteq \mathbb{R}$, find all x for which $f(x) = 0$. In practice, the root finding might be limited to a finite interval that is a subset of the domain. In many cases, the interval is determined via *root bounding*. That is, you search D for intervals of the form $[a, b]$ for which $f(a)$ and $f(b)$ have opposite sign. The *intermediate value theorem* says that the function must attain any value between $f(a)$ and $f(b)$. In particular, if the signs of these numbers are opposite, then 0 is between $f(a)$ and $f(b)$, so there must be a number $x \in (a, b)$ for which $f(x) = 0$. The intermediate value theorem guarantees at least one root for $f(x)$ on $[a, b]$, but there may be others.

The practical challenge is to find an interval on which $f(x)$ has a unique root. Techniques exist for computing root-bounding intervals for polynomial functions, although some of these are sensitive to the use of floating-point arithmetic, so you need to implement them very carefully. One such method is recursive, computing the roots of derivatives of the polynomial. Another related one but more robust involves Sturm sequences of polynomials; for example, see [8].

7.2.2 Bisection

If $f(x)$ is defined in $[a, b]$ and has opposite signs at the endpoints ($f(a)f(b) < 0$), then the simplest method for computing a root is bisection. For the sake of argument, suppose $f(a) < 0$ and $f(b) > 0$. Compute the interval midpoint $m = (a + b)/2$ and evaluate $f(m)$. If $f(m) < 0$, then the intermediate value theorem guarantees $f(x)$ has a root on $[m, b]$. This subinterval is half the length of the original. If $f(m) > 0$, then $f(x)$ has a root on $[a, m]$. In either case, you can repeat the algorithm on the subinterval. Of course if you get lucky and find that $f(m) = 0$, you have your root.

In theory, the bisection algorithm usually does not converge in a finite number of steps, so in practice you need to limit the number of iterations. Based on the discussion of Section 2.5.5, root finding can be badly behaved if you were to terminate the iterations based on how close to zero the current $f(m)$ is. Instead, you can terminate based on the length of the current subinterval. Current generation floating-point units are fast enough that an alternative is to repeat bisection until the midpoint equals one of the endpoints. The termination is guaranteed, because there are only a finite number of floating-point numbers and at some time the rounding of the average of the endpoints will be to one of those endpoints:

```
Real x0, x1;  // interval [x0,x1] with x0 < x1, Real is float or double
Real f0 = f(x0), f1 = f(x1);
int s0 = Sign(f0), s1 = Sign(f1);  // s0*s1 < 0
Real root;
for (;;)
{
    Real xmid = (x0 + x1)/2;
    int smid = Sign(f(xmid));
    if (x0 == xmid || x1 == xmid || smid == 0)
    {
        root = xmid;
        break;
    }
    if (smid == s0)
    {
        x0 = xmid;
    }
    else
    {
        x1 = xmid;
    }
}
```

If the loop terminates because smid is zero, then you have a root for which the function evaluates exactly to zero. However, be aware that with floating-point arithmetic, the expression you use to evaluate the function can influence the outcome. For example, consider a quadratic polynomial $f(x) = ax^2 + bx + c$. With floating-point, you can get two different values,

```
float a = 0.1234f;
float b = −0.56f;
float c = −122840.000f;
float x = 1000.0f;
float f0, f1;
```

```
f0 = a*x*x + b*x + c;   // f0 = 0.0f
f1 = x*(a*x + b) + c;   // f1 = 0.00781250000f
```

The computed numbers are indeed different. If the loop terminates with distinct x0 and x1 and where f0 and f1 have opposite signs, you have a root-bounding interval (given the way you have decided to evaluate the function), no matter how small or large in magnitude the endpoint function values. As mentioned in Section 2.5.5, *this is the best you can do* with 32-bit floating-point arithmetic.

7.2.3   Newton's Method

One of the most popular root-finding methods is Newton's method, which requires the function to be continuously differentiable. It is based on having an estimate x_i of a root and then choosing the next estimate x_{i+1} as the point of intersection between the tangent line to the graph of f at $(x_i, f(x_i))$. This point is

$$x_{i+1} = x_i - \frac{f(x_i)}{f'(x_i)} \tag{7.1}$$

It is essential that you have a good initial estimate x_0 for the root in order for the iterates to converge to the root. In practice, the iterations are repeated until you meet some termination criterion.

As mentioned in Section 2.5.5, choosing a criterion based on how close $f(x_i)$ is to zero usually is not advised. Even if the function values are on order one (i.e., reasonably sized floating-point numbers) you can run into problems. A typical attempt at coding the root finder is

```
float x;   // initial guess
float functionEpsilon;   // positive number close to zero
float derivativeEpsilon;   // worries about dividing by zero
int maxIterations;   // limit iterations when the unexpected happens
for (int i = 0; i < maxIterations; ++i)
{
    float f = Function(x);
    if (std::abs(f) < functionEpsilon)
    {
        return x;   // f small, so we will call this a root
    }
    float df = FunctionDerivative(x);
    if (std::abs(df) < derivativeEpsilon)
    {
        // This leads to division by (nearly) zero.  WHAT TO DO?
        return aargh;
    }
    x -= f/df;
}
return x;   // Failed to converge, so return current best guess?
```

Let us ignore the problem for now of the derivative nearly zero, assuming you have a function whose derivative does not have this behavior near a root. The comparison to functionEpsilon can fail; consider the quadratic polynomial of Section 2.5.5 for which you have a root bound of two consecutive floating-point numbers but their magnitudes well exceed the epsilon test. Most likely, you will continue to loop until maximum iterations, never obtaining estimates better than the previous iterations.

One of the classical root-finder breakers you see in a course on numerical methods is a function for which the iterates cycle around the root but never converge. For example, $f(x) = x/(1 + x^2/3)$ has this property at $x = \pm 1$. The iterates are

$$x_{i+1} = x_i - \frac{f(x_i)}{f'(x_i)} = -\frac{2x_i^3}{3 - x_i^2} \tag{7.2}$$

For initial guess $x_0 = 1$, the next iterate is $x_1 = -1$ and yet the next iterate is $x_2 = 1$. You can iterate as much as you want but you will not find the root $x = 0$. The same cyclical behavior can happen due to numerical roundoff errors if you are near a root. My suggestion for a solution with a computer-science flavor rather than a purely mathematical one is to store the iterates and trap the cycles,

```
float x;  // initial guess
float functionEpsilon;  // positive number close to zero
int maxIterations;  // limit iterations when the unexpected happens
std::set<float> visited;
visited.insert(x);
for (int i = 0; i < maxIterations; ++i)
{
    float f = Function(x);
    if (std::abs(f) < functionEpsilon)
    {
        return x;  // f small, so we will call this a root
    }
    float df = FunctionDerivative(x);
    x -= f/df;
    if (visited.find(x) == visited.end())
    {
        // We have not yet seen this iterate.
        visited.insert(x);
    }
    else
    {
        // We have seen this iterate, so there is a cycle.  One possible
        // response is to return the iterate whose function value is
        // smallest.
        float fmin = std::numeric_limits<float>::max();
        float root = std::numeric_limits<float>::max();
        for (auto y : visited)
        {
            float fabs = std::abs(Function(y));
            if (fabs < fmin)
            {
                fmin = fabs;
                root = y;
            }
        }
        return root;
    }
}
return x;  // Failed to converge, so return current best guess?
```

Finally, in practice you probably want to implement a hybrid of Newton's method and bisection. Given a root-bounding interval $[a, b]$, compute a Newton's iterate starting at $x_0 = a$. If the resulting x_1 is inside $[a, b]$, then accept this value and compute another Newton's iterate. But if x_1 is outside $[a, b]$, reject x_1 and apply a bisection step.

7.2.4   Exhaustive Evaluation

If you want a (presumably) robust computation for float roots of any function $f(x)$ with no worries about computation time, a simple but slow algorithm is to iterate over all finite float numbers and evaluate the function. Let x_0 and x_1 be two consecutive finite floating-point numbers. If $f(x_0)f(x_1) < 0$, then the interval $[x_0, x_1]$ bounds a root. However, there are no floating-point numbers between x_0 and x_1, so the best you can do is estimate the root with x_i for which $|f(x_i)|$ is the minimum absolute value of the two function values. In fact, the test should be $f(x_0)f(x_1) \leq 0$, allowing for either of the x-values to be exactly a root with the understanding that the function evaluation involves potentially roundoff errors—with exact arithmetic, f is not exactly zero at the rational-valued input.

A sample application illustrating the root finding is located at

GeometricTools/GTEngine/Samples/Numerics/RootFinding

In the previous paragraph, I parenthesized "presumably" because there are some potential problems with the GPU output. These are mentioned at the end of the discussion.

7.2.4.1   CPU Root Finding Using a Single Thread

The inner-loop costs depend on the function evaluation. To give you an idea of how expensive the approach is, consider the code in Listing 7.5 that computes the roots of $f(x) = (x - 1.1)(x + 2.2)$. On my machine with an Intel Core i7-3930K 3.20 GHz core, the execution time was approximately 10.5 seconds. In general, the polynomial function may be replaced by any other function whose domain is the set of real numbers; that is, the algorithm is not specific to polynomials, but of course the execution time increases as the cost of evaluating $f(x)$ increases. If your function's domain is a subset of the real numbers, you will need to modify the code to visit only those floating-point numbers in the domain.

```
float MyFunction (float x) { return (x − 1.1f)*(x + 2.2f); }

void FindRootsCPUSingle(std::set<float>& roots)
{
    std::set<float> roots;
    unsigned int const supTrailing = (1 << 23);
    for (unsigned int trailing = 0; trailing < supTrailing; ++trailing)
    {
        for (unsigned int biased = 0; biased < 255; ++biased)
        {
            unsigned int exponent = (biased << 23);
            unsigned int encoding0 = exponent | trailing;
            unsigned int encoding1 = encoding0 + 1;
```

```
float z0 = *(float*)&encoding0;
float z1 = *(float*)&encoding1;

float f0 = MyFunction(z0);
float f1 = MyFunction(z1);
if (f0*f1 <= 0.0f)
{
    roots.insert(std::abs(f0) <= std::abs(f1) ? z0 : z1);
}

z0 = -z0;
z1 = -z1;
f0 = MyFunction(z0);
f1 = MyFunction(z1);
if (f0*f1 <= 0.0f)
{
    roots.insert(std::abs(f0) <= std::abs(f1) ? z0 : z1);
}
        }
    }
}
```

LISTING 7.5: Root finding on the CPU using an exhaustive search with a single thread.

The same approach for double roots is a lot slower. Do not try this at home. You have 2^{32} times more numbers to process, so the total execution time is on the order of 1430 years!

7.2.4.2 CPU Root Finding Using Multiple Threads

The exhaustive processing for finite float numbers may be reduced by distributing the work across cores. Each core handles a subset of the inputs. Listing 7.6 shows an implementation of this.

```
void FindSubRootsCPU(unsigned int tmin, unsigned int tsup,
    std::set<float>& roots)
{
    for (unsigned int trailing = tmin; trailing < tsup; ++trailing)
    {
        for (unsigned int biased = 0; biased < 255; ++biased)
        {
            unsigned int exponent = (biased << 23);
            unsigned int encoding0 = exponent | trailing;
            unsigned int encoding1 = encoding0 + 1;
            float z0 = *(float*)&encoding0;
            float z1 = *(float*)&encoding1;

            float f0 = MyFunction(z0);
            float f1 = MyFunction(z1);
            if (f0*f1 <= 0.0f)
            {
                roots.insert(std::abs(f0) <= std::abs(f1) ? z0 : z1);
            }

            z0 = -z0;
            z1 = -z1;
            f0 = MyFunction(z0);
            f1 = MyFunction(z1);
            if (f0*f1 <= 0.0f)
            {
                roots.insert(std::abs(f0) <= std::abs(f1) ? z0 : z1);
            }
```

```
            }
        }
    }

void FindRootsCPUMultithreaded(std::set<float>& roots)
{
    int const numThreads = 16;
    unsigned int const supTrailing = (1 << 23);
    std::set<float> subRoots[numThreads];

    std::thread process[numThreads];
    for (int t = 0; t < numThreads; ++t)
    {
        unsigned int tmin = t * supTrailing / numThreads;
        unsigned int tsup = (t + 1) * supTrailing / numThreads;
        auto rootFinder = std::bind(FindSubRootsCPU, tmin, tsup,
            std::ref(subRoots[t]));

        process[t] = std::thread([&rootFinder](){ rootFinder(); });
    }

    for (int t = 0; t < numThreads; ++t)
    {
        process[t].join();
    }

    for (int t = 0; t < numThreads; ++t)
    {
        for (auto const& z : subRoots[t])
        {
            roots.insert(z);
        }
    }
}
```

LISTING 7.6: Root finding on the CPU using an exhaustive search with multiple threads.

The performance depends on the number of cores your machine has available. My machine has six cores (twelve logical processors). Running sixteen threads, the execution time for the root finding is approximately 1.7 seconds, which is faster than the 10.5 seconds for root finding in a single thread.

7.2.4.3   GPU Root Finding

You can even perform this experiment using a GPU. The number of trailing significands is 2^{23}, so I chose to partition these into a $2^{12} \times 2^{11} = 4096 \times 2048$ grid. The trailing significand mapping is $i = x + 4096y$. Listing 7.7 contains the compute shader and the GTEngine application code that creates and executes it.

```
// RootFinding.hlsl

// The macro FUNCTION_BODY must be declared by an HLSLDefiner object.
float Function(float z) { return FUNCTION_BODY; }

// The number of elements in the append buffer must be sufficiently large.
AppendStructuredBuffer<float4> rootBounds;

[numthreads(8, 8, 1)]
void CSMain(uint2 t : SV_DispatchThreadID)
```

```
{
    uint trailing = t.x + 4096 * t.y;
    for (uint biased = 0; biased < 255; ++biased)
    {
        uint exponent = (biased << 23);
        uint encoding0 = exponent | trailing;
        float z0 = asfloat(encoding0);
        uint encoding1 = encoding0 + 1;
        float z1 = asfloat(encoding1);
        float f0 = Function(z0);
        float f1 = Function(z1);
        if (sign(f0) * sign(f1) <= 0.0f)
        {
            rootBounds.Append(float4(z0, f0, z1, f1));
        }
        z0 = -z0;
        z1 = -z1;
        f0 = Function(z0);
        f1 = Function(z1);
        if (sign(f0) * sign(f1) <= 0.0f)
        {
            rootBounds.Append(float4(z1, f1, z0, f0));
        }
    }
}

// C++ application code
void FindRootsGPU(std::set<float>& roots)
{
    DX11Engine engine;

    std::shared_ptr<StructuredBuffer> acBuffer(new StructuredBuffer(
        1024, sizeof(Vector4<float>)));
    acBuffer->MakeAppendConsume();
    acBuffer->SetCopyType(Resource::COPY_STAGING_TO_CPU);
    acBuffer->SetNumActiveElements(0);

    HLSLDefiner definer;
    definer.SetString("FUNCTION_BODY", "(z - 1.1f)*(z + 2.2f)");
    std::shared_ptr<ComputeShader> cshader(
        ShaderFactory::CreateCompute("RootFinder.hlsl", definer));
    cshader->Set("rootBounds", acBuffer);

    engine.Execute(cshader, 512, 256, 1);

    engine.CopyGpuToCpu(acBuffer);
    int numActive = acBuffer->GetNumActiveElements();
    Vector4<float>* rootBounds = acBuffer->GetAs<Vector4<float>>();
    for (int i = 0; i < numActive; ++i)
    {
        Vector4<float> const& rb = rootBounds[i];
        if (std::abs(rb[1]) <= std::abs(rb[3]))
        {
            roots.insert(rb[0]);
        }
        else
        {
            roots.insert(rb[2]);
        }
    }

    acBuffer = nullptr;
    cshader = nullptr;
}
```

LISTING 7.7: Root finding on the GPU using an exhaustive search with 512×256 thread groups, each group containing 8×8 threads.

The execution time for the GPU version of the root finder was measured to be approximately 1.4 seconds. This is faster than the CPU single-threaded time (10.5 seconds) and the CPU multithreaded time (1.7 seconds). The speed up of the GPU version over the CPU multithreaded version is not that much, but if the function is more complicated and expensive to compute, the GPU version should be much faster.

Several comments are in order about the GPU root finder.

1. The HLSL function asfloat is extremely handy for allowing you to interpret bit patterns differently. This feature was not available in Shader Model 3 (D3D 9). A similar function asdouble allows you to assemble double values from input resources that store uint values.

2. The body of the function is delivered to the HLSL compiler via an HLSLDefiner object that is part of the design of GTEngine. You can see where this is set in the C++ application code.

3. Because sorting is not a natural thing to do in a shader, I choose to compute root-bounding intervals and store them in an append buffer. The GPU memory for this buffer must be copied back to the CPU in order to construct the (sorted) set of roots. The read-back from the GPU is the most expensive part of the computation.

4. The GPU floating-point arithmetic might use flush-to-zero semantics for subnormals, potentially leading to differences in the sets of roots reported by the CPU and by the GPU.

5. The number of root-bounding intervals is generally unknown, although in this example we know that the quadratic polynomial has two roots. The append buffer must be created with enough storage for the intervals; otherwise, we may miss some intervals once the buffer is full. If r is a floating-point number for which the floating-point computation of $F(r)$ is exactly zero, we will actually get two bounding intervals, $[r_0, r]$ and $[r, r_1]$ where r_0, r, and r_1 are three consecutive floating-point numbers. In worst case all roots lead to function values of exactly zero, so to be safe we need the append buffer to have twice as many roots. In fact, the situation can be worse when extraneous roots are generated, typically when the GPU uses flush-to-zero semantics for subnormal floating-point numbers. If you want to ensure you have enough storage for a general root finder, you can make multiple passes. The first pass does not append the intervals; rather, it keeps track of the number of intervals, storing this counter in a RWStructuredBuffer<uint> that has exactly one element. The counter is read back to the CPU and an append buffer is created to store that many intervals. The second pass uses the compute shader as shown in Listing 7.7.

6. When a function is nearly zero, floating-point roundoff errors during function evaluation can cause a lot of spurious root-bounding intervals.

For example, when experimenting with the minimax approximation to the inverse sine function, I used the GPU-based exhaustive approach to compute root bounds for $g(x)$ and $g'(x)$ mentioned in the minimax construction, using 32-bit float. I knew from plotting the graphs that $g'(x)$ had three roots, but the GPU output reported approximately fifty root-bounding intervals. An analysis of the output showed that the intervals were clustered about 3 different floating-point values. The spurious intervals were a result of sign changes caused by the rounding errors. I performed the same experiment on the CPU and had approximately 40 root-bounding intervals reported. When I switched to 64-bit double, the CPU code reported 3 root-bounding intervals. I could not switch to double on the GPU because there is no sqrt function available in double precision. The message here is that you cannot just blindly use the GPU output. You might have additional work to do, say, regarding clustering of the output intervals.

7. The root-bounding intervals have float endpoints. If you want a higher-precision estimate for the root, you can convert the endpoints to double and use bisection or Newton's method on the CPU to polish the root.

7.3 Least Squares Fitting

A common algorithm for fitting data with a parameterized function is *least squares fitting*. This section shows algorithms for fitting of lines and planes.

A GPGPU version of plane fitting is provided to show how to estimate normal vectors of height-field samples. The vectors can be used for lighting or they can be used to identify flat portions of the height field. The latter is typical of LIDAR, where lasers are used to illuminate a target and the reflected light can be measured to estimate distances to the target. For example, one might want to identify sections of roofs in a scene with LIDAR generated from an airplane.

7.3.1 Fit a Line to 2D Points

The classical introduction to least squares fitting involves fitting a set of points $\{(x_i, y_i)\}_{i=0}^{n-1}$ by a line $y = Ax + B$. The assumption is that the y-values are measurements that are dependent on the x-values.

The selection of A and B is based on minimizing the sum of squared errors between the samples and the corresponding points on the fitted line. The errors are measured only in the y-direction. Define the error function $F(A, B) = \sum_{i=0}^{n-1} [(Ax_i + B) - y_i]^2$, a nonnegative function whose graph is a paraboloid with vertex occurring when $\nabla F(A, B) = (0, 0)$. Thus, the global minimum of F occurs at the vertex. The gradient equation leads to a system of two linear equations in the unknowns A and B, namely, $(0, 0) = \nabla F = 2\sum_{i=0}^{n}[(Ax_i + B - y_i](x_i, 1)$. The linear system is listed next, where we use the statistical concept of expected value of a uniformly distributed random variable U, namely, $E[U] = (\sum_{i=0}^{n} u_i)/n$;

$$\begin{bmatrix} E[X^2] & E[X] \\ E[X] & 1 \end{bmatrix} \begin{bmatrix} A \\ B \end{bmatrix} = \begin{bmatrix} E[XY] \\ E[Y] \end{bmatrix} \tag{7.3}$$

The solution to this system provides the coefficients for the least squares fit.

$$\begin{bmatrix} A \\ B \end{bmatrix} = \frac{1}{E[X^2] - E[X]^2} \begin{bmatrix} E[XY] - E[X]E[Y] \\ E[X^2]E[Y] - E[XY]E[X] \end{bmatrix} \tag{7.4}$$

Although the construction is mathematically correct, in practice when using floating-point numbers to solve the system, ill conditioning can cause problems. Typically, the ill conditioning manifests itself via subtractive cancellation; see the example presented later.

To avoid the ill conditioning, it is better to fit the data with a line $y - \bar{y} = A(x - \bar{x}) + C$, where $\bar{x} = E[X]$ and $\bar{y} = E[Y]$ are the averages of the sample channels. The error function $F(A, C)$ for this version has zero gradient that leads to the linear system

$$\begin{bmatrix} E[(X - \bar{x})^2] & E[X - \bar{x}] \\ E[X - \bar{x}] & 1 \end{bmatrix} \begin{bmatrix} A \\ C \end{bmatrix} = \begin{bmatrix} E[(X - \bar{x})(Y - \bar{y})] \\ E[Y - \bar{y}] \end{bmatrix} \tag{7.5}$$

Observe that $E[X - \bar{x}] = 0$ and $E[Y - \bar{y}] = 0$, so in fact the matrix of coefficients is diagonal and the last entry of the right-hand side is zero. The solution is

$$A = E[(X - \bar{x})(Y - \bar{y})]/E[(X - \bar{x})^2], \quad C = 0 \tag{7.6}$$

and the fitted line is $y - \bar{y} = A(x - \bar{x})$. The line has slope A and passes through the average point $(\bar{x}, \bar{y})$. Compared to the previous version, it can be shown that $B = \bar{y} - A\bar{x}$, so mathematically the two formulations produce the same line. However, the second formulation does not suffer from the ill conditioning that the first formulation does when computing numerically.

Listing 7.8 is a program that fits a line to four samples.

```
int main()
{
    // Random samples.  Case 1: The x-values are not ordered, but
    // mathematically this is not required.  Case 2: Swap sample[2]
    // and sample[3] to order by x-value.
    int const numSamples = 4;
    Vector2<float> sample[numSamples] =
    {
        Vector2<float>(1.00001252f,  156.358536f),
        Vector2<float>(1.00193310f,  180.874054f),
        Vector2<float>(1.00585008f,  147.987305f),
        Vector2<float>(1.00350296f,  189.596252f)
    };
```

```
    // Compute linear system elements.
    float sumX = 0.0f, sumY = 0.0f, sumXX = 0.0f, sumXY = 0.0f;
    float sum1 = (float)numSamples;
    for (int i = 0; i < numSamples; ++i)
    {
        sumX += sample[i][0];
        sumY += sample[i][1];
        sumXX += sample[i][0]*sample[i][0];
        sumXY += sample[i][0]*sample[i][1];
    }
    Matrix2<float> A(sumXX, sumX, sumX, sum1);
    Vector2<float> B(sumXY, sumY);
    float det = A[0][0]*A[1][1] - A[0][1]*A[1][0];
    float invDet = 1.0f/det;

    // Solve by computing the inverse of A first; that is, the adjoint
    // of A is divided by the determinant before the multiplication of B.
    Vector2<float> solution1;
    solution1[0] = (A[1][1]*invDet)*B[0] - (A[0][1]*invDet)*B[1];
    solution1[1] = (A[0][0]*invDet)*B[1] - (A[1][0]*invDet)*B[0];

    // Solve by multiplying B by the adjoint of A and then dividing by
    // the determinant.
    Vector2<float> solution2;
    solution2[0] = (A[1][1]*B[0] - A[0][1]*B[1])*invDet;
    solution2[1] = (A[0][0]*B[1] - A[1][0]*B[0])*invDet;

    // Compute the mean of the samples and subtract before computing the
    // sum of squared terms.
    Vector2<float> mean(sumX/numSamples, sumY/numSamples);
    float rsumXX = 0.0f;
    float rsumXY = 0.0f;
    for (int i = 0; i < numSamples; ++i)
    {
        float dx = sample[i][0] - mean[0];
        float dy = sample[i][1] - mean[1];
        rsumXX += dx*dx;
        rsumXY += dx*dy;
    }
    Vector2<float> solution3(rsumXY/rsumXX, 0.0f);

    // Compute the least squares error functions for the three cases.
    float error1 = 0.0f, error2 = 0.0f, error3 = 0.0f;
    float diff;
    for (int i = 0; i < numSamples; ++i)
    {
        diff = solution1[0]*sample[i][0] + solution1[1] - sample[i][1];
        error1 += diff*diff;
        diff = solution2[0]*sample[i][0] + solution2[1] - sample[i][1];
        error2 += diff*diff;
        diff = solution3[0]*(sample[i][0] - mean[0]) -
            (sample[i][1] - mean[1]);
        error3 += diff*diff;
    }

    return 0;
}
```

LISTING 7.8: Program to illustrate ill conditioning in line fitting when the mean is not subtracted from the samples.

The linear system $A\mathbf{S} = \mathbf{B}$ is ill conditioned. Recall that the inverse of a matrix is $A^{-1} = \mathrm{adjoint}(A)/\det(A)$. The first approach solves the system by computing the inverse first and then multiplying $\mathbf{B}$, $\mathbf{S}_1 = A^{-1}\mathbf{B}$. The second approach multiplies by the adjoint matrix first and then divides by the

TABLE 7.1: Numerical ill conditioning for least squares

	Case 1	Case 2
sumX	4.01129866	4.01129818
sumY	674.816162	674.816162
sumXX	4.02264738	4.02264738
sumXY	676.697632	676.697632
det	7.24792480e−005	7.62939453e−005
invDet	13797.0527	13107.2002
solution1	(−1360.00000, 1536.00000)	(−1288.00000, 1460.00000)
solution2	(−1360.84216, 1532.63159)	(−1289.59998, 1459.20007)
rsumXX	1.83162738e−005	1.83162738e−005
rsumXY	−0.0246384665	−0.0246384628
solution3	(−1345.16809, 0.000000000)	(−1345.16785, 0.000000000)
error1	1180.78613	1133.57544
error2	1135.34753	1163.27869
error3	1133.04541	1133.04553

determinant, $\mathbf{S}_2 = (\text{adjoint}(A)\mathbf{B})/\det(A)$. The third approach subtracts the mean from the samples and then computes solution $\mathbf{S}_3$ directly. Two cases are presented to illustrate how sensitive the first two approaches are to even something as simple as swapping a pair of samples. The numerical results are shown in Table 7.1. Solution $\mathbf{S}_3$ is better than the other two, and it is robust to swapping the order of two of the samples. Solution $\mathbf{S}_1$ has integer components due to computations that produce floating-point numbers in the range for which the numbers are nonconsecutive integers (the numbers are larger than 2^{24}).

Using exact rational arithmetic to compute the coefficients A and B for the fitted line $y = Ax + B$ and to compute the least squares error $F(A, B)$, and then converting to the nearest **double** values, we obtain $A = -1345.1678879586245$, $B = 1517.6715721342564$, and $F = 1133.0455049651985$.

7.3.2   Fit a Plane to 3D Points

Given a set of points $\{(x_i, y_i, z_i)\}_{i=0}^{n-1}$, where it is presumed that the z-values are measurements that depend on the x- and y-values, a plane of the form $z = Ax + By + C$ may be fitted to the data. The construction is similar to that for fitting 2D points by a line.

The selection of A, B, and C is based on minimizing the sum of squared errors between the samples and the corresponding points on the fitted plane. The errors are measured only in the z-direction. Define the error function $F(A, B, C) = \sum_{i=0}^{n-1}[(Ax_i + By_i + C) - z_i]^2$, a nonnegative function whose graph is a paraboloid with vertex occurring when $(0, 0, 0) = \nabla F(A, B, C) = 2\sum_{i=0}^{n}[(Ax_i + By_i + C) - z_i](x_i, y_i, 1)$. The linear system is listed next, where the $E[]$ notation refers to expected value mentioned in the section on line fitting,

$$
\begin{bmatrix}
E[X^2] & E[XY] & E[X] \\
E[XY] & E[Y^2] & E[Y] \\
E[X] & E[Y] & 1
\end{bmatrix}
\begin{bmatrix}
A \\
B \\
C
\end{bmatrix}
=
\begin{bmatrix}
E[XZ] \\
E[YZ] \\
E[Z]
\end{bmatrix}
\tag{7.7}
$$

The solution to this system provides the coefficients for the least squares fit.

As in the case of fitting a line, the linear system can be ill conditioned. To avoid this, it is better to fit the data with a plane $z - \bar{z} = A(x - \bar{x}) + B(y - \bar{y}) + D$, where $\bar{x}$, $\bar{y}$, and $\bar{z}$ are the averages of the sample channels. The error function $F(A, B, D)$ for this version has zero gradient that leads to the linear system

$$
\begin{bmatrix}
E[(X - \bar{x})^2] & E[(X - \bar{x})(Y - \bar{y})] & 0 \\
E[(X - \bar{x})(Y - \bar{y})] & E[(Y - \bar{y})^2] & 0 \\
0 & 0 & 1
\end{bmatrix}
\begin{bmatrix}
A \\
B \\
D
\end{bmatrix}
$$

$$
=
\begin{bmatrix}
E[(X - \bar{x})(Z - \bar{z})] \\
E[(Y - \bar{y})(Z - \bar{z})] \\
0
\end{bmatrix}
\tag{7.8}
$$

The solution for (A, B) is obtained by solving a 2×2 linear system, and it is the case that $D = 0$. The fitted plane is $z - \bar{z} = A(x - \bar{x}) + B(y - \bar{y})$. The plane has unit-length normal vector $(-A, -B, 1)/\sqrt{A^2 + B^2 + 1}$ and passes through the average point $(\bar{x}, \bar{y}, \bar{z})$.

Even in the well-conditioned formulation, you can still have numerical problems—when the 2×2 block of the coefficient matrix is nearly singular. This can happen if you have a collection of points that are nearly collinear, which makes it difficult to fit with a plane.

If the covariance $E[(X - \bar{x})(Y - \bar{y})]]$ is zero, then the coefficients are easily determined because the matrix of coefficients is diagonal. In particular, this case happens on a rectangular grid of samples, say, where $(x_i, y_j) = (a + ci, b + dj)$ for $0 \le i \le i_{\max}$, $0 \le j \le j_{\max}$, $c > 0$, and $d > 0$.

A practical example is provided in Section 7.3.4 with implementations both for the CPU and GPU.

7.3.3 Orthogonal Regression

The line and plane fitting previously discussed had one variable dependent on the others. It is possible to fit the points with lines and planes when all variables are independent.

7.3.3.1 Fitting with Lines

Section 7.3.1 is about fitting samples (x_i, y_i) with a line $y = Ax + B$. The y-value is assumed to be dependent on the x-value. The least squares fitting uses errors measured in the y-direction. I refer to this as *height line fitting* to emphasize that errors are measured in the dependent variable (the height of the graph). If the x- and y-values are independent variables, we may measure errors in the direction orthogonal to the postulated line. This is referred to as *orthogonal line fitting.*

Because the variables are independent, orthogonal line fitting may be used in any dimension m. Let the m-dimensional samples be $\{\mathbf{X}_i\}_{i=0}^{n-1}$. The fitted line is parameterized as $\mathbf{L}(t) = \mathbf{A} + t\mathbf{D}$ where $\mathbf{D}$ is unit length and $\mathbf{A}$ is a point on the line. The squared distance from a sample point to the line is obtained by projecting out the $\mathbf{D}$ component of $\mathbf{X}_i - \mathbf{A}$ and computing the squared length,

$$\ell_i^2 = |(\mathbf{X}_i - \mathbf{A}) - \mathbf{D} \cdot (\mathbf{X}_i - \mathbf{A})\mathbf{D}|^2 = (\mathbf{X}_i - \mathbf{A})^\mathsf{T} P(\mathbf{X}_i - \mathbf{A}) \qquad (7.9)$$

where $P = I - \mathbf{D}\mathbf{D}^\mathsf{T}$ is a projection matrix onto a plane containing the origin and whose normal is $\mathbf{D}$. The matrix has the property $P^2 = P$. The least squares error function is the sum of the squared lengths,

$$F(\mathbf{A}, \mathbf{D}) = \sum_{i=0}^{n-1} \ell_i^2 = \sum_{i=0}^{n-1} (\mathbf{X}_i - \mathbf{A})^\mathsf{T} P(\mathbf{X}_i - \mathbf{A}) \qquad (7.10)$$

A minimum of F must occur its derivative with respect to the components of $\mathbf{A}$ is zero, namely,

$$\mathbf{0} = \frac{\partial F}{\partial \mathbf{A}} = -2\sum_{i=0}^{n-1} P(\mathbf{X}_i - \mathbf{A}) = -2P\sum_{i=0}^{n-1}(\mathbf{X}_i - \mathbf{A}) \qquad (7.11)$$

Therefore, $(\sum_{i=0}^{n-1} \mathbf{X}_i)/n = \mathbf{A} + \tau\mathbf{D}$ for some scalar τ. Regardless of choice of τ, the right-hand side is a point on the line whose location cannot change the value of F because the line itself is invariant regardless of its parameterization; that is, $F(\mathbf{A} + \tau\mathbf{D}, \mathbf{D}) = F(\mathbf{A}, \mathbf{D})$ for all τ. We might as well choose $\tau = 0$, so

$$\mathbf{A} = \frac{1}{n} \sum_{i=0}^{n-1} \mathbf{X}_i \qquad (7.12)$$

is the average of the sample points.

Define $\mathbf{Y}_i = \mathbf{X}_i - \mathbf{A}$ and observe that F may be factored as

$$F(\mathbf{A}, \mathbf{D}) = \mathbf{D}^\mathsf{T} \sum_{i=0}^{n-1} \left(\mathbf{Y}_i^\mathsf{T}\mathbf{Y}\, I - \mathbf{Y}_i\mathbf{Y}_i^\mathsf{T} \right) \mathbf{D} = \mathbf{D}^\mathsf{T} S \mathbf{D} \qquad (7.13)$$

where I is the identity matrix and where the last equality defines the symmetric matrix S. The problem is now one of minimizing a quadratic form over the set of unit-length vectors. The minimum occurs for a unit-length vector $\mathbf{D}$ whose corresponding eigenvalue is the minimum of all the eigenvalues. We may use an eigensolver to compute $\mathbf{D}$.

7.3.3.2 Fitting with Planes

Section 7.3.2 is about fitting samples (x_i, y_i, z_i) with a plane $z = Ax + By + C$. The z-value is assumed to be dependent on the x- and y-values. The least squares fitting uses errors measured in the z-direction. I refer to this as *height plane fitting* to emphasize that errors are measured in the dependent variable (the height of the graph). If the x-, y-, and z-values are independent variables, we may measure the errors in the direction orthogonal to the postulated plane. This is referred to as *orthogonal plane fitting*.

Because the variables are independent, orthogonal plane fitting may be used in any dimension m. Let the m-dimensional samples be $\{\mathbf{X}_i\}_{i=0}^{n-1}$. The fitted hyperplane is represented implicitly by $\mathbf{N} \cdot (\mathbf{X} - \mathbf{A}) = 0$ where $\mathbf{A}$ is a point on the hyperplane and $\mathbf{N}$ is a unit-length normal for the hyperplane. The squared distance from a sample point to the hyperplane is obtained by projecting $\mathbf{X}_i - \mathbf{A}$ onto a normal line and computing the squared length,

$$\ell_i^2 = |\mathbf{N} \cdot (\mathbf{X}_i - \mathbf{A})|^2 = (\mathbf{X}_i - \mathbf{A})^\mathsf{T} P (\mathbf{X}_i - \mathbf{A}) \tag{7.14}$$

where $P = \mathbf{N}\mathbf{N}^\mathsf{T}$ is a projection matrix onto a normal line containing the origin and whose direction is $\mathbf{N}$. The matrix has the property $P^2 = P$. The least squares error function is the sum of the squared lengths,

$$F(\mathbf{A}, \mathbf{N}) = \sum_{i=0}^{n-1} \ell_i^2 = \sum_{i=0}^{n-1} (\mathbf{X}_i - \mathbf{A})^\mathsf{T} P (\mathbf{X}_i - \mathbf{A}) \tag{7.15}$$

A minimum of F must occur its derivative with respect to the components of $\mathbf{A}$ is zero, namely,

$$\mathbf{0} = \frac{\partial F}{\partial \mathbf{A}} = -2 \sum_{i=0}^{n-1} P (\mathbf{X}_i - \mathbf{A}) = -2P \sum_{i=0}^{n-1} (\mathbf{X}_i - \mathbf{A}) \tag{7.16}$$

Therefore, $(\sum_{i=0}^{n-1} \mathbf{X}_i)/n = \mathbf{A} + \mathbf{D}$ for some vector $\mathbf{D}$ that is perpendicular to $\mathbf{N}$; that is, $\mathbf{D}$ lies in the hyperplane. Regardless of choice of $\mathbf{D}$, the right-hand side is a point on the line whose location cannot change the value of F because the hyperplane itself is invariant regardless of the location of its origin; that is, $F(\mathbf{A} + \mathbf{D}, \mathbf{N}) = F(\mathbf{A}, \mathbf{N})$ for all $\mathbf{D}$ for which $\mathbf{D} \cdot \mathbf{N} = 0$. We might as well choose $\mathbf{D} = \mathbf{0}$, so

$$\mathbf{A} = \frac{1}{n} \sum_{i=0}^{n-1} \mathbf{X}_i \tag{7.17}$$

is the average of the sample points.

Define $\mathbf{Y}_i = \mathbf{X}_i - \mathbf{A}$ and observe that F may be factored as

$$F(\mathbf{A}, \mathbf{N}) = \mathbf{N}^\mathsf{T} \sum_{i=0}^{n-1} \mathbf{Y}_i \mathbf{Y}_i^\mathsf{T} \mathbf{N} = \mathbf{N}^\mathsf{T} S \mathbf{N} \tag{7.18}$$

where the last equality defines the symmetric matrix S. As for lines, the problem is now one of minimizing a quadratic form over the set of unit-length vectors. The minimum occurs for a unit-length vector $\mathbf{N}$ whose corresponding eigenvalue is the minimum of all the eigenvalues. We may use an eigensolver to compute $\mathbf{N}$.

7.3.4   Estimation of Tangent Planes

The sample application

GeometricTools/GTEngine/Samples/Numerics/PlaneEstimation

shows how to estimate tangent planes to points on a bicubic Bézier height field. The surface points are stored in a 32-bit RGBA texture image of size 1024×1024. The (x, y) values are the indices into the texture. The z-value is computed using Bézier control points. The tangent plane at each surface point $(x, y, f(x, y))$ is estimated using a least-squares fit as described previously. The estimation is computed for a 7×7 neighborhood centered at (x, y). The neighborhood size is a parameter to the shader that does the least-squares fitting, so you can experiment by modifying the size.

The points are chosen so that most of the height values are positive but some are negative or zero. When computing the height field, any nonpositive value is deemed to be *missing data*. This makes the plane fitting interesting in that the neighborhood does not always contain forty-nine points.

The application visualizes both the surface and the normals to the surface. Points for which the height is positive are drawn in shades of green that are proportional to height. Missing data is drawn in solid blue. This visualization appears in the left half of the application window. The fitted planes are of the form $z = Ax + By + C$ and are reported as 4-tuples $D(A, B, -1, C)$, where D is the determinant of the covariance matrix built by the fitting algorithm. In theory, $D > 0$, so you can extract unit-length normals by normalizing the 3-tuple $(DA, DB, -D)$ to obtain $\mathbf{N} = (A, B, -1)/\sqrt{A^2 + B^2 + 1}$. In this example, A and B are relatively small compared to one, so instead of pseudocoloring the normal vectors, I pseudocolor using normalized (A, B) and then map to the unit square $[0, 1]^2$ to obtain valid red and green colors. Missing data is drawn as solid blue.

The HLSL compute shader for least-squares fitting is shown in Listing 7.9. Currently, I have the number of threads in each dimension set to eight and the radius to three. I stripped the comments from the listing to keep the listing short. The discussion about the shader design occurs after the listing. The actual HLSL file has the comments embedded in it.

```
Texture2D<float4> positions;
RWTexture2D<float4> planes;

[numthreads(NUM_X_THREADS, NUM_Y_THREADS, 1)]
void CSMain (int2 t : SV_DispatchThreadID)
{
```

```
float4  position  =  positions[t];
if (position.w > 0.0f)
{
    float4  center  =  float4(position.xy,  0,  0);
    float4  sums0  =  0.0f;    //  (sumXX,  sumXY,  sumX,  sumXZ)
    float4  sums1  =  0.0f;    //  (sumYX,  sumYY,  sumY,  sumYZ)
    float4  sums2  =  0.0f;    //  (sumX,   sumY,   sum1,  sumZ )
    int2  offset;
    [unroll]
    for (offset.y = −RADIUS;  offset.y <= RADIUS;  ++offset.y)
    {
        [unroll]
        for (offset.x = −RADIUS;  offset.x <= RADIUS;  ++offset.x)
        {
            float4  diff  =  positions[t + offset] − center;
            float  valid  =  sign(diff.w);
            sums0  +=  valid*diff.xxxx*diff.xywz;
            sums1  +=  valid*diff.yyyy*diff.xywz;
            sums2  +=  valid*diff.xywz;
        }
    }

    if (sums2.z >= 3.0f)
    {
        float3  V0xV1  =  cross(sums0.xyz,  sums1.xyz);
        float3  V1xV2  =  cross(sums1.xyz,  sums2.xyz);
        float3  V2xV0  =  cross(sums2.xyz,  sums0.xyz);
        float  determinant  =  dot(sums0.xyz,  V1xV2);
        float3  DABC  =  sums0.w*V1xV2 + sums1.w*V2xV0 + sums2.w*V0xV1;
        planes[t]  =  float4(DABC.xy,  −determinant,  DABC.z);
    }
    else
    {
        planes[t]  =  0.0f;
    }
}
else
{
    planes[t]  =  0.0f;
}
};
```

LISTING 7.9: HLSL shader for least-squares plane fitting.

Valid positions are of the form $(x, y, z, 1)$, where $z > 0$ and missing data are of the form $(x, y, 0, 0)$. The shader first tests the w-component to see whether the incoming point is valid. If not, the returned 4-tuple for the plane is $(0, 0, 0, 0)$ as an indication to the application that no plane is available for a missing datum.

The center of the neighborhood is chosen to occur at (x, y) of the incoming point. For the height field of this example, this point is the xy-mean when the neighborhood has no missing values. However, it is only the approximate xy-mean when the neighborhood has missing values. Subtracting the approximate xy-mean will still help us avoid the catastrophic cancellation mentioned previously.

The covariance matrix is computed by iterating over the neighboring points. Notice that as a 4-tuple the center is $(x, y, 0, 0)$. When computing the covariance matrix, we subtract the center from each neighbor. Having a w-value of zero means that we will not destroy the validity information stored in the points' w-channel. The sign of the w-channel of the difference is either one or zero.

The summation is computed efficiently using vectorization. The matching swizzles indicate the particular sum. For example, the swizzle pairs of diff.xxxx*diff.xywz are xx, xy, xw, and xz. For valid positions, the w-channel is one, so the pair xw corresponds to an x-sum. For diff.yyyy*diff.xywz the pairs are yx, yy, yw, and yz. For valid positions, the w-channel is one, so the pair yw corresponds to a y-sum. For diff.xywz and valid positions, the w-channel corresponds to a sum of the numbers one, in which case sums2.z is the number of valid positions in the neighborhood. No valid positions mean no estimated plane, but to obtain a plane fit we should have at least three noncollinear points. Thus, sums2.z needs to be at least three. Even this might not be enough if your missing data is such that the valid neighborhood points lie on a line. When not enough valid data is available, the returned plane is $(0, 0, 0, 0)$ as an indication to the application that no plane is available.

At this time we have enough valid sample points to solve the linear system for the coefficients (A, B, C). Abstractly, the system of Equation (7.7) is $M\mathbf{P} = \mathbf{R}$, where M is the matrix of summations, $\mathbf{P}$ represents the coefficients of the plane equation, and $\mathbf{R}$ is the right-hand-side column of summations. The HLSL shader could explicitly solve the equation using Cramer's rule and scalar computations, but to take advantage of the vectorization of the cross product, I use the following fact. We can write M as a matrix of row vectors and the inverse as a matrix of column vectors,

$$M = \begin{bmatrix} \mathbf{V}_0^\mathsf{T} \\ \mathbf{V}_1^\mathsf{T} \\ \mathbf{V}_2^\mathsf{T} \end{bmatrix}, \quad M^{-1} = \frac{1}{\det(M)} \begin{bmatrix} \mathbf{V}_1 \times \mathbf{V}_2 \mid \mathbf{V}_2 \times \mathbf{V}_0 \mid \mathbf{V}_0 \times \mathbf{V}_1 \end{bmatrix} \quad (7.19)$$

where $\mathbf{V}_i$ are 3×1 column vectors and $\det(M) = \mathbf{V}_0 \cdot \mathbf{V}_1 \times \mathbf{V}_2$ is the determinant of M.

If you were to convert the shader to using double rather than float, be aware that there are no double versions of cross or dot. You will need to write your own. You can do so in a scalar-like manner but you could also mimic the Intel SSE2 SIMD approach that is implemented in class SIMD in the files GteIntelSSE.{h,inl,cpp}.

Executing the two shaders—one for Bézier evaluation and one for least-squares fitting—in each pass of OnIdle leads to approximately 186 frames per second.

7.4   Partial Sums

Given a sequence of n numbers $\{a_i\}_{i=0}^{n-1}$, the goal is to compute the partial sums $\{s_j\}_{j=0}^{n-1}$ where $s_j = \sum_{i=0}^{j} a_j$. Although perhaps not interesting by itself,

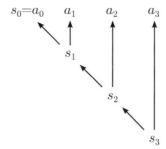

FIGURE 7.1: The binary expression tree for computing partial sums on the CPU.

applications might have partial sums as a subproblem. An example is provided in Section 7.6 for computing the shortest path through a weighted graph on a rectangular grid.

Computing partial sums on a CPU is simple, as shown in Listing 7.10.

```
float a[n] = <the numbers to sum>;
float s[n];  // the partial sums
s[0] = a[0];
for (int i = 1; i < n; ++i)
{
    s[i] = s[i-1] + a[i];
}
```

LISTING 7.10: A CPU implementation for computing partial sums.

This algorithm is sequential, because each partial sum is computed only after the previous partial sum is computed. It is possible to implement this algorithm for the GPU using a single thread; however, n must be small, otherwise the GPU execution time might exceed the maximum allowed before the display driver must gracefully shutdown, and a single thread of execution is definitely not recommended for hardware designed for embarrassingly parallel computation.

To motivate how you would make better use of the GPU, note that the CPU algorithm generates an expression tree that is binary. For example, let $n = 4$. The binary tree is shown in Figure 7.1. Each interior node is a sum of the numbers in the two child nodes to which the arrows point. The tree represents a parenthesizing of the sums, namely, $s_0 = a_0$, $s_1 = (a_0) + a_1$, $s_2 = (a_0 + a_1) + a_2$, and $s_3 = ((a_0 + a_1) + a_2) + a_3$.

If we can construct a different binary tree to represent the expression, but one that allows us to compute in parallel, such a tree will be a good candidate for computing the partial sums on the GPU. In fact, there are many ways to do this, all according to *dynamic programming*. Define $S(i,j) = \sum_{k=i}^{j} a_j$ for all relevant indices i and j with $i \leq j$. The input numbers are $a_i = S(i,i)$. We can decompose such a sum as $S(i,j) = S(i,k) + S(k+1,j)$ for any index k with $i \leq k$ and $k + 1 \leq j$. As is the case in dynamic programming, there

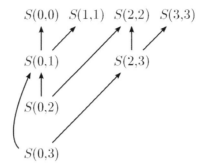

FIGURE 7.2: A DAG for computing partial sums of four numbers.

are many subproblems we could solve but we want to select a small set of subproblems, memoize the results, and combine them to solve the original problem. One such approach is illustrated as a directed acyclic graph (DAG) when $n = 4$, shown in Figure 7.2. Each node in the graph has two arcs pointing to the nodes whose values are summed. The inputs are $S(i, i) = a_i$ for $0 \le i \le 3$. The first sums to compute are $S(0, 1) = S(0, 0) + S(1, 1)$ and $S(2, 3) = S(2, 2) + S(3, 3)$. These may be computed simultaneously, so we have our first hint at parallelism. The next sums to compute are $S(0, 2) = S(0, 1) + S(2, 2)$ and $S(0, 3) = S(0, 1) + S(2, 3)$.

The pattern of decomposing is more obvious when $n = 8$, as shown in Figure 7.3. The first sums to compute in parallel are $S(0, 1)$, $S(2, 3)$, $S(4, 5)$, and $S(6, 7)$. The second sums to compute in parallel are $S(0, 2)$, $S(4, 6)$, $S(0, 3)$, and $S(4, 7)$. The third sums to compute in parallel are $S(0, 4)$, $S(0, 5)$, $S(0, 6)$, and $S(0, 7)$. Observe that each subset of sums has four numbers that can be computed in parallel. If we were to compute the partial sums using the CPU algorithm discussed first, the number of additions is seven because the loop executes seven times. Using the DAG approach, we use twelve additions, but unlike the CPU algorithm, some of these happen in parallel. Each subset of four terms are computed simultaneously, so four additions occur in a single unit of time. We have three subsets, so effectively we use three units of time for addition on the GPU but seven units on the CPU. Of course, in practice you have start-up costs to take into account, so as always—profile your results.

The DAG pattern extends to larger $n = 2^m$. The decomposition is

$$S(2^p x, 2^p x + 2^{p-1} + y)$$
$$= S(2^p x, 2^p x + 2^{p-1} - 1) + S(2^p x + 2^{p-1}, 2^p x + 2^{p-1} + y) \quad (7.20)$$

for $0 \le x < 2^{m-p}$, $0 \le y < 2^{p-1}$, and for each p increasing from 1 to m. This equates to m shaders called in succession, each shader having a single group of $n/2 = 2^{m-1}$ threads. The CPU version of the algorithm uses $n - 1$ additions. The GPU version makes $log_2(n)$ passes, $n/2$ additions computed in

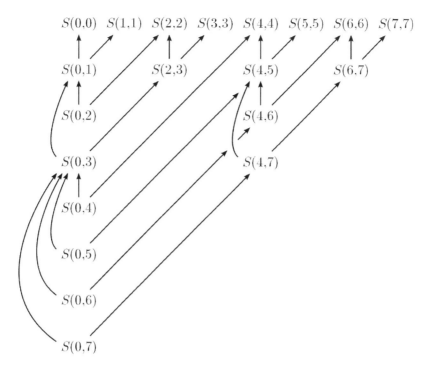

FIGURE 7.3: A DAG for computing partial sums of eight numbers.

parallel per pass, so asymptotically the GPU performance is superior. That is the theory, but as always you need to profile the algorithm to measure the real speedup.

The number of threads per dimension in a D3D11 HLSL program is limited to 1024, so the sample code presented next is set up for $n = 1024$. The numbers $S(i, j)$ are stored in an array, but the set of relevant numbers is sparse in the array. This allows the program to remain simple. The HLSL program can be redesigned to handle $n > 1024$ and to be more efficient about memory usage, but I leave this as an exercise. Listing 7.11 shows the HLSL code.

```
// Code contains contents of PartialSums.hlsl.
#define NUM_X_THREADS (1 << (LOGN-P))
#define NUM_Y_THREADS (1 << (P-1))
#define TWO_P (1 << P)
#define TWO_PM1 (1 << (P-1))
RWTexture2D<float> sum;
[numthreads(NUM_X_THREADS, NUM_Y_THREADS, 1)]
void CSMain(int2 t : SV_GroupThreadID)
{
    float input0 = sum[int2(TWO_P * t.x, TWO_P * t.x + TWO_PM1 - 1)];
    float input1 = sum[int2(TWO_P * t.x + TWO_PM1,
        TWO_P * t.x + TWO_PM1 + t.y)];
    sum[int2(TWO_P * t.x, TWO_P * t.x + TWO_PM1 + t.y)] = input0 + input1;
}
```

```
// The application code is executed on the CPU.  Create the compute shader
// objects.  The diagonal of sum(*,*) is set to the numbers whose partial
// sums are required.
std::mt19937 mte;
std::uniform_real_distribution<float> unitRandom(0.0f, 1.0f);
int const logn = 10;
int const n = (1 << logn);
std::shared_ptr<ComputeShader> partialSumShader[logn];
std::shared_ptr<Texture2> sum(new Texture2(DF_R32_FLOAT, n, n));
float* data = sum->GetAs<float>();
for (int i = 0; i < n; ++i)
{
        data[i + n*i] = unitRandom(mte);
}
sum->SetUsage(Resource::SHADER_OUTPUT);
sum->SetCopyType(Resource::COPY_STAGING_TO_CPU);
HLSLDefiner definer;
definer.SetInt("LOGN", logn);
for (int i = 0; i < logn; ++i)
{
    definer.SetInt("P", i + 1);
    partialSumShader[i].reset(
        ShaderFactory::CreateCompute("PartialSums.hlsl"), definer);
    partialSumShader[i]->Set("sum", sum);
}

// Execute the shader.  Each call involves one group of threads.
DX11Engine* engine = <your engine object>;
for (int i = 0; i < logn; ++i)
{
    engine->Execute(partialSumShader[i], 1, 1, 1);
}

// Read back the data.  If this is one stage in a longer GPU pipeline and
// you plan on consuming the partial sums in a later stage, there is no
// need to read back the data.
engine->CopyGpuToCpu(sum);
float partialSum[n];
for (int i = 0; i < n; ++i)
{
    partial[i] = data[0 + n*i];  // The elements sum(0,i).
}
```

LISTING 7.11: The HLSL program for computing partial sums of numbers.

7.5 All-Pairs Triangle Intersection

Let us look at the problem of computing whether two 3D triangles intersect, a *test-intersection* query, so to speak. In such a query, we care only about knowing the triangles intersect (or not). A *find-intersection* query involves computing the actual set of intersection, which in the case of two triangles is either a point or a line segment. For simplicity, I will consider the two triangles to intersect only when the set of intersection is a line segment. Such an intersection is said to be *transverse*, whereas the point-contact case is said to be *tangential*.

Let the first triangle have vertices $\mathbf{U}_i$ and the second triangle have vertices $\mathbf{V}_i$ for $0 \le i \le 2$. The planes that contain the triangles have (not necessarily unit-length) normal vectors

$$\mathbf{N} = (\mathbf{U}_2 - \mathbf{U}_0) \times (\mathbf{U}_1 - \mathbf{U}_0), \ \ \mathbf{M} = (\mathbf{V}_2 - \mathbf{V}_0) \times (\mathbf{V}_1 - \mathbf{V}_0) \qquad (7.21)$$

and the plane equations are $\mathbf{N} \cdot (\mathbf{X} - \mathbf{U}_0) = 0$ and $\mathbf{M} \cdot (\mathbf{X} - \mathbf{V}_0) = 0$.

A necessary condition for the second triangle to intersect the first is that the second triangle must intersect the plane of the first. A transverse intersection of triangle and plane requires that at least one vertex is on the side of the plane in the direction of $\mathbf{N}$ and at least one vertex is on the opposite side of the plane. In terms of the plane equation, we need $d_{i_0} = \mathbf{N} \cdot (\mathbf{V}_{i_0} - \mathbf{U}_0) > 0$ for some i_0 and $d_{i_1} = \mathbf{N} \cdot (\mathbf{V}_{i_1} - \mathbf{U}_0) < 0$ for some i_1. The remaining vertex $\mathbf{V}_{i_2}$ can be on either side of the plane or even on the plane itself. The edge connecting $\mathbf{V}_{i_0}$ and $\mathbf{V}_{i_1}$ intersects the plane at a point $\mathbf{P} = \mathbf{V}_{i_0} + t(\mathbf{V}_{i_1} - \mathbf{V}_{i_0})$ for some $t \in (0, 1)$. Because the intersection point is on the plane, we know

$$
\begin{aligned}
0 &= \mathbf{N} \cdot (\mathbf{P} - \mathbf{U}_0) \\
&= \mathbf{N} \cdot (\mathbf{V}_{i_0} - \mathbf{U}_0) + t\mathbf{N} \cdot (\mathbf{V}_{i_1} - \mathbf{V}_{i_0}) \\
&= \mathbf{N} \cdot (\mathbf{V}_{i_0} - \mathbf{U}_0) + t\mathbf{N} \cdot ((\mathbf{V}_{i_1} - \mathbf{U}_0) - (\mathbf{V}_{i_0} - \mathbf{U}_0)) \\
&= d_{i_0} + t(d_{i_1} - d_{i_0})
\end{aligned} \qquad (7.22)
$$

Solving for t and substituting in the parametric equation for $\mathbf{P}$, the intersection point is

$$\mathbf{P} = \frac{d_{i_1} \mathbf{V}_{i_0} - d_{i_0} \mathbf{V}_{i_1}}{d_{i_1} - d_{i_0}} \qquad (7.23)$$

If two edges of the triangle intersect the plane transversely, we can compute the points of intersection using Equation (7.22), say $\mathbf{P}_0$ and $\mathbf{P}_1$. In the event that only one edge transversely intersects the plane, call the intersection $\mathbf{P}_0$, then call the remaining vertex on the plane $\mathbf{P}_1$. In either case the line segment of intersection has endpoints $\mathbf{P}_0$ and $\mathbf{P}_1$. A direction of the line segment is, of course, the difference of endpoints. However, a line direction is also the cross product of normals, $\mathbf{N} \times \mathbf{M}$. Choose a unit-length direction $\mathbf{D} = \mathbf{N} \times \mathbf{M}/|\mathbf{N} \times \mathbf{M}|$.

For the triangles to intersect transversely, we need each triangle to intersect the plane of the other triangle, thereby producing two segments with four endpoints: $\mathbf{P}_0$, $\mathbf{P}_1$, $\mathbf{Q}_0$, and $\mathbf{Q}_1$. Both segments must be contained by the same line, but we do not yet know whether the segments overlap (triangles intersect) or are separated (triangles do not intersect). For numerical robustness, choose $\mathbf{A}$ to be the average of the four points. We may compute scalars s_i and t_i so that $\mathbf{P}_i = \mathbf{A} + s_i \mathbf{D}$ and $\mathbf{Q}_i = \mathbf{A} + t_i \mathbf{D}$. The triangles intersect transversely whenever the intervals $[\min(s_0, s_1), \max(s_0, s_1)]$ and $[\min(t_0, t_1), \max(t_0, t_1)]$ overlap. They do overlap when

$$\max(s_0, s_1) > \min(t_0, t_1) \ \text{ and } \ \max(t_0, t_1) > \min(s_0, s_1) \qquad (7.24)$$

In fact, this is a find-intersection query because the interval of intersection determines the line segment of intersection of the two triangles.

The exhaustive algorithm for determining where two triangle meshes intersect is to iterate over all pairs of triangles, one from each mesh, and compute the intersection of the two triangles of the pair. This is generally not the approach one should take when computing on a CPU, because it is extremely slow and inefficient. A spatial data structure is typically used to localize the search for intersecting pairs. For example, a tree of bounding volumes may be precomputed for a nondeformable triangle mesh—usually the bounding volumes are spheres, axis-aligned boxes, or oriented boxes. The intersection query involves testing for overlap of the root bounding volumes, one from each tree. If they do not overlap, then the triangle meshes cannot intersect. If they do overlap, a double recursion is applied, once for the first tree and then for each visited node, once for the second tree. At any time when two bounding volumes do not overlap, the depth-first traversal stops for those tree branches. Assuming the meshes do intersect, you will eventually reach two overlapping bounding volumes, each one at a leaf of a tree. Assuming that the leaf nodes represent single triangles, at that time you can apply the triangle-triangle intersection query. I have a description of this algorithm in [9] and a Wild Magic sample application called CollisionsBoundTree that implements it for two cylinder meshes.

When you have a massively parallel GPU, you might very well have enough computing power for all-pairs triangle intersections, assuming that the number of triangles is not too large. The sample application that illustrates this is

GeometricTools/GTEngine/Samples/Geometry/AllPairsTriangles

The triangle-triangle intersection query described previously is implemented in the files TriangleIntersection.{h,cpp}. A mesh-mesh intersection query is implemented both for the CPU and for the GPU. In this sample, the first mesh is a cylinder with 4416 triangles and the second mesh is a torus with 4608 triangles. Initially, the two meshes are not intersecting. The cylinder triangles are drawn in blue and the torus triangles are drawn in red. You can use the virtual trackball by left-click-and-drag to rotate the torus so that it intersects the cylinder. When a pair of triangles intersect, the cylinder triangle is drawn in cyan and the torus triangle is drawn in yellow. Figure 7.4 shows a screen capture of the intersection.

The performance difference is quite noticeable on my AMD 7970 graphics card. The GPU version runs at 175 frames per second, allowing you to rotate the torus and see the intersection results in real time. The CPU version runs so slowly that the frame rate counter I display always shows zero frames per second. Thus, you might as well measure seconds per frame for the CPU.

You can certainly choke the GPU by increasing the triangle count. Possible alternatives to improve performance are:

1. Decompose the meshes into submeshes and call the GPU triangle-triangle intersector for each pair of submeshes.

FIGURE 7.4: Intersection of a meshes for a cylinder and a torus.

2. Precompute a tree of bounding volumes and perform the localized search on the CPU to generate sets of triangles that you know do intersect. Then process those sets with the GPU triangle-triangle intersector.

3. Precompute the tree of bounding volumes on the GPU and use the GPU triangle-triangle intersector.

I leave these alternatives as exercises.

7.6 Shortest Path in a Weighted Graph

Consider a directed graph $G = (V, E)$, where V is the set of vertices and E is the set of directed edges connecting vertices. Assuming V is finite, we may index the n vertices as $V = \{V_i\}_{i=0}^{n-1}$ and the m edges as $E = \{E_j\}_{j=0}^{m-1}$, where $E_j = \langle V_{i_j}, V_{k_j} \rangle$ for a pair of vertices. Each edge is assigned a positive weight w_j. Given a beginning vertex V_b and an ending vertex V_e, the problem is to compute a path from V_b to V_e whose sum of weights along the path is the minimum for any path connecting the two vertices.

Standard textbooks on algorithms (for example, [6]) discuss this type of problem in the general context of graph algorithms. In particular, this is known as a single-pair shortest-path problem. Variations include single-source shortest-path (shortest paths from a beginning vertex to all other vertices), single-destination shortest-path (shortest path to an ending vertex from all other vertices), and all-pairs shortest-paths (shortest paths for all pairs of vertices). Methods of solving such problems include relaxation, Dijkstra's algorithm, and the Bellman-Ford algorithm. For the single-pair shortest-path problem in a directed acyclic graph, we can use a topological sort of the vertices and compute the shortest path on order $O(n+m)$, where n is the number of vertices and m is the number of edges.

This section provides an example of such a problem for a graph that is a square grid of dimensions $S \times S$. The grid points are located at the integer points (x, y), where $0 \leq x < S$ and $0 \leq y < S$. The directed edges starting at (x, y) are limited to $E_1(x, y) = \langle (x, y), (x+1, y) \rangle$, $E_2(x, y) = \langle (x, y), (x, y+1) \rangle$, and $E_3(x, y) = \langle (x, y), (x + 1, y + 1) \rangle$. Each point has an associated function value, $F(x, y) > 0$.

Think of the grid and function values as an image that represents a terrain where the function values are altitude (height). To walk between two points on the terrain with minimum effort, you want to minimize the total change in altitude. For example, if you are at a point facing a tall mountain peak and you want to get to a point directly ahead but on the other side of the mountain, you have the option of walking straight up the mountain, over the top, and down to your destination. Climbing can be a lot of effort, so you can instead try to walk around the mountain because the path keeps you on relatively flat terrain. However, if the path around the mountain is on the order of ten kilometers but the path up and over the mountain is on the order of one kilometer, it is not clear which path minimizes your effort. On a small scale, you will consider the altitudes between your current location and a location to which you want to walk taking into account the distance between the locations.

In the abstract, the weight w assigned to an edge of the grid is the sum of the altitudes along the straight-line path connecting the vertices but multiplied by the length of the path. In the continuous formulation, consider vertices (x_0, y_0) and (x_1, y_1) and the linear path connecting them, $(x(t), y(t)) = (x_0, y_0) + t(x_1, y_1)$ for $t \in [0, 1]$. The weight is an integral that we can approximate using the trapezoid rule,

$$
\begin{aligned}
w &= \sqrt{(x_1 - x_0)^2 + (y_1 - y_0)^2} \int_0^1 F(x(t), y(t)) \, dt \\
&\doteq \sqrt{(x_1 - x_0)^2 + (y_1 - y_0)^2} \left(F(x_0, y_0) + F(x_1, y_1) \right)/2
\end{aligned}
\tag{7.25}
$$

where the right-hand side is an application of the trapezoid rule for approximating an integral. Thus, the weights w_i associated with the edges E_i defined

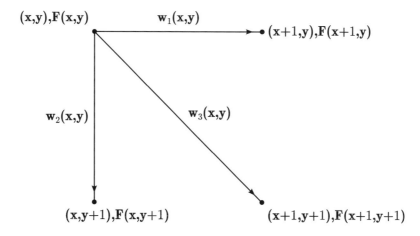

FIGURE 7.5: The directed edges from a point in the grid graph. Each vertex stores the altitude $F(x, y)$ and the weights $w_1(x, y)$, $w_2(x, y)$, and $w_3(x, y)$.

previously are

$$w_1(E_1) = (F(x, y) + F(x + 1, y)) / 2$$

$$w_2(E_2) = (F(x, y) + F(x, y + 1)) / 2 \qquad (7.26)$$

$$w_3(E_3) = (F(x, y) + F(x + 1, y + 1)) / \sqrt{2}$$

Figure 7.5 shows point (x, y) and the three neighbors to which you can walk. The weights are labeled with the beginning point, indicating that a data structure for the vertex at (x, y) stores the altitude $F(x, y)$ and three weights $w_1(x, y)$, $w_2(x, y)$, and $w_3(x, y)$ for the outgoing edges.

The beginning vertex for our example is $(0, 0)$ and the ending vertex is $(S - 1, S - 1)$. We need to compute a path of minimum total weight. I will refer to the sum of weights for a path between two vertices as the *distance* between the vertices, but keep in mind this is not the Euclidean distance between the xy-values. Let $d(x, y)$ denote the distance from $(0, 0)$ to (x, y). The vertices are sorted topologically in the sense that a vertex located at (x, y) also has three incoming edges, as shown in Figure 7.6. If the distances $d(x - 1, y - 1)$, $d(x - 1, y)$, and $d(x, y - 1)$ are known, we can compute $d(x, y)$ in a recursive manner as

$$d(x, y) = \min \left\{ \begin{array}{lcl} d(x - 1, y) & + & w_1(x - 1, y), \\ d(x, y - 1) & + & w_2(x, y - 1), \\ d(x - 1, y - 1) & + & w_3(x - 1, y - 1) \end{array} \right\} \qquad (7.27)$$

Initially we know that $d(0, 0) = 0$; that is, the distance from a vertex to itself is zero. The recursion in Equation (7.27) requires us to know the distance

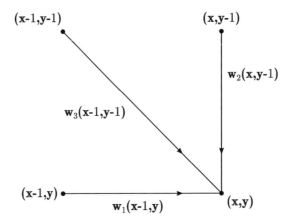

FIGURE 7.6: The directed edges to a point in the grid graph.

for the three predecessors show in Figure 7.6. Consequently, we must compute next the values $d(x, 0)$ for $1 \le x < S$ and $d(0, y)$ for $1 \le y < S$. Finally, we can compute $d(x, y)$ for $x \ge 1$ and $y \ge 1$, but not just at any selected (x, y). The distance computation effectively is a breadth-first process. Once we know the distance at the top and left edges of the grid, we can solve for distances along grid lines of the form $x + y = z$ for $2 \le z \le 2(S - 1)$, as shown in Figure 7.7. Once we have computed the distances for all grid points on a line $x + y = z$, we can use those distances for computing grid points on the next line $x + y = z + 1$. For $z = 2$, we have previously computed $d(2, 0)$ and $d(0, 2)$,

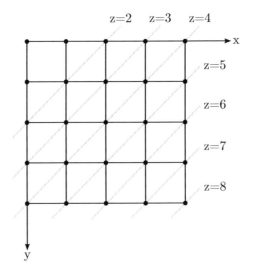

FIGURE 7.7: The breadth-first update of distances in a 5×5 grid.

so we need only compute $d(1,1)$. For $z = 3$, we must compute $d(1,2)$ and $d(2,1)$. Pseudocode for the breadth-first search on an $S \times S$ grid is shown in Listing 7.12.

```
d(0,0) = 0;
for (x = 1; x < S; ++x)
{
    d(x,0) = d(x-1,0) + w1(x-1,0);
}
for (y = 1; y < S; ++y)
{
    d(0,y) = d(0,y-1) + w2(0,x-1);
}
for (z = 2; z < S; ++z)
{
    for (x = 1, y = z-x; y > 0; ++x, --y)
    {
        d1 = d(x-1,y) + w1(x-1,y);
        d2 = d(x,y-1) + w2(x,y-1);
        d3 = d(x-1,y-1) + w3(x-1,y-1);
        d(x,y) = min(d1,d2,d3);
    }
}
for (z = S; z <= 2*(S-1); ++z)
{
    for (y = S-1, x = z-y; x < S; --y, ++x)
    {
        d1 = d(x-1,y) + w1(x-1,y);
        d2 = d(x,y-1) + w2(x,y-1);
        d3 = d(x-1,y-1) + w3(x-1,y-1);
        d(x,y) = min(d1,d2,d3);
    }
}
```

LISTING 7.12: Breadth-first update of distances in an $S \times S$ grid.

It is not sufficient to compute the distances. We need to keep track of the actual path. Whatever weight was used in computing the minimum distance, its grid location must be stored. The data structure for each grid point is therefore

```
struct Node
{
    float distance;
    int xPrevious, yPrevious;
};
```

At $(0,0)$, the previous location is set to $(-1,-1)$ as a flag indicating there is no previous neighbor. For $x > 0$, the previous location for $(x,0)$ is $(x-1,0)$. For $y > 0$, the previous location for $(0,y)$ is $(0,y-1)$. For $x > 0$ and $y > 0$, the innermost loop logic must be replaced by

```
dmin = d(x-1,y) + w1(x-1,y);
previousmin = (x-1,y);
dcandidate = d(x,y-1) + w2(x,y-1);
if (dcandidate < dmin)
{
    dmin = dcandidate;
    previousmin = (x,y-1);
}
dcandidate = d(x-1,y-1) + w3(x-1,y-1);
```

```
if (dcandidate < dmin)
{
    dmin = dcandidate;
    previousmin = (x-1,y-1);
}
d(x,y) = dmin;
previous(x,y) = previousmin;
```

Once the distances have been computed, the path is generated by

```
stack<intpair> path;
x = S - 1;   y = S - 1;
while (x != -1 && y != -1)
{
    path.push(x, y);
    (x, y) = previous(x, y);
}
```

and you can pop the stack to visit the path nodes from $(0,0)$ to $(S-1, S-1)$.

The algorithm for shortest path is straightforward to implement for the CPU. However, implementing a GPU version that has decent performance is more difficult. The first problem is implementing the partial sums via the loops for $d(x,0)$ and $d(0,y)$. A single GPU thread could be dedicated per loop, but that sequential operation is not efficient. Instead, we can use the dynamic programming solution discussed in Section 7.4. The second problem is implementing the inner loops of the z-loops. Because of the dependency that the $z+1$ line cannot be computed until the z line is computed, we do not have much workload that can be distributed across GPU threads. Fortunately, though, the order of computation in the inner loops is irrelevant, so each distance $d(x,y)$ on a line $x+y=z$ can be computed in parallel with the others. Thus, we can take advantage of some parallelism, but the GPU is not fully utilized.

The sample algorithm that implements both the CPU and GPU versions is

GeometricTools/GTEngine/Samples/Geometry/ShortestPath

A height field (for the altitudes) of size 512×512 is generated from a bicubic polynomial and then perturbed by small random numbers. This could be done on the CPU, but I have chosen to create it on the GPU. The values must be read back to the CPU in order for the CPU-based shortest-path algorithm to consume it. The GPU version has quite a few shaders to create in order to use the partial-sum algorithm and have the results for $d(x,0)$ stored in the first row of a distance texture and the results for $d(0,y)$ stored in the first column of the same texture. Also, a previous texture is required, a two-channel integer-valued texture whose first row and first column must be initialized properly. The z-line shader has a constant buffer that stores the starting (x,y) and the number of pixels on that line to update. This buffer is updated for each z-value in the loops.

The height field is recomputed each frame. The performance measurements are comparable for my AMD 7970 graphics card. The CPU performance is 57 frames per second and the GPU performance is 60 frames per second. This is not that significant a speed up. However, the need for a shortest-path algorithm with the grid as described here arose in a stereo vision application. Signals (digital curves) for two corresponding scan lines in rectified left and right images needed to be matched to locate corresponding points. The function $F(x, y)$ was a cost function for matching a point (and neighborhood) at row-index x on the left signal to a point (and neighborhood) at row-index y on the right signal. The cost function is expensive to compute on a CPU, so it was computed instead on the GPU; this is why I recompute the height field in the sample application—to mimic the vision application. Reading back the results to the CPU, computing the shortest path on the CPU, and uploading the path to the GPU for downstream computations was not an option because we wanted the vision computations to stay always on the GPU. This is an example of the performance guidelines I mentioned in Section 5.3.3: it is not always necessary to have each task in a GPU-based application run faster than its counterpart on the CPU. The important performance measurement is end-to-end speed.

7.7   Convolution

Consider a 2D image, whether color or grayscale, that must be filtered by convolution. This process computes a pixel at location (x, y) in the output image as a weighted sum of pixels in a rectangular region centered at (x, y) in the input image. Let the input image be represented as an $N_0 \times N_1$ array with elements A_{i_0, i_1}, where $0 \leq i_0 < N_0$ and $0 \leq i_1 < N_1$. The output image is the same sized array and has elements B_{i_0, i_1}. The weights are represented as a $(2M_0 + 1) \times (2M_1 + 1)$ array with elements W_{j_0, j_1} where $0 \leq j_0 \leq 2M_0$ and $0 \leq j_1 \leq 2M_1$. For simplicity, the weight array is chosen with odd dimensions. The convolution of image A with weights W is

$$B_{i_0, i_1} = \sum_{j_0 = -M_0}^{M_0} \sum_{j_1 = -M_1}^{M_1} W_{j_0 + M_0, j_1 + M_1} I_{i_0 + j_0, i_1 + j_1} \tag{7.28}$$

The typical example is blurring using a radially symmetric Gaussian distribution to generate the weights in a square filter of size $2M + 1$,

$$G(x, y, \sigma) = \frac{1}{2\pi\sigma^2} \exp\left(-\frac{x^2 + y^2}{2\sigma^2}\right) \tag{7.29}$$

where σ^2 is the variance and the mean is $(0, 0)$. The distribution is formulated in terms of continuous variables but you need the weights on a discrete grid. Therefore, you need a relationship between the desired standard deviation σ and M; see the discussion later in this section about one way to do this.

The sample application

GeometricTools/GTEngine/Samples/Imagics/Convolution

shows several methods for computing a convolution for a 2D image. Two of these compute the convolution natively in 2D. Three of these use the fact that the Gaussian distribution is *separable*:

$$G(x, y, \sigma) = \frac{1}{\sqrt{2\pi\sigma^2}} \exp\left(-\frac{x^2}{2\sigma^2}\right) \frac{1}{\sqrt{2\pi\sigma^2}} \exp\left(-\frac{y^2}{2\sigma^2}\right) = g_0(x, \sigma) g_1(y, \sigma) \tag{7.30}$$

where the last equality defines the functions g_0 and g_1. In continuous terms with images defined for all real numbers, the convolution is defined by

$$B(x, y) = [G \otimes I](x, y) = \int_{-\infty}^{\infty} \int_{-\infty}^{\infty} G(u, v) I(x - u, y - v) \, du \, dv \tag{7.31}$$

Turns out that separability means you can convolve with each of the functions in the factorization,

$$B(x, y) = [G \otimes I](x, y) = [g_1 \otimes [g_0 \otimes I]](x, y) \tag{7.32}$$

In discrete terms, the convolution of an image with a separable filter of size $N \times M$ is equivalent to convolving first with a filter of size $N \times 1$ and then by a filter of size $1 \times M$. The number of arithmetic operations is greatly reduced, so it is more efficient to use separability. The sample application demonstrates this and shows the frame rates associated with each method.

The sample application also shows how to use group-shared memory in a compute shader. The memory is declared using an identifier groupshared, and it is shared by all threads in the thread group currently executing. In image processing algorithms such as convolution, the neighborhood image lookups can be a bottleneck in the memory system. A large amount of time is spent on looking up the same pixel value but in different threads when those threads all need access to the pixel. The idea of group-shared memory is to allow each thread to load one image value, have all threads wait until the entire group has loaded its values (via a synchronization call), and then proceed with the computations by accessing values in group-shared memory.

Listing 7.13 shows the straightforward implementation of a convolution of an image with a filter kernel of size $(2R + 1) \times (2R + 1)$ where the radius $R > 0$.

```
cbuffer Weights { float weight[2*R+1][2*R+1]; };
Texture2D<float4> input;
RWTexture2D<float4> output;

[numthreads(NUM_X_THREADS, NUM_Y_THREADS, 1)]
void CSMain(int2 dt : SV_DispatchThreadID)
{
    float4 result = 0.0f;
    for (int y = -R; y <= R; ++y)
```

```
    {
        for (int x = -R; x <= R; ++x)
        {
            result += weight[y+R][x+R]*input[dt+int2(x,y)];
        }
    }
    output[dt] = result;
}
```

LISTING 7.13: Convolution with a square filter kernel.

The filter kernel weights are supplied via a constant buffer. The default HLSL packing rules will store each weight in the x-swizzle of a register, so the constant buffers uses $(2R+1)^2$ registers and the application must pack the weights accordingly. Each thread will load all $(2R + 1)^2$ image values in the neighborhood centered at the thread ID (dt.x,dt.y). No attempt is made to avoid accessing the input image using out-of-range indices. According to the HLSL specifications for the ld instruction for a texture, out-of-range reads will return zeroed memory. If you execute this shader for a large radius, you will see darkening around the blurred image boundary. The zeroed memory is averaged with the image values, causing the darkening.

We do not know the order of execution of threads, but imagine that if thread (dt.x + 1, dt.y) were to execute immediately after thread (dt.x,dt.y), we would again load $(2R + 1)^2$ image values. However, only $(2R + 1)$ of them are new compared to the previous set, so will have loaded redundantly many image values from memory to registers. In an attempt to avoid the redundant loads, you may use group-shared memory. Listing 7.14 shows a shader that does so.

```
cbuffer Weights { float weight[2*R+1][2*R+1]; };
Texture2D<float4> input;
RWTexture2D<float4> output;
groupshared float4 samples[NUM_Y_THREADS + 2 * R][NUM_X_THREADS + 2 * R];

[numthreads(NUM_X_THREADS, NUM_Y_THREADS, 1)]
void CSMain(int2 dt : SV_DispatchThreadID, int2 gt : SV_GroupThreadID)
{
    // Load the texels from the input texture, store them in group-shared
    // memory, and have all threads in the group wait until all texels
    // are loaded.
    samples[gt.y + R][gt.x + R] = input[dt];
    if (gt.y >= R)
    {
        if (gt.y < NUM_Y_THREADS - R)
        {
            if (gt.x >= R)
            {
                if (gt.x < NUM_X_THREADS - R)
                {
                    // No extra inputs to load.
                }
                else
                {
                    samples[gt.y+R][gt.x+2*R] = input[dt+int2(+R,0)];
                }
            }
            else
```

```
                {
                    samples[gt.y+R][gt.x] = input[dt+int2(-R,0)];
                }
            }
            else
            {
                if (gt.x >= R)
                {
                    if (gt.x < NUM_X_THREADS - R)
                    {
                        samples[gt.y+2*R][gt.x+R] = input[dt+int2(0,+R)];
                    }
                    else
                    {
                        samples[gt.y+2*R][gt.x+2*R] = input[dt+int2(+R,+R)];
                        samples[gt.y+2*R][gt.x+R] = input[dt+int2(0,+R)];
                        samples[gt.y+R][gt.x+2*R] = input[dt+int2(+R,0)];
                    }
                }
                else
                {
                    samples[gt.y+2*R][gt.x] = input[dt+int2(-R,+R)];
                    samples[gt.y+2*R][gt.x+R] = input[dt+int2(0,+R)];
                    samples[gt.y+R][gt.x] = input[dt+int2(-R,0)];
                }
            }
        }
        else
        {
            if (gt.x >= R)
            {
                if (gt.x < NUM_X_THREADS - R)
                {
                    samples[gt.y][gt.x+R] = input[dt+int2(0,-R)];
                }
                else
                {
                    samples[gt.y][gt.x+2*R] = input[dt+int2(+R,-R)];
                    samples[gt.y][gt.x+R] = input[dt+int2(0,-R)];
                    samples[gt.y+R][gt.x+2*R] = input[dt+int2(+R,0)];
                }
            }
            else
            {
                samples[gt.y][gt.x] = input[dt+int2(-R,-R)];
                samples[gt.y][gt.x+R] = input[dt+int2(0,-R)];
                samples[gt.y+R][gt.x] = input[dt+int2(-R,0)];
            }
        }
    }

    GroupMemoryBarrierWithGroupSync();

    float4 result = 0.0f;
    for (int y = 0; y <= 2*R; ++y)
    {
        for (int x = 0; x <= 2*R; ++x)
        {
            result += weight[y][x] * samples[gt.y+y][gt.x+x];
        }
    }
    output[dt] = result;
}
```

LISTING 7.14: Convolution with a square filter kernel and using group-shared memory.

You will notice that the shader program is much longer than the direct approach. The first part of the program loads the input image values to group-shared memory. But why is this so complicated? The test image is 1024×768. For the sake of simplicity in the presentation, suppose $R = 1$ in which case we are convolving with a 3×3 kernel. Suppose that the number of x-threads is 512 and the number of x-groups is 2. To produce an output at pixel (x_0, y_0) requires accessing pixels with x-value satisfying $x_0 - R \leq x \leq x_0 + R$ and with y-value satisfying $y_0 - R \leq y_0 + R$. If (x_0, y_0) is within R pixels of the pixels represented by the thread group, we would access neighborhood values outside that set of pixels. Thus, the group-shared memory samples must be larger than the number of group threads in order to store the image values outside the group. The nested if-then-else statements are designed to distribute the loading responsibility among those pixels near the group boundaries. This is preferable to assigning the responsibility of a large number of loads to a small number of threads because threads not loading a lot of data will be stalled until the other threads can load theirs.

The function GroupMemoryBarrierWithGroupSync is for synchronization and specifies that all threads in the group wait until they get to that point in the code. Once they do, all data in the thread group has been loaded into samples and each thread can read the shared memory as needed to compute its weighted sum.

Now you might ask why bother choosing more than one x-group. The problem is that in D3D11, group-shared memory is limited to 32,768 bytes and the number of threads in a group is limited to 1024. In most cases you have to decompose the domain into small groups so that the shared data fits in memory. In Listing 7.14, we need

```
(NUM_X_THREADS+2*R)*(NUM_Y_THREADS+2*R) <= 32768/sizeof(float) = 2048
```

In the application code, I selected the number of x-threads and y-threads each to be sixteen and the radius can be no larger than eight. The radius eight case uses 16,384 bytes of shared memory.

The application also implements a shader that uses the separability of the Gaussian kernel. Two passes are required, one for a convolution with a $(2R+1) \times 1$ filter and one for a convolution with a $1 \times (2R+1)$ filter. Listing 7.15 shows the HLSL code.

```
cbuffer Weights { float weight[2*R+1]; };
Texture2D<float4> input;
RWTexture2D<float4> output;

[numthreads(NUM_X_THREADS, NUM_Y_THREADS, 1)]
void HorizontalPass(int2 dt : SV_DispatchThreadID)
{
    float4 result = 0.0f;
    for (int x = -R; x <= R; ++x)
    {
        result += weight[x+R] * input[dt+int2(x,0)];
    }
    output[dt] = result;
}
```

```
[numthreads(NUM_X_THREADS, NUM_Y_THREADS, 1)]
void VerticalPass(int2 dt : SV_DispatchThreadID)
{
    float4 result = 0.0f;
    for (int y = -R; y <= R; ++y)
    {
        result += weight[y+R] * input[dt+int2(0,y)];
    }
    output[dt] = result;
```

LISTING 7.15: Convolution with a square filter kernel and using separability.

The code is concise and runs faster than the code in Listings 7.13 and 7.14. I have also implemented the separable filters using group-shared memory, but I will not include the code here.

As always, you want to profile the results. Using simple frame rates (in convolutions per second), Table 7.2 is a comparison of the implementations. The method is 0 for Listing 7.13, 1 for Listing 7.14, and 2 for Listing 7.15. Method 3 is a convolution using separability and group-shared memory where the number of x-groups is 1. Method 4 is a convolution using separability and group-shared memory where the number of x-groups is 4. The numbers were somewhat surprising when comparing a method with and without group-shared memory. I expected the group-shared performance to be better for large radii. The only win for shared memory appears to be for 2D convolution with radius one. Apparently, the memory reads for the AMD 7970 are good enough that the groupshared mechanism does not help in this application. You should compare the methods anyway on other hardware.

In this example, the hope for group-shared memory was to avoid redundant memory lookups. Shared memory can be used also to cache numbers that are expensive to compute; that is, if you had to recompute expressions many times, causing a bottleneck in the scalar or vector arithmetic logic units, you should consider storing them in shared memory.

A final concept about convolution with square filter kernels is in order. The Gaussian kernel is separable. Thinking of the kernel as a $(2R+1) \times (2R+1)$ matrix M, the matrix can be factored as $M = \mathbf{V}\mathbf{V}^\mathsf{T}$ where $\mathbf{V}$ is a $(2R+1) \times 1$ vector. A 2D convolution by M may be obtained by convolving with $\mathbf{V}^\mathsf{T}$

TABLE 7.2: Performance comparisons for convolution implementations

radius	method 0	method 1	method 2	method 3	method 4
1	2834	3012	2238	1746	1750
2	2407	1860	2245	1743	1773
3	1442	1168	2233	1830	1929
4	1045	779	2275	1804	2086
5	701	544	2305	1705	1948
6	545	396	2244	1584	1780
7	399	306	2135	1495	1530
8	323	241	2033	1396	1500

(horizontal pass) and convolving the result with $\mathbf{V}$ (vertical pass). The vector $\mathbf{V}$ has symmetry to it. If v_i are the components of $\mathbf{V}$ for $0 \leq i \leq 2R$, then the center element is v_R and $v_{R+j} = V_{R-j}$ for $0 \leq j \leq R$. As a consequence, M is *symmetric about its center*; I will use the term *fully symmetric* to describe M. If $m_{i,j}$ are the elements of M for $0 \leq i \leq 2R$ and $0 \leq j \leq 2R$, then $m_{R+j,R+k} = m_{R-k,R-\ell}$ for $0 \leq k \leq R$ and $0 \leq \ell \leq R$. For example, consider $R = 2$ and $\sigma = 0.538079560$; then the vector is the following, written as a tuple

$$\mathbf{V} = (0.00073656, 0.13098156, 0.73656368, 0.13098156, 0.00073656) \quad (7.33)$$

and the matrix is

$$M = \begin{bmatrix} 0.00000054 & 0.00009647 & 0.00005425 & 0.00009647 & 0.00000054 \\ 0.00009647 & 0.01715617 & 0.09647627 & 0.01715617 & 0.00009647 \\ 0.00005425 & 0.09647627 & 0.54252612 & 0.09647627 & 0.00005425 \\ 0.00009647 & 0.01715617 & 0.09647627 & 0.01715617 & 0.00009647 \\ 0.00000054 & 0.00009647 & 0.00005425 & 0.00009647 & 0.00000054 \end{bmatrix} \quad (7.34)$$

If you were given a $(2R+1)^2$ fully symmetric matrix M without knowledge of how it was generated, how can you factor it in order to take advantage of separability? As it turns out, not all fully symmetric matrices can be factored into a product of a vector with itself. To see this, consider

$$M = \begin{bmatrix} a & b & a \\ b & c & b \\ a & b & a \end{bmatrix} \overset{?}{=} \begin{bmatrix} u \\ v \\ u \end{bmatrix} \begin{bmatrix} u & v & u \end{bmatrix} = \begin{bmatrix} u^2 & uv & u^2 \\ uv & v^2 & uv \\ u^2 & uv & u^2 \end{bmatrix} \quad (7.35)$$

where the question mark suggests it might or might not be possible to equate the left-hand and right-hand sides. For equality to occur, we need $a \geq 0$ and $c \geq 0$. This already places constraints on the elements of M, so not all fully symmetric matrices can be factored this way. As an attempt to allow negative a or c, we could introduce a scalar factor $\sigma < 0$ on the right-hand side so that $a = \sigma u^2$ and $c = \sigma v^2$; however, it is clear that the signs of a and c must agree. A matrix M with $a = -1$ and $c = 1$ cannot be factored as desired. When a and c are nonnegative, we obtain $u = \sqrt{a}$, $v = \sqrt{c}$, and $b = \sqrt{ac}$ which implies $b \geq 0$; however, if $b < 0$, we can choose u or v to be the negative square root.

It is possible, though, to factor M into a linear combination of at most $R+1$ vector products. The matrix is symmetric in the classical linear algebraic sense, $M^\mathsf{T} = M$, so it has $(2R + 1)$ linearly independent unit-length eigenvectors, say, $\mathbf{U}_i$ for $0 \leq i \leq 2R$, and corresponding eigenvalues λ_i. The eigenvalues are not necessarily distinct; in fact, zero is an eigenvalue of algebraic multiplicity at least R. The matrix can be decomposed into

$$M = \sum_{i=0}^{2R} \lambda_i \mathbf{U}_i \mathbf{U}_i^\mathsf{T} \quad (7.36)$$

which is derivable algebraically from $MR = RD$, where R is a rotation matrix whose columns are the $\mathbf{U}_i$ and D is a diagonal matrix whose diagonal entries are the corresponding eigenvalues. Let the eigenvalues be ordered so that the zero eigenvalues occur from indices n to $2R$, where $n \leq R$; then

$$M = \sum_{i=0}^{n-1} \lambda_i \mathbf{U}_i \mathbf{U}_i^\mathsf{T} \qquad (7.37)$$

The convolution of M with an image can be computed by convolving the image $2n$ times and then summing outputs. The input image is convolved with $\mathbf{U}_i$ (horizontal pass) and then $\mathbf{U}_i^\mathsf{T}$ (vertical pass), the result stored in an output image T_i. The final output image T is the linear combination $T = \sum_{i=0}^{n-1} \lambda_i T_i$.

For example, the derivative-like filter

$$M = \begin{bmatrix} -1 & -2 & -1 \\ -2 & 12 & -2 \\ -1 & -2 & -1 \end{bmatrix} = \lambda_0 \mathbf{U}_0 \mathbf{U}_0^\mathsf{T} + \lambda_1 \mathbf{U}_1 \mathbf{U}_1^\mathsf{T} \qquad (7.38)$$

where $\lambda_0 = 5 + \sqrt{57}$, $\lambda_1 = 5 - \sqrt{57}$, and

$$\mathbf{U}_0 = \frac{(2, -7 - \sqrt{57}, 2)}{\sqrt{8 + (7 + \sqrt{57})^2}}, \quad \mathbf{U}_1 = \frac{(2, -7 + \sqrt{57}, 2)}{\sqrt{8 + (7 - \sqrt{57})^2}} \qquad (7.39)$$

More factorizations for 5×5 general matrices (not necessarily fully symmetric) are proved in the PhD dissertation [24], where M is a sum of products with terms not necessarily generated by vector products. The hope is that a linear combination by convolutions of smaller filters will perform faster than a convolution by the original filter.

7.8 Median Filtering

Consider a 2D grayscale image that has a small number of pixel values that you wish to modify because they are extremely large or small compared to what you expect pixel values to be. For example, you might have a generally dark image that contains a small number of very bright pixels. At first you might consider using convolution with a filter kernel that performs a weighted average in each pixel's neighborhood to produce an output image for which the noise has been visually reduced. However, if a pixel is very bright and its neighbors very dark, a weighted average might not be enough to remedy the contrast at that pixel.

Instead, we can apply a *rank-order filter* that sorts the neighborhood of pixels by intensity and chooses as output one of the ordered values in a specified location. The most common is to choose the *median* of the pixel values.

The idea is that the very bright or very dark pixels are outliers and the sorting places them at the tail ends of the sorted pixels. Selecting the median reduces greatly the chance that a noisy pixel will still remain in the neighborhood in the output image.

Although the output is via selection, the rank-order filters are image smoothers just as weighted-average convolution filters are when you apply them repeatedly to an image. This is no surprise, because for sets of numbers with not a lot of variation of intensity, the mean and the median are similar. In fact, the fixed-point sequences from the repeated application of a one-dimensional median filter are completely known [7].

Rank-order filters may be extended by computing the output to be a weighted average of the ordered neighbors, but these filters are also smoothers. A more sophisticated extension is a *weighted majority minimum range* (WMMR) filter [22]. A set of $N + 1$ nonnegative weights are chosen that sum to one. After sorting a neighborhood of $(2N + 1)$ intensities, the weighted average is computed for each subset of $N + 1$ contiguous numbers. There are $N + 1$ such averages, the minimum chosen as the output of the filter. The fixed-point sequences from the repeated application of one-dimensional WMMR filter are also completely known. These demonstrate that the filter has smoothing behavior in regions where the intensities have small variation but has edge-preserving behavior in regions where the intensities have large variation.

In this section I discuss how to implement median filtering on two-dimensional images for high performance on the GPU. The sample application is

GeometricTools/GTEngine/Samples/Imagics/MedianFiltering

The WMMR filters may also be implemented on the GPU, but the implementations are not provided here. The median filtering is implemented for 3×3 and 5×5 neighborhoods using repeated applications of the min and max operators. The 3×3 approach is discussed in *Median Finding on a 3-by-3 Grid* by Alan Paeth in [13]. An optimal extension to 5×5 neighborhoods is not immediately obvious from the 3×3 case. For comparison, a shader program that uses an insertion sort for the neighborhood is provided. The min-max approach clearly outperforms the insertion sort approach.

7.8.1 Median by Sorting

I used an insertion sort for computing the median value of a neighborhood of dimensions $(2R + 1) \times (2R + 1)$, where R is the radius of the neighborhood. Listing 7.16 contains the HLSL code.

```
#define SIZE (2*RADIUS+1)
#define NUM_DATA (SIZE*SIZE)
Texture2D<float> input;
RWTexture2D<float> output;
[numthreads(NUM_X_THREADS, NUM_Y_THREADS, 1)]
```

```
void CSMain(int2 dt : SV_DispatchThreadID)
{
    // Load the neighborhood of the pixel.
    float data[NUM_DATA];
    int i = 0;
    int2 offset;
    [unroll]
    for (offset.y = -RADIUS; offset.y <= RADIUS; ++offset.y)
    {
        [unroll]
        for (offset.x = -RADIUS; offset.x <= RADIUS; ++offset.x)
        {
            data[i] = input[dt + offset];
            ++i;
        }
    }

    // Use an insertion sort to locate the median value.
    for (int i0 = 1; i0 < NUM_DATA; ++i0)
    {
        float value = data[i0];
        int i1;
        for (i1 = i0; i1 > 0; --i1)
        {
            if (value < data[i1 - 1])
            {
                data[i1] = data[i1 - 1];
            }
            else
            {
                break;
            }
        }
        data[i1] = value;
    }

    output[dt] = data[NUM_DATA / 2];
}
```

LISTING 7.16: A shader that uses insertion sort to compute the median.

The radius and number of x- and y-threads is provided via an HLSLDefiner object in the application code. The first pair of loops has compact code for reading the neighborhood of the pixel, but the unroll directives cause the HLSL compiler to generate sequential code for loading the values. The second pair of loops is standard code for an insertion sort of a set of numbers. I unit-tested the code by applying the filter on the GPU, reading back the output image, and comparing to an output image generated by the same code on the CPU. I also compared the insertion sorts of neighborhoods to sorted values obtained by std::sort. On my AMD 7970 graphics card for a 1024×1024 image, the 3×3 filter runs at 1370 frames per second and the 5×5 filter runs at 60 frames per second.

I also added unroll directives to the loops of the insertion sort, but the output was incorrect in both cases. The Microsoft Direct3D shader compiler version is 6.3.9600.16384. I did not investigate further to determine the correctness (or not) of the generated assembly instructions. When you unroll the loop manually, you have a long sequence of nested if-then expressions, so even if the loop were to be unrolled correctly, you have a lot of branching that can occur. Most likely that branching is as expensive as the loop construct.

7.8.2   Median of 3×3 Using Min-Max Operations

To avoid branching and looping in the shader, the key observation is that if you have a set S of $2n + 1$ numbers, any subset T of $n + 2$ numbers has the property $\min(T) \leq \operatorname{median}(S) \leq \max(T)$. The proof is by contradiction. Suppose that $\operatorname{median}(S) < \min(T)$. If you were to sort S, say, $x_0 \leq \cdots \leq x_n \leq \cdots \leq x_{2n}$, then $x_n = \operatorname{median}(S)$. However the $n + 2$ elements of T, presumed to be larger than x_n must be in the sorted set as x_{n-1} through x_{2n}, which overlaps x_n, a contradiction. Similarly, if it were the case that $\operatorname{median}(S) > \max(T)$, then the $n + 2$ elements of T must be in the sorted set as x_0 through x_{n+1}, which overlaps x_n and is again a contradiction.

A 3×3 neighborhood has $2n + 1 = 9$ numbers ($n = 4$). If we choose a subset T of $n + 2 = 6$ numbers and locate the minimum and maximum *without* fully sorting T, we can discard those numbers because they cannot be the median. This leaves us with a set of seven numbers. We can repeat the process and discard two more numbers, leaving us with a set of five numbers, and then again leaving us with a set of three numbers. The median is obtained by ordering the three numbers and selecting the middle one.

The algorithm for locating the minimum and maximum is performed within the array. We swap elements so that the minimum bubbles toward the beginning of the array and the maximum bubbles toward the end of the array. Only swapping is allowed, because elements that are not the extreme must be preserved for repetition of the algorithm on the next smallest set. Although a direct GPU implementation may manipulate the subsets as arrays of scalars float, we can additionally take advantage of vectorization and store the numbers in 4-tuples float4. This allows us to perform swaps of the channels of float4 numbers in parallel.

The nine elements of the neighborhood are stored in three float4 tuples where only the first channel of the last tuple is used. Although we can set up the float4 values manually by assigning one channel at at time, the HLSL compiler will unroll a double loop and set up the swizzling properly. Listing 7.17 shows the HLSL code for this.

```
void LoadNeighbors(
    in Texture2D<float> input, // the image to be filtered
    in int2 dt, // the neighborhood center (dt.x,dt.y)
    out float4 e[3]) // nine elements copied to e[0].xyzw, e[1].xyzw, e[2].x
{
    uint i = 0;
    int2 offset;
    [unroll]
    for (offset.y = -1; offset.y <= 1; ++offset.y)
    {
        [unroll]
        for (offset.x = -1; offset.x <= 1; ++offset.x)
        {
```

```
        // The HLSL compiler determines the correct swizzle (.s) for
        // e[i / 4].s knowing that i started at 0 and increments on
        // each pass.
        e[i / 4][i % 4] = input[dt + offset];
        ++i;
      }
    }
}
```

LISTING 7.17: Initialization of data for vectorized median filtering.

The operation that is at the heart of the min-max searching is to swap two k-tuples u and v so that the minimum is in u and the maximum is in v. The minimum and maximum are computed in the SIMD sense, applying to all channels of the tuples. The generic function for this operation is

```
void minmax(inout vector<float,k> u, inout vector<float,k> v)
{
    vector<float,k> save = u;
    u = min(save, v);
    v = max(save, v);
}
```

Let us now locate the minimum and maximum in the subset of six numbers stored in e[0].xyzw and e[1].xy. Listing 7.18 shows the function that bubbles the minimum to e[0].x and the maximum to e[1].y.

```
void minmax6(inout float4 e[3])
{
    minmax(e[0].xy,e[0].zw);  // min in {e0.xy,e1.xy}, max in {e0.zw,e1.xy}
    minmax(e[0].xz,e[0].yw);  // min in {e0.x,e1.xy}, max in {e0.w,e1.xy}
    minmax(e[1].x, e[1].y);   // min in {e0.x,e1.x}, max in {e0.w,e1.y}
    minmax(e[0].xw,e[1].xy);  // min in e0.x, max in e1.y
}
```

LISTING 7.18: Extracting the minimum and maximum from six numbers with swaps.

The comments in the code make it clear the subsets of numbers that contain the minimum and the maximum. Similar functions for smaller subsets are named minmax5, minmax4, and minmax3. These are all designed to minimize the number of swaps needed to bubble the extremes to the first and last swizzles.

The compute shader for the median filtering is shown in Listing 7.19. The subset of six elements has its minimum moved to e[0].x and its maximum moved to e[1].y by the function minimax6. The minimum is discarded by moving an unvisited element of the neighborhood into e[0].x. The maximum is discarded implicitly, because the next subset of five elements has the last element in the channel immediately before the maximum's channel.

```
#include "MedianShared.hlsli"
Texture2D<float> input;
RWTexture2D<float> output;
[numthreads(NUM_X_THREADS, NUM_Y_THREADS, 1)]
void CSMain(int2 dt : SV_DispatchThreadID)
{
    float4 e[3];  // 12 slots, we use the first 9
```

```
    LoadNeighbors(input, dt, e);
    minmax6(e);           // Discard min/max of v0..v5 (2n+1=9, n+2=6).
    e[0].x = e[2].x;      // Copy v8 to v0 slot.
    minmax5(e);           // Discard min/max of v0..v4 (2n+1=7, n+2=5).
    e[0].x = e[1].w;      // Copy v7 to v0 slot.
    minmax4(e);           // Discard min/max of v0..v3 (2n+1=5, n+2=4).
    e[0].x = e[1].z;      // Copy v6 to v0 slot.
    minmax3(e);           // Sort v0, v1, and v2.
    output[dt] = e[0].y;  // Return the median v1.
}
```

LISTING 7.19: The compute shader for 3×3 median filtering.

The LoadNeighbors and minmaxN functions are defined in the included hlsli file to be shared by all median filter shaders. Although this example shows hard-coded numbers for radius three, the actual shader code uses macros to generate these.

On my AMD 7970 graphics card for a 1024×1024 image, the 3×3 filter runs at 2540 frames per second, which is faster than the 1370 frames per second for the insertion-sort approach.

7.8.3   Median of 5×5 Using Min-Max Operations

The generalization of the algorithm from 3×3 to 5×5 neighborhoods has many paths. When you have a larger set of numbers, the possibilities for swapping channels increases greatly. The goal is to minimize the swaps. The number of float4 required is seven, where we use only the first twenty five of the twenty eight available channels.

Given $2n + 1 = 25$ elements ($n = 12$), the largest subset to process is the first one with $n + 2 = 14$ elements. As a first attempt to generalize, you might consider defining functions minmax7 through minmax14 and apply them one at a time and then copying an unprocessed element into e[0].x as we did in Listing 7.19. The problem, though, is that when the last float4 is not fully filled, the number of minmax operations increases due to (1) a need for swizzling involving single channels and (2) the limit of two float4 per minmax call. For example, minmax6 in Listing 7.18 has four minmax operations. A function for seven elements is shown in Listing 7.20 and uses six minmax operations.

```
void minmax7(inout float4 e[7])
{
    minmax(e[0].xy,e[0].zw); // min in {e0.xy,e1.xyz}, max in {e0.zw,e1.xyz}
    minmax(e[0].xz,e[0].yw); // min in {e0.x,e1.xyz}, max in {e0.w,e1.xyz}
    minmax(e[1].x, e[1].y);  // min in {e0.x,e1.xz}, max in {e0.w,e1.yz}
    minmax(e[1].x, e[1].z);  // min in {e0.x,e1.x}, max in {e0.w,e1.yz}
    minmax(e[1].y, e[1].z);  // min in {e0.x,e1.x}, max in {e0.w,e1.z}
    minmax(e[0].xw,e[1].xz); // min in e0.x, max in e1.z
}
```

LISTING 7.20: Extracting the minimum and maximum from seven numbers with swaps.

A function for eight elements is shown in Listing 7.21 and uses five minmax operations, one fewer than that for the smaller subset of seven elements.

```
void minmax8(inout float4 e[7])
{
    minmax(e[0],    e[1]);      // min in e0, max in e1
    minmax(e[0].xy,e[0].zw);    // min in e0.xy, max in e1
    minmax(e[0].x,  e[0].y);    // min in e0.x, max in e1
    minmax(e[1].xy,e[1].zw);    // min in e0.x, max in e1.zw
    minmax(e[1].z,  e[1].w);    // min in e0.x, max in e1.w
}
```

LISTING 7.21: Extracting the minimum and maximum from eight numbers with swaps.

This pattern occurs for larger numbers, and it appears that the largest number of minmax operations occurs when the last float4 uses only three channels.

The first attempt was based on wanting to apply the key observation that the minimum and maximum of a subset of $n + 2$ elements can be discarded. But the same is true even when the subset has more than $n + 2$ elements. The trick to reducing the number of calls to minmax is to use subsets whose numbers of elements are multiples of four. The idea is to take advantage of the vectorization and swap as many channels in parallel at the same time. In particular, we want to swap fully filled float4 objects. For an initial set of twenty-five elements, we need only two more functions, namely, minmax12 and minmax16, shown in Listing 7.22.

```
void minmax12(inout float4 e[7])
{
    minmax(e[0], e[1]);        // min in {e0, e2}, max in {e1, e2}
    minmax(e[0], e[2]);        // min in e0, max in {e1, e2}
    minmax(e[1], e[2]);        // min in e0, max in e2
    minmax(e[0].xy, e[0].zw);  // min in e0.xy, max in e2
    minmax(e[0].xz, e[0].yw);  // min in e0.x, max in e2
    minmax(e[2].xy, e[2].zw);  // min in e0.x, max in e2.xy
    minmax(e[2].xz, e[2].yw);  // min in e0.x, max in e2.y
}

void minmax16(inout float4 e[7])
{
    minmax(e[0], e[1]);        // min in {e0, e2, e3}, max in {e1, e2, e3}
    minmax(e[2], e[3]);        // min in {e0, e2}, max in {e1, e3}
    minmax(e[0], e[2]);        // min in e0, max in {e1, e3}
    minmax(e[1], e[3]);        // min in e0, max in e3
    minmax(e[0].xy, e[0].zw);  // min in e0.xy, max in e3
    minmax(e[0].xz, e[0].yw);  // min in e0.x, max in e3
    minmax(e[3].xy, e[3].zw);  // min in e0.x, max in e3.xy
    minmax(e[3].xz, e[3].yw);  // min in e0.x, max in e3.y
}
```

LISTING 7.22: Extracting the minimum and maximum from twelve or sixteen numbers with swaps.

Not only will this reduce the number of minmax calls compared to the first attempt, you have fewer new functions to implement (two versus eight). This is helpful in the event you want larger neighborhoods. By the way, in each function the first block of minmax calls that take float4 inputs are essentially a parallel sort of the four channels. For example, after the first three calls in minmax12, you know that $e[0].x \le e[1].x \le e[2].x$, $e[0].y \le e[1].y \le e[2].y$, $e[0].z \le e[1].z \le e[2].z$, and $e[0].w \le e[1].w \le e[2].w$.

In the second (and optimal) attempt, we will use minmax8, minmax12, and minmax16 multiple times. Each time, though, we must copy two unprocessed elements rather than one in order to set up for the next smaller subset. The compute shader for the median filtering is shown in Listing 7.23.

```
#include "MedianShared.hlsli"
Texture2D<float> input;
RWTexture2D<float> output;
[numthreads(NUM_X_THREADS, NUM_Y_THREADS, 1)]
void CSMain(int2 dt : SV_DispatchThreadID)
{
    float4 e[7];           // 28 slots, we use the first 25
    LoadNeighbors(input, dt, e);
    minmax16(e);           // Discard min/max of v0..v15 (2n+1=25, n+2<16).
    e[0][0] = e[6][0];     // Copy v24 to v0 slot.
    e[3][3] = e[5][3];     // Copy v23 to v15 slot.
    minmax16(e);           // Discard min/max of v0..v15 (2n+1=23, n+2<16).
    e[0][0] = e[5][2];     // Copy v22 to v0 slot.
    e[3][3] = e[5][1];     // Copy v21 to v15 slot.
    minmax12(e);           // Discard min/max of v0..v11 (2n+1=21, n+2=12).
    e[0][0] = e[5][0];     // Copy v20 to v0 slot.
    e[2][3] = e[4][3];     // Copy v19 to v11 slot.
    minmax12(e);           // Discard min/max of v0..v11 (2n+1=19, n+2<12).
    e[0][0] = e[4][2];     // Copy v18 to v0 slot.
    e[2][3] = e[4][1];     // Copy v17 to v11 slot.
    minmax12(e);           // Discard min/max of v0..v11 (2n+1=17, n+2<12).
    e[0][0] = e[4][0];     // Copy v16 to v0 slot.
    e[2][3] = e[3][3];     // Copy v15 to v11 slot.
    minmax12(e);           // Discard min/max of v0..v11 (2n+1=15, n+2<12).
    e[0][0] = e[3][2];     // Copy v14 to v0 slot.
    e[2][3] = e[3][1];     // Copy v13 to v11 slot.
    minmax8(e);            // Discard min/max of v0..v7 (2n+1=13, n+2=8).
    e[0][0] = e[3][0];     // Copy v12 to v0 slot.
    e[1][3] = e[2][3];     // Copy v11 to v7 slot.
    minmax8(e);            // Discard min/max of v0..v7 (2n+1=11, n+2<8).
    e[0][0] = e[2][2];     // Copy v10 to v0 slot.
    e[1][3] = e[2][1];     // Copy v9 to v7 slot.
    minmax6(e);            // Discard min/max of v0..v5 (2n+1=9, n+2=6).
    e[0].x = e[2].x;       // Copy v8 to v0 slot.
    minmax5(e);            // Discard min/max of v0..v4 (2n+1=7, n+2=5).
    e[0].x = e[1].w;       // Copy v7 to v0 slot.
    minmax4(e);            // Discard min/max of v0..v3 (2n+1=5, n+2=4).
    e[0].x = e[1].z;       // Copy v6 to v0 slot.
    minmax3(e);            // Sort v0, v1, and v2.
    output[dt] = e[0].y;   // Return the median v1.
}
```

LISTING 7.23: The compute shader for 5×5 median filtering.

The LoadNeighbors and minmaxN functions are defined in the included hlsli file to be shared by all median filter shaders. Although this example shows hard-coded numbers for radius five, the actual shader code uses macros to generate these.

On my AMD 7970 graphics card for a 1024×1024 image, the 5×5 filter runs at 2500 frames per second, which is orders of magnitude faster than the 60 frames per second for the insertion-sort approach. Clearly, the absence of looping and branching in the min-max approach is superior and shows you just how expensive looping and branching can be on the GPU.

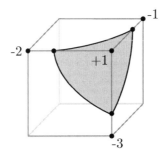

FIGURE 7.8: A level surface for a single voxel.

7.9   Level Surface Extraction

Consider a continuous function $F(x, y, z)$ defined on a domain that is an axis-aligned solid box $[x_{\min}, x_{\max}] \times [y_{\min}, y_{\max}] \times [z_{\min}, z_{\max}]$ and with range $[f_{\min}, f_{\max}]$. A *level set* is defined by the implicit equation $F(x, y, z) = L$ for $L \in [f_{\min}, f_{\max}]$. The number L is said to a *level value*. The level set contains topological objects, potentially of mixed dimension. For practical purposes, though, we are interested in those objects that are locally two-dimensional; these are referred to as *isosurfaces* or *level surfaces*.

In image processing, the function $F(x, y, z)$ is built from a 3D regular lattice of function samples. For example, in medical imaging the samples can be magnetic resonance images (MRI) or computed tomography (CT). In other application domains, the samples can be scalar measurements from physical processes. The regular lattice has size $N_0 \times N_1 \times N_2$ with integer points (i_0, i_1, i_2), where $0 \le i_j < N_j$ for all j. A *voxel* is a rectangular solid whose corners are eight neighboring lattice points (i_0, i_1, i_2), (i_0+1, i_1, i_2), (i_0, i_1+1, i_2), $(i_0 + 1, i_1 + 1, i_2)$, $(i_0, i_1, i_2 + 1)$, $(i_0 + 1, i_1, i_2 + 1)$, $(i_0, i_1 + 1, i_2 + 1)$, and $(i_0 + 1, i_1 + 1, i_2 + 1)$. Figure 7.8 illustrates the level surface contained by a single voxel. Each corner of the voxel has an associated function value. Four of these are shown in Figure 7.8, one positive and three negative. Assuming the function values vary continuously, each edge connecting a positive and negative value must have a point where the function is zero. The level surface $F(x, y, z) = 0$ necessarily passes through those zero points, as illustrated by the triangularly shaped surface drawn in gray.

A standard isosurface extraction algorithm for a 3D image is the Marching Cubes algorithm [23][**?**]. The algorithm analyzes each voxel in the image and determines whether the isosurface intersects it. If so, the algorithm produces a triangle mesh that approximates the isosurface inside the voxel. To simplify the algorithm, the function values at the corners are required to be positive or negative and the level value is required to be zero. The latter constraint is not restrictive, because you can always reformulate the level set $F(x, y, z) = L$ as the zero level set of $G(x, y, z) = F(x, y, z) - L$. The former constraint of nonzero function values prevents the isosurface from containing voxel corners. This leads to a table lookup for the triangle meshes with 256 entries (two possible signs at the eight corners). The constraint is generally not an issue. For example, medical image data tends to be integer valued. The isosurfaces produced by a level value that is exactly an integer I are usually not much different from those produced by a level value that is a floating-point number $I + \varepsilon$ for a small number ε.

The strength of this algorithm is the speed in which the triangle meshes are generated for the entire isosurface, the performance due to the simplicity of the table lookups. The original algorithm had a topological flaw. Two voxels sharing a face with alternating signs at the four corners might lead to triangle meshes that do not form a continuous mesh across the face. This problem can be fixed by carefully implementing the table to deal with meshes and reflections of them, depending on the sign data. The consequence, though, is that the triangle mesh produced for the level set $F = L$ can be different from the triangle mesh produced by the level set $-F = -L$. The meshes are not always consistent with those produced by truly assuming the voxel corners produce a function via trilinear interpolation, but in practice this is usually not a problem. If it is, you can use an ear-clipping algorithm that is consistent with a trilinear function, one that I described in [9]. The ear-clipping algorithm, though, is more complicated to implement on a GPU.

The table lookup leads to twenty-one distinct triangle-mesh configurations. Each configuration can occur with different orientations depending on the signs at the corners. Figures 7.9 through 7.10 show the configurations, each labeled with a name to describe the sign patterns at the corners. In the source code, the signs are stored in an 8-bit quantity, where a 0-bit denotes a positive sign and a 1-bit denotes a negative sign. The cubes that are shown are oriented so that the corners are 3-tuples with components either zero or one. The corner $(0, 0, 0)$ is the one farthest from view. The z-axis is upward, the y-axis is rightward, and the x-axis points out of the plane of the page although it is drawn askew at a 45-degree angle for perspective. The indexing is: $(0, 0, 0)$ has index 0, $(1, 0, 0)$ has index 1, $(0, 1, 0)$ has index 2, $(1, 1, 0)$ has index 3, $(0, 0, 1)$ has index 4, $(1, 0, 1)$ has index 5, $(0, 1, 1)$ has index 6, and $(1, 1, 1)$ has index 7.

GTEngine has a class called MarchingCubes that is used to generate a table of information about the vertices and triangles in a voxel determined by the 8-bit sign index for the voxel corners. The maximum number of vertices for a voxel mesh is twelve, because the voxel has twelve edges. The maximum number of triangles is five, which you can count for yourself in Figures 7.9 through 7.10. The table is stored as a 2D array of integers, table[256][41], where the row index represents the 256 possible 8-bit sign indices. For the configuration i, table[i][0] stores the number of vertices and table[i][1] stores the number of triangles.

The twenty-four entries table[i][2] through table[i][25] store up to twelve pairs of voxel corner indices. Each pair identifies a voxel edge that contains a vertex,

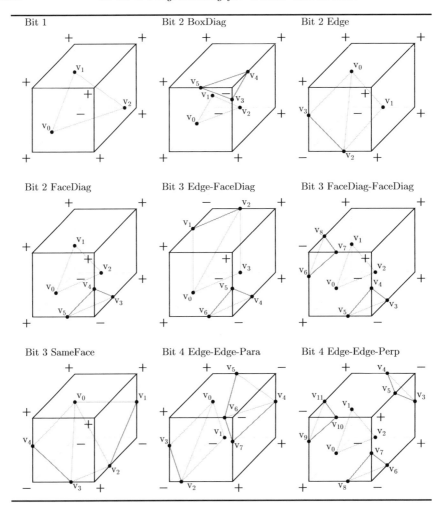

FIGURE 7.9: Triangle mesh configurations (part 1).

so the number of pairs is the same as the number of vertices. The pair of indices are always listed with smallest first and largest second. These numbers are used for linear interpolation of the function values at the voxel corners in order to identity where on the edge the mesh vertex lives.

The fifteen entries table[i][26] through table[i][40] store up to five triples of indices that represent triangles in the mesh. The indexing is for the pairs of voxel corner indices, effectively telling you which vertices form the triangle. The index ordering is such that the triangle is counterclockwise oriented when viewed from the negative side of the zero-valued level surface.

For example, the configuration *Bit 5 FaceDiag-FaceDiag* has nine vertices and five triangles. Vertex $\mathbf{v}_0$ is associated with the pair $(0, 1)$, where 0 is

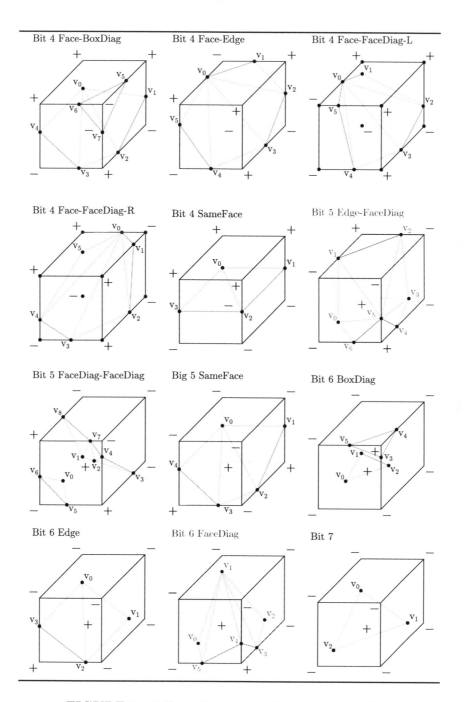

FIGURE 7.10: Triangle mesh configurations (part 2).

associated with corner $(0, 0, 0)$ and 1 is associated with corner $(1, 0, 0)$. Vertex $\mathbf{v}_5$ is associated with pair $(1, 3)$ and vertex $\mathbf{v}_6$ is associated with pair $(1, 5)$. The triple of indices for the triangle formed by these three vertices is $(0, 5, 6)$. The ordering is counterclockwise when viewed from the negative side of the level surface, say, from the corner $(1, 0, 0)$ that has a negative function value. The table in full is

```
int  i = 0x29;  // sign  bits,  binary  00101001  (—+—+——+)
table[i][0] = 9;
table[i][1] = 5;
table[i][2..25] = {0,1,0,4,0,2,2,3,3,7,1,3,1,5,5,7,4,5,x,x,x,x,x,x};
table[i][24..40] = {0,5,6,1,8,7,1,7,2,2,7,4,2,4,3};
```

The sample application illustrating the concepts is

GeometricTools/GTEngine/Samples/Imagics/SurfaceExtraction

Two different algorithms are presented for the extraction, the second one the preferred one for optimal performance. A function is generated as a sum of Gaussian distributions in order to produce multiple components for various level values.

The first algorithm uses the compute shader in ExtractSurface.hlsl. The inputs are the Marching Cubes lookup table (structured buffer), the 3D image from which level surfaces will be extracted (3D texture), and a constant buffer with the level value of interest. The buffer also had the dimensions of a voxel, because some image applications require this; for example, medical images usually have a real-world measurement for the voxel size, say, in millimeters per dimension. The output is an append buffer, because it is unknown how many voxels actually contain the level surface. The append buffer uses a data structure that stores the bit-sign index and the information obtained from the Marching Cubes table lookup. It also stores the linearly interpolated function values along the edges so that we know where the vertices lie on the voxel edges. Keep in mind that the order of GPU thread execution is not deterministic, so the order of the voxels in the append buffer can vary for each call using the same level value. If you need a spatially organized set of voxels that contain the level surface, you can always allocate a structured buffer that has the same number of elements as the original image, but this can consume a large amount of GPU memory. The compute shader cannot produce index buffer outputs directly, so the append buffer is read back from the GPU so that the CPU can construct the triangle mesh, this using the sample application CreateMesh function. The triangle mesh is then uploaded to the GPU for drawing. The memory transfer between the GPU and CPU is a bottleneck in the application.

The second algorithm uses the SV_VertexID semantic in D3D11 so you can use the drawing subsystem to pass the indices of the index buffer representing the triangles instead of the actual vertices. This mechanism facilitates the interoperability of compute shaders with vertex, geometry, and pixel shaders; that is, compute shaders can generate information in structured buffers and

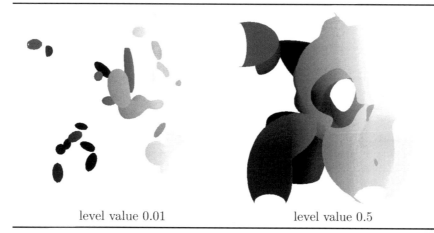

level value 0.01   level value 0.5

FIGURE 7.11: Surface extraction for two level values.

textures, and these resources can be attached to vertex, geometry, and pixel shaders to be accessed via the indices passed to the vertex shader. The compute shader in ExtractSurfaceIndirect.hlsl is similar to the previous compute shader except that the only information returned in the voxel buffer is the 1D index of the voxel relative to the 3D image and the bit-sign index that is used in the Marching Cubes table lookup.

In this algorithm, the append buffer is *not* read back to the CPU. However, the number of elements in the append buffer is read back—this is a single 4-byte integer, so the memory transfer is not a bottleneck. We have vertex, geometry, and pixel shaders in the file DrawSurfaceIndirect.hlsl. The drawing call specifies that we will draw points, but in this case the indices are just those between zero and the number of elements in the append buffer. The append buffer is attached to the vertex shader. When the vertex shader receives an index, it extracts the voxel index and bit-sign index and passes them to the geometry shader. The geometry shader does the work of interpolating the edges for the voxel at hand in order to generate 3D points for the vertices, and then it creates the triangles using information from the Marching Cubes table.

The performance between the two methods is noticeable, mainly because the large GPU-CPU memory transfers are not present in the second method. On my AMD 7970, the first method runs at 612 frames per second for level value 0.5 and at 80 frames per second for level value 0.01. The program slows down for smaller level values, because there are more voxels that contain portions of the triangle mesh and so the GPU-CPU transfer involves more data. The second method runs at 1375 frames per second for level value 0.5 and at 914 frames per second for level value 0.01. Either method produces the same output, shown in Figure 7.11. The figures are drawn in grayscale. The actual program displays them with various colors, and you can toggle between solid display and wireframe display.

7.10   Mass-Spring Systems

A deformable body can be modeled as a system of particles (point masses) connected by springs. One-dimensional arrays are good for modeling hair or rope, two-dimensional arrays are good for modeling cloth or water surfaces, and three-dimensional arrays are good for modeling solid blobs, say, of gelatinous material.

Arbitrary topologies are also allowed, so in general suppose you have a mass-spring system of p particles where particle i has mass m_i (possibly infinite) and location $\mathbf{X}_i$. The system has springs, modeled using Hooke's law. The spring attaching particle i to particle j has spring constant c_{ij} and resting length L_{ij}. Let $\mathcal{A}_i$ denote the set of indices j for which particle j is connected to particle i by a spring. The equation of motion for particle i is

$$m_i \ddot{\mathbf{X}}_i = \mathbf{I}_i + \mathbf{E}_i = \sum_{j \in \mathcal{A}_i} c_{ij} \left(|\mathbf{X}_j - \mathbf{X}_i| - L_{ij} \right) \frac{\mathbf{X}_j - \mathbf{X}_i}{|\mathbf{X}_j - \mathbf{X}_i|} + \mathbf{E}_i \qquad (7.40)$$

where the terms of the summation for $\mathbf{I}_i$ are the internal forces due to the springs. The external forces $\mathbf{E}$ are generated by wind, gravity, or simply pulling on the particles. The particle positions may be listed in a single tuple

$$\mathbf{X} = (\mathbf{X}_0, \ldots, \mathbf{X}_{n-1}) \qquad (7.41)$$

and the internal and external forces divided by the masses may be listed in a single tuple,

$$\mathbf{F} = ((\mathbf{I}_0 + \mathbf{E}_0)/m_0, \ldots, (\mathbf{I}_{n-1} + \mathbf{E}_{n-1})/m_{n-1}) \qquad (7.42)$$

If you want a particle to be immovable, you can assign it infinite mass. In practice, you assign zero to the inverse mass $1/m$. Equation (7.40) is concisely written as a system of second-order differential equations,

$$\ddot{\mathbf{X}} = \mathbf{F}(t, \mathbf{X}, \ddot{\mathbf{X}}) \qquad (7.43)$$

where the right-hand side indicates that $\mathbf{F}$ can vary with time, position, and velocity. This can be reduced further to a system of first-order differential equations by choosing $\mathbf{V} = \dot{\mathbf{X}}$, in which case $\dot{\mathbf{V}} = \ddot{\mathbf{X}}$ and

$$\dot{\mathbf{S}} = \begin{bmatrix} \dot{\mathbf{X}} \\ \dot{\mathbf{V}} \end{bmatrix} = \begin{bmatrix} \mathbf{V} \\ \mathbf{F}(t, \mathbf{X}, \mathbf{V}) \end{bmatrix} = \mathbf{G}(t, \mathbf{S}) \qquad (7.44)$$

where $\mathbf{S}$ is the state vector of positions and velocity and $\mathbf{G}(t, \mathbf{S})$ is a concise representation of the right-hand side of the system of differential equations.

To simulate the mass-spring system, we need to implement a numerical solver for the first-order system of differential equations. I choose to use a

Runge–Kutta fourth-order method whose input is the current time t_i and current state $\mathbf{S}_i$ and whose output is the state $\mathbf{S}_{i+1}$ at the next time $t_{i+1} = t_i + h$ for a small time step $h > 0$:

$$
\begin{aligned}
\mathbf{K}_1 &= \mathbf{G}(t_i, \mathbf{S}_i) \\
\mathbf{K}_2 &= \mathbf{G}(t_i + h/2, \mathbf{S}_i + h\mathbf{K}_1/2) \\
\mathbf{K}_3 &= \mathbf{G}(t_i + h/2, \mathbf{S}_i + h\mathbf{K}_2/2) \\
\mathbf{K}_4 &= \mathbf{G}(t_i + h, \mathbf{S}_i + h\mathbf{K}_3) \\
\mathbf{S}_{i+1} &= \mathbf{S}_i + h(\mathbf{K}_1 + 2\mathbf{K}_2 + 2\mathbf{K}_3 + \mathbf{K}_4)/6
\end{aligned}
\tag{7.45}
$$

Equation (7.40) can be specialized for arrays of particles. For a 1D array, each particle has two neighbors. Let the spring connecting particle j to particle $j+1$ have spring constant c_j and resting length L_j. Define the Hooke's law term

$$
\mathbf{H}_j = c_j \left(|\mathbf{X}_{j+1} - \mathbf{X}_j| - L_j \right) \frac{\mathbf{X}_{j+1} - \mathbf{X}_j}{|\mathbf{X}_{j+1} - \mathbf{X}_j|}
\tag{7.46}
$$

The equation of motion for the particle is

$$
m_i \ddot{\mathbf{X}}_i = \mathbf{H}_{i-1} + \mathbf{H}_i + \mathbf{E}_i
\tag{7.47}
$$

For a 2D array, each particle has four neighbors. Let the spring connecting particle (j_0, j_1) to particle (k_0, k_1) have spring constant c_{j_0, j_1} and resting length L_{j_0, j_1}. Define the Hooke's law term

$$
\mathbf{H}_{j_0, j_1} = c_{j_0, j_1} \left(|\mathbf{X}_{k_0, k_1} - \mathbf{X}_{j_0, j_1}| - L_{j_0, j_1} \right) \frac{\mathbf{X}_{k_0, k_1} - \mathbf{X}_{j_0, j_1}}{|\mathbf{X}_{k_0, k_1} - \mathbf{X}_{j_0, j_1}|}
\tag{7.48}
$$

The equation of motion for the particle is

$$
m_{i_0, i_1} \ddot{\mathbf{X}}_{i_0, i_1} = \mathbf{H}_{i_0-1, i_1} + \mathbf{H}_{i_0+1, i_1} + \mathbf{H}_{i_0, i_1-1} + \mathbf{H}_{i_0, i_1+1} + \mathbf{E}_{i_0, i_1}
\tag{7.49}
$$

For a 3D array, each particle has six neighbors. Let the spring connecting particle (j_0, j_1, j_2) to particle (k_0, k_1, k_2) have spring constant c_{j_0, j_1, j_2} and resting length L_{j_0, j_1, j_2}. Define the Hooke's law term

$$
\begin{aligned}
\mathbf{H}_{j_0, j_1, j_2} = & \\
c_{j_0, j_1, j_2} & \left(|\mathbf{X}_{k_0, k_1, k_2} - \mathbf{X}_{j_0, j_1, j_2}| - L_{j_0, j_1, j_2} \right) \frac{\mathbf{X}_{k_0, k_1, k_2} - \mathbf{X}_{j_0, j_1, j_2}}{|\mathbf{X}_{k_0, k_1, k_2} - \mathbf{X}_{j_0, j_1, j_2}|}
\end{aligned}
\tag{7.50}
$$

The equation of motion for the particle is

$$
\begin{aligned}
m_{i_0, i_1, i_2} \ddot{\mathbf{X}}_{i_0, i_1, i_2} = & \ \mathbf{H}_{i_0-1, i_1, i_2} + \mathbf{H}_{i_0+1, i_1, i_2} + \mathbf{H}_{i_0, i_1-1, i_2} \\
& + \mathbf{H}_{i_0, i_1+1, i_2} + \mathbf{H}_{i_0, i_1, i_2-1} + \mathbf{H}_{i_0, i_1, i_2+1} + \mathbf{E}_{i_0, i_1, i_2}
\end{aligned}
\tag{7.51}
$$

The sample application

GeometricTools/GTEngine/Samples/Physics/MassSprings3D

is an implementation of Equation (7.51) using the numerical method of Equation (7.45) for both the CPU and GPU in order to compare performance. The graphics are not particularly pretty. The mass-spring system has size $32 \times 32 \times 32$. The outer shell of particles are set to have infinite mass so that they cannot move. This prevents the cube of masses from collapsing into its center. The faces of the cube of masses are vertex colored, each face having a distinct color. The only external force is viscous friction, where each particle's velocity is dampened by the coefficient of viscosity whose value is 0.1. As the simulation is executed, you can see the particles on the cube faces move about slightly. A more visually interesting application is the gelatin cube of [9], where the cube has semitransparent textured faces and only $6 \times 6 \times 6$ particles. However, the particle positions are used as control points for a Bézier volume function, which adds smoothness to the motion. And that application runs on the CPU. As an exercise, you can modify the mass-spring application of this book to have the same visual appearance.

The differential equation update occurs as eight separate loops to compute in order: $\mathbf{K}_1$, $\mathbf{S}_i + h\mathbf{K}_1/2$, $\mathbf{K}_2$, $\mathbf{S}_i + h\mathbf{K}_2/2$, $\mathbf{K}_3$, $\mathbf{S}_i + h\mathbf{K}_3$, $\mathbf{K}_4$, and $\mathbf{S}_i + h(\mathbf{K}_1 + 2\mathbf{K}_2 + 2\mathbf{K}_3 + \mathbf{K}_4)$. This is encapsulated by class CpuMassSpringVolume for CPU computing. The GPU version is in class GpuMassSpringVolume but the differential equation solver is contained in eight different HLSL shaders. These shaders have no tricks to deal with CPU-GPU differences. The Runge–Kutta solver is a straightforward implementation for either processor.

As expected, the performance difference is striking. The CPU version of the mass-spring system executes at 33 frames per second. The GPU version runs on my AMD 7970 graphics card at 2300 frames per second.

7.11 Fluid Dynamics

Consider a fluid in space (2D or 3D) that has velocity $\mathbf{u}(\mathbf{x}, t)$ and density $\rho(\mathbf{x}, t)$, each dependent on spatial location $\mathbf{x}$ and time t. A simplified model of fluid flow is presented in [54], and a detailed derivation of the model from conservation laws and with simplifying assumptions is provided in [9]. The model is suitable for computing on a GPU, thus providing real-time fluid simulations. The modeling equations are

$$
\begin{aligned}
\frac{\partial \mathbf{u}}{\partial t} + (\mathbf{u} \cdot \nabla)\mathbf{u} &= \nu_{\text{vel}}\nabla^2\mathbf{u} + \mathbf{F}_{\text{vel}}, & \text{conservation of momentum} \\
\frac{\partial \rho}{\partial t} + (\mathbf{u} \cdot \nabla)\rho &= \nu_{\text{den}}\nabla^2\rho + F_{\text{den}}, & \text{conservation of mass} \\
\nabla \cdot \mathbf{u} &= 0, & \text{incompressible fluid}
\end{aligned}
\tag{7.52}
$$

where ∇ is the gradient operator, $\nabla^2 = \nabla \cdot \nabla$ is the Laplacian operator, ν_{vel} and ν_{den} are viscosity coefficients (positive constants), $\mathbf{F}_{\text{vel}}(\mathbf{x}, t)$ is an external source of acceleration (for example, due to wind or gravity), and $F_{\text{den}}(\mathbf{x}, t)$ is an external source (or sink) of density.

The fluid is confined to a bounded region of space R that has boundary B. The initial conditions for velocity and density must be specified within the region,

$$\mathbf{u}(\mathbf{x}, 0) = \mathbf{u}_0(\mathbf{x}), \quad \rho(\mathbf{x}, 0) = \rho_0(\mathbf{x}), \quad \mathbf{x} \in R \tag{7.53}$$

for user-defined functions $\mathbf{u}_0$ and ρ_0.

The boundary conditions must be specified also for all time. For simplicity, the density is required to be zero on the boundary and the velocity is required to have zero component in the normal direction to the boundary. These conditions are based on the requirement of confinement. No mass is at the boundary of the region (density is zero) and no mass may escape the region due to motion (velocity has zero component normal to the boundary):

$$\mathbf{n}(\mathbf{x}) \cdot \mathbf{u}(\mathbf{x}, t) = 0, \quad \rho(\mathbf{x}, t) = 0, \quad \mathbf{x} \in B, \ t \geq 0 \tag{7.54}$$

where $\mathbf{n}(\mathbf{x})$ is the unit-length outer-pointing normal vector to the boundary point $\mathbf{x}$.

7.11.1 Numerical Methods

The classical approach to solve the first two of Equations (7.52) uses finite difference estimates for the derivatives. The time derivative is estimated by a forward difference and the spatial derivatives are estimated by centered differences. The numerical method is usually conditionally stable, requiring small time steps in the simulation. Creating an implicit equation with the right-hand-side terms involving $t + \Delta t$ (the time we want new state information) rather than time t is a reasonable alternative that may be solved using Gauss-Seidel iteration. In the case at hand, the terms $(\mathbf{u} \cdot \nabla)\rho$ and $(\mathbf{u} \cdot \nabla)\mathbf{u}$ lead to a complicated set of equations to iterate.

A third possibility takes advantage of the left-hand-sides of the first two of Equations (7.52) being *material derivatives*. The fluid flow may be thought of as particles traveling along curves with time-varying positions, say, $\mathbf{x}(t)$. These curves are referred to as *flow lines* where the particles travel along the curves with velocity $\mathbf{x}'(t) = \mathbf{u}(t)$. The time-varying density is related to how the particles move: $h(t) = \rho(\mathbf{x}(t), t)$. The time derivative is

$$h'(t) = \frac{\partial \rho}{\partial t} + \mathbf{x}'(t) \cdot \nabla \rho = \frac{\partial \rho}{\partial t} + (\mathbf{u} \cdot \nabla)\rho = \left(\frac{\partial}{\partial t} + \mathbf{u} \cdot \nabla \right) \rho = \frac{D\rho}{Dt} \tag{7.55}$$

where $D/Dt = \partial/\partial t + \mathbf{u} \cdot \nabla$ is the material derivative operator. Similarly, if $\mathbf{g}(t) = \mathbf{u}(\mathbf{x}(t), t)$, then $\mathbf{g}'(t) = D\mathbf{u}/Dt$. Define the *state vector* that consists of density and velocity to be $\mathbf{S}(t) = (\mathbf{g}(t), h(t))$, define the differential operator $\mathbf{L} = (\nu_{\text{vel}}\nabla^2, \nu_{\text{den}}\nabla^2)$, and define the external source $\mathbf{F} = (\mathbf{F}_{\text{vel}}, F_{\text{den}})$. The initial condition is $\mathbf{S}(0) = (\mathbf{u}_0, \rho_0)$. In vectorized form, Equations (7.52) are then

$$\frac{\partial \mathbf{S}(\mathbf{x}, t)}{\partial t} = \mathbf{L}\mathbf{S}(\mathbf{x}, t) + \mathbf{F}(\mathbf{x}, t), \ \nabla \cdot \mathbf{u}(\mathbf{x}, t) = 0, \quad \mathbf{x} \in R, \ t \geq 0$$
$$\mathbf{S}(\mathbf{x}, 0) = (\mathbf{u}_0(\mathbf{x}), \rho_0(\mathbf{x})), \quad \mathbf{x} \in R \tag{7.56}$$
$$(\mathbf{n}(\mathbf{x}), 1) \cdot \mathbf{S}(\mathbf{x}, t) = \mathbf{0}, \quad \mathbf{x} \in B, \ t \geq 0$$

We use the following estimate for the material derivative of $\mathbf{S}$:

$$\mathbf{S}'(t) \doteq \frac{\mathbf{S}(\mathbf{x}(t), t + \Delta_t) - \mathbf{S}(\mathbf{x}(t - \Delta_t), t)}{\Delta_t} \qquad (7.57)$$

The right-hand side in the limit as Δ_t approaches zero becomes $\mathbf{S}'(t)$. This allows us to compute the next state at the current position using the current state at the last position, thus simplifying the numerical computations. Let $\hat{\mathbf{L}}$ represent the operator corresponding to centered differences for estimates of spatial derivatives. The numerical method for solving the first two of Equations (7.52) is

$$\mathbf{S}(\mathbf{x}(t), t + \Delta_t) = \mathbf{S}(\mathbf{x}(t - \Delta_t), t) + \Delta_t \left(\hat{\mathbf{L}} \mathbf{S}(\mathbf{x}(t), t) + \mathbf{F}(\mathbf{x}(t), t) \right) \qquad (7.58)$$

The left-hand side of the equation is the state vector we want to compute for the next time $t + \Delta_t$. The right-hand side of the equation requires computing the sources at the current time t. It also requires looking up the state vector at the previous time $t - \Delta_t$ but *along flow lines*. This mechanism is referred to as *advection*. We can estimate the previous state by using the backward difference $\mathbf{u}(\mathbf{x}(t), t) \doteq (\mathbf{x}(t) - \mathbf{x}(t - \Delta_t))/\Delta_t$; that is, $\mathbf{x}(t - \Delta_t) \doteq \mathbf{x}(t) - \Delta_t \mathbf{u}(\mathbf{x}(t), t)$. Given the current position and time, we can estimate the previous position and look up the state vector at that position at the previous time. On a regular grid, the previous position is usually not at a grid point, so we will use linear interpolation to approximate the previous state vector. The final formulation of the numerical method is listed next, where we have dropped the notation about position depending on time:

$$\mathbf{S}(\mathbf{x}, t + \Delta_t) = \mathbf{S}(\mathbf{x} - \Delta_t \mathbf{u}(\mathbf{x}, t), t) + \Delta_t \left(\hat{\mathbf{L}} \mathbf{S}(\mathbf{x}, t) + \mathbf{F}(\mathbf{x}, t) \right) \qquad (7.59)$$

The left-hand side is the new state (time $t + \Delta_t$) at a grid position $\mathbf{x}$, and it depends on the right-hand side that contains information only about the current state (time t) in a neighborhood of the grid position.

The update of the state vector has approximation errors, so the estimated velocity does not necessarily have a divergence of zero. A velocity vector field $\mathbf{u}$ may be decomposed as $\mathbf{u} = -\nabla\phi + \nabla \times \mathbf{g}$; this is referred to as the *Helmholtz decomposition*. Dotting the decomposition with the gradient operator, the function ϕ must be a solution to $\nabla^2 \phi = -\nabla \cdot \mathbf{u}$. If $\mathbf{u}$ is the output from the state vector update, we need to modify it to have divergence of zero, $\hat{\mathbf{u}} = \mathbf{u} + \nabla\phi$. Observe that $\nabla \cdot \hat{\mathbf{u}} = \nabla \cdot \mathbf{u} + \nabla^2 \phi = 0$. Thus, we must solve the Poisson equation $\nabla^2 \phi = -\nabla \cdot \mathbf{u}$ for ϕ, compute its gradient, and update the velocity to $\hat{\mathbf{u}}$. The numerical method for solving the Poisson equation involves centered difference estimates for the spatial partial derivatives and Gauss-Seidel iteration to solve the set of linear equations produced by the estimates. We need a boundary condition for the Poisson equation. In the theoretical case of $\nabla \cdot \mathbf{u} = 0$, we can choose $\phi = 0$, which suggests that the boundary values for

ϕ should be zero. This process is summarized next but with the dependence on t not shown,

$$\begin{aligned}
\nabla^2 \phi(\mathbf{x}) &= -\nabla \cdot \mathbf{u}(\mathbf{x}), \ \ \mathbf{x} \in R \\
\phi(\mathbf{x}) &= 0, \ \ \mathbf{x} \in B \\
\hat{\mathbf{u}}(\mathbf{x}) &= \mathbf{u}(\mathbf{x}) + \nabla \phi(\mathbf{x}), \ \ \mathbf{x} \in R \\
\mathbf{n}(\mathbf{x}) \cdot \hat{\mathbf{u}}(\mathbf{x}) &= \mathbf{0}, \ \ \mathbf{x} \in B
\end{aligned} \tag{7.60}$$

High-level pseudocode for the numerical solver is shown in Listing 7.24.

```
t = 0;
dt = <small positive time step>;

// any setup for F(x,t) in Equation (7.56)
InitializeSources();

// Compute S(x,0) in Equation (7.56).  To support advection on the
// first update, set S(x,-dt) = S(x,0).
InitializeVelocityAndDensity();

// constraint in Equation (7.56) for S(x,0) and S(x,-dt)
EnforceVelocityAndDensityBoundaryConstraint();

DoForever
{
    // Compute S(x,t+dt) from S(x,t) and S(x,t-dt).
    ComputeNextState();

    // constraint for S(x,t+dt)
    EnforceVelocityAndDensityBoundaryConstraint();

    // Update the velocity to have a zero divergence.
    ComputeDivergenceOfVelocity();
    SolvePoissonEquationForPhi();
    EnforcePhiBoundaryConstraint();
    AddGradientPhiToVelocity();
    EnforceVelocityBoundaryConstraint();

    t += dt;
};
```

LISTING 7.24: Pseudocode for the high-level fluid simulation.

Actual implementations for 2D and 3D are provided in the source code that accompanies the book. They are described in the next sections.

7.11.2 Solving Fluid Flow in 2D

The sample application is found at

GeometricTools/GTEngine/Samples/Physics/Fluids2D

In the application, the 2D fluid is be confined to a square $R = \{(x,y) : 0 \le x \le 1, 0 \le y \le 1\}$. The boundary B consists of points for which $x = 0$, $x = 1$, $y = 0$, or $y = 1$. The velocity is (u,v). The velocity boundary conditions are $u(0,y,t) = 0$, $u(1,y,t) = 0$, $v(x,0,t) = 0$, and $v(x,1,t) = 0$.

We partition R into an $N_0 \times N_1$ grid, each grid cell a rectangle of dimensions $\Delta_x = 1/N_0$ and $\Delta_y = 1/N_1$. Centered finite differences are used for $\hat{\mathbf{L}}$ in

Equation (7.59),

$$\mathbf{S}_{xx}(x, y, t) \doteq \frac{\mathbf{S}(x + \Delta_x, y, t) - 2\mathbf{S}(x, y, t) + \mathbf{S}(x - \Delta_x, y, t)}{\Delta_x^2} \qquad (7.61)$$

and

$$\mathbf{S}_{yy}(x, y, t) \doteq \frac{\mathbf{S}(x, y + \Delta_y, t) - 2\mathbf{S}(x, y, t) + \mathbf{S}(x, y - \Delta_y, t)}{\Delta_y^2} \qquad (7.62)$$

The update for state information is

$$\begin{aligned}
\mathbf{S}(x, y, t + \Delta_t) = {} & \mathbf{S}(x - \Delta_t u, y - \Delta_t v, t) \\
& + \boldsymbol{\lambda}_x * (\mathbf{S}(x + \Delta_x, y, t) - 2\mathbf{S}(x, y, t) + \mathbf{S}(x - \Delta_x, y, t)) \\
& + \boldsymbol{\lambda}_y * (\mathbf{S}(x, y + \Delta_y, t) - 2\mathbf{S}(x, y, t) + \mathbf{S}(x, y - \Delta_y, t)) \\
& + \Delta_t \mathbf{F}(x, y, t)
\end{aligned} \qquad (7.63)$$

where $\boldsymbol{\lambda}_x = (\Delta_t/\Delta_x^2)(\nu_{\text{vel}}, \nu_{\text{vel}}, \nu_{\text{den}})$, $\boldsymbol{\lambda}_y = (\Delta_t/\Delta_y^2)(\nu_{\text{vel}}, \nu_{\text{vel}}, \nu_{\text{den}})$, and the $*$ operator denotes componentwise multiplication of tuples: $(a, b, c) * (d, e, f) = (ad, be, cf)$.

In the compute shaders of the sample application, a constant buffer is used to store the various physical parameters. The declaration in the shaders and the creation and initialization are listed next. The naming conventions to relate the two are clear. Listing 7.25 shows the setup code.

```
// From various HLSL files:
cbuffer Parameters
{
    float4 spaceDelta;      // (dx, dy, 0, 0)
    float4 halfDivDelta;    // (0.5/dx, 0.5/dy, 0, 0)
    float4 timeDelta;       // (dt/dx, dt/dy, 0, dt)
    float4 viscosityX;      // (velVX, velVX, 0, denVX)
    float4 viscosityY;      // (velVX, velVY, 0, denVY)
    float4 epsilon;         // (epsilonX, epsilonY, 0, epsilon0)
};

// From Smoke2D.cpp:
// Create the shared parameters for many of the simulation shaders.
float dx = 1.0f/static_cast<float>(mXSize);
float dy = 1.0f/static_cast<float>(mYSize);
float dtDivDxDx = (dt/dx)/dx;
float dtDivDyDy = (dt/dy)/dy;
float ratio = dx/dy;
float ratioSqr = ratio*ratio;
float factor = 0.5f/(1.0f + ratioSqr);
float epsilonX = factor;
float epsilonY = ratioSqr*factor;
float epsilon0 = dx*dx*factor;
float const denViscosity = 0.0001f;
float const velViscosity = 0.0001f;
float denVX = denViscosity*dtDivDxDx;
float denVY = denViscosity*dtDivDyDy;
float velVX = velViscosity*dtDivDxDx;
float velVY = velViscosity*dtDivDyDy;
mParameters.reset(new ConstantBuffer(sizeof(Parameters), false));
Parameters& p = *mParameters->GetAs<Parameters>();
p.spaceDelta = Vector4<float>(dx, dy, 0.0f, 0.0f);
p.halfDivDelta = Vector4<float>(0.5f/dx, 0.5f/dy, 0.0f, 0.0f);
```

```
p.timeDelta = Vector4<float>(dt/dx, dt/dy, 0.0f, dt);
p.viscosityX = Vector4<float>(velVX, velVX, 0.0f, denVX);
p.viscosityY = Vector4<float>(velVY, velVY, 0.0f, denVY);
p.epsilon = Vector4<float>(epsilonX, epsilonY, 0.0f, epsilon0);
```

LISTING 7.25: Setup of constant buffers for the 2D fluid simulation.

The fluid grid has mXSize columns and mYSize rows, which are both 256 in the application. The time step dt is chosen to be 0.001.

7.11.2.1 Initialization of State

The initialization of velocity and density is implemented in the class InitializeState. The assignments are in the constructor for the class. The initial velocities are set to zero and the initial densities are set to random numbers in $[0, 1]$. Textures storing state information at current time and previous time are also created by the constructor. Listing 7.26 shows the pseudocode.

```
// Initial density values are randomly generated.
std::mt19937 mte;
std::uniform_real_distribution<float> unirnd(0.0f, 1.0f);
mDensity.reset(new Texture2(DF_R32_FLOAT, xSize, ySize));
float* data = mDensity->GetAs<float>();
for (int i = 0; i < mDensity->GetNumElements(); ++i, ++data)
{
    *data = unirnd(mte);
}

// Initial velocity values are zero.
mVelocity.reset(new Texture2(DF_R32G32_FLOAT, xSize, ySize));
memset(mVelocity->GetData(), 0, mVelocity->GetNumBytes());

// The states at time 0 and time -dt are initialized by a compute shader.
mStateTm1.reset(new Texture2(DF_R32G32B32A32_FLOAT, xSize, ySize));
mStateTm1->SetUsage(Resource::SHADER_OUTPUT);
mStateT.reset(new Texture2(DF_R32G32B32A32_FLOAT, xSize, ySize));
mStateT->SetUsage(Resource::SHADER_OUTPUT);
```

LISTING 7.26: Selection of initial state for 2D fluids.

The compute shader is trivial as is the GTEngine code that creates an instance and executes the shader, as shown in Listing 7.27.

```
// From InitializeState.hlsl:
Texture2D<float> density;
Texture2D<float2> velocity;
RWTexture2D<float4> stateTm1;
RWTexture2D<float4> stateT;
[numthreads(NUM_X_THREADS, NUM_Y_THREADS, 1)]
void CSMain(uint3 c : SV_DispatchThreadID)
{
    float4 initial = float4(velocity[c.xy], 0.0f, density[c.xy]);
    stateTm1[c.xy] = initial;
    stateT[c.xy] = initial;
}

// From InitializeState.cpp:
// Create the shader for initializing velocity and density.
HLSLDefiner definer;
definer.SetInt("NUM_X_THREADS", numXThreads);
definer.SetInt("NUM_Y_THREADS", numYThreads);
```

```
mInitializeState.reset(
    ShaderFactory::CreateCompute("InitializeState.hlsl", definer));
mInitializeState->Set("density", mDensity);
mInitializeState->Set("velocity", mVelocity);
mInitializeState->Set("stateTm1", mStateTm1);
mInitializeState->Set("stateT", mStateT);

// From InitializeState.cpp (in a wrapper for execution):
engine->Execute(mInitializeState, mNumXGroups, mNumYGroups, 1);
```

LISTING 7.27: Initial state computations 2D fluids, both for the CPU and the GPU.

7.11.2.2 Initialization of External Forces

The external density control in Equation (7.52) has a source, a sink, and is constant for all time. Thus, fluid is added at one location in the square and removed at another location.

$$
\begin{aligned}
F_{\text{den}}(x, y) = \quad & A_0 \exp\left(-\frac{|(x - x_0, y - y_0)|^2}{2\sigma_0^2}\right) \\
& - A_1 \exp\left(-\frac{|(x - x_1, y - y_1)|^2}{2\sigma_1^2}\right)
\end{aligned}
\tag{7.64}
$$

where $A_i > 0$, $\sigma_i > 0$, and $(x_i, y_i) \in (0, 1)^2$ are user-defined constants.

The external velocity control has three types of components. A constant gravitational force $\mathbf{G}$ is applied. A wind force $\mathbf{W}$ is applied at the middle of the left side of the square but is distributed as a Gaussian through a small portion of space with direction towards the right. Finally, a sum of vortices $\mathbf{V}_i$ gives the fluid local swirling effects. All external forces are constant over time.

$$
\begin{aligned}
\mathbf{F}_{\text{vel}}(x, y) \; = \; & \mathbf{G} + \mathbf{W}(x, y) + \sum_{i=0}^{n-1} \mathbf{V}_i(x, y) \\[2mm]
= \; & \begin{bmatrix} g_0 \\ g_1 \end{bmatrix} + M_0 \exp\left(-\frac{(x - \xi_0)^2}{2s_0^2}\right) \begin{bmatrix} 1 \\ 0 \end{bmatrix} \\[2mm]
& + \sum_{i=1}^{n} M_i \exp\left(-\frac{|(x - \xi_i, y - \eta_i)|^2}{2s_i^2}\right) \begin{bmatrix} (y - \eta_i) \\ -(x - \xi_i) \end{bmatrix}
\end{aligned}
\tag{7.65}
$$

where g_i, $M_i > 0$, $s_i > 0$, and $(\xi_i, \eta_i) \in (0, 1)^2$ are user-defined constants.

The class InitializeSource manages the setup and evaluation of the external forces. The constructor does the work, but the initialization is more complicated than that for state initialization. If the number n of vortices is small, we can generate the vortex contribution rapidly on the CPU. However, if n is large, the start-up time for the application can be quite lengthy because of the triple loop necessary to sum the n contributions at each pixel in the image. In the application, I have chosen to use 1024 vortices. Unlike the density that is initialized to random numbers on the CPU, the parameters of the external forces are selected on the CPU but the computations of the initial source are all performed on the GPU. The InitializeSource constructor contains code shown in Listing 7.28.

```
// Create the resources for generating velocity from vortices.
mVortex.reset(new ConstantBuffer(sizeof(Vortex), true));
mVelocity0.reset(new Texture2(DF_R32G32_FLOAT, xSize, ySize));
mVelocity0->SetUsage(Resource::SHADER_OUTPUT);
mVelocity1.reset(new Texture2(DF_R32G32_FLOAT, xSize, ySize));
mVelocity1->SetUsage(Resource::SHADER_OUTPUT);

// Create the resources for generating velocity from wind and gravity.
mExternal.reset(new ConstantBuffer(sizeof(External), false));
External& e = *mExternal->Data<External>();
// (x,y,variance,amplitude)
e.densityProducer = Vector4<float>(0.25f, 0.75f, 0.01f, 2.0f);
// (x,y,variance,amplitude)
e.densityConsumer = Vector4<float>(0.75f, 0.25f, 0.01f, 2.0f);
// no gravity for this sample
e.gravity = Vector4<float>(0.0f, 0.0f, 0.0f, 0.0f);
// (x,y,variance,amplitude)
e.wind = Vector4<float>(0.0f, 0.5f, 0.001f, 32.0f);
mSource.reset(new Texture2(DF_R32G32B32A32_FLOAT, xSize, ySize));
mSource->SetUsage(Resource::SHADER_OUTPUT);
```

LISTING 7.28: Setup code for initialization of source forces for 2D fluids.

The mSource texture is initialized with the external forces.

The vortex generation occurs first and is passed to the initialization shader so that gravity and wind forces may be added. The Parameters constant buffer was mentioned previously and is omitted from the listings. The relevant HLSL code is shown in Listing 7.29.

```
// From GenerateVortex.hlsl:
cbuffer Vortex
{
    float4 data;  // (x, y, variance, amplitude)
};
Texture2D<float2> inVelocity;
RWTexture2D<float2> outVelocity;
[numthreads(NUM_X_THREADS, NUM_Y_THREADS, 1)]
void CSMain(uint3 c : SV_DispatchThreadID)
{
    float2 location = spaceDelta.xy*(c.xy + 0.5f);
    float2 diff = location - data.xy;
    float arg = -dot(diff, diff)/data.z;
    float magnitude = data.w*exp(arg);
    float2 vortexVelocity = magnitude*float2(diff.y, -diff.x);
    outVelocity[c.xy] = inVelocity[c.xy] + vortexVelocity;
}

// From InitializeSource.hlsl:
cbuffer External
{
    float4 densityProducer;  // (x, y, variance, amplitude)
    float4 densityConsumer;  // (x, y, variance, amplitude)
    float4 gravity;          // (x, y, *, *)
    float4 wind;             // (x, y, variance, amplitude)
};
Texture2D<float2> vortexVelocity;
RWTexture2D<float4> source;
[numthreads(NUM_X_THREADS, NUM_Y_THREADS, 1)]
void CSMain(uint3 c : SV_DispatchThreadID)
{
    // Compute the location of the pixel (x,y) in normalized [0,1]^2.
    float2 location = spaceDelta.xy*(c.xy + 0.5f);
    // Compute an input to the fluid simulation consisting of a producer
    // of density and a consumer of density.
    float2 diff = location - densityProducer.xy;
    float arg = -dot(diff, diff)/densityProducer.z;
```

```
float density = densityProducer.w*exp(arg);
diff = location - densityConsumer.xy;
arg = -dot(diff, diff)/densityConsumer.z;
density -= densityConsumer.w*exp(arg);
// Compute an input to the fluid simulation consisting of gravity,
// a single wind source, and vortex impulses.
float windDiff = location.y - wind.y;
float windArg = -windDiff*windDiff/wind.z;
float2 windVelocity = { wind.w*exp(windArg), 0.0f };
float2 velocity = gravity.xy + windVelocity + vortexVelocity[c.xy];
source[c.xy] = float4(velocity.xy, 0.0f, density);
}
```

LISTING 7.29: HLSL code for generating vortices and other forces in 2D fluids.

The creation of instances of the shader and the execution of them is shown in Listing 7.30.

```
// From InitializeSource.cpp:
HLSLDefiner definer;
definer.SetInt("NUM_X_THREADS", numXThreads);
definer.SetInt("NUM_Y_THREADS", numYThreads);
mGenerateVortex.reset(
    ShaderFactory::CreateCompute("GenerateVortex.hlsl", definer));
mGenerateVortex->Set("Parameters", parameters);
mGenerateVortex->Set("Vortex", mVortex);
mGenerateVortex->Set("inVelocity", mVelocity0);
mGenerateVortex->Set("outVelocity", mVelocity1);
mInitializeSource.reset(
    ShaderFactory::CreateCompute("InitializeSource.hlsl", definer));
mInitializeSource->Set("Parameters", parameters);
mInitializeSource->Set("External", mExternal);
mInitializeSource->Set("source", mSource);

// From InitializeSource.cpp (in a wrapper for execution):
// Compute the velocity one vortex at a time. After the loop terminates,
// the final velocity is stored in mVelocity0.
std::mt19937 mte;
std::uniform_real_distribution<float> unirnd(0.0f, 1.0f);
std::uniform_real_distribution<float> symrnd(-1.0f, 1.0f);
std::uniform_real_distribution<float> posrnd0(0.001f, 0.01f);
std::uniform_real_distribution<float> posrnd1(128.0f, 256.0f);
memset(mVelocity0->GetData(), 0, mVelocity0->GetNumBytes());
Vortex& v = *mVortex->GetAs<Vortex>();
for (int i = 0; i < NUM_VORTICES; ++i)
{
    v.data[0] = unirnd(mte);
    v.data[1] = unirnd(mte);
    v.data[2] = posrnd0(mte);
    v.data[3] = posrnd1(mte);
    if (symrnd(mte) < 0.0f) { v.data[3] = -v.data[3]; }
    engine->CopyCpuToGpu(mVortex);
    engine->Execute(mGenerateVortex, mNumXGroups, mNumYGroups, 1);
    std::swap(mVelocity0, mVelocity1);
    mGenerateVortex->Set("inVelocity", mVelocity0);
    mGenerateVortex->Set("outVelocity", mVelocity1);
}

// Compute the sources for the fluid simulation.
mInitializeSource->Set("vortexVelocity", mVelocity0);
engine->Execute(mInitializeSource, mNumXGroups, mNumYGroups, 1);
```

LISTING 7.30: Shader creation and execution for initializing sources in 2D fluids.

The vortex parameters are randomly generated on the CPU, one vortex at a time. The negation of **v.data[3]** reverses the direction of spin for the vortex— also randomly selected. These parameters are uploaded as constant buffers and then the shader is executed. The loop ping-pongs between two textures for efficiency (no GPU-to-CPU copies). When all vortices are computed, the result is in **mVelocity0**, which is then attached to the shader that computes the gravity and wind forces. The vortex velocities are added to those.

The design for the remaining shader wrapper classes is similar to that for InitializeState and InitializeSource. Resources are created, shaders are loaded from disk and compiled, and an execution wrapper is provided for the simulation. The remainder of the discussion focuses on the HLSL files themselves.

7.11.2.3   Updating the State with Advection

The update of state using advection and derivative estimation is encapsulated in the class UpdateState, as shown in Listing 7.31. The Parameters constant buffer is omitted from the listing.

```
// From UpdateState.hlsl:
Texture2D<float4> source;
Texture2D<float4> stateTm1;
Texture2D<float4> stateT;
SamplerState advectionSampler;   // bilinear, clamp
RWTexture2D<float4> updateState;
[numthreads(NUM_X_THREADS, NUM_Y_THREADS, 1)]
void CSMain(uint3 c : SV_DispatchThreadID)
{
    uint2 dim;
    stateT.GetDimensions(dim.x, dim.y);

    int x = int(c.x);
    int y = int(c.y);
    int xm = max(x-1, 0);
    int xp = min(x+1, dim.x-1);
    int ym = max(y-1, 0);
    int yp = min(y+1, dim.y-1);

    // Sample states at (x,y), (x+dx,y), (x-dx,y), (x,y+dy), (x,y-dy).
    float4 stateZZ = stateT[int2(x, y)];
    float4 statePZ = stateT[int2(xp, y)];
    float4 stateMZ = stateT[int2(xm, y)];
    float4 stateZP = stateT[int2(x, yp)];
    float4 stateZM = stateT[int2(x, ym)];

    // Sample the source state at (x,y).
    float4 src = source[int2(x, y)];

    // Estimate second-order derivatives of state at (x,y).
    float4 stateDXX = statePZ - 2.0f*stateZZ + stateMZ;
    float4 stateDYY = stateZP - 2.0f*stateZZ + stateZM;

    // Compute advection.
    float2 tcd = spaceDelta.xy*(c.xy - timeDelta.xy*stateZZ.xy + 0.5f);
    float4 advection = stateTm1.SampleLevel(advectionSampler, tcd, 0.0f);

    // Update the state.
    updateState[c.xy] = advection +
        (viscosityX*stateDXX + viscosityY*stateDYY + timeDelta.w*src);
}
```

LISTING 7.31: HLSL code for updating the 2D fluid state with advection.

The resources for compute shaders are accessed directly by index. The dimensions of the texture are conveniently accessed by the HLSL function GetDimensions. The SV_DispatchThreadID system-value semantic provides a natural tuple into a grid. If a compute shader is called with (x_t, y_t, z_t) threads (the parameters in the [numthreads] statement) and (x_g, y_g, z_g) groups (the parameters passed to the Dispatch call), then the dispatch ID (c_x, c_y, c_z) satisfies

$$(0,0,0) \leq (c_x, c_y, c_z) < (x_t, y_t, z_t) * (x_g, y_g, z_g) = (x_t x_g, y_t y_g, z_t z_g) \quad (7.66)$$

In our case, the thread counts are NUM_X_THREADS, NUM_Y_THREADS, and 1. The group counts are dim.x/NUM_X_THREADS, dim.y/NUM_Y_THREADS, and 1. The dispatch thread ID c satisfies (0,0,0) <= (c.x,c.y,c.z) < (dim.x,dim.y,1). We are guaranteed that the x and y values in the shader are within bounds for the state texture. We need to access the four immediate neighbors to compute centered finite differences, so the computation of xm, xp, ym, and yp must be clamped to the image domain.[1]

The external force contributions are provided by the lookup into the source texture. The finite difference approximations are stored in stateDXX and stateDYY; observe that these computations are vectorized for speed—the first two components are for the velocity and the last component is for density.

Recall that advection involves estimating the previous state at a subpixel location; see Equation (7.63). That location is $(x, y) - \Delta_t(u, v)$, where (x, y) is the current pixel center and (u, v) is the current velocity. Texture sampling, though, requires a normalized texture coordinate in $[0, 1]^2$. The shader code float2 tcd = spaceDelta.xy*(c.xy - timeDelta.xy*stateZZ.xy + 0.5f) is the conversion to such a coordinate. For an image of width W and height H, the standard graphics mapping for a pixel $(x_p, y_p) \in [0, W) \times [0, H)$ to a texture coordinate $(x_t, y_t) \in [0, 1]^2$ is

$$(x_t, y_t) = \left(\frac{x_p + 1/2}{W}, \frac{y_p + 1/2}{H} \right) \quad (7.67)$$

The term c.xy - timeDelta.xy*stateZZ.xy is in pixel coordinates. Adding 0.5f and multiplying by spaceDelta.xy = (1/dim.x, 1/dim.y) = (1/W,1/H) converts the pixel coordinates to texture coordinates. As always in compute shaders, you must specify the miplevel, which requires a call to the HLSL function SampleLevel rather than Sample.

The final statement is the update step and is also vectorized for speed.

7.11.2.4　Applying the State Boundary Conditions

The compute shaders are allowed to compute values on the image boundaries. Because we cannot guarantee the order in which GPU threads are called, we cannot enforce boundary values until all state information is computed on

---

[1] Alternatively, we could have use nearest-neighbor sampling of the state texture using the HLSL SampleLevel function call, which requires computing first a texture coordinate. The sampler can then take care of the clamping to image domain.

the image domain. Thus, enforcing the boundary conditions is a postprocessing task. Multiple shaders are used for this task and use ping-pong buffers. The shaders are executed in pairs.

The boundary condition $\mathbf{n}(\mathbf{x}) \cdot \mathbf{u}(\mathbf{x}, t) = 0$ may be applied on the grid solely by setting the appropriate velocity components to zero at the boundary cells. However, this introduces some discontinuity in the velocity near the boundary. To counteract this, a zero-derivative condition is also applied. The grid cells adjacent to the boundary are copied to the boundary first, then the appropriate components are set to zero.

One shader of the pair is responsible for copying the velocity information from boundary-adjacent rows and columns adjacent to temporary buffers. The other shader writes the information from the temporary buffers to the boundary rows and columns and sets various components to zero. The process is illustrated next using a small grid.

$(u_{00}, v_{00}, \rho_{00})$	$(u_{01}, v_{01}, \rho_{01})$	$(u_{02}, v_{02}, \rho_{02})$	$(u_{03}, v_{03}, \rho_{03})$
$(u_{10}, v_{10}, \rho_{10})$	$(u_{11}, v_{11}, \rho_{11})$	$(u_{12}, v_{12}, \rho_{12})$	$(u_{13}, v_{13}, \rho_{13})$
$(u_{20}, v_{20}, \rho_{20})$	$(u_{21}, v_{21}, \rho_{21})$	$(u_{22}, v_{22}, \rho_{22})$	$(u_{23}, v_{23}, \rho_{23})$
$(u_{30}, v_{30}, \rho_{30})$	$(u_{31}, v_{31}, \rho_{31})$	$(u_{32}, v_{32}, \rho_{32})$	$(u_{33}, v_{33}, \rho_{33})$

Copy v of columns 1 and 2:
$\rightarrow$

Write v to columns 0 and 3 and zero u and ρ:
$\rightarrow$

$(0, v_{01}, 0)$	$(u_{01}, v_{01}, \rho_{01})$	$(u_{02}, v_{02}, \rho_{02})$	$(0, v_{02}, 0)$
$(0, v_{11}, 0)$	$(u_{11}, v_{11}, \rho_{11})$	$(u_{12}, v_{12}, \rho_{12})$	$(0, v_{12}, 0)$
$(0, v_{21}, 0)$	$(u_{21}, v_{21}, \rho_{21})$	$(u_{22}, v_{22}, \rho_{22})$	$(0, v_{22}, 0)$
$(0, v_{31}, 0)$	$(u_{31}, v_{31}, \rho_{31})$	$(u_{32}, v_{32}, \rho_{32})$	$(0, v_{32}, 0)$

(7.68)

Copy u of rows 1 and 2:
$\rightarrow$

0	u_{11}	u_{12}	0

0	u_{21}	u_{22}	0

Write u to rows 0 and 3 and zero v and ρ:
$\rightarrow$

$(0, 0, 0)$	$(u_{11}, 0, 0)$	$(u_{12}, 0, 0)$	$(0, 0, 0)$
$(0, v_{11}, 0)$	$(u_{11}, v_{11}, \rho_{11})$	$(u_{12}, v_{12}, \rho_{12})$	$(0, v_{12}, 0)$
$(0, v_{21}, 0)$	$(u_{21}, v_{21}, \rho_{21})$	$(u_{22}, v_{22}, \rho_{22})$	$(0, v_{22}, 0)$
$(0, 0, 0)$	$(u_{21}, 0, 0)$	$(u_{22}, 0, 0)$	$(0, 0, 0)$

The class EnforceStateBoundary encapsulates the boundary handling for velocity and density. The compute shaders are listed next and executed in the order specified. The shaders are compiled one at a time using conditional defines to expose the main functions. Listing 7.32 has the relevant shader code.

```
// From EnforceStateBoundary.hlsl:
Texture2D<float4> state;
RWTexture1D<float> xMin;
RWTexture1D<float> xMax;
[numthreads(1, NUM_Y_THREADS, 1)]
void CopyXEdge (uint3 c : SV_DispatchThreadID)
{
    uint2 dim;
    state.GetDimensions(dim.x, dim.y);
    xMin[c.y] = state[uint2(1, c.y)].y;
    xMax[c.y] = state[uint2(dim.x-2, c.y)].y;
}

Texture1D<float> xMin;
Texture1D<float> xMax;
RWTexture2D<float4> state;
[numthreads(1, NUM_Y_THREADS, 1)]
void WriteXEdge (uint3 c : SV_DispatchThreadID)
{
    uint2 dim;
    state.GetDimensions(dim.x, dim.y);
    state[uint2(0, c.y)] = float4(0.0f, xMin[c.y], 0.0f, 0.0f);
    state[uint2(dim.x-1, c.y)] = float4(0.0f, xMax[c.y], 0.0f, 0.0f);
}

Texture2D<float4> state;
RWTexture1D<float> yMin;
RWTexture1D<float> yMax;
[numthreads(NUM_X_THREADS, 1, 1)]
void CopyYEdge (uint3 c : SV_DispatchThreadID)
{
    uint2 dim;
    state.GetDimensions(dim.x, dim.y);
    yMin[c.x] = state[uint2(c.x, 1)].x;
    yMax[c.x] = state[uint2(c.x, dim.y-2)].x;
}

Texture1D<float> yMin;
Texture1D<float> yMax;
RWTexture2D<float4> state;
[numthreads(NUM_X_THREADS, 1, 1)]
void WriteYEdge (uint3 c : SV_DispatchThreadID)
{
    uint2 dim;
    state.GetDimensions(dim.x, dim.y);
    state[uint2(c.x, 0)] = float4(yMin[c.x], 0.0f, 0.0f, 0.0f);
    state[uint2(c.x, dim.y-1)] = float4(yMax[c.x], 0.0f, 0.0f, 0.0f);
}
```

LISTING 7.32: HLSL code for enforcing the boundary conditions for the 2D fluid state.

The minimum and maximum buffers are created and managed by the class but not exposed to the application.

7.11.2.5 Computing the Divergence of Velocity

The class ComputeDivergence manages the simple shader for computing the divergence of the velocity vector. This involves centered finite difference estimates. Listing 7.33 shows the compute shader; the Parameters constant buffer is omitted.

```
// From ComputeDivergence.hlsl:
Texture2D<float4> state;
RWTexture2D<float> divergence;
[numthreads(NUM_X_THREADS, NUM_Y_THREADS, 1)]
void CSMain(uint3 c : SV_DispatchThreadID)
{
    uint w, h;
    state.GetDimensions(w, h);

    int x = int(c.x);
    int y = int(c.y);
    int xm = max(x-1, 0);
    int xp = min(x+1, w-1);
    int ym = max(y-1, 0);
    int yp = min(y+1, h-1);

    float2 velocityGradient =
    {
        state[int2(xp, y)].x - state[int2(xm, y)].x,
        state[int2(x, yp)].y - state[int2(x, ym)].y
    };

    divergence[c.xy] = dot(halfDivDelta.xy, velocityGradient);
}
```

LISTING 7.33: HLSL code for computing the divergence of the velocity for 2D fluids.

7.11.2.6 Solving the Poisson Equation

The class SolvePoisson manages the shaders for solving the Poisson equation $\nabla^2\phi = -\nabla \cdot \mathbf{u}$ with boundary condition $\phi = 0$. As noted previously, the solver is implicit and uses Gauss-Seidel iteration with ping-pong buffers. The first buffer must be zeroed, which is accomplished by a compute shader ZeroPoisson.hlsl. The compute shader SolvePoisson.hlsl is called thirty-two times, each time swapping buffer pointers to avoid memory copies. Listing 7.34 shows the compute shaders for solving the equation; the Parameters constant buffer is omitted.

```
// From ZeroPoisson.hlsl:
RWTexture2D<float> poisson;
[numthreads(NUM_X_THREADS, NUM_Y_THREADS, 1)]
void CSMain(uint3 c : SV_DispatchThreadID)
{
    poisson[c.xy] = 0.0f;
}

// From SolvePoisson.hlsl:
Texture2D<float> divergence;
Texture2D<float> poisson;
RWTexture2D<float> outPoisson;
[numthreads(NUM_X_THREADS, NUM_Y_THREADS, 1)]
void CSMain(uint3 c : SV_DispatchThreadID)
```

```
{
    uint2 dim;
    divergence . GetDimensions ( dim . x ,  dim . y );

    int  x = int ( c . x );
    int  y = int ( c . y );
    int  xm = max( x −1,  0);
    int  xp = min ( x +1,  dim . x −1);
    int  ym = max( y −1,  0);
    int  yp = min ( y +1,  dim . y −1);

    // Sample the divergence at (x,y).
    float  div = divergence [ int2 ( x ,  y )];

    // Sample values at (x,y), (x+dx,y), (x−dx,y), (x,y+dy), (x,y−dy).
    float  poisPZ = poisson [ int2 ( xp ,  y )];
    float  poisMZ = poisson [ int2 ( xm ,  y )];
    float  poisZP = poisson [ int2 ( x ,  yp )];
    float  poisZM = poisson [ int2 ( x ,  ym )];

    float4 temp = { poisPZ + poisMZ ,  poisZP + poisZM ,  0.0 f ,  div  };
    outPoisson [ c . xy ] = dot ( epsilon ,  temp );
}
```

LISTING 7.34: HLSL code for solving the Poisson equation for 2D fluids.

The boundary conditions are enforced via postprocessing shaders. These are simple, writing zeros to the desired locations and using temporary buffers to avoid memory copies. Listing 7.35 shows the shader code.

```
// From EnforcePoissonBoundary. hlsl :
RWTexture2D<float> image;
[numthreads (1,  NUM_Y_THREADS,  1)]
void WriteXEdge ( uint3 c :  SV_DispatchThreadID)
{
    uint2 dim;
    image . GetDimensions ( dim . x ,  dim . y );
    image [ uint2 (0,  c . y )] = 0.0 f ;
    image [ uint2 ( dim . x −1,  c . y )] = 0.0 f ;
}

RWTexture2D<float> image;
[numthreads (NUM_X_THREADS,  1,  1)]
void WriteYEdge ( uint3 c :  SV_DispatchThreadID)
{
    uint2 dim;
    image . GetDimensions ( dim . x ,  dim . y );
    image [ uint2 ( c . x ,  0)] = 0.0 f ;
    image [ uint2 ( c . x ,  dim . y −1)] = 0.0 f ;
}
```

LISTING 7.35: HLSL code for enforcing the boundary conditions after solving the Poisson equation.

7.11.2.7 Updating the Velocity to Be Divergence Free

The gradient of ϕ, the solution to the Poisson equation, must be added back to the velocity vector. This process is managed by class AdjustVelocity. The shader code is shown in Listing 7.36; the Parameters constant buffer is omitted.

```
// From AdjustVelocity.hlsl:
Texture2D<float4> inState;
Texture2D<float> poisson;
RWTexture2D<float4> outState;
[numthreads(NUM_X_THREADS, NUM_Y_THREADS, 1)]
void CSMain (uint3 c : SV_DispatchThreadID)
{
    uint2 dim;
    inState.GetDimensions(dim.x, dim.y);

    int x = int(c.x);
    int y = int(c.y);
    int xm = max(x-1, 0);
    int xp = min(x+1, dim.x-1);
    int ym = max(y-1, 0);
    int yp = min(y+1, dim.y-1);

    // Sample the state at (x,y).
    float4 state = inState[c.xy];

    // Sample Poisson values at immediate neighbors of (x,y).
    float poisPZ = poisson[int2(xp, y)];
    float poisMZ = poisson[int2(xm, y)];
    float poisZP = poisson[int2(x, yp)];
    float poisZM = poisson[int2(x, ym)];

    float4 diff = { poisPZ - poisMZ, poisZP - poisZM, 0.0f, 0.0f };
    outState[c.xy] = state + halfDivDelta*diff;
}
```

LISTING 7.36: HLSL code for updating the velocity to be divergence free.

The gradient is estimated using centered finite differences and the result is structured to use vectorized computations for speed.

7.11.2.8 Screen Captures from the Simulation

The 2D fluid simulation is clamped to run at 60 frames per second. The screen captures shown in Figure 7.12 were taken every second. The coloring of the density is based on the velocity vectors and modulated by the density. The pixel shader is shown in Listing 7.37.

```
// From DrawDensity.hlsl:
Texture2D<float4> state;
SamplerState bilinearClampSampler;
struct PS_INPUT { float2 vertexTCoord : TEXCOORD0; };
float4 PSMain (PS_INPUT input) : SV_TARGET
{
    float4 current = state.Sample(bilinearClampSampler,
        input.vertexTCoord);
    float3 color = 0.5f + 0.5f*current.xyz/(1.0f + abs(current.xyz));
    return float4(current.w*color, 1.0f);
}
```

LISTING 7.37: The pixel shader for visualizing the density of the 2D fluid.

Naturally, screen captures are not sufficient to convey the actual real-time behavior. You will have to run it yourself.

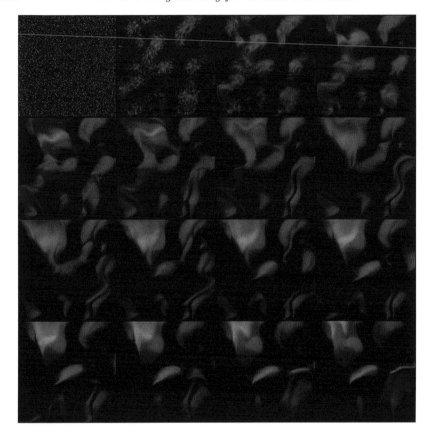

FIGURE 7.12: Screen captures from the 2D fluid simulation. The upper-left image is the initial random density with initial zero velocity. The captures were taken at 1-second intervals, left to right and then top to bottom.

7.11.3 Solving Fluid Flow in 3D

The sample application is found at

GeometricTools/GTEngine/Samples/Physics/Fluids3D

In the sample application, the 3D fluid is confined to a cube $R = \{(x, y, z) : 0 \le x \le 1, \, 0 \le y \le 1, \, 0 \le z \le 1\}$. The boundary B consists of points for which $x = 0$, $x = 1$, $y = 0$, $y = 1$, $z = 0$, or $z = 1$. The velocity is (u, v, w). The velocity boundary conditions are $u(0, y, z, t) = 0$, $u(1, y, z, t) = 0$, $v(x, 0, z, t) = 0$, $v(x, 1, z, t) = 0$, $w(x, y, 0, t) = 0$, and $w(x, y, 1, t) = 0$.

We partition R into an $N_0 \times N_1 \times N_2$ grid, each grid cell a rectangular solid of dimensions $\Delta_x = 1/N_0$, $\Delta_y = 1/N_1$, and $\Delta_z = 1/N_2$. Centered finite differences are used for $\hat{\mathbf{L}}$ in Equation (7.59),

$$\mathbf{S}_{xx}(x,y,z,t) \doteq \frac{\mathbf{S}(x+\Delta_x,y,z,t) - 2\mathbf{S}(x,y,z,t) + \mathbf{S}(x-\Delta_x,y,z,t)}{\Delta_x^2} \quad (7.69)$$

and

$$\mathbf{S}_{yy}(x,y,z,t) \doteq \frac{\mathbf{S}(x,y+\Delta_y,z,t) - 2\mathbf{S}(x,y,z,t) + \mathbf{S}(x,y-\Delta_y,z,t)}{\Delta_y^2} \quad (7.70)$$

and

$$\mathbf{S}_{zz}(x,y,z,t) \doteq \frac{\mathbf{S}(x,y,z+\Delta_z,t) - 2\mathbf{S}(x,y,z,t) + \mathbf{S}(x,y,z-\Delta_z,t)}{\Delta_z^2} \quad (7.71)$$

The update for state information is

$$\begin{aligned}
\mathbf{S}(x,y,z,t+\Delta_t) = & \; \mathbf{S}(x-\Delta_t u, y-\Delta_t v, z-\Delta_t w, t) \\
& + \boldsymbol{\lambda}_x * (\mathbf{S}(x+\Delta_x,y,z,t) - 2\mathbf{S}(x,y,z,t) + \mathbf{S}(x-\Delta_x,y,z,t)) \\
& + \boldsymbol{\lambda}_y * (\mathbf{S}(x,y+\Delta_y,z,t) - 2\mathbf{S}(x,y,z,t) + \mathbf{S}(x,y-\Delta_y,z,t)) \\
& + \boldsymbol{\lambda}_z * (\mathbf{S}(x,y,z+\Delta_z,t) - 2\mathbf{S}(x,y,z,t) + \mathbf{S}(x,y,z-\Delta_z,t)) \\
& + \Delta_t \mathbf{F}(x,y,z,t)
\end{aligned} \quad (7.72)$$

where $\boldsymbol{\lambda}_x = (\Delta_t/\Delta_x^2)\boldsymbol{\nu}$, $\boldsymbol{\lambda}_y = (\Delta_t/\Delta_y^2)\boldsymbol{\nu}$, and $\boldsymbol{\lambda}_z = (\Delta_t/\Delta_z^2)\boldsymbol{\nu}$ with $\boldsymbol{\nu} = (\nu_{\mathrm{vel}}, \nu_{\mathrm{vel}}, \nu_{\mathrm{vel}}, \nu_{\mathrm{den}})$. Also, $(a,b,c,d) * (e,f,g,h) = (ae,bf,cg,dh)$ is componentwise multiplication of tuples.

In the compute shaders of the sample application, a constant buffer is used to store the various physical parameters. The declaration in the shaders and the creation and initialization are listed next. The naming conventions to relate the two are clear. Listing 7.38 shows the setup code.

```
// From various HLSL files:
cbuffer Parameters
{
    float4 spaceDelta;      // (dx, dy, dz, 0)
    float4 halfDivDelta;    // (0.5/dx, 0.5/dy, 0.5/dz, 0)
    float4 timeDelta;       // (dt/dx, dt/dy, dt/dz, dt)
    float4 viscosityX;      // (velVX, velVX, velVX, denVX)
    float4 viscosityY;      // (velVX, velVY, velVY, denVY)
    float4 viscosityZ;      // (velVZ, velVZ, velVZ, denVZ)
    float4 epsilon;         // (epsilonX, epsilonY, epsilonZ, epsilon0)
};

// From Smoke3D.cpp:
// Create the shared parameters for many of the simulation shaders.
float dx = 1.0f/static_cast<float>(mXSize);
float dy = 1.0f/static_cast<float>(mYSize);
float dz = 1.0f/static_cast<float>(mZSize);
float dtDivDxDx = (dt/dx)/dx;
float dtDivDyDy = (dt/dy)/dy;
float dtDivDzDz = (dt/dz)/dz;
float ratio0 = dx/dy;
float ratio1 = dx/dz;
float ratio0Sqr = ratio0*ratio0;
float ratio1Sqr = ratio1*ratio1;
float factor = 0.5f/(1.0f + ratio0Sqr + ratio1Sqr);
```

```
float epsilonX = factor;
float epsilonY = ratio0Sqr*factor;
float epsilonZ = ratio1Sqr*factor;
float epsilon0 = dx*dx*factor;
float const denViscosity = 0.0001f;
float const velViscosity = 0.0001f;
float denVX = denViscosity*dtDivDxDx;
float denVY = denViscosity*dtDivDyDy;
float denVZ = denViscosity*dtDivDzDz;
float velVX = velViscosity*dtDivDxDx;
float velVY = velViscosity*dtDivDyDy;
float velVZ = velViscosity*dtDivDzDz;
```

LISTING 7.38: Setup of constant buffers for the 3D fluid simulation.

The fluid grid has mXSize columns, mYSize rows, and mZSize slices, which are both 128 in the application. The time step dt is chosen to be 0.002.

7.11.3.1   Initialization of State

The initialization of velocity and density is implemented in the class InitializeState. The assignments are in the constructor for the class. The initial velocities are set to zero and the initial densities are set to random numbers in $[0, 1]$. Textures storing state information at current time and previous time are also created by the constructor. Listing 7.39 shows the pseudocode.

```
// Initial density values are randomly generated.
std::mt19937 mte;
std::uniform_real_distribution<float> unirnd(0.0f, 1.0f);
mDensity.reset(new Texture3(DF_R32_FLOAT, xSize, ySize, zSize));
float* data = mDensity->GetAs<float>();
for (int i = 0; i < mDensity->GetNumElements(); ++i, ++data)
{
    *data = unirnd(mte);
}

// Initial velocity values are zero.
mVelocity.reset(new Texture3(DF_R32G32B32A32_FLOAT, xSize, ySize, zSize));
mVelocity->SetUsage(Resource::SHADER_OUTPUT);
memset(mVelocity->GetData(), 0, mVelocity->GetNumBytes());

// The states at time 0 and time -dt are initialized by a compute shader.
mStateTm1.reset(new Texture3(DF_R32G32B32A32_FLOAT, xSize, ySize, zSize));
mStateTm1->SetUsage(Resource::SHADER_OUTPUT);
mStateT.reset(new Texture3(DF_R32G32B32A32_FLOAT, xSize, ySize, zSize));
mStateT->SetUsage(Resource::SHADER_OUTPUT);
```

LISTING 7.39: Selection of initial state for 3D fluids.

The compute shader is trivial as is the GTEngine code that creates an instance and executes the shader, as shown in Listing 7.40.

```
// From InitializeState.hlsl:
Texture3D<float> density;
Texture3D<float4> velocity;
RWTexture3D<float4> stateTm1;
RWTexture3D<float4> stateT;
[numthreads(NUM_X_THREADS, NUM_Y_THREADS, NUM_Z_THREADS)]
void CSMain(uint3 c : SV_DispatchThreadID)
{
    float4 initial = float4(velocity[c.xyz].xyz, density[c.xyz]);
```

```
        stateTm1[c.xyz] = initial;
        stateT[c.xyz] = initial;
}

// From InitializeState.cpp:
// Create the shader for initializing velocity and density.
HLSLDefiner definer;
definer.SetInt("NUM_X_THREADS", numXThreads);
definer.SetInt("NUM_Y_THREADS", numYThreads);
definer.SetInt("NUM_Z_THREADS", numZThreads);
mInitializeState.reset(ShaderFactory::CreateCompute(path, definer));
mInitializeState->Set("density", mDensity);
mInitializeState->Set("velocity", mVelocity);
mInitializeState->Set("stateTm1", mStateTm1);
mInitializeState->Set("stateT", mStateT);

// From InitializeState.cpp (in a wrapper for execution):
engine->Execute(mInitializeState, mNumXGroups, mNumYGroups, mNumZGroups);
```

LISTING 7.40: Initial state computations 3D fluids, both for the CPU and the GPU.

7.11.3.2 Initialization of External Forces

The external density control in Equation (7.52) has a source, a sink, and is constant for all time. Thus, fluid is added at one location in the square and removed at another location.

$$
\begin{aligned}
F_{\text{den}}(x,y,z) \;=\;& A_0 \exp\left(-\frac{|(x-x_0, y-y_0, z-z_0)|^2}{2\sigma_0^2}\right) \\
& - A_1 \exp\left(-\frac{|(x-x_1, y-y_1, z-z_1)|^2}{2\sigma_1^2}\right)
\end{aligned}
\tag{7.73}
$$

where $A_i > 0$, $\sigma_i > 0$, and $(x_i, y_i, z_i) \in (0,1)^2$ are user-defined constants.

The external velocity control has three types of components. A constant gravitational force $\mathbf{G}$ is applied. A wind force $\mathbf{W}$ is applied at the middle of the left side of the square but is distributed as a Gaussian through a small portion of space with direction towards the right. Finally, a sum of vortices $\mathbf{V}_i$ gives the fluid local swirling effects. All external forces are constant over time.

$$
\begin{aligned}
\mathbf{F}_{\text{vel}}(x,y,z) =\;& \mathbf{G} + \mathbf{W}(x,y,z) + \sum_{i=0}^{n-1} \mathbf{V}_i(x,y,z) \\[2mm]
=\;& \begin{bmatrix} g_0 \\ g_1 \\ g_2 \end{bmatrix} + M_0 \exp\left(-\frac{(x-\xi_0)^2 + (z-\xi_2)^2}{2s_0^2}\right) \begin{bmatrix} 0 \\ 1 \\ 0 \end{bmatrix} \\[2mm]
& + \sum_{i=1}^{n} M_i \exp\left(-\frac{|(x-\xi_i, y-\eta_i, z-\zeta_i)|^2}{2s_i^2}\right) \mathbf{N}_i \times \begin{bmatrix} x-\xi_i \\ y-\eta_i \\ z-\zeta_i \end{bmatrix}
\end{aligned}
\tag{7.74}
$$

where g_i, $M_i > 0$, $s_i > 0$, $(\xi_i, \eta_i, \zeta_i) \in (0,1)^3$ are user-defined constants. The normal vectors $\mathbf{N}_i$ are unit length and act as the axis directions for the planar vortices.

The class InitializeSource manages the setup and evaluation of the external forces. The constructor does the work, but the initialization is more complicated than that for state initialization. If the number n of vortices is small, we can generate the vortex contribution rapidly on the CPU. However, if n is large, the start-up time for the application can be quite lengthy because of the triple loop necessary to sum the n contributions at each pixel in the image. In the application, I have chosen to use 1024 vortices. Unlike the density that is initialized to random numbers on the CPU, the parameters of the external forces are selected on the CPU but the computations of the initial source are all performed on the GPU. The InitializeSource constructor contains code shown in Listing 7.41.

```
// Create the resources for generating velocity from vortices.
struct Vortex { Vector4<float> position, normal, data; };
mVortex.reset(new ConstantBuffer(sizeof(Vortex), true));
mVelocity0.reset(new Texture3(DF_R32G32B32A32_FLOAT, xSize, ySize, zSize));
mVelocity0->SetUsage(Resource::SHADER_OUTPUT);
mVelocity1.reset(new Texture3(DF_R32G32B32A32_FLOAT, xSize, ySize, zSize));
mVelocity1->SetUsage(Resource::SHADER_OUTPUT);

// Create the resources for generating velocity from wind and gravity.
struct External
{
    Vector4<float> densityProducer;   // (x, y, z, *)
    Vector4<float> densityPData;      // (variance, amplitude, *, *)
    Vector4<float> densityConsumer;   // (x, y, z, *)
    Vector4<float> densityCData;      // (variance, amplitude, *, *)
    Vector4<float> gravity;
    Vector4<float> windData;
};
mExternal.reset(new ConstantBuffer(sizeof(External), false));
External& e = *mExternal->GetAs<External>();
e.densityProducer = Vector4<float>(0.5f, 0.5f, 0.5f, 0.0f);
e.densityPData = Vector4<float>(0.01f, 16.0f, 0.0f, 0.0f);
e.densityConsumer = Vector4<float>(0.75f, 0.75f, 0.75f, 0.0f);
e.densityCData = Vector4<float>(0.01f, 0.0f, 0.0f, 0.0f);
e.gravity = Vector4<float>(0.0f, 0.0f, 0.0f, 0.0f);
e.windData = Vector4<float>(0.001f, 0.0f, 0.0f, 0.0f);
mSource.reset(new Texture3(DF_R32G32B32A32_FLOAT, xSize, ySize, zSize));
mSource->SetUsage(Resource::SHADER_OUTPUT);
```

LISTING 7.41: Setup code for initialization of source forces for 3D fluids.

The mSource texture is initialized with the external forces.

The vortex generation occurs first and is passed to the initialization shader so that gravity and wind forces may be added. The Parameters constant buffer was mentioned previously and is omitted from the listings. The relevant HLSL code is shown in Listing 7.42.

```
// From GenerateVortex.hlsl:
cbuffer Vortex
{
    float4 position;   // (px, py, pz, *)
    float4 normal;     // (nx, ny, nz, *)
    float4 data;       // (variance, amplitude, *, *)
};
Texture3D<float4> inVelocity;
RWTexture3D<float4> outVelocity;
[numthreads(NUM_X_THREADS, NUM_Y_THREADS, NUM_Z_THREADS)]
```

```
void CSMain (uint3 c : SV_DispatchThreadID)
{
    float3 location = spaceDelta.xyz*(c.xyz + 0.5f);
    float3 diff = location - position.xyz;
    float arg = -dot(diff, diff)/data.x;
    float magnitude = data.y*exp(arg);
    float4 vortexVelocity = float4(magnitude*cross(normal.xyz, diff), 0.0f);
    outVelocity[c.xyz] = inVelocity[c.xyz] + vortexVelocity;
}

// From InitializeSource.hlsl:
cbuffer External
{
    float4 densityProducer;    // (x, y, z, *)
    float4 densityPData;       // (variance, amplitude, *, *)
    float4 densityConsumer;    // (x, y, z, *)
    float4 densityCData;       // (variance, amplitude, *, *)
    float4 gravity;            // (x, y, z, *)
    float4 windData;           // (variance, amplitude, *, *)
};
Texture3D<float4> vortexVelocity;
RWTexture3D<float4> source;
[numthreads(NUM_X_THREADS, NUM_Y_THREADS, NUM_Z_THREADS)]
void CSMain (uint3 c : SV_DispatchThreadID)
{
    // Compute the location of the voxel (x,y,z) in normalized [0,1]^3.
    float3 location = spaceDelta.xyz*(c.xyz + 0.5f);
    // Compute an input to the fluid simulation consisting of a producer
    // of density and a consumer of density.
    float3 diff = location - densityProducer.xyz;
    float arg = -dot(diff, diff)/densityPData.x;
    float density = densityPData.y*exp(arg);
    diff = location - densityConsumer.xyz;
    arg = -dot(diff, diff)/densityCData.x;
    density -= densityCData.y*exp(arg);
    // Compute an input to the fluid simulation consisting of gravity,
    // a single wind source, and vortex impulses.
    float windArg = -dot(location.xz, location.xz)/windData.x;
    float3 windVelocity = { 0.0f, windData.y*exp(windArg), 0.0f };
    float3 velocity =
        gravity.xyz + windVelocity + vortexVelocity[c.xyz].xyz;
    source[c.xyz] = float4(velocity.xyz, density);
}
```

LISTING 7.42: HLSL code for generating vortices and other forces in 3D fluids.

The creation of instances of the shader and the execution of them is shown in Listing 7.43.

```
// From InitializeSource.cpp:
HLSLDefiner definer;
definer.SetInt("NUM_X_THREADS", numXThreads);
definer.SetInt("NUM_Y_THREADS", numYThreads);
definer.SetInt("NUM_Z_THREADS", numZThreads);
mGenerateVortex.reset(
    ShaderFactory::CreateCompute("GenerateVortex.hlsl", definer));
mGenerateVortex->Set("Parameters", parameters);
mGenerateVortex->Set("Vortex", mVortex);
mGenerateVortex->Set("inVelocity", mVelocity0);
mGenerateVortex->Set("outVelocity", mVelocity1);
mInitializeSource.reset(
    ShaderFactory::CreateCompute("InitializeSource.hlsl", definer));
mInitializeSource->Set("Parameters", parameters);
mInitializeSource->Set("External", mExternal);
```

```
mInitializeSource ->Set("source", mSource);

// From InitializeSource.cpp (in a wrapper for execution):
// Compute the velocity one vortex at a time.  After the loop terminates,
// the final velocity is stored in mVelocity0.
std :: mt19937 mte;
std :: uniform_real_distribution<float> unirnd(0.0f, 1.0f);
std :: uniform_real_distribution<float> symrnd(-1.0f, 1.0f);
std :: uniform_real_distribution<float> posrnd0(0.001f, 0.01f);
std :: uniform_real_distribution<float> posrnd1(64.0f, 128.0f);
memset(mVelocity0->GetData(), 0, mVelocity0->GetNumBytes());
Vortex& v = *mVortex->GetAs<Vortex>();
for (int i = 0; i < NUM_VORTICES; ++i)
{
    v.position[0] = unirnd(mte);
    v.position[1] = unirnd(mte);
    v.position[2] = unirnd(mte);
    v.position[3] = 0.0f;
    v.normal[0] = symrnd(mte);
    v.normal[1] = symrnd(mte);
    v.normal[2] = symrnd(mte);
    v.normal[3] = 0.0f;
    Normalize(v.normal);
    v.data[0] = posrnd0(mte);
    v.data[1] = posrnd1(mte);
    v.data[2] = 0.0f;
    v.data[3] = 0.0f;
    engine->CopyCpuToGpu(mVortex);
    engine->Execute(mGenerateVortex, mNumXGroups, mNumYGroups,
        mNumZGroups);
    std :: swap(mVelocity0, mVelocity1);
    mGenerateVortex->Set("inVelocity", mVelocity0);
    mGenerateVortex->Set("outVelocity", mVelocity1);
}

// Compute the sources for the fluid simulation.
mInitializeSource->Set("vortexVelocity", mVelocity0);
engine->Execute(mInitializeSource, mNumXGroups, mNumYGroups, mNumZGroups);
```

LISTING 7.43: Shader creation and execution for initializing sources in 3D fluids.

The vortex parameters are randomly generated on the CPU, one vortex at a time. These parameters are uploaded as constant buffers and then the shader is executed. The loop ping-pongs between two textures for efficiency (no GPU-to-CPU copies). When all vortices are computed, the result is in mVelocity0, which is then attached to the shader that computes the gravity and wind forces. The vortex velocities are added to those.

The design for the remaining shader wrapper classes is similar to that for InitializeState and InitializeSource. Resources are created, shaders are loaded from disk and compiled, and an execution wrapper is provided for the simulation. The remainder of the discussion focuses on the HLSL files themselves.

7.11.3.3   Updating the State with Advection

The update of state using advection and derivative estimation is encapsulated in the class UpdateState, as shown in Listing 7.44. The Parameters constant buffer is omitted from the listing.

```
// From UpdateState.hlsl:
Texture3D<float4> source;
Texture3D<float4> stateTm1;
Texture3D<float4> stateT;
SamplerState advectionSampler;  // trilinear, clamp
RWTexture3D<float4> updateState;
[numthreads(NUM_X_THREADS, NUM_Y_THREADS, NUM_Z_THREADS)]
void CSMain (uint3 c : SV_DispatchThreadID)
{
    uint3 dim;
    stateT.GetDimensions(dim.x, dim.y, dim.z);

    int x = int(c.x);
    int y = int(c.y);
    int z = int(c.z);
    int xm = max(x-1, 0);
    int xp = min(x+1, dim.x-1);
    int ym = max(y-1, 0);
    int yp = min(y+1, dim.y-1);
    int zm = max(z-1, 0);
    int zp = min(z+1, dim.z-1);

    // Sample states at (x,y,z) and immediate neighbors.
    float4 stateZZZ = stateT[int3(x, y, z)];
    float4 statePZZ = stateT[int3(xp, y, z)];
    float4 stateMZZ = stateT[int3(xm, y, z)];
    float4 stateZPZ = stateT[int3(x, yp, z)];
    float4 stateZMZ = stateT[int3(x, ym, z)];
    float4 stateZZP = stateT[int3(x, y, zp)];
    float4 stateZZM = stateT[int3(x, y, zm)];

    // Sample the source state at (x,y,z).
    float4 src = source[int3(x, y, z)];

    // Estimate second-order derivatives of state at (x,y,z).
    float4 stateDXX = statePZZ - 2.0f*stateZZZ + stateMZZ;
    float4 stateDYY = stateZPZ - 2.0f*stateZZZ + stateZMZ;
    float4 stateDZZ = stateZZP - 2.0f*stateZZZ + stateZZM;

    // Compute advection.
    float3 tcd =
        spaceDelta.xyz*(c.xyz - timeDelta.xyz*stateZZZ.xyz + 0.5f);
    float4 advection = stateTm1.SampleLevel(advectionSampler, tcd, 0.0f);

    // Update the state.
    updateState[c.xyz] = advection +
        (viscosityX*stateDXX + viscosityY*stateDYY +
        viscosityZ*stateDZZ + timeDelta.w*src);
}
```

LISTING 7.44: HLSL code for updating the 3D fluid state with advection.

The resources for compute shaders are accessed directly by index. The dimensions of the texture are conveniently accessed by the HLSL function GetDimensions. The SV_DispatchThreadID system-value semantic provides a natural tuple into a grid. If a compute shader is called with (x_t, y_t, z_t) threads (the parameters in the [numthreads] statement) and (x_g, y_g, z_g) groups (the parameters passed to the Dispatch call), then the dispatch ID (c_x, c_y, c_z) satisfies

$$(0,0,0) \leq (c_x, c_y, c_z) < (x_t, y_t, z_t) * (x_g, y_g, z_g) = (x_t x_g, y_t y_g, z_t z_g) \quad (7.75)$$

In our case, the thread counts are NUM_X_THREADS, NUM_Y_THREADS, and NUM_Z_THREADS. The group counts are dim.x/NUM_X_THREADS, dim.y/NUM_Y_THREADS, and dim.z/NUM_Z_THREADS. The dispatch thread ID c satisfies (0,0,0) <= (c.x,c.y,c.z) < (dim.x,dim.y,dim.z). We are guaranteed that the x, y, and z values in the shader are within bounds for the state texture. We need to access the four immediate neighbors to compute centered finite differences, so the computation of xm, xp, ym, yp, zm, and zp must be clamped to the image domain.

The external force contributions are provided by the lookup into the source texture. The finite difference approximations are stored in stateDXX, stateDYY, stateDZZ; observe that these computations are vectorized for speed—the first three components are for the velocity and the last component is for density.

Recall that advection involves estimating the previous state at a subvoxel location; see Equation (7.72). That location is $(x, y, z) - \Delta_t(u, v, w)$, where (x, y, z) is the current voxel center and (u, v, w) is the current velocity. Texture sampling, though, requires a normalized texture coordinate in $[0, 1]^3$. The shader code float3 tcd = spaceDelta.xyz*(c.xyz - timeDelta.xyz*stateZZ.xyz + 0.5f); is the conversion to such a coordinate. For an image of width W, height H, and thickness T, the standard graphics mapping for a voxel $(x_p, y_p, z_p) \in [0, W) \times [0, H) \times [0, T)$ to a texture coordinate $(x_t, y_t, z_t) \in [0, 1)^3$ is

$$(x_t, y_t, z_t) = \left(\frac{x_p + 1/2}{W}, \frac{y_p + 1/2}{H}, \frac{z_p + 1/2}{T} \right) \tag{7.76}$$

The term c.xyz - timeDelta.xyz*stateZZ.xyz is in voxel coordinates. Adding 0.5f and multiplying by spaceDelta.xyz = (1/dim.x, 1/dim.y,1/dim.z) = (1/W,1/H,1/T) converts the voxel coordinates to texture coordinates. As always in compute shaders you must specify the miplevel, which requires a call to the HLSL function SampleLevel rather than Sample.

The final statement is the update step and is also vectorized for speed.

7.11.3.4 Applying the State Boundary Conditions

The compute shaders are allowed to compute values on the image boundaries. Because we cannot guarantee the order in which GPU threads are called, we cannot enforce boundary values until all state information is computed on the image domain. Thus, enforcing the boundary conditions is a postprocessing task. Multiple shaders are used for this task and use ping-pong buffers. The shaders are executed in pairs.

The boundary condition $\mathbf{n}(\mathbf{x}) \cdot \mathbf{u}(\mathbf{x}, t) = 0$ may be applied on the grid solely by setting the appropriate velocity components to zero at the boundary cells. However, this introduces some discontinuity in the velocity near the boundary. To counteract this, a zero-derivative condition is also applied. The grid cells adjacent to the boundary are copied to the boundary first, then the appropriate components are set to zero. The details are tedious and mimic those shown in Equation (7.68), so they are not discussed here. You can go directly to the HLSL file to see the shader implementations.

7.11.3.5 Computing the Divergence of Velocity

The class ComputeDivergence manages the simple shader for computing the divergence of the velocity vector. This involves centered finite difference estimates. Listing 7.45 shows the compute shader; the Parameters constant buffer is omitted.

```
// From ComputeDivergence.hlsl:
Texture3D<float4> state;
RWTexture3D<float> divergence;
[numthreads(NUM_X_THREADS, NUM_Y_THREADS, NUM_Z_THREADS)]
void CSMain(uint3 c : SV_DispatchThreadID)
{
    uint3 dim;
    state.GetDimensions(dim.x, dim.y, dim.z);

    int x = int(c.x);
    int y = int(c.y);
    int z = int(c.z);
    int xm = max(x-1, 0);
    int xp = min(x+1, dim.x-1);
    int ym = max(y-1, 0);
    int yp = min(y+1, dim.y-1);
    int zm = max(z-1, 0);
    int zp = min(z+1, dim.z-1);

    float3 velocityGradient =
    {
        state[int3(xp, y, z)].x - state[int3(xm, y, z)].x,
        state[int3(x, yp, z)].y - state[int3(x, ym, z)].y,
        state[int3(x, y, zp)].z - state[int3(x, y, zm)].z
    };

    divergence[c.xyz] = dot(halfDivDelta.xyz, velocityGradient);
}
```

LISTING 7.45: HLSL code for computing the divergence of the velocity for 3D fluids.

7.11.3.6 Solving the Poisson Equation

The class SolvePoisson manages the shaders for solving the Poisson equation $\nabla^2\phi = -\nabla \cdot \mathbf{u}$ with boundary condition $\phi = 0$. As noted previously, the solver is implicit and uses Gauss-Seidel iteration with ping-pong buffers. The first buffer must be zeroed, which is accomplished by a compute shader ZeroPoisson.hlsl. The compute shader SolvePoisson.hlsl is called thirty-two times, each time swapping buffer pointers to avoid memory copies. Listing 7.46 shows the compute shaders for solving the equation; the Parameters constant buffer is omitted.

```
// From ZeroPoisson.hlsl:
RWTexture3D<float> poisson;
[numthreads(NUM_X_THREADS, NUM_Y_THREADS, NUM_Z_THREADS)]
void CSMain(uint3 c : SV_DispatchThreadID)
{
    poisson[c.xyz] = 0.0f;
}

// From SolvePoisson.hlsl:
Texture3D<float> divergence;
```

```
Texture3D<float> poisson;
RWTexture3D<float> outPoisson;
[numthreads(NUM_X_THREADS, NUM_Y_THREADS, NUM_Z_THREADS)]
void CSMain (uint3 c : SV_DispatchThreadID)
{
    uint3 dim;
    divergence.GetDimensions(dim.x, dim.y, dim.z);

    int x = int(c.x);
    int y = int(c.y);
    int z = int(c.z);
    int xm = max(x-1, 0);
    int xp = min(x+1, dim.x-1);
    int ym = max(y-1, 0);
    int yp = min(y+1, dim.y-1);
    int zm = max(z-1, 0);
    int zp = min(z+1, dim.z-1);

    // Sample the divergence at (x,y,z).
    float div = divergence[int3(x, y, z)];

    // Sample Poisson values at (x,y) and immediate neighbors.
    float poisPZZ = poisson[int3(xp, y, z)];
    float poisMZZ = poisson[int3(xm, y, z)];
    float poisZPZ = poisson[int3(x, yp, z)];
    float poisZMZ = poisson[int3(x, ym, z)];
    float poisZZP = poisson[int3(x, y, zp)];
    float poisZZM = poisson[int3(x, y, zm)];

    float4 temp = { poisPZZ + poisMZZ, poisZPZ + poisZMZ,
        poisZZP + poisZZM, div };
    outPoisson[c.xyz] = dot(epsilon, temp);
}
```

LISTING 7.46: HLSL code for solving the Poisson equation for 3D fluids.

The boundary conditions are enforced via postprocessing shaders. These are simple, writing zeros to the desired locations and using temporary buffers to avoid memory copies. Listing 7.47 shows the shader code.

```
// From EnforcePoissonBoundary.hlsl:
RWTexture3D<float> image;
[numthreads(1, NUM_Y_THREADS, NUM_Z_THREADS)]
void WriteXFace (uint3 c : SV_DispatchThreadID)
{
    uint3 dim;
    image.GetDimensions(dim.x, dim.y, dim.z);
    image[uint3(0, c.y, c.z)] = 0.0f;
    image[uint3(dim.x-1, c.y, c.z)] = 0.0f;
}

RWTexture3D<float> image;
[numthreads(NUM_X_THREADS, 1, NUM_Z_THREADS)]
void WriteYFace (uint3 c : SV_DispatchThreadID)
{
    uint3 dim;
    image.GetDimensions(dim.x, dim.y, dim.z);
    image[uint3(c.x, 0, c.z)] = 0.0f;
    image[uint3(c.x, dim.y-1, c.z)] = 0.0f;
}

RWTexture3D<float> image;
[numthreads(NUM_X_THREADS, NUM_Y_THREADS, 1)]
void WriteZFace (uint3 c : SV_DispatchThreadID)
{
```

```
    uint3 dim;
    image.GetDimensions(dim.x, dim.y, dim.z);
    image[uint3(c.x, c.y, 0)] = 0.0f;
    image[uint3(c.x, c.y, dim.z-1)] = 0.0f;
}
```

LISTING 7.47: HLSL code for enforcing the boundary conditions after solving the Poisson equation.

7.11.3.7 Updating the Velocity to Be Divergence Free

The gradient of ϕ, the solution to the Poisson equation, must be added back to the velocity vector. This process is managed by class AdjustVelocity. The shader code is shown in Listing 7.48; the Parameters constant buffer is omitted.

```
// From AdjustVelocity.hlsl:
Texture3D<float4> inState;
Texture3D<float> poisson;
RWTexture3D<float4> outState;

[numthreads(NUM_X_THREADS, NUM_Y_THREADS, NUM_Z_THREADS)]
void CSMain(uint3 c : SV_DispatchThreadID)
{
    uint3 dim;
    inState.GetDimensions(dim.x, dim.y, dim.z);

    int x = int(c.x);
    int y = int(c.y);
    int z = int(c.z);
    int xm = max(x-1, 0);
    int xp = min(x+1, dim.x-1);
    int ym = max(y-1, 0);
    int yp = min(y+1, dim.y-1);
    int zm = max(z-1, 0);
    int zp = min(z+1, dim.z-1);

    // Sample the state at (x,y,z).
    float4 state = inState[c.xyz];

    // Sample Poisson values at immediate neighbors of (x,y,z).
    float poisPZZ = poisson[int3(xp, y, z)];
    float poisMZZ = poisson[int3(xm, y, z)];
    float poisZPZ = poisson[int3(x, yp, z)];
    float poisZMZ = poisson[int3(x, ym, z)];
    float poisZZP = poisson[int3(x, y, zp)];
    float poisZZM = poisson[int3(x, y, zm)];

    float4 diff = { poisPZZ - poisMZZ, poisZPZ - poisZMZ,
        poisZZP - poisZZM, 0.0f };
    outState[c.xyz] = state + halfDivDelta*diff;
}
```

LISTING 7.48: HLSL code for updating the velocity to be divergence free.

The gradient is estimated using centered finite differences and the result is structured to use vectorized computations for speed.

7.11.3.8 Screen Captures from the Simulation

The 3D fluid simulation is clamped to run at 60 frames per second. The screen captures shown in Figure 7.13 were taken at various times during the

FIGURE 7.13: Screen captures from the 3D fluid simulation. The captures were taken at various time intervals with increasing time from left to right and then top to bottom.

simulation. The coloring of the density is based on the velocity vectors. The semitransparency is obtained via alpha blending, where the geometric primitives are nested boxes and the boxes are drawn from innermost to outermost.

Naturally, screen captures are not sufficient to convey the actual real-time behavior. You will have to run it yourself.

Bibliography

[1] Milton Abramowitz and Irene A. Stegun. *Handbook of Mathematical Functions with Formulas, Graphs, and Mathematical Tables.* Dover Publications, Inc., New York, NY, 1965.

[2] Martin Braun. *Differential Equations and Their Applications : An Introduction to Applied Mathematics, Texts in Applied Mathematics*, volume 11. Springer-Verlag, New York, NY, 4th edition, 1992.

[3] Bengt Carlson and Max Goldstein. Rational approximation of functions. Technical Report LA-1943, Los Alamos Scientific Laboratory, August 1995.

[4] Jr. Cecil Hastings. *Approximations for Digital Computers.* Princeton University Press, Princeton, NJ, 1955.

[5] Bernard Chazelle. Triangulating a simple polygon in linear time. *Discrete & Computational Geometry*, 6:485–524, 1991.

[6] Thomas H. Cormen, Charles E. Leiserson, Ronald L. Rivest, and Clifford Stein. *Introduction to Algorithms.* The MIT Press, Cambridge, MA, 3rd edition, 2009.

[7] David Eberly, Harold Longbotham, and Jorge Aragon. Complete classification of roots to one-dimensional median and rank-order filters. *IEEE Transactions on Signal Processing*, 39(4):197–200, 1991.

[8] David H. Eberly. *3D Game Engine Design.* Morgan Kaufmann, San Francisco, CA, 2nd edition, 2007.

[9] David H. Eberly. *Game Physics.* Morgan Kaufmann, San Francisco, CA, 2nd edition, 2010.

[10] David H. Eberly. A fast and accurate algorithm for computing slerp. *The Journal of Graphics, GPU, and Game Tools*, 15(3):161–176, 2011.

[11] H. ElGindy, H. Everett, and G.T. Toussaint. Slicing an ear using prune-and-search. *Pattern Recognition Letters*, 14(9):719–722, 1993.

[12] Erich Gamma, Richard Helm, Ralph Johnson, and John Vlissides. *Design Patterns: Elements of Reusable Object-Oriented Software.* Addison-Wesley, Boston, MA, 1995.

[13] Andrew S. Glassner, editor. *Graphics Gems I.* Academic Press, San Diego, CA, 1990.

[14] David Goldberg. What every computer scientist should know about floating-point arithmetic. *ACM Computing Surveys*, 23(1):5–48, March 1991.

[15] Robert E. Goldschmidt. Applications of division by convergence. Master's thesis, Massachusetts Institute of Technology, 1964.

[16] Gene H. Golub and Charles F. Van Loan. *Matrix Computations.* Johns Hopkins University Press, Baltimore, MD, 3rd edition, 1996.

[17] Markus Gross and Hanspeter Pfister. *Point-Based Graphics.* Morgan Kaufmann, San Francisco, CA, 2007.

[18] Roger A. Horn and Charles R. Johnson. *Matrix Analysis.* Cambridge University Press, Cambridge, England, 1985.

[19] W. Kahan and J. D. Darcy. How Java's Floating-Point Hurts Everyone Everywhere. http://www.cs.berkeley.edu/~wkahan/JAVAhurt.pdf, 1998.

[20] Elmar Langetepe and Gabriel Zachman. *Geometric Data Structures for Computer Graphics.* A K Peters, Ltd., Wellesley, MA, 2006.

[21] Chris Lomont. Fast inverse square root. http://www.math.purdue.edu/~clomont/Math/Papers/2003/InvSqrt.pdf, 2003.

[22] Harold Longbotham and David Eberly. The WMMR filters: A class of robust edge enhancers. *IEEE Transactions on Signal Processing*, 41(4):1680–1685, 1993.

[23] William E. Lorensen and Harvey Cline. Marching cubes: A high resolution 3D surface construction algorithm. *Proceedings of SIGGRAPH 1987*, pages 163–169, 1987.

[24] Zohra Z. Manseur. *Decomposition and Inversion of Convolution Operators.* PhD thesis, University of Florida, 1990.

[25] Robert Mayans. The Chebyshev Equioscillation Theorem. *Journal of Online Mathematics and its Applications*, 6:Article ID 1316, December 2006.

[26] G.H. Meisters. Polygons have ears. *American Mathematical Monthly*, 82:648–651, 1975.

[27] Microsoft Developer Network. Append function. http://msdn.microsoft.com/en-us/library/windows/desktop/bb205069(v=vs.85).aspx, 2014.

[28] Microsoft Developer Network. D3D11_CREATE_DEVICE_FLAG enumeration. http://msdn.microsoft.com/en-us/library/windows/desktop/ff476107(v=vs.85).aspx, 2014.

[29] Microsoft Developer Network. D3D11_MAP enumeration. http://msdn.microsoft.com/en-us/library/windows/desktop/ff476181(v=vs.85).aspx, 2014.

[30] Microsoft Developer Network. D3D11_MAP_FLAG enumeration. http://msdn.microsoft.com/en-us/library/windows/desktop/ff476183(v=vs.85).aspx, 2014.

[31] Microsoft Developer Network. D3D11_MAPPED_SUBRESOURCE structure. http://msdn.microsoft.com/en-us/library/windows/desktop/ff476182(v=vs.85).aspx, 2014.

[32] Microsoft Developer Network. Debugging directx graphics. http://msdn.microsoft.com/en-us/library/hh315751.aspx, 2014.

[33] Microsoft Developer Network. DXGI Overview. http://msdn.microsoft.com/en-us/library/windows/desktop/bb205075(v=vs.85).aspx, 2014.

[34] Microsoft Developer Network. Floating-point rules. http://msdn.microsoft.com/en-us/library/windows/desktop/jj218760(v=vs.85).aspx, 2014.

[35] Microsoft Developer Network. ftod (sm5 - asm). http://msdn.microsoft.com/en-us/library/windows/desktop/hh447074(v=vs.85).aspx, 2014.

[36] Microsoft Developer Network. ID3D11DeviceContext::CopyResource method. http://msdn.microsoft.com/en-us/library/windows/desktop/ff476392(v=vs.85).aspx, 2014.

[37] Microsoft Developer Network. ID3D11DeviceContext::CopySubresourceRegion method. http://msdn.microsoft.com/en-us/library/windows/desktop/ff476394(v=vs.85).aspx, 2014.

[38] Microsoft Developer Network. ID3D11DeviceContext::Dispatch. http://msdn.microsoft.com/en-us/library/windows/desktop/ff476405(v=vs.85).aspx, 2014.

[39] Microsoft Developer Network. ID3D11DeviceContext::Map method. http://msdn.microsoft.com/en-us/library/windows/desktop/ff476457(v=vs.85).aspx, 2014.

[40] Microsoft Developer Network. ID3D11DeviceContext::Unmap method. http://msdn.microsoft.com/en-us/library/windows/desktop/ff476485(v=vs.85).aspx, 2014.

[41] Microsoft Developer Network. ID3D11DeviceContext::UpdateSubresource method. http://msdn.microsoft.com/en-us/library/windows/desktop/ ff476486(v=vs.85).aspx, 2014.

[42] Microsoft Developer Network. IDXGISwapChain1::Present1 method. http://msdn.microsoft.com/en-us/library/windows/desktop/hh446797 (v=vs.85).aspx, 2014.

[43] Microsoft Developer Network. imm_atomic_alloc (sm5 - asm). http: //msdn.microsoft.com/en-us/library/windows/desktop/hh447116(v=vs .85).aspx, 2014.

[44] Microsoft Developer Network. ld (sm4 - asm). http://msdn.microsoft. com/en-us/library/windows/desktop/hh447172(v=vs.85).aspx, 2014.

[45] Microsoft Developer Network. Packing Rules for Constant Variables. http://msdn.microsoft.com/en-us/library/windows/desktop/ bb509632(v=vs.85).aspx, 2014.

[46] Microsoft Developer Network. Resource Limits. http://msdn.microsoft. com/en-us/library/windows/desktop/ff819065(v=vs.85).aspx, 2014.

[47] Microsoft Developer Network. Shader Constants. http://msdn.microsoft. com/en-us/library/windows/desktop/bb509581(v=vs.85).aspx, 2014.

[48] Microsoft Developer Network. Subresources. http://msdn.microsoft. com/en-us/library/windows/desktop/ff476901(v=vs.85).aspx, 2014.

[49] Michael L. Overton. *Numerical Computing with IEEE Floating Point Arithmetic*. Society for Industrial and Applied Mathematics, Philadelphia, 2001.

[50] Carl E. Pearson, editor. *Handbook of Applied Mathematics: Selected Results and Methods*. Van Nostrand Reinhold, New York, NY, 2nd edition, 1985.

[51] Raimund Seidel. A simple and fast incremental randomized algorithm for computing trapezoidal decompositions and for triangulating polygons. *Computational Geometry: Theory and Applications*, 1:51–64, 1991.

[52] Ken Shoemake. Animating rotation with quaternion calculus. *Computer Animation: 3-D Motion, Specification, and Control (ACM SIGGRAPH Course Notes)*, 10, 1987.

[53] Alexey V. Skvortsov and Yuri L. Kostyuk. Efficient algorithms for Delaunay triangulation. *Geoinformatics: Theory and Practice (Tomsk State University)*, 1:22–47, 1998.

[54] Jos Stam. Real-Time Fluid Dynamics for Games. Game Developer Conference, San Jose, CA, March, 2003.

[55] Herb Sutter and Andrei Alexandrescu. *C++ Coding Standards: 101 Rules, Guidelines, and Best Practices*. Addison-Wesley, Boston, MA, 1st edition, 2005.

[56] Chuck Walbourn. Games for Windows and the DirectX SDK. http://blogs.msdn.com/b/chuckw/, 2014.

[57] Jason Zink, Matt Pettineo, and Jack Hoxley. *Practical Rendering & Computation with Direct3D11*. CRC Press, Taylor & Francis Group, Boca Raton, 2011.

Index

accuracy, 19
advection, 402
Append, *see* HLSL functions
append-consume buffer, *see*
　　resources, buffers
AppendStructuredBuffer, *see* HLSL
　　types
approximation
　　cosine, by minimax, 116
　　exponential, by minimax, 120
　　inverse cosine, by minimax, 119
　　inverse sine, by minimax, 117
　　inverse square root
　　　by minimax, 114
　　　by Newton's method, 110
　　inverse tangent, by minimax,
　　　119
　　least-squares algorithm, 107,
　　　355, 362
　　logarithm, by minimax, 120
　　minimax algorithm, 82, 109, 355
　　orthogonal fitting, 360
　　sine, by minimax, 116
　　square root
　　　by minimax, 111
　　　by Newton's method, 111
　　tangent, by minimax, 117
asfloat, *see* HLSL functions
asint, *see* HLSL functions
asuint, *see* HLSL functions

back buffer, 169
　　clearing, 173
　　color, 172
　　creating, 172
　　depth-stencil, 172
　　resizing, 173

barycentric coordinates, 131
Bellman-Ford algorithm, *see* shortest
　　path in graph
binary encodings, 32
　　general format, 45
binary scientific notation, 24
binary scientific number
　　definition, 24
　　implementation (BSNumber), 24
　　implementation of ratios
　　　(BSRational), 30
　　properties
　　　algebraic, 30
　　　arithmetic, 27
ByteAddressBuffer, *see* HLSL types

Cayley-Hamilton theorem, 293
change of basis, 338
characteristic polynomial, 293
Chebyshev
　　equioscillation theorem, 82, 109,
　　　116, 303
　　polynomials, 109, 302
conservation laws, 400
constant buffer, *see* resources, buffers
Consume, *see* HLSL functions
ConsumeStructuredBuffer, *see* HLSL
　　types
conversion
　　binary32 to rational, 64
　　binary64 to rational, 66
　　integer to floating-point, 60
　　narrow format to wide format,
　　　70
　　　general implementation, 73
　　rational to binary scientific
　　　number, 24

conversion *(continued)*
    rational to binary32, 67
    rational to binary64, 70
    wide format to narrow format, 73
        general implementation, 81
coordinate system
    converting between right-handed and left-handed, 336
    handedness, 319, 333, 335
    orthonormal basis
        left-handed, 124
        right-handed, 124
    orthonormal set, 263
counting drawn pixels, 205

D3D interfaces
    ID3DBlob, 161, 203, 226
    ID3DInclude, 160
D3D11 device, 168
    creating, 169
    reference, 170
D3D11 interfaces
    ID3D11BlendState, 202
    ID3D11Buffer, 181
        dynamic update, 208
    ID3D11ComputeShader, 203
    ID3D11DepthStencilState, 202
    ID3D11DepthStencilView, 173
        creating, 178
    ID3D11DeviceContext, 169
    ID3D11Device, 169
    ID3D11GeometryShader, 203
    ID3D11InputLayout, 184, 230
    ID3D11PixelShader, 203
    ID3D11Query
        counting drawn pixels, 205
        performance measurements, 243
        wait for GPU to finish, 207
    ID3D11RasterizerState, 202
    ID3D11RenderTargetView, 173
        creating, 178
    ID3D11SamplerState, 202

ID3D11ShaderReflection, 161
ID3D11ShaderResourceView, 177
ID3D11UnorderedAccessView, 177
ID3D11VertexShader, 203
hierarchy, 174, 228
dadd, *see* HLSL functions
ddiv, *see* HLSL functions
DecrementCounter, *see* HLSL functions
deferred context, 168
depth-stencil texture, *see* resources, textures
depth-stencil view, *see* resources, views
deq, *see* HLSL functions
dfma, *see* HLSL functions
dge, *see* HLSL functions
Dijkstra's algorithm, *see* shortest path in graph
division
    of binary scientific numbers, 30
    by multiplicative division, 82
    by Newton's method, 81
dlt, *see* HLSL functions
dmax, *see* HLSL functions
dmin, *see* HLSL functions
dmov, *see* HLSL functions
dmul, *see* HLSL functions
dne, *see* HLSL functions
drcp, *see* HLSL functions
dtof, *see* HLSL functions
DXGI interfaces
    IDXGIAdapter
        device creation, 169
        enumerating adapters, 215
    IDXGIDevice, creating swap chains, 170
    IDXGIFactory1
        copying between GPUs, 217
        creating swap chains, 170
        enumerating adapters, 215
    IDXGIOutput, enumerating displays, 215
    IDXGIResource, sharing textures, 195

IDXGISwapChain
   creation, 170
   resizing the back buffer, 173
   toggling between windowed
      and full-screen, 171
dynamic programming, 365, 376

error
   absolute, 19
   relative, 19
   rounding, 26
   truncation, 26
Euler angles
   body coordinates, 306
   world coordinates, 306

finite difference estimation, 401
floating-point
   adjacent number
      next-down, 47
      next-up, 47
   biased exponent, 33, 37, 39, 41
   classification, 45
   narrow format, 51
   normal, 33, 37, 39, 41
   not-a-number (NaN), 32
      payload, 33
      quiet, 32
      signaling, 32
   pseudocode for parsing, 34, 38,
      40, 42, 45
   sign, 33, 36, 39, 41
   signed infinities, 32
   signed zeros, 32
   significand, 33, 37, 39, 41
   subnormal, 33, 37, 39, 41
   trailing significand, 33, 37, 39, 41
   wide format, 51
front buffer, 169
ftod, *see* HLSL functions

Gauss-Seidel iteration, 401
Gaussian distribution, *see* image
      processing

geometric algorithm
   definition, 16
   robust, 16
   stable, 16
geometric problem
   constructive, 15
   convex hull of disks, 15
   convex hull of points, 15
   definition, 14
   distance between points, 17
   intersection of line segments, 15
   selective, 15
Gram-Schmidt orthonormalization,
      263, 265, 267, 268, 328, 330
graph
   directed, 371
   directed acyclic, 372
   topological sort, 372
group-shared memory, in compute
      shader, 378
GroupMemoryBarrierWithGroupSync, *see*
      HLSL functions

handedness, *see* coordinate system
Helmholtz decomposition of vector
      fields, 402
HLSL functions
   decrementcounter, 188
   incrementcounter, 188
   Append
      behavior when buffer full, 187
      in compute shader, 186
      in geometry shader, 139
   asdouble, 188, 354
   asfloat, 188, 221, 352, 354
   asint, 188
   asuint, 188
   Consume, 186
   dadd, 221
   ddiv, 221
   deq, 221
   dfma, 221
   dge, 221
   dlt, 221

HLSL functions *(continued)*
    dmax, 221
    dmin, 221
    dmov, 221
    dmul, 221
    dne, 221
    drcp, 221
    dtof, 221
    ftod, 221
    Load4, 189
    mul, 134, 135
    RestartStrip, 139
    Store4, 189
HLSL loop unrolling, 158
HLSL registers
    constant buffer (cb#), 149
    input (v#), 149
    output (o#), 149
    output stream (m#), 155
    sampler (s#), 152
    temporary (r#), 149
    temporary indexable (x#), 158
    texture (t#), 152
    unordered access view (u#), 158
HLSL types
    AppendStructuredBuffer, 186
    ByteAddressBuffer, 188
    ConsumeStructuredBuffer, 186
    RWByteAddressBuffer, 188
    RWStructuredBuffer, 185, 186
    StructuredBuffer, 185
    TriangleStream, 139

IEEE 754-2008 Standard, 22–23
    binary interchange formats, 32
        binary8, 33
        binary16, 36
        binary32, 39
        binary64, 41
        binaryN, 42
    GPU conformance, 218
    SIMD conformance, 103
image processing
    convolution, 377
    filter kernel, 378

Gaussian distribution, 377
    median filter, 384
        using insertion sort, 385
        using min-max swapping, 387
    rank-order filter, 384
    separable filter, 378
immediate context, 168
    creating, 169
IncrementCounter, *see* HLSL functions
index buffer, *see* resources, buffers
input assembly stage, 185
input layout, 184, *see* resources
intermediate value theorem, 346
intersections
    bounding volume trees, 370
    find query, 368
    tangential, 368
    test query, 368
    transverse, 368

l'Hôpital's Rule, 294
Laplace expansion theorem, 284
Laplacian operator, 400
least-squares, *see* approximation
left-handed, *see* coordinate system
level set, 392
level surface, 392
level value, 392
Load4, *see* HLSL functions

mass-spring system, 398
matrix
    column-major order, 274
    row-major order, 274
    vector-on-the-left convention, 274
    vector-on-the-right convention, 274
median filter, *see* image processing
memory mapping, 182, 208, 211
minimax, *see* approximation
mul, *see* HLSL functions
multiple render targets, 201

output merger stage, 206

ping-pong buffers, 143, 411, 414, 425, 426
Poisson equation, 402, 414, 426
precision
    definition, 19
    of floating-point numbers, 43
processing unit
    CPU (central processing unit), 1
    FPU (floating-point processing unit), 22
    GPU (graphics processing unit), 1
    SIMD (single-instruction-multiple-data), 2, 93
programming pattern
    adapter, 174
    bridge, 174
    listener, 230

rank-order filter, *see* image processing
register
    shuffling (swizzling), 94
    splat, 95
relaxation, *see* shortest path in graph
Remez
    algorithm, 109, 303
    iteration, 112–114, 116
render-target texture, *see* resources, textures
render-target view, *see* resources, views
resources
    buffers
        append-consume, 186
        byte-address, 188
        constant, 182
        index, 138, 185
        indirect argument, 190
        raw, 188
        structured, 185
        structured with internal counters, 186

        texture, 182
        vertex, 138, 183
    indexless primitive, 138
    input layout, 138
    limit on bind points, 191
    staging, 175
    texture arrays, 196
        1-dimensional, 196
        2-dimensional, 197
    textures, 190
        1-dimensional, 193
        2-dimensional, 194
        3-dimensional, 195
        automatic mipmap generation, 191, 193, 195, 196
        creation, 191
        cubemap, 198
        cubemap arrays, 199
        depth-stencil, 200
        render target, 199
        sharing between devices, 195
    views, 176
        depth-stencil, 176
        render target, 176
        setting render targets and unordered access views together, 206
        shader resource, 176
        unordered access, 176
RestartStrip, *see* HLSL functions
right-handed, *see* coordinate system
Rodrigues rotation formula, 292
root polishing, 85
rounding
    correctly rounded result, 50
    floating-point to integral floating-point, 54
    ties-to-away, 51, 52, 56
    ties-to-even, 26, 51, 54
    toward negative, 51, 53, 59
    toward positive, 51, 52, 58
    toward zero, 51, 52, 57
Runge–Kutta fourth-order method, 399

RWByteAddressBuffer, *see* HLSL types
RWStructuredBuffer, *see* HLSL types

semantics, 136
    COLOR, 135, 149
    POSITION, 135, 148
    TEXCOORD, 136, 151
shader compiling, 144
    using D3DCompile, 160
    using FXC, 144
shader reflection, 138, 161
    determining buffer packing, 163
    skeleton code wrapper, 163
    using D3DReflect, 161
shader resource view, *see* resources,
        views
shaders
    compute
        dispatch thread ID, 143
        for Gaussian blurring, 142
        group ID, 143
        group thread ID, 143
        groups of threads, 142
    geometry
        for billboards, 139
        for splatting, 141
        for surface extraction, 396
    out-of-range resource accesses,
        160
    pixel
        for texturing, 137
        for vertex coloring, 135
    vertex
        for texturing, 137
        for vertex coloring, 135
shortest path in graph, 372
slerp (spherical linear interpolation),
        300
spaces
    model, 123
    projection (clip), 125
        perspective divide, 129
        view frustum, 127
        view plane, 125

view (camera), 124
window, 129
    normalized device
        coordinates, 129
    viewport, 129
world, 123
SSE instructions
    arithmetic
        _mm_add_ps, 100
        _mm_div_ps, 100
        _mm_mul_ps, 100
        _mm_rcp_ps, 100
        _mm_rsqrt_ps, 100
        _mm_sqrt_ps, 100
        _mm_sub_ps, 100
    comparison
        _mm_cmpeq_ps, 99
        _mm_cmpge_ps, 99
        _mm_cmpgt_ps, 99
        _mm_cmple_ps, 99
        _mm_cmplt_ps, 99
        _mm_cmpneq_ps, 99
        _mm_cmpnge_ps, 99
        _mm_cmpngt_ps, 99
        _mm_cmpnle_ps, 99
        _mm_cmpnlt_ps, 99
    floating-point control registers
        _mm_getcsr, 103
        _mm_setcsr, 103
    logical
        _mm_and_not_ps, 99
        _mm_and_ps, 99
        _mm_or_ps, 99
        _mm_xor_ps, 99
    matrix transpose
        _MM_TRANSPOSE4_PS, 102
    memory allocation
        _mm_free, 93
        _mm_malloc, 93
    memory loading and storing
        _MM_SHUFFLE, 94
        _mm_load_ps, 96
        _mm_loadu_ps, 96
        _mm_set_ps1, 94

_mm_set_ps, 94
_mm_setr_ps, 94
_mm_shuffle_ps, 94
_mm_store_ps, 96
_mm_storeu_ps, 96
selection (flattening), 104
Store4, *see* HLSL functions
structured buffer, *see* resources,
        buffers
structured buffer with counter, *see*
        resources, buffers
StructuredBuffer, *see* HLSL types
Sturm polynomial sequence, 346
subresources, 179
        numbering of mipmaps, 179
        numbering of texture arrays,
        179
subtractive cancellation, 84
swap chain, 169
        creating, 170
system value semantics, 136
        SV_Depth, 201
        SV_DispatchThreadID, 143
        SV_GroupID, 143
        SV_GroupIndex, 143
        SV_GroupThreadID, 143
        SV_Position
            clip position in vertex shader,
            136
            pixel center in pixel shader,
            136
        SV_Target, 136
        SV_VertexID, 396

texture buffer, *see* resources, buffers
texture sampling modes, 152
top-left rule for rasterization, 131
trade-offs, 20–22

transformation
        affine, 322
            decomposition, 327
            rotation, 325
            scaling, 324
            shearing, 325
            translation, 323
        composition, 326
        model-world, 123
        orthographic projection, 127
        perspective projection, 127
        projection-window, 129
        rigid, 327
        scaled rigid, 327
        view-projection, 128
        world-view, 125
        world-view-projection, 226, 232,
        236
            HLSL storage order, 150
            used in vertex shaders, 137
trapezoid rules, 372
TriangleStream, *see* HLSL types

unordered access view, *see* resources,
        views

vertex buffer, *see* resources, buffers
video streams, 341
        parallel processing, 343
        producer-consumer model, 341
        serial processing, 343
voxel
        definition, 392
        use in 3D fluid flow, 417
        use in surface extraction, 392

wait for GPU to finish, 207
world-view-projection matrix, *see*
        transformation

Printed and bound by CPI Group (UK) Ltd, Croydon, CR0 4YY

30/10/2024

01781310-0002